Lead Me On

FRANK GOAD CLEMENT AND TENNESSEE POLITICS

Lead Me On

FRANK GOAD CLEMENT

AND TENNESSEE POLITICS

by Lee Seifert Greene

THE UNIVERSITY OF TENNESSEE PRESS / KNOXVILLE

Frontispiece: Painting of Frank Goad Clement, by Martin Kellogg.
Reproduced by courtesy of Tennessee State Museum.

Library of Congress Cataloging in Publication Data
Greene, Lee Seifert, 1905–
  Lead me on.
  Bibliography: p.
  Includes index.
  1. Clement, Frank Goad. 2. Tennessee—Politics and
government—1951– . 3. Tennessee—Governors—Biography. I. Title.
F440.3.C57G73   976.8'053'0924 [B]   81-11459
ISBN 0-87049-335-3   AACR2

Contents

Illustrations

CARTOONS

MAPS

Foreword

BY EDWARD J. BOLING

Were he alive today, Senator Herbert S. Walters would be the logical one to write the introductory paragraphs to a book about Frank Clement, for he was the individual, aside from the author, most responsible for its having been written. As much as anyone, Senator Walters set Frank Clement upon the political highway, and as chairman of the Democratic party in Tennessee, he helped clear the way for Clement victories in three gubernatorial elections. For months before his own death, Senator Walters repeatedly cited a need for a biography of Frank Clement, and his persistence resulted in the present volume.

The choice of a scholar to chronicle the life of Frank Clement was indeed a fortunate one. As a University of Tennessee professor, Lee S. Greene demonstrated a rare ability as a writer in his field of political science, and the combination of his broad knowledge of politics and mastery of the pen has produced a volume that is analytical, historically accurate, and readable.

Few of us have an opportunity to observe at first hand the day-to-day work of a great public servant. For four years I had the privilege of working, as state budget director, in the cabinet of Frank Goad Clement. In those few years, the first four-year term for a Tennessee governor, I saw the government modernized and the state's future reshaped and redirected—mainly through the efforts of its energetic young governor. When I joined his cabinet in 1954, Frank Clement was a vigorous young man, filled with a vision of progress, eager to serve his native state and its people. The common faults of youth were evident, but whatever weaknesses he had were far outweighed by his strengths: his devotion to honest government, his fearlessness in espousing unpopular legislation that would bring long-range benefits to the people of Tennessee. If taxes were needed to move the state ahead in education or transportation or some other vital area, he did not hesitate to take the none-too-popular route. When disorder erupted in Tennessee in the early months of school desegregation, Governor Clement chose to uphold the law of the land, not an altogether popular stand in those volatile times. Because of his unwavering strength of purpose and character, I am convinced that history will remember Frank Clement as one of the great modern Tennessee governors, if not the greatest.

High on his list of improvements in state administration when Clement first became governor in 1953 was the modernization of the state's fiscal affairs. He inherited an antiquated record-keeping and budget-making system for the largest financial operation in Tennessee; and when he reached out to the University of Tennessee for fiscal experts such as Bill Snodgrass and Harold Read, and to the business and industrial and professional world for assistants, he was more concerned with performance than with partisanship. When he appointed me to his cabinet, he did not ask my politics. In fact, he did not know if I were a Democrat or a Republican or if I had voted for or against him. This demand for competence in public servants and the desire for results were evident in his appointments throughout the fabric of government—in education, in agriculture, in conservation, in mental health.

No governor has demonstrated a greater awareness of the importance of health and education to the progress of Tennessee than Frank Clement did. He brought mental patient care out of the Dark Ages, and his concern for schools at all levels was constant and productive. He realized that only by developing its resources—and that includes the intellects of its people—can Tennessee reach its potential for growth and productivity. His abiding interest in young people and the educational process extended beyond the state's borders. As chairman of the Southern Regional Education Board, and as a member of various educational task forces at regional and national levels, he made his beliefs about the importance of education known throughout the land.

No one can truly assess the loss to Tennessee implicit in the untimely death of Frank Clement at the age of forty-nine. In one tragic moment, the state and its people were deprived of any further service that he might have rendered, whether in governmental office or by his wise counsel. His monument stands in the service he gave as governor, in better schools and safer roads, in mental hospitals and state parks. An-

other monument, we believe, has been raised by Lee Greene in the pages
that follow.

Knoxville   EDWARD J. BOLING
1982   President
                                                The University of Tennessee

Preface

From time to time, during the composing of this biography, I have been asked, particularly by people not especially friendly to Frank Clement and his memory, why do you want to write on Governor Clement?

The simplest answer to this query is that I was commissioned to do so. The circumstances of this commission can be recounted briefly. Senator Herbert Walters, whose interest in and affection for Governor Clement will be clear in the account of the governor's career that follows, wanted a biography of the former chief executive published. He approached the University with his proposal, and I was invited by President Edward Boling, Louis Iglehart, director of the University of Tennessee Press, and Julian Harriss, director of public relations, to meet with them and Senator Walters, Judge Robert S. Clement, and Noble Caudill to discuss the project. At this meeting, in the late spring of 1973, I was invited to undertake the present work. As a member of the board of the University of Tennessee Press for many years, I had been constantly concerned that the Press should publish material on Tennessee government and politics. Among other things, I had read for the Press a number of manuscripts dealing with Tennessee political figures, and it was known to Mr. Iglehart that I thought the Press should promote biographies of Tennessee governors whenever possible.

In the summer of 1973, while preliminary plans were being made, Senator Walters died. At the suggestion of President Boling, the Board of Trustees decided to continue with the project, partly as a means of memorializing Senator Walters and his financial support of this project.

There were, however, other compelling reasons for my interest in this biography. When the matter first reached my attention, I had retired as head of the Department of Political Science and was in the last months of my life as a teacher. I had plans for further writing in the field of politics in Tennessee. The preparation of a biography of a major political figure in Tennessee history was a task entirely to my taste, and the proposal made to me by the University was thoroughly welcome.

If anyone should get the impression that the preceding paragraphs indicate that my interest in this project was entirely personal or mercenary, that impression would be wrong. I believe that politics should be studied up close, and I believe that one good way of doing this is to read biography. I would like to see a burst of biographies of Tennessee political figures. I am glad to have had a chance of contributing to such a development, and I regret that I did not have the opportunity earlier in my life.

And, finally, there remains the subject. It is not difficult to justify an interest in Frank Clement. He was a lively and attractive personality in life; he remains so in memory. His brief and active career, with its victories and defeats, was lent a tragic element by his early death. His three terms as governor were filled with important events and several major crises. His uneasy alliance with Buford Ellington continued a faction in Tennessee politics that could reasonably be said to have dominated Tennessee affairs from the days of Prentice Cooper to the administration of Governor Dunn, except for the Browning interim. To study Frank Clement is to study Tennessee affairs, and those affairs have long been my major interest.

I have tried to write this book objectively. I became deeply interested in Clement, but I am not a hero-worshiper, and I am aware of some of the faults of my subject. I hope that I am a charitable man (although I am aware that many of my friends will find this rather unbelievable), and I hope also that I approach the subject of politics with some understanding of the Tennessee voter. I know that this account of the former governor will be found lacking by some of my readers, but I must accept that with whatever grace I can muster. This life of Clement is concerned chiefly with his public career, and some of his private life and business affairs have not been treated. His interests were always concentrated on public concerns and on the strife and triumph of politics; the role of an unobtrusive private person was not congenial to him. It is impossible to avoid the conviction that had he been compelled to live out the normal span as a private citizen he would have been intensely unhappy. In this respect, his tragic early death may have been disguised good fortune.

Although I have tried to verify facts by any means open to me, I am all too aware that errors cannot be avoided. I am sorry for them—in advance. I have not hesitated to express my own opinions and judgments. For example, many people believe that Governor Clement could have been elected governor again in 1970. That might have come about. I think otherwise and have said so. I believe this will be recognized as my own opinion, not as inevitable fact. Although I hate to admit it, I have been known to make mistakes.

My indebtedness to others who have helped me with this book is very large; I seek to acknowledge my benefactors as fully as space and memory permit. Frances Kunstling, Susan Haddock, Linda Parker, and Heloise Shilstat helped me immensely with the examination of the Clement papers in the Tennessee State Library and Archives. Mrs. Kunstling studied the papers at Dickson, Tennessee. Douglas R. Dadisman searched the Kefauver collection at the University of Tennessee, Knoxville. Wallace B. Katz examined the papers in the Vanderbilt University Library and at Middle Tennessee State University at Murfreesboro, and Stanley A. Cook searched the Walters papers in the UT library. Michael K. Goodwin examined the Browning papers in the Tennessee State Library and Archives. I would not have been able to write the biography without their assistance. I have relied on typists drawn largely from the students of UT Knoxville. I am unable to mention them all by name, but I wish to express especial gratitude to Mary H. Clarke, Sonia Muzzall, Patricia Hyatt, and JoAnn Randolph, who helped me with research as well as with the onerous typing work. My debt to librarians is substantial. I wish I could mention them all. Especial thanks are tendered to Cleo Hughes, Jean Waggener, and John Thweatt of the Tennessee State Library and Archives, Marice Wolfe of the Vanderbilt University library, and the Reference and Special Collections staffs of the University of Tennessee library at Knoxville.

The uncertain policy of the University of Tennessee on the subject of offices for retired faculty can only be described in administrative law terms as "arbitrary and capricious." But UT has always been hard-pressed for office space, and retired scholars cannot always be fully accommodated, even though the University's good will can safely be taken for granted. Over the long years as an administrator I grew used to working in the confusion of an ordinary campus day, and I needed that atmosphere during my retirement. For some years I was able to retain my reasonably luxurious quarters in the McClung Tower; when that was no longer possible, I was provided, through the assistance of Chancellor Jack Reese, with adequate (and sunny) space in the Hoskins Library. For some time, Professor Thomas Ungs was able to eke out some space for my secretary in the increasingly crowded McClung Tower, and thereafter John Dobson made room for my secretary and the growing bulk of Clement papers in the Special Collections stacks at the library. Officials at UT Nashville aided me in various ways. I am grateful to all of these people; I have tried to give them as little trouble as possible.

A great many individuals have contributed to this project. It has enjoyed the sustained interest and support of President Edward J. Boling and Chancellor Jack Reese of UT. Professor Sam Smith assisted me with advice on research assistants. The staff of the Press have aided me, including the former director, the late Louis Iglehart, and his successor, Carol Orr. Sue English has managed the budget and employed aides. Katherine Holloway has edited the book. Jim Billingsley has contributed the design. My indebtedness to persons who have granted me interviews is substantial. I have enjoyed the support of members of the Clement and Goad families, particularly Robert S. Clement (who died in October 1981, as this book was being printed), former TVA Director Robert N. Clement, State Senator Anna Belle Clement O'Brien, and Judge Frank Goad.

Many people have read all or parts of the manuscript, and aided me with counsel, including Dr. Boling, Dr. Roy Nicks, Dr. Joseph Johnson, Mr. Edward Jones, Mr. Noble Caudill, Judge Goad, Chancellor Reese, Judge Ray Brock, Mr. William Wilson, Professor Robert S. Avery, the late Dr. Herman Spivey, Professor Sam B. Smith, Wilma Dykeman, and Professor T. McNider Simpson. Dr. Stephen D. Boyd has permitted me to use records of his interviews made during his study of the 1954 campaign. My wife and children have aided me with praise and loyalty.

To all of these people and many others I express my warm thanks and my hope that they will approve the resulting work.

Knoxville, 1982   LEE S. GREENE

Lead Me On

FRANK GOAD CLEMENT AND TENNESSEE POLITICS

♪ *The morning light is breaking,*
The darkness disappears.

SAMUEL FRANCIS SMITH, 1808–1895

1. The Morning Light Is Breaking

CHILDHOOD AND YOUTH

I hope that someday the opening paragraph of a Tennessee history yet to be written will say of my administration: "During the humane administration of Frank G. Clement, Democrat of Dickson, from 1953–59, the aged, the needy, the lame and the halt, the blind and the mentally ill citizens of Tennessee were the beneficiaries of unprecedented recognition and advancement. Clement was known as the humane governor."

With this wish (here in some degree fulfilled) Frank Goad Clement closed his opening speech at Lebanon in 1954. The birth of the speaker, thirty-four years earlier, had been recorded in a terse announcement in the *Dickson County Herald* of June 4, 1920: "Born, to Mr. and Mrs. Robert S. Clement, June 2, a son." This laconic observation was tucked into a column, along with other items, including one other birth, labeled "Local and Otherwise"; the second item in the miscellany offered the information: "Wanted—Second Hand Trunk."

The small male whose advent was noticed in this offhand way, typical of the juxtapositions of small town newsheets, was to live a hasty life of forty-nine years, that life crushed out by a motor disaster on Nashville's Franklin Pike in the early evening of November 4, 1969. But in those forty-nine years, he would be governor of Tennessee three times, for a total span of ten years, and, he and his uneasy political ally, Buford Ellington, would dominate the executive branch of the state for a period of eighteen years.

Tennessee is severe with its governors. Their brief periods of power, limited first by law and second by practice, have been followed by the deepening obscurity that few men surmount. John Sevier, James Polk, Andrew Johnson are remembered, but most of the men who have

3

The Halbrook Hotel, Dickson, in 1981. Photograph courtesy Robert S. Clement.

tenanted the executive office are not long recalled, whatever their deserts, and most of them do not succeed in advancing from the rank of governor to greater offices. By reason of frontier political power, Polk could become President. John Wilkes Booth's murdering weapon gave Johnson a presidency he would not have attained by better and less violent means. But the Washington glory lies beyond the hopes of most Tennesseans. Time's passage will no doubt dim the memory of Frank Clement as it does the remembrance of most men, but his brief life has interest for students of human destinies. In the manner and circumstances of his early death, his life was tragic. The spectacular youthful rise to the governorship was succeeded by sharp repudiations that brought an end to his political hopes shortly before the smash that ended his life. Had he lived, he would have been retired to a private life that could never satisfy his deepest wishes. But while he lived, his days were filled with significance and excitement.

Clement arrived at the governorship on his first try. He reached and occupied the office at a crucial time, when Tennessee was faced with dramatic and emotion-invoking change: the approach of desegregation, the expansion of city population, the slow and reluctant decline of rural power, the professionalization of the state bureaucracy, a sudden burst of higher education, and a widening role for state government. It was a time of troubles—the 1950s and the 1960s—when a governor, sniffing the shifting political winds in the hope of political survival, would not always know which way to turn. The responses of Governor Clement, roundly condemned by his bitter opponents, emotionally applauded by his ardent supporters, often the butt of cynicism and disbelief, helped to produce the Tennessee of the seventies and left in the minds of a generation of Tennesseans the image of a charismatic and controversial figure.

Frank Clement was the descendant of pioneers of English and Scottish stock who had come into Tennessee through Virginia eventually to take up residence on the borderlands between Middle and West Tennessee. Among the early settlers who sought their livelihood just beyond the boundaries of what is now called Middle Tennessee was Aaron Clement. This Clement had come into Benton County as had three of his brothers, Nathan, Isaac, and Stephen; in Benton and Henry counties they became the forebears of Clements still found in that region.

Benton County, divided between the Highland Rim and the East Gulf Coastal Plain, was no place for plantations. It is a rolling country, cut by sharp ridges, with narrow flood plains bordering sluggish streams. Even today it is heavily wooded. In pioneer times thick forests of oak, hickory, dogwood, sourwood, sycamore, and beech faced the farmer with an obstacle and a challenge; but even when the trees were cleared away, the soil was not promising. Benton County never became a slave economy; in 1850, when its population had reached almost 6,000 whites, only 363 slaves could be counted. By contrast, Haywood County, south and west of Benton where the plantation economy flourished, had about 8,500 black slaves to some 8,700 whites. The farmers of Benton did not sit on Greek revival porches reading Sir Walter Scott while their happy slaves sang spirituals in the cotton fields. Benton was a rough country where life was maintained by hard scrabbling.

Aaron Clement was born in 1814. His wife, two years younger, bore the unusual first name of Christian. She was a daughter of the legendary Daniel Buchanan, who had built a cabin on Sugar Creek before 1818 (when West Tennessee was opened to settlement) without filing a claim to land. When he did file, he was among the first to stake out land, after the western third of the state was dedicated to the invading whites, laying claim to 160 acres on the banks of the Big Sandy River. He claimed added acreage in 1841 and 1846. Daniel was a reputed "strong man"; when he pummeled an attacking bear to death, with flailing arms, fists, and feet, he made himself into a local legend. Christian, his daughter, eventual great-grandmother to a governor, was born in 1816 in what is now Benton County.

Local and uncertain rumor has it that Daniel Buchanan was the descendant of a Buchanan who accompanied James Robertson up the Cumberland River to the site of Nashville, and for those who value dramatic coincidence it would be pleasant to think the report is true. Be that as it may, there were certainly Buchanans among the increasing families of Scots then penetrating the thick hardwood forests of Middle Tennessee. Tangible traces of these early settlers have been long since lost. Graves were not well marked or well preserved in those times, and whatever markers commemorated Daniel Buchanan and Aaron Clement have vanished totally. Even the burial grounds that supposedly held them can no longer be found. Their times fade away into the remote and half-forgotten.

The eighth child of Aaron and Christian Clement was James Archibald Clement, born by the "strong man's" daughter on August 1, 1853, in Benton County. James A. Clement was married three times and fathered two families; by the second he became the grandfather of the future governor of the state. A small stone obelisk in the City Cemetery not far from the court square in Camden, Tennessee, hard by the busy highway

Will C. Goad, Sr. and Belle S. Goad. Photograph courtesy Judge Frank Goad.

70-S, marks the grave of "Sallie F. wife of J.A. Clement." The first wife, she had been Sallie Stockdale. Beside her grave are markers for two infant sons, who died, one in 1891, the other in 1895. Sallie, who had been born January 28, 1858, followed her infant boys in death on January 27, 1899, but six other children of this first marriage survived.

Life for J.A. Clement had many rough edges. He had little schooling — only fourteen days, all told, and even that secured under harsh conditions. But he managed to acquire some learning. For a time, after farming, he practiced the trade of blacksmith in Camden, but in that small town he made the acquaintance of one of the town's lawyers, Tom Rye, and read law in Rye's office. (Rye was to become governor of Tennessee in later years.) Admitted to practice in 1890, J.A. Clement maintained a law office on the courthouse square in Camden, where he remained until 1903. Even before the Civil War, Clement men had begun to appear among the officialdom of Benton County, and, true to a growing family tradition, James A. Clement went to the state Senate for the term 1897 to 1899, representing Benton, Decatur, Hardin, and Humphreys counties.

In Nashville, Senator Clement, his first wife now dead, encountered a young widow, who excited his interest. Born Agnes Anne Work on January 17, 1866, she had married "Dock" Shipp of Hickman County. She was a Dickson County girl, the daughter of R.J. Work and his wife, Malissa (or Melissa) T. (Bingham). R.J. Work was a proper great-grandfather for a political figure. His gravestone in the old Union cemetery near the center of Dickson records him as a Mason, and a Confederate soldier. He became a member of the county court and General Assembly. He had served in the 11th Tennessee Infantry, advancing to third lieutenant, and had been wounded at Murfreesboro. "Look," he would say to his grandson, Robert S. Clement, showing his leg wound, "look at what those damned Yankees did — shot me through the leg there, but, by God, they didn't get me, though." Born in August 1841, the old man, having survived the Civil War, the military occupation of Tennessee, and the trials of reconstruction, lived on until August 9, 1920, long enough by two months to overlap the life of his great-grandson. His wife, Malissa, born on February 25, 1842, lived until January 3, 1926.

"Dock" and Agnes Anne Shipp had only one child, born in 1894, shortly after the death of her father. This daughter was "Auntie Dockie" to Frank Clement and his two sisters. She was their teacher in public speaking, and so a major figure in Frank Clement's career as a public

Camden, courthouse square, west side. Clement spoke from the four-story building, July 5, 1952. Next door, the old bank, dating from 1889, housing law office of J.A. Clement. Photograph courtesy Jonathan K.N. Smith.

speaker and a politician. In maturity, Dockie became the wife of Joe B. Weems, who became a county judge of Dickson County.

Neither of the marriages of Agnes Anne Shipp—first to Dock Shipp and, after his death, to James A. Clement—kept her from an active public career in the communities where she lived. Like most of her contemporaries, she had little formal education, but she learned enough to become a school teacher, and eventually she was elected to the post of county superintendent of schools in Dickson County. Possibly she was the first woman in the state to be chosen by the voters as a superintendent of schools; in any case, she was unusual enough to attract attention. She held the office from 1895 to 1897 at a salary of $25.00 a month, tending to her duties by riding horseback from one school to another.

Some strategy went into the courtship of Mrs. Shipp. The young widow was a candidate for a post within the gift of the legislature. A few remember it to have been a job as state librarian; others recall it as state superintendent of schools. The documents are silent on the subject. But, in any case, J.A. Clement had a vote in the matter and a vote in her favor would have taken her to Nashville, away from his attentions. Quietly he voted for someone else, an action he kept to himself, at least until, after her defeat, she left Nashville and he married her. What she may have said when she learned all this no one now remembers.

James A. Clement and the widow Shipp were married in December 1899, a union that lasted until February 6, 1913, when Agnes Shipp Clement died at age forty-seven. Agnes Clement bore four children to her second husband. The oldest, Robert Samuel Clement, the governor's father, was born November 6, 1900. The others were Jesse Archie, Malcolm, and Ida. Jesse Archie, a lawyer, and Malcolm, a druggist, died in the 1950s. Ida became Mrs. Carl Nicks and spent much of her life in the state service.

The political interests of Agnes Clement were stimulated by her growing family. When her oldest son, Robert, was still a boy, she made up her mind that he should serve as a page in the state Senate. In those days, the Senate was served by two pages, both elected by the Senate, and both paid four dollars a day, the same pay that was prescribed for members of the legislature by the 1870 constitution. James Clement was a lawyer for the railroads, which had the useful habit of retaining a large number of country lawyers and politicians on a regular basis, and he and his family traveled on passes. It was easy for Mrs. Clement to take her eldest to see influential politicians, and the boy and his ambitious mother traveled to Memphis to see Senator Hubert Fisher and to Nash-

(*Top*) Agnes Work. Photograph courtesy Robert S. Clement. (*Bottom left*) James A. Clement, Senator, 1913, 1915. Photograph courtesy Lt.-Gov. John Wilder. (*Bottom right*) Robert S. Clement, Senate page, 1913–1916. Photograph courtesy Lt.-Gov. John Wilder.

ville to capture the aid of Senator Hill McAlister. These men helped young Robert Clement to a post as page of the Senate, where he served in the sessions of 1913, 1915, and 1916. Each legislative day he took an early morning train ride from Dickson to Nashville, returning that night. In 1913 Governor Ben Hooper, a Republican of Newport was beginning his second term; the Democratic party was torn in two by their disputes over the liquor question, and Robert Clement remembered in his latter days that as page, he had the reputation of being the only Democratic candidate who got 100 percent of the votes. Legislative errand-running was an informative and entertaining experience for a teenage boy and helped to lay the foundations for a lifelong canny understanding of Tennessee politics. The boy's father was again in the state Senate, this time from a district that included Dickson. He had moved with his new wife and the second family from Camden to Dickson in 1903. His second stint in the General Assembly lasted from 1913 to 1917.

While the Buchanans and the Clements were establishing themselves along the Big Sandy in Benton and Henry counties, another family, the Goads, were moving into the farmlands along Goose Creek in the hills of Macon County on the Highland Rim between what are now the towns of Lafayette and Hartsville. The Goad family, of Scottish origin, had come from Virginia. Their neighbors, Taylors, Burrows, Roarks, and Wrights, were English and Scottish; graves marked with these names can be seen in the old burial grounds of the area.

When they first moved into Macon County the Goads, like most of their pioneer neighbors, sought their living from the farms they cleared in the forests, but later generations left that hard occupation for the law. Will C. Goad (who was to become Will C., Sr.), after having spent some time as an employee of country newspapers in Hartsville and Westmoreland, was introduced to the law by an uncle who carried the intriguing name of Idle Roark. Roark had practiced law in Lafayette, for a period dating back to the years before the Civil War. His nephew passed his bar examination at Lafayette in 1889 when he was twenty-one. In 1891, Will Goad, attracted by the construction of the Louisville and Nashville Railroad from Gallatin, Tennessee, to Scottsville, Kentucky, moved to Scottsville in Allen County just north of the Tennessee-Kentucky line. There his descendants still live. The family disappeared from Macon County, Tennessee, but the lawyers in the Goad family still practiced in the Tennessee courts, a circumstance that Frank Clement could use effectively in opening his campaigns in Middle Tennessee. The Goads, like the Clements further west, were Democrats in areas strongly

Democratic, although Macon County at times deserted the Democrats in presidential elections. Macon County was no more a plantation county than was Benton. When the Goads moved north to Allen County, Kentucky, they moved into a similar economy, a region of small towns and small farmers, overwhelmingly white. Things were not too much different in 1920, when Frank Clement was born, but change was in the air.

Belle S. Goad, the wife of Will Goad, Sr., was made a widow on July 28, 1915, when her husband died of a sudden heart attack while he was pleading a case in Lafayette. She was left with five children. Her struggles to feed and shelter her family were aided by a decided flair for business. She acquired real estate. One of her business ventures took her to Dickson, Tennessee, accompanied by her daughter Maybelle. There she operated a commercial hotel, the Halbrook, a two-story brick building with rows of rooms along two sides of its central corridor, beside the much-used tracks of the N.,C., and St.L. Railway (the Nashville, Chattanooga, and St. Louis). The hotel probably catered principally to commercial travelers, but it also provided shelter and food for Mrs. Goad and her family.

Robert Clement, then nineteen, came to join this family when he and Maybelle eloped on August 20, 1919. His bride (born March 27, 1895) was almost six years older than he. The couple's resources were meager and their opportunities restricted; they moved into a back bedroom of the first floor, some distance behind the public reception room, and there Frank Goad Clement, their first child, was born on June 2, 1920.

Dickson, in the 1920s, was a typical small Middle Tennessee town. Although then—and now—it was the largest town in Dickson County, the county seat was the old village of Charlotte, seven miles away, its one-time importance underlined by the name of one of Nashville's principal streets, Charlotte Pike. The county is one of the older units of Tennessee, but by 1920 it had lost some of its original territory to the formation of other counties. The present Dickson County lies on the edge of the Highland Rim to the west of Nashville. In 1920, it numbered over 19,000 people, a figure already down from the 1910 showing. The town of Dickson contained 2,200 persons; it had grown in the past decade. Over 87 percent of the county's people were white, mostly native Americans. The foreign-born numbered no more than three-tenths of 1 percent of the total, a figure that included 2 Irish, 5 Italians, 3 Scots, 1 Russian, 1 Dane, 1 Greek, and 1 Czech. There was no problem of

Americanization, no ethnic politics, and, for the moment, no racial tension. Black Americans were small in number, even less as a proportion of the total population than they were ten years earlier.

The town's economy and its two banks (assets for one, slightly over one million; for the other, $630,000) were focussed on a rural surrounding. Advertisements in the weekly *Herald* featured the new model Dodge, Maxwell cars, Wintersmith's Chill Tonic, Hunt's Lightning Oil for Rheumatism, wood-burning stoves, and a real estate venture at the nearby resort of Bon Aqua.

Movies (still silent) were a principal means of entertainment, and one of the chief items in the weekly newspaper was the fare at the single movie-house, the Patriot (America's first world war had only lately ended). On the day of Clement's birth the movie was *Dawn,* with J. Stewart Blockton, actor and script long since forgotten. But during that month of June, some more enduring figures dominated the screen, including Mary and Jack Pickford, Anita Stewart, and Constance Talmadge. The dramas of 1920 offered such titles as *Human Desires, Heart of the Hills,* and *The Double Squeeze* (a serial thriller). Aside from the pantomime thrown silently on the screen, entertainment was offered during these early June days at Tolbert's Big Tent Theatre, with a performance of a drama daringly entitled *Wife in Name Only.* Admission to this intrigue could be had for 25 to 35 cents. Radio was beginning; television, which was to have its effect on Clement's political future, was still years away.

The Clement infant must have had an early introduction to human bustle and commotion. The hotel, just across the tracks from the depot, and just off the main business street, would have been busy. On the day of his birth, eight passenger trains arrived in Dickson, not counting four trains on the branch that ran to Centerville. The era of the automobile that was to become so important in the political career of Clement was just dawning, but sales were picking up. In 1916, cars had been open to the weather; ten years later new models were taking passengers out of the rain and cold.

Outside the protecting walls of the back bedroom in the Halbrook Hotel, the wide, wide world was in its usual trouble. The United States had begun to suffer the aftermath of the first war to save democracy. In 1919, the United States attorney general, A. Mitchell Palmer, had been pursuing Reds and suspected Reds, and the *Dickson County Herald* carried an advertisement in June 1920: "Mitchell Palmer for President." But by then, the leading newspapers were growing weary of Palmer and his activities. In the middle of January 1920, prohibition became effective — legally — across the country. In March, the United States Senate killed the Versailles Peace Treaty, as far as this country was concerned. The country's decisive repudiation of Woodrow Wilson was in train, even though he was to leave a mass of legislation that would foretell the New Deal of Clement's boyhood.

Tensions that would continue into Clement's political career were already abroad. Negroes and whites fought on the Chicago beaches in 1919, the Boston police strike had started Coolidge on the road that led him to the White House, and Eugene V. Debs was convict 9653 in the federal prison in Atlanta — landed there by a guilty verdict on a charge of violating the Espionage Act of 1917. (Harding freed him in 1921, without restoring his civil rights.)

Life was not easy for the young Clement family in the 1920s, and when the frenetic prosperity of the twenties was followed by the Great Depression, times grew hard indeed. Life at the Dickson hotel was exchanged, when Clement was still small, for a short period in Vermont and thereafter residence in Kentucky. Belle Goad, her daughter and son-in-law, and her small grandson all returned to Scottsville, where the family lived for some time. Clement's two sisters, first Anna Belle and then Emma Gene, were born in Kentucky, Anna Belle on May 6, 1923 and Gene on March 16, 1925. Robert Clement had obtained a job as bookkeeper with the Kentucky Rock Asphalt Company of Kyrock, Kentucky, near Scottsville. The company and its products played a role in the downfall of Rogers Caldwell and Governor Horton in the frenzied financial developments of the late 1920s. During part of the time when Robert Clement worked at Kyrock, not only as bookkeeper, but as manager of the company commissary and assistant postmaster, the family lived at Scottsville where the small boy was much in the company of his grandmother. In Scottsville, he entered grade school and made the close acquaintance of his cousin, Frank Goad. He was surrounded by other relatives in the Goad family, who remained close to him in later years — his uncle, Goebel Goad, named for the controversial Kentucky political figure, and an aunt, Emma Goad Johnson. He was a peaceful and quiet child, more quiet than might have been expected from his later personality, good looking with his black hair and blue eyes, but marked by an abnormally large head. In a grandmother's candid way, Belle Goad would say: "Well, either you'll make a mighty big man — you'll be governor—or President—or something, or you just won't have any sense at all." Perhaps the remarks, repeated at intervals, put ideas in the boy's head, but, if so, he kept them to himself.

His sisters were welcomed additions to his circle and he developed an affectionate and protective attitude toward them. It was a family that had to watch the pennies, but the children had no sense of serious deprivation. Although Maybelle Clement knew how to obtain her way in matters that were important to her, the father was clearly the household's head and made most of the decisions. On matters of religion, important to father and mother alike, a split was worked out. In Benton County, the Clements had been Methodists; Robert Clement clung to his family's denomination. But Maybelle Goad had been a Southern Baptist and, after marriage, remained so. When the children arrived, it was arranged that Robert Clement and his son would attend the church of the Methodists; Maybelle Clement and her daughters went to the Baptists.

When Jimmy Carter ran for the presidency in 1976, it seemed a surprise to newsmen that numbers of Christians subscribed to a doctrine of rebirth. In truth the idea is as venerable as the gospel. According to John, Jesus said to Nicodemus, a ruler of the Jews, "I say unto thee, Except a man be born again, he cannot see the kingdom of God." The ancient tradition of conversion and rebirth was believed and observed by both Methodists and Baptists, a rebirth marked by personal dedication and confirmed by a baptism. "Except a man be born of water and of the Spirit, he cannot enter into the kingdom of God. That which is born of the flesh is flesh; and that which is born of the Spirit is spirit." For Methodists in the years when Frank Clement was growing up, baptism followed as the result of a conviction reached by the individual. Often this conversion takes place in early adolescence and so it was with Frank Clement. When he was eight or nine years old, the boy indicated his wish to join the church that he had been attending at Kyrock, and he asked to be baptized—immersed—in the Green River. He could have achieved membership by sprinkling, but to his way of thinking more was needed. Robert Clement, although he had already been sprinkled— dry-cleaned, as he put it in later years—in a perceptive and touching union with his small son, walked with him into the water to be baptized a second time, this time by immersion, and the two were symbolically cleansed by Reverend H.C. Ogles in the Green River near the ferry at Brownsville, Kentucky.

The conversion and the baptism were not isolated events. Clement remained a religious boy and man, both privately and in public. The constitution puts church and state asunder, but politics have always reunited them. Clement was to undergo repeated attacks for "Bible-toting," but, encouraged by his family and particularly by his mother, he stuck to his beliefs and to their public expression. The Clement family, and the governor himself, frequently recalled the occasion when a young Sunday school teacher said that a man could not be a sincere Christian and a politician. The statement was made when Clement's grandfather happened to be present with his grandson, and the elder Clement immediately challenged the teacher, forcing him to retract the statement, at least in words if not in secret belief. The scene involved something of a family confrontation with the teacher, for grandfather, father, and grandson were all present. The occasion left a lasting imprint in the family's consciousness.

This small, if fundamental, contest occurred in Bowling Green, Kentucky where the family had migrated in 1929, following a period of ill health for the mother. Robert Clement purchased a home on Park Street. Frank Clement was then in the fourth grade, Anna Belle was starting the second. In the fall the stock market crashed and as the depression worsened, so did the fortunes of the young Clement family. The father found the payments on the house harder and harder to raise. The job at Kyrock disappeared, and money Robert Clement had invested in the Kentucky Rock Asphalt Company was lost. In the autumn of 1932 the Bowling Green home was given up, and the family returned to Scottsville and in 1933 briefly to Dickson. There Robert Clement's half-brother, W.A. Clement who operated the Clemore Drug Store, was in poor health, and Robert operated the store in his place for a time. He then possessed a 1931 Chevrolet but little else. The family rented a three-room apartment in Dickson. The drug store job disappeared. In the meantime the old Halbrook Hotel had suffered a decline and was about to be vacated. Robert Clement rented the entire structure, furnished, for $40.00 a month, and moved his family back to rooms 3, 5, and 7. Maybelle Clement reopened the hotel, rented rooms for 75 cents per night and sold meals for 25 cents, prices fairly standard for those deflated days.

During these hard times Robert Clement wandered downtown where a store was being sold, bid $95.50 for the contents of the store—a successful bid that did not disclose the fact that he then had no more than the $2.50 in his pocket—and promptly auctioned off the contents to the waiting crowd for about $300. By such desperate and ingenious stratagems, the family was sheltered and fed.

Frank Clement entered high school in Dickson in 1933. His grade school days had passed without special mark, except the nagging economic hardships, mitigated by family solidarity and courage. The boy was rather quiet, peaceful, little inclined to fights with other children, rarely punished, and strongly attached to his younger sisters. Certainly he had the potential for being a good student, except for poor mechanical aptitude, but if there were any signs of his later quick grasp of facts and his prodigious memory, they remain unremembered.

The freshman high school year at Dickson (and Lebanon) introduced him to algebra, English, civics, and Latin. His grades were unremarkable: B in algebra and English, and, ironically, B minus in civics.

In 1933, James A. Clement died and was buried in Dickson, in the old cemetery near the center of the present town, where many of his relatives found their graves. He had been interested in his grandson, although the Kentucky sojourn had kept them separated. Oddly, the elder Clement had never wanted his sons to practice law or to get involved with politics; somehow he must have found his own career unsatisfying. All the same, two of his children, Robert and Archie did become lawyers and did pursue political careers. Robert Clement determined to study law, after his father's death. He was now over thirty years old, with a wife and three minor children, leading an existence, like so many of his contemporaries, on the verge of want. But 1933 marked the advent of the Roosevelt years, and the new President attacked the depression with a variety of weapons. The economy began to look up. Fortunately for Robert Clement a law school was available that could offer opportunity to a man in his position.

At Cumberland University, a small school long established in Lebanon, Tennessee, a law degree could be acquired in one year. Tuition was low. Students, many of them destined to be significant political figures in Tennessee, attended classes in the morning, studied their cases in the afternoon, and managed by the year's crash program to prepare for the bar examination. It was a slight advance in the ancient system of reading in some law office—a limited education, certainly, but an opportunity for men situated as Robert Clement was. He moved to Lebanon in the fall of 1933; the family followed in January 1934, acquired a temporary home where Maybelle Clement took in boarders, the children went to school, and Frank peddled newspapers; and after the school year had passed, the family returned first to Scottsville and then to Dickson and the father started a law practice, aided by city employment.

Frank Clement's high school sophomore year was spent in Scottsville High; grades began to look up: a 99 in algebra, B's in English, A's in Latin. He did well enough in geography. High school marked the passing of the quiet, retiring child remembered in Scottsville and Bowling Green. In the final two high school years in Dickson County High School, after the return to Dickson from Scottsville, the future orator began to emerge. The diet in those two years included English, French, geometry, history, public speaking, and physics. Grades were normal and largely unspectacular, ranging from a low of 83 in French to 98 in public speaking. Clement took a year and a half of typing. His reports show an outside reading list that includes *The Heart of Washington, The Last of the Mohicans, Left End Edward, Hamlet,* and *Tom Sawyer.* There is no evidence that he read much beyond his requirements, but we know that his interest in public affairs picked up.

He did not participate very actively in high school athletics, although there is some record of football ambitions. But he watched the basketball matches, particularly one player, a blond and beautiful girl of Swedish blood, Lucille Christianson, who played for Erin High School. And he studied public speaking with Aunt Dockie.

It seems improbable that Clement would have become governor of Tennessee if it had not been for oratory; certainly he believed this himself, and publicly admitted as much. The development of this talent was the work of Dockie Shipp Weems, Robert Clement's half-sister, the single child of the first marriage of Agnes Work to "Dock" Shipp of Hickman County, where Dockie was born. Aunt Dockie was educated in Dickson County. She was graduated from the Dickson Normal School, one of the many small schools in the state devoted to the training of teachers. Dickson Normal had grown out of Edgewood Normal that started at Yellow Creek in 1885. Originally a private school, Dickson Normal reached an enrollment of 800 students after the 1891 move to Dickson. When public education was pushed by the legislation of 1909, the school declined, and it ceased existence in 1919. Dockie Shipp was listed as an honor student there in 1909. After her graduation from Normal, Dockie Shipp began to teach public speaking and followed this calling through the remainder of her life and her marriage to Joe Weems. In her later years she acquired a bachelor of oratory from the Vanderbilt School of Expression, and in 1944 she went to Peabody College as a graduate student, where she directed the Peabody Players.

Dockie Weems embodied a standard feature of the culture of the small American town in her day — the development of elocution, sometimes called "expression." Debating, extemporaneous speaking, oratory, humorous readings, dramatic readings, amateur acting — these constituted the fare that often plagued small fry who would rather have been on the baseball diamond, and incidentally served as an outlet for many a country town woman who wanted something more than home and church. In this movement, whose overtones can be sensed in Booth Tarkington's stories of Penrod, for those who never went through the experience on their own, Dockie Weems was a star. She made Dickson debate-conscious; she attracted statewide recognition and even was made the subject of stories in *Life* and *Time*. On the side she wrote plays. Her educational activity would have had an eye on political affairs, for her grandfather Work had been a member of the county court, her husband became county judge of Dickson, and, in due course, her son, Jimmy Weems, became county judge in his father's footsteps. She lived to watch her nephew deliver the keynote address to the Democratic National Convention of 1956.

Mrs. Weems was solidly in the stream of American cultural history. Oratory had been cultivated in America since colonial times and many of its great figures — the preachers, the statesmen, the lawyers — trained for oratorical careers and based their lives on their voices and their spoken words. Clement was to follow along trails set by Webster, Clay, Edward Everett, Calhoun, Charles Sumner, Bryan, and Woodrow Wilson. It was a tradition supported by universities and other statewide organizations. At the University of Georgia a tradition of debating societies was cherished since its earliest days, and two of the oldest buildings on the Athens campus still house the two leading debating fraternities. At the University of Tennessee in Knoxville, Ayres Hall, constructed in 1921, made provision for rooms and stages for the use of debate groups. A Tennessee Interscholastic Literary League was established in the late 1920s, with headquarters at the University at Knoxville. The league divided the state into districts for the conduct of competition in debate, original oratory, extempore speaking, and declamation, sometimes augmented by contests in humorous and dramatic readings.

Aunt Dockie and her pupils were in District III. There the Dickson contestants were always much in evidence, and they made their impact on the state contests held in Knoxville. Clement's training by his aunt was constant and intense during his years in Dickson high school. Before that he lived in Scottsville, Bowling Green, and Lebanon; in any case his voice would not have developed much before his junior year. But during the last two years in Dickson he practiced oratory and extempore speaking, working with his aunt in the early darkness of evenings, reading other speeches, particularly, so far as can be remembered now, the speeches of Bryan. Whether he read the speeches of the father of orators, Cicero, with the refrain, "How long, O Cataline", that has echoed down the centuries, no one now remembers, but the phrase appeared again in the famous words of the keynote speech of 1956: "How long, O Lord how long?"

Frank, or Frank Goad, as his Goad relatives often called him, specialized in extemporaneous speaking, cultivating a talent for the election to the governorship that he had already begun to think of, in private. In 1936 and 1937, he placed first in District III in extempore speech and thus competed in the state matches. In 1936 he failed to place in the state contest, but in 1937 he won second prize in the state, falling second to Stuart Maher of Knoxville. The contest held moments of astonishment for the judges. The extempore procedure gave each candidate a few moments alone with some source material dealing with the subject—the proposed child labor amendment—that came to them as a surprise. The candidates drew lots for their order of appearance. Maher came first and so was allowed to listen to the others. Young Clement came in one or two contestants later. His style was formal—in language and gesture —already somewhat traditional and old-fashioned from Maher's point of view, who cultivated a more modern, conversational manner. Clement opened with an introductory paragraph that moved smoothly. Two contestants later, another speaker—to the profound astonishment and disquietude of the judges—delivered exactly the same paragraph. What the judges did not immediately realize was that they had before them two boys endowed with photographic recall; both had remembered exactly—and independently—the opening paragraphs of a news story on their subject, just read in preparation for their extempore speeches. Other Dicksonians did well in the speech contests, both in 1936 and 1937; Jimmy Weems wangled a first in declamation in District III.

Public speaking absorbed Clement's complete attention during his high school days. He was not athletic. In later years, he liked to follow baseball games. As a politician he had to show interest in football, but he could have lived without it. His parents were musical; his mother played piano and organ, serving as organist for her Baptist churches in Scottsville and Dickson. Robert Clement had a gift for music; even in his middle seventies he possessed a pleasing and full baritone. But Clement seems to have had little interest in music, although he liked group singing. His tastes always ran to the simple fundamental harmonies and plaintive nostalgic melodies of gospel hymns and country music. Clement once said he took up public speaking when his father advised him to quit singing out loud. He commanded no instrument.

The drive to the governorship was awakened during those last months in high school. No doubt many a boy, particularly if raised in a political family, dreams of that office. For many of them this is no more than a fancy that passes with the waning of childhood; for most of the others the dream can never become reality. It was to be otherwise with Frank Clement. For the most part, he kept his own counsel on the matter; this, in itself, is an indication of the serious nature of his thinking. He did tell his sister, Anna Belle, to whom he was always strongly attached, of his thoughts on several occasions, and as early as his sixteenth year he must have offered his sweetheart, Lucille Christianson, his promise to make her the first lady of Tennessee, if she would have him for a husband. We do not know why, as a high school boy, he wanted the governorship. At times, in conversation with his family, he would indicate his wish to right wrongs at Nashville, but he could not have had, in his high school days, vivid ideas of conditions there. The ambition to reach the governorship was a personal drive, nurtured in a family active in Kentucky and Tennessee politics for several generations and helped by living in a time and place where political rivalries must have furnished a major object of attention and entertainment.

♪ *There is a time, we know not when,*
A point, we know not where,
That marks the destiny of men
To glory or despair.

JOSEPH ADDISON ALEXANDER, 1809–1860

2. There Is a Time
That Marks the Destiny of Men

EDUCATION AND EARLY CAREER

Frank Clement enrolled in Cumberland University at Lebanon, on September 14, 1937; he was seventeen. In campaign publicity, where he always accented youth, he liked to say that he finished high school when he was sixteen; it was true, ceremonially, but he reached his seventeenth birthday on June 2, shortly after acquiring the Dickson High School diploma. The national economy, under the impact of the New Deal, had begun to stir into activity again, and in the previous year's election Franklin Roosevelt had buried Alfred M. Landon of Kansas under an avalanche of approval for the Democrats. But the Clement family, still not thoroughly established, had suffered from bouts of ill health, and it was well understood—and accepted—in the household that the two girls would be allowed one year of college each but probably no more. The full preparation for a profession was to be provided for the only boy. That the boy's sisters could have benefited from college or university life was not questioned, but the money was not in sight.

It was a natural consequence of the family history that Frank Clement would look to the law for a profession; his political ambitions were already forming. It was natural, too, that he would enter Cumberland. His father and his uncle Archie had been there, and it was a school that bred politicians. Cumberland was a modest, even if old, institution, certainly not the best the state had to offer, but it was inexpensive, and it possessed traditions.

Cumberland was organized under Presbyterian auspices in 1842. At first a liberal arts college only, the Board of Trustees resolved in February 1845 to establish a chair of law, and Nathan Green was appointed profes-

23

sor of law and political economy. When he declined the appointment, Abram (or Abraham) Caruthers, then a judge of the circuit court, accepted the post but was unable at that time to assume his duties. Finally, in 1847, a Department of Law was set up, and in the years that followed many well-known lawyers of Tennessee, including Nathan Green and Abram Caruthers, served as teachers there. The liberal arts program continued, but it was the law curriculum that attracted attention. Cumberland has enjoyed a remarkable history of training the lawyers and politicians of Tennessee. Cordell Hull, from a neighboring county, was one of its famous graduates, as was James V. Allred, a governor of Texas. Joe Evins, later a powerful member of Congress, is an alumnus. The law faculty included persons subsequently prominent in political and judicial service. Albert Williams, who served three governors of Tennessee as a cabinet member, had been a professor of law there during the period of Robert Clement's attendance in the law school, although he had left by the time Frank Clement enrolled as a freshman in the college. A.B. Neil, later chief justice of the Supreme Court of Tennessee and presiding judge in the sensational trial of Raulston Schoolfield on impeachment in Clement's second term, was on the law faculty when Clement entered school.

Dickson County boys had often gone to Cumberland. Altogether, five Dickson boys were in the freshman class of 1937, when Frank Clement and his cousin, Jimmy Weems, entered the college. Weems remained two years at Cumberland, moved then to Vanderbilt and eventually the University of Virginia law school.

The 1937 roster is rich with later political associations. Dortch Oldham, from the nearby town of Hartsville, in the neighborhood of the old home of the Goad family, was a sophomore in 1937. In later years he would be a Republican candidate for the governorship and state chairman of the Republican party in Tennessee during the crisis year of 1976. Ramon Davis of Lebanon was a freshman; in the not too distant future he would be a Clement cabinet official. Moreau P. Estes, later a Nashville real estate dealer and a minor political figure during the years of Clement power, was studying law. James Bomar, future speaker of the Tennessee House of Representatives and later of the Senate and one of Tennessee's most successful lawyers, was a student (and a member of the cast in a college performance of *Charlie's Aunt*). The school was small enough so that Clement, by this time noted for his open friendliness, could have known most of his young colleagues. The associations formed there were significant for him.

We have no record of youthful commitments to politics by Clement or his contemporaries, but the atmosphere of the school was congenial to political concerns. Politicians appeared there as speakers from time to time (Gordon Browning spoke there during Clement's student days), in a period when the University of Tennessee at Knoxville, led by the ultra-cautious James Dickson Hoskins, discouraged the appearance of political speakers on campus. Public figures were invited to speak at Cumberland commencements; at UT, President Hoskins himself monopolized the platform. Cumberland felt easy with Democratic politicos; UT, a struggling institution in the Republican end of a Democratic state, was jittery.

When Clement entered Cumberland, the president of the institution was Ernest L. Stockton. His son, Ernest, Jr., who was to succeed his father as president, was a student. Although the institution sported the name of "university," it was in reality a small college, with a faculty of twenty-two teachers. They guided studies in chemistry, philosophy and religion, psychology, law, mathematics, English and journalism, political and social science, commerce, ancient language, and history. Piano, French, Spanish, and German were taught. Courses in biology helped to round out the sciences. It was fairly standard fare for the time, primarily cultural, with small obeisances to the vocational. The faculty held baccalaureate and masters' degrees; doctors of philosophy were rare.

Of necessity, the curriculum was narrow and firmly set. Few electives could be afforded. Clement was to remain in the arts college for two years, where the bachelor of arts curriculum included in the freshman year, English, foreign language, mathematics, and social science. Sophomores were offered religion, English, foreign language, and social science, and, in that second year, natural science replaced the freshman course in mathematics. A slight variation of Latin, economics, and philosophy was available for pre-law students. Within some of the field requirements, a limited choice of electives was offered. Courses in political science in 1937–38 included American national government, European governments, international government, political parties, and state and local government. In a small college, the teacher occupies not so much a chair, as a bench, on which he must slide from one course to another.

Tuition of $57.50 each semester was modest even by 1937 standards. A double room, with board, in the men's dormitory could be secured for $90.00 each semester; students furnished their own linens and electric light bulbs. They paid their own electricity bills. (It might be remembered that as yet, there was no national Fair Labor Standards Act; even after it came into existence in 1938 the minimum wage was not to rise above 45 cents an hour until the entrance of the United States into the Second World War.)

Like most colleges of its time, Cumberland had been founded as a religiously oriented school, and this persuasion remained. Three mornings a week the students gathered in the chapel. By contrast, at the University of Tennessee, chapel, once compulsory, had been abandoned, although an annual religious week was still observed. At Cumberland a similar religious emphasis week was celebrated each year by the students.

During the two years that Clement spent at Cumberland, he followed the prescribed liberal arts curriculum, with the addition of public speaking. His grades were average—no especial disaster, no particular brilliance. One D was chalked up in chemistry, and one C. His one encounter with mathematics produced a D, which, had it been known, should have been good for a few sympathetic votes. Some overly cautious or misguided teacher gave him a B+ in the first semester of public speaking, but sophomore public speaking produced an unequivocal A throughout the year. (For some curious reason, the record shows no grade for the second semester of freshman public speaking.) In the remaining courses, Clement achieved predominantly B's and B+'s, with one C+ in history, and one A− in Bible. Considering the youth's possession of the photographic memory that was a part of his Goad inheritance, one must assume that his studies were pursued with typical student moderation. Some of his time was spent on the long trip to Erin to see Lucille Christianson. Some of it was spent in social life and other college activities, although he left comparatively little trace in the college yearbook. He joined Sigma Alpha Epsilon. He was in the YMCA, where the other future politician, Dortch Oldham, was also a member. He, and his cousin Weems, were in the Public Speaking Club and on the debate team. His name is not listed among those in the international relations club or in the American government club.

The debate team, coached by Ralph T. Donnell, a teacher of mathematics, was a member of the Tennessee Forensic League; the league sponsored debate for both men and women, after-dinner speaking, oratory, declamation, and humorous reading—all a continuation of the regimen guided by Aunt Dockie. Curiously, neither Clement nor his cousin held an office in the Public Speaking Club, although Weems became president of the freshman class, and Clement was a member of the student council. But for the most part, whatever campus politics occupied young Clement's attention left no trace. Professor Donnell generally managed to avoid placing Frank Clement in direct competition

(*Top left*) Frank Clement, freshman, Cumberland University. (*Top right*) Jimmy Weems, freshman, Cumberland University. (*Bottom left*) Robert S. Clement as law graduate, Cumberland University. (*Bottom right*) James Bomar, senior, Cumberland University. Photographs courtesy Mr. Lillard Barrett, Seat's Studio, Lebanon, Tennessee.

with his cousin, but on the one occasion when the two met in contest, Weems lost to his cousin. But Weems was, in general, a brilliant student.

The *Phoenix,* the college yearbook for 1937–38, includes small photographs of Clement and his cousin. Family resemblance between the two boys is detectable; although, on the whole, Clement took his features from the Goads, his image can be seen in the youthful face of the grandmother the two boys shared. Young Weems was never as strikingly handsome as his cousin. At seventeen, Clement showed the penetrating blue-eyed gaze, the glossy black hair, straight long nose, high forehead, and generous mouth that, with his six feet of height, made him a notable physical figure throughout his life.

On September 10, 1939, the college registrar forwarded a copy of the two-year transcript to Vanderbilt University, where Clement, now nineteen years old and in his characteristic hurry to get on with the business of living, was about to enter law school.

Fifteen days later, Clement entered the law school (at the time the second great world war began in Europe), on the basis of 33 and ½ yearly hours of academic credit. No entrance examinations were required for entrance into Vanderbilt in those days, and, very probably, competition for admission to law school was less competitive than the sharp scramble of the 1970s. Nonetheless, Vanderbilt was a prestigious school, and Clement was taking a step higher on the ladder than his father or grandfather had been able to manage. The law faculty of that period consisted of six professors and one assistant professor. Classes were small and students were intimately acquainted with one another. One of Clement's particular friends there was Dave Alexander; he was to share closely in Clement's experiences, to become his personal attorney, and was probably the last person to speak to him shortly before his tragic death. Of the sixteen students, two of them women, who made up the graduating class when Clement was awarded his degree, only six were Tennesseans. Of the sixteen graduates, only ten had finished baccalaureate degrees. These neophyte attorneys had varying backgrounds. Six had attended Vanderbilt as undergraduates, two had come south from the University of Cincinnati, and the remainder had come from Ohio State, William and Mary, Howard (in Georgia), Davidson, Murray State, Sweetbriar, and the University of Arizona—altogether a small but somewhat cosmopolitan group. No Negroes were admitted to Vanderbilt in those days.

Vanderbilt's law school had the same vocational bent that most such schools had (and have) and the curriculum was the usual cut-and-dried preparation for practice. In the first year Clement and his colleagues concentrated on personal property, contracts, real property, torts, and criminal law, with some constitutional law and common law procedure — the same grind familiar to every law school freshman. Clement's scores in that first year were a mixture of C's and B's (the latter clearly predominating). Then, and now, a B record in law college, particularly in the first year, represents a thoroughly respectable achievement of professional quality; A's are bestowed grudgingly by law professors. In his second year, Clement turned in one C, in real property, a course of recognized complexity; all else was B: evidence, municipal corporations, federal jurisdiction, equity, and the rest. In his final year, Clement again produced B's, except for a C in business associations, and two A's, in appellate practice court and insurance. A good record — not spectacular, and not the top.

Still in a hurry, he and Lucille eloped to be married at Hopkinsville, Kentucky, on January 6, 1940, and he took and passed the bar examination, both before graduating from law school. In Hopkinsville, the bride and groom gave their ages as twenty-one; they were, in fact, nineteen.

Young Clement first set eyes on Lucille Christianson during a basketball tournament in Waverly, Tennessee, three years earlier. Lucille was playing for Erin High School. She was the "girl with the flaxen hair," a brown-eyed beauty with the fair complexion traditionally associated with Swedish women, and the trim, coordinated grace of the born sportswoman. Clement paid little attention to the game. His eyes were on the single player. Abruptly he turned to the boy who was with him. "There is the girl I am going to marry," he announced. After the game, as Lucille relaxed over a soft drink at the drugstore, Clement, pretending to be looking for her brother (quite unknown to him), began a conversation with her and shortly, the brother abandoned, got around to asking what she was doing that evening. Lucille had a date, but Clement was not to be put off. He showed up that evening at Lucille's Waverly residence — early — and talked her into breaking the date (the only time, she said, that she ever stood anyone up). Her future was determined.

Clement the boy was as aggressive in love as Clement the man was to be in politics. Pushing his luck relentlessly, he gradually hunted down all the pictures of his sweetheart that other young men had collected and talked them away from their owners. He urged his girl to marry him when they were sixteen, when they were seventeen, and when they were eighteen. (Clement once said that his first experience in public speaking came when he put his proposals to Lucille over a party-line telephone). Lucille, more circumspect and realistic then her young man, braked his impetuosity, but finally, when they were both nineteen, she decided that the hour had arrived. During his two years at Cumberland, Clement made frequent trips to Erin, driving a huge old Chrysler convertible that he had acquired for $50.00. When, on occasion, the gas ran out, Lucille's father came to the rescue, for there was no parental opposition to the persistent suitor. On the night when the couple finally decided to elope, the old car had broken down, and Clement appeared in Erin in a brand new car that a kind-hearted—and perhaps far-sighted— gas salesman had lent him. He cashed two checks, for five dollars each, and the two set out for Hopkinsville, to be married there by a Methodist minister. "Long ago, these lovers fled away."

Lucille Christianson was born in Erin and lived there—always in the same home—until her marriage. She had been educated in grade and high school in Erin, and, as she inherited a musical and artistic bent from her mother, she had studied violin briefly and later piano, and, in the fashion of those times, "expression" and tap-dancing. Her background and her youthful life were similar to her husband's, minus the economic tribulation that had plagued the Clement family. Her Christianson grandparents, Nelson Edwin and Ena Johanna Christianson, had migrated, by separate ways and unknown to each other, from Sweden to Kentucky and then to West Tennessee. Probably they had come from Lutheran families, but Erin could not support a Swedish Lutheran congregation, and somewhere along the line of their lives they had joined the Baptists. Lucille's father, Nelson Christianson, had been born in 1886 in Houston County and as an adult had engaged in the lumber business and in politics. Her mother was Mary Laverne Mitchum, married to Nelson Christianson in 1913. Nelson Christianson's interest in politics was strong. He was the mayor of Erin from 1938 to 1944 and he served two eight-year terms as county judge of Houston County. In the later years of his life he would be a local cog in the political organization of his son-in-law. Lucille, as a girl, was interested in her Swedish grandparents and made some attempt to learn their native language, but learning a foreign language in a small American town was never easy. Lucille's maternal grandfather was Albert Jackson Mitchum, born in 1860 in Carroll County, a descendant of Virginians and North Carolinians, as were so many of his contemporaries. He had been engaged in various business activities in Erin.

There was no opposition to young Clement as a suitor in the Christianson household, and the elopement was an act born of romantic impulse, not parental disapproval, although marriage at nineteen, with education incomplete, involved risk and certainly hardship. After a few days of secrecy, Lucille disclosed her marriage to her mother, who took her to Nashville to buy clothes and to help find a home. A job also had to be found, for Lucille went to work while her husband slugged away at law school; two and one-half years of residence in law college lay ahead of them.

Marriage for Lucille Clement began a period of sacrifice for the political career of her husband. She had graduated from high school and had taken a business course, but hopes for college were given up. Frank was not especially keen on subjecting himself to the competition of other young males that college would most certainly have involved.

Lucille, having lived all her life, with her two brothers, in one home in Erin, now became a partner in a household constantly on the move, both by reason of the couple's straightened circumstances and the restlessness of the world during their young life together. Lucille longed for a permanent home such as her husband's military and political career could not provide. The frequent moves were difficult for her.

Through the years she faithfully made public appearances that would support her husband's political ambitions, but it was not a life that appealed to her. She was wearied by the constant speech-making, the public appearances at occasions that meant little to her, the long barnstorming trips to win and hold the voters' affections, the problems of rearing her sons amid the turmoil of political life. It was an experience that other wives of politicians went through, and many, like Lucille, found the constant round of public affairs a wearisome and profitless undertaking.

After the marriage was disclosed, Clement's close friend and fellow student, Dave Alexander, was made chairman of a law students' committee to buy a present for the Clements. He set up a beer bust one afternoon and used the occasion to assess each student one dollar to finance the gift—and he made Clement contribute like the rest. Alexander remembers the work and the "moonlighting" to keep young couples alive. "Most of us," he recalls, "were riding our wives' coattails through law school. My wife was working, Frank's wife was working—most of them were. In addition to that, I picked up laundry and worked in a filling station. What Frank did, I don't remember. I seems to me he worked in the library some at law school. . . . Frank lived on Terrace Place," his memory says. "You know we lived in boarding houses. I lived on Terrace Place, and, I think, next door to Frank. We used to study together. We were staying at a fine house, my wife and I, and the monthly room and board for the two of us, two fine meals a day, full breakfast, full dinner at night, room and board for the two of us for a big corner, sunny room in this boarding house, was $40 apiece, no—$40 for the two of us, $20 apiece."

The young Clement couple rented a bedroom, with a small pantrylike kitchen, and shared the bathroom with some ten other people. The accommodations were limited, but Frank, at least, was confident that they were on the way to the executive mansion. Whether his wife always believed as deeply as he in his destiny is uncertain, but, if she had doubts, they did not deter her husband. He knew where they were going. Lucille worked at various stenographic jobs, including a period of work for the Tennessee General Assembly. She was paid $7.00 a day, seven days a week, a pay scale larger by $3.00 a day than the legislators themselves were paid. To a generation used to prices in the 1970s this sounds impossible, but then groceries for a childless couple could be found for $20.00 a month in those days. The two Clements collected their groceries and brought them home on the streetcars; at times the sacks broke and discharged their comestibles on the floor, sometimes to the young husband's acute discomfort. There was little money for entertainment; the Clements managed to afford the Vanderbilt home football games, and that was all. But the governor's mansion was less than fifteen years in the future.

Clement passed the bar examination when he was a junior at Vanderbilt and was thus able to take any cases that came his way in his senior year. In these days that seems remarkable, and of course it was, but it was by no means unheard of. Others did the same from time to time.

Clement's photographic memory and his quick grasp of the essentials of any problem would have stood him in good stead for the ordeal of the bar tests. The law was a means to an end for Clement—a basic economic foundation for his real goal, politics. He was not interested in becoming a profound student of the law. But he remembered what he read. "It used to make me mad as hell," said Alexander, "because he could read a complicated case that we knew the professor was going to ask on the examination and that damned rascal could practically quote it verbatim."

A rumor got around that Clement made the highest grade in the bar examination when he took it, and some have built this rumor into an assertion that he made the highest grade ever made in a Tennessee bar examination. It could have been true; probably it was not. The origins of the story go back, apparently, to a telephone call from Robert Clement to a member of the examining committee, inquiring anxiously about the younger man's fate with the examiners. He was told that the junior law student had passed, indeed that he had made the highest grade. But bar examinations and their results are surrounded by a tight secrecy. Apparently, numerical scores are given, but all that is publicly announced is pass or failure, and no one is allowed to examine the scores. And, even considering Clement's quick intelligence, it does not seem that he could have achieved the highest score, given a record in law college that was respectable but not spectacular. One must relegate the story to legend, useful in campaigns but entirely inessential to a career that was to offer other more congenial achievements.

In the first semester of Clement's final year in Vanderbilt, the destinies of young and old Americans were drastically altered by the sneak attack of the desperate Japanese on Pearl Harbor. It was now evident that most young American men would be called to war; but Clement was married and a student, and deferment was possible for a time. Fresh from his graduation in 1942, Clement entered training as an FBI agent, which also would have involved a temporary postponement of military service. In reply to an inquiry from a friend on the progress of the new FBI recruits, the officer in charge of Clement and his class of trainees, stated: "Fine, but I have one crazy young fellow who thinks he is going to be governor of Tennessee." Anna Belle, in the meantime, after one year of college, had gone to work for the Capitol Chevrolet Company in Nashville. Her employers had given her a serious talk about staying on the job; too much had been lost, they said, by training young women who then left for better jobs. Anna Belle promised to stay, but she said she would have to leave when the time came for her brother to run for governor; he would need her help. This seemed no threat to her bosses; they laughed and promised to help in the election campaign. (They did.) It is clear that Clement's goal was now firmly established in his mind and that he was beginning to talk about it.

Clement spent three months in the FBI Training School at Quantico, Virginia, in 1942. From July 1942 until November 1943, Clement was an FBI agent, assigned to the investigation of espionage, sabotage, problems of internal security, selective service investigations, and general criminal investigations. These were standard FBI duties. Clement remained interested in internal security against the threat of Communist subversion and was to make speeches on the subject in the future, but he was never a rabble-rouser in the traditon of extreme rightwingers.

There is no absolutely clear road to political preferment in American political life, but the tradition of military service has always been strong.

In Tennessee, a political base has long been available in a combination of military service, the American Legion, the Young Democrats Clubs, and charitable drives of every sort. Clement was to use them all. Military service came to him unsolicited. He left law school as his country faced its greatest military challenge. Inevitably he would be drawn into the service.

Clement was taken into the military when he was twenty-three. His military records describe him, at the time of his entrance, as blue-eyed, with black hair and ruddy complexion, six feet tall. By the time of his separation in 1946 the army noted his weight at 162 pounds. It is evident that he was in first-rate physical condition. He was inducted November 12, 1943, at Fort Oglethorpe, Georgia, as a private. In July 1944, he was promoted to corporal. In November 1943 after induction, he was placed in the Military Police School at Fort Custer, Michigan, a post for which his short FBI experience had given him background. He remained in basic training at that post until November 11, 1944. He was discharged, in the words of his military records, "at the convenience of the government," on November 11, 1944, to enable him to accept a post as second lieutenant with the Military Police Battalion at Fort Sam Houston, Texas. From January 1945 to the end of that year, as the war was winding down, he was with the Military Police Battalion at Camp Bullis, Texas. He had been promoted to first lieutenant, effective June 4, 1945. Between that date and his relief from duty on March 28, 1946, he had been promoted to commanding officer of Company C of the Military Police Battalion at Camp Bullis. He was released officially from active service at the Separation Center at Fort Sam Houston. In addition to his rank as first lieutenant, it was noted that he was a rifle expert (the highest rank for measuring command of a weapon), submachine gun expert, and carbine sharpshooter (the next to highest rank). But, in all this time, he never saw overseas service and never fought in a battle. Lucille went with him to many of his assignments and accepted willingly, as did other wives, the makeshift arrangements for living that were available.

Clement's involvement with the military was a useful feature in his political life, but the absence of combat was a potential embarrassment, inevitably attracting the attention of Gordon Browning, who was never at loss for a bitter witticism. (Clement repeated his World War II experiences in the Korean engagement.) Browning had been an authentic war hero, participating overseas in both world wars. In the 1952 campaign, Joe Hatcher, the persistent gadfly of Clement in the columns of the *Nashville Tennessean,* called the attention of his readers to the nature of Clement's military experience and chronicled a reading by his friend of those days, "Honest Eddie" Friar, of statements of defenders of Clement's military record. The Hamilton County Veterans for Browning attacked Clement's war history. But Clement's lack of a battle record never appeared to do much for his opponents. Such are the uncertainties of politics.

The war had come to an end and all over the country young GI's were returning, many of them to claim immediate recognition in politics. In McMinn County, Tennessee, young veterans from all over East Tennessee, using weapons surreptitiously "liberated" from defeated Germans, converged on Athens, Tennessee, on election night in August 1946 and drove the local Cantrell machine out of office, backing up local ballots with their bullets. Two years later it would be the time for ousting the machine of Burch Biggs in neighboring Polk County. In Anderson County, twenty-six-year-old Buford Lewallen, returning from the war, determined not only to go to the state House of Representatives, but to become its speaker (which he did), an achievement unusual both for his age and his East Tennessee location, but one aided by the support of Ed Crump and his Shelby County machine. Frank Clement was only six years away from the governorship; his determination to grasp that prize was no secret from family and friends. Further employment in the FBI would not serve. His base in Tennessee had now to be established and a living had to be made. He returned to Dickson early in 1946 to start a law practice.

But private law practice was never to content Clement. In October 1946, a few months after returning to Dickson, Clement was named general counsel for the Railroad and Public Utilities Commission (later renamed the Public Service Commission), a prestigious and politically significant appointment for a twenty-six-year-old beginner. During the 1952 campaign, the *Nashville Tennessean* was to claim that Clement's appointment had been made with the consent and influence of the *Tennessean*'s principal target, Ed Crump, the "Red Snapper" of Memphis. Very possibly the charge was true, for Crump was still a power in Shelby County and the state. The governor at that time was Jim Nance McCord and his predecessor had been Prentice Cooper; both men were acceptable to Crump. The commission is elected by popular vote and is not, necessarily, dominated by the governor, but at this date official opposition to Crump, outside the columns of the *Tennessean,* was muted.

It is certain that Clement was recommended for the post by Herbert Walters of Morristown. Walters was already launched on the career that was to make him a major power in the Democratic party of Tennessee, a power that he retained until his death. Walters was a building and road contractor in Hamblen County, who rose to local political influence and on that foundation became an increasingly significant figure, officially and unofficially, in statewide Democratic affairs. He was clearly tied to the conservative elements in the party—to McKellar, Prentice Cooper, Tom Stewart, Jim McCord—but he received appeals for support from numerous elements of the party. He thought well of Clement as a young contender for future advancement, and Clement kept in close touch with him while he was counsel for the commission, and in the Korean War period a short time later when he clearly had his aim fixed on the governorship. Walters assisted Clement in the development of his early law practice, and Clement helped to get medical treatment for Walters' niece.

Walters was much attracted to Clement; he became his friend and devoted follower. Indeed, his attachment to Clement was strongly emotional, for Clement became a surrogate for the son that Walters never had. In this appointment and Walters' relation to it, present-day national commentators would see a pronounced conflict of interest, for Walters was interested in a company that marketed natural gas, and this concern would have been subject to the Railroad and Public Utilities Commission. But this kind of interest conflict has been widespread in Tennessee and elsewhere and to this day has never aroused much public criticism. Apparently none was forthcoming in 1946.

Clement was the youngest man to become chief counsel in the history of the commission. It was the only public office he ever held other than the governorship. In every way it was a significant step in his career. He was given some visibility. He was freed from the consuming anxieties of a beginning law practice; he had an assured and regular income. He was in a position to attract the attention of the state's political figures, particularly Governor McCord whose machine he was to build on later. He could gain experience in the law and in administration. Above all, he had time to make speeches and engage in other activities pertinent to his real goal. His work with the commission was successful enough that he was subsequently given legal assignments for similar commissions in Alabama and Georgia. He remained with the commission until 1950.

In the meantime he began the process of acquiring statewide recognition the chief weapon his growing reputation as a public speaker. He was given a leg up in this career by a new found friend whose office was just down the hall from his own. This was Andrew David Holt ("Andy" to everyone, high and low), a Milan, Tennessee, product, then serving on the staff of the increasingly powerful lobby, the Tennessee Education Association. Holt's homespun and inspirational speeches, longer on good humor than intellectual stress, were in heavy demand, particularly at high school commencement time, and Andy was more than glad to delegate some of this unrewarding effort to Clement. Clement, like Barkus, "was willin." The fees were small, and, in any case, Clement either would not take fees or would have them passed on to some church or charity. But the high school graduates were soon to vote, and their parents were present in large numbers. Moreover, Clement enjoyed speaking; it was "his thing." Both Clement and his close acquaintance, Andy parlayed their gifts of speech into significant careers.

Clement's personality and speaking style were already clearly established. He had outgrown completely the quiet, somewhat withdrawn character he had as a child. No longer did he acknowledge the existence of strangers. Even as a high school student he would stop to speak to people in the street, and his typical manner of sticking out his hand with the words "Frank Clement" were undoubtedly in full operation in his twenties. He was completely gregarious—the perfected politician to whom quick friendship with others had become his basic nature. Such an attribute—like his constant reference to religious themes—invite the suspicion of the sceptic, but there can be little doubt that both phases of his outgoing nature were quite genuine. Years later, when in 1955 Clement visited the operations of the University of Tennessee at the University of San Andres in La Paz, Bolivia, during a trip he made on behalf of the Cordell Hull Foundation, he charmed and fascinated his Latin hearers by the same gesture of extended hand and the "Frank Clement" that brought him votes in Tennessee.

Other steps of political importance could now be taken. In 1946, Clement was elected president of the Dickson County Young Democrats Club and later in the year he grasped the presidency of the Young Democrats Clubs of the state. The clubs have had an up and down history in Tennessee, but they furnish a convenient springboard for politically ambitious persons. Clement was helped to his statewide position by people who were to be influential in his career, especially by Joe Carr, Lipe Henslee, and Sam Coward. Joe Cordell Carr, often called "Mr. Democrat," came from a political family (his father had been a campaign manager for Cordell Hull) and was then well established in a career of state office-holding. He was to hold the national presidency of the Young

Young Democrats with Truman (second left, Joe C. Carr; President Truman; Frank Clement; others unidentified). Photograph courtesy Joe C. Carr.

Democrats. Lipe Henslee, a citizen of Dickson County, was a part of the federal revenue bureaucracy. Dr. Sam Coward was an experienced political figure of Overton County; he was to become a strong supporter of Frank Clement in his later years. These three now united to make Clement the president of the Young Democrats of Tennessee, and Sam Coward stepped out of the running in order to make the choice of Clement unanimous. The Young Democrat's group put Clement in contact with Joe Henry of Pulaski and with Charlie Lockett of Knoxville, both crucial figures in Clement's later life.

The presidency of the Young Democrats expanded Clement's scope as a public speaker, and, as he cast the spell of long practiced voice and gesture over increasingly interested audiences, it became clear to many informed listeners that a new star was rising. In 1948, Clement was one of the alternate delegates-at-large to the national Democratic convention that launched Harry Truman on a quest for the presidency that looked dubious until the last-minute surprise upset of Dewey in November. In 1948–49, Clement was state chairman for the March of Dimes, and in 1949, Red Cross chairman for the campaign among state employees, adding a connection with drives that gives exposure in the cause of charity. In 1949, he became state chairman of the Legislative Committee of the Junior Chamber of Commerce, an assignment that brought him into occasional contact with Gordon Browning, who, following the adoption of a state sales tax, had ousted Jim Nance McCord from the governorship, in spite of Crump. By this time, the experienced Browning must have recognized in the budding orator a potential threat to his own career. In that same year, the Junior Chamber of Commerce unanimously selected Clement for its Distinguished Service Award as the Outstanding Young Man from Tennessee. The award produced letters of congratulation from a number of political figures, including Andrew "Tip" Taylor, Congressman Percy Priest, and Robert "Fats" Everett, whose antennae for political probabilities were no doubt in a state of extreme sensitivity. The Dickson County Jaycees nominated Clement for inclusion among the nation's ten outstanding young men.

In 1949, Clement was elected state commander of the American Legion and thus added the third leg of the three-legged platform for future political activity: charity drives, the Young Democrats, and the Legion. He had already served as chairman of the Legion's committee on subversive activity and as a district commander. The Legion membership was widespread, and of course it contained a number of active politicians whose friendship was important to Clement. One could include in any list of such persons Donald McSween of Newport, who had been state commander for a term ending in 1948, Roane Waring, Jr., George T. Lewis of Memphis, and Cayce Pentecost, who was to become a member of the Railroad and Public Utilities Commission. All were to become political allies of Clement. Support for Clement as state commander had been building for some months, but Clement held off acceptance until he could get the backing of the Dickson County post. When this was forthcoming, his election was assured. The rules of the Legion restrict the political activity of the state commander, and during his term Clement scrupulously absented himself from formal party meetings, but the Legion post gave him still other platforms and wider audiences for his oratorical art and intensified his visibility as a political figure.

In 1950, Clement left the Railroad and Public Utilities Commission. Two sons had been added to the family; Robert N., on September 23, 1943, and Frank, Jr., on August 1, 1949. (Frank, Jr., had arrived just as Daddy was being elected state head of the legion.) By pooling their still meager resources—some desks, chairs, a small law library, and a few hundred dollars—father Robert S. Clement and Frank, Sr., formed a law partnership. Letters from early candidates for seats on the bandwagon commenced to reach Clement, asking him to announce for the governorship. Valerius Sanford was asked to join the firm, not as partner but as an active junior in the firm. Robert Clement was to continue headquarters in Dickson, but a Nashville office was established for Frank Clement and Sanford. Sanford had recently completed law school at Vanderbilt and had been with the firm of Waring, Walker, Cox, and Lewis in Memphis. Waring and Lewis had become friends with Clement. When Frank Clement was again called to active military duty, Sanford remained in Nashville reporting regularly to Clement from offices in the Stahlman Building on details of a general practice, largely civil, which included motor carriers suits and a religious dispute involving the right to her chair of Bishop Mattie Lou Jewell, the black true chief overseer of the House of God, which is the Church of the Living God, the Pillar and Ground of the Truth and Without Controversy, Incorporated.

Clement might have been tempted to make his first try for the governorship in 1950, but Korea intervened. He had remained in the reserves, and on call he reentered active service on September 17, 1950. He was again assigned to the military police, serving as instructor for policing, with his rank of first lieutenant. His wife and the two little boys went with him to his station at Augusta, Georgia. Clement remained on active duty until late December 1951, when he was released with a very high rating in which his personality, enthusiasm, and resourcefulness were mentioned in the most generous terms by his superior, Lieutenant-Colonel Virgil P. Foster, Jr. Again, he saw no foreign duty, no combat. Indeed, he was allowed off post from time to time for speeches back in Tennessee and elsewhere when the army found his talents useful. Val Sanford and Clement's sister, Anna Belle, kept political fires simmering at home, for, before he returned to the army, Clement had taken an unusual early step on the governorship. Overly eager friends had placed his name among the candidates for governor. He asked the state chairman of the Democratic party, Jack Norman, to withdraw his name, but he publicly declared himself a candidate for the election of 1952.

3. Precious Lord, Take My Hand

THE FIRST CAMPAIGN

When Clement announced in 1950 that he would be a candidate for governor in the spring and summer of 1952, he broke the behavior pattern normal for gubernatorial aspirants. Usually, such hopefuls would take a stance of coy caution until the early months of election year. Clement felt unable to do that. He had to go into the army again, and he needed to throw his hat into the ring before the military swallowed him up in an uncertain future that might leave little opportunity for politics. In truth, although he said confidently that he would be in the 1952 campaign, he could not know for sure that the Korean venture would by then be over. Some of his good friends held the private opinion that the war in the Far East would extend much beyond 1952. Others suspected that his political rivals had taken steps to see that he was taken out of the state at this time, although no proof of such moves was ever forthcoming.

The portraits of modern governors that grace the walls of the capitol building make the best of their subjects; few warts there. The painters unabashedly present stalwart figures, clothed in properly creased suits, showing frank, pleasant, and dignified countenances. In actuality the artists did not need to depart too far from the truth, for at least from Prentice Cooper onward they were a good-looking lot; Browning could not be thought exactly handsome (a fact that his own campaign literature reluctantly recognized), but his rugged face with its solid pugnacious jaw was certainly not in the least repulsive. All of these men could carry the governorship with appropriate dignity. But the striking physical beauty of Clement with his deep set blue eyes and brilliant coloring set him apart in a group of handsome contemporaries. This physical attractiveness was clearly at its zenith in the days when Clement entered

Cumberland University; then he had youth on his side, but although time coarsened his features and added weight, he always had the decided political advantage of a handsome, lively, mobile face, a long and robust body. He would never miss political office because, like Stephen Douglas, "the seat of his pants was too close to the ground."

The office that Clement was now to seek had been held by forty men before him, beginning with John Sevier, who started his first term in March 1796. The post they occupied was weak constitutionally, and often weak in actuality. Until 1953, the term was two years. Governors could succeed themselves for a total period of six years, and after being out of the office for a single term, could run again, although only a few succeeded in acquiring the office for a second run of one or more terms. Most of the men who became governor left the office to return to obscurity. Very few attained any national prominence. James K. Polk gained the presidency and became a leader in the forcible annexation of former Mexican territory, a representative of the expansionist sentiments of early Tennesseans. Andrew Johnson (whose occupation is listed in the *Tennessee Blue Book* as "Tailor, President of the United States") attained notoriety as the intelligent and crafty blocker of the harsh measures of Radical Republicans and as the only President ever impeached (or even close to it—until Richard Nixon). Sam Houston was a romantic figure, who suddenly quit the job to become a hero in the Republic of Texas. Robert Love Taylor is remembered as a populist governor, and William G. "Parson" Brownlow is recalled for his bitter personality and his corruption of democratic processes in his enmity for the Confederates. All of the men who occupied the post, from Sevier onward, were born Southerners, with the exceptions of Archibald Roane, Joseph McMinn, and William Carroll, representative of the Pennsylvania settlers who made their way down toward Tennessee through the long valleys and across the sharp forest-covered ridges that stretch from western Pennsylvania to northern Alabama. A few of them were Virginians, North Carolinians, or Kentuckians. The greatest number were native Tennesseans. Clement is highly representative of his predecessors. He was a native Tennessean, with ancestors rooted in Tennessee and Kentucky, whose own forebears migrated from Virginia.

Overwhelmingly, beginning with Sevier, the governors of Tennessee were Democrats. In the 1830s, forties, and fifties, four Whigs made it to the office, for the Whig party secured the support in those days of voters led by wealthy city dwellers and some of the substantial planters of the state. After the disasters of the Civil War, three governors bear the Whig label in the *Blue Book,* two Whig-Republicans, one Whig-Democrat. Under the impact of the war and racial controversy, the Whig Party disappeared. Republican national racial policies pushed most of Tennessee into the Democratic party, and henceforth the Republicans, their strength based on East Tennessee, could capture the governorship only when Democratic infighting reached the stage of an open split. Rarely did matters come to that pass. Victory in the Democratic primary of 1952 was an almost certain assurance of a runaway in the general election.

Tennessee politics has never been dominated by planter aristocrats; its leaders have been men of the people, for the most part. Most of them have been lawyers. Most of the governors have been in their forties and fifties when elected; a few reached the office in their thirties. The youngest of them all, "Lean Jimmy" Jones, beat Clement to the youth record by a few months. Clement emphasized his youth until the campaign for his third term, when he began to refer to himself, with considerable exaggeration, as "ole" Frank.

Tennessee has been, since the Civil War, a divided state, with one dominant party in each of the Grand Divisions into which the state is officially separated. Even now that official and unofficial separation exists, although mitigated somewhat by the growth of Democratic voting in East Tennessee and Republican voting in the suburbs of Shelby County. From the Civil War onward, East Tennessee has been a Republican fief (with a Democratic enclave in Sullivan County). Middle and West Tennessee have been Democratic property, with the exception of a few ridge counties along the western reaches of the Tennessee River, where poor soil blocked the growth of a rich planting economy. Only in the last decade has the Republican party shown strength in Shelby County, a sign of a white suburban backlash. We are talking here of state affairs, for, in national politics, Tennessee had sometimes been captured by Republican presidential candidates, when national Democratic candidates represented persons and policies that Tennessee voters rejected. But in state and congressional matters, the state has been divided into two one-party areas, with the Democrats ordinarily dominant, both in the legislature and in the governorship. Until the late years of Clement's administrations, this condition was fostered by a legislature that had defied reapportionment from 1901 on. Even the apportionment of 1901 was faulty.

Tennessee has been, generally, an open state politically. Local bosses, rural and urban, could seize and hold power, although none of them could completely dominate the state, and most of them did not try. The local rural machines in the years just before the Clement era included those of Paul Cantrell in McMinn County and Burch Biggs in Polk; their activities had some relation to Clement's fortunes, but they were in decline as his star rose. While in Clement's childhood, Luke Lea and Austin Peay were powers, would-be bosses, in state affairs, as Clement came to prominence only Ed Crump remained as a statewide political power, and his life overlapped only the first term served by Clement. Even in the high noon of Crump's influence, he could not always pick statewide candidates. In fact, as a conscious technique, he frequently sat back while he watched the contest, attempting to spot winners. Often enough, he picked winners with whom he subsequently fell out. Such was the case with Senator Tom Stewart; the falling-out process that year elected Kefauver to the Senate of the United States. He parted company with Gordon Browning, and the long drawn-out struggle between Browning and Crump redounded to Clement's advantage. Not far into Clement's first term, the old boss objected openly and sharply to some of Clement's policies, but by that time the aging Memphis leader's life had almost run its course. He was never to be a threat to Clement's fortunes.

Since the establishment of the direct primary in the reform years of the early 1900s, party nominations have been open to any able politician who could grasp them, as well as to any obscure persons whose hopes surpassed reality. Each candidate is compelled to build his own organization, although there has been a sort of continuity of factions within the Democratic party that enabled candidates to take over organizations already developed by some predecessor. Decisions to run are made by candidates partly on the basis of who else is running or likely to run, either because of personal ties or judgments as to the likelihood of success. Campaign money plays a great part; if it is not forthcoming, all hope of a successful campaign withers. Nominations are not strictly up for purchase because success calls for more than money, but money must be there. Members of the official machine of the parties, state chairmen, committeemen, and public officials feel free to endorse particular candidates, and the party machinery is likely to be divided between clearly identified supporters of rival individuals. No pretense of non-alignment is allowed to spoil the fight. A victorious candidate tries to capture the party machine and the administrators of elections. And a good deal of this infighting is unnoticed or little understood by the average voter, who is largely indifferent to the whole show.

The absence of a primary runoff invites candidacies, for in a field split between a number of runners, anyone of even minimum prominence can slip into a plurality, and a plurality is enough. In the last quarter-century, multiple candidacies and plurality nominations have been the rule in the Democratic party. Both Clement and Ellington faced more than one opponent in some of their battles, and both of them came in, at times, with pluralities, not majorities, in the August election. Had the opposition been concentrated, the outcomes could have been different.

Candidates seek factions; factions seek candidates. It is when the two find each other, as they did in the 1952 election, that victory becomes a strong possibility.

Politics in Tennessee is highly personal. W.S. Gilbert could write on British politics

> How Nature always does contrive
>   That every boy and every gal
>   That's born into this world alive
>   Is either a little Liberal
>   Or else a little Conservative.

But a reckless librettist could say of Tennessee politics:

> Every man that's now alive
>   To get some votes must make his pitch
> But liberal or conservative
>   No one can tell just who is which.

In Tennessee (as well as elsewhere in America), family connections and the ties of uneasy and changing friendships are the cement that, together with the lively expectation of favors to come, bond the political mixture into a structure. Issues mean little. Frequently, they have to be found—or dug up. There are no party platforms. Each candidate puts together a rickety collection of planks of his own, sufficient only to hold his own candidacy. The shifting rivalries furnish no key to the ideas of the candidates, for alliances are based on happenstance and temporary convenience, without much regard for ideology. Ideological incompatibles can be accommodated for years in the same bed. Wildly dissimilar individuals may maintain long-term political communion. The young Estes Kefauver started his career in the cabinet of Governor Prentice Cooper; they remained personal and political friends in spite of wide divergence in their fundamental views. Cooper was conservative to the point of reaction. ("I do not want college professors around," he said, as president of the constitutional convention of 1953, to one of the delegates. "They believe in the greatest good for the greatest number, and I do not believe in that.") Kefauver, whatever his early beliefs, became a populist and a reformer, both in Hamilton County and in the Senate of the United States. Indeed, Kefauver's views could have been easily adopted by Clement, whose humanitarian impulses could fit in well with Kefauver's philosophy, but fate and time cast Clement as a rival of Kefauver, and Kefauver, dependent on Browning support, was forced to support, sometimes unofficially only, the conservative Browning's ambitions. What has been said about candidates applies equally well to some of the great newspapers of the state—not to all of them.

Clement's career is a beautiful illustration of Tennessee political culture. His family background, on both sides, led him naturally to politics. The young man's great-grandfather Work had held political office. His grandfather, James Archibald Clement, whom he knew well in childhood, had been in the state Senate on different occasions, from two different districts; his admonitions to his own sons not to get involved with politics probably made no impression on his grandson. His father, Robert, had held local political office and would doubtless have aimed higher had opportunity offered. Aunt Dockie's husband was a county judge. His Goad relatives were active in Kentucky politics, as he must have been able to see when he lived near them in Scottsville and Bowling Green. Conversation in the Clement household was very probably politically informed, particularly as the economic hardships of Clement's boyhood time led people to think of political solutions and political jobs. Grandfather J.A. Clement saw to it that political figures visited the Clement home.

No royal road leads to the governor's office on the first floor of the beautiful Greek Revival capitol in the center of Nashville, but most governors have had some encounters with a fickle electorate, as legislators, as local officials, or even, as in Browning's case, as congressmen, before they make a try at the head executive office. Clement had encountered none of these experiences. True, for four years he had been general counsel of the Railroad and Public Utilities Commission, and in a sense therefore a member of the McCord administration, and, for a short time, as was occasionally remarked, a member of the Browning administration. He had also held office in statewide organizations of an open or indirect political significance. But he had held no office bestowed by the electorate.

In 1952 Gordon Browning was serving out his third two-year term as governor, his second since his return to office in 1949. He was eligible for candidacy. Very probably he was not immediately clear as to his own plans, but he had no more fondness for private life than Clement had. Undoubtedly, a thought of a Senate term flitted through Browning's thinking, although if he were to run for that post in 1952, he would probably face Senator Kenneth McKellar, who, though old and ill, could still have been a formidable vote-getter. Browning was eligible for one more consecutive term as governor. In the end, he became a candidate once more.

Browning coupled a fiery temper with a formidable obstinacy, a combination offering rich potential for self-destruction, but he was nonetheless a stout opponent for anyone and particularly for a newcomer such as Frank Clement. He had served twelve rather routine years in the national House of Representatives, starting at the early age of thirty-four. Even in the lower house, he had cast a longing eye on a senatorship, but timing was never quite right. Crump had become dissatisfied with the weak Hill McAlister as governor and had decided late in the campaign to throw support to Gordon Browning, leaving his Shelby County ally, Senator McKellar, to back Burgin Dossett. Browning, after he was elected in 1936, proved no more satisfactory to Crump than McAlister had, and the two staged a bitter shoot-out in front of the entire state. Browning attempted to trim Crump's power by a so-called county unit election law, modeled after a system long used in Georgia. Many political leaders in Tennessee considered the law unfair and unwise, and not a few forecast the decision of the state Supreme Court which found the act unconstitutional. But Browning was always a bitter scrapper, particularly when he was angered. He lost the court case, and he lost the subsequent campaign for reelection. He was replaced by bachelor Prentice Cooper, a mild-mannered, soft-spoken, irascible, and determined former legislator from Shelbyville, who secured Crump's backing. Cooper, notable for both his honesty and his conservatism, served three consecutive terms. He was succeeded by Jim Nance McCord, who also had the blessing of the Shelby County boss.

Tennesseans have made a habit of defeating governors who add taxes to their burdens. Browning had advocated the imposition of a personal income tax, but an earlier attempt to impose such a charge had been ruled unconstitutional by the state Supreme Court. McCord, like most of his successors, was under heavy pressure from the teachers, and he sponsored and approved the imposition of the state's first general sales tax. Very probably for this reason he was denied a third term. Browning returned to office as governor in 1948, still the bitter enemy of Crump. In that same year, because Crump shifted his support from Senator Tom

Stewart to Judge John Mitchell of Cookeville, without succeeding in getting Stewart out of the race, Estes Kefauver slipped into the Senate. Crump's decline was thus prepared, although he had still six years of life. The election of 1948 made allies of Browning and Kefauver; they were to remain such through many of the Clement-Ellington years, and the alliance continued to play a role even after Kefauver's death.

Any opponent of Browning would have to contend with a formidable political machine and with a colorful and agile campaigner who had a solid record of achievement in office. In his first term in 1937 Browning had updated the administrative organization of the state that had been created for the first time by the able and austere governor, Austin Peay. Browning's reorganization was not innovative; what he did was to return to the Peay administrative principles that Hill McAlister had weakened. The merit system was cautiously upgraded, although neither Browning nor any of his successors, including Clement, was as devoted to merit appointments as to sound fiscal administration. Educational appropriations were improved during the second and third terms of Browning, but it was not in the nature of the educational establishment to be content. They were not always happy with Clement, in his turn. The cities began to press for more state money; Browning put them off.

Browning was an ardent spokesman for rural-road building. A major campaign plank for him was the promise to put a paved road in front of every farm house in Tennessee. But Browning was less keen on big highways and city streets, partly because the railroad lobby of Tennessee was one of his main sources of campaign funds, and big roads were a basic threat to railway health. Browning touted, as his major achievement, and with good reason, the proper funding and control of the state debt, and he later observed the increase of the state debt in the Clement administration with exasperated loathing. Basically, he held a pay-as-you-go philosophy, even for capital expenditures for which debt could be properly incurred. Since he was unable to get the income tax, Browning did not dare to get rid of the sales tax. To do so would have required a roll-back of state expenses and state services, and it has to be a desperate governor who would try that.

Browning was fiercely loyal, always, to his friends, many of whom were military companions from the two world wars. This loyalty, admirable in itself and necessary, to a degree, to a politician, can still land a man in trouble, as many an American executive can bear witness, and for Browning it was to prove a step to defeat. Browning, like most other governors, played the game of patronage according to long estab-

lished rules, rewarding his friends and punishing his enemies. He had reorganized the primary election system in order to give his friends control of the machinery, a gimmick used before and after him.

Through 1950 and 1951, Clement was busy building his own machine. While he sought allies, remnants of the McCord organization,
turned out of office by Browning, were seeking out ways, means, and
persons to make a comeback. A key figure in this intended rebirth was
G. Hilton Butler, an intelligent and able politician long associated politically with McCord, and, before him, with Prentice Cooper. Butler's
dislike for large crowds did not prevent him from being highly effective
in small groups; he was a power. Butler had been adjutant general in the
McCord administration, and he had no intention of remaining in private life. He sensed a winner in the young Clement. "Come on down,"
he wrote to Brainard Cheney (naturally, called Lon), former newsman,
author of novels, and friend of some of the group of Vanderbilt scholars
and writers known as the Fugitives; "I've got a real candidate and I want
you to get in on this." Cheney, at the moment, was in Washington doing free-lance writing; he gave it up and became one of the first men on
the Clement campaign payroll, where then and later he was key technician in the speechwriting staff that turned out material for the Clement
oratory. Joe Carr, forced for a short period into private employment (in
the insurance business, that ever present help in time of trouble), had
been able to notice Clement's rapport with crowds of listeners from a
background with the Young Democratic Clubs, and he also got behind
Clement as a challenger to Browning. Frank Hobbs of Lawrenceburg, a
central figure in the state party, joined with Clement forces. Joe Henry
of Pulaski became a major speechwriter, and adjutant general in the later
crucial years. Henry had managed the statewide campaign in 1946 for
McCord, McKellar, and "Tip" Taylor. Eddie Friar, a close friend of
Clement ("ole buddy" to each other in those early days), had worked for
McCord. McCord himself was on friendly terms with Clement, but he
did not clearly commit himself as yet; it is reasonable to assume, from
his later actions, that he continued to nurse some ambitions of his own.
And, on the banks of the Mississippi, the Red Snapper, still wary from
the wounds of 1948, bided his time—for the moment.

Clement was certainly not without his own coterie of friends. These
included, at that time, Whit LaFon at Jackson, the brother-in-law of
Albert Gore. At the moment Gore was in the national House of Representatives from the old district that had once sent Cordell Hull to Washington, but he was shortly to retire the aging McKellar to the Gayoso

Hotel in Memphis. Donald McSween of Newport, a young past commander of the state Legion, was in touch with Clement. He had been a campaign manager of Clifford Allen in his race for the governorship in 1950, but he was about to desert Allen for a better prospect. R.G. Crossno, mayor of the once "model" TVA town of Norris, who was to play a role in the Anderson County desegregation drama, joined Clement forces. Jared Maddux, a Cookeville attorney with gubernatorial dreams of his own, began a support of Clement that was to ripen into lasting and devoted friendship. Clement's cousin and schoolboy companion, Jimmy Weems, was a backer. Ramon Davis, another Cumberland University colleague, joined the movement.

The year of 1951 was filled with rumors, maneuvers, and unease. Clement was still in the army (although he was allowed to make frequent speeches). He could not be sure how long the Korean action would last and did not actually know whether he could be back in civilian life by 1952. As it turned out he was released from active duty on December 21, 1951, in plenty of time to make the campaign. Meanwhile, the Clement law firm continued in operation, and back in Nashville, Val Sanford and their secretary, Ellyn Warth, took pains to keep Clement informed of both business and political concerns. Anna Belle, now employed by Capitol Chevrolet Company in Nashville, was waiting for the leave of absence she had been skeptically promised by her employers when her brother ran for the governorship. She wrote detailed, penetrating, and amusing observations to her brother in Georgia, reporting on the developing political scene. She had joined two women's organizations — the American Business Women's Association and the League of Women Voters. The league, in particular, aroused her interest and respect. "Those gals," she wrote her brother, "really know about State laws." Clement, reading these and similar lines, drew correct conclusions; his organization and his administrations were to pay close attention to the interests and votes of women.

In the freely competitive atmosphere of Tennessee's personal politics, it was not at all clear who might run. The whisper factory spread the word that Clement would not be out of the army in time; Clement was urged to counteract the report and did what he could to respond, although he could not give any sure promise on the future military commitments of his country. Browning's own intentions took time to form. It seems likely that even in 1950 he was thinking of the Senate and would have liked to see Albert Gore eliminated politically, and he saw in Gore a possible rival for national office. But by 1952 not only was Gore not eliminated, but neither was McKellar, and Browning did not think well of a candidacy that involved opposition to McKellar. Furthermore, Browning's own camp could not agree on a possible successor for him. Walter Haynes, generally known as "Pete," Jim Cummings, Charles Wayland, Jr., and Robert L. Taylor were all possible candidates. Their support of Browning could turn into a faction-destroying rivalry, if Browning were not a candidate. Browning himself, surveying the field, thought that Clifford Allen, Frank Clement, and Clifford Pierce of Memphis were all possible candidates. Browning had them all tagged as Crump men, and battle with Crump and all his allies was the overriding principle of Brownings politics. If his candidacy were essential to the defeat of Crump, he would be a candidate. The whole scenario was typical of Tennessee Democratic politics, where every private feels the marshall's baton in his knapsack. In the end, there were four candidates, not one of them a crackpot nonentity, and the contest took on the usual Democratic aura of a free-for-all. The *Tennessean*'s Hatcher could see no sign of coalitions; "each political tub," he opined, "would be standing on its own bottom."

Interest groups, already in at least standby readiness, began to stir in 1951. Three were fundamental forces in the politics of the time—the teachers, the truckers, the cities. Since its reorganization in the days of World War II, the Tennessee Municipal League had been pushing for a share of the state gas tax. Browning had made them some reluctant promises, but he was slow to deliver. Instead he tried to put them off and on one occasion tried to get them in a good humor with a story to illustrate the basic poverty of the state's fisc. Two old men, who had been friends in youth and who had never married, he told the mayors in the digestic afterglow of a Municipal League banquet, decided in retirement to pool their resources in a common household. "One had been a mariner," the governor continued, "the other, a minister. Each of the old parties owned a parrot, and, as they were both frugal, the two old friends decided to put the two parrots in a single cage. That they did. The ministerial parrot eyed the seafaring parrot with a speculative eye and said, 'What shall we do to be saved?' 'Pump like Hell, or we'll all go down,' shouted the sailor's parrot." The mayors did not find the story funny. The league had employed an aggressive young man, Herbert Bingham, as executive secretary, and Bingham was determined that municipal power would now be brought decisively to bear on the gubernatorial candidates. He was not to be put off with jokes.

Under the direction of Herbert Bingham and Mayor Bill Baird of

Lebanon, the pressure of the TML was purposefully developed. Cards were distributed to municipal officials soliciting their pledges to vote only for candidates who backed the league's demands. Only Allen held out against those demands, but undoubtedly Clement was the principal beneficiary of the league's campaign.

The truckers were equally determined that the legislature should increase the weight allowed for trucks on Tennessee highways. Browning had the backing of the railroads, long active and powerful in state affairs. Browning, thought the truckers, was in the railway pocket, and they would seek to defeat him. Already, in 1951, Robert M. Crichton, whose company was the Super Service Motor Freight Company of Nashville, was emerging as one of the leaders of the truckers. He was to become the financial manager for the Clement campaign.

As always, the teachers, through the Tennessee Education Association, were a power to be reckoned with; some observers of Tennessee affairs have considered them the most powerful and the most ruthless lobby in the state. What they wanted in the way of greater education appropriations was likely to become a nonissue, for most candidates would not buck them.

Organized labor was vocal but weak in Tennessee, and in the early 1950s the blacks were ill-organized, not very active, and generally disregarded. Union support, however, was worth having, and, aided by Charles Houk, secretary-treasurer of the Tennessee Federation of Labor, Clement reached for the endorsement of labor organizations, many of whom had become somewhat disenchanted with the Browning performance. Clement was equivocal on the question of repealing the open shop law, saying that he opposed its repeal but thought it should be amended to provide for freedom of the employers and employees to do what they wanted. Like all candidates he found the issue uncomfortable. Clement organizers also made contacts with the Veterans of Foreign Wars, with county judges, and with legislative leaders and personalities, such as Forrest Ladd of Shelby, Senator Charles Everhart from Sullivan and Hawkins Counties (Everhart incidentally was an accountant employed by the Mason and Dixon trucking line), and Harlan Dodson of Davidson, who in addition to his legislative activity, was a partner in the important law firm of Walker and Hooker. The Hooker in this firm was John J., Sr., whose son John J., Jr., was in the Clement years to become a political personage, the assistant prosecutor in Raulston Schoolfield's trial on impeachment, and, later, twice a candidate for governor and once a candidate for the United States Senate. Mark Hays, state commander of the American Legion, was lending support. Other Legion backing came through George T. Lewis, associated with the prestigious law firm of Roane Waring, a Legion personality of national significance.

Newspapers cannot deliver a Tennessee public office to candidates, but their endorsements are useful and are eagerly sought. Press backing is especially important for a young candidate who needs wide recognition — visibility. Probably Clement's most important partisanship came from the *Nashville Banner,* the afternoon daily long associated with the Stahlman family. The well-known *Banner* columnist, Leslie T. Hart, assigned to state affairs and to his daily column, "Capitol Hill," was an early disciple of Clement. Hart, who thought of himself as the "discoverer" of Clement, started to push him in his column as far back as 1949. Hart ran stories on Clement's education, his family, his Legion activities, and his public speaking. He described him selling hamburgers at the Methodist booth at the state fair. He continually prophesied his future political eminence. The *Banner* continued to support Clement throughout most of his career, in spite of occasional but severe disagreements between the publisher, James G. Stahlman, and Clement—disagreements that remained private and that were patched up, partly because of Clement's consistently conciliatory attitude toward criticism.

The *Banner* was Nashville's conservative voice. Since the resurgence of the Republican party in Tennessee, the newspaper has often backed Republican candidates; it supported Howard Baker for reelection to the Senate in 1978. But in 1952, the Republicans had neither hope nor prospects, and the *Banner* had to make do with the most conservative of the Democrats. Such conservatives were not easy to find, and, in fact, Clement was not conservative enough to suit the *Banner,* but alternatives to him were unpalatable.

The *Banner's* Nashville rival is the *Tennessean,* the morning broadside. What the one is for, the other must be against. So it has been for years. The *Tennessean* has had an interesting history, a history that goes far to explain attitudes that, on strictly logical grounds, are not always comprehensible. The *Tennessean* had been established by Luke Lea, the flamboyant would-be boss of Tennessee, who became involved in the financial collapse of the Caldwell fortunes in the Great Depression. (Lea's most remarkable exploit had been an almost successful attempt to capture the Kaiser at the end of World War I.) The paper fell on evil days, and in the early New Deal period it was purchased by Silliman Evans, with the aid of a loan from the federal Reconstruction Finance Corporation. Evans, a Texan, came to Nashville with the intent of making the

Tennessean a major force in Tennessee politics. He made opposition to Boss Crump the touchstone of his newspaper policies and mounted a sustained attack on the poll tax as a prerequisite for voting. Anyone backed by Crump had the *Tennessean's* opposition; Crump's enemies could count on *Tennessean* support, provided they had some hope of success. Evans was not interested in losers as a steady proposition. The newspaper therefore supported Gordon Browning and Estes Kefauver and helped to keep the two united, in spite of the fact that Browning was basically conservative. It would have made sense if Browning had been pushed by the *Banner,* and Clement by the *Tennessean,* but good sense could not reverse the chance alignments of factional politics.

Joe Hatcher was the principal *Tennessean* columnist, assigned to state affairs. His column was (without imaginative innovations) simply entitled "Politics." When Kefauver's national fortunes were involved, Hatcher traveled the country, but mostly he stuck to state and local affairs. Throughout his career, Clement faced the fundamental opposition of the morning newspaper, with the exception of some occasions when the paper accorded some of his actions a grudging approval. Hatcher carried on a campaign to build up Browning and to denigrate Clement. Both he and Hart indulged in election prophecies; when the voters subsequently proved them wildly wrong, no disturbance to their natural aplomb was visible. In April 1952, Hatcher stated confidently that Clement was "sinking under the clammy Crump hand into third place in the field." As it turned out, Hatcher was more often wrong than Hart, for Hart had turned to private business before the days of Clement's defeats. Hatcher's views of Clement were dictated by the policy of the paper, for in private he was not as contemptuous of Clement's record as he appeared to be in print.

In 1952, Clement gained the backing of the *Commercial Appeal* of Memphis, while the Scripps-Howard outlet of that city, the *Press-Scimitar,* endorsed Browning, as did the independent and respectable *Chattanooga Times.* But endorsements of small dailies and weeklies in the state were also important, and Clement managed to gather in substantial support there.

The 1952 campaign developed into a clear contest rather earlier than had been usual. Clement had been an announced candidate since 1950. If Browning's plans were initially uncertain, it was fairly clear that the race would include Clifford Allen, who had been a candidate in 1950, and Clifford Pierce of Memphis, less well known but apparently determined to run, with or without Crump support. By early 1952, all candidates were beginning to be heard on the issues, even though, according to the sometimes strange rituals established by politics, official campaign openings were still some months away.

These rituals might recall the cautious and formalized courtship of birds. At first the candidates strut circumspectly, treading warily, showing plumage to best advantage. Rumors are floated, by the candidates, by their friends, their enemies, and those ubiquitous foster-fathers of speculation, the newspaper-column writers. Then the really interested parties begin "hand-shaking tours," descending suddenly on surprised and humble citizens around the courthouses (later to be superseded by shopping centers), while less publicized visits may be paid on potential financial "angels." Encouraged by the handshakes, and the commitment of money (if it is forthcoming), the candidate may indicate his detection of a ground swell of opinion demanding his candidacy, and he may even admit that he will announce on a later date. Meanwhile, qualifying petitions will be circulated by the candidate's friends, and indeed, those friends may circulate such petitions without the candidate's initiative, or even consent. In due course, the candidate will make an official announcement, selecting a strategic location for a statement that by this time surprises nobody, and sometime later the candidate will open his campaign with his first major speech, always in those days in a medium-sized town on the courthouse square, usually in Middle or West Tennessee, and from then on the tempo builds up, the remarks get more pointed and less dignified and objective, until the voter gets his chance to bring it all to end on the first Thursday in August.

As matters turned out, Browning, unable to run for the Senate, tried for a third term as governor (or a fourth, if we count the term he had enjoyed in the late 1930s). Of course, he had his own machine, and most of his troops stuck to their guns in 1952; not until 1954 did the desertions mount up. The Browning forces included Jack Norman (who six years later, by Clement's appointment, became the prosecutor in Schoolfield's trial); John J. Hooker, Sr., whose law partner, Harlan Dodson, was supporting Clement (law firms frequently manage to walk along the top of the fence with great agility), and McAllen Foutch, a leading legislator, who was to continue in key opposition to Clement in subsequent sessions of the General Assembly. James Cummings was secretary of state in the Browning administration. This long-time Assembly leader from the tiny town of Woodbury in Cannon County had formed, with "Pete" Haynes and I.D. Beasley, a trio, sometimes called "the Unholy Trinity," that led the powerful rural bloc in the legislature. Cummings remained loyal to Browning in 1952; in time he was to become a legislative leader for Clement. Charles Wayland, who became Browning's manager, was a veteran politician of Knoxville, mentioned himself as a possible candidate for governor. A Browning partisan in 1952, he was to show up in later years as a campaign manager for Ellington. The transition from Browning to Clement was accompanied by shifts in the *dramatis personae* that contributed to the general bewilderment of the uninitiated.

The Democratic primary of 1952 offered a complication for Browning that does not often plague candidates for governor in Tennessee; Estes Kefauver, senator from Tennessee, was making his first run for the presidency of the United States. Harry S Truman, triumphantly elected in 1948, after an uphill battle against Thomas Dewey (the little man on the wedding cake to Alice Roosevelt Longworth, who thought you had to know Dewey well to dislike him), appeared uncertain about running in 1952. Possibly, Truman could have had another nomination. While he hesitated, Kefauver solved his problem by announcing himself — on January 23, 1952. Kefauver offices were set up in Washington early that month; Charles Neese, later to be rewarded with a federal judgeship, became temporary chairman of a Tennessee Kefauver-for-President Club; Mrs. Tom Ragland was named vice-president of the club. Truman, sensing his inability to combat Kefauver, particularly after Kefauver's victory in the New Hampshire presidential primary, bowed out with public grace — and private annoyance. The feisty chunky little man from Independence maintained a persistent animosity to Kefauver thereafter, an animosity crudely revealed in his reference to the Tennessee senator as "Senator Cowfever." It was an enmity that helps to explain Truman's subsequent receptivity to Clement's friendship. Kefauver took a lead over other candidates in a number of important presidential primaries, although, significantly for the southern view of the Tennessean, Senator Russell of Georgia defeated him in the Florida primary in May 1952. Nevertheless, Kefauver was the front runner down to the convention of the Democrats, which convened on July 21, 1952.

Kefauver's activities put both Browning and Clement on the spot. Browning and Kefauver had been allies against Crump; they had united to defeat his candidates in 1948. Certainly they were not alike in their political views, and the alliance carried a cost for Browning, for Kefauver was increasingly associated with a civil rights movement that, although it had not fully surfaced, was most unwelcome to conservatives in Middle and West Tennessee. Kefauver was by no means universally popular in his home state, and he was far from having the full support of

The *Tennessean* views Clement as a Crump puppet; Little, *Tennessean.*

Southerners, as the Florida victory of Senator Russell clearly indicated.

Kefauver's position in Tennessee, and hence Browning's reputation there, must be viewed in the light of events at the national Democratic convention of 1948. As a result of platform decisions there relating to civil rights, a number of Southerners defected from the Democratic candidate, Harry Truman, to support the candidate of the "Dixiecrats," Strom Thurmond of South Carolina. As a third party movement, it was short lived but represented a continuing split in Democratic ranks.

But Browning loyally aided in shoring up Kefauver's presidential ambitions. A brief and somewhat ridiculous flurry of support for Browning for President had developed in 1951; early in 1952, Browning put this movement to rest in favor of Kefauver's campaign. The Browning-for-President clubs were dispatched with the same lack of fanfare that had greeted their birth. Browning was to head the Tennessee delegation to the 1952 convention.

As a Browning opponent, Clement could be expected to treat Kefauver with coolness, even though, in their political ideals, the two were quite similar. Kefauver was always an embarrassment to Clement. A fiction of friendship was publicly maintained; in fact the two always walked around each other like two opponents, unable to shake hands and reluctant to strike out in open hostility. The *Tennessean*, deeply committed to Kefauver (Joe Hatcher followed him on his national campaign trail), constantly heckled Clement on the subject, saying that he was withholding support from a fellow Tennessean. Clement replied — he had to take some sort of position — by announcing his support for Kefauver — but he added that his own campaign was not tied to Kefauver's coattails. Surely the *Tennessean* was as much interested in embarrassing Clement as it was in supporting Kefauver.

On April 15, 1952, Clement announced the selection of Buford Ellington as his state campaign manager. It was one of the most significant events for the state for the twenty years of the fifties and sixties. Ellington was again campaign manager in 1954, and twice he succeeded Clement as governor, in a "leap-frog" arrangement that held power for the better part of a generation. The alliance of Clement and Ellington was one of convenience, not friendship. The two belonged to somewhat different generations. Before the development of the campaign organization they had not been acquainted personally. They became political allies but never close friends. Robert Clement was taking an active part in planning his son's strategy; he felt, and he convinced his son, that victory could be secured only if the rural areas were carried. This had been true in the past, and urban growth had not yet reached the point where urban power would be decisive. Frank Clement himself had friendships and contacts both in the four big cities and in the small towns. Rural leadership could have been a problem for him because there was little of the farm in his background. Ellington seemed made to order for the needs that the elder Clement sensed in the situation. Born in Mississippi, he had migrated to Tennessee, where he began his career as a county farm agent, starting in Jefferson County in East Tennessee. He had served for a short time in the General Assembly. From his base in a small business in Verona, a small Marshall County town, Ellington had developed a wide acquaintance with rural people; at the time of his appointment as Clement's manager he was field representative of the Tennessee Farm Bureau Federation. His residence in a medium-size Middle Tennessee county was an advantage.

Clement and Ellington conferred in Dickson for the first time early in 1952. Aside from the two main actors in this private and significant episode, Robert Clement, Hilton Butler, Joe Carr, and, possibly, Leslie Hart, were present. Robert Clement remembers not being especially impressed by Ellington on his first meeting, but an offer of the managership of the campaign was eventually made and Ellington accepted. It was, from almost any angle, a wise move.

The selection of Ellington as Clement's manager was a fateful decision for both men. They were not fully compatible and the strains of their association increased as Ellington's own ambitions matured. Both men were intelligent, and both were consummate politicians. Clement's nature was a more trusting one than Ellington's, and Clement was more inclined to forgiving forgetfulness than his campaign manager, who chose his friends with caution and seldom relaxed his watch on his enemies. Ellington was not the old-fashioned and evangelistic orator that Clement now had become, but with work and coaching, he learned to speak well. Fundamentally he was more cautious and conservative than the man he was now to pilot to the Capitol.

Ellington was an indefatigible worker. He arrived at the office very early in the morning and worked until late at night. In a single day he would sometimes take as many as three hundred telephone calls. A campaign committee was organized in each county — four or five persons in most counties, ten to twelve in the big counties. Ellington ran a tight ship; schedules were carefully worked out and faithfully observed (Clement was expected to move from one town to another in accordance with plans); local activities were closely coordinated.

The *Banner* views Browning as the ally of Humphrey and the "liberal" wing of the Democratic party; Knox, *Banner.*

Under Ellington's wing, the organization took shape, with personalities later to be important in Clement's future career. Anna Belle Clement, following plans long since made, became Ellington's secretary in the central office in the Hermitage Hotel. Eddie Friar came on the campaign payroll early in 1952; Brainard Cheney followed soon after. Cheney's job was to work on speeches; he was especially valued as a research man. Speechwriters included Hilton Butler and Joe Henry—both highly valued by Ellington as effective phrasemakers. Butler had long served as a speechwriter for various governors, and Joe Henry had experience from earlier campaigns. Both of them could imitate Clement's speechwriting style, but Clement depended heavily on their initiative, even though, as an experienced extempore speaker, he could depart effectively from a prepared text when he felt like it.

Full publicity for campaign contributions was still twenty-five years in the future. In 1952, no firm figures could be established for campaign expenditures. Experienced observers have estimated that a campaign for governor in the early fifties could cost $250,000, but these were dollars not yet cheapened by the rapid inflation of the late sixties and the decade that followed. Browning had the backing, financial and otherwise, of the railroads, and Ellington frankly said in later years that the contest was one between the railroads and the truckers. In addition, Browning undoubtedly collected contributions, with the usual amount of arm-twisting, from state employees. Naturally, Clement forces raised a great outcry against these "shakedowns," although of course such shakedowns were used by Clement organizations when their turn came to hold power. Clement benefitted from numerous small, unpublicized contributions—ten dollars up to a thousand—and undoubtedly he got trucker money. Browning said the truckers gave Clement "fabulous sums" and claimed they had offered Browning himself $150,000. This is probably greatly in excess of what was actually put up. Help was received in kind—transport, free billboards, and so on. Without question, aside from employee contributions (and some civil servants with an eye to the future may have contributed to the challenger), Clement and Browning got the same kind of financial undergirding throughout the campaign. And, most certainly, many such contributions were made in the expectation of future rewards.

The air of Tennessee was already full of charges and countercharges and issues, real or trivial, when Browning formally opened his campaign at his home town of Huntingdon, in Carroll County, on May 24. Browning was a formidable stump speaker, a tough in-fighter whose

On to Nashville

Crump in the driver's seat for the truckers; Bissell, Little, *Tennessean.*

pugnacious jaw (one of the Clement staff privately called him "Gargantua") indicated little inclination to charity or moderation; his opener
gave due notice of a no-holds-barred scrap. His natural rivalry with
Clement had been raised to a boiling point by Crump's endorsement of
his opponent, and the formation of a committee to aid Clement in
Shelby County that included District Attorney John Heiskell, State Senator Forrest Ladd, and George T. Lewis. "Clement," said Browning,
"went to Memphis and got E.H. Crump to blow his breath on him."
Clement, in Browning's announced opinion was a "loud mouth." In later low moments of the campaign, Browning, according to the *Banner,*
would refer to Clement as a liar, a pipsqueak, a demagogue—depending
on what word seemed best at the moment—a "loud-mouthed traducer
of character who is told what to say," "a loud-mouthed character assassin," "a pliable puppet of the Shelby machine." He held the view that
Clement "had been picked too green."

Clement opened officially in the square at Gallatin on May 31, 1952.
He and his speech writers had worked out a lengthy speech, formally
structured into a florid introduction, a statement of his political principles, a ten count "indictment" of the Browning administration, and a
sixteen-point program of his own, all to be elaborated and reiterated as
the campaign progressed. Clement always had a fondness for lists of
programs or indictments; he was to return to the form in the 1956 keynote speech. First, the poetic Clement: "I am a son of the Volunteer
State; I was born beneath the ambient blue of her arching skies; I was
rocked in the cradle of her beauty and glory; I am proud of her priceless
contribution to the building of this nation . . . We must once again return our magnificent heritage to . . . the people of Tennessee." Then he
rejected any thought of personal animosity toward Gordon Browning,
"in spite," he noted in passing "of his mud-slinging . . . the vile names
he has bitterly spewed in my direction . . . merely because I have had
the temerity to seek the office he considers his own. . . ."

Clement did not often formalize his political theory, but he stated a
sort of credo on this occasion—a combination of religious feeling, devotion to democratic rights, a belief in economy and efficiency, the preservation of free enterprise, limits on government, and an independent legislature, a somewhat mixed bag of the eternal and the contingent. And
this material out of the way he promptly moved to an indictment of
Browning and his works—rather general in nature but generally pointing to waste, favoritism, neglect of the aged, blind, dependent, and
handicapped, a loose pardoning policy, and flagrant disregard for com-

petitive bidding. And then he moved into the Memorial Hotel issue that was to become a major feature of the campaign.

His own sixteen-point program pledged no new taxes, but promised improved benefits in health and welfare, a sharing of road and other money with the municipalities (naturally without neglecting rural roads), improvement in education at all levels, a hint at the revision of the open-shop law, and a reduction in the number of executive agencies and employees. He was vague on the issue of truck weights. A peroration returned to the religious theme—an invitation to join the campaign to all "who remember Mother's tears as the silver tide upon which the ship of state can most safely sail . . . to all who could say precious Lord take my hand, lead me on." There were passages here to make intellectual critics cringe, but, much as they would balk at admitting it, there was content, too—and promises, some to be kept, some never fulfilled.

And now the speechmaking spread across the state in earnest. The pace was gruelling for all four candidates. Allen worked as hard as Clement and Browning, with the added burden of preparing his own speeches. Clement rushed from one engagement to another, changing his sweaty clothes between stands, and keeping his emotions inspired by gospel hymns and country music. He came to rely heavily on a favorite: "Precious Lord, take my hand and lead me on." When he was criticized for mixing hymns with the dirty mess of politics, his mother urged him not to abandon his public profession of his religious conviction. "Precious Lord" took on the character of a signature; he was to use it repeatedly throughout his early career.

The campaign was not without its serious themes, but these lacked drama, and in not a few instances the candidates could find no grounds for disagreement. They were all imprisoned by the state's interest groups. They could not fight it out on teacher pay, on good roads, or taxes, for all of them had to back educational benefits of various sorts; no one in his right mind could take a stand against the constant expansion of the highway system; and proposals for new taxes were in the class of obscenities, not to be mentioned in the hot sunlight of the courthouse squares. Only on minor details were the candidates in disagreement, and minor details do not make good campaign speeches.

When Clement was finally in the governor's chair, one of his major achievements—certainly one that gave him the greatest satisfaction—was the improvement of mental health care. But this kind of improvement lacks campaign drama. Clement mentioned his hopes for advance in this sector a few times, but the issue never became a fiery one. Browning maintained that his administration had a good record in mental health, but the candidates never came to close grips in the matter.

But Browning's administration delivered an understandable issue to Clement, as though on a silver salver. This was the lease of the Memorial Hotel. In tune with the times and the rest of the country, the Tennessee state bureaucracy was steadily expanding; it became increasingly difficult for the budding bureaucrat to find a place to hang his hat, park his briefcase, and shuffle his papers, reports, and interoffice memoranda. Long since, the state offices had filled up the restricted space in the Capitol (completed, against considerable public opposition, shortly before the Civil War), flowed out of the Capitol to fill up the state office building across the street, and swamped old row houses that stood around Capitol Hill. (The Planning Commission was said to occupy quarters once devoted to love-for-hire, and old clients were reported to have wandered in from time to time in search of girls instead of filing cabinets.) Southwest of the Capitol stood the Memorial Hotel, a slightly decayed hostelry that looked like a good bet for state office space; in the summer of 1951 the building was acquired by a new corporation, Cumberland Properties, with the hopeful likelihood that it could be leased to the state as an office building for the Department of Employment Security, with, naturally, the federal government footing the bill. In late summer, the *Nashville Banner,* sniffing the ambient air for the sweet scent of corruption, suggested that the owners of the corporation and the building were, or included, Karl Martin and R.S. Doggett, who went by the obvious nickname of "Pup." Now Karl Martin, as the *Banner* must have noted with satisfation, was a young Knoxville man busied in the construction industry, and Pup Doggett was head of the Southern States Paving Company of Nashville. Their activities impinged on the activities of state government. The *Banner* duly noted that both Karl Martin and R.S. Doggett were friends and backers of Browning, and it observed that they had been particularly close to W.N. McKinney, known to friend and foe as "Rube." McKinney had been "the man to see" (the typical phrase used for a patronage dispenser) in Browning's camp, at least according to the *Banner.* That much was publicized in August 1951. Further explorations now disclosed that the incorporators of Cumberland Properties were J. Marshall Ewing, Andrew Ewing, and J.H. Talbot of Nashville. Andrew Ewing had been an attorney for Doggett, but of course this proved nothing, although it could be worked to the full for those wanting to smell a rat. Martin and Doggett denied they had any connection with the enterprise.

Browning lampooned for the hotel "deal"; Knox, *Banner.*

Throughout September, accompanied by the constant attention of the *Banner,* the Browning administration went ahead with its plans to use the building. The *Banner* was not alone in sensing a possible scandal. Clifford Allen asked for more publicity. There was talk of possible legal action, and Attorney General Roy Beeler was rumored to have issued an adverse opinion on the proposed transaction. But Browning was never one to turn aside because of a little opposition; he went ahead with his plans. (In the meantime, in Knoxville, George Dempster, the hardy perennial of Knoxville city politics who had once run for governor against Prentice Cooper and who was in the process of shifting his former support of Browning over to Frank Clement, defeated Jimmy Elmore for mayor; Elmore was reputedly a friend of Karl Martin.)

The hotel issue continued to simmer on the backburner during the warming-up months of 1952. In March the *Banner* carried a story that Cumberland Properties had purchased the hotel for $625,000 and stood to realize $1,769,040 through lease to the state. Figures were becoming too precise to be mere fabrications. On March 14, the *Banner* headlined a story—a story in which they had already been scooped by the morning newspaper, the *Tennessean*—that Browning's friends, Martin and Doggett, were in truth involved in the hotel transaction, denials to the contrary notwithstanding. The *Banner* noted triumphantly that Martin had managed Browning's East Tennessee campaigns in 1948 and 1950.

The affair was a God-send to the Clement forces. Browning, characteristically stubborn, aided the Clement case by going ahead with the lease, maintaining that the state was getting a good deal. On this score, it was not easy to prove him wrong. Over the subsequent years, not a few political observers, many in the Clement camp, willingly conceded that the arrangement may have been advantageous. Unfortunately for his image, Browning had said that he had not known who the owners were, that he still did not know, and that it made no difference anyhow. It was never easy to convince the average voter that Browning did not know what was going on. In any case he should have known, and, politics duly considered, he should have pulled out of the affair as rapidly as a retreat could be sounded. He did not do so, and at last the voter had an issue that was both entertaining and understandable. Clement made the most of it.

During the summer months, the challenger who had attacked the Memorial Hotel agreement in detail during his Gallatin opener, returned repeatedly to the subject, duly noting the benefits accruing to Browning's friends (there was never any suggestion that Browning himself was to gain any profit from the arrangement) and promising an early investigation of the Browning adminstration after his inaugura-tion. (Had the governor been addicted to puns, he could have toyed with the coincidence of Clement's middle name—Goad.) Publicly, Browning responded with characteristic enraged sarcasm. The young ex-FBI agent, opined the governor, could not track a bleeding elephant in six feet of snow; he had been in two wars without ever locating a battle. The young man, said Browning, would not be able to locate the right end of a horse for a halter. Clement, who often ignored campaign witticisms (he had little taste and perhaps little talent for this sort of quick cut), al-lowed that he knew enough about anatomical extremities to put both collars and muzzles on Doggett and Martin. Clement attacked Brown-ing purchasing policies generally. Whatever the effect on candidacies, public entertainment was stepped up as June and July wore on.

The whiplash on battle experience stung. It seems unlikely that many votes were changed by this oblique reference to the fact that Clement re-mained in continental United States in both World War II and the Korean engagement. There is no evidence that any wires were pulled by Clement or his friends to avoid battle service; it was natural enough that he would be drawn into the military police, given his past experience. His record was good, and his service ratings were high. All the same, letters were secured from former commanders to indicate that Clement went where he was sent and that he sought no special favors. The only practice that could be clearly questioned—and this got no attention—was that Clement was released from time to time during the Korean war to make speeches, after he had already announced his candidacy.

In East Tennessee, decisions in the Browning administration on higher educational policy received some consideration. During Brown-ing's 1949–50 term, a move had developed, not probably on Browning's personal initiative, to attach Memphis State College to the University of Tennessee. Memphis State had formerly been one of the state's several normal schools for the training of teachers. At the time it had become, as had the other normal schools, a college, but in enrollment, buildings, equipment, and faculty it remained a far less significant educational in-stitution than the University of Tennessee, with its principal campus at Knoxville, just then experiencing the beginnings of its subsequent spec-tacular growth. The University of Tennessee maintained its sizeable medical school and attendant institutions at Memphis (where, inciden-tally, they had the strong support of Crump). Given the clear likelihood of the growth of Memphis, it seemed certain that Memphis State would grow willy-nilly, and educational leaders in Memphis sought ways of elevating Memphis State College to university status. Rowlett Paine, a former mayor of Memphis, was active in promoting plans of this sort. Some Knoxvillians saw in these schemes traces of Crump's ambitions for his home town; East Tennesseans had always been a little fearful that Crump would manage to move UT to the banks of the Mississippi. In 1948 both McCord and Browning had denied that they had any plans for "splitting" UT or for moving it. But in the late months of 1950 a proposal was offered to the University of Tennessee Board of Trustees to bring about a union of Memphis State with the Knoxville institution under the administration of the University of Tennessee. To those who approved the idea it seemed that the proposed merger would be good for both institutions. The state college would be elevated, the needs of the fast-growing and largest metropolitan area of the state would be served, and the University of Tennessee would be protected from the almost certain growth of a rival institution. The whole move could be interpreted as a step in the direction of improved coordination of higher education in the state, where institutional and regional rivalries had been the regular order of behavior.

Whatever may have been Browning's connection with the origins of the scheme, he now gave it his hearty backing, as it was presented to the board of Trustees on October 20, 1950. The idea of a merger seemed to be a bit of a surprise to the East Tennessee members of the board, and they took a little time before organizing their opposition. In October the board authorized a study of the proposal; reports were brought in to a meeting of the board in the first week of December, and at this time the board by a vote of 10 to 7 recommended the merger, which would require action by the General Assembly. President Brehm voted for the proposal, as did Governor Browning and the ex officio members of the board. The substantial opposition came principally from East Tennesseans on the board, a line-up that emphasized the long-standing regional divisions in the state. Browning was tagged with responsibility for the decision.

The University of Tennessee, as an institution in the Republican end of a Democratic state, functioned under a faint cloud of paranoia, not entirely without historical reason. Many of the faculty worried about the ambitions of Memphians, reinforced by horror stories of the Crump machine. What could have been interpreted as a union of Memphis and Knoxville interests was thought to be a continued "split-UT" movement. Sam McAllester, a Chattanooga industrialist who was a member of the Board of Trustees, took a lead in a successful move to kill the proposal in the General Assembly in 1951. The merger did not take place. In the years that followed, Memphis State College became Memphis State University and did, in fact, become something of a rival to the University of Tennessee, with some duplication of both undergraduate and graduate programs. In 1952, this was still in the future, and Clement took occasion to assail the plan in his East Tennessee speeches, even though the merger plan had already failed. Clifford Allen also joined in, assailing the proposed "split" as one of Crump's pet schemes.

Attacks on the use of the pardoning power are almost a standard part of campaign fare. The challengers and their newspaper backers hit Browning and his pardon record. A free-wheeling dispensation of clemency, according to one newspaper, had included the pardon of a rapist who subsequently gave a repeat performance of his offense. Browning's defense in this case was that the man had been unfairly convicted as the result of the activities of attorney Will Gerber, widely known as Crump's hatchet-man. In several speeches, Clement sharply attacked Browning's pardon record. The governor was aroused by the charge. "If it had not been for the pardoning power of God Almighty," shouted the angered Browning, "Frank Clement would have been in Hell long ago." This premature damning of a thirty-two-year-old man, however entertaining after a twenty-five-year cooling of political heat, is not likely to have had as bad an effect on Clement as on Browning himself. Browning was defending his record by sweeping personal name-calling. There is no way of telling what effect it had, except that it kept the campaign from becoming humdrum.

Even the unsophisticated voter knows enough of human behavior to realize that criticism is easier than performance; he has a jaundiced view of political promises. As things turned out, the pardon and commutation record of Clement was, in some ways, more generous to prisoners than that of Browning. The old records of pardons and commutations as kept by the Board of Pardons and Paroles look much like the ledgers of a nineteenth-century country grocery, but, as nearly as one can make out from looking at them, Browning pardoned 131 persons from 1949 to 1953. Clement was far more restrained. From 1953 to 1959, he pardoned only 13 people, and in his final term only 18. But commutations are another story. From 1949 to 1953, Browning commuted 256 sentences, whereas Clement, in his first two terms, lightened the sentences of almost 500 persons, and in his final four years, commuted about the same number. The Clement commutations peaked at 168 in 1965. Only Governor Blanton had a higher number of commutations down to the year 1979, although even Blanton's pardons (he was much criticized for his pardoning record) were far from equal to Browning's. Of course, raw numbers such as these take no account of the rising population, the rising prison population, the nature of the crimes involved, nor the recommendations that the governor receives. It seems clear only that Clement slowed the pace of pardoning, while increasing clemency through commutation.

When all else fails, a candidate can always accuse his opponent of extravagance. Evidence is not usually required; the voter is predisposed to belief, and some justification can always be found in the chance uncertainties of administration. The charge fits in well with one of standard promises of politics: economy and efficiency. Clement was able to make a case for extravagance against Browning on three counts, none of them significant, but all easily understood and not without some appeal. Count one was the mounting number of official cars. Twenty-five years later the public would be asked to vote against the use of jet airplanes. In the more plodding 1952, Clement promised to sell off the surplus cars, and later he did, with great fanfare, but it is safe to say that the retrenchment had little permanent effect. Clement's count two was to point to the increased number of state employees. On this count he was on slippery turf; after his election and the years to follow, the number of state employees increased with relentless persistence.

Count three attacked the extravagance of a cherished practice of the General Assembly. Tennessee was still operating under the unamended constitution of 1870, which set the pay of legislators at the miserable pittance of $4.00 a day. To make up for this anachronism, the solons had recourse to a variety of petty contrivances. One such was the appointment of hoards of legislative doorkeepers, none of them with anything much to do. There were more doorkeepers than legislators. Some appointees showed up in the state capitol for the sole purpose of getting their pay checks; otherwise they never cluttered the legislative chambers with their presence. The Clement campaign tacticians decided to move in on this practice (for which, of course, Browning had little responsibility). With the advice of Clement's father, a major counselor on strategy and tactics, long scrolls were prepared, listing the doorkeepers by name and their home towns or counties and showing the pay they received for services that obviously amounted to nothing. Scroll in hand, Clement would mount the rostrum, describe for his listeners the number of legislative doors—reaching a grand total of three—and then fling the scroll

Down Campaign Highway

On the excessive number of state-owned cars; Clement promised to hold an auction; Knox, *Banner.*

out in a long streamer into the crowd, inviting inspection of the door-keeper pay list. It was an effective and funny gesture; sooner or later the crowd would study the locals and their pay. (Why, look there—there's old Jones, $240—look at that!) Browning would get the blame; blame could not be pinned on the legislators—there were too many of them—and it could always be assumed that Browning could have made the legislature behave if he wanted to. The scroll-tossing had another advantage: it was too patently ridiculous to be answered adequately. Browning kept mum about the whole matter, although it is safe to think he fumed quietly to himself and his cronies.

As the campaign cranked up, enmities were nursed and feelings harshly rasped, but nowhere did tensions reach the pitch they attained in Polk County. Formed largely out of part of Bradley County in East Tennessee and named for James K. Polk while he was still governor, Polk County has a long history of pioneer independence, anti-Negro sentiment, frontier violence, and bootlegging. At the edge of that portion of the state that was pro-Union and subsequently Republican, Polk County was anti-Union. It voted secessionist, and Democrats, who had carried the county for their presidential nominee in the years from 1844 to 1856, usually carried it again in the post-Civil War years. The county's fertile northern valleys lay at the base of spectacularly beautiful mountains; its southern portion had been given over to the copper industry, whose noxious fumes had denuded the country around Copperhill and Duck-town of every blade of vegetation. The copper industry controlled the politics of the county whenever it needed to; it still does. For some twenty years prior to the middle 1940s, the county had been dominated by Burch Biggs and his sons, who were in and out of the office of sheriff by turns. (The state constitution put a limit on self-succession by sheriffs.) Biggs maintained a loose alliance with the Crump crowd in distant Shelby County and with the Paul Cantrell machine in neighboring Mc-Minn. He watched his fences, maintained friends with other Tennessee politicians, and built connections with other counties, with the state, and with Tennesseans in the Washington establishment. He fought for keeps, using all the tactics associated with political machines elsewhere, not needing or caring to preserve any especial secrecy about his power or his actions. He could deliver majorities, somewhat in the manner of Crump, even if subject to the handicap of the small population of his county (although there was no necessary relationship between the votes turned in and the number eligible). During much of Crump's time in power, Tennessee had no effective voter registration, and, in any case, election machinery was (and still is for the most part) under local control.

Democrats were in the majority in Polk County, but Republicans were still numerous enough to give dissident Democrats some support. Frequently in the past, the county had voted for a Whig or Republican for President. As elsewhere in state affairs, the Republican chance was rosiest when Democrats had a falling out, and Biggs' eventual doom was forecast by the return of the GIs from Europe, for they carried erstwhile German sidearms with them into civil life. In 1946, the Paul Cantrell machine in McMinn County, trying for business as usual by seizing ballot boxes and manipulating results, had been ousted in a wild nighttime gun battle around the courthouse in Athens. The local GIs, assisted by friends and relatives from the ridges and valleys of East Tennessee, expelled Cantrell and his machine from power for good. In 1948, it was the turn of the aging Biggs.

The Republicans of Polk County, together with some of the dissident Democrats, formed the Good Government League, but the choice of name indicated little about the nature of the group. This was no ordinary middle-class, uppercrust "goo-goo" association; it was composed of the same sort of determined men who had built the Biggs machine, and its tactics differed little from the opposition. Probably some of the returning veterans were involved in the GGL, but the association was not dependent upon the GI. Indigenous dissidents were numerous enough, for the differences in the county reached back to the Civil War. As usual, the copper company had an interest in events. A prominent leader of the GGL was R.E. Barclay, a high official in the company. Biggs men found it impossible to steal the election this time, for Barclay and the GGL kept a close watch on affairs, but they tried to stall. Governor McCord felt impelled to send in troops. The upshot was the final fall of Biggs; he was ousted from office and never again recovered power.

One of the members of the GGL was August Lewis, a dissident Democrat who subsequently became a member of the county court. Lewis, having become a member of the GGL, defected, an action likely to be taken seriously in a community in earnest about its local politics. In the night of May 11, 1951, he was murdered from ambush—felled by shotgun blasts in the dark—as he tried to make his way from his garage to his home. His death in Benton was matched several years later by nighttime murders near Turtletown. There is no way of knowing that these were political murders, for the killers have never been identified. Lewis had been a deputy sheriff for several years, and probably he had made enemies; no doubt existed in the minds of local people that his murder was political. Browning had been urged to intervene in the county in order to find the murderers, but he refrained from further action. He said he personally would not go to Polk unless he had to—and maybe not then. Once he was enough irritated to say that he would abolish Polk County and distribute it among its neighbors, and no doubt he genuinely wished he had the power to do so.

In this stormy setting, Clement campaigned in Polk, and in a speech (written by Brainard Cheney) delivered in the courthouse square in Benton, Clement promised to bring the murderers of Lewis to justice. "I come to Benton this afternoon," he began, "to let the people of Polk County know, and the people of Tennessee know that Polk County's trouble is Tennessee's trouble. If the bells toll in Polk County, they toll also, for me—and verily, they toll for every one of you, my fellow citizens of Tennessee's other 94 counties." Clement went on to charge Browning with failure to enforce the law, and he outlined in detail the violent disturbances that had characterized Polk County politics for some years past. He attacked Robert Barclay by name. "But violence," he said, "begets lust and there is no lust like the lust for power. . . . The lust for power became the consuming passion of one R.E. "Bob" Barclay, a Colonel on the staff of Governor Gordon Browning. This passion developed in Bob Barclay, burst the thongs of respect for life and property and under the benign protection of Governor Browning, took over the people and the Government of Polk County in a form of anarchy theretofore unknown in the democratic boundaries of America."

Clement reviewed the history of the GGL (from his point of view, of course) and castigated Browning for his refusal to intervene. He drew a harrowing picture of the efforts of August Lewis to secure Browning's protection for himself and his cause. He pointedly challenged the GGL sheriff, John A. Edwards, who stood a few feet from him during the speech. And he promised to bring the murderers of Lewis to justice. "I hope," he said, "that the murderers of August Lewis are present here this afternoon or that they are within the sound of my voice by radio. To them I say—with every strength at my command and with the help of a just God, you will be found out, prosecuted and punished for the crime you have committed . . . Murderers of August Lewis, defilers of democracy, your days are numbered! Justice is as inevitable as is the arrival of August 7, 1952 and January 17, 1953."

As these fierce threats were shouted in the small town of Benton, Clement was surrounded by armed men, friends, and enemies. Sheriff

Edwards, who stood near the speaker, was shadowed by a Clement friend, Lynn Bomar, a man "who couldn't spell fear." Bomar's presence doubtless aided Edwards to maintain an amused tolerance; Edwards said the "boy" was a good campaigner, but that he was doing Edwards more good than harm.

Subsequently, Clifford Allen campaigned in Polk County and criticized Clement for "grandstanding," but no gathering of armed men in Polk was to be considered a joking matter. The Clement family was anxious for the son's safety; to them the occasion was a display of personal bravery — not grandstand bravado.

Browning's own hard-hitting campaign specialized in sharp attacks on his rivals. Neither he nor anyone else paid much heed to Clifford Pierce, who was more of a nuisance than a serious contender. But now and then Browning turned his ever ready wrath on Clifford Allen. "Allen," he said, "is a demagogue who distorts the truth." Sometimes, in a lighter vein, Browning obliged with a rendition of the Tennessee Waltz.

It was clear from the beginning of the campaign that Clement was the real threat, and Browning gave his main attention to the young man from Dickson. Fully backed by the *Tennessean*, the then governor zeroed in on Crump's endorsement of Clement. In 1950, Crump had refrained from backing anyone for the governorship, but early in 1952, he approved Clement, and allies of Crump formed a Shelby County organization for Clement. Nothing more was needed to assure the bitter enmity of Browning and the *Tennessean*. The paper ran a cartoon showing Crump winding up little toy figures all looking like Frank Clement. Another showed Crump handing bouquets to Clement and McKellar, with the caption: "I love you, too, Frankie." In June the *Tennessean* ran an old picture showing Willie Gerber, a Crump henchman, in conversation with Clement who was then counsel for the Public Utilities and Railroad Commission, and the *Tennessean* said that Clement obtained the job with Crump's backing (which indeed is not unlikely). In July the paper editorially called Clement "Crump's talkative little stooge."

Enmity to Crump had become the centerpiece of Browning's political being, and the *Tennessean* had made a career of attacking the Shelby County boss. In fact Crump's power had been seriously damaged in 1948, and he was getting old — in the summer of 1952 Crump had only two more years of life left. His help was still valuable, but he was not quite the issue that Browning forces tried to make him.

Overlooking his own commitment to the railroads, Browning at-

1952—Clement goes to radio for thanks to voters. Photograph courtesy Robert S. Clement.

Greetings from the Red Snapper — Crump and Clement. Photograph courtesy Mrs. Lucille Clement.

tacked the trucking interest's endorsement of Clement, stating that the truckers had offered him money, but that he had turned them down. Browning had lost some labor support, not only because he had not been able to deliver what they wanted from the General Assembly, but also because he had sent troops into Hamblen County to maintain order during a strike of the Enka plant. Browning tried to tie radical labor support to both Clement and Allen, and he staunchly defended his maintenance of law in Hamblen. The governor was never fond of apologies.

Stubbornly, he defended his actions on the Memorial Hotel, insisting that it was a good arrangement for the state, and he continued to assert that he had not known who the owners were during the initial stages of negotiation. Browning cultivated a "folksy" style, appearing without coat among crowds of people, eating at hamburger stands, carrying a battered old Panama hat, and inviting his hearers "into town tonight for a hog-callin' and peafowl pickin'." He declined Clement's proposals for a debate.

Allen worked hard. He endured a demanding speaking schedule, even heavier than Clement's, and, in addition, he used no speechwriters. Then, and later, Allen was a great promiser—tax reductions, free textbooks for school children (which he had advocated for several years), full earmarking of the gas tax for roads, four big superhighways, and a popular referendum on a soldiers' bonus. The *Tennessean* ran a cartoon showing Allen (who was in the restaurant business) behind a large smorgasbord table marked "Everything Free—Come and Get It." Allen took time to attack Crump and stated that Crump had offered to make him senator if he would get out of the race for governor. Crump, who seldom let any charge go unanswered, called this an outrageous lie; Allen, he said, "wanted to get in bed with us, but when we said, 'No,' he wants to burn the house down—says bad people live in it." Throughout the campaign, rumors floated that Browning wanted Allen to stay in to defeat Clement, and that Clement wanted him in to deprive Browning of votes. In fact, both men were probably worried about the unpredictable effects of Allen's presence. Certainly in private the Clement forces worried that Allen might shove the victory to Browning.

Some of Allen's past backers had shifted to Clement, most notably Donald McSween of Newport, who had been Allen's campaign manager in 1950. McSween had announced for Clement in November 1951, accompanied by some public quarreling with Allen. Allen had always had some support from the split labor forces, and he retained such support in 1952. Labor was never united, either in this or in later elections.

As the primary election day came nearer, the Democrats had now to turn aside from state affairs to choose candidates for the presidency and the vice presidency. In those days, twenty years before the reforming drive of McGovern and his backers, delegations to the national convention were under the control of the state machines, with little regard for wide popular participation in their choice and no thought of quotas for women, young voters, or racial minorities. In Tennessee, the delegation was under the chairmanship of Browning, but this did not necessarily mean that the governor could have his own way. The delegation was controlled by the unit rule and Browning would have to act as the delegation determined. Kefauver had the backing of the delegates and also the support of Browning, but the governor was forced at times to take actions that he disliked and that did him some harm back in Tennessee.

Kefauver was making his first bid for the presidential nomination. He had campaigned in the presidential primaries, elections that were then not as significant and controlling as they later came to be, but still significant enough to give Kefauver a temporary lead that he would never have been able to secure by other means. Kefauver was the front runner when the Democratic forces met in Chicago on July 21. But he was not popular in the South, for he was tied into the wrong side of the growing conflict over civil rights. Senator Richard Russell of Georgia had defeated him in Florida primary in May, thus slowing down a bandwagon that up to then had been crashing through all barriers.

The Democrats had been split on civil rights in 1948, and some Southerners had dropped their Democratic allegiance to turn to the "Dixiecrat" candidate for the presidency, Governor Strom Thurmond of South Carolina. Those defections had not kept Harry Truman from the White House, but they were troublesome all the same, and liberals in the 1952 convention hoped to find ways to hold down party dissidents. A loyalty oath was proposed to be administered to state delegations, requiring them to pledge future allegiance to the convention's choice. Kefauver saw the loyalty oath as a strategy that would aid him to stop Adlai Stevenson, and he and Averill Harriman formed an alliance to make the oath requirement a reality. The argument started over the seating of delegations from Texas and Mississippi; an attempt was made to seat loyalist delegations from these states, but that attempt failed in a convention vote. After Stevenson had been placed in nomination, attacks were mounted on the seating of delegations from Virginia, South Carolina, and Louisiana, who claimed that the laws of their states made it impossible to give the loyalty pledge that was required; Stevenson forces thought the challenges to these three delegations were a ploy to force Southern delegations to walk out of the convention, a walk-out that might have revived the waning chances of Kefauver. Another struggle on the floor of the convention seated the challenged delegations (the main test coming on the vote to seat Virginia), and Browning, as chairman of the delegation bound by the unit rule, was compelled to cast the Tennessee vote against Virginia. Within the delegation he actually voted against Kefauver's request to reject Virginia, but, as chairman, he did what he had to do, and it hurt him politically. Kefauver, too, was hurt, for he did not get the nomination, and his disloyalty to the traditions of the South were remembered in the crucial state convention of 1956.

Browning had earned the loyalty of Kefauver, and, in return for his support, Kefauver (who doubtless would have preferred to remain neutral in the race for the governorship) endorsed Browning; the endorsement, however, came late in an election where Browning's victory became increasingly doubtful as the campaign wore on.

The final day drew near. Clement completed the weary round of speech-making, preceded by the constant singing of the old hymn: "Precious Lord, take my hand, lead me on." Desperately Browning observed that the Lord could not find Clement's hand, even if He wanted to, for Crump had hold of one hand and Willie Gerber firmly held the other. It was all hopeless; the wheel of fortune had turned down for Gordon Browning.

The Democratic primary of August 7, 1952, was decisive, but it was not a landslide. Browning mustered 38 percent of the Democratic vote; Clement was comfortably ahead with 47 percent; Clifford Allen was far behind with 12 percent; and Clifford Pierce managed no more than 4 percent. A plurality was enough. Had Browning been able to gather in all the votes that went to Allen and Pierce, he could have had another term, though there is no basis for thinking that this would have happened. In a straight contest between Clement and Browning, it seems likely that Clement would still have been the victor. Even though the Clement record would always be clouded by this small uncertainty, the fact that he was a plurality, not a majority, governor would never do him any real harm. Tennessee was used to living with this sort of doubt.

Browning's principal strength was in East Tennessee, an area where Clement remained comparatively weak throughout his career. In all likelihood, East Tennessee Republicans were poaching as usual in Democratic territory. As one correspondent put it, "A Republican [who sticks] close by his party has no more privilege in Tennessee . . . than a 'stray hound dog.'" They may have moved into the Democratic primary to vote for Browning as they later did to favor Clement in the contest with Bass for the United States Senate. Browning carried 30 of the state's 95 counties; 18 of these were in East Tennessee. He carried 6 counties with 60 percent or more of the vote, a very high figure; these 6 were East Tennessee counties, and in one of these, Sevier, he took a whopping 72 percent of the ballots. Sevier County is a long-time stronghold of ultraconservative Republicanism. Browning carried Knox County with 45 percent of the vote to Clement's 44, and he did well in Hamilton County, even though he lost here. In fifteen counties of the state, Browning had an absolute majority, and he had at least the satisfaction of carrying his home county, Carroll. But even here his majority while comfortable was not spectacular, and his satisfaction must have been dashed if he noted that Clement carried his home county of Dickson by 76 percent.

Middle and West Tennessee became Clement country; particularly was that true of West Tennessee, although in 1952 Clement lost some interesting counties such as Hardin and Hardeman. Hardeman, in particular, had an old-South style. So did Haywood, and there Clement took the election. Black power was not much in evidence in 1952, and no clear pattern of black activity emerged.

Clement, heavily influenced by his father's political sense, had felt that he needed rural support. Probably this was true enough, but, in fact, he did well in the metropolitan counties. He did not carry Knox, but he was only 1 percent behind Browning even there. He carried Hamilton, 46 to 41 percent; Davidson, 40 to 31 percent; and Shelby by 54 percent to 33. Crump was still alive and, apparently, well. The 54 percent gave Clement his only absolute majority in the metropolitan counties.

For all his courage (Allen would have said: grandstanding), Clement lost Polk, which at the same time it defeated Clement, elected as sheriff the object of his attack, John Edwards. The murders in Polk County were never solved.

There is no way to tell how labor voted. It is strongest in the metropolitan areas, and Clement was victorious there, generally. Could be that labor had decided to try to win with Clement, but other elements in the voting population could just as easily have given him his margins. Certainly in Shelby County, labor could not have been decisive.

The election did not especially alter the voting patterns so long established in Tennessee, but one significant change was made: the aged and ill senior senator from Tennessee, Kenneth McKellar, was brought down by the youthful Albert Gore, who had hitherto represented the fourth congressional district around Carthage. All over the state Mc-Kellar had posted small signs, reading "Thinking Feller, vote for Mc-Kellar"; under each such sign, Gore had caused to be posted a second bit of advice: "Think once more, and vote for Gore." Second thoughts carried the day. McKellar carried twenty-four counties, by far the most of them being in East Tennessee, where McKellar and Crump had long maintained friendly rapport with like-minded Republicans. McKellar retained Shelby county, but even here, Gore was close on his heels — only 3,000 votes behind him. The truth was that McKellar, like many another senator addicted to life at the nation's power centers, had stayed too long. Loneliness, sickness, and old age had come to him. Feebly he tried to maintain his interest in political affairs for few years, but he was never again a power.

In Tennessee, little relationship can be discerned between the senatorial and gubernatorial races. The Browning-Clement contest was carried out independently of the McKellar-Gore rivalry. Gore and Clement carried on essentially separate campaigns, although on occasion Clement and Gore supporters cooperated, quite inattentive to Crump support of a combination of Clement and McKellar.

The day for Republican resurgence had not yet dawned in Tennessee. The minority party held a partial and half-hearted contest for the useless nomination for governor, in which the only candidate was Beecher Witt, an East Tennessee attorney. The Republicans recorded primary votes in 39 counties, most of them in the East. It is one of the curiosities of this election that the Republican contestant garnered 18 votes in Clement's home county, and 402 in Browning's. Voices in the wilderness!

♪ *Work, for the night is coming,*
   Work through the morning hours,
   Work while the dew is sparkling,
   Work mid springing flowers;
   Work when the day grows brighter,
   Work in the glowing sun;
   Work for the night is coming,
   When man's work is done.

ANNA LOUISE COGHILL, 1836–1907

4. Work Through the Morning Hours

THE TWO-YEAR TERM

The primary won, it was a foregone conclusion that Clement would be the next governor. (About twelve months later, Frank, Jr., aged four, sped some parting Dickson County guests from the executive mansion with the words: "Thanks for helping us get this big house to live in.") But there was still a campaign to wage; the November general election was important to the Democrats, for a president was to be elected. They lost.

Through the early fall, Clement, Gore, and J.B. Avery, the candidate for the Railroad and Public Utilities Commission, campaigned together for the Democratic ticket. Ellington was made chairman of the Democratic State Executive Committee and coordinated the campaign of the combined Democratic slate. Clement, Ellington, Crichton, Carr, and Friar trekked to Springfield, Illinois, to confer with Adlai Stevenson, and Clement spoke repeatedly for Stevenson and his running mate, Senator John Sparkman from Alabama. Two Memphis groups worked for the national ticket, one group attached to the Crump organization, the other, independent, but allied to Gore, Kefauver, Browning, and McKellar. Clifford Pierce could not stomach the Stevenson candidacy; he bolted to Eisenhower.

Eisenhower and Nixon carried the state with 446,147 votes to 443,710 for Stevenson and Sparkman, a narrow margin to be sure, but a portent of coming Republican strength in Tennessee and a harbinger of trouble for Clement's fortunes in later years. As usual, the Republicans retained East Tennessee, including Hamilton and Knox counties, but—

85

more of a portent—Shelby gave Eisenhower 65,170 votes to Stevenson's 71,779. Conservative forces were evidently shifting in that county from Democrats to Republicans, and, in the not distant future, the outer reaches of the Memphis area would be numbered more or less permanently among the Republicans.

In the gubernatorial contest Clement rolled up 642,290 votes. In the hard fought primary, the combined Democratic vote had numbered no more than 647,117, so his backers, whether Democratic or Republican, had stuck to him pretty well, and his erstwhile opponents had apparently reentered the Democratic fold. And this has some added significance, for nationally it was a Republican year in Tennessee. The little-known Republican candidate, Beecher Witt, corralled 166,377 votes over the entire state. He carried eight counties, all of them in East Tennessee; five of them had been carried by Browning in the Democratic primary. But Witt's vote in Hamilton, Davidson, and Shelby counties was pitifully low, and even in Knox County he had only about a third of the total ballots. Clement had good reason to be pleased with his November mandate. It strengthened his growing confidence that people liked him as he liked them.

Albert Gore overwhelmed Hobart Atkins in the race for the United States Senate, and thus began a long career as a senator that always impinged on Clement's own fortunes.

The newly chosen governor-elect began immediately to prepare for his first term, slated to begin about the middle of January (the exact date in Tennessee is left up to the legislature.) Like most other men who succeed to the governorship, Clement had no concise or consistent political theory to guide his policies. Nor was any such set of principles likely to fill the demands of the office. The governor, even more than the legislature, had to respond to the day-to-day pressures and emergencies as they arose; he was a troubleshooter, not a reformer or a revolutionary. He was not a man given to wide theorizing on governmental programs. He had made some promises in order to be elected; he would seek to make good on those commitments, and, for the rest, one would have to see what developed. He was certain about one thing; he intended to stay in politics and to run for other offices, but for the moment he was not certain of his political goals. The new governor did have a youthful urge to set some things right; this ideal he had mentioned in his early musings about the governorship to his sister and to his sweetheart. He was always a compassionate man, and as his life went on he gave expression to the hope that he would be known as a humane governor.

In the fall of 1952 Clement began to tour the state institutions. He gave particular attention to the mental health facilities, for he had an especial interest because of a family tragedy. W.A. Clement, a half-brother of his father, one of the sons of J.A. Clement by his first wife, had been shot in the head in an accident; the bullet could never be recovered from his brain, and as he lived on his condition worsened. Finally he had been compelled to go into a mental health center. As a boy, Frank Clement had been fond of his uncle and had worked for him; the man's misfortune led the young Clement to consider the plight of the mentally ill, and he carried this interest into the governorship. It was a case of the triumph of policy over votes, for in those days the mentally distressed and their friends had little political power. The autumn visits included the asylums, and often when Clement left them, he would sit on the hospital steps, weeping bitterly for the unfortunates whose grim troubles he had just witnessed. Clement was an emotional and a religious man (as Brainard Cheney remarked: in his extrovertive way)—a man easily moved to tears, and visits to the hospitals dealt him a severe shock.

Clement worked on the building of his cabinet and the designation of the men and women he was to back for election to the state constitutional offices. Aside from the state's judges, the constitution of Tennessee provides for the selection of five important officials besides the governor. The adjutant general is appointed by the governor. The secretary of state, the treasurer, and the comptroller of the treasury are elected by the General Assembly. The attorney general is elected by the Supreme Court, which he also serves as recorder.

The attorney general is the creature of the Supreme Court, both in law and in actuality. But since the early 1930s, it had been customary for the Assembly to elect persons backed by the governor to the offices of secretary of state, treasurer, and comptroller. These offices were part of the important patronage at the executive's disposal (he never had enough offices to pass around to satisfy all the demands), and the acceptance of his choices by the Assembly was a necessity of prestige. The Assembly itself readily acquiesced in the arrangement; even the defeated faction accepted the arrangement as entirely proper. Under Browning, the secretary of state had been James Cummings of Woodbury, a man whose long experience of state politics had been started with his youthful acquaintance with Governor Patterson. Cummings knew that his term as secretary would end with Clement's first term. He never fumed about it (useless struggle against the rules of politics was not part of his canny behavior) but accepted the inevitable quietly while he waited for a better day. W.N. Estes was Browning's treasurer and Cedric Hunt his comptroller. They, like Cummings, were politicians, not technicians primarily, and, like Cummings, they were clearly identifiable Browning men. It was taken for granted—by everyone—that they would go.

In those days, the governor's power went further than the bestowal of offices legally committed to the Assembly; it was equally taken for granted that the governor would dominate the legislature, and the domination was expressed through the governor's control of the legislative machinery. The arrangement did not rest on any firmly established political machine that elected both governor and Assembly. There was no evidence of a coattail effect in Tennessee elections. The governor and the majority of the legislature would be Democrats, but it was all highly individual. Particularly was this true when a new face appeared among the roster of governors. Turnover in the legislature was high, and the new men (few or no women in those days) would not have allied themselves clearly with either faction that contended for the governorship. Of course, there were exceptions. Certain friends and supporters of Gordon Browning were returned to the legislature; most of them would be earmarked for opposition. And there would be a few persons who were decidedly independent; they would be with Clement on some issues, not on others. The Clement machine in the Assembly still was to be constructed, however, and it would never give a governor absolute power.

For day-to-day purposes, the power Clement had was sufficient. It rested on the governor's control of the speakers of the two houses and on the selection of floor leaders, not majority and minority leaders, as in later days, but on administration leaders selected by the Assembly according to the governor's wishes. Minority leaders did not exist officially, although leaders of the opposition could be identified.

Tennessee has no clearly defined cabinet. The governor has the power to appoint his principal administrators, without Senate approval; they serve without term and may be dismissed at the governor's pleasure, although this rarely happens. Of course, the governor does not have an absolutely free hand. He must duly consider the demands of party patronage, geographic distribution (Tennesseans are highly conscious of the division of their state in three Grand Divisions—East, Middle, and West), interest group representation, and individual capacity. Clement added another dimension; he developed in his own mind an image of certain posts where technical competence, not political or geographical consideration, would play the major role in selection. Such technicians had not been unknown in earlier administrations, but Clement added a new urgency to this type of selection, an urgency so strong that it has persisted for a quarter of a century, through change of faction and change of party.

The new governor-elect had two particular posts — budget director and commissioner of education — for which he sought technical competence. Young as he was, Clement had few connections with specialists outside the legal profession. His first choice for commissioner of education was not too difficult for him because he used a friendship formed during his years with the Railroad and Public Utilities Commission, with Andrew D. Holt, "Andy" to firm friend and casual acquaintance alike. When Clement was counsel for the commission, Andy Holt had been executive secretary of the politically powerful Tennessee Education Association. The two had nearby offices, and it was easy for two such out-going personalities to form a quick rapport. Holt, meanwhile, had been administrative assistant to the president of the University of Tennessee, placed there by the board, according to faculty rumor, despite the reluctance of President C.E. Brehm, who correctly perceived in Holt a possible rival and intended successor. Holt had technical qualifications: he earned a Ph.D. from Teachers' College of Columbia University in New York, and he had written a comprehensive dissertation on the growth of public school education in Tennessee. Holt had worked and lobbied for the TEA. He was not a technician alone, however — he was an engaging personality and a popular public speaker. He had been an active Democrat and thoroughly understood the forces and personalities of Tennessee politics. He would have bridged the gap between politics and technocracy as well as anyone. Clement asked him to become commissioner of education.

Holt's position at UT was not exactly easy, but it was safe. Andy wanted none of the uncertain troubles of the state Department of Education. He turned his old friend down, kindly but firmly. "Listen, son," he paraphrased the conversation in later years, "I don't *want* the job; I've got a job." The words may not have been exactly remembered, but the style was Andy's style, as it was then, and was always to be. When Clement was finally convinced that Andy could not be budged, he asked Holt to name someone else, and Holt proposed Quill Cope. Cope, a Tennessean (Clement had not extended his search for talent beyond the state), was associate professor of education at the University of Tennessee; he had just completed a master's degree in education at New York University. He had formerly been superintendent of education of White County, with headquarters at Sparta. Cope was approached and accepted the offer. No political clearance was demanded; he was appointed for his specialist qualifications, but he was not without political background. He was a Tennessean and he had occupied a local post that is never far from local political affairs. In turning to Cope, Clement passed over a supporter who had wanted the job; this was Howard Warf, a powerful political leader in Lewis County. Warf remained attached to Clement and eventually succeeded in becoming a cabinet member in spite of the opposition he faced. Cope served Clement loyally during the difficult desegregation controversies that still lay in the future, and he was able to report to friends that he had been left free from political pressure during his years in office.

The second post that Clement thought required technical capacity was that of budget director; the governor was determined to have a thoroughly competent fiscal agent at his right hand. That presence became a hallmark of his administration. Again, he had to find a lead. Through a mutual acquaintance Clement's attention was called to Harold Read, professor of accounting in the College of Business of the University of Tennessee. Read, unknown to Clement, was somewhat remote from the political world, but he had made it a point to keep in touch with the fiscal officers of the state over his years as a teacher. President Brehm had made Read the budget director of the university, and Read had acquired a thorough knowledge of the university's fiscal affairs and their relation to state finance. Read was interviewed by Robert S. Clement, who was actively advising his son in recruitment affairs, and Read was subsequently approached by Buford Ellington and Eddie Friar jointly; Friar and Ellington were already vying for the post of top adviser to the governor. Read, like Holt, declined to leave the stable atmosphere of the university for the stormier climate of state affairs; he did agree to assist Clement as a temporary budget director during the transition between governors, although he did not want the job permanently.

Browning's budget director, Robert G. Allison, died in November, and Browning made no attempt to find a replacement for the few weeks remaining in his term. He made it clear to Clement, however, that he would provide him with every facility he required for the preparation of the budget proposal that was due in the legislature in January, and, in spite of the bitterness of the campaign, was completely cooperative with Read and his associates as they dug into the state's fiscal affairs. The fact that Read, as budget officer of the university, might suffer some conflict of interest in serving as the state's chief fiscal adviser seemed to occur to no one, with the exception of the university's rival colleges, which must have felt some anxiety. Even they might have reflected that Read's interest in higher education might be beneficial to others than UT alone.

As Read went to work planning for the opening of the new administration, he took as his principal assistant a former student, William Snodgrass. Snodgrass hailed from Sparta (Cope's home town); in late 1952 he held a post with the Municipal Technical Advisory Service of the University of Tennessee, where his job was to assist the cities of the state with accounting and fiscal problems. He had worked as a consultant for the Community Services Commission of Nashville and Davidson County, which in 1951 and 1952 was preparing a study of Nashville-Davidson relations that eventually led to consolidated government. When Read was asked for suggestions for a permanent budget director, Snodgrass' name was offered to Clement, along with a few others.

Snodgrass was a quiet man, by no means a high-pressure artist, although friendly enough in his self-contained way. He had had no connection with party politics, which indeed is somewhat foreign to his nature, even though in time he learned to work with political figures. At the initial conferences between Read, the elder Clement, and Snodgrass, Read tended to dominate the conversations, and Robert Clement's initial impression of Snodgrass was not highly favorable. Nonetheless he correctly sensed that he was not seeing all that was there. He engaged Snodgrass in later conversations, only the two being present, and gradually began to see in Snodgrass a future budget director. Eventually, Frank Clement named Snodgrass to the budget directorship, but it was the last major appointment he made in his first administration. Read thought that Clement might have held off on Snodgrass because of his youth. Snodgrass was even younger than Clement, and Clement's obvious pride in having come to the governorship very early in his thirties was somewhat dimmed by Snodgrass.

The appointment finally came through, and it proved to be one of the most significant moves Clement ever made. Snodgrass was a thorough technician. His appointment signalled the beginning of a lengthy history of appointments, particularly in fiscal and administrative areas, solely for purposes of competence, without regard for political backgrounds. These appointments continued throughout the Clement and Ellington regimes, extending beyond those years to provide Tennessee with a corps of professional bureaucrats, free, at least in considerable measure, from the entanglements and pressures of factional and party politics. Not only was Snodgrass the first of these, but he became a force in quietly pushing considerations of competence in the state's higher civil service. He quickly gained Clement's full confidence, and Clement made him a key figure in the control of administration. Snodgrass came to occupy in Clement's administrative structure the power of the budget administrators at the national level and of the treasury in British affairs. Whether or not he did it consciously, Clement had grasped the most essential feature of sound governmental administration.

Snodgrass thought, without knowing it clearly, that he received a routine political check, but he was never subjected to unwanted political pressure from Clement. When he went into the office, he knew no one in the Clement administration, except Commissioner Cope. He *had* been a college friend of Howard Bozeman, a backer of Clement. Snodgrass attributes some of the protection from pressure that he enjoyed in the Clement administration to the shrewd operations of Robert Clement, who had a keen appreciation of what was needed by his son, if his administration was to avoid political and administrative pitfalls.

But if Clement insisted on having as his budget director a man of non-political technical capacity, his choice of an individual for the post of comptroller of the treasury was guided by more traditional considerations. Jeanne Stephenson Bodfish announced her candidacy for the job in November, and Clement promptly endorsed her. Mrs. Bodfish came from a family concerned with political activity. She had been the head of the women's division in Clement's campaign organization and had filled a similar role for the entire Democratic ticket in the general election. But she had other qualifications as well. She was trained as a political scientist and held a post as instructor in government at Vanderbilt. She was active in the League of Women Voters. She was not, clearly, a trained accountant, but her predecessors in the comptrollership had often been lawyers, and, as the office had been run in the past, the position had been more political than technical. Moreover, important for her as well as for the Clement administration, Snodgrass was to be available to help Mrs. Bodfish learn her job; she proved a willing and quick learner. Politically, the appointment turned sour; she was to break with the governor before the two-year term had passed. Nonetheless, her regime saw the beginning of a growing importance for the office in Tennessee affairs.

Clement's choice for treasurer was James B. Walker, a Henderson banker, who had no more than a limited commitment to politics. The treasurer's functions are rather routine, but the office does have political significance — the treasurer has often been a fiscal official in the campaign organization and has the power to distribute money among the banks of the state, a form of patronage that goes more or less unnoticed by the general public. Walker also had the assistance of Snodgrass, and Walker became one of Snodgrass' staunchest backers within the Clement organization.

The filling of the post of secretary of state was a purely political matter, as the requirements of the office call for no highly developed or specialized skills, unless it be those appropriate for a lawyer. James Cummings held the post under Browning; he was an avowed Browning man, and he acknowledged, entirely without resentment, that Clement would need to put his own man in the post. Cummings was a lawyer; his successor was to be Eddie Friar, another lawyer. Friar had been a close friend of Clement; he had succeeded Clement as counsel for the Railroad and Public Utilities Commission. In the warm correspondence exchanged between Clement and Friar, they had been "ole buddies" to each other. Friar had boosted Clement at every opportunity and Clement's letters to Friar were filled with expressions of grateful friendship. But Friar nursed political ambitions of his own. He hoped to be Clement's principal adviser and the dispenser of patronage—the "man to see" —and unquestionably he had the governorship in mind for the future, when Clement, supposedly, would have gone on to higher things. Ellington, the campaign manager, stood athwart Friar's path. Their rivalry for power surfaced at once.

The transition from Cummings to Friar as secretary of state was made with typical good grace and wisdom on Cummings part. But this appointment, like that of Jeanne Bodfish, ended in recrimination for, within the first term, Friar fell out publicly with the governor, and the old friendship ended in bitterness, frustration, and suspicion. Clement was unfortunate in his choice of two constitutional officers. The treasurer remained loyal until ill-health forced him from office. As adjutant general, Clement, who had the appointment in his own hands by constitutional provision, named Joe Henry, his able phrase-making speechwriter.

The selections for the constitutional posts were made public during the late autumn and early winter; during the same period, selections of the commissioners—the cabinet proper—were announced. Typically, Clement coupled his announcements of prospective appointments with the statement that he had sought the men; they had not sought the jobs. That can hardly be fully true. Tactics may have impelled some candidates to temper the candor of their ambitions. Individual choices may have been made without too much consideration of personal campaigns.

Some applicants were necessarily rejected. But it is certainly not true that pressures were absent; that would be too much to expect. Clement had to distribute some rewards; the hope of preferment is the principal cement of party loyalty. Geography had to be regarded. Interest groups must be placated, particularly in such areas as insurance, banking, conservation, and labor. And technical competence played a traditional role, particularly in departments such as health and education. Young as he was, Clement was fully aware of all these forces, and, if his attention to such matters had ever faltered, his father was always present to set him right.

Very likely the most important political appointment of Clement's first administration was that of Buford Ellington as commissioner of agriculture. Presumably Ellington could have had any post he wanted; his contributions to the governor's election had been notable. Agriculture was a natural choice. Ellington's professional and business career had been tied to agriculture; aside from politics that was the field he knew. Furthermore, the state Department of Agriculture was one of the hunting grounds for patronage, in spite of the technical nature of some of its activities. But, in addition to becoming commissioner of agriculture, Ellington, throwing aside the rivalry of Friar, became the principal patronage dispenser of the first two Clement terms (and clearly the "one most likely to succeed" in the contest to come six years later). Ellington's selection was made public by the middle of November.·

Other cabinet appointments came along in rapid-fire. The highly important post of commissioner of highways went to W.M. Leech, a friend of Clement throughout his life and the county judge of Dickson County for sixteen years. Leech was an active politician—president of the statewide County Judges Association in 1941–42 and an elected delegate to the constitutional convention that was to meet in 1953, a post he had to resign to become highway commissioner; like so many Tennessee politicians, Leech held a law degree from Cumberland University. The commissioner of conservation was to be Glen Nicely. Nicely was a former newsman, who had gone into business for himself (he had an automobile agency in Unicoi County, on the extreme eastern boundary with North Carolina), but for a time he had been an agricultural agent in Hamblen and Union counties. Nicely was something of a newcomer in the Clement organization; he had not been acquainted with Clement before the campaign and had been recruited for work in his area. Nicely was to become significant in the first two Clement administrations, enough so to advance from his commissionership to a post as the governor's administrative assistant.

Hilton Butler, the intelligent and somewhat aloof mentor and aide of governors before Browning and the "discoverer," in a sense, of Clement and his extraordinary talent for oratory, was made commissioner of safety. He became again, as he had been in the past, a man to reckon with in the formation of state cabinets — so long as they were not headed by the Browning faction.

In early December 1952, the *Banner* featured a cartoon captioned: It's A Girl. Young doctor Clement was pictured presenting a newborn daughter to a delighted (and goateed) father Tennessee. The cartoon celebrated the announcement of the selection of a woman to a cabinet post — the first in Tennessee's history. Clement, relying partly on the political savvy of his sister, had been careful to give women's organization a high priority in his strategy, and Jeanne Bodfish was to be the comptroller. Now, Mrs. Christine Reynolds was tapped as commissioner of public welfare. Mrs. Reynolds was a resident of Paris in West Tennessee, just beyond the Tennessee River; she and her husband were engaged in real estate and insurance, but she had worked in the Department of Public Welfare in years past, resigning in the McCord administration to return to business. Business and public service were combined with political activity in her career; she had been a West Tennessee vice-president of the Young Democratic Clubs.

Another significant politician was named commissioner of employment security; this was Donald McSween of Newport, also a graduate of Cumberland University. McSween, who had been state commander of the American Legion, nursed political ambitions of his own (as did an embarrassing number of the future cabinet), and his constant communications to Clement during the months to come showed him as a hyperactive patronage dispenser. McSween, who was only thirty-seven years old, had been the state campaign manager for Clifford Allen in 1950, but he had broken with him (Allen and McSween publicly differed on whose initiative) and had gone over to Clement. McSween, like Butler, was destined to remain cabinet material for some years.

All through December, selection news poured from the temporary Clement offices in the Hermitage Hotel. Geography had already been paid its due respect. Now the interest group choices began to emerge, mixed, however, with factional loyalty, friendship, and residential considerations. The commissioner of labor (a secondary department in the

Blessed Event In Tennessee Government

The first woman cabinet member in Tennessee history; Knox, *Banner.*

scale of Tennessee affairs) was to be William Parham of Jackson, Tennessee, whose own union was the International Alliance of Theatrical Stage Employees and Motion Picture Operators. Parham was president of Jackson's Trades and Labor Council, but in addition he had been a member of the Madison County Court, the county's governing body; his brother, Chester Parham, the Jackson commissioner of education—a municipal elective post—had managed Clement's campaign in Madison County, a pivot in West Tennessee affairs.

The appointment of a commissioner of banking and insurance raised, as always, the specter of possible conflicts of interest—conflicts that, in those days, received only passing comments from the opposition but that were to be increasingly pressed as time went on. Arch Northington was awarded this post; he himself was in the insurance business, and in the future his private and public activities were to be made the brunt of sharp attacks by Clifford Allen. During the campaign, Joe Hatcher, writing in the *Tennessean*, had stated that Crump had handpicked commissioners of insurance in past years. Crump's own business was insurance, and the implication had been left that Crump would choose the Clement insurance commissioner, as—so the *Tennessean* asserted—he had since the days of Governor Hill McAlister, except, of course, when Browning was in office for his final two terms. But, the *Tennessean* and Hatcher both publicly admitted that Crump played no part in the Northington appointment, and it may be that Clement was quietly demonstrating his independence of the old Memphis boss, even before his inauguration.

The governor-elect passed up a chance to name another technician for the Department of Purchases, which had come under his attack during the campaign. To this job he named William Luttrell, a former UT football hero and currently Knox County commissioner of finance. Luttrell had been Clement's Second Congressional District manager, but his qualifications were not on the order of those of Snodgrass and Cope. But Clement returned to technical considerations in his retention of Dr. Hutcheson as commissioner of public health and when the new Department of Mental Health was established, technical qualifications were to be paramount there. The selection of the cabinet was virtually complete by the last days of December. The *Tennessean,* avowedly pro-Browning and hence anti-Clement, nevertheless spoke approvingly of the Clement cabinet and praised him for the early announcement of his choices.

The anointment of prospective leaders of the General Assembly did not proceed with the calm that, at least outwardly, distinguished the choice of the cabinet. Contests for the speakerships were quite open, and disappointments were severe enough to cause talk of floor fights—fights that looked less desirable by the time the Assembly got down to organization. The senate speakership was eyed by Jim Camp, legislator from White County, by Carl Hardin of Davidson, Charles Everhart of Sullivan (an employee of the trucking firm Mason and Dixon), Fleming Hodges of Dyersburg, Forrest Ladd of Shelby, and Jared Maddux of Cookeville. Temporarily, it was something of an open race, but Maddux got the nod early in December, and the talk of a floor fight gradually disappeared. Such talk was definitely dampened by the award of the post of floor leader to Jim Camp. Camp was a member of the Kefauver machine. Hardin and Everhart withdrew from the race but not without some publicly put harsh words from Hardin.

Maddux was a freshman legislator, but he was no raw newcomer to public affairs. He had been assistant clerk and clerk of the House under Prentice Cooper and comptroller of the treasury in the administration of Jim McCord. Maddux was a former district commander of the American Legion and, perhaps more to the point, a long-time friend of Clement, one of those who remained loyally attached to the governor until Clement's early death.

The names of several prominent legislators were tossed around in press circles as possible speakers of the House, including James Bomar, Hoyt Bryson (from "Mr. Jim" Cummings' tiny home town, Woodbury), and Harry Lee Senter of Bristol. Bomar was endorsed publicly by Clement by the middle of December. It was a significant choice; Bomar (who had been an upper classman at Cumberland University when Clement was a freshman there) became an effective and loyal Clement leader during all three Clement terms. Hoyt Bryson was named floor leader. Bryson was an independent person, formally a Democrat but not allied to the Clement forces, and he felt no especial loyalties to the governor. In fact, he and the governor did not always agree, and he was not to remain in the Assembly during succeeding Clement years. His appointment is illustrative of the basic conditions surrounding the governor's relationship to the legislature in those days. In the public eye, the governor was in control of the legislature; in reality, his control was subject to limits. He could exercise some choice on legislative leaders— speakers and floor leaders— but his choices were hedged with restrictions, and typically his floor leaders were— had to be— permitted some independence. On some issues—taxation, the death penalty—they would not follow the governor, and Clement was always wise enough not to push his friends too far, combining in this attitude both personal generosity and political wisdom.

Although Clement exercised the patterns of control over the Assembly that he found to hand, he showed some interest in upgrading legislative performance, and he took steps that eventually helped to build the legislature into the really independent branch of government that it became after his tenure. One of the independent members of the House, and a potential opponent of Clement's forces, was the young Democrat, Tom Johnson of Manchester, a former Browning floor leader. Johnson was interested in improving legislative procedure and performance, and during the fall and early winter he and Clement had become involved in discussing proposals to set up calendar committees in the legislature, as a means of better organization. Such committees would be useful to any organization seeking to control legislation. During their conversations, Clement had raised with Johnson the idea of instituting a legislative council, such as had existed in a few legislatures over the country, particularly in Indiana and Kansas. Johnson prepared a draft of legislation to establish such a council, with the aid of political scientists from the University of Tennessee, another evidence of the growing contacts between the University professionals and the state's political figures. In due course, when the Assembly got down to business in 1953, Johnson's proposals became law, and Johnson subsequently resigned his seat in the legislature to become the council's first executive director and a close collaborator with the governor and his successor.

Clement's successful overtures to Johnson were characteristic of his ability to win over the opposition, a trait highly useful to a politician but one grounded firmly in Clement's basic disposition. The council, officially termed the Legislative Council Committee, became a useful tool for Clement. Its membership represented the majority forces in the legislature, forces that were allied to Clement and Ellington, to be sure, but in the council one could find a germ of the independence that finally began to come to full flower in Clement's third and final administration. During the Clement-Ellington years the council was the source of many useful studies on state policy and sometimes a means for putting under study — and delay — policies that were too sensitive for immediate action.

The General Assembly convened on January 5, 1953, and promptly ratified the choices of the governor for constitutional posts and for leadership of the legislature. On the first day, the Senate elected Maddux to the speakership without opposition. Charles Everhart, who for a time

had been a candidate, made the nominating speech. The Republicans
went through their hopeless ceremonial. Sterling Roberts nominated
Senator Ernest Guffey for speaker, and Guffey requested that his name
be withdrawn. On the House side, McAllen Foutch, a prominent
Browning backer, nominated Bomar, Clement's man, for the speakership. The Republicans nominated Judd Acuff of Knoxville, and Bomar
was elected with all due dispatch. Two days later, Bodfish, Friar, and
Walker were unanimously placed in the constitutional offices — "all systems were go."

On the fourth day of the legislative session, Governor Browning appeared before a joint session of the two houses to deliver an accounting
of his last four years in office. He made no budgetary proposals, but he
did offer a lengthy analysis of his achievements, and what he had to say
was important for judging where the state had been and where it stood
as Clement came to power. Had no new programs been enacted,
Browning noted, the number of state employees would have declined.
But the new programs had been created and the number of employees
was up. Among those new services he cited the new tuberculosis hospitals (a quarter-century later those hospitals were being closed down, for
drugs had almost completely killed the disease), the rural road program,
and the passage of a motor-vehicle title law. He called attention to the
new state library, an elegant and spacious building across the street and
down the slope of Capitol Hill, the rebuilding and refurnishing of the
capitol itself, and he noted that further steps would be necessary to replace the rotting outer stone that had been falling from the building. Already mindful of his successor's interest in mental health, he noted the
increased appropriations in that area. He pointed to the reduction of certain taxes. He justified his ways to labor, noting the comprehensive
mine safety law, the improved child labor law, and the requirement of
prevailing pay on state construction. He paid his respects to improved
forest fire protection, to the growth of the state parks, and the rise in
tourism. During the campaign, the policy of putting liens on the property of recipients of old-age assistance had been attacked by his opponent, and Browning vigorously defended the policy. He asked for general police powers for the highway patrol. He spoke with pride and
conviction of his reorganization of the state debt. The speech was built
up, as gubernatorial accounts always are, from departmental reports
that "accentuate the positive." It was a forerunner of the more vigorous
and dramatic defense of his administration that was to accompany the
inaugural address of Clement.

The inauguration was set for January 15. Clement arranged that the ceremony be preceded by a religious service in McKendree Methodist Church on Church Street in downtown Nashville. At noon, the traditional hour, the Senate and House members moved out of the Capitol to the space in front of the War Memorial Building to hear the final message of Governor Browning and the inauguration speech of his successor. Browning had cooperated fully in the transition to the new administration; in particular he had been as helpful as he could be to Read and Snodgrass as they prepared the new budget. But on January 15, the relations between Browning and Clement were frigid; the campaign had been a bitter one, and no doubt Browning was already turning over in his mind the prospect of a return bout two years hence. Browning spoke first, beginning — perhaps unconsciously — on a note of irony; his mission was difficult, he said; not that the occasion was a burden to him "but because I've been in and out of this office so many times it is hard to find anything not already said either coming or going." Politicians are not always so candid. What he did do was to list his promises and to place alongside them his performance. He had made good on his pledges, he claimed; repeatedly he said, "This I have done." But first he warned of the difference "between the lavish impulses of aspiration and the chilling and sobering hand of responsibility," and he noted the undoubted (and all too frequently unnoticed) fact that state expenditures rise from the provision of services, not from the overhiring of state employees, corruption, or maladministration. He stubbornly defended the Memorial Hotel contract. Browning was never one to strike his colors.

Religious overtones were not lacking in Browning's speech, but, as often was so with him, they tended toward warning references to a day of judgment. "In God's law of retributive justice I verily believe," said the old fighter. Browning's speaking style was simpler than Clement's, less emotional and florid, but he was in full and forceful command of the English language.

Browning's farewell makes better reading than Clement's inaugural address, which, unlike Browning's parting shot, was lacking in specific content, relying principally on religious and emotional appeal — an inspirational speech in every way. The new governor was saving his specifics for the budget message to the legislature. Clement's address ended, as so many of his speeches ended, with the hymnal words: "Precious Lord, take my hand, lead me on."

In the early days of the legislative session, Clement made Snodgrass the budget director, and in the middle of February he completed the roster of his official family by naming Ramon Davis, an insurance dealer of Lebanon, as his director of personnel. Davis was another college friend; he had attended Lebanon High School where Clement had been a student for some months, and he had been the governor's classmate at Cumberland. Davis had no technical training for the post he was now to occupy. The contrast between Davis and Snodgrass is illustrative of Clement's attitude toward administration; indeed it is an approach that has been followed by most governors, both preceding and succeeding Clement. Clement made Snodgrass a confidential and powerful non-political adviser and controller in the interest of sound fiscal procedure. The post of director of personnel has never been used in this fashion. Its occupants have usually been straight-out politicians, more concerned with the partisan aspects of patronage than with the ethical niceties of the merit system. Personnel management, in a technical sense, has never had the same appeal for Clement or other governors that fiscal management has enjoyed. Nor have the personnel directors ever held the same status in the affairs of the state that the fiscal managers have retained since Clement's first entrance into office.

For a few days the legislature more or less marked time while it waited for initiation of important action from the governor's office. Local bills appeared in their usual uncontrolled flood. A mildly embarrassing investigation of college textbooks—obscure in origin—started up. Clement, as an official of the American Legion, had been somewhat active in antisubversive affairs of various sorts, and he had been an FBI agent in a period when the agency was especially hot on the trail of disloyalty; the measure authorizing the investigation in Tennessee, however, was not an administrative measure and may even have been regarded by Clement with mild distaste. After all, the governor had far more important items on the agenda. Certainly the governor took no part in the affair.

Senator Sterling Roberts of Roane County was made chairman of the investigating committee, and it seems quite clear that Roberts used his position to prevent the investigation from becoming the extensive witch hunt that some of the legislators wanted. Some hearings were held. Mrs. Winston Caldwell, chairwoman of the Americanism Committee of the Tennessee Federation of Women's Clubs, testified that her committee was preparing a list of objectionable texts. Mrs. Eric Bell, chairwoman of the Davidson County Young Republicans Club, listed some objectionable books in sociology and democratic problems courses, and Sims Crownover made an attack on a high school text in Tennessee history written by Mary Utopia Rothrock, a widely known and highly respected librarian, whose other qualifications included a father who had served under Fust-with-the-Most Nathan Bedford Forrest. Donald Davidson, Vanderbilt professor of English, appeared before the committee. Both Crownover and Davidson were to play prominent roles in the desegregation arguments that were then but a few years in the future. The committee came to Knoxville for a day of quizzing of faculties in the social sciences.

The investigation fizzled like a half-wet firecracker. Symptomatic of the uninformed fumbling of all parties to the probe was the single adverse finding of the committee on UT that the economics department had used a textbook that stated that the capitalistic system was founded on debt — private debt. So it was — and had been since the days of Florentine bankers and the Augsburg Fuggers. Clearly committee members somehow confused this necessary feature of capitalism with a justification for the deficit-ridden federal budget, and they did not like it. The administrators and faculty of UT, no doubt despairing of a role as adult educators for assemblymen, contented themselves with a statement that the book had been used only in its Extension Division and had already been withdrawn. In any case, the affair petered out, perhaps fortunately all the way round, for the Clement administration was now about to embark on a six-year program of expanded spending and state service, accompanied by a drastic climb in the state debt.

During the campaign, Clement had promised that his first piece of legislation would be an act to share the gasoline tax with cities; it was a promise that had much to do with his victory. Chapter One of the Public Acts of 1953 now fulfilled that commitment. The campaign of the Tennessee Municipal League for a portion of the gas tax was one of long standing, going back to the years just before the Second World War. Of the four candidates for governor in 1952, only Clifford Allen had refused to endorse the proposal. But of the other three, Clement had managed to be the most convincing, and the League was now to reap what it had so long and laboriously cultivated.

The statute provided that municipalities should receive from the gasoline tax and motor vehicle fuel tax, one cent per gallon (the counties already received two cents) distributed to each city on the basis of its share of the total city population, to be spent on highways and related items. There can be little doubt of the justification of this statute, but the new governor was fully aware that he was thus opening up the prospect of demands on the state's central collections that would be pressed still fur-

Cartful of boys—Gary, Bob, and Frank Jr., with parents and Pip and Polly.
Photograph courtesy Mrs. Lucille Clement.

Father-son combination—Bob with his father. Photograph courtesy Bob Clement.

ther. Indeed, the insistence of the League and its aggressive secretary, Herbert Bingham, on further concessions from the state has never ceased, from that day to this. The counties had long fed at the trough of the state treasury; this statute opened up a new era of city demands at a time when urban population was beginning its steady growth at the expense of rural.

Approval of the measure was overwhelming. For a short period, the organized county officials had flirted with the notion of asking more state money for the counties, but the time was rightly judged to be unpropitious, and the flirtation stopped. The gas tax legislation sailed through an Assembly that acted with the facility of a perfectly functioning rubber-stamp. In the lower house, the vote was 93 for, 1 against; the nay vote was apologetically explained on the basis of pre-election promises made locally. In the Senate the vote was 32 to 0!

It was February 25 before Clement delivered his budget message to the two houses. There was no religious note in this speech, but it was delivered at the same level of intensity that characterized all his major speeches, and the lengthy analysis of the state's needs must have been exhausting to more than one Assemblyman. The speech was all content. Rumors had been afloat in the month of January, or so the *Tennessean* reported, that Clement was thinking of asking one cent increase in the general sales tax. But if there was any key theme of the budget message, it was the firm rejection of any new taxes, a theme emphasized in the printed version by italics and capital letters presumably called for in the copy submitted by the governor. "*I am against increasing taxes,*" said the governor. "So [at another point] I plead for NO NEW TAXES." The *Banner* picked up the theme with a headline: NO NEW TAXES. The message was clear, and the Assembly had no trouble reading it. But it was a theme to which Clement did not return in later administrations. Both in the second and third terms he became firmly associated with tax increases and the broadening of the tax base. This association was followed finally (and probably partly for that reason) by defeat at the polls.

Immediately after taking this stand against new taxes, Clement noted that gas-tax sharing had already been enacted, and he continued his verbal support of the legislation, but nonetheless his disquiet was clearly revealed, for he noted the state's heavy participation in local expenditures. His language reveals a sense of the plagues that would follow him in the future, as the teachers, the cities, and the counties continued their demands upon him.

Clement now went on to charge that waste and corruption had sub-

First ladies—Lucille Clement and Mrs. Jim Folsom at a governors' conference.
Photograph courtesy Mrs. Lucille Clement.

Allies—Clement with Herbert Bingham. Photograph courtesy Tennessee State Library and Archives.

Legislative amity—Clement with Tom Johnson. Photograph courtesy Tennessee State Library and Archives.

Jeanne S. Bodfish, comptroller. Photograph courtesy Tennessee State Library and Archives.

stantially bankrupted the highway and conservation departments, surely an exaggeration left over from the campaign. He outlined his legislative proposals: the creation of a separate department of mental health, the improvement of purchasing procedures, authorization of some form of the union shop, reform of the election laws (that ever-present must for many governors), and industrial development, the favorite end-of-the-rainbow for all hard-pressed executives. Without mentioning the widely-known source of campaign contributions, he asserted that he had no commitment to the trucking industry, but his remarks indicated support for trucking interests. He cited county figures to show the industry's importance for Tennessee.

Like the cities, the truckers were to have their reward, but life was not made so easy for them. The gas tax bill had carried the signature of floor leader Hoyt Bryson, a sure sign, if any were needed, of administration backing. The increase in the allowable truck weights, which became Chapter 3 of the Public Acts of 1953 carried the signature of Bryson and six other persons. There was never any doubt that the truck measure was an administration bill, and Clement must bear his full share of responsibility for the statute, which, like all truck bills, was highly controversial and politically dangerous. The maximum weight allowable was raised from 42,000 to 55,980 pounds, a modest figure when compared with the behemoths that customarily exceeded the speed limits on the interstates in the 1970s. The legislation also contained figures on the distribution of weights on the axles, and it raised license fees.

One day after the budget message was delivered, the truck weight bill passed the House on third reading. On the following day, February 27, the House bill was substituted in the Senate for the Senate version and passed on third reading there. No hearings had been held on the bills, and no conference committee was necessary. In both House and Senate, members of the governor's administrative entourage worked openly on the floor for the truck measure.

Opposition papers promptly stressed the lack of hearings and the on-the-floor activities of nonmembers of the Assembly. They were rediscovering virtues that had never been practiced by the legislature. Committees did not hold many hearings in the 1950s. Indeed, they had no place to meet except in hotel rooms. And the legislative floors were never closed to nonmembers; the administration and other lobbyists mingled freely with the Assembly, on and off the floor. Only the losing side found the procedures objectionable in those days. But the loud and clear chugging of the steamroller was bound to raise objections.

The truck weight bill passed the House, 68 to 25. In the Senate the vote was 21 to 12, a comfortable enough margin in a house where 17 votes are required by the constitution for all legislation. The votes showed clearly that party lines mean little in the General Assembly. In the House of Representatives, McAllen Foutch and Tom Johnson were highly vocal in the opposition. Clement himself publicly noted that some of his friends voted against him, and he mentioned Harry Lee Senter of Bristol as one of them. In the Senate the parties were split. That body contained only five Republicans; three of these voted against the bill. But the most notable of Clement's supporters were solidly behind the truck legislation.

The fight—and the adverse publicity—gave the governor a case of cold feet. He held the bill on his desk for several days, saying he needed to study the act. Clifford Allen, a persistent heckler of the governor then and later, called for a veto. Crump was critical, and Clement wired him a sharp rejoinder. In the end Clement signed the bill, but he echoed the criticism that no hearings had been held, a disingenuous position surely, considering the governor's hold on the Assembly. Indeed, the failure to hold hearings had been a tactical error because the bill would have passed in any case without the necessity for such open disregard of legislative properties. Some observers have seen in this episode the beginnings of the quarrel between the governor and his campaign finance man, Robert Crichton. The public has long since forgotten these initial storms over truck weights, but the issue itself has never died, for the truckers, like other interest groups, are never content with temporary victories.

March was now at hand, and in that month and the first few days of April (the legislature adjourned on April 10) the administration floor leaders poured into the flood of local legislation a steady stream of significant public proposals. Clement had promised to support free textbooks for school children, an idea that Clifford Allen had put forward earlier and that Clement, he claimed, had stolen from him. It was a popular measure, but the governor ran into more trouble with it than could have been anticipated. Read and Snodgrass in working up the budget had somehow counted an item of $5 million on the revenue side that was earmarked for welfare programs. When, late in the budgetary process, the mistake was spotted, Clement was strongly impelled to seize upon the dramatic possibilities in the situation by calling for sharp cuts through an appeal to his cabinet members. The governor's father, supporting Read's views on strategy, opposed such action, and the gover-

Could Tie Up Traffic Considerably—

Even the *Banner* worries about the truck weight issue; Knox, *Banner.*

nor backed away from his idea. As it turned out later $5 million were borrowed to start the free text program. The borrowing was a dubious maneuver. Crump, whose sensitivity on fiscal affairs was always highly developed, called the action financial quackery, and, as Crump had not liked the truckers' bill very well, a fairly sharp rift developed between Crump and the governor. Clement publicly informed Crump that he, not Crump, was governor, and Crump, according to report, gave serious thought to backing Walter Chandler for governor in the future. But, in any case, the row made it clear the Crump could not give orders to the governor, and that, in itself, may have been a political plus for Clement.

Ironically, a major source of opposition to the free text bill was the Tennessee Education Association, which evidently feared that the cost of the service would come out of funds that they hoped would go for salary increases. Pressure was freely applied in the Assembly by the administration. The general education bill had not yet been passed, and charges were made that it was held up until the textbook question was settled. Republican support was rumored to be based on promises offered for more Republican power in a revised election commission. In any case, the textbook bill became law, with an adequate margin in the House, but with no more than the constitutional minimum of 17 in the State. Deficit financing split both parties, as they were usually split.

Although the administration had its way—just barely—with free texts, it could not deliver on another campaign promise: the modification of the open shop law. The governor duly advocated that modification and bills were introduced to bring it about, but the pressure exerted on the truck measure and the textbook bill was not repeated. But even had it been, the anti-open-shop measures would probably not have passed. Opposition was widespread and intense, organized labor was more vocal than powerful, and, at the most, had Clement persisted, he would have alienated much of his legislative support, perhaps irremediably. It is interesting that some Negroes opposed the legislation on the grounds that they had been frozen out of union membership. The bill received its come-uppance on April 8, two days before adjournment, when the Senate, by a vote of 20 to 12, tabled the measure. The only Republican who voted against tabling was Chester Coker, who represented seven counties in the Upper Cumberlands where miners' votes are significant. Speak Maddux and floor leader Jim Camp stuck with the official Clement position. The metropolitan vote, where labor should have had strength, was split.

Election machinery in Tennessee had long been under the direction of state and local boards, whose composition was the frequent subject of factional fights. The partisan interest that these structures aroused has to be explained on the theory that control of the machinery would either permit corrupt elections, or would permit the factions to watch each other. The Republicans received minimal consideration in the alterations that took place periodically as the Democratic factions changed the machinery whenever one succeeded the other in power. When Browning took office in 1948, Crump forces controlled the three-man board that administered general elections. (Primaries were run by party boards, authorized by state law.) In 1948, only a single Republican member for the state board was up for choice (the General Assembly elected the board members), and Browning forces in the 1949 Assembly, in order to seize power, had increased the size of the state board from three to six, giving themselves the chance to select two more Democrats. That same legislature had put an additional Republican on the board, favorable to Browning, without giving the Republican legislative caucus any choice in the matter. In 1951, when the board had been increased to eight members, Browning captured control of all five Democratic members, but dissension among the Republicans weakened the governor's control.

Clement now set about to reorganize the Browning board out of existence. Apparently the legislature considered this proposal an entirely appropriate exercise of administrative power; the proposed legislation passed 78 to 1 on third reading in the House and 30 to 1 in the Senate. Possible Republican opposition was eliminated by increasing Republican power slightly. The new legislation, which bore the sponsorship of Hoyt Bryson, provided for the election of three state board members for terms of six years, two from the majority party, one from the minority, elected by the General Assembly on the basis of choices by the party caucuses. This was as much as the Republicans could expect in the early 1950s. The *Tennessean* charged that Clement had secured victory by working with the Guy Smith-Carroll Reece faction of the Republican party, which, like the Democrats, was split into two groups.

The members of the new state board were, of course, friends of the governor—Sam Coward of Livingston, an early friend and backer of Clement, and James Alexander of West Tennessee, who was to play an important role in later Clement campaigns. Guy Smith, editor of the sharply conservative *Knoxville Journal,* was chosen Republican member. Among other things Smith and his ally, B. Carroll Reece of upper East Tennessee, were close friends of the increasingly powerful Democrat,

Herbert Walters—"Mr. Hub"—of Morristown. The alliance between Walters and East Tennessee Republicans was always an important element in Clement's rise to fortune.

The new state board now met to seal the Clement control of the statewide election machinery by selection of the county boards. At times, amid the pressure that now was brought to bear on the governor, Clement tried to maintain that he was keeping hands off the state board. In fact he did not—and probably could not—do so. Wrote one candid correspondent to the governor: "My friends are your friends here in Sullivan. We want to name the Election Commission and the Primary Board." There was no mealy-mouthed reticence here, but just to make things perfectly clear the writer went on: "You know, that was one of the numerous reasons we broke with Browning." Stand—and deliver; such was the message that came through succinctly. And the state board's choices are a roster of Clement friends: McPheeters Glasgow, Clement's Davidson County campaign manager; Thomas W. Jarrell, associate of Joe Carr in the Jarrell Insurance Company, Bayard Tarpley of Bedford County, later one of the attorneys in the Schoolfield trial, T.H. Avery of Alamo, of a family strongly attached to the governor, Hugh Abercrombie of Hamilton, Dr. Sam Jones in Morgan County, and Pryor Crowe in troubled Polk.

The major action of the General Assembly is the appropriation of funds. Clement's appropriation proposals were readied for the legislature in late February, and, of course, they passed without too much controversy in spite of objections to the amounts involved and to what some legislators regarded as deficit financing. The debt was raised. Tennessee now stood on the threshold of a steady twenty-five years of expansion of services and a national inflationary economy. The Seventy-eighth General Assembly set an all-time record for state spending—up to that date. But, as the legislature went home in the second week of April (governors did not tolerate long sessions in those times), even the opposition found words of praise. As accomplishments, the *Tennessean* listed the creation of the new Department of Mental Health, the sharing of the gas tax with cities, the revision of the motor title law, the revision of state purchasing laws (on this score the *Tennessean* had to admit some laxity in the Browning record), the increase in teachers' pay to a ten-month minimum, increased funds for old-age pensions, and greater aid to the blind, the disabled, dependent children, and the victims of tuberculosis. Clement and his legislature created a Division of Services for the Blind, and the blind still revere him for his friendship.

But the *Tennessean*, calling the Assembly a "mere rubber stamp" of the governor (perhaps no more than a slight exaggeration), listed as demerits the truck weight increase, the elimination of the lien on the property of persons on old-age relief, too liberal new pensions for attorney generals, the six-year terms of the new state board of elections (that, to be sure, could have hampered Browning had he been able to make a comeback), and the use of bonds to start the textbook program. Joe Hatcher of the *Tennessean* referred to the increased appropriations and the issuance of new bonds as the "wildest spending orgy" in the state's history. The Assembly had authorized $14 new million for rural roads, another $10 million to match federal funds for highways, $5 million for the new mental health program, $2 million for other institutions, and $4,050,000 for various public works, including repair of the state Capitol (in fact that building threatened to fall, parts of it, on the passers-by).

Indeed the state was taking leave of the cautious fiscal policy of Browning. He suffered — and not in silence. "It's a disheartening thing," he said to the Nashville Civitan Club in July 1953, "to fight your soul out to establish a sound financial system and then see it butchered to make a political holiday."

The legislators left the labors and entertainments of Nashville on April 10, 1953. Eleven days later the first constitutional convention held in Tennessee since 1870 convened in the chamber of the House of Representatives under a mandate to undertake a strictly limited revision of what was the oldest unamended written constitution in the United States — and probably in the world. The calling of the convention was neither a party nor a factional matter, and the issues it would consider were not clearly soluble on a partisan basis. Both Browning and Clement had supported the call for the convention. Neither had had much to say about the constitutional issues involved. Cautiously, Clement had indicated that he favored some revision of the difficult amending process imbedded in the 1870 document, and he admitted to a bias in favor of municipal home rule.

The governor and his close associates did become involved in a close three-cornered race for the presidency of the convention between former Governor Prentice Cooper, Cecil Sims of Nashville, and Raymond Denney of Nashville. Both Sims and Denney had worked hard for the calling of the convention, and both wanted the presidency. Cooper campaigned over the state for the presidency, perhaps as a preparation for his reentry into a candidacy for the governorship or a seat in the United States Senate. Denney ran a rather poor third on the first ballots, attributing his defeat to his being caught in a crossfire between the Browning forces that backed Sims and the Clement forces that favored Cooper. Denney was certainly correct in seeing in the Cooper-Sims contest a continuation of the struggle between Clement and Browning, but, as usual in Tennessee affairs, lines were not rigidly drawn, for Sims, in the past, had supported men who were not Browning backers. Cooper won, by a margin of one vote, after intense campaigning on the floor by Clement men, but once the headship of the convention was settled, Clement and his subordinates had little to do with subsequent proceedings.

What the convention did—once ratified by popular vote—had important effects on the Clement career. Most notably, the convention proposed an increase in the governor's term, and Clement became the first governor in the history of Tennessee to serve a four-year term. As amended, the constitution then required him to retire from that office, and he spent four years in somewhat painful exile before returning for his final term in 1963. The convention proposed, and the people adopted, an item veto; this probably strengthened Clement's power in his later years, when legislative control commenced to slip from his grasp. The convention proposed—and the people agreed to—a sharp restriction on the passage of local legislation, and the Assembly gradually shifted its major attention away from local squabbles to general legislation; very possibly this served to enhance legislative power at the expense of the governor's authority.

The legislature once out of the way—accompanied by sighs of relief from the lowlands along the Mississippi to the Unakas in the east—the governor was able to concentrate on the details of administration (and to prepare for the election of 1954 now once more just around the corner).

Patronage was Item Number One. It had been a constant concern of the governor since the primary victory, and it continued to be so. Just a year and a half later, Ellington dispatched a memorandum to Glen Nicely, the governor's administrative assistant, with the desperate note: "There are 10,000 trying to get jobs."

Patronage is the bond that holds the factions of Tennessee together in alliances that continually threaten to come unglued. The gubernatorial files contain some discussions of high policy, but mostly it is made up of appeals for jobs, conciliatory replies, peremptory demands for dismissals, pitiful appeals for help, and occasional condemnations. Ellington's note evidences the nuisance that surrounds the bestowal of employment. The patronage system is annoying enough at the top level of jobs, but its methods are used all the way down the hierarchy to the unskilled workers at the bottom of the pecking order. The state faction rests on county organizations, and the county machines must be fed with jobs if they are to remain in existence. The governors of Tennessee have never shown a deep devotion to the principles of the merit system, quite possibly because they cannot be elected if they do. Tennessee had a merit system when Clement came to office. It could have formed a logical part of the administrative reorganization of Governor Austin Peay, but the time was not then ripe. The expanding national social services instituted by the New Deal called for a state merit system, and one was created, but it was strictly limited and not always rigidly observed where it existed. State jobs, whether in Nashville or in the field, were still distributed with close attention to the county campaigns just past and just ahead. This was the system that Clement inherited, and he did little to change it, aside from those areas, such as fiscal administration or health, where technical competence was his first consideration. In those areas, where Clement insisted on the appointment of technicians, he usually did not ask, and sometimes did not know, what political loyalties his appointees recognized.

The mechanism for the spreading of patronage follows the imperatives of size and place. In spite of opposition criticism, there must be "a man to see." Clement campaigners made what they could of "Rube" McKinney, the "man to see" in Browning's headquarters. McKinney was lampooned accordingly. But Clement had to have his own man, and individuals close to the governor aspired to the post. Frank Clement was deeply attached to his father, and the elder Clement was influential in many ways during all three administrations, but he was not acknowledged as the chief patronage dispenser. Friar and Ellington were the principal rivals for this role, and in the end Ellington won, a sensible arrangement given the close ties between jobs and vote-getting. Friar did not lose easily or gracefully; Bob Crichton was thought by some to want the post as well, and Friar and Crichton split sharply with Clement before the second campaign was mounted.

Jobs at the local level were distributed by the committees that had been used to carry on the campaign. Sometimes known as the patronage committee, the campaign committee, or simply "the committee," Clement and Ellington cleared appointments with them and listened to their complaints, for rivalries and rows were frequent, particularly in smaller counties. Rural intimacies made for sharp enmities, particularly where jobs were not plentiful. "The personnel your administration is hiring is embarrassing to me," wired one local supporter, and the copy of the telegram that reached the governor's desk bore the urgent secretarial gloss, "He has been calling for days."

Perhaps the constant nagging of local committees was the burden heaviest to endure, but other appeals rolled in. Both senators wrote the governor on job appeals or recommendations, well-known members of the House of Representatives, both Democratic and Republican chimed in, mayors, councilmen, ministers of the gospel—all offered advice. Even the governor's staff lent a hand occasionally. On one letter from a persistent applicant, the staff member noted that he had been trying for months to land a job with the state. "Poor man," she wrote.

Given the frantic scramble for employment, it is surprising that so little trace exists in the correspondence of the use of patronage for controlling the legislature. The governor did not put warnings to recalcitrant legislators on paper, and yet it is difficult to believe that no such pressure was ever exerted. Perhaps the presence of the threat was recognized without its being clearly stated. A few legislators did not hesitate to ask the governor for favors, and occasionally the governor lost friends because he would not—or could not—honor the appeals. Occasionally a legislator would land a post for himself.

Such was the demand side; how about the supply? Ellington's despairing note indicated that the supply fell short. Leaving the judiciary aside for the moment, the big jobs were the cabinet posts, the constitutional offices, and the leadership posts in the General Assembly. These had been settled early, with careful attention to all criteria. What was needed below this level was a large reservoir of jobs, either unskilled or capable of being learned with a minimum of training. These were to be found chiefly in those areas where extensive public services were offered. One of the largest areas of employment was in public education, but that area was fairly well—although not entirely—closed to political choice because of the professionalization of teaching and the power of accrediting associations, to say nothing of public attitudes on the matter. The other big service areas, statewide and local, and the prime targets for the distribution of spoils, were the departments of highways, agriculture, finance and taxation, the highway patrol, welfare and employment security, and conservation—particularly, in the latter, those activities associated with parks and park concessions. In some of these departments, if jobs were distributed, the applicants had to be filtered through the merit system, and in all the departments some degree of expertise had to be considered. Highway engineering requires technical competence; but the building of highways also requires large amounts of labor, and transportation has always been a happy hunting ground for the spoilsman. Health, welfare and employment security had federally imposed merit systems to observe, but applicants could be steered in that direction. "[Name withheld], the widow of our late friend [name withheld] is in desperate need of employment," wrote a supplicant to the governor. "I am not sure of her exact qualifications except that we do know she is quite intelligent and capable." It takes no great effort to imagine the need that produced this letter. Clement replied: "Mr. Ellington and I concluded that perhaps the department in which she would be happiest and for which she might be best suited would be Employment Security. Don [the commissioner] is contacting Mrs. [name withheld] . . . and will place her in some position on an emergency basis, pending her subsequent qualification and certification, based on a Civil Service examination which will be given June 13." This could be labeled more of an act of charity than of politics, but in another exchange the same commissioner gave the governor notice of his intention to appoint [name withheld] as intermediate male clerk [mail clerk, assuredly, except for the minor slip]. "[Name withheld] was our sound truck driver during the General Election campaign and several of us have been committed to him . . . since then." Charity, too, perhaps, but the politics are frankly acknowledged. Boards and commissions, always tending to multiply out of control, offered another source of jobs.

But in any case, there were not enough jobs to go round. Posts of honor, rather than of power or pay, were used to satisfy the cravings of both donor and donee. "How on earth do you get to become a Tennessee Colonel?" queried one candid candidate. "I play the Tennessee Waltz every Sunday night on the piano for Mr. Hanky of the Marietta Eagles Club . . . Is that enough qualifications?" The governor's assistant, Glen Nicely, acknowledging this unabashed inquiry, noted that out-of-state colonels were appointed from a list of contributors to state or national welfare, and Nicely offered to place the aspirant on the list; it seems unlikely that he ever made it to a group that came to include Harry Truman and Alben Barkley. Most of the colonels were friends and allies within the state, and careful analyses were made of their distribution by counties. The governor wanted a limit set on the number; as W.S. Gilbert had once written, in a place where everybody is somebody, nobody is anybody.

The reverse of hiring is firing; "the man to see" may become "the hatchet man," the man designated metaphorically to bury the small deadly weapon in the skull of the appointed victim. Changes in party faction in Tennessee are the occasion for the forced retirement of big fish and small fry from public employment to private enterprise. Significant retirements of this kind, such as those of Joe Cordell Carr and Hilton Butler by the Browning administration, are matters of wide public understanding. No dishonor is involved; it is all part of the game. But dismissals of smaller jobholders can mean serious trouble for the people involved, and the threat is one of the burdens borne daily by the minor officeholder. While it is difficult to estimate the extent of this kind of turnover, it is easy, given his personality, to think that Clement would try to mitigate such hardship where he could. He knew that he was expected to give jobs to the faithful and that dismissals had to be made. Grievances were often most bitterly expressed, and defenses had to be offered. Wrote the spokesman of one "Clement committee," who described a résumé of the balloting that took place to mark those destined for lay-off, "Have always had your interests at heart and have tried to handle matters of this kind on a majority rule of the Committee. I feel this is the only fair way to do it." Dismissals were sometimes checked with Friar, sometimes with Ellington, but gradually Friar had to relinquish his role.

As this flood of trouble and heartache overwhelmed him, the governor was compelled to find ways to turn some of it aside. Typically, he dispatched a friendly letter to the jobseeker, pointing out that he did not interfere in the prerogatives of his commissioner, to whom he was passing the letter on. Some of this was assuredly "buck-passing," but sheer necessity made such delegation inevitable (and Clement was known for delegating thoroughly, with no strings attached.) What was not said was that the governor or "his man to see" would not hesitate to override lower-level decisions when necessary. Governor Clement could become peremptory when pushed to it. "Why shouldn't this man be dismissed?" he demanded in one note to a commissioner. To Eddie Friar, he wrote, "Please see that this man is not dismissed unless and until [name withheld] has been consulted," referring to an employee in the Department of Finance and Taxation. And once at least he ordered Ellington, "Work out something for him [referring to a personal friend] as soon as he is able and wants to go to work." Essential details did not escape the governor's attention.

Clement gave unusually close attention to judicial appointments. Although judges in Tennessee are elected by popular vote, the constitution gives the governor the power of interim appointments—and illness, death, and resignation give him more actual authority than might be expected. The power covers all levels of courts, from the minor general sessions to the Supreme Court. The total number of such jobs is not large, but the offices are eagerly sought. The pay then was not good but it was regular, the work is interesting, and the honor is substantial. Even if questions of public policy do not figure largely in selection, for the state courts have relatively little impact on controversial political matters, to the extent that public weal is bound to judicial competence, the governor's actions are important. Endorsements for candidates come principally from lawyers and other judges; at least one endorsement for a lower judicial post came from the chief justice of the Supreme Court himself. Bar association polls were frequently taken. Usually Clement appointed Democrats, although appointments of Republicans were not ruled out automatically. Close attention was paid to geography — the trinity of East, Middle, and West pervades all Tennessee affairs. Clement himself described the pressure on him as "severe," but it was largely quiet and unpublicized. In addition to heeding advice from bench and bar, the governor kept an eye on political and personal ties.

Early in his first term, Clement had to fill a post on the Court of Appeals. Andrew "Tip" Taylor was seriously considered, until he withdrew his name. The notion was interesting because Taylor was to become a serious contender for the governorship at the end of Clement's second term. In April 1954, Clement put John E. Swepston of Memphis on the Supreme Court. The appointment was widely approved, even gaining the grudging acceptance of Joe Hatcher in the *Tennessean*. Hatcher also approved the appointment of Lois D. Bejach to the Court of Appeals, although he observed that both Bejach and Swepston had Crump's approval. There is no reason to doubt the statement. In Sevier County, David Pack was made chancellor temporarily; Pack was subsequently to become a Clement cabinet member. Clement's first appointment to the bench, made in March 1953, was that of J.B. Avery of Alamo. The Averys of Alamo were notably faithful backers of the governor throughout his career.

Patronage is not confined to jobs. The ardent backers of candidates include car dealers, road contractors, oil and gas vendors, bankers, insurance salesmen, and architects. The correspondence that reached the young governor showed clearly that his backers were not looking for treasures in Heaven alone. Bankers wanted a share of the state funds, and letters asking for such shares received prompt and favorable action.

Quite frequently the governor's replies were put in terms of his promised improved standards of state purchasing, coupled with assurances that every business firm would have a fair chance to bid.

The new governor was dealing with an old phenomenon, but his administration had promised an improvement. The most dramatic element in the 1952 campaign had been the controversial Memorial Hotel transaction; Clement had attacked the "deal," had promised to undo it, and had pledged an investigation of the Browning administration. The promises were followed up. On the day following the inauguration, the governor had signed Senate Joint Resolution No. 12, authorizing an investigation into the hotel contract and other aspects of purchasing under the Browning administration. The presence, particularly in the House, of administration lobbyists, including Friar, Cayce Pentecost, Ellington, Robert Clement, and cabinet members Atkins, Pierce, and Butler, all duly catalogued by the *Tennessean*, indicated unmistakably the high importance that the administration attached to the resolution. It was passed with strong majorities.

The investigating committee consisted of five senators and six representatives, including both speakers and both floor leaders. Joe Hatcher praised the committee choices, saying the members were men of experience with reputations for fair play and independence, although he thought some good friends of Browning should have been included; his paper editorially labeled the committee as hand-picked by the governor.

Whether stacked or not, the committee was ordered to do a quick job; in fact the committee missed the deadline of February 23 by only one day. Although its proceedings were not public (how shocking this might have appeared twenty-five years later!), testimony got into the news, and again Hatcher, long a partisan of Browning, was impelled to express shock at the loose and improper purchasing procedure disclosed by some of the witnesses. The committee reported that its study had no more than scratched the surface of an unwholesome situation existing in all the departments it had looked at. Some of the witnesses could not be found; some had sought to avoid the service of papers, and at least one had succeeded.

It could come as no surprise that the committee attacked the hotel contract. No criminality was uncovered or alleged, but the transaction was criticised as unnecessary, and, under the conditions prevailing, the agreement was held to be illegal and void. "The finger" was clearly pointed at Martin and Doggett, and the report left Browning, even if innocently victimized, tinged with culpability and incompetence.

Browning was never charged with having profited from the contract.

The report then turned to the Highway Department, described in words that, in those days, if used by an academic researcher would have landed him in trouble. "It is the one department of State Government," said the committee members — who were in a position to know — "which because of its very nature is perhaps more susceptible to outside pressures and influence or more subject to collusive and fraudulent practices than any other Department." "Perhaps" is no more than a minor softening of these strong words. But then the committee became even more pointed: "Undoubtedly during the past four years, the Department of Highways and Public Works of the State of Tennessee has been generally speaking mismanaged and misused." Specifics were added: dummy companies, accommodation addresses, collusive and fictitious bidding, closed specifications, excessive purchases, and unnecessarily high prices. Expansion joints, paint thinner, and guard rails were the convenient commodities that facilitated these tax-burdening practices.

Having blanketed Highways and Public Works with these damning charges, the committee paid similar respect to the Department of Conservation, bestowing special mention on the park system. This time the specifics included improper sales practices, obvious forgery, fraud and collusive bidding, and the committee specified a particular Knoxville furniture company by name. In passing, the committee side-swiped a former commissioner of conservation for his use of state employees for work on his private property, a practice that perenially troubles public officials, big and small. Similar exploratory surgery was then applied to the department of purchasing and the penal institutions.

Conflict of public with private interest is a plaguey kind of thing for the public official. Obviously it is offensive for a public man to use his office for private gain, and yet the system itself fosters exactly that. Public life is a part-time and temporary affair for most of those in it. Clement was unusual among the governors in holding office for ten years. Even he, devoted as he was to running and holding office, was compelled to spend some of his short life in private pursuits. Men do not grow rich on their official pay. And the numerous small folk who make up the campaign organization across the state must live as private persons where doing business with the state or taking advantage of public decisions offers opportunities that cannot be resisted. But such connections, even if quite legal, give the political opposition issues that appeal to the voter far more forcibly than sober assessments of public policy.

The legislation passed by the Clement-dominated legislature of 1953 took some steps to meet the issue. Chapter 160 of the Public Acts of that year, sponsored by Clement's floor leader, Hoyt Bryson, made it unlawful for any state employee or official to bid on or sell or offer to sell any merchandise or equipment to the state during his tenure of employment or six months thereafter, or to have any interest in such sale. Penalties, civil and criminal, were imposed. Chapter 161, also backed by Bryson, made it unlawful for an employee of the Highway Department working in the Division of Materials and Tests to encourage the purchase of any particular material or product, or to assist in the preparation of requisitions for any state department. Chapter 163 reorganized the purchasing department, creating a Board of Standards within the renamed department, to consist of the commissioners of highways, public health, institutions, and conservation, and the director of the budget, with the director of purchases as secretary, to approve standard specifications, an obvious move to cut off the rigged specifications that the investigating committee had discovered. Methods of bidding were specified with some care; increases in purchase beyond the original bid were limited. A permanent register of bidders was established to cut down the fly-by-night firms. But the act was devoid of penalties, and it did not apply to contracts for highways, bridges, and public buildings. It was a step in the right direction; to say that it eliminated the threat of corruption and influence would be to claim too much. Patronage committees continued to interest themselves in the allocation of contracts. The writing of insurance for state operations was particularly troublesome as the approaching 1954 campaign was to show.

In due time the Memorial Hotel issue approached an end. The process of invalidating the deal began its slow march through the chancery court of Davidson County in March 1953. Late in the summer, despite efforts to keep the state to the deal, state employees started moving out of the hotel. Periodically through 1954, maneuvers were undertaken by the parties, and the court took evidence. In late August 1954, Chancellor Wade ruled that the making of the lease was beyond the powers of the state, since the action had not been based on a statute. The arrangement was brought to an inconclusive end; the issue had served its political purpose. In the meantime the hotel had gone under receivership. Stubborn as ever, Browning maintained throughout the 1954 campaign that the proposed lease would have been a good arrangement for the state, but this only contributed more votes against him. And so the hotel and the deal gradually passed away into the limbo of forgotten trivialities.

The location of highways was a constant occasion for pressure and trouble, and requests were sometimes unreasonable. As one comment put it, "The short route from [_____] is a dream route that has been kicking around for years. It looks good on a map, but the terrain in them hills is something else again."

Clement had set himself the task of creating a department of mental health, separating the treatment of the lot of unfortunate Tennesseans from the ministration of those who were charged with the correction of criminals. The enabling legislation sailed through the legislature without opposition, and Clement selected a professional man, Dr. C.J. Ruilman, to head the new agency. Browning claimed to have improved the lot of the mentally ill, and probably he had, but Clement started the sharp growth of state activity in this area that has since continued. Clement's reorganization and his promises to put technicians in charge of this service did not automatically provide a guarantee from the intrusions of the politicians, as the allegations of 1975–76 were to indicate.

The governor, like many another candidate before and since, had stressed his devotion to law and order, a law and order that was always threatened by illegal liquor, gambling, political violence, and labor unrest. He had to struggle with these forces then and in the future. In the early fifties, Polk County had furnished the most dramatic example of political violence. Clement had promised justice. He ordered an investigation by the Tennessee Bureau of Identification, and rewards were offered. The promises of 1952 had to be repeated in 1954, but today the murders in Polk remain unsolved—and forgotten. Time and death must soon conceal the truth forever.

In the scheme of things in Tennessee, the control of the liquor traffic and gambling is primarily the task of local police and prosecutors. Together with prostitution, and now, pornography, they constitute a mixture of annoyance and opportunity to local enforcers. By and large governors stay out of this quagmire, where, for the most part, their attention is not welcomed. Clement, however, in his first administration, showed an initial disposition to "crack down." He picked out certain counties where "night-spot" activity seemed especially flagrant and informed sheriffs in those areas that state raids would take place if the sheriffs were derelict. Some state action did follow. Suppression of this unrespectable although highly durable activity requires something steadier and more unremitting than crusades. Perhaps the governor's actions helped to keep things under a kind of control—that is the most that can be claimed for it.

A telling, although insignificant, feature of Clement's attack on

Browning had been the excessive use of state cars. With the instincts of a showman in full operation. Clement now arranged to sell a number of these vehicles at public auction. It was all part of the entertainment, as the governor no doubt fully appreciated.

Clement has been remembered as a good friend to education, and to the University of Tennessee in particular. For many years, the University had maintained some distance from gubernatorial patronage, and Clement showed no disposition to alter this relationship. Before Clement's time, the University faculty remained aloof from party politics, an attitude that was fostered by the attitudes of the administrators. Even the administrators themselves stayed out of party squabbles so far as they could. President James D. Hoskins, had never so much as met Edward Crump and did not want to, although the medical units of the University at Memphis did not hesitate to ask Crump's help when they needed it. With the accession of C.E. Brehm to the presidency, the fear of and animosity of the University toward the professional politician began to erode, and by the time Clement became governor, the administration and the faculty were interested in establishing relationships with the state government wherever suitable opportunities arose. Clement's early appointments clearly showed a disposition to use the talents of the University, but his contacts tended to be filtered through a small group of University administrators and researchers. Neither the governor nor the administration seemed to sense how to make a prolonged and determined effort to draw the faculty into participation with the top state administrators. Lacking a clearly articulated policy of this kind, individual faculty members were left to make their own contacts, as best they could, but inevitably the associations between the faculty and state officialdom slowly grew. Obviously the relationship involved dangers as well as opportunities; still, abuses did not develop, and relationships were generally amicable and fruitful for both sides.

The campaign of 1952 had featured the "split-UT" issue, as the thoroughly sensible proposal to unite Memphis State to the University was erroneously dubbed. Memphis State went its own way, developing programs that UT regarded suspiciously, and the University of Tennessee was deprived of a chance to grow. Echoes of the controversy arose again in a proposal to build a teaching hospital at the University in Knoxville.

At the conclusion of the Second World War, a group of Knoxville physicians led by Dr. R.B. Wood and the Acuff Clinic secured backing from the Tennessee Medical Association for a proposal of state participation in the financing of a hospital at Knoxville that would combine the functions of a charity hospital with cancer research. The once secret operations at Oak Ridge, besides producing a monstrous threat to civilization, held forth hope for peaceful uses of atomic energy. One such possible use involved treatment of cancer. At the same time the old and dilapidated General Hospital at Knoxville, where indigent patients received treatment, was due for replacement. The University of Tennessee, a struggling institution of some 3,500 students, was on the verge of postwar growth; its infirmary was small. The private hospitals of Knoxville could furnish no more than a limited number of inadequate facilities for specialist study. The Acuff group needed a new building and an additional hospital for practice. They sought to put all these needs together; a new hospital was suggested, to be attached to UT at Knoxville, to be paid for by state, county, and city, to provide specialized teaching, cancer-oriented research, and private and indigent care.

Of course, the proposal aroused opposition, as all such proposals do. McCord's blessing was secured and, later, Browning's, but Browning regarded all public expenditures with sentiments of suspicion; as he wrote to Senator Albert Gore who was interested in a similar hospital for Oak Ridge: "When a phobia breaks out for trying to get money out of the state treasury, rabies is not a circumstance." In many ways, the hospital issue was a parallel to the "split-UT" issue that had troubled Browning. Opposition came from within the Board of Trustees and the UT faculty at Knoxville, many of whom feared that a hospital would eat the heart out of the struggling UT's budget. The medical units at Memphis could see in the proposal the beginnings of a rival hospital in East Tennessee, and some faculty members thought the East Tennessee development might be countered by withdrawing the medical units in Memphis from UT and transferring them to Memphis State College. What was at issue here was the familiar rivalry between the geographical sections of Tennessee, always a major feature of Tennessee policy.

The plea that the hospital should be build near Oak Ridge to make use of fast-decaying isotopes was never very convincing, and less and less was heard of it as time went on. The prospect that the state would be led into a policy of paying for local indigents was one that had little appeal for some state leaders, particularly those who, like Browning, did not want to burden the state budget with charges that ought to be borne locally.

Despite opposition, the proposal went forward, pushed by the mobilization of Knoxville pressure groups, medical and otherwise. In Browning's final administration the proposal was brought to a temporary halt by a suit instituted by Colonel Harry S. Berry, a member of the UT Board of Trustees. Berry had tried to stop the project cold; he succeeded only in delaying it until Clement came into power.

Clement's initial impulse seems to have been to drop the project, but the same forces that organized the project in the first place were now brought to bear on him. Sam McAllester of Chattanooga, the Hamilton County member of the UT Board who had done so much to stop the union of UT with Memphis State, became a leading proponent for the new hospital. George Dempster, mayor of Knoxville, a long-time Kefauver supporter who was developing ties to Clement also, and Knox County Judge Howard Bozeman, who had strong ties to Clement, both pushed the project. The combination was a powerful one, and after a public hearing stage-managed by Eddie Friar, who knew the Knoxville political situation intimately, Clement announced his decision to proceed with the project. The hospital was built and became a successful institution—the center of several facilities, with a good training program and a sound hospital practice which Knoxville certainly needed. A research program was mounted, and over the ensuing years some advances were made in the widening fight against malignancies.

The governor is almost certain to be the object of attempts to get educational favors. Applicants for entrance into medical educational institutions frequently sought the governor's intercession. Requests of this sort rarely developed in other areas, partly because, presumably, the entrance requirements were not as hard to meet, as in the medical units. Clement responded to these requests courteously but vaguely, turning the letters over to the established educational officers. There is no evidence of administrative subservience to the governor or of undue favoritism, although the letters must have exerted some quiet pressure at least.

The governor's aid was occasionally asked for locating jobs in the higher educational units; these jobs were usually of a minor character, not impinging on the teaching posts, although a few would-be academicians tried the political route. The University of Tennessee had come to be too large and too prestigious to suffer any interference in appointments and other personnel actions of an academic kind, but some of the smaller institutions were not completely immune from such pressure.

Appointments to top-level administrative posts in the higher scholastic units had never been entirely independent of personal connections with political powerholders, and were not to be during Clement's tenure, but party regularity was not an element in appointments. For example, it has been said that the career plans of Andrew Holt were damaged temporarily by Governor Prentice Cooper's animosity. It was rumored that Browning had put people in administrative posts whom he liked and trusted, and in later years many significant figures in educational administration in Tennessee were persons who had served Clement and Ellington in important state posts. But most of these persons were not mere political hacks. They could show substantial qualifications for their jobs, including appropriate educational achievement. Still the desire of some faculties for a significant role in selection of administrators, and the appointment of administrators who had no connection with other state functions went largely unappeased.

Membership on the boards of the educational institutions were within the governor's gift and were valued prizes, particularly membership on the Board of Trustees of the University. Appointments were subject to local, party, and professional pressures, and Governor Clement had to give attention to these forces, but he always kept President Brehm and his successor Holt fully informed as to his probable choices.

The Clement cabinet was generally stable during the two years of the first term. Glen Nicely left the commissionership of conservation to become the governor's administrative assistant. Former Governor Jim McCord now in his middle seventies succeeded Nicely in the conservation post. Douglas Fisher, who had been a Clement law firm associate, joined the governor's staff as his counsel, one of his chief chores being the analysis of legislative proposals. Franklin Pierce succeeded Luttrell in the Department of Standards and Purchasing as Luttrell moved to Safety as a commissioner and Keith Hampton, a political leader in Marion County, took Pierce's former spot as commissioner of institutions.

As 1953 passed in 1954, certain portents of future problems began to emerge. Labor violence intensified: roadbuilding equipment was dynamited in Gallatin; barber shops were dynamited in Nashville. A troublesome municipal strike developed in Weakley County. Strikes occurred in Oak Ridge; Clement was called upon to intervene but declined to move. Racial issues had played no more than a submerged role in the politics of 1952, but black dissatisfaction became more open as the first term neared its end. A desegregation case was pending in Clinton, and the landmark case on school desegregation was decided by the United States Supreme Court in 1954. Whites became vocal against the placement of black blind persons in the white blind school at Donelson, and privately a few blacks commenced to express dissatisfaction with black progress under Clement. Labor violence and black agitation were to spell trouble for Clement in the future, as he now headed into one of the bitterest campaigns of Tennessee history. It was to be a campaign that would produce his most sweeping victory.

5. Lead Me On

THE SECOND CAMPAIGN

The 1953 convention, its work ratified by popular vote, had altered the ground rules of Tennessee politics. The governor's term, formerly two years with two successions allowed, had been changed to four years with no immediate succession permitted. Tradition in Tennessee had long favored at least one succession—a governor, it was thought, was entitled to his second term. Some governors had managed to stay in for six continuous years, and a few had returned for added years, after returning to private life for a short period. Clement was the first governor to have a chance at a four-year term.

The two-year term left little time free from speculation about the succession. No sooner had the governor been through the stresses of a campaign than he had to meet the tensions of the legislative session. After the Assembly had gone home, he might have a few short months free from the formation of plans, but late in his first year he had to begin to maneuver for the succession. Much of his second year would be given to campaigning for the second term, if he wanted one.

So it was that in the fall of 1953, before the ink was long dry on legislative acts, political writers began to float names for the 1954 campaign. Joe Hatcher, in the *Tennessean* in September 1953, mentioned "Rudy" Olgiati, mayor of Chattanooga, as a possibility. A couple of months later he reported that a trial balloon for the return of Prentice Cooper had been deflated. Qualifying petitions were said to be circulating for Clifford Pierce, the distant fourth-runner in 1952, and Clifford Allen's ambition showed no signs of weakening. Carl Fry, a Kefauver supporter, eyed the first floor office in the Capitol. Hatcher tossed in the names of McAllen Foutch, Walter Haynes, and John R. Long.

There was some speculation—and it strikes the observer as realistic—

that Clement was tempted at this time to abandon politics for the life of an evangelist. Politics always had strong appeal for him, but that career made serious demands at the expense of family life with his wife and small sons. Lucille, although she gamely supported her husband in public, did not fully share his taste for crowds of devoted or curious people. Political life even for the governor carried its full load of disappointment and frustration. He could never manage to do all that he wished to do.

Public speech was Clement's art form. He was stimulated by audiences; he loved crowds. The drive to speaking was coupled to a deep religious fervor. For years, he had given money freely (and privately) to various Protestant churches. He frequently served as a lay preacher. He had formed a wide circle of friendships with ministers of various denominations; his enduring friendships with evangelist Billy Graham and with the Dr. Ira North, the lively leader of the Madison Church of Christ, were widely known. Repeatedly he had helped to raise funds for Graham's crusades. It seems certain the life of the evangelist beckoned to him, but, whatever his thoughts may have been, in the end he remained with his political career.

In 1954, Clement faced one of those painful choices that plague professional office-seekers. Estes Kefauver's first term was approaching an end. Kefauver's first attempt to grasp the presidency had come to nothing in 1952 (and another chance at that would not arise until 1956), so it was a "lead-pipe cinch" that the senator would run again in 1954. In 1948 he had slipped in partly because Crump had miscalculated. In early 1954, Crump was still alive, and even if his power was waning, he could be counted on against Kefauver. The prospect that Kefauver could be ousted was enough to tempt any man of ambition.

Before the 1954 primary took place, Clement would have passed his thirty-fourth birthday. That he nursed national ambitions cannot be doubted. It was alleged that he and Eddie Friar had worked out a Clement time schedule that would lead to the presidency, possibly half as a joke, but a joke with considerable seriousness behind it in any case. Herbert Bingham of the Tennessee Municipal League was only one of many who thought hopefully of making Clement president; Clement's correspondence files included many a letter predicting such a culmination of his career. If that was to be his goal, he had to be thinking of getting on with it.

But there were arguments against an immediate challenge to Kefauver. The governor was young. That was not a particular disadvantage in Tennessee, but he had been in office only a year and a half, and a race for the Senate so soon might have seemed overly presumptuous to the average voter. More important, Clement must have suspected that Kefauver would be a much harder man to beat than Browning. Clement's own support, in spite of the informal alliance between Browning and Kefauver, contained a growing number of persons such as George Dempster and Rudy Olgiati, who happened also to be Kefauver people. In a contest with Kefauver, Clement could not count on them. All in all, a challenge to Kefauver did not look entirely promising.

Casting about for means of coming to some decision, Clement circularized his cabinet members: should he run for reelection as governor or should he try the Senate? Overwhelmingly they counseled him to seek a second term as governor. Not one person advised running for the Senate, and one or two of them came out specifically against the Senate. No doubt some of this was pure self-interest—cabinet members do not tag after an ex-governor to Washington—but much of it can be attributed to plain good sense. The time was not ripe, and Kefauver would be hard, perhaps impossible to beat. Joe Hatcher maintained that Clement's financial backers would not stake him to a Senate contest, and the notion makes considerable sense even though Hatcher cited no sources. Nevertheless, during 1953, Clement played his hand close to the vest. He made it clear he would be a candidate for something—this was always his position—but he declined to say what. But Clement clearly recognized his need to run for office. As he once wrote, "If a man wants to buy an automobile, get married or run for political office, he will do just that regardless of advice."

Doubts were resolved early in January 1954 when Ellington announced that around March 1, he would leave the cabinet to serve as Clement's campaign manager for reelection. At the same time, Ellington took himself out of the running as a possible candidate for the Senate. Ellington's announcement also was a final indication that he had been the victor in his rivalry with Friar, although the extent of Friar's falling-out with the governor had not yet come clearly into public view.

That there would be a return bout between Browning and Clement was made certain by Browning's announcement of his own candidacy on January 19, 1954. Many of Browning's friends, including some on the *Tennessean* staff, had urged Browning not to run. Browning, however, was as devoted to public office as Clement was. He had been running so long for something, said the *Banner's* Leslie Hart, that the babies he had kissed in his first campaign were now old enough to vote for him. Browning was a determined fighter and the wounds he had sustained in

1952 went deep. It is galling to any man to see his program overrun by a successor, and Clement's spending policies went sharply against the fiscal caution that had been the hallmark of Browning policies. But Fortune's wheel was turning down for Browning; he was entering his last campaign for his own candidacy, and the results were to be disastrous.

Browning had announced on January 19; Clement made his candidacy official on February 1. Both announcements, coming somewhat earlier than is often the case, guaranteed a long as well as a hard-fought campaign. Clement's announcement brought swift and enthusiastic endorsements, both from newspapers and individuals, a sure sign that he was riding a victory wave. The *Commercial Appeal* endorsed him as early as February, and as the campaign developed during the next several months other influential newspapers came over to him, including some that, like the *Chattanooga Times,* had backed Browning in 1952. Of the big dailies over the state only the *Tennessean* stuck to the ex-governor.

In the 1952 campaign, Clement had found it necessary to build his own organization on the remnants of the McCord machine. In 1954, this organization, tightly managed by Ellington and fed on past patronage and burgeoning hopes for the future, was undoubtedly in top form. Local squabbles had been at least partially resolved, and rivalries at the top had either been put aside or partially subdued. Bill Baird of Lebanon and Rudy Olgiati of Chattanooga, firmly established municipal leaders, continued to back the governor. The Tennessee Municipal League was highly pleased with Clement. McCord was now in the Clement cabinet, his own ambitions not yet revived. Some in the Clement camp, already satisfied that the 1954 results would be flattering, were looking forward to the national events of 1956.

A few defections were in process. Although the falling away of Crichton, Friar, and Bodfish had become known in the winter of 1953–54, the split got little attention until late in the campaign. Crichton was no longer in charge of finance (Russell Brothers had succeeded him), and Mrs. Bodfish was replaced in the women's organization by Mrs. Albert Hill, whose later election to the national Democratic committee signaled the triumph of the conservative wing of Tennessee Democrats over the Kefauver forces, represented by Mrs. Tom Ragland. The roster of Clement supporters evident through this campaign is a catalog of the political notables of the time: "Hub" Walters of Hamblen County (veteran party officeholder of conservative views and friend of East Tennessee Republicans, who were switching from Browning to Clement), Ross Dyer and his wife (from West Tennessee), Hugh Abercrombie (wealthy "fat cat" of Hamilton, where the Clement contingent also included the former county official, Will Cummings). In Hamilton County, the Clement-Browning rivalry was reflected in local politics, for young Wilkes Thrasher, son of a Cummings rival, became Browning's state manager.

The Clement organization included numbers of people who in the years ahead would be prominent in state affairs. Charles Lockett of Knoxville, who broke his law partnership with Eddie Friar to remain loyal to Clement, was to become a member of the University of Tennessee Board of Trustees; in 1978 Lockett backed Jake Butcher rather than Clement's oldest son, Bob, for the governorship. J.N. Doane of Jefferson County was to become Blanton's commissioner of personnel. Howard Warf of Lewis County remained loyal to Clement despite his disappointment in not being named commissioner of education in the first cabinet (he made it, later). John Bragg of Murfreesboro and David Pack of Sevier County were to be significant state officials in later years. Established friends stuck with the governor: Don McSween, Chester Parham, the devoted Sam Coward of Livingston, Sam Ridley of Smyrna, and cabinet member Arch Northington. Jim Alexander in Carroll County and Jimmy Peeler were to continue their careers throughout the Clement-Ellington years.

It was inevitable, even if futile, that Browning would attempt once more to tie Clement to Crump. Opposition to Crump gave meaning to life for Browning. Although Crump had not always approved of Clement's policies, after some initial tiffs, Clement and Crump had been seen together in Memphis, and this was enough for public condemnation by Browning and the *Tennessean*. Crump announced his backing of Clement in early February 1954, and the backing was undoubtedly welcome to Clement. But it was no longer crucial. Crump was to die not long after the primary, and his machine suffered some temporary disarrangement. Clement's career remained unaffected by these events.

The campaign of that year was bound to be something of a rehash of 1952. Only two years had passed and the two principal contenders were the antagonists of 1952. Both Allen and Pierce were qualified as candidates, but neither made the race. Governor Clement had put a considerable portion of his announced platform into legislation, and it was a platform that often parted company with Browning's deepest instincts. This was especially the case with deficit financing, or what Browning chose to call deficit financing, for in a proper sense, with the exception of the $5 million for textbooks, the Clement additions to the debt were not improper, or even ill-advised. But Browning never liked debt; his idea of proper procedure was to pay for the future out of the surplus he could scrape up from the present. It was a safe program, but a program that was not entirely fair to the present generation. With respect to other matters, Clement's actions were not greatly different from what might have been expected from Browning. Browning was still anti-truck, but that he could have held the line on increasing truck weights, given the technology of the time, is highly doubtful. Clement's charges of corruption cut Browning deeply, and he was bound to defend his record.

Two big issues loomed—desegregation and reapportionment. They were nettles that neither candidate was eager to grasp. Reapportionment could be put off, for a short time, but desegregation had to be dealt with in some way.

Desegregation was a no-win affair, whoever tried to handle it. The two Brown decisions handed down by the United States Supreme Court, in 1954 and 1955, must have made it perfectly clear to the discerning that the old days of complete separation of the races in public schools were coming to an end. Resistance to any change whatever could at best be no more than a rear-guard action, although at the moment no one could say with absolute certainty how far federal action would be pushed. Southern candidates, even those in the states of the Upper South, had a limited range of choices. Straight out support for the court's decision and for immediate compliance with its guidelines were realistically impossible for any candidate who genuinely hoped to be elected. Certain academic liberals advised Clement to adopt this position, but they were not running for office, and the governor naturally discounted their views. Outright defiance of the court was popular in the more hare-brained sectors of southern opinion, even though such attitudes had little prospect of producing anything except confusion and trouble. The days of secession were a hundred years in the past. It seems probable that all the major political figures in both parties in Tennessee would have been quite willing to maintain segregation in the schools, and that many of them believed sincerely that segregation was both correct and right.

Two realistic positions were possible. A public official—or a candidate—could pronounce against desegregation, without threatening disobedience to court orders. Or, he could indicate that the law had to be obeyed but that compliance would be as cautious and limited as possible. Between these possibilities there was little to choose. Browning tended to take the first option; Clement, the second. Browning went so far as

Man in the white suit—courthouse square crowd in 1954. Photograph courtesy Tennessee State Library and Archives.

to say that desegregation would not be allowed if he were elected, but he did not say how he would prevent it. Clement, challenged by Browning to take a clear position, said that he would not desegregate, noting, however, that the state had not been ordered to do anything. It took little imagination, although this was left unsaid, to suppose that in due course the state would be ordered to do something. The two men were not far apart, and there is no reason to suppose that either was insincere. They both came from small towns to the west of Nashville, where desegregation had been a way of life as long as the area had been occupied by whites and blacks. They had lived in association with Negroes all their lives in a social situation where the black man had occupied an inferior status, but where relations were normally friendly, at least in outward ways. The black was in no position to change things in those small towns without the intervention of the federal judiciary. Neither candidate took quite the "no compromise" position that was assumed by governors to the south of Tennessee, and neither man fully satisfied the die-hards among the Tennessee people.

The bitter-end attitude was taken up by Criminal Court Judge Raulston Schoolfield of Hamilton County, who entered the race for the governorship on a segregation program. Schoolfield's candidacy had no discernible influence on the election, but he himself became a significant figure in Clement's life, for his impeachment and conviction by the House of Representatives and the Senate were to prove a major event in the history of the second Clement administration.

In honor of the long established practice of opening a campaign in the courthouse square of a small town, Browning officially opened at Trenton on June 4, 1954. He was introduced by his erstwhile opponent, Clifford Pierce of Memphis, who had abandoned his hopes of another try for the governorship in order to make common cause with other elements in the Clement opposition. Browning's campaign manager, Wilkes Thrasher, Jr., of Hamilton, was present along with other dignitaries. They and the crowd, who craved entertainment rather more probably than enlightenment, listened first to Gene Steele and His Roundup Boys of Memphis.

Browning's opening words—in a speech that was well written and forcefully delivered—were typical of his aggressive style. "It is not my nature mutely to stand by and let an immature and incompetent and deceptive official butcher a great state program, fill the Capitol with corruption and fraud—just to make himself a political holiday." The words clearly foretold a no-holds-barred battle; not all the entertainment was to be provided by the Roundup Boys.

The entire speech was principally an attack on Clement and a defense of the former governor's past record. Little new was offered by way of a program for the middle 1950s. Browning conceded no mistakes (few politicians do). He continued to defend the idea of toll roads. He attacked the truckers for their monster vehicles, many of which he said were overweight even by the new standards. He was clearly most pained by the debt policies of Clement. Clement had no monopoly on Holy Writ; Browning had complete command of Scripture, particularly those verses that hint of fire and brimstone. He quoted Job, 15-6: "Thine own mouth condemneth thee, and not I; yea, thine own lips testify against thee." With these ominous words as an opener, he then went on to review the promises made by Governor Clement in his opening Gallatin speech in 1952.

From the challenger's account, it was clear that the young candidate had been too hopeful in 1952. He had, Browning observed, promised a free and independent legislature, appointment of election officials free from partisanship or personal loyalties, conduct of business in the open, fairly awarded contracts, no new taxes, no state employees to be used as political pawns, and so on. The promises, except for the one of no new taxes, flew directly in the face of political reality; Browning did not claim that he could or would do differently. Browning went on to belittle Clement's achievements; he down-graded Clement's claims for improved mental health care, asserting that he had started the state's training of psychiatrists back in 1937.

Clement's opening salvo was fired at Lebanon, on the same day that Browning opened at Trenton. (Candidates in those days did not think of opening in Republican East Tennessee). Joe Hatcher had already tried to forecast the character of the Clement campaign as "another one of emotional appeal." The governor, Hatcher said, would promise a new state institution to treat alcoholics, lavish new old age pensions, and similar state aids. No promises were to be made about means of paying for these bounties.

The lines that inaugurated the governor's campaign were vintage Clement, sweet to the listening Lebanon ears: "From the historic rotunda of the Wilson Count Courthouse—'far from the madding crowd's ignoble strife' . . . in the center of the tranquil and serene city of Lebanon . . . a city of culture and learning, located in a county which has

enriched the public life of Tennessee by a host of statesmen and warriors.
. . . I open my campaign for a second term with pride, confidence and
enthusiasm."

He promised a dignified campaign free of rancour (a promise that
could not be kept as Browning harshly attacked the governor and his
father) and he listed a number of beneficial conditions in the state, such
as the good condition of agriculture, adequate forest fire fighting, and
good civil defense that not even the most accomplished orator could
make very exciting. Then he went on to note the large appropriations
for education, including improved teacher retirement and free textbooks. He endorsed TEA's 4-point program. He mentioned the cities'
new one-cent share of the gas tax. The governor stuck to his guns on
truck weights, but shifted—or tried to—some of the blame to legislative shoulders. He talked about improved purchasing procedures and
said gamblers and racketeers were coveting his scalp.

The governor skirted the segregation issue, asking for calm and cautious waiting. At this stage the Supreme Court had not yet issued its order for all deliberate speed on desegregation, having decided only that
segregation was unconstitutional. The governor's moderate position,
justified well enough on this score, was in itself an act of good sense and
courage, but it left him a target for the lunatic fringe on both wings.

In the peroration that begins this book and that must be credited as
completely sincere, the governor hoped that in the future people would
say that, during the humane administration of Frank Clement the aged,
the needy, the lame, the halt, and the blind—and the mentally ill—had
received unprecedented recognition and advancement. "Precious Lord,
take our hands," he said, " and lead us on." It was the core of Clement's
political theory and of his emotional response to life.

In 1954, as with most such campaigns, persons, not issues, interested
the voters. There were some issues, but not too much disagreement.
Real controversies were kept below the surface, for candidates could not
risk the voter alienation that always results from forthright positions.

Segregation could have been made into a red hot issue, but Clement
and Browning were both too canny to use it ruthlessly. Only Schoolfield, who entered the race as an independent, sought to make it the
overriding concern of the campaign. The civil rights issue, shortly to
loom larger in state and national affairs, was foreshadowed in the arguments over segregation in schools, but the bitter fights that surfaced in
the earlier national Democratic conventions were relatively toned down
in 1954. The between-convention meeting of the Democrats held in

Clement family — campaign flyer, 1954. Courtesy Tennessee State Library and Archives.

Chicago in late 1953 attracted little notice in Tennessee. Kefauver had lost his first bid for the presidency. Now, in this campaign, he was running again for the Senate. Browning had backed Kefauver's ambitions in the past, often to his own cost, and Kefauver might now have been expected to return the support. He did not do so—publicly, at least. Kefauver's connections with Browning were, in any case, calculated to lose Browning some votes, for the Tennesseans who disliked Kefauver's civil rights stands were quite numerous enough to damage Browning and benefit Clement. The anti-Kefauver vote had no place to go other than Clement, for Schoolfield was not a convincing possibility.

Other issues remained, more hum-drum, but they were issues that the two main candidates could talk about—and they did, often finding themselves on the same side. Labor had its own perennial issue: repeal of the right-to-work law. Clement promised in 1952 to seek its modification, but when he tried, the Assembly had snubbed his proposals. He promised to try again. Browning, too, sought labor support, but for him it was an up-hill fight, partly because during his final term he had used the national guard to keep order at the Enka plant. He defended himself, vigorously, noting quite correctly his paramount obligation to preserve law and order. He took broad swipes at agitators. For the moment, at least, Browning was on the wrong side, and Clement probably looked better then to labor, although before Clement's life was closed he was to find himself involved, as Browning had been, in the conflict between the claims of the law and the demands of organized labor. Then, he did what Browning had once done.

The teachers were campaigning for more money; TEA had a new program. Neither candidate was prepared to make an enemy of this powerful lobby. Both backed the TEA program, but here Clement had a slight advantage, for he had supported the teachers more recently than his opponent and had been able to finance his free textbook program without depriving the teachers of a raise.

The cities and their mayors were pretty well rounded up in the Clement corral. Although Browning had agreed to the mayors' program, Clement had been the one to deliver, and the Municipal League, officially nonaligned, was almost certainly in the Clement camp. On the same day that the *Banner* reported Clement's opener, it listed fifty-one mayors who had announced support for Clement; some of these were making the switch from Browning to Clement, a switch that became general throughout the state during the next two months. The *Banner's* roll of mayors included the big, the little, and the middle-sized. Chattanooga and Memphis mayors were included, places like Morristown, Bristol, Covington, and Pulaski came along, and many a crossroad municipality chimed in. Among other matters, the list indicated that the Browning hold on East Tennessee was loosening.

The big trucks were rolling. Browning attacked them, claiming the trucks were knocking the roads to pieces. No doubt he was right, but it was all a lost cause. And his proposals for toll roads did no better.

Finance was always in the background of all issues, for the state had become primarily a mechanism for the dispensation of goods and services and the partial transfer of the means of existence from the fortunate to those left out. Browning worried about the increasing debt, but the voters were not interested. Browning and others hinted from time to time that Clement wanted to raise the sales tax. Clement said this was all propaganda, and he and some of his campaigners threw the same charge at the other side. In fact, the sales tax was to go up in the next administration, but for the moment the Clement campaign avoided this dangerous subject as best it could. The benefits were accentuated; the cost was thought of as little as possible. It was, all-in-all, the typical mode in which popular campaigns are conducted.

However nobly campaigns start by concentrating on the issues, what really engages the voter is unfortunately personal attributes, some good but many bad. In 1952 Browning had endured the misfortunes of the Memorial Hotel deal. In 1954 he sought to dramatize some of Clement's mistakes. Just as Clement entered office in 1953, he acquired a new Cadillac—a new Cadillac or something like it had become a customary badge of office for Tennessee governors, financed by contributions from the Tennessee corps of colonels or from contributions from state employees. Browning had possessed such cars during his terms without exciting much comment, but Clement's Cadillac brought trouble. In the 1954 campaign, Robert Crichton, who had been Clement's finance manager in 1952 but who had fallen out with him in early 1954, asserted that he had given Clement the money for the automobile; it was suspected, at least, that the money came from surplus campaign funds. Clement became alarmed by the stories; he insisted that he had bought the Cadillac for his wife, using his savings. He offered proof of various sorts, without succeeding in killing the stories off. The opposition press, particularly the *Tennessean*, played up the Cadillac story wherever it could but without any noticeable effect. The matter never attained the significance of the Memorial Hotel deal, where the key figures ran into more than a million.

Browning's bitterest shafts were directed at Clement's father. The elder Clement had become inured to criticisms and misfortunes. Both he and his own father had suffered their full share of ill luck. The attacks must have hurt Frank Clement deeply; his admiration for his father was deep and strong. Browning satirized the elder Clement as Pappy Clementine, and a song on the subject was prepared to be sung obviously, to the tune of "Darling Clementine." The ex-governor's attacks were downright brutal. Clement senior, said Browning, had never practiced law before any court higher than a j.p. A fee of $240 was a fortune, Browning said, to Robert Clement. Browning attacked Clement's credit rating in his own home town. The *Banner* reported Browning's remarks in detail, no doubt thinking—quite properly—that they would harm Browning more than Clement. The *Tennessean* thought the elder Clement had played too large a role in state affairs in the past two years; it remained silent on the fact that Browning's father, F.L. Browning, had been that governor's trusted administrative assistant until ill health and approaching death had forced him from the Capitol.

Clement vigorously defended his father. Mutual loyalty was strong in the Clement family, an appealing emotion and perfectly genuine indeed, that the governor could nevertheless use to his political advantage. He put his parents on the platform at political rallies; he said: "I love and respect my daddy and I am not ashamed of the fact that I go to him for counsel and advice." This at Brownsville. At Cookeville: "I have sought the counsel of my father many times. You probably have too, if you have a father." Clement could have justifiably added that the adviser was a shrewd and intelligent man, whose advice was worth taking, but he did not need to. Familial attachment sat well with his Tennessee listeners.

Tennessean reporters attacked the insurance policies of the state and claimed that the elder Clement had played a major role in allocating lucrative insurance contracts to friends and backers. Information on the awarding of these contracts was at first denied, but newspaper pressure could not be ignored, and the governor released information on the awards. In fact, the awarding of insurance contracts in both the Browning and the Clement administrations showed that business was routed to political allies. Such awards were part of the patronage system of the state that had been and continued to be a set feature of the state's political system. Browning extended his attacks to Mrs. Reynolds, the woman cabinet official, whose husband was in the insurance business. The cabinet included former governor—presently commissioner—McCord, now a widower who was later to marry Mrs. Reynolds' mother.

As usual, Browning's remarks were far from gentle; he derided McCord as an old man in love. But the ex-governor always stopped short of criticism of the governor's immediate family. Lucille was no Eleanor Roosevelt or Rosalynn Carter; her own quiet nature gave her immunity. Lucille and the young boys, Browning said, were the only decent things about the governor.

Browning's seeming natural talents for invective, by no means latent, were consciously fostered by Clement's campaign staff who tried to think up ways of provoking their rough-tongued opponent. They sensed that Browning's outbursts would be self-wounding. In any case Browning needed little stimulus for the release of energy. Indeed the maddened ex-governor made some serious mistakes. One of these was his sudden attack on Mayor Olgiati of Chattanooga, a power in the state Municipal League, and a present friend and future rival of Clement. In a burst of passion, Browning promised to help the Chattanooga voters to remove Olgiati from city hall. Even in states less localized than Tennessee, governors do not publicly offer to oust mayors, and other Tennessee mayors flocked openly to Olgiati's support. The whole sorry episode was a minor replay of Browning's historic attack on Shelby County back in the late thirties when he temporarily foisted a unit rule system on state elections. The Olgiati episode was no more than a flurry, but it added votes, quite probably, to the approaching Clement landslide.

In 1952, Clement had promised vigorous law enforcement, particularly against the liquor and gambling spots that cluttered the sleazy outskirts of some towns and cities. During his first term, he had pressured some sheriffs into action and had reaped some approving publicity. Raids of this kind have at most a temporary success, and the "joints" crept back into operation. The governor's opposition now sought to make use of one of these operations to discredit the governor's law enforcement image. An offer was made to the *Chattanooga Times* by persons connected to the 400-Club outside Cleveland, Tennessee, to photograph some of the gaities the club afforded in the hours after midnight. The *Times* declined to play, and the offer was transferred to the *Tennessean*, whose management found the proposition attractive. Photographs were made, according to the Clement version of the episode, purportedly in the very early morning hours but actually in the afternoon, and newspaper readers across the state were offered pictures of the bar in operation on "two successive nights" in a locale that had supposedly been under padlock.

The pictures jarred the Clement camp. The governor later claimed that he had sought guidance in prayer. The governor's father, shrewd and observant, studying the photographs with care, noticed that the bottles displayed back of the bar presented an unusual character: the liquor was all of the same brand. The pictures seemed unreal; prearrangement was suggested. The Clement campaign headquarters attacked the bona fides of both the club owner and the *Tennessean*. The owner was on probation; operation of the club would have violated his parole (actually, it was claimed the club was closed). It seemed odd that the owner would invite public attention to a breach of his own parole. He explained the action by saying he was tired of making payoffs to the Clement administration—if so, his weariness produced immediate results. He was picked up for parole violation, and his club was padlocked once more. Judge Sue Hicks (non-Tennesseans should be warned that Judge Sue Hicks was a male), after judicially closing the club permanently, observed in off-the-bench remarks that the whole affair looked like a frame-up. The *Tennessean* categorized Judge Hicks as a Clement backer and ran the pictures again, pictures that carried the neat touch of showing Governor Clement's portrait hanging behind the bar, almost too much of a touch of artistry to be convincing. The *Times,* which had declined all interest in the 400-Club affair, ended by endorsing Clement, although it had backed Browning in 1952. The newspaper deplored the way in which the truck bill had been jammed through the Assembly, but it endorsed Clement's record in general.

Shortly after the unexpected furor over nightspot operations, the break between Governor Clement and his erstwhile close friends, Bob Crichton, Eddie Friar, and Jeanne Bodfish was brought into open view by Browning. The break had occurred some months before the active campaign and had resulted in changes in the campaign organization, but it had attracted little attention until, in the middle of July, Browning announced that he now had the support of three of Clement's closest friends. That there was such a break was quite clear; its underlying causes are still obscure, and the exchanges that now took place between the principals produced more questions than answers. Eddie Friar had been a close friend of Clement in the years immediately before the election of 1952. Their letters to each other have a youthful touch of friendship like little else in the Clement correspondence. Friar had planned and plotted to make Clement governor, and his imagination leaped far beyond that first office to peaks of national prominence. Now all this was swept away in mutual recrimination.

Robert Crichton's ties with Clement were less binding. As a prominent figure in the truck lobby, Crichton needed a favoring candidate while Clement needed financial backing. Their interests coincided. Jeanne Bodfish had been Clement's representative before the women voters. Young in political experience (although her father was a well-known political figure), Mrs. Bodfish had been an instructor in political science at Vanderbilt and a prominent member of the League of Women Voters. It is safe to attribute to her a zest for reform, clean government, and social welfare. Why the break?

Rumors floated around the gossip-charged atmosphere of Nashville, which, like all capitals, relishes personal foibles and clashes. Clement had his own version of the conflict, a version at odds with some other reports. Friar's motivations seem easiest to divine. It is not difficult to credit Friar's early friendship with Clement as genuine; it was always easy to establish friendship with Clement. Friar was not merely a Colonel House or a Harry Hopkins, however; he cherished ambitions of his own, and everyone knew that Frank Clement had no life tenure as governor. After 1957, Clement could not succeed himself, and most observers expected him to try for something higher. Friar looked toward the governorship, and indeed he later made an abortive try for it. Even before Clement took office in 1953, it was evident that Friar's ambitions were about to collide with Ellington's drive for office, and in this collision Friar soon lost out. In any case, as all too often in politics, friendship was destroyed by unsatisfied ambition, and the loyalties of early youth turned sour and was replaced by bitter and public recrimination.

Clement provided a public explanation of the break with Crichton; his reasons have the ring of conviction, but they are ex parte. Crichton's own ambitions were not as patent as Friar's, but it does not seem improbable that he used his record as a successful campaign financier to promote his own influence within the administration. Perhaps he pushed further than the governor would endure. One rumor had it that Crichton craved an appointment to the Board of Trustees of the University of Tennessee, an appointment the governor would have been unwilling to grant, but the rumor was unverified. Crichton and his two colleagues were reported to have objected to the elder Clement's influence and to his alleged use of political power to foster his law practice.

Jeanne Bodfish's motives for the break with Clement are the most obscure of all, for she kept them to herself, took no part in the 1954 campaign, and quietly left political life. For some years she lived outside the state.

Browning's use of the break within the governor's official family forced Clement to make some sort of public response to the rumors. He released to the press two letters that bore the date of January 28, 1954, one addressed to Friar ("Dear Eddie") and the other to Crichton ("Dear Bob"). To "Dear Eddie" he wrote: "This letter is perhaps the most difficult I have ever been called upon to write." To "Dear Bob" the version went: "Next to the letter I have just finished writing Eddie Friar, this is the most difficult I have ever undertaken." It is not difficult to believe that the letters were in fact painful, in every way.

The letter to Friar is a bit short on specific charges of a serious nature. Friar is castigated for decorating his office luxuriously, without competitive bidding, and for installing a record player in the back room of his office. He is charged, more seriously, with attempts to influence the awarding of state contracts. The governor has no power to remove the secretary of state; Clement called on Friar to resign.

The communication to Crichton is slightly more circumstantial. The governor said Crichton had been a major factor in rushing the truck weight bill through the legislature without the hearings that the governor had requested. It is not to be credited that the governor, familiar as he was with legislative procedure, could have been denied hearings that he may have requested, although it is not hard to believe that Crichton and other trucking representatives, including influential members of the Assembly, were glad enough to see the truck bill move rapidly and to do whatever was necessary to put it through in a hurry. Hurry was the usual order of the day in the brief sessions of the General Assembly in those days, and only those in the path of the steamroller were likely to complain of legislative speed.

But Clement's letter goes on to complain of Crichton's attempts to get state business for firms he was interested in and charges him and his friends with efforts to control the departments of highways, finance and taxation, and safety. Near the end of the long letter Clement wrote: "You have several million dollars to leave to your children and you would not permit me or anyone else to rob them of this wealth. I have only a good name to leave my children, and it is worth far more than your millions and neither you nor anyone else in or out of politics, regardless of how rich and powerful you may be, will be permitted to take away from my family the only thing I have to leave."

The correspondence of the governor includes a long statement, printed in capital letters and evidently used for a public statement, entitled "The Crichton Story." This statement lists more specific charges against Crichton, alleging his attempt to control state deposits, to influence Commissioner Leech, and, this having failed, to have him fired, to influence appointments of truck weight inspectors in the Department of Finance and Taxation, and to interfere in contract awards. The statement ends with the observation that, as Jesus had his Judas, Caesar his Brutus, so Clement had his R.M.C., G.E.F., and J.B.

Jeanne Bodfish, J.B., declined to fight back in public. She acknowledged the break, and once said she had been threatened if she made the break known. She supported no one for governor in 1954. Friar and Crichton fought back. Friar held a news conference late in July. He said he had never received the letter, and he claimed that Clement had written the account post facto, backdating his letter. He retained the services of a handwriting and typewriting expert and asked facilities for determining the date the letter was written. The governor declined to see the expert, and the *Tennessean* made what it could of the issue. Actually the date of the letter was somewhat irrelevant. What mattered most was the charge of influence peddling against Friar and Crichton, for, if true, they had risked putting Clement in the position that Browning had occupied in the matter of the Memorial Hotel. Both the charge and the actuality of influence peddling was always a possibility as long as the state's business was subject to influence, as it was then, had been, still is (even if somewhat reformed), and may ever be.

Nothing was ever proved, one way or the other; the voters believed the governor, or they disregarded the break. Charles Lockett dissolved his law partnership with Friar; he felt that Friar had failed to keep him informed and he thought his conduct incompatible with a friendly partnership. Crichton disappeared from Democratic councils. Bodfish finished her term as comptroller and retired from politics. Friar refused to resign and finished his four-year term. Loose talk and small moves to impeach him came to nothing. He attempted to run for governor in 1958 but had to withdraw from the race just before the primary; after a period of law practice in Knoxville, Friar emigrated to the West Coast. The whole episode furnished grist for newspapers, magazines, and biographers and cast a light on the old connections between state politics and the world of contractors.

The murder of August Lewis still haunted Polk County. Clement had failed to locate the killer or killers, and the Lewis kin were deeply disappointed. A poem, "Waiting for the Answer," was dispatched to the governor:

August Lewis was shot from ambush,
   And you said in fifty-two
That the blame was all on Gordon,
   And we certainly thought you knew.

No answer ever came. Clement appeared again in Polk County, accompanied by armed supporters and equally well-equipped opponents. Luckily, the peace was maintained.

The grinding campaign in summer's humid heat took its toll from everyone. Lucille Clement was exhausted, and her distaste for politics grew. The governor, in those days before TV was quite the mainstay it has since become, tried to touch base in as many counties and small towns as possible. Browning adopted the same tactics, and the two put in long hours moving from town to town, accompanied by country musicians. Clement began to appear in a white suit and a broad-brimmed white hat, a costume that contrasted with his dark handsomeness, and, as he warmed to his own words, excited and stimulated, as he always was, by the responsive audiences, he would shed his coat and give his speech the full accompaniment of vigorous arm and shoulder movements characteristic of the evangelist and the melodramatic actor. Those were performances to be remembered.

His detractors would always note that he spoke with effect, but they would charge that he had little to say. The comment is simply not true; it reflects the sophisticate's distaste for florid English, which Clement used constantly, and for the use of Scripture. American politicians have always used the Bible, and to good effect; like Shakespeare, the Bible is "full of quotations," and both Clement and Browning knew the Scriptural language and used it to the full. But there was content, too, for Clement took care to list point by point (he and his speechwriters loved points — in one speech the points amounted to seventeen) what he had achieved for Tennesseans, particularly the disadvantaged and what he had done for the community he was then visiting. Almost always, the governor insisted that he was conducting a high-level campaign, but he generally allowed a word or two to describe the opposition's "viciousness" or its "hymn of hate." Repeatedly, his administration's quality of "humaneness" was stressed. The voters of the state — and whenever he was close to the state line, the out-of-state nonvoters — flocked to savour the oratory, for both candidates were gifted speakers and the attacks and counterattacks rated above fried chicken, cornbread, and catfish.

Money was needed, and it was found. State law required no proper reporting in those days, and information on amounts and sources is fragmentary. Contributions came from many sources and in both large and small amounts. Joe Hatcher said that Clement would be able to count on a minimum of half a million dollars, and labeled the truckers and heavy equipment vendors as probable big contributors.

This time, as chief executive, Clement benefitted from the contributions from state employees. The *Tennessean* went through the time-honored ritual of condemning employee shakedowns, and Clement issued a memorandum relieving employees from the obligation of making contributions, but it is certain that they did contribute. It is probable that in some departments the contributions were tabulated and checked against the employee rosters. It is not so clear that reprisals were threatened or taken, but it is certainly true that they must have been feared. It is equally certain, however, that a lot of employee contributions were made willingly; those who had jobs were not likely to favor Browning's return and the uncertainties that could bring. Services in kind were given in various ways—advertising space, automobiles, free entertainment (Clement was always something of a favorite in the world of country music).

Most of the newspapers, large and small, declared for Clement. The *Tennessean* was fully committed to Browning and, up until the last hours before the primary vote, stubbornly predicted his victory, although it is difficult to believe that experienced reporters could not sense how things were going. For Browning the wheel of Fortune now made its final disastrous turn. The vote on August 5 was an astonishing mandate for Frank Clement. He carried 94 of the state's 95 counties, a record seldom attained, although Prentice Cooper had turned in such an accomplishment in earlier years. The county majorities were staggering. In the state as a whole, Clement brought in 68 percent of the votes cast. In 79 counties the governor secured 60 percent or more of the total vote for governor, and in many counties his majorities reached the upper seventies or eighties. Even Polk County, where his enemies were strong and his failure to solve the Lewis murder may have hurt him, gave him a majority of 67 percent. Polk County was quiet on election day (some had feared violence), but pro-Clement election commissioners seized election boxes from the office of Sheriff Edwards.

The vote in the four metropolitan counties was lop-sided. Knox and Hamilton counties voted 72 percent for Clement; Shelby County delivered a heart-warming 78 percent. And even Davidson County, where Clifford Allen had vainly backed Browning, surrendered to Clement by a 62 percent majority. Browning was spared the final humiliation of losing his home county, Carroll, but even here Clement received 45 percent of the vote. Raulston Schoolfield, the avowed segregationist candidate, acquired something less than 30,000 votes in the entire state, a fact that says much about the values held by Tennesseans. Close to 5,000 of Schoolfield's votes were in his home county of Hamilton, which aside from being his base was a county that showed a considerable segregationist bias.

The elections for the General Assembly showed some changes in the form of retirements or losses of important Clement personalities: Hoyt Bryson, Jim Camp, Everhart, Sterling Roberts, and Harry Mansfield. But both houses remained strongly pro-Clement, and it seemed apparent that his control of the legislature in the next four years would be stronger than ever.

Browning's defeat spelled the virtual end of a long political career. He suffered the repudiation that seems to be the all too common tragedy of democratic political life. In spite of his harsh attacks on his opponents, he had been a man of achievement in Tennessee affairs, a man loyal to his friends, sometimes to his own harm, and a man of upright personal life. He had quite simply been around too long. He tasted the defeat that was to be Clement's own portion only ten to twelve years in the future. Browning retired to private life, to business, to local judicial office, and to continued participation in political life as a backer, not a candidate. In his later years, he suffered from Parkinson's disease, but, increasingly enfeebled, he outlived many of his friends and political enemies— Cooper, McCord, Clement, and Ellington.

Clement could afford to be magnanimous toward Browning, and he was. Indeed, magnanimity came easy to the governor, for it was deeply engrained in his nature. Browning was given various courtesies, and the two met from time to time. Even the elder Clement, who had been the butt of Browning's astringent sarcasm, established more cordial relations with Browning in the evening of his life. But all this did not keep Browning from further attempts to aid in Frank Clement's defeat, an attitude that could be anticipated easily in the context of factional politics in Tennessee. Clement and Gordon Browning never again came into a direct two-man confrontation.

While the Democratic primary was disposing of Browning's future, other political fates were dispensed by the same means. Kefauver was nominated for his second term. He was challenged by Pat Sutton, a member of the lower house of Congress. Characteristically, Senator Gore refused to become involved in the Kefauver-Sutton contest. Kefauver, although some of his followers ran scared, defeated Sutton without much trouble, 440,497 to Sutton's 186,363. Sutton obtained about 9,000 less votes than Browning, but Kefauver was about 40,000 behind Clement. Sutton carried or came close to carrying only a few counties, but the votes indicated that Kefauver's strength lay strongly in the east, his weaknesses in the west. The election placed Kefauver in a secure position in the Senate and ended Sutton's officeholding. Kefauver was to face one more senatorial challenge six years later, this time from "Tip" Taylor of West Tennessee; in the meantime his career had fateful consequences for Frank Clement.

Primaries for seats in the lower house of Congress also carried portents for Clement's future. County Judge Howard Bozeman of Knox County, won an uncontested Democratic nomination for Congress in the Second Congressional District; Clement campaigned for him before the general election. Districts four through nine in those days were safely Democratic, and some of the incumbents had these seats firmly tied down. In the Sixth District, a close race developed between Ross Bass, former postmaster of Pulaski, and John R. Long, one of the powerful mayors of the state. Bass defeated Long by a small margin and laid the basis for later contests with Clement for the United States Senate.

The underdog Republicans staged a modest primary, mostly undistinguished by contests. Presumably large numbers of Republicans chose to vote in the Democratic primary, and probably a great many of them, by deserting Browning, helped to bring him down. Knoxville's colorful and successful criminal lawyer, Ray Jenkins, who had obtained a brief notoriety as counsel in the Army-McCarthy hearings, was nominated for a useless race for the Senate. Carroll Reece, the Republican leader in the First District and the good friend of Herbert Walters of Morristown, retained his power and his office in the First Congressional District and in Congress. For governor, and in the Fourth, Fifth, Seventh, and Eighth districts, there were no Republican contests at all.

The primary over, the Democrats did what they could for the general election. In the period between elections, on October 16, 1954, the old Red Snapper—Boss Crump—who had reached eighty on October 2, died.

The November outcome was never in any doubt. Clement worked for Bozeman in East Tennessee; some unkind critics of the judge said Clement worked harder for Bozeman than Bozeman had worked for Clement. Be that as it may, the Second District could not be moved from its traditional loyalties to the Republicans. Since the Civil War, the district has never sent a Democrat to Congress. Bozeman made a creditable showing, but he could not erase the unsullied Republicanism of the mountains. One of history's small ironies is that the winner, Representative Howard Baker, was the father of the Howard Baker, Jr., who was to deliver the final defeat to Frank Clement only twelve years later. In the Democratic districts of Middle and West Tennessee, very few voters bothered to go to the polls; all the issues had been disposed of in the primary. Tom Wall was the Republican candidate against Senator Kefauver, and, although Kefauver secured a heavy majority, Wall's vote of over 100,000 indicated that Kefauver still aroused substantial opposition in the state. Much of the Wall vote came from East Tennessee (even though Kefauver was an East Tennessean), but the undercurrents of Kefauver's opposition elsewhere was a sign of the future struggle that helped to wreck Kefauver's second bid for the presidency, a bid and a defeat in which Clement forces played a significant role.

Clement had been returned. Two months thereafter he entered his dramatic second term, in which he would face some of his most serious tests. The sunny noon of his career was now at hand.

♪ Work, for the night is coming,
Work through the sunny noon;
Fill brightest hours with labor,
Rest comes sure and soon.
Give every flying minute,
Something to keep in store:
Work for the night is coming,
When man works no more.

ANNA LOUISE COGHILL, 1836–1907

6. Work Through the Sunny Noon

THE FIRST FOUR-YEAR TERM

The term served by Governor Clement from January 1955 to January 1959, the first four-year term in the history of Tennessee, was the high point of his short and spectacular career. His political power was at a peak. He had been returned to office by one of the most sweeping victories in Tennessee history. The tensions and frustrations that were to mark him, as they eventually mark most if not all the objects of public favor, had not yet become evident. The legislature was generally under his control. Of course, the Democratic party was not. There he had great power, but it was a power he had to share with the senators, both of whom — Gore and Kefauver — saw in the governor an ever-present threat to their own incumbency. His reputation as an orator — all the snide comments of newspaper critics notwithstanding — had spread far beyond the courthouse squares of Tennessee; he was in demand over the length and breadth of the country. In this second term he was to serve as the keynote speaker for the 1956 Democratic National Convention, a goal that would engage the hopes of anyone as committed to the art of public address as Clement always was.

Conflicts of great historic significance faced the state in this second term. The national investigation of illegal and violent behavior within organized labor was to lead to the impeachment and conviction of a criminal court judge in the state, in Tennessee history an unusual and distressing event made possible by the governor's decision to call the Assembly into special session to deal with the issue. Reapportionment of the Assembly became a more pressing issue, even though no resolution

157

was attained in this second term. And above all, the state and its governor faced the traumatic first experiences of desegregation as they struggled with the demands presented by the national judiciary on a puzzled,
divided, and reluctant people. Clement's moral commitments and his
political skills were fully engaged in these momentous four years.

The transition from the first to the second term was made smoothly,
with comparatively few changes in personnel. A new team of constitutional officers was necessary. Treasurer Walker had been forced by ill-
health to leave his office, and Ramon Davis, who had been director of
personnel, succeeded him. The open conflict between Clement and
Friar meant that Friar would no longer be regarded as part of the team,
but the term of the secretary of state was four years, and Friar remained
to fill out his allotted time. Jeanne Bodfish retired as comptroller of the
treasury.

The vacancy in the comptrollership led Clement to several of his
most significant appointments; he offered William Snodgrass the choice
of remaining as budget director or assuming the position of comptroller.
Snodgrass took the office of comptroller (officially, however, he still had
to be elected by the Assembly), and thus began the long career in that office that has carried through the succeeding years of Ellington, Clement
(in the third term), Ellington again, Dunn, Blanton, and Alexander.
The choice was highly significant, for Snodgrass himself and for the
state. Snodgrass was never a professional politician; he was always the
technician living and working with political figures, whose imperatives
he could appreciate but not really share. His long tenure established a
tradition of competence for this key office, which over the years he expanded into the kind of agency it was meant to be.

The decision by Snodgrass to assume the office of comptroller left a
vacancy in the budget director's position, and Clement continued the
practice he had adopted two years earlier in appointing a technician to
this significant post. Snodgrass was asked for a recommendation. He advised the governor to appoint Edward Boling. Boling had been, as
Snodgrass was, a student of Harold Read, and as students Boling and
Snodgrass were good friends. Boling was unknown to Clement. He had
served briefly as an instructor in the College of Business Administration
at the University of Tennessee, Knoxville, and at the time of his appointment was holding a position as a fiscal officer for Union Carbide at
Oak Ridge. His political allegiances were unknown to the governor,
and he was not asked about them. The governor interviewed Boling,
and the two young men proved to be sympathetic to each other, but

Capitol Press Corps—(left to right) John Harris, AP; Howard Anderson, WSM; Les Hart, *Banner*; Tom Kesterson, UP. Photograph courtesy Tennessee State Library and Archives.

Boling took pains to warn the governor that, if appointed, he would be his own man, not a creature of the new comptroller, an attitude that the governor thoroughly approved. Not until many weeks after the appointment did the governor become aware, so far as Boling knew, where his budget director's political loyalties lay.

Boling's service as budget director led him into a career as a fiscal officer of the state, later the vice-president for development, and eventually the president of the multi-campus University of Tennessee. Boling, with the aid and support of Snodgrass, was to bring other young technicians into the fiscal and administrative structure of the state by the appointment of such persons as Harlan Mathews, Joseph Johnson, Roy Nicks, and Gerald Adams to positions in what became the Department of Finance and Administration. Mathews had been educated in political science at Vanderbilt, and had entered state employment first as a staff member of the Planning Commission. Johnson, Nicks, and Adams, and a number of others brought into the state service at this period and later, had been graduate students in public administration in the Southern Regional Training Program in Public Administration founded in the middle 1940s at the universities of Alabama, Kentucky (Georgia, in the first year), and Tennessee. Johnson, Boling, and Nicks all reached high administrative posts in the state educational system. Nicks' career took him into a cabinet post in Clement's third term and into active participation in Clement's campaigns. Nicks was the only one of these primarily technical people who made a visible transition from the world of administration to the world of political campaigns, but Nicks has never run for political office himself.

The cabinet remained stable; both technicians and politicians retained their posts as the second term began. Bomar remained as speaker of the House, and Maddux was reelected speaker of the Senate, both as a matter of course and with the governor's support. Some flurries of competition quickly died. Changes in the floor leadership were necessary as both Senator Jim Camp and Representative Hoyt Bryson had decided not to run again. Some tensions had developed between Clement and Bryson, but Clement had vainly urged Bryson to stay in the legislature, and Bryson, while not wishing to continue to public life, had offered to help the governor if he could. Camp remained active in patronage matters and eventually ran unsuccessfully for one of the three posts on the Railroad and Utilities Commission.

T. Robert Acklen of Shelby County became the floor leader of the Senate, and the youthful Eugene Collins of Hamilton County was chosen as floor leader of the House. Collins had served in the preceding session of the legislature when he had been a protegé of Hoyt Bryson; Bryson had gone to school to Collins' mother. Clement's relationships with Collins disclose the nature of the governor's powers in the Assembly, as well as his limitations, as they existed during the 1950s. Collins was still in his twenties. His campaign in Hamilton County was a low-keyed and inexpensive venture; in the primary and general election both he spent not more than $500. Moved no doubt by his friendship with Bryson, Collins decided that he wanted a significant position in the 1955 General Assembly, and he actively sought leadership, with the backing of political powers in Hamilton County, including Rudy Olgiati, Hugh Abercrombie, Ben Cash, J. Fred Johnson, and Leonard Aymon, all allied more or less with the Clement organization. He also enjoyed some support from surrounding counties whose leaders wanted friends for East Tennessee in positions of authority.

Collins enjoyed a slight acquaintance with Clement but had no strong part in Clement's own campaign. Nonetheless, Clement felt impelled to support Collins for the floor leadership, and Collins was happy enough to accept—but he also felt able to impose one highly significant condition on his acceptance. Although Clement had soft-pedalled the issue of an increase in the sales tax during the campaign, it was clear to students of the state's needs and its resources that the sales tax issue would arise in the legislature, and there was more than a little suspicion that the governor would back an increase. Collins had deep-seated ideological objections to the sales tax; he told the governor so and told him he could not support an increase in the rate if the matter came up. It is a tribute to Clement's gift for toleration as well as his feel for political reality that the governor accepted the condition without hesitation; it was agreed that when the issue came up, Collins would step aside for the temporary leadership of Damon Headden of Lake County, who was to be co-leader. This scenario was duly played through when the time came. Collins voted openly against the tax, and Clement accepted the defection, with no more than a little strain for a few days, although the *Tennessean* gave the episode all the publicity that could be wrung from the unlikely situation. There was no break in the cordial relations of Collins and his chief. Collins abandoned his legislative career after this term because he thought it could not be combined with the kind of success he looked for in his law practice, as many other legislators before and after him have done.

The leadership of the floor was no sinecure. Collins had to work

(*Top*) Charm for UT Latin American students—The governor and Comptroller Snodgrass, far left; author, fifth, back row. Photograph in author's collection. (*Bottom*) Speakers Maddux and Bomar with Latin American diplomats. Photograph courtesy Tennessee State Library and Archives.

hard, up early, to bed late. He had to study the legislation at night and attend the daily early morning conferences in the governor's office on the legislative program, attended by the governor, the key members of his staff, the two speakers, and the two floor leaders. The attendance at the morning conferences disclosed, as did those of the first term, the firm control which the governor and his legislative leaders exerted on the General Assembly. The state was still in the period when policy emanated principally from the governor, not from the individual members or party caucuses or committees of the legislature. On one occasion, Collins, worn-out by the pace of the few preceding days, simply dropped off to sleep while the governor was in the middle of a statement that failed to hold the floor leader's attention. Clement, who spotted the quiet slumber of his floor leader, walked over and shook him awake, and in the middle of the hilarity at Collins' abashed apologies, told him he was the first man ever to go to sleep during one of his speeches. It happened only that one time.

Collins was an adroit floor leader. He sponsored, for that was a major portion of his job, about 80 percent of the administration's proposals. Damon Headden took responsibility for the remainder, including the controversial sales tax increase. As in the earlier term, the administration had some legislation it wanted, and some it did not want. Collins watched especially for bills that some administrators had proposed to increase their own power. The governor's general control of the Assembly was assisted by the fact that the speakers, floor leaders, and other allies of the governor held membership on the Legislative Council Committee, whose executive director continued to be Tom Johnson.

When the legislature convened in January, it faced one new condition of some significance. Crump had died; Senate Joint Resolution Number One took note of his death and lauded his wisdom and business judgment, his devotion to clean and efficient government, his lowering of taxes, and his broadening of services and benefits. Not all of this encomium would have been endorsed by everyone, but resolutions memorializing politicians normally are not expected to be coldly objective; the resolution was duly passed, and a motion to reconsider was tabled. Such a motion to reconsider a memorial to a passing life must come as a shock to the uninformed reader of the Tennessee legislative journals. The truth is that a record of such motions to reconsider, and their prompt tabling, is applied to everything that goes through the legislature, and the result often makes surprising, inaccurate, and somewhat hilarious reading.

Crump's death was a symbol of the slowly but surely changing conditions of Tennessee politics. As has so often been the case with boss rule, he left no successor, and his machine was in some disarray in the years that followed. The Shelby County delegation to the General Assembly, which had once been carefully chosen to represent all interests although acting as a unit, commenced to break into fragments and ceased to exercise the extensive authority it had once possessed. Candidacies for the governorship would no longer be fought out with the endorsement or nonendorsement of the boss in view. Other leaders would arise in the state. One of those was Herbert Walters of Morristown, in whom some have discerned the successor to Crump, but, if he was a successor, he was decidedly different—quiet, reserved, and prepared to compromise without undue publicity, although undeniably conservative. In any case, Walters was more solidly loyal to Clement, and much closer to him, than Crump had ever been. But Clement had never been under the Crump thumb, and Crump's departure from the stage left Clement's situation relatively unchanged.

As always in Tennessee, the Assembly opened shortly before the inauguration date set by legislative resolution. This time the Assembly had to deal with two unusual questions of eligibility for Assembly membership. Richard Fulton, in later years to become a member of Congress, mayor of Nashville-Davidson County, and candidate for governor, had been elected to the state Senate from Davidson County although he was under the constitutional age. His elder brother, who had been the nominee, had died of cancer before the general election, and by party action Richard Fulton took his place. To Fulton's deep disappointment, the Senate, by a vote of 28 to 0, refused to seat him. The other question of eligibility arose under that article of the Tennessee constitution (borrowed from North Carolina—and years later, in 1978, held unconstitutional by the United States Supreme Court) that made ministers of the gospel ineligible for seats in the Assembly. Representative Sam Jenkins was a part-time minister. He was seated.

The refusal to seat Fulton had consequences for Governor Clement, for the man who was elected to fill the place left by Fulton's ineligibility was Clement's old opponent, Clifford Allen. Allen remained throughout his legislative career a persistent and annoying heckler of Clement and his policies. If there was any man in politics who gained Clement's clear enmity, that man was Allen (although even in this case, reconciliation was eventually achieved).

Clement was inaugurated a second time on January 18, 1955, but already he had presented his budget on January 11, in two hours and eight minutes of intense oratory that must have exhausted the legislators. The governor always gave his budget messages the same fervent oratorical pitch that he would use for an inspirational address. The two hours plus made it clear that expansion of services and heavier taxation were to be the keynotes of his second term. Gone was the cry "No More Taxes" that had punctuated the opening speech of two years earlier. The governor faced increasing demands from the teacher and highway lobbies, and he nursed his own vision of himself as a humane governor. He asked the Assembly members for $55 million in new revenue and presented them with appropriation proposals that reached a new high of $450,680,000. The legislators must have been overwhelmed by the figures as well as by the oratory.

Clement had already written the heads of the higher educational institutions of the state, who were not backward about asking for more money, for advice on where to find it. Although UT's Andy Holt remained evasive, many of the educators did not hesitate to ask for a rise in the sales tax, and the TEA came out for an increase shortly before the inauguration. Clement had expressed resentment when his opponents in 1954 had charged him with thinking of an increase in the sales charge—and Ellington disliked the idea of an increase—but the sales tax remained the most likely source; in short order, the chips came down that way.

Some teachers began to feel that the governor's former support had cooled down. One teacher, with a sense of irony, sent the governor a get-well card; to the printed text wishing the stricken person a speedy recovery, had been added, in writing: "Of the trust of the teachers of Tennessee." The governor filed this and another similar card away, and in due course it came to rest in the state's archives, a small memento of the fickleness of pressure groups.

Before the nasty bullet of added taxation had to be chewed, the Assembly took time out for the inaugural ceremonies. The Democratic clan gathered on the steps of the War Memorial Building in full force. All the past and present notables were on hand, with the striking exception of Gordon Browning: Gore, Kefauver, Prentice and Mrs. Cooper, Mr. and Mrs. Herbert Walters; Jim Nance and Mrs. McCord; several Stahlmans; George Lewis, the Legion friend from Memphis; Russell Brothers; Max Friedman; Joe Carr; and the family connections of the governor and Lucille Clement—'Cille to her husband and friends. Ross Bass, who was to hand Clement his first defeat in the next decade, was on the platform. The governor's colleague among the ten outstanding young men of 1954, Billie Sol Estes, occupied a place, yet to face the

(*Top*) Political powers—(left to right) Holt, Walters, Ellington. Photograph
Walters Papers, UT Library, Special Collections. (*Bottom*) Administrators—
Boling and Snodgrass, standing, second, third, left. Photograph courtesy Edward J. Boling.

Friend and aide—Harlan Mathews. Photograph courtesy Edward J. Boling.

building and eventual collapse of a business empire that would land him in prison. Fate was to turn, as it often does, the jubilation of that day into sadness and irony.

The fun completed, the legislature returned to the unpleasantness of revenue needs. A move to create a committee to study state finances, signed, among others, by long-time Browning backer McAllen Foutch and by Ben Cash, who was, at least off and on, a Clement man, died aborning; generally senators shied away from any idea of extensive fiscal exploration. Clifford Allen attacked the idea of an increase in the sales tax as soon as he got into the Senate, although he had been and contin- ued to be a persistent spender throughout a career that led him into Congress before his death in 1978. Finally in the early days of February, the administration grasped the prickly issue firmly and proposed a three- cent sales tax, a pay raise for teachers — to cost $10,700,000 — and a hike in motor vehicle license fees. The sales tax was to be extended to beer and whiskey, parking lot charges, and transient rental units, but pre- scription medicine and burial caskets were to be exempt. Henceforth, it was to be cheaper to go than to stay. The extra cent was to be dumped into the general fund rather than allocated to specific purposes.

The fight, such as it was, lasted no more than a few days. Former Governor McCord, whose administration had adopted the two-cent tax and whose subsequent defeat followed, publicly backed the increase, and when Jim Cummings, long a lynchpin of the Browning machine, came over, the battle was ended. Since Eugene Collins was committed against the increased tax, the bill was herded through the House by Damon Headden, whose motions to table one amendment after another were passed, usually with something around a two-thirds majority. The House voted final approval on February 10, by a vote of 67 to 30. On February 16, the Senate followed suit by a one-sided vote of 24 to 7. Sen- ator Ben Cash, who was committed against the sales tax to his constitu- ents in Hamilton County, as Eugene Collins was, voted against the tax. Clifford Allen voted "no."

A change in the original plans had been made. As the act emerged from the Assembly, all of the added one cent was earmarked for educa- tion, a tribute to the power of the education lobby, and a justification for some of the assemblymen placing an added burden on the taxpayer. In the Senate, McAllen Foutch had persuaded his colleagues to provide that the yield of the one cent beyond a set point should be distributed to the cities and counties, but when the House refused to go along, the Senate backed down. Foutch voted for the added one cent. The record appropriations went through without significant desertions; some abstentions and some absences were recorded in the journals, but otherwise unanimity was the rule. After all, in the legislature it is more blessed to give than to demand.

The tax and the appropriations were the major events of the legislature. Once again Governor Clement made a gesture to labor; he asked again for a revision of the open shop law and for the requirement of a minimum railway crew. On both counts, he was denied. The *Tennessean* carefully emphasized the disappointment that labor felt with Clement, but no governor could have secured the repeal of the open shop legislation; it was too popular with the legislature, who felt they were reflecting public opinion. Joe Henry, adviser and speech-writer for the governor, had persuaded the administration to introduce an anti-injunction law modeled on the Norris-LaGuardia federal act, but the proposal died in a popular storm that embarrassed both Henry and the governor.

The legislature, pushed by the Tennessee Municipal League, with the enthusiastic support of Eugene Collins, enacted a general annexation law, acting under the 1953 constitutional amendments, which, by allowing annexations by municipal ordinance, subject to a court review, opened up the way to a quarter century of readjustment of municipal boundaries.

Legislative reapportionment began to come alive, but neither the Assembly nor the governor was ready to more. The legislature continued to be dominated by the rural bloc, the governor had worked comfortably with the rural leadership, and even the Municipal League felt easy under the regime as it was functioning. Reapportionment was to come, with significance for the entire nation, through the appeal of dissatisfied Tennesseans to the state and federal judiciary. For the moment, that time had not yet arrived.

With the legislature safely away from the work and the diversions of the capital, the governor concentrated on administrative and political problems. Judicial appointments were given Clement's usual careful attention. Douglas Fisher collected information on candidates and the local bar was duly consulted. The illness of Judge John Swepston of the Supreme Court created a temporary vacancy, and the governor named his father as temporary judge to the state's highest tribunal. A similar temporary appointment of his father was made in his final term. Surprisingly enough, these appointments aroused little opposition in the state, although the governor's use of his father's advice in the first term had been severely chastised by the opposition. The opportunity that the governor had to cherish his father was a deep satisfaction to both men.

The governor made a significant choice in the selection of Wardlaw Steele as chancellor in Davidson County, for Steele was later to hold that the legislature was improperly apportioned, a courageous decision that forecast the epochal federal decision of *Baker* versus *Carr*.

In his first long term, Clement came face to face with the searing problems of capital punishment. Clement was too sensitive and too emotional not to have hated the death sentence. His family history included stories of his grandfather's opposition to the penalty. The legislative journals show that in the regular session of 1915, when James Archibald Clement was a member of the Senate, chapter 181 of the Public Acts abolished the penalty. The abolition had originated as House Bill No. 94, sponsored by Seldon L. Maiden and T.K. Reynolds. When introduced in the Senate it was referred to the Committee on the Penitentiary, of which Senator J.A. Clement was the chairman. The committee reported the bill without recommendation, but the Senate passed the repealer, 20 to 11, with Clement voting for repeal. A motion to reconsider was tabled on motion of Senator Clement, and the death penalty was abolished. It remained abolished for only two years: in 1917, following a highly publicized crime, it was once more instituted, and was in full force when Senator Clement's grandson came to the executive chair.

In Tennessee executions are ordered and dates set by the courts; the governor is spared the painful duty of signing death warrants, but he knows all too clearly that the death can be stayed or stopped by his action — and by his action alone. Since 1915, sentences of death had been carried out by electrocution, instead of the hanging that had before then been the method used, and executions, although not carelessly allotted, were still frequent enough to be a burden to a conscientious governor. Between July 13, 1915, and November 7, 1960, 85 colored men and 39 white men were put to death for the crimes of murder, rape, and assault with intent to ravish.

The number of persons to suffer death in the chair had been steadily diminishing, and Governor Clement faced fewer decisions of the sort than had plagued his predecessors, but he reluctantly — and often with tears — allowed a few men to walk that "last mile," for he felt that he had sworn to uphold the law of which the imposition of death was a part. But the governor never allowed a man to go to execution until he had gone to death row to talk to him, and in those deeply private final conversations there can be no doubt that the governor sought to reconcile the condemned man to his punishment and to his God. Governor Clement always said that he had sent no man to death who had not in those final moments confessed his guilt to him. To a national press animated by scepticism and hatred of the fundamentalist evangelical religion that Clement followed, such conversations would appear cynical and hypocritical. But there was no publicity, no show, no votes to be garnered, nothing but unhappiness and misery, and it is not believable that the governor could have gone through those sad encounters as a publicity stunt. The most moving of these confrontations came when the governor, by chance, met with the wife and children of Harry Kirkendall, a black man, who with a white, Charley Sullins, had been sentenced to death for the brutal slaying of a filling station attendant during the course of a robbery in Lebanon, Tennessee, that netted them $600.

The station attendant, sixty-three-year-old Eddie Collins, was killed in March 1953. The trial began the following January. In Clement's second term the life-or-death issue reached the governor. Feelings on the crime ran high, and the governor was pressured from both sides. In particular, the governor's good political friend, William Baird, a power in Wilson County, opposed clemency and wrote the governor that he had urged the Collins family to oppose the mob violence that was a possibility in Wilson County after the crime. Baird said he had moved the prisoners to Murfreesboro to guarantee that due process would be observed. Congressman Joe Evins asked for a delay for Sullins on ground that actual murder was done by Kirkendall. Clement repeatedly visited the prisoners. On one occasion, Billy Graham was present. In the end, both men confessed their guilt to the governor. Let the governor describe in his own words what happened when he encountered the prisoners on death row:

> My wife went with me one day and I interviewed a white man and a colored man who were scheduled to die in the electric chair for cold blooded murder: Charley Sullins, white man; Harry Kirkendall, colored man. And I might add that aside from the four who've died thus far—there were five and I saved one—all four denied their guilt in the courtroom; all four . . . have absolutely confessed their guilt to me and all four according to the belief of their clergy—all four gave their heart to God before they died. There's never been a record like it in the history of Tennessee. All four walked to the chair without any assistance, without any outcry, without any trouble and sat down it it, which showed they had placed their faith in God. Well, when I saw Harry Kirkendall the last time—I went to see him a second time—a colored man, I spent about an hour and a half with him this time and I'd spent some time with him before. As I walked through the

front of the prison my wife with me, I saw this colored woman and six of the neatest little children I've ever seen in my life . . . And as I passed by them I knew who they were. I'd never met them, but there couldn't be any question . . . As I went on by them I rationalized my thoughts. I thought —well, they may not want to see me at a time like this . . . I got to the front gate and I stopped and told my wife that I can't do it. She said, "What?" I said, "You know who those children were?" She said, "I think I do; I'm afraid to say." I said, "Why that was Mrs. Kirkendall and her six kids. I can't do it, I've got to go back and talk to her."

The governor and Mrs. Kirkendall went into the warden's office, and, as the governor later described the scene,

I said, "Now, Mrs. Kirkendall, I've got the power to save your husband, but I haven't got the right to do it." And she didn't argue with me. She sat there and tears would come down her cheek, with no outcry, no nothing. Finally, I just broke down completely, just completely, and my wife came over and comforted me til I got stabilized again. And the chaplain prayed with us. Then I said, "Mrs. Kirkendall, do you want me to talk to your kids?" I took the youngest one on my lap and I talked to them. "There are some things that the State cannot forgive you for, but God can forgive you for anything." . . . I talked to them and . . . kept my composure. I promised their daddy . . . that I'd see that they got the best Christmas they ever had and everything my boys got we shared with them. Then I sent her a little bed, bed clothing and everything else and we've been in touch with them since then and helped them.

The encounter with Sullins was scarcely less difficult. Sullins made one request of the governor. As the governor told it: "'I know everybody thinks I'm going to crack up and I'm scared to death . . . Tell them not to put any handcuffs on me and let my arms swing free.' We walked down and I said, 'Sure we'll do that.' He walked down and sat in the chair. After they started putting on the straps he said, 'Let me stand up again please.' They let him up again, he knelt down, put his head in the chair, and prayed, got back up and said, 'I'm ready to go.'"

The sentences were carried out.

Clement's second term was marked by the passing of significant political leaders of an earlier generation. Funeral services were held on Monday, June 27, 1955, at Brentwood Methodist Church, south of Nashville, for the publisher of the *Nashville Tennessean*, Silliman Evans. The death of Evans removed one of the most persistent opponents of the governor and his forces, but the policy of the newspaper that Evans had directed remained basically unchanged. Evans, sixty-one, died suddenly of heart failure in Fort Worth, Texas, where he had gone to mourn the death of an old and close friend, Amon G. Carter, publisher of the *Fort Worth Telegram*, for whom Evans' son, Amon, had been named. Evans had been a power in Tennessee Democratic affairs. He had pursued a career with newspapers in Texas, Chicago, and Washington, D.C., and had played a key role in the nomination of John Nance Garner for the vice-presidency in 1932. He had been assistant postmaster-general under Jim Farley, that master dispenser of patronage in the New Deal. Eighteen years before his death, he had put together enough money to buy the *Tennessean*, once the political mouthpiece of Luke Lea. Through various financial stresses, the paper had come under the control of the Reconstruction Finance Corporation, and it was from the RFC that Evans acquired ownership. Immediately upon coming to Tennessee, Evans had set out on a reform career; the immediate objects of his attention were the poll tax and Boss Crump. He fought them both with considerable effectiveness. By reason of his opposition to the Memphis satrap, he came to be a supporter of Gordon Browning and, in due course, of Estes Kefauver, once Kefauver had demonstrated that his ham-like out-stretched hand could garner votes in large quantities. Since by the nature of Tennessee rivalries Clement had to seek office through opposition to Browning, and by implication to Kefauver, Evans and his paper became the center of newspaper opposition to the governor. Evans' death changed nothing in the policy of the paper or in the politics of Tennessee.

Cordell Hull died on July 23, 1955. He was by that time in retirement, but students of personal histories could reflect that his early campaigns had been managed by the father of Secretary of State Joe Cordell Carr, whose name testified to the friendships of the past.

On October 26, 1955, I.D. Beasley died at Carthage. Beasley, Jim Cummings, and "Pete" Haynes had formed the triumvirate called by its enemies the "Unholy Trinity" that had controlled the state legislature in the interests of the rural communities of the state. Like so many other Tennessee political lights, Beasley had attended Cumberland University. In the legislature he had been noted for his gift of mimicry and his love of practical jokes. His old partner Cummings was still in the General Assembly, a canny and respected leader of small town and rural interests who was determined as ever to stop the moves to reapportion the legislature that were even then beginning to build.

The next three years were to witness the end of life for other Clement friends and allies. The governor's first treasurer J.B. Walker, out of office because of ill health, died in September of 1956. In the following month, Mrs. Albert Hill, at the time national Democratic committee-woman for Tennessee and a consistent backer of the governor, died suddenly of a heart attack. That same month, a year later, former Senator McKellar, old, ill, and frail, died in Memphis; he was 88. Lipe Henslee, a fellow Dickson County political figure and a warm friend of the young governor, died in 1958. The pre-Clement leaders were dropping away, one after another.

Clement's terms in office were marked with labor conflicts that he was relatively powerless to deal with. The first of these was the bitter and prolonged strike of the L&N Railway that began in March 1955. Disorder accompanying the railroad strike spread to the coal fields. In April, employees of the Southern Bell Telephone Company struck. Neither court action nor the intervention of Clement and Governor Wetherby of Kentucky succeeded in bringing the railroad strike to an end. The governors suggested arbitration, and Clement asked both Southern Bell and the L&N to discharge all employees who unlawfully carried arms. Clement managed to avoid calling out troops. After some weeks of turmoil, the strikes came to an end.

The year 1956 had passed in the crisis atmosphere of desegregation and the Democratic National Convention. The convention and election ended, and Eisenhower had been returned. Clement's national ambitions remained unfulfilled. The 1957 legislative session began, with the crisis of desegregation begun in 1956 now intensified.

The Eightieth General Assembly convened in January 1957 with substantial stability in leadership. In late 1956 Bomar and Maddux had again received the blessing for continuation in the offices of speaker. Jim Cummings had indicated some interest in running for the Senate speakership, but true to a tradition that had benefitted him in the past, he withdrew from a contest with the governor's choices without resentment or fuss. It was rumored that Cummings was offered the Senate floor leadership but declined. In any case, his amiability was to be rewarded in the future. When the legislature met, even the Republican candidates for speaker withdrew, as the governor's mastery of the legislature was affirmed—or so it appeared; some conflicts still lay ahead.

Eugene Collins had retired from the legislature to nurse his law practice, and Damon Headden of West Tennessee, who had been co-leader with Collins in order to guide the sales tax increase through the House because Collins would have none of it, was put in Collins' place. Ross Dyer and Lyndon Jennings shared honors in the State.

A significant change occurred in the office of the secretary of state.

Edward Friar's term expired in January, and there was no chance of his reelection during the incumbency of his old friend from whom he was now completely estranged. Well aware that he had no hope of reelection as secretary, Friar announced his candidacy for governor on January 14, 1957, a year and half away from the contests of 1958. He attacked Clement, charging him with dishonesty, indecency, and immorality — all unspecific and unsupported charges. Bob Crichton, he said, would back his candidacy.

Friar's successor as secretary of state was Joe Cordell Carr, who now entered a post that he continued to occupy until 1977. Carr was in the process of becoming "Mr. Democrat." He had been a page in the state Senate in 1923; his father had been a member of the legislature in 1919, chief clerk in the office of the secretary of state, and trustee for Putnam County. Joe Carr had been elected national president of the Young Democratic Clubs in 1941. He had previously served as secretary of state but was ousted from that post during the final two terms of Browning. In his first period as secretary he had taken a leave to enter the military service during the Second World War, and his wife had served in his place. He and Lipe Henslee had aided the young Clement to start his career, by picking him for the state presidency of the Young Democrats. Now he was returning to a job that had become almost family property. He remained a devoted cog in what was to be known as the Clement-Ellington machine.

Snodgrass remained comptroller of the treasury, Ramon Davis continued as treasurer, and Joe Henry, Clement's longtime speech writer and phrasemaker par excellence (and incidentally the object of some of Clement's practical jokes), continued to serve as adjutant general. The discord between the constitutional officers and the chief executive that marred the first term was put aside.

The legislature settled to business. Except for the new and insistent troubles of desegregation and reapportionment, the problems faced by the Assembly bore a wearisome familiarity. The teachers wanted more money. The Tennessee Municipal League had the same idea.

In November 1956 the League and the Tennessee County Services Association had laid the groundwork for their 1957 legislative program by holding a series of conferences over the state. The League had used its muscle to put Clement in the governor's chair; now he was to find these friends as insistent on more money as the teachers were. Funds were not unlimited, even though the advancing economy and the increase in the sales tax were pouring more millions into the state pocketbook, and the two groups—teachers and cities (aided by the counties)—eyed each other quite accurately as formidable competitors. The local municipal and county officials, among other matters, were pressing for a bond issue of $45 million to match funds for the proposed federal interstate highway system. The local officials proposed the establishment of a state agency to help the counties equalize property assessments. They came out again for industrial development, that ever-present aid for increasing the tax base, and they spoke favorably for enabling legislation to help municipalities solve their pressing problems, a catch phrase to cover the hope of increased power to levy local taxes. Clement was keenly aware of the pressure that the local officials were exerting on his fiscal policy.

The governor was set to make one last attempt to repeal or modify the open shop law. This attempt was to fail, too, and the repeated rejection of repeal finally convinced subsequent candidates for governor, including even the former labor leader, Olgiati, that repeal was hopeless. Unable to secure open shop repeal, Clement had tried to assuage labor discontent by pointing to other achievements: the boiler safety law, amendments to the child labor laws, better workmen's compensation, and an announcement of a minimum wage on state employment. When labor objected to prison labor, he pointed to the need of rehabilitation programs. The repeal of the open shop always eluded him.

The governor was now prepared to put up some resistance to the increasing demands of the teachers. Even in his first term, as he had supported increased benefits for the teachers and the hard-pressed cities, he had observed that the state's budget could be endangered by increased demands from the localities. Again in January 1956, in his address on "the state of the state" to newspaper representatives, he warned that the financial structure of the state placed a limit on the degree to which the central government could take over the support of the schools. It was an open challenge to a pressure group that many observers considered the most powerful in Tennessee, not excepting the truckers and the farmers. But the Tennessee Education Association was not to be put off by any considerations of the state's limited resources, and Clement's most persistent legislative gadfly, Senator Clifford Allen, rushed to introduce a bill in the Eightieth Assembly to raise teacher pay by $400 annually, even before Clement could deliver his message to the legislators. Doubtless Allen reflected that Clement had gained the credit for free textbooks, a benefit that Allen considered Clement had stolen from him. Allen continued throughout the session to push for higher teacher pay, coupling his posture with an insouciant opposition to added taxes. Added taxes at this point were clearly an equivalent of political suicide, but the governor was saved by the steady increase in state revenues that accompanied good times and a slowly mounting inflation.

Clement spelled out his general program to the legislature on January 16. He offered a total program whose cost would reach close to a biennial figure of three quarters of a billion dollars, more than $125 million in excess of the expenditure of the previous biennium (how Browning must have squirmed), but the governor said he would not recommend or sponsor added taxes. He allotted an annual increase of $150 for 1957–58 and an additional $50 for 1958–59 to teachers; this allocation, less than half of what they demanded, furnished — aside from desegregation — the main controversy of the legislative days that followed, a conflict which the governor did not fully win.

The demand for a reapportionment of legislative seats was building up, and the governor, although he had correctly pointed out that the problem was one for legislative action, asked for a study of the matter by the Legislative Council. He had made the same suggestion in 1955, but the Assembly had allowed the matter to slide, as usual. Clement again alluded to the need for repeal or revision of the open shop law, and he asked again for the railway minimum crew law. He wanted an increase for the Industrial and Agricultural Development Commission; like his predecessors and his successors, he saw a solution to his economic problems if further development could be kept coming. He asked for legislation to permit teachers and other state employees to go on federal social security.

It would be tedious to chronicle the teacher pay conflict in great detail. Clement would not have risked alienating the teachers, for he had further political ambitions, had he not felt keenly that the teacher lobby had grown too demanding. The issue split the Assembly, and Clement faced a harder fight than in earlier legislatures. In the wisdom acquired by later events, one can see in this session the beginnings of the reasserted legislative independence that was to come to full flower some fifteen or twenty years in the future. The Shelby delegation split — the Red Snapper was no more — with some of the delegation backing the governor, others supporting the teachers. Snodgrass and Boling challenged the accuracy of the teachers' estimates of future income. Allen, thick in the fight for the teachers, suffered a heart attack and was forced into temporary absence; in the final voting he had himself carried into the Senate chamber on a stretcher to deliver an impassioned appeal for meeting the teachers' terms. McAllen Foutch, a consistent opponent of the Clement forces, led the TEA fight. A bloc of Republicans took the opportunity of supporting the teachers and confounding the Democrats.

The governor was weaker in the House than in the Senate, and in the end the issue had to be settled by a conference committee, a procedure that had been little used during the days of strong gubernatorial control of the Assembly. The conference committee was heavily dominated by Clement forces, but nonetheless some compromise was necessary. The teachers were to have a raise of $150 in the first year that followed plus an additional $50 subsequently, but, if the collections in taxes were larger than the state fiscal officials had predicted so firmly, the "overage" was to go for teacher salary increases unless local legislation allocated that overage to educational costs generally. The compromise, which had been drafted by Clement's Senate floor leader, L.B. Jennings, was adopted in both houses by overwhelming majorities. In the House, only two loners, both Republican, voted "No." Clement had won but only by giving a little. As a matter of fact, overages were produced, and the teachers made another modest gain. The governor lost, almost surely, as some of the TEA's attachment to him eroded.

Right on schedule, the legislature struck down the minimum crew bill and the open shop repeal. The action had taken on the routine character of a time-worn legislative procedure. The rural bloc duly killed off all overtures on reapportionment. The Assembly's firm refusal to obey the mandates of the state constitution was to force the whole issue of reapportionment into the federal judiciary, with fateful alterations in the relationship of the judiciary to other branches and a thoroughgoing reform of state and local legislative bodies throughout the United States. The legislature was once more demonstrating how difficult it is for an institution to reform itself.

The final months of Clement's second term were agitated by a choice of his successor and the question of Clement's own future plans. Under the constitutional amendment of 1953 Clement could not succeed himself. It was natural that he should think of the Senate, as Gore's first term was coming to an end. Gore's friends gave a good deal of worried attention to Clement; by early 1958, however, it became increasingly clear that Clement would not challenge Gore. Clement's friends had considerable respect for Gore, and on occasion the governor's speechwriters had called Clement's attention to the fact that Gore's speeches had content as well as form. In retrospect it may be doubted that Clement could have unseated Gore, and he evidently reached that conclusion himself, for certainly he had no taste for private life.

The gubernatorial gladiators were put on early notice by the announcement of Eddie Friar in January 1957, well over a year before such definite commitments are normally made. The cap so prematurely flung into the ring by Friar gave rise to immediate speculations about other candidates. As late as October 1957, no clear choice had emerged in the Clement machine, where potential candidates sprouted like wild marijuana in a Kansas fencerow. In many ways, Buford Ellington was the logical front runner in the Clement camp. He had grown a powerful organization in 1952 and 1954 on the stumps of the old McCord underbrush, keeping a sharp eye on his own future even as he took care of Clement's interests. Clement had reason to be grateful to the hardworking and hard-headed Ellington for two highly successful campaigns. But there were plenty of vaulting ambitions within the Clement organization, as well as among older members of that wing of the Democratic party. As one observer put it: you couldn't throw a brick without hitting a candidate. Glen Nicely, former cabinet commissioner and the governor's administrative assistant, saw no reason why he should not sit in the boss' seat. Joe Henry, Joe Carr, Hilton Butler, William Leech were all mentioned, and all of them were men of recognized ability. Speakers Maddux and Bomar had every right to be considered. Rudy Olgiati, Clement backer and a power in the Municipal League, had ill-concealed ambitions. Outside the immediate Clement entourage, but within that faction of the party were other potentialities such as Judge Andrew "Tip" Taylor and Prentice Cooper, who found retirement not enough for a still active person. Judge Schoolfield, who had run for governor as a straight-out segregationist, was considered a possible candidate, but before Clement's term came to a close Schoolfield was to be impeached and convicted.

The plethora of possibles within the Clement camp was a source of embarrassment and conflict, and Clement attempted to dampen ambitions by using Boling as an example of a highly able person who nevertheless could not be elected governor. Clement warned Boling he would make him the "goat" just before a cabinet meeting in which the governor would attempt to quell discussion of possible candidacies. But the "sacrifice" of Boling brought no lasting results; the rivalries continued strong as ever.

Ellington grew restless at Clement's failure to give him an early endorsement, and he determined to force the issue by taking a strong seg-regationist stand. This Ellington did in a speech to the Memphis Rotary Club in November 1957. It was a position he continued to maintain until 1962. Ellington ruled out mob violence, but he stated that he would use every legal means available to maintain the separation of blacks from whites. He attacked the decision of President Eisenhower to use federal troops to enforce the integration of the Little Rock schools.

During 1957, Prentice Cooper and Tip Taylor announced their candidacies. In January 1958, Glen Nicely resigned from Clement's staff to announce his candidacy, the fourth person to enter the lists. The *Banner* greeted the Nicely announcement with studied contempt, and Clement, having failed to dissuade his executive assistant from entering, issued a statement of nonsupport. The *Banner* insultingly called Nicely "a peanut politician," hailed his departure from the Clement staff as good news, and said he had been a disturbing element in the Clement political family. It may be assumed that the *Banner* was already committed at least privately to Ellington.

The formal candidacy of Ellington was announced in mid-February 1958. It was promptly endorsed by Clement, but Clement's earlier silence was apparently resented by Ellington, whose anxieties had been compounded by Clement's unwillingness or inability to quiet rivalries within the inner conclave. Ellington's ties in the past had included friendships with Congressman Joe Evins and former governor McCord, but in 1958 both of them had seriously thought of the governorship. Evins decided against trying, but eventually McCord became an ineffectual opponent of Ellington in the general election. In supporting Ellington, Clement announced that he would run for no office in that year, thus putting to rest the notion that he might take Gore on.

Ellington had built the Clement organization thoroughly and well, and he took it over almost intact for his own purposes. He was endorsed promptly by such Clement backers as J.N. Doane of Jefferson County, Judge Sue Hicks of Madisonville, Howard Warf, boss of Lewis County, Ross Dyer, member of the Senate and one of Clement's Senate leaders, and Jimmy Peeler of Covington. Although he withheld formal endorsement, Herbert Walters stated publicly that Ellington would be the next governor, and he made a few careful statements on political matters. Shortly thereafter he extended a formal endorsement.

With no signs of regret, the *Banner's* Capitol Hill columnist noted the difficulty the Browning-Kefauver forces were facing in picking a candidate. Joe Evins would have been acceptable, but he declined to run.

"Tip" Taylor, like Ellington a segregationist and perhaps a more committed one, was unacceptable to the group. Prentice Cooper furnished no answer, in spite of his long personal friendship with Kefauver. Clifford Allen was already in the race, but he was not part of the Kefauver-Browning community. Nicely and Friar were dismissed by the writer as political lightweights, as indeed they turned out to be before long.

A candidate was about to emerge in Shelby County, urged to the race by Kefauver, according to the *Commercial Appeal*. Edmund Orgill, a prominent merchant of Memphis, had been elected mayor of his city in 1955, after the death of Crump. In the years following the Second World War Orgill had been a member of a small group of prominent citizens of Memphis who became interested in Clarence Streit's efforts to promote a union between the United States and Great Britain. The group had solicited Kefauver's interest and support, and Kefauver, on the lookout for a base in Crump's home town, had managed to cock a favorable eye on this rather naïve concept. Orgill had helped to run Kefauver's first crucial campaign for the Senate in 1948. His attachment to the new senator was at one with his espousal of "liberal" or "progressive" causes of various sorts, including the reform of local government in Shelby County and Memphis, where he continued for years to push local betterment, not without some very considerable success. Orgill was pressured to run for governor by various Kefauver friends, including William C. Wilson of Knoxville (later to be a manager for Ross Bass and, still later, an aspirant himself for the governorship) and by Mayor Frank Gray of Franklin. (Gray was to become a federal district judge in Tennessee, under Kefauver's sponsorship, and the author of some drastic desegregation orders before his retirement and death.) Kefauver's own support of Orgill had to be publicly toned down, for other Kefauver friends were interested in the job, and their support would be needed in the Kefauver campaign for return to the Senate in 1960. But Orgill continued to be interested, and various Memphians, including Lucius Burch, Jr., and George Crider, finally pushed him to a commitment.

Judge Andrew "Tip" Taylor eyed with distaste the Orgill waltz with candidacy; Orgill could split the anti-Ellington vote. Ellington could have murmured a prayer that Orgill stay in. Late in April, Kefauver, his neutrality strongly reinforced by self-interest, said that if Orgill made the race, he would make it on his own; he had not, said the senator, urged Orgill to the contest. Almost immediately after this declaration of benevolent neglect, Orgill formally committed himself to the candidacy, the seventh hopeful to enter a race where elbow room was becoming scarce. In all this complicated and circumspect maneuvering, no great issues are to be discerned. The Tennessee political system was once again demonstrating its essential features of a career open to talents, where personal ambitions and unstable loyalties overshadowed other aspects of statecraft.

Although Ellington had been anointed by the outgoing governor, and undoubtedly carried most of the machine with him, there were defections. Speechwriter "Lon" Cheney left the former commissioner of agriculture, for he thought he detected in one of Ellington's speeches a favorable allusion to the Ku Klux Klan. Only later did he find out that the offending passage had been inserted in one of Ellington's speeches by someone else, without Ellington apparently realizing the implications of the words. In the process of leaving Ellington, Cheney also broke with Clement, and, in 1962, his support was given to Olgiati.

Ellington had already plumped for segregation; he labeled himself an "old-fashioned segregationist," a phrase supposedly invented by one of his speechwriters, and a tag he subsequently had to get rid of. It must have been clear to Ellington—certainly it was to most able politicians, and Ellington was assuredly such—that some desegregation was coming. But it was only 1958, and it was by no means clear how far the judiciary would go to force desegregation, nor how long-drawn-out the attempt was to be. The *Banner* columnist said that Orgill would get a large share of the black vote in Shelby County because of his liberal stand on desegregation, but at a talk to the UT Political Science Club in Knoxville, Orgill had declined to take a firm position in favor of desegregation. Both Ellington and Orgill knew quite well that the prevailing white feeling in the state was not flamingly revolutionary. In spite of his genuine idealism, Orgill could not have survived too close an identification with the black cause, and he tip-toed around the troublesome issue of race relations, as did Clement and every other Tennessee politician of moderating instincts. Taylor was an acknowledged segregationist and that plus his residence in West Tennessee was good for thousands of votes. He could be counted on to eat into some of the Ellington support.

All the candidates had difficulty finding issues. Orgill tried to tag Ellington as the representative of a powerful and sinister machine; it was a sort of low-keyed replay of the Browning attacks on Crump. But, of course, Kefauver also had a machine, albeit an ill-organized and quarrelsome one, and Orgill was associated with that loose aggregation. Ellington had one plank of time-tested and deep appeal; he took an unequivocal stand against new taxes, and it was a plank that he could safely offer, as Clement's raised taxes and the burgeoning economy of the state were about to present Ellington with a lush surplus. New taxation gets few votes, and the history of Tennessee shows that it loses a great many.

As spring heated up into summer, the campaign added to public entertainment. A *Banner* cartoonist depicted Orgill moving about under a dark shadow labelled Kefauver, recalling the childhood poetry with the line: "I have a little shadow that moves in and out with me." Late in July, the paper ran another masterpiece of satire, showing three candidates under one coat, with the caption: "Edmund G. Estes Kefriar."

In the middle of the campaign, the whole process was complicated by the convening of a special session of the General Assembly to consider the impeachment of Criminal Court Judge Raulston Schoolfield. As nearly as can be told, this diversion had no effect on the outcome of the primary, although it constituted a temporary distraction from the duller drama of the election.

As the candidates' organizations were gradually perfected in late spring and early summer, Orgill's ties to the Kefauver organization became quite clear. Carl Fry became Orgill's manager. Lucius Burch of Memphis, M.M. Bullard of Newport, and Noble Caudill of Nashville, all Kefauver friends, were active in raising funds for the Orgill campaign. Caudill, a business leader with a deep interest in politics, had, with Sam Fleming, Nashville banker, been a financial supporter of Kefauver for a long period. In due course he was to become a close friend and advisor to Frank Clement, without cutting his strong ties to the Senior Senator. Frank Wilson of Oak Ridge handled Orgill's East Tennessee campaign; he had managed the Stevenson-Kefauver campaign in Tennessee in 1956. Other backers of Orgill included Mrs. Martha Ragland, long associated with Kefauver forces, Jim Camp of Sparta, once a legislative floor leader for Clement, Max Friedman, Knoxville jeweler and totally commited Kefauver friend. One of the rumors that found its way into the *Banner* had Kefauver, assisted by G. Mennen ("Soapy") Williams and Averill Harriman, providing Orgill with a slush fund of $300,000 collected from northern liberals and national labor tycoons. True or not—and skepticism is certainly in order—it was a damaging tale; Tennesseans do not like foreign money in party fights.

By early June, the overly crowded field commenced to thin out. It became increasingly evident that Nicely and Friar were not attracting support, financial or otherwise. Rumors began to float through the politically polluted air that Prentice Cooper would withdraw and run for the Senate against Gore. The former governor denied it, but, in fact, that is

Edmund C. Estes Kefriar

The *Banner* notes the alliance of Orgill, Kefauver, and Friar—and adds the Americans for Democratic Action and the National Association for the Advancement of Colored People, for good measure; Knox, *Banner.*

what he did. Newspaper reports indicated that his financial backers compelled him to make the shift. Whether true or not, the story had a ring of conviction. Clifford Allen's support was limited, but Allen did not quit easily, and this time, he stayed in until the bitter end, attacking Clement, Ellington, and Orgill, severally and collectively.

Nicely withdrew in early June, throwing his support, so far as he could, to Taylor. He became Taylor's state manager. Friar, in his opener, had charged Clement with supporting both Ellington and Taylor. Nicely's candidacy, Friar averred, was a plot, and later he said that Taylor gave Nicely $12,000 to gain his support, together with a promise of a cabinet post and control of the state insurance business. Taylor said Friar was a liar. Friar said Ellington was owned "body, boots, and britches" by Clement, a neatly alliterative statement thoroughly belied by what is known of the true uneasy relations between Clement and Ellington. Friar also charged that a whiskey ring was running illegal liquor into the dry counties. Whatever the effect of these charges and replies, Friar had to withdraw late in July; he announced his support of Orgill. His withdrawal came so late that his name could not be removed from the ballot in all counties.

And so, to the accompaniment of country music, the campaign came to a close.

The Democratic primary of August 7, 1958, was a near thing for the Ellington-Clement combination. Ellington managed to come in first, but Taylor was breathing on the back of his neck, with Orgill close behind. Allen was far, far in the rear. The vote was 213,415 for Ellington, 204,629 for Taylor, and 204,382 for Orgill. Allen managed to get only 56,854 votes, a large part of these in Davidson and Cheatham counties. He carried only Cheatham; even Davidson, where he had always had strength, went to Orgill by a narrow margin. Had a very few thousand people shifted their votes, Ellington could have lost, and the subsequent history of both Clement and Ellington could have been much different. The past close alliance of these two extremely different personalities, already tense, was now to be put under increasing strain as the next few years went by.

The election evidenced a certain regional pattern characteristic of many of Tennessee's political decisions. Taylor's areas of strength show this most clearly. He carried every county west of the western reaches of the Tennessee River, with the exception of Tipton and Dyer counties, which, somewhat surprisingly, went for Ellington. In addition, Taylor carried Rhea, Hamilton, and Bradley in the lower valley of East Tennessee, as well as Washington, Carter, and Unicoi counties along the high mountains of the East. It is not easy to see why. Judge Schoolfield had been convicted on several of numerous impeachment charges during the course of the campaign in a session called by Clement, and the action may have offended his friends in Hamilton. The three upper East Tennessee counties lie in an area once dominated by the Taylor brothers of Happy Valley, and some of the aura of the Taylor name may have helped the modern West Tennessean. Taylor's strong segregationist position may have carried weight in Hamilton County, just then entering the pangs of desegregation. Segregationists have been visible and vocal in that county. Taylor showed considerable strength in all the metropolitan counties.

The remainder of the state was divided between Ellington and Orgill. Ellington's appeal was basically rural and centered in Middle and East Tennessee. The *Banner* said that Republican crossovers helped Ellington. That is believable but not easily proved. Ellington carried none of the metropolitan counties; Orgill took Knox and Davidson, and Taylor carried off Hamilton and Shelby—in spite of the fact that Shelby was Orgill's home county. White backlash and the still lively distaste for Kefauver and all his friends help to account for Shelby's repudiation of its own.

Some of Orgill's triumphs could have been attributed to Kefauver forces. He carried Knox and Monroe counties. Monroe was the site of the old Kefauver home, and important Knox County leaders had long been associated with Kefauver. There were miners' counties—such as Campbell and Morgan—that went for Orgill, but the similar counties of Scott, Fentress, and Pickett (neighbors of Campbell and Morgan) helped Ellington to victory.

But pluralities in the counties do not tell the whole story. Throughout the state, the three candidates ran close to each other. Ellington had absolute majorities in ten counties; Orgill in three; Taylor in thirteen. In certain segregationist counties (where blacks were probably not voting in great numbers) such as Fayette, Hardeman, and Haywood, Taylor rolled up lopsided majorities; in his home county of Madison, he gathered 81 percent of the vote. Given these heavy votes in the west and remembering that Ellington was associated with the racial views of Taylor, it seems likely that in a straight-out fight between Ellington and Orgill, Ellington would have won. That such would have been the likely outcome is made more believable by Ellington's defeat of John J. Hooker, Jr., eight years later.

In the race for the nomination for senator, Gore won handily over Prentice Cooper. Cooper became another politician who tried once too often; he carried only twenty-five counties. These included Hamilton County, some West counties, and a handful in East and Middle Tennessee. The great bulk of Middle Tennessee went for Gore, including Bedford, Cooper's home. It was a bad year for local loyalties. In the general election that followed Gore swamped the veteran, Hobart Atkins, Republican of Knoxville, and was safely in the Senate for what was to be twelve more years.

Ellington's narrow margin fed hopes that he could still be defeated, through an independent candidacy in the general election. The *Banner*'s Capitol Hill column reported that Glen Nicely and Mrs. Christine Reynolds had actively sought independents. Mrs. Reynolds' mother had become the second Mrs. Jim Nance McCord, and McCord looked like a possible independent. Add to this the fact that McCord was no friend to Ellington. Rumors were also floated that Taylor might go on the general election ballot as an independent. But one by one most of the leading Democrats repudiated all proposals for a revolt against Ellington within the party. Ellington and Taylor met in September and buried the hatchet. Taylor asked that his name be removed from consideration as an independent. Carl Fry, who had been Orgill's manager, announced in that same month that he would support Ellington. In the next month in a speech at Kingsport, Gore blasted away at all notions of independence and announced that he would support Ellington. His formal attachment to the Ellington candidacy was a useful gambit, aside from party loyalty, to a candidate who wished to temper his liberalism with a dash of conservative association. Gore admitted openly in his memoirs published some years later that he had deliberately campaigned with Ellington as a means of courting conservative Democrats. It is possible that the group that sought independent candidates approached Friar, but if so he turned them down.

Pushed by persons opposed to Ellington, some of whom had been Browning backers of earlier years, Jim Nance McCord announced as an independent in early October. It was a final political act, based on bad judgment, of a man long prominent in Tennessee affairs, an act sharply opposed by many of his own friends. McCord said he wished to give the voters a new chance, in response to the wishes of over two-thirds of the voters who had expressed their dissatisfaction with Ellington. McCord attacked machines in general and said he wished to prevent the formation of one, a slap at the Ellington-Clement combination with which he himself had been long associated. McCord was now seventy-nine years old.

In the general election that followed, Ellington was elected without trouble. McCord carried only the three small East Tennessee counties of Meigs, Campbell, and Hancock. All the same he did poll 136,399 votes; and although this was far behind Ellington's 248,000 plus, it did indicate the considerable depth of Ellington's opposition. In Macon, Mc-Cord tied Ellington. The relatively little known Republican candidate, Thomas P. Wall, received less than 36,000 votes. While this was going on, the first and second congressional districts were going Republican on their regular schedule, and the remaining districts went Democratic with no significant signs of opposition. Two years later the state was to be carried by Richard Nixon against John F. Kennedy.

♪ *On Jordan's stormy banks I stand*
And cast a wishful eye
To Canaan's fair and happy land
Where my possessions lie.

SAMUEL STENNETT, 1727–1795

7. On Jordan's Stormy Banks I Stand

THE RACE QUESTION

Twenty-five years of struggle with desegregation have made it clear that racism is not a strictly southern problem. Slavery, however, was primarily a southern institution, and Tennessee was and is a southern state. As a unit in the Upper South, Tennessee could boast of an antislavery movement of its own, before 1820, but after that time it became increasingly impossible for Tennesseans to find a way out of a system that held the black men and women in a bondage whose ill effects were in part visited upon the whites. The institution had its economic uses, but, in addition, emancipation would have sent a horde of black free people into a civilization that could see no way of absorbing them.

The slaves were most numerous in West Tennessee, least numerous in East Tennessee; this essential difference in the two regions had colored the politics of the state from 1820 on. In 1818 West Tennessee was opened to settlement, and some of its terrain, particularly the alluvial plains along the Mississippi, would fit in securely into the plantation economy of the Deep South. But not all of West Tennessee territory was so hospitable to the slave-based economy, and, notably for the Clement family history, Benton County was not plantation country.

Slaves were held throughout the state. Free Negroes lived here as well, but after the close of the first quarter of the nineteenth century, the lot of these freemen became progressively more difficult. Laws were enacted to make emancipation harder, immigration of free blacks into the state was restricted, and attempts were made to require the deportation of recently freed blacks.

By the time of the crucial election of Abraham Lincoln to the presidency, the institution of slavery was as firmly implanted in Tennessee as in its neighbors to the South. Nevertheless, the election of Lincoln did

189

not immediately trigger a vote for secession. The first referendum on the subject produced a vote in favor of remaining in the Union, and it was not until the South Carolinians attacked Fort Sumter that sentiment in the state shifted in favor of leaving it. Even then East Tennessee voted in favor of continuing in the Union and became a stronghold of Union sentiment, remaining so throughout the war and reconstruction.

Tennessee was a major battleground of the disastrous conflict of 1861–65. Its railroads and waterways were vital links in southern communications. Its possession was essential to both northern and southern strategy. Major conflicts took place in or near the state—the capture of Fort Donelson and Fort Henry, the battles of Shiloh, Stone's River, and Nashville, and the blood-letting of Chickamauga and Missionary Ridge. When the armies of the North finally and firmly possessed the state, the end was in sight.

Tennessee underwent no military reconstruction of the sort experienced by other southern states. Before the war was ended elsewhere, Andrew Johnson, a citizen of the state, had been made its military governor. From 1865 to the adoption of the new constitution of 1870, Tennesseans lived in ready fear of military intervention, but intervention never came. It was fended off in part by a series of concessions to the blacks—freedom, particularly, and the grant of the franchise. The concessions were given grudgingly and they remained incomplete because various forms of disability were preserved, disabilities reflected in the terms of the 1870 constitution and in the statutes that were to dictate the nature of race relations until the desegregation decisions of the 1950s.

Several basic provisions of the constitution of 1870 set the rights and privileges of "persons of color." Article 1, section 5 stated (and still does) that "The elections shall be free and equal, and the right of suffrage, as hereinafter declared, shall never be denied to any person entitled thereto, except upon conviction by a jury of some infamous crime." The historic decision of the war between the states was confirmed in sections 33 and 34 of the same article: "Slavery and involuntary servitude . . . are forever prohibited in this State" and "The General Assembly shall make no law recognizing the right of property in man." But now came some provisos. Section 28 of Article II stated that "all male citizens over the age of twenty-one . . . shall be liable to a poll tax of not less than fifty cents nor more than a dollar per annum." A county or municipal corporation could levy a similar tax. No qualification was to be attached to the suffrage except that each voter was to give evidence of payment of the poll tax, for such period as the legislature should direct.

The miscellaneous sections of the constitution contained two of the most significant restrictions. Section 14 of Article XI stated: "The intermarriage of white persons with negroes, mullatos [sic], or persons of mixed blood, descended from a negro to the third generation inclusive or their living together as man and wife in this State is prohibited. The legislature shall have power to enforce this section by appropriate legislation." A clause of Section 12, which deals with education, provided: "No school established or aided under this section shall allow white and negro children to be received as scholars together in the same school." These clauses (not including the poll tax) remained in the state constitution until 1978, although they had lost validity through decisions of the Supreme Court before that date.

The constitutional requirements of segregation were supplemented by state statutes, local regulations, and business and social practice. The statutes provided that children of persons of color living together as man and wife could inherit, but a child of color could not inherit the estate of his mother's husband, unless the mother or husband was a person of color. Colored insane were to be housed in buildings separate from the white insane. Housing was segregated throughout the state, often enforced by deed restrictions, although in certain areas the colored shanties would be close to white dwellings, sometimes in adjoining alleys. Blacks rode in the rear portions of streetcars; in theaters, if they were admitted at all, they sat in high galleries — "nigger heavens." Few people passing the side entrance to the old Bijou Theater on Cumberland Avenue in Knoxville still recognize the separate entrance to that "heaven." White hotels, motels, retaurants, and barbershops were closed to blacks, except as servants to the whites. The professions were not formally closed to blacks nor was ownership of land and other property, but few Negroes made their way into the professions, or acquired substantial property, or even moderate wealth. It was not easy for blacks to get medical attention; some physicians refused to treat them. Blacks were segregated from whites in the hospitals. Throughout the state, they had to use separate drinking fountains, washbasins, and toilets. Surely to be black in Tennessee in those decades was something less than heaven.

The separation was not complete and it was changing, but the pace of change was painfully slow. In the late 1930s Negroes served on the Knoxville police force (not however in the firefighting forces, for firemen slept in the stations while on duty). The city conducted its somewhat rudimentary civil service examinations in an atmosphere of integration. Throughout the state, segregation in housing was the general rule, but there were spots where blacks and whites lived side by side; such spots were particularly likely to exist in the kind of small towns in which Frank Clement and his sisters spent their childhood. Negroes voted, but their votes were used to foster the fortunes of rival whites. Blacks held a few — a very few — local elective offices, and they were not to be found in the upper levels of the state or local bureaucracies.

Frank Clement passed his boyhood in small Kentucky and Tennessee communities where the Negro population was not large and prejudices were usually not violent, partly no doubt because the black men and women accepted the submerged role assigned them. There was nothing in Clement's background to lead him toward racial animosity, but at the same time nothing in his experience would have caused him to question seriously the policies of separation that pervaded southern life. Clement's sister, Anna Belle, recalls her years in Dickson, when she and her brother and sister walked a short distance from their home on Main Street to a small black church adjacent to the back of their home, where, sitting on the back row of the church, they joined in the singing. It was a form of integration that could be seen in certain gatherings even in the large cities, but it was a fraternization on white terms, the whites condescending to the Negro congregation, not the other way round.

Faint beginnings of school desegregation could be detected in the 1940s. Segregation prevailed generally at the college level. Indeed, it was mandated by the constitution for schools that received state aid. A Negro university at Nashville, called the Agricultural and Industrial University, was maintained by the state; like the University of Tennessee, A&I received land grant funds, but its physical plant was not impressive, and its standards were not up to the level of some white institutions. Black graduate students were required to attend black schools, unless specific programs were not available in the black schools; in that event, graduate students could be admitted to the University of Tennessee. A few such students were admitted before the 1950s, but they did not live in university residence halls, did not use the swimming pools or other recreational facilities, and, in general, were scarcely seen. There were, of course, no Negro faculty members, and indeed blacks were not invited to speak in University buildings. University officials became increasingly conscious of the tight-rope they were walking.

As it turned out, the first violent conflict over school desegregation in Tennessee occurred in the small town of Clinton in a school operated by Anderson County. Clinton was a typical East Tennessee town perched on the edge of the mining communities of the Cumberlands, communities primarily white and mostly poor. A few blacks lived there, settled in poor houses on the higher borders of the town. Their number was too small to support a high school, and, in the manner of those days, the black high school students were transported to neighboring towns where black schools were available. First, they were sent north to the town of LaFollette or west to Rockwood. Later, Clinton made a more economical contract for the Clinton blacks to be received in Austin High at Knoxville. The Negro youngsters had to travel farther under this arrangement, but a least they were enrolled in a school possibly superior to that in LaFollette or Rockwood.

Early in the 1950s, some of the black parents in Clinton had filed a class action suit in the federal district court in Knoxville asking for the desegregation of the High School in Clinton. Judge Robert Taylor of that court ruled against the black ligitants, who appealed his decision to the Court of Appeals in Cincinnati. In the meantime, similar cases had been filed involving the states of Kansas, South Carolina, Virginia, and Delaware, and these controversies having reached the Supreme Court of the United States, the Clinton case was held up, pending a resolution of the issue in what was to be captioned "the Brown case."

The Brown case caught Tennessee with racist legislation in its code; it did not catch the state by surprise. It was apparent to many far-sighted observers in Tennessee that steps to desegregate would probably be ordered by the Supreme Court, and in his first term Clement was urged to prepare for the steps that would be required. His replies were noncommittal, although he noted that steps were being taken to improve Negro schools. The governor generally took the view that most blacks were satisfied with the existing situation. The first pace-setting decision in the Brown case was handed down in May 1954, as the campaign for the second Clement term was warming up. The decision made it clear that some sort of desegregation would be ordered, but it was not yet plain how far or how fast the states might have to move. Many whites probably hoped for prolonged delays, and some clearly stood for massive resistance.

Browning had been an announced proponent of segregation, and Clement was certainly not opposed to this view, but the Supreme Court decision was taken calmly enough in Tennessee. Most of the state's political leaders were middle-of-the-road, law-and-order men and women. Attorney General Roy Beeler criticized the Supreme Court for legislating, but he said he had expected the decision. Clement himself made a cautious, non-committal, wait-and-see statement. Judge Schoolfield of

Hamilton County, representative of the limited number of hardliners in the state, was dissatisfied with the attitudes of Browning and Clement; in 1954 he ran for the Democratic nomination for governor as a hard-line segregationist, but he had next to no effect on the outcome of the election. Still, it was evident that the Supreme Court's decision would give rise to disputes in the legislature that convened in 1955.

In the meantime, the first Brown decision was accompanied or followed by demands for the admission of blacks into several previously all-white institutions. On June 10, 1954, a petition reached the Nashville school board for admission of three white children to all-black schools. The fathers of these children were white professors of mathematics at Fisk University. The petition was naturally denied, and City Superintendent W.A. Bass said the segregated system of Nashville would not change until some overall statewide change had been started. Bass' statement was in conflict with what would be the chief thrust of the Clement administration that desegregation was a local problem on which the state as a whole would make no move. On June 29, 1954, the Reverend Charles M. Williams, chancellor of the Roman Catholic diocese of Nashville, announced that the parochial schools of Nashville would desegregate in the following fall. On July 23, 1954, a committee representing the NAACP petitioned the Davidson County School Board to open its schools on a desegregated basis in the fall. That request was refused in the following month, but a committee of the board was appointed to consider desegregation at some future date. Petitions were received from Negroes for admission to Middle Tennessee State College and Memphis State. The State Board of Education denied the petitions on the grounds that no definitive order had been issued by the Supreme Court of the United States. In general the public institutions, which in fact were sworn to obey the state constitution and state statutes, were acting properly until the federal rulings had been made clear, although their actions no doubt gave the impression to some impatient souls of administrative caution to the point of cowardice. There was to be no federal ruling until the following year, but it was certainly clear that something — one did not know quite what — would happen.

In the summer primary, Clement smashed his political opposition. His attitude on school desegregation remained watchful and uncommitted. Some opinion in the state favored an attempt by Tennessee to become a part of the Brown litigation still pending in the Court, but the Clement administration made no such move. Attorney General Beeler supported the policy of staying out of the suit until his death in September 1954, and his successor George F. McCanless took the same position. Had Tennessee become a party to the suit, it could have come under the Court's jurisdiction before it needed to; cautious delay was the favored tactic. School opened in the fall of 1954 as it had in the long past—the whites in one place, the blacks in another.

Delays became more difficult when 1955 brought the seventy-ninth General Assembly into session. In the month of its opening, the Atomic Energy Commission announced that the public schools of Oak Ridge would be desegregated in autumn 1955, but of course Oak Ridge was highly untypical. It was a federally controlled community, heavily populated by atomic scientists, most of them not native to the state, with high IQs and agreeably high incomes. Still, the action brought the first desegregation to Anderson County, where, a few miles away from Oak Ridge, the first violence was soon to occur.

In the 1955 General Assembly, the first of the segregation bills was introduced by Senator Charles A. Stainback of Somerville, whose legislative proposition was backed by seven other senators, all from Middle and West Tennessee—Columbia, Shelbyville, Selmer, Lewisburg, Friendship, and other points. One of the backers of the legislation was Justin Thrasher, who figured as a major opponent of the Clement regime. Senator Stainback was the very prototype of the unreconstructed segregationist. His habitat was Somerville, seat of government of Fayette County, east of Memphis, where cotton had been king for many long years. In 1952–53, Fayette counted 4,000 black students in its public schools, as against 1,600 whites. In neighboring Haywood County, which Stainback also represented, there were some 3,900 blacks to 1,800 whites. Haywood and Fayette were to be a focal point of segregationist resistance for some years to come. In Anderson County, in the east, where the first serious conflict actually developed, white students outnumbered blacks, 6,660 to 116. The governor had some good reasons to consider that desegregation was a local, not a statewide problem.

Senate Bill No. 62—Stainback's bill, reported out of the Senate education committee on February 22 with a recommendation for passage—authorized local school boards to assign pupils on an individual basis without regard to established school attendance boundaries. The basis for the bill was the state's police power to protect public health, morals, and safety; Stainback indicated he would support the bill by citing attention to the higher rate of illegitimate births among Negroes of West Tennessee—a danger to white morals—and the prevalence of tuberculosis among blacks.

The bill had been approved by the committee by a vote of 6 to 1. Stainback was a member of the committee. He had the support of Mc-Allen Foutch of Smithville in Middle Tennessee, as well as that of Landon Colvard from the Sequatchie Valley. The only negative vote was that of Dr. J.H. Gammon, a veteran Knoxville Republican. During the hearings on the bill the arguments were those that might be expected. Whites from West Tennessee claimed that both whites and blacks in Fayette and other West Tennessee counties were satisfied with things as they were (which may have been true of some of the blacks, and were certainly true of most of the whites). Opposition to the bill stemmed principally from Negroes, including some students, chiefly from the Nashville area. Mrs. C.M. Hayes, speaking as a representative of the Nashville Colored Parent Teachers Association, declared the bill to be in every sense against the will of God. Avon Williams, at the beginning of his career as a crusader for Negro rights, spoke against the bill but managed to ease tensions by a timely joke.

Governor Clement received correspondence both for and against the legislation. As he often did on public matters, he sought the views of university and college presidents in the state. Most of the replies were thoughtful and cautious, but the presidents were in general unfriendly to the bill, thinking its constitutionality doubtful. Nashville pastors were officially unfriendly to the legislation. After having won the approval of the Senate Education Committee, the bill had to run the gauntlet of the Calendar Committee, composed of the speaker and the chairmen of the standing Senate committees. Here Clement most assuredly had control. The committee met secretly late in February and buried the bill. It was reported, although the vote was not made public, that the decision to suppress the bill was overwhelming, and it subsequently became clear that Senator Colvard supported the suppression. To his indignation, Stainback was not allowed to be present when the Calendar Committee was acting, and he subsequently tried to force the bill out of the committee. He secured the support of a majority of those senators who voted, but he did not quite reach the necessary majority of seventeen. His bill was dead.

Promptly following this defeat, Stainback introduced a similar local bill that would have covered only Haywood and Fayette counties. Passage of such local acts that have the support of the local delegation are normally accepted by the remaining legislators without difficulty, and Stainback's local bills passed both houses—as did other local bills permitting pupil assignment in Tipton County in West Tennessee, and in

Sumner County, northeast of Davidson. Usually the governor does not attempt to veto local bills, and if he does, he courts the danger of overrides, but Clement vetoed every one of these local segregation bills, and neither Stainback nor other segregationists could ever muster the votes necessary to overrule the vetoes. Attempts to attach amendments to the educational appropriations to prevent expenditures on integrated schools also failed.

Senator Stainback had moved too fast in a shadowed area where the legislators, many of them, were as eager to put off confrontation as the governor was. Clement's veto message on the two Stainback bills was measured and reasoned; he took no position for or against segregation, but hints are there to indicate what his future position would be.

> It is my understanding, [he wrote,] that this measure represents an attempt to circumvent the efficacy of the recent opinion handed down by the Supreme Court of the United States. [He noted that no final decree had been issued by the Court; segregation, he said, was still the law of the state.] This bill, [he continued,] can produce no desirable result. Its only possible effect can be to foment racial hatred and disorder where none exists, and to precipitate disputes to the detriment of all concerned. [He quoted his own public statement made] within a matter of minutes after the Supreme Court handed down its decision. The problems, [he had said at that time] presented by the Supreme Court's decision must be solved only after careful study, deliberation, and judicious appraisal. They will not be solved immediately and must not be considered hastily or in a disturbed or excited atmosphere. . . . I call upon all God-fearing citizens of our beloved State to pray for all of us that our thoughts, words and actions may be worthy of our religious and political heritage. . . . I have considered this bill from every conceivable angle, [the veto message went on,] and am of the opinion that I have only one course of action open to me which is honorable and that course is the one which, in the light of conscience and reason, appears to be consistent with Christian convictions and will reflect pure regard for the welfare of all the people of Tennessee. . . . I have made my decision and have done my duty as I see it. The matter is now in your hands. May the same God who watches over us all guide you in your deliberations.

Clement sent letters announcing and explaining his veto to a number of his fellow governors.

One irate Memphian wrote the governor: "The State of Tennessee and its true Southern citizens would be a lot better off if you spent more time trying to prevent integration in our schools and less time trying to get nominated for V.P." But plenty of commendations came in. Ministers in considerable number praised his action. The *Louisville Courier-Journal* commented favorably, and Governor Lawrence Wetherby of Kentucky wrote: "Dear Frank, / It is easy to understand the feelings you endured in vetoing your Senate bill 671. I think you acted correctly."

The governor was staking his political future on a course that would infuriate radicals on both wings. But his own secret convictions were well conveyed to Sam Morris, a Jewish friend in Hamilton County, when Morris reported in 1954 on a small anti-Semitic rally in that county that "these race haters will apparently stop at nothing." In his speech and in his actions, Clement was putting distance between himself and his die-hard brother governors farther south.

On the last day of May 1955, the Supreme Court issued its implementation order in the Brown case. The district courts were to enter such orders and decrees as were proper to enforce the basic principle of integration "with all deliberate speed." Considering the complications of altering a course that had been pursued by state and local officials for close to a century, the rubric of "deliberate speed" was the best the Court could come up with, but the vagueness of the phrase invited further delay. In fashioning decrees, the lower courts, said the Supreme Court, were to be guided by considerations of equity, showing practical flexibility in shaping and adjusting and reconciling public and private needs. More uncertainty. The decree inaugurated years of legal maneuver—a period still far from ended—on principles even not yet completely detailed nor thoroughly accepted.

The implementation order made it clear that some kind of action was required, but no one knew how much and how soon. Moreover, Tennessee was not a party to the suits in the Brown case, and Tennessee local officials, for the most part, felt the need for court orders before they moved, for Tennessee constitutional and statutory law still called for obedience. The governor asked his commissioner of education, Quill Cope, for advice; Cope told him to say nothing, unless he had to, but, if he was forced to speak, to say nothing that would imply that the state would attempt to tell local education authorities what to do. The governor also took counsel with the state attorney general, who told him that desegregation was a local problem; the state should not intervene. This became the firm position of the state administration.

Resistance to the implementation order began to build up during the remainder of 1955. A Ku Klux Klan rally was held in Marion County, west of Chattanooga. A Federation for Constitutional Government was born in Davidson County, and an organization for resistance developed

in Hamilton County, where some of the labor unions also took segregationist positions. Governor Clement was criticized by Eugene Cook, attorney general of Georgia, who was critical of some of plans for integration being worked out in Chattanooga. No massive integration was
foreseen for the fall of 1955, but a number of school systems and state
colleges began to prepare plans for slow but sure desegregation.

On January 14, 1956, federal judge Robert L. Taylor issued his order
requiring desegregation in the school system of Clinton. Judge Taylor
was an East Tennessean, the son of a former governor of the state, the
nephew of another, a member of the famous Taylor family of Carter
County, where the two Taylor brothers of Happy Valley had fought out
their contest for the governorship. He was an experienced party politician and friend and supporter of Gordon Browning. Nothing in his
background would have made him a proponent of desegregation, but
there was plenty in that background to make him a defender of federal
law and the federal judiciary. His January order, which came at the end
of five years of litigation, specified that integration in the Anderson
County high schools should begin not later than the beginning of the
fall term of 1956.

By most criteria one thinks of, desegregation was fully justified in
Clinton. The town was overwhelmingly white. The number of black
students was quite insignificant; in no way could they have been
thought of as a danger to white children. By no stretch of the imagination could their presence have diluted whatever educational advantages
the white children had. The blacks had been bussed for years, first to
black schools in LaFollette, and Rockwood and then, miles further, to
Knoxville.

On the other hand, Clinton was a mountain community of the east,
where blacks are comparatively rare and not especially welcome. But in
spite of local wishes, the leadership of the small town realized quite
clearly that integration was on the way and that it could be accepted.
That it could be peaceful was their hope. And so, probably, it would
have been, had they been let alone. This was not to be.

While the Clinton authorities made their plans, resistance to Clement and his policies were being organized in other parts of the state.
A.A. Canada of Chattanooga became president of the Tennessee Society
to Maintain Segregation. His group organized a caravan to descend on
Nashville to pressure the governor into calling a segregationist special
session of the legislature. The march moved into Nashville on January
23, 1956, but found the governor quite unwilling to call the Assembly to

Nashville or to interfere with local actions on desegregation. In that same month, Vanderbilt Professor Donald Davidson and fifteen other persons asked a chancery court to enjoin officials from giving funds to Austin Peay State College as long as Negro students were attending there. Clement ask the court to dismiss the suit.

In March 1956, members of Congress—House and Senate—presented the famous Southern Manifesto to the country. Of all the senators from eleven of the southern states, only Lyndon Johnson, Albert Gore, and Estes Kefauver refused to sign. The political temper of Tennessee, if the two senators were to be thought of as representative politicians, was conciliatory. In the House, however, the story was quite different: Tennesseans Joe Evins, Ross Bass, Clifford Davis, Jere Cooper, Tom Murray, and James Frazier all signed. They were all Democrats. Ross Bass by his signature introduced complications into his two races for the Senate a decade later.

As events had developed, Clinton was to be the only desegregated public school system in Tennessee in the autumn of 1956. There things were quiet during the heat of the summer, but the town's elite lived with an undercurrent of worry. The high school superintendent, D.J. Brittain, a native of nearby Oliver Springs, anticipated trouble. He talked with Horace Wells, publisher of the *Clinton Courier-News,* with Sidney Davis, a leading attorney, and with Mayor W.E. Lewallen and his son, Buford. The Lewallens were close friends of the governor. Meetings were organized to prepare the town for the change. Talks were made to civic clubs, PTA groups, and teachers and students in the schools that would feed students into the county high school in Clinton. But the talk reached the wrong people. This kind of sweet reasonableness never influenced those who were to cause the violence and disorder in the later summer.

High school registration in Clinton was set for August 20. On that day three Negro children were added to the 12 previously enrolled. Had Clinton been left alone, it is probable that the enrollment of the black students would have gone through without too much difficulty. The young blacks were told that they could participate in athletics, a matter of major importance in high school, although they could be members of teams only if opposing teams raised no objection. They were to be allowed to attend social events in the high school, but they were instructed that there would be no mixing. These rules gave warning of possible future difficulties, but gradual local adjustments might have been worked out without disturbance. Unfortunately, Clinton's small affairs, usually of no great moment to the rest of the world, were now news, and the media, always on the lookout for trouble and by no means unwilling to foment controversy to relieve the tedium of existence, began to pinpoint this usually obscure small town. The stories attracted the attention of Frederick John Kasper, who determined to come to Clinton to organize forceful resistance to the court-ordered actions of the school authorities.

John Kasper emerged briefly in the 1950s from a life of obscurity to become a roving ambassador of trouble. He was then a young man of few attainments and limited prospects. He worked for a time in a Washington bookstore. The crackpot social theories and attitudes of the poet, Ezra Pound, had greatly influenced him. Racism in the United States had frequently coupled Jews and blacks as inimical in some way to white America, and Pound's racist attitudes toward Jews were taken over by Kasper and applied to blacks. Kasper had no organization behind him at the moment, but he determined to conduct a single-handed opposition in Clinton; late in August he appeared in the town to begin a door-to-door campaign against school policy.

Classes opened on Monday, August 27, and, during the week following, conditions grew steadily more threatening. A small group of the town's leaders, including Mayor Lewallen and editor Wells, vainly attempted to persuade Kasper that they had no choice but to obey the law. On Sunday night, August 26, Kasper held a mass meeting in front of the courthouse; some fifty persons attended. The local authorities, puzzled and apprehensive, arrested Kasper on charges of vagrancy and incitement to riot, but the charges could not be upheld on the evidence so far available, and he was released. The arrest brought him some of the publicity he sought, and his audience grew. Kasper's muddle-headed insistence that the people could lawfully resist court orders on the basis of their rights under common law appealed to the emotions of listeners of limited education who could not have understood either the law or the attitudes of judges.

Local police conditions were not encouraging. The county was in the middle of a transition from one sheriff to another, as new terms began in early September, and the new sheriff, Glad Woodward, had not had time to assemble a complete force of deputies. The police force of Clinton was small, no match for a fully developed invasion of interested or curious outsiders. The school board, seeking further means of forestalling opposition, secured a sweeping injunction from Judge Taylor prohibiting interference with the process of integration in Clinton. His order

The Guard in Clinton. Photograph courtesy *Knoxville Journal.*

Attack in Clinton. Photograph courtesy *Knoxville Journal.*

was read on the school steps and on the courthouse steps; the county attorney read the order to the assembled students. Kasper, in a grandstand gesture, tore the order up. All of these moves were given first-page space.

A small picket line of students and other teenagers formed on Monday, August 27, as school opened. On Tuesday, Kasper, with about twenty-five companions, went to the school, where Superintendent Brittain told them he would obey the court order. That night Kasper harangued a crowd of about five hundred at the courthouse. Pickets appeared at the school the following morning, and police arrested two fighting teenagers. Kasper began to attract backers from outside the state. Admiral Cromelin, a well-known member of the right wing, appeared on the scene from Alabama.

Local authorities looked toward the up-coming weekend with growing apprehension. A high school football game was scheduled for Friday, and the crowds attracted by that game could be turned to trouble-hunting marauding. Labor Day was to follow on September 3, and holiday crowds could find Clinton's troubles more interesting than vacation spots. A principal highway from the north to the Smokies ran down Clinton's main street, and holiday traffic would complicate local police problems. The town elite and their allies formed a home guard.

A major crisis now loomed in East Tennessee, and Clement was faced with what he was to describe as the hardest decision of his life. Should he intervene in Clinton? with the highway patrol? with the young and inexperienced citizen soldiers of the National Guard? Turning out the state's military forces on their own people was distasteful, dangerous, likely to invite political reprisals. No governor takes such a step lightly. Browning had turned out troops to keep order at the strike-bound Enka plant near Morristown and earned a permanent black mark with organized labor. If Clement were to turn troops on Clinton, he would be labeled an integrationist; if he refrained, he would court disaster of another kind. For most of that crucial week he dodged the issue, managing to be unreachable.

The crisis came to a peak on Saturday, September first. A rally was scheduled for eight that night by the Tennessee Federation for Constitutional Government, the Tennessee Society to Maintain Segregation, the States Rights Council of Tennessee, the Pro-Southerners, and the White Citizens Council. Raulston Schoolfield was slated to be the principal speaker, but in fact he did not appear. Arthur A. Canada of Chattanooga spoke, as did Jack Kershaw of Nashville, representing the Federation for Constitutional Government. On the preceding Friday night, a crowd of 2,000 had milled around a town flooded with rumors, including reports that the courthouse and mayor's house were to be burned. Members of the hastily organized home guard were assigned to protect the house.

Under Tennessee procedure, the governor does not ordinarily move into an area until the sheriff certifies that he is losing control, and word was relayed to Clinton that Governor Clement would insist on receiving a request for aid from the sheriff. On September 1, three telegrams were sent to the governor. In one Horace Wells said: "Lives and property are threatened by mobs that rage out of control. Local law enforcement officers are exhausted. Some have been on duty more than 40 hours without relief. . . . We need immediate relief." W.E. Lewallen, the mayor, and Paul Horton, city recorder, forwarded to the governor a resolution of the board of mayor and aldermen calling on the executive for help. And, finally, the official request from Sheriff Woodward was sent, containing the key words: "I therefore formally request that you direct State Assistance be sent to Anderson County Immediately and to remain during the Emergency. Please give me your decision by telephone or telegram at the earliest possible moment." The written requests of Mayor Lewallen and Sheriff Woodward were flown to Clement by special plane.

The buck had now come to rest on the governor's desk. Saturday afternoon some twenty persons convened at the governor's mansion on Curtiswood Lane in south Nashville to map strategy and tactics; there was no longer any doubt that troops were going in. The governor's mansion was crowded with the executive leadership of the state, with Adjutant General Joe Henry a key figure. Assistant Adjutant General Van Nunally was present, along with Secretary of State Joe Carr, Attorney General George McCanless, and others of equal importance. Actions were to be taken that brought danger of bloody confrontation. Some of the participants wanted Henry to excuse all soldiers less than twenty-one years of age. "I'm just *not* going to do that," said Henry. "I'm not going to tell these fellows that we are trying to train—I'm not going to tell them that we've been training you and now you can't come —because when I take the National Guard, I'm going to take *all* of them." McCanless backed him up. Some timid soul wanted Henry to take the troops in with without ammunition—a sure recipe for disaster. Henry flatly refused. "We went in with loaded guns," he remembered later. "It was not a sham or pretense. We were ready in Clinton."

At 5:45 the highway patrol was ordered to proceed to Clinton; they arrived just at the moment on Saturday evening when the mob showed signs of attacking the home guard—the lawyers, football and basketball coaches, teachers, businessmen. "Just at the most crucial moment," recalled Wells years later, "around the hill, you heard the sirens, and you saw the lights flashing. . . . They had been organized from all over Tennessee. They drove up across the bridge with their sirens going, and they came down to the courthouse, and Greg O'Rear, nearly eight feet tall—he stepped out—he stepped out—and, I mean, order was restored."

The following Monday was Labor Day; the patrol would be needed elsewhere to control the slaughter by automobile that usually took place across the state. And so on Sunday afternoon, the National Guard took over, led personally by Henry, who without changing clothes, had started for Clinton immediately following the breakup of the conference at the mansion. The force consisted of 633 battle-equipped men, 7 M-41 tanks, and 3 armored personnel carriers. Henry intended to overawe any resistance from the very first. At nine in the evening, two platoons moved into the courthouse square and dispersed a crowd of about 1,000. Henry set up road blocks and turned the curiosity seekers away. Nine out of every ten cars were turned around and headed out of Clinton. On September 3, Henry prohibited outdoor assemblies in Clinton, outdoor public speaking, parking, or assembly in the courthouse square after six in the evening, or use of any public address system out of doors. The troops at Clinton were drawn from various sections of the state. The tank battalion came from Cookeville, and troops were drawn from Sparta, Crossville, Livingston, and from other units in East and Middle Tennessee. No troops were moved in from the areas west of Nashville. Fifteen officers were in command of the more than six hundred soldiers, most of them very young.

On Saturday night as the highway patrol was establishing control, the governor took to the air waves to explain his action. Privately he called nine religious leaders—pastors and a rabbi—to the Capitol where they prayed with him for the safety of the young men in the Guard. The governor was racked with anxiety, and the aid of the ministers gave him solace and confidence. The session was not a publicity stunt; there no reporters, no news reports, and few people ever learned of the session.

Clement always maintained that he sent the patrol and the Guard to Clinton, not to enforce integration but to preserve order. Henry does not remember receiving written orders from the governor; but he knew what to do, and he knew that Clement, in his usual administrative style, had put him in charge and given him authority.

The National Guard, during their stay, camped in the middle of the town; they were well behaved. During their period in Clinton, two of the tanks made a side trip to nearby Oliver Springs, where the evidence of their guns cooled off some local hotheads who threatened to get out of hand. The town was overrun with newsmen — some 125 of them from all over the world. *Time* was on hand; the black press was represented — the Chicago *Defender,* the *Amsterdam News,* and others. The press was anything but helpful. When things threatened to get too quiet, the newsmen looked around for ways to get some action. "Help me," said Henry to Loye Miller of the *Knoxville News-Sentinel,* "help me get them out of here."

Within a week, order was pretty well restored. Nine of the dozen blacks enrolled in the school attended class on the first day after Labor Day, an action that called for extraordinary courage. Out of 806 white students, only 257 students attended. But the following day, all twelve Negroes were in school and the total attendance was up to 324. Some 394 students attended class on Thursday, and the figure mounted steadily in the days that followed. All but 250 of the Guard left for home that weekend, and these left in the middle of the following week.

Peace settled temporarily on an uneasy community. Clement and the sheriff exchanged somewhat acrimonious letters, for the governor felt the sheriff was reluctant to take responsibility for maintaining order. A news note quoted Woodward as saying he had never asked for help; if he made the statement, the documents give him the lie. Henry sent the story to Clement with a note: "This takes the cake." Gradually the sheriff was forced to accept the governor's view of his responsibility; he organized a special force of some two hundred local citizens to keep the peace. The newsmen left, on the alert for trouble elsewhere.

In fact, Clinton's troubles were not yet over. The battles of words and decisions being fought through the courts were accompanied by fistfights in the streets. Late in August, as the Clinton crisis built up, a group of Anderson County citizens and the Tennessee Federation for Constitutional Government had sought an injunction in Anderson County chancery court to prevent admission of black students to Clinton High. Chancellor Joe M. Carden denied the petition. On October 5, on appeal from that denial, the Tennessee Supreme Court held unanimously that the Tennessee segregation laws had been rendered void by the Brown decisions of 1954 and 1955. On August 31, Judge Robert Taylor had found John Kasper in contempt of his court and had sentenced him to one year in prison and fined him $10,000, but Kasper remained free on bond pending appeal. Kasper had also been charged, under an old Tennessee law, with sedition and incitement to riot, but in a November trial, to the cheers of the crowd, an Anderson county jury had found him not guilty. By way of celebration, Kasper marked his acquittal with a free-wheeling speech of thirty minutes, attacking the United States Supreme Court, the "dirty press," and the "Jew-led" NAACP. In later months a piece of polemic writing printed over Kasper's name used words reminiscent of Pound's cantos to describe his opposition: pink punks, flat-chested highbrows, homos, poodledogs, hot-eyed Socialists, Fabians, and scum.

The acquittal of Kasper by the Anderson County twelve may have given some new hope to the bitter-enders in Clinton. Harrassment of black children in the high school increased; eggs were thrown. At the end of November, two of the Negro students withdrew, and the remaining ten were staying out of school. The school board offered to pay tuition and transportation for any black students who wished to return to Austin High in Knoxville, but there were no takers.

By early December, Superintendent Brittain had had enough; he said that further disturbances would call for expulsions. A municipal election was scheduled for December 4, and the White Citizens Council put candidates in the field. Sixteen residents of Clinton and Anderson County were arrested for contempt of the federal district court in Knoxville. The Anderson County School Board sent a letter to United States Attorney General Herbert Brownell, saying it could not enforce integration.

Superintendent Brittain was fighting a hard battle, but he was by no means alone. Clinton numbered other citizens of high courage and independence. One of these lone individualists was the Reverend Paul W. Turner of the First Baptist Church of Clinton, who, no doubt remembering prayerfully his Christian vows and beliefs, rose in his pulpit on December 1, and to a capacity congregation that on this day got more than the usual exhortations announced that on Monday he would accompany to the school any black child that needed his help. Turner had spent his youth in West Tennessee, and he thought that more time was needed — up to five years — to adjust to the changes in race relations, but he was not prepared to stand by while abuse of black children continued. He invited any of his congregation who felt as he did to join him. No black student appeared on Monday. On Tuesday, in the clear cold air of Clinton at eight in the morning, white adults began to gather near the school. Shortly after 8:30, six black children, escorted by Reverend Turner, Sidney Davis, a white attorney, and Leo Burnett, a white accountant at Magnet Knitting Mills, entered the school. When Turner left the school, he was set upon a group of whites, both men and women, and his nose bloodied, but he was a big man and escaped serious injury. Some scuffling occurred inside the school, Mrs. Brittain was shoved against a wall, and one white student said that if Brittain came after him he would "cut his guts out." Shortly before noon, Brittain closed the school indefinitely.

Those who wished to obey the law in Clinton had already appealed to the Attorney General of the United States for aid. Having received no immediate reply, they turned again to the courts. A delegation of Clinton citizens, including Mayor Lewallen, now went to the office of Judge Taylor in Knoxville to ask for enforcement of his injunction. Late that same afternoon, before Brownell announced in Washington that the administration would enforce orders of the federal courts, the United States attorney in Knoxville, John C. Crawford, Jr., formally asked Judge Taylor to order the arrest of sixteen persons in Anderson County for violation of his injunction. Meanwhile, in the election for the city council of Clinton, all the candidates of the White Citizens Council were defeated. The forces of moderation in the town were regaining power.

In the next two days, thirteen men, two women, and a teen-age boy were rounded up by the United States marshal and his deputies. They were, on the whole, a pitiable contrast to the law-abiding citizens of Clinton. Several were unemployed; there were painters, grocery clerks, utility workers, and others of like stations in the hierarchy of occupations. One was a fireman, and another was a school bus driver who had once been a deputy sheriff. The arrests brought an immediate and predictable response from the segregationists of Tennessee. These were quite probably less numerous than in the states to the south, and they were less vocal, but even so they were a troublesome element in Clinton and elsewhere in the state. Several organizations had been put together rather hurriedly against the approach of integration, but perhaps one of the most vocal was the Tennessee Federation for Constitutional Government. Three of its most prominent leaders were Donald Davidson, professor of English at Vanderbilt, Jack Kershaw, a Nashville lawyer, and Sims Crownover, another Nashville attorney. Kershaw had been present in Clinton during the troubles there, particularly on the Saturday when the highway patrol first entered the town. Crownover was active then and later during the legal battles of that transitional period.

In many ways, Donald Davidson was the most prominent man associated with this group. He had a long record of attachment to the conservative traditions of the South. He was one of the young writers at Vanderbilt University who called themselves "the Fugitives," a set comprising novelists and poets; many of them later reached great eminence — several became internationally famous. Some of the Fugitives initially pledged their loyalty to the ideal of an agrarian South, resistant to the urbanization and industrialization that was remaking their southern world in a fashion they disliked. Most of them left Vanderbilt as their lives moved on, but Davidson remained. And Davidson remained true to his original views. His poetry clearly expresses his deep-seated conservatism. In the 1940s he had written articles friendly to the traditional southern attitudes on race. His two-volume work on the Tennessee in the Rivers of America Series was sharply critical of TVA and its promotion of change in the Tennessee Valley. He was outspokenly anti-Communist and tended to view liberals as thinly disguised leftists, if not worse.

In 1948, at the height of the States Rights controversy inside the Democratic party, he wrote to W.T. Couch, director of the University of Chicago Press: "The Southern political situation is what interests me most. I am no prognosticator. I will simply put down what I notice. Without exception, every person who has expressed himself to me, on and off campus, has said he will vote for the States Rights ticket. The exception, a sulky New Dealer, says he'll stay at home. The Nashville Banner runs the Confederate flag on its masthead every day . . . Roy Acuff stands a good chance, it seems, to be governor, and he may carry Reese with him to the Senate and thus knock out Kefauver, who is a weak liberal hypocrite . . . I shall take the greatest pleasure in voting for Thurmond. This is the first time in my life that I have had a chance to vote for a real Southerner."

The extremity of Davidson's views is matched by his failure to sense the realities of politics. This fault of judgment continued throughout the segregation controversy, but Davidson did not quit trying. He did have periods of discouragement, when realities were sensed more clearly. "I get the impression," he wrote in late 1953, "that Tennesseans in general are too busy listening to Kefauver, TVA, Dinah Shore, Liberace, Hodding Carter, Ralph McGill, the New York Times, Winston

Churchill, and Company, to listen to whatever feeble words I might have to utter."

During 1955 and 1956 Davidson worked to form an organization in Tennessee that would represent the conservative point of view, not on segregation alone, but on other matters as well. Davidson became the chairman of the Tennessee Federation for Constitutional Government formed in response to the directions taken by the federal courts. Jack Kershaw was made vice-chairman, and Dudley Gale, a prominent insurance executive in Nashville, became treasurer. None of the officials of the Federation possessed any stature within the main stream of Tennessee politics.

Kershaw was in Clinton during the troubles there. At that time Davidson was not in Tennessee, but from his temporary residence at Bread Loaf Rural Station in Middlebury, Vermont, he provided a member of the publishing firm of Charles Scribner's Sons with a version of the Clinton struggle sharply at variance with other reports. He wrote:

> For your information I want to assure you that the N.Y. newspapers, also the radio reports, are miserably incorrect and incomplete in various respects. . . . The *Times* has so far played up only the outsider from Washington [Davidson always maintained his distance from Kasper] a "professional" who barged in and got arrested and sentenced. We have had a strong local unit of the Federation in Anderson County, including Oak Ridge, Clinton, and other points, since about this time last year. Our state leaders arranged and held an entirely peaceable and successful public meeting at Clinton on Saturday night. Permission was given by the Judge to hold this meeting at the Clinton court-house. But at the last moment the judge, probably under pressure from the radical element in that area, weakened and withdrew his permission. The meeting was . . . held in the open. . . . It was decided to launch a campaign to raise funds for establishing a private school in Clinton. . . . Prior to this meeting, the Clinton people picked up the news that Gov. Clement was sending in the state police, etc. They promptly went and got their guns and prepared to fight. Our leaders persuaded them to leave the guns at home and take a peaceful course. When they arrived, finding nobody else to hustle, they went around shooting off tear-gas bombs at a few lingering groups, mostly children, scattered about the Clinton streets. Gov. Frank Clement, in sending in state police and now two battalions of the National Guard, is just making a silly and dangerous grandstand play, in order to get national attention for himself. . . . In fact, he will make everybody in the state of Tennessee, except the radicals and his own gang of lickspittles and flatterers, as mad as all hell — and they were already pretty mad

at Clement, for his performance at Chicago, and his switching to the detested Kefauver."

This letter, with its strange views on Tennessee affairs, was dated September 2, 1956, before the Clinton crisis had subsided. On December 24, another letter was dispatched to the Scribner representative, giving further reactions to Tennessee affairs. "Back here," wrote Davidson, now from his Nashville home, "we are preparing to go into the difficult battle with the Tennessee Legislature, with our poltroon of a Governor and leftist-liberal cohorts (including the Kefauverites, the NAACP, the One-Worlders, etc.) already playing tricks to block sensible and forthright action. . . . Meanwhile, too, we are organizing the legal defense for the 16 defendants who were so cruelly arrested and mistreated under Judge Taylor's fool order in the Clinton case."

Clement received sundry notes of condemnation during the year of the Clinton riot. "Your political future is now practically hopeless," wrote one irate citizen. One newspaper writer, remembering his Dickens, dubbed the governor the "artful dodger." Wilkes Thrasher, Jr., suggested changing the state constitution to preserve desegregation, although how this was to be done was far from clear. And, of course, at least one letter called him a "nigger lover." Ordinarily, the governor answered his letters, including those of critics, but the office note on this particular insult was marked "No reply." The governor, attempting to keep an even keel in stormy weather, was taking his blows from the right. Those from the left were soon to follow.

Now that the Supreme Court had issued implementation instructions to the lower federal courts and now that plans for compliance were already taking form, it was clear that the General Assembly of 1957 would have to come to grips with this stormy issue. Clinton had already gone through the first painful steps of integration. Larger communities, where blacks were more numerous, were planning moves to comply with expected court orders. A plan for grade-by-grade desegregation in Nashville, beginning with the first, was submitted to federal judge Miller in Nashville. The plan included provisions for transfer of students from one school to another that would have made voluntary segregation possible, and Negro groups attacked the scheme in court and out. Vanderbilt admitted two blacks to its law school; one Negro had already been graduated from its divinity school. Both the admissions and the graduation were new precedents for Vanderbilt. In the fall, Roy Wilkins, executive secretary of the NAACP, in Nashville for the funeral of

Charles Johnson, former president of Fisk University, said that more progress would be made to desegregate if decisions were left up to local boards, without state politicians mixing in the matter. The opinion is especially interesting in its agreement with what was emerging as the settled policy of the Clement administration.

The Federation for Constitutional Government, from which Davidson had hoped so much, prepared legislative proposals for the 1957 Assembly, designed to relax the compulsory attendance law, to establish pupil assignment systems, and to provide administrative appeals from enforced integration that might delay the process. The Tennessee Baptist Convention, meeting in Knoxville, dodged the issue. Clement's staff were fending off all notions of crippling the state public school system, while Commissioner Quill Cope stated clearly that integration was a local problem and that the state would keep hands off. Complete inaction on the part of the state was not, however, politically feasible, and legislative action could not be avoided.

In this atmosphere the governor addressed the General Assembly on January 9, 1957, delivering what some of his staff considered his finest speech. The address was more than the usual virtuoso performance of a master orator. Clement faced a crisis of conscience and statecraft. He could not satisfy either side completely. The manner and tone of the speech was emotional and appealing. In the end he came down for a compromise and indeed a compromise that did not work, but in seeking that compromise he turned his back on the die-hards on both sides, at great risk to his political future. Moderate groups in the state were pleased, and there can be no doubt that Clement correctly sensed the mood of the great mass of his people. He must be given credit for defusing the bomb that in the states around him was allowed to explode.

"Lieutenant Governor Maddux, Mr. Speaker Bomar, Distinguished Senators and Representatives of the 80th General Assembly, My Friends and Fellow Citizens," began the governor, "The words I speak to you today represent a decision I must live with the rest of my days on this earth and through all Eternity. . . . I come before you to speak the truth. I come to suggest that course of action which, under prevailing circumstances, I honestly believe to be in the best interests of all of you in general—and Tennessee's children in particular." The governor went on to describe the bitter history of race relations, and then continued: "I am not so concerned with what the extremists on either side think of what I shall say here today—nor those out-of-staters of both races who come into our midst stirring up trouble and strife where none existed in order to further their own gains. I shall not attempt to please them. But I am greatly concerned with what our God-fearing law abiding citizens think." He appealed for internal unity and warned that America could not be trusted with world peace if it could not preserve its own. He described the process by which slavery was fastened on the South and the war that caused its end.

"We must face the problems of today," he continued, "in the light of the past. We must accept the fact that no law, no judicial decree can erase three hundred years of history. *But in recognition of the existence of different backgrounds for white and negro, we must not overlook that the negro is equal to the white in the eyes of the law and in the sight of God.*" [The emphasis is the governor's.]

The Negro, the governor observed, is a citizen. He pays taxes, "even as the white." He serves in the armed forces. He is entitled to equality of opportunity. "Whether we like it or not, the Negro will never willingly keep an assigned place in society if that place is set in shame and degradation"; and with these words the governor stated the whole crux of the issues before them.

But then he shifted ground. Tennessee, he noted, had required separate schools in recognition of historic differences between the races. Some of the white and negro schools were good; some, bad. "The great Tennessee Agricultural and Industrial University is comparable to the institution maintained for the whites," a claim that was most certainly not true, whatever the extent of the efforts put forth for A&I. The governor went on to analyze the decisions of the Supreme Court, emphasizing that it had outlawed statutes *compelling* segregation, but leaving the administration of the schools where it had been. However true this view may have seemed at the time, it underestimated the future drive of the federal courts and federal administrators not only to outlaw deliberate segregation, but to compel integration. But at the moment when Clement was speaking, a limited correction of segregation seemed possible. This was to be the thrust of Clement's compromise proposals, which now followed.

"*I am . . . convinced,*" he said, "*that extreme measures will not help us reach the goals we seek, but rather will lead to a worsening of our difficulties.*" Clement took his stand on five principles; the basic purpose must be the preservation and promotion of peace between the races; adequate educational chances must be provided for all children; the people of the state must be given an opportunity of choosing without force the course that best suits their desires and needs; an inflexible system must not be im-

Segregation —

quote in chapter head (?)

Insert 1

There comes a time in the life of every public official when a decision must be made as to a controversial issue. Usually the official can choose sides and feel certain of substantial support.

Today I face an entirely different & rather unique situation. On the one hand we have radical elements who claim they support our negro citizens and who obviously will be satisfied with nothing less than an all-out drive to force negroes & whites into the classrooms together at any cost at the earliest possible moment.

On the other side we have radical elements among our white citizens who declare the negro to be little about & and who declare they will fight have demonstrated that they will oppose with everything at their command illegal, violent & otherwise any effort to have an integrated school.

From Clement's draft of the desegregation speech.

posed throughout the state; and local officials must have the fullest power compatible with a democratic government. If a key is sought to Clement's basic philosophy of government, it can probably be found in these guides.

The governor now went on to propose five pieces of legislation to meet the court's instructions: an act to authorize local school systems to provide separate schools for children whose parents voluntarily wished them to attend separate schools; an act to give local school boards full power to place or assign students, with due regard to their background and with adequate administrative and judicial review; an act to permit transfer of students from one school to another; an act authorizing school systems to maintain schools jointly; and an act to amend the existing law on transportation of school children, to back up the other statutes. The governor rejected any amendment of the compulsory attendance laws.

And the governor summed up his proposals with these words. *"I would be the last to say that this program is a panacea to cure all our ills. BUT IT IS AN HONEST PROGRAM. It is not compounded of the medicine of political quackery. . . .* If we are to succeed in our purpose, if we are to live, work and go to school in peace and harmony, we will need, we must have, white and negro alike, the greatest gift of them all—the charity which our Lord and Master commanded us to bear in our hearts and souls for one another. And now," as his voice dropped to a quiet close, "may God Almighty be with you one and all."

It was a great speech; applause was prompt, vigorous, and prolonged. Before the speech, large crowds milled through the capitol. The galleries in the House were filled—and they were desegregated. No demonstrations occurred, and the crowd was fully dispersed within thirty minutes after the governor had left the chamber. It was a great speech, but it may have fallen short of being a great state paper, for the proposals that the governor offered seemed an anti-climax to his ringing description of black rights. What Clement was proposing was freedom of choice for the whites, a freedom that the federal courts would not allow, and a freedom that would most certainly have continued a large measure of de facto segregation. There can be little doubt that the governor was speaking the wishes and views of the great mass of white Tennesseans.

In making his proposals, Clement offended those who wished to take a posture of defiance of the court, as a number of southern governors did. A telegram bearing the signatures of John Kasper and others purporting to represent county white citizens' councils in Knox, Anderson, Roane, Campbell, Blount, Sevier, Jefferson, and Union reached the governor, under the dateline of January 9. Among other matters the telegram said that the Communist party, Kefauver, Gore, and Franklin Roosevelt [already dead since the last months of World War II] had a continuing program to turn Tennessee and all of us over to the "Chosen People, Jews, Kikes, Yidds, Hebrews and Negro stooges."

On the opposing side, blacks were to oppose the proposed legislation, which, in fact, would have permitted an evasion of integration. A group of UT scientists wrote the governor in some disappointment that he had not gone further toward integration. There is no way of telling whether Clement really believed that his proposals, if enacted, would have stood up under court attack. He was himself a lawyer, and he was surrounded with men who could give him competent legal advice: most certainly it must have seemed doubtful whether evasive legislation would be held valid. Clement was on better ground when he proposed to leave decisions to individual localities, as even black militants agreed, for such action would recognize the differences in the racial distribution in the state. Today, in Clement's home town, blacks and whites peacefully attend the same high school, and black boys can be seen with whites in the school swimming pool, an unthinkable arrangement when Clement was a student there. And the governor's hope for peace was not completely unjustified, in spite of serious difficulties that arose in some sections of the state.

Clement's speech was followed by the introduction of bills carrying out his program, and their passage some two weeks later without significant dissent. The bills were given extensive hearings, contrary to usual legislative practice in those days, but no substantial alterations were made in the proposals. Quite probably the passage of the administration's bills deadened attempts to enact other legislation, some of which could have been less reasonable. The Assembly did pass an act permitting segregation by sex, a virtual dead letter. Acts were passed regulating and curbing actions of the NAACP, by defining and interdicting barratry, compelling the filing of information, and requiring registration with the secretary of state. These swept through the legislature with scarcely any dissent, but they were of more than dubious constitutionality. As to the administration bills, however sane they may have looked in these early months of desegregation, their validity was soon successfully challenged. Their import was to maintain voluntary segregation, and before long it became clear that the federal judiciary would not tolerate voluntary segregation any more than it would accept enforced segregation.

The legislation had some justification in that it compelled the federal courts to define objectives.

The resolutions of the General Assembly are a mixture of the serious, the futile, and the absurd. Aside from the resolutions of condolence for sickness and death (those where-as clauses that recognize the inscrutable wisdom of the Almighty), the 1957 legislature passed joint resolutions of all three types, including one that recognized Bristol as the music capital of Appalachia. Among those that were serious but utterly futile, and therefore absurd, were several condemning the actions of the Supreme Court on segregation. House Resolution No. 1, sponsored by fifty-five members of the lower chamber and signed by Speaker Bomar on January 17, 1957, condemned the Supreme Court for usurpation of power and pledged support for a constitutional amendment to preserve the state's power to segregate. The view was duplicated by Senate Resolution No. 3, sponsored by fourteen senators. Senate and House resolutions do not require the governor's signature. Although the legislature thus expressed sentiments regarding segregation and the court, that rang like sentiments expressed throughout the South, it stopped short of any suggestion of extra-legal or illegal action. To this degree at least, legislative forces were in accord with Governor Clement's cautious avoidance of defiance of the national government.

In June the Tennessee Federation for Constitutional Government, through a statement signed by its chairman Donald Davidson, hit out at the governor and Attorney General McCanless for their failure to assert the right to nullification, as well as for failing to intervene in the contempt trial of citizens of Clinton in the federal district court. The federation's divorce from reality, even though shared by others in the Deep South, was nothing short of bizarre.

The remaining months of 1957 witnessed a very slow but none-the-less steady process of desegregation. In January, twelve black students and their parents had filed suit for desegregation in the Knoxville schools. Nashville made plans to begin desegregation in the fall, and as a counter move a group called the Parents School Preference Committee was formed to pressure the Nashville school administrators to permit placement according to parental preferences under the statute passed by the General Assembly. School authorities, perhaps thinking the statute unlawful in any case, showed no disposition to change their plans. They were acting under a specific court order and could not give credence to any contrary statute passed by the Assembly.

John Kasper and fifteen residents of Anderson County faced trial for contempt of the court of Judge Taylor in Knoxville. This annoyance, however, did not inhibit his continued activity, an activity that was becoming increasingly unwelcome to Tennessee residents and newspapers that were themselves unfriendly to court rulings. Kasper was more and more viewed as a troublesome interloper in a situation that he could only make worse. In late June he announced that he had helped to form a White Citizens Council in Nashville, but he was reticent about the details of this venture. He called on the Knoxville school board to resign.

The contempt trial of Kasper and the fifteen residents of Anderson County was held in July. Four lawyers were retained for the defense by the Federation for Constitutional Government; one of them was Thomas P. Gore of Nashville, first cousin of Senator Albert Gore. Altogether eighteen defense attorneys were occupied in the case. The trial opened on July 8, 1957; on that same day debate was opened in the United States Senate on the civil rights bill of 1957 and on the question of abandoning jury trials in criminal contempt cases arising from racial issues. That debate would hinge around the difficulty of getting convictions through juries, an issue that once more would put the country's prominent political figures in an embarrassing situation.

In the Clinton case, after a trial lasting about two weeks, the jury brought in verdicts of guilty for seven persons, including Kasper. Four dependents were acquitted. Charges against four others had been dropped before the issue was sent to the jury. Kasper was subsequently sentenced to one year in federal prison; the remaining six defendants were placed on probation for periods ranging from twelve months to two years. The six convicted defendants included two used car dealers, a carpenter who was a part-time preacher, an Oak Ridge fireman, a machinist, and a housewife.

In the late summer of 1957, Hattie Cotton School in Nashville was bombed, and other disorders occurred in that city. Later, in nearby Arkansas, President Eisenhower used troops to quell the attempts of Governor Orville Faubus to halt the integration of the Little Rock High School, an action with which Governor Clement publicly disagreed, but the people of Tennessee could have noted that his own cautious actions had saved their state experiences of this sort.

Governor Clement's second term was drawing to a close (the primary had already given the Democratic nomination to Buford Ellington) when on October 5, 1958, racial tensions were once more raised by a dynamite explosion that wrecked the Clinton High School. The dynamiters were never identified. Dynamite is a familiar substance in a mining and farming community; any number of persons could have set the charge. Anderson County has never been reluctant to call on other governments for financial aid, and this time local officials called on the federal government to foot the repair bills, a gesture almost as futile as a proposal to nullify a court order. President Eisenhower declared that the federal government could not step in every time anything went wrong locally, from a leaky water faucet on up. Governor Clement, who had never wasted any love on the General, was annoyed, and R.G. Crossno, a local school board member said the group that asked for federal aid got an official "run-around, heave-ho, and pass-the-buck."

In the meantime the school was continued in other buildings, and the high school was eventually rebuilt aided by funds collected under the leadership of the widely known columnist, Drew Pearson. His help was memorialized in a bronze plaque attached to the building. A notable feature of the new building was its connection by a sensitive warning system to the police station across the street. As one observer put it, even a rat running across the floor would sound an alarm.

Kasper's welcome wore paper-thin. In November of 1958 he was convicted for inciting to riot in Nashville. At his trial on this charge he was represented by Raulston Schoolfield, who had recently been convicted by the state Senate on impeachment charges based on some of his activities as judge of the criminal court in Hamilton County. In October, Kasper had attempted to hold a rally in McMinn County and had been escorted to the county line by police officers, who also ousted a Knoxville resident. "We've got a nice, quiet town here," said the Athens police chief, "and we don't want any trouble."

As Governor Clement's significant second term neared its end, Tennessee was clearly at the beginning of desegregation. Some close friends of the governor thought they detected in the governor's thinking an increasing conservatism nursed by others of his close advisers. Nevertheless change was in the wind. Institutions of higher learning in the state at five locations were opening up to black students, and three local school districts had started on the thorny path to integration. Violence had broken out in Clinton and Nashville, but the desegregation moved slowly forward.

The great push of that desegregation still lay some years ahead, and the governor would face its problems once more in his final term.

♪ *Why should I shrink at pain and woe?*
Or feel at death dismay?
I've Canaan's goodly land in view,
And realms of endless day.

JAMES MONTGOMERY, 1771–1854

8. I've Canaan's Goodly Land in View

THE DEMOCRATIC NATIONAL CONVENTION OF 1956

Perhaps it was not his best speech, but nonetheless the keynote address that Frank Clement used to open the Democratic National Convention of 1956 was the height of Clement's oratorical career, merely because of the nature and size of his audience. Whether good or not, the speech had a countrywide impact, and his famous words, "How long, O Lord, how long," have been remembered for years by both detractors and friends. The keynoter's job was one that he wanted, and his close friends, especially Joe Carr and Herbert Walters, worked assiduously to get it for him. In their minds, and those of other Clement friends, there was always the chance that a rousing keynote might catapult the speaker into a nomination, and things were reasonably fluid and open to surprises in the 1956 conclave. After all, Bryan's famous Cross-of-Gold appeal had made him the leader of the Democrats for several tries at the presidency, and Democrats always remembered that. In 1948, Alben Barkley's keynote oratory made him the vice-presidential choice. It could happen again.

Clement's staff had long pondered the national possibilities open to him, and they worked hard to build him up. Brainard Cheney tried to interest magazine publishers in the governor, and the possibility of biographies and autobiographies was studied. Through the middle fifties, Kefauver, Gore, and Clement were all in demand for speechmaking throughout the country. Kefauver was a bumbling, plodding speaker, but his efforts carried conviction. Gore was an able speaker, and his speeches had content. Clement's reputation as an orator bloomed. He spoke in Indianapolis, in Michigan, Connecticut, Ohio, and Missouri.

221

He clicked particularly in Indianapolis and Springfield, Missouri, and hints of the vice-presidency were stirred up.

Clement's first Indianapolis speech, in September 1954, was a rousing success. In describing it, the *Saturday Evening Post* author flung restraint to the winds like the winter garments of repentence. "Mr. Clement", he said, "a handsome, dreamy-eyed, full-lipped young man with the mobile, fine boned face of a Shakesperian actor, strode to the rostrum and, in a voice which alternately boomed like a siege gun, sang like a mountain fiddle and died away, in moments of emotion, to a dramatic whisper, tore passion to tatters as he heaped scorn, contumely and obloquy upon the Republicans." He said a new star was rising in the political firmament, unless Clement's larynx failed him. *Time* magazine, with its usual slangy superciliousness, referred to the speech as "corn" delivered by a "cornball governor."

Clement, Gore, and Kefauver all yearned for the presidency, and each was quite prepared to settle for second place, could that much be secured. Until Eisenhower's heart attack, the first place lost some of the appeal it could have had in a normally promising Democratic year.

The fortunes of all Democratic hopefuls in Tennessee were conditioned by the ambitions of Estes Kefauver and his stance on the racial issues of that day. Kefauver had won the race for the Senate in the fateful year of 1948, when the civil rights issue had begun to make Democratic party history. In doing so, he had administered the first of the final blows to Crump's ascendancy, aided by the wound that Crump inflicted on himself by his failure to back Senator Tom Stewart. Kefauver's second term had been assured by the events of 1954. Clement had decided not to challenge him, but the senator had many enemies inside the Tennessee Democratic party, enemies because of Kefauver's position on civil rights and enemies because of the divisive quarrels in the 1952 national convention, when Kefauver made his first bid for the presidency.

By 1952, Kefauver's activities in the Senate had won him national attention as a liberal fighter against corruption, but his Senate colleagues did not always find his lone efforts endearing. Truman was uncertain about running again for the presidency, reluctant, as Coolidge once was, to say either yes or no. While Truman teetered on the fence, Kefauver rushed in and announced his own candidacy, on January 23, 1952. Browning said he immediately put a coonskin cap on the capitol. But even if Browning was enthusiastic, the announcement was greeted with noticeable coolness by the President, who said that Kefauver was a nice man and a good senator. Privately, his comments were more acerbic.

Kefauver was "that fella from Tennessee that was aching to President and went around getting his picture taken in a coonskin cap." The President's dislike of Kefauver was clearer by the day; as time wore on, he would think Clement increasingly attractive as a foil to Kefauver, and Clement found Truman a good friend in the years ahead.

Kefauver won a number of victories in the 1952 presidential primaries, just then beginning to give promise of their future importance, although he lost, significantly, in Florida to Senator Richard Russell of Georgia. Those primary victories lent him a sort of hollow publicity. Some of them were preferential only, where Kefauver could secure no pledged or obligated delegates. In certain others, the senator had been the sole candidate. True, when the convention met, Kefauver could count more delegates than any other candidate, but he was still far from a majority, and he faced plenty of rivals. Richard Russell was strongest of all candidates in the South, where Kefauver had little support and plenty of opposition — opposition strong enough to split the party. Barkley, Harriman, and, above all, Adlai Stevenson were possibilities. Kefauver formed a team with Averill Harriman, and together they led the liberal wing of the party. Stevenson was seen by many as the candidate who could avoid a split in the party, but, with characteristic indecision, Stevenson was not absolutely certain he wanted to run; repeatedly he said he was content with the governorship of Illinois. The personal arrangements of Tennessee internal politics had placed Kefauver and Browning in an unlikely alliance. In those days, the governor had control of the delegation to the national convention, and Browning loyally took the delegation along for Kefauver, in actions that cost him dearly in the late summer primary.

The dispute in Democratic ranks at the national convention came to a sharp focus in the struggle to require pledges of loyalty from southern delegations, where defections had occurred in 1948 over the party platform's favorable position toward civil rights. The convention wrestled with the issue of seating the Virginia, South Carolina, and Louisiana delegations. Virginia could not, or would not, give a clear pledge of loyalty to the Democratic nominee and on a crucial vote of seating that delegation, Tennessee became the only southern state to vote against seating. Browning led the twenty-eight Tennessee delegates in this move, following the Kefauver-Harriman strategy, which Stevenson supporters viewed as means of forcing the South out of the party, in order to improve Kefauver's chances. In the end the Southerners were seated, Kefauver was isolated, and his supporters angered. Kefauver did not improve his standing in Tennessee. Stevenson was nominated, Sparkman was made the vice presidential nominee, and Browning returned to his own contest in Tennessee under a cloud as the tool of the too-liberal senior senator from his state.

Now in 1956, Kefauver wanted a second chance at the nomination. Adlai Stevenson was a defeated candidate and some party leaders said that if he wanted the nomination a second time, he would have to work for it. On November 15, 1955, Stevenson made his candidacy public and official. One month later, Kefauver threw his own hat in. Harriman held off officially until June 1956, but he was always an evident candidate. So the convention of '56 was to be essentially a replay of the '52 scenario. The plot was slightly, but only slightly, complicated by a clutter of minor candidacies, including Senators Lyndon Johnson, Stuart Symington, Richard Russell, Paul Douglas, and Harry Byrd. Governors who longed for the top spot included Frank Lausche, Mennen Williams —"Soapy"—Robert Myner, and "Happy" Chandler, the flamboyant personality from the Blue Grass. Speaker Sam Rayburn's eye showed a gleam.

Kefauver's strength, such as it was, lay, as it had in 1952, in the presidential primaries. His entrance into those contests forced a reluctant Stevenson onto the battleground. As always, Kefauver was weak on organization, strong on personal appeal. He selected fourteen primaries as contests to be entered, and in Minnesota, Oregon, Florida, California, Alaska, and the District of Columbia he took on Adlai Stevenson. He was conceded to have New Hampshire, where he had made his first big splash in 1952. He planned to enter New Jersey. He was the only candidate (a weakness again) in Wisconsin, Maryland, Indiana, Nebraska, Montana, and South Dakota, and write-ins were attempted in Illinois, Pennsylvania, and Massachusetts.

New Hampshire was again the scene of the first state primary, in March. In spite of some Stevenson attempts to cripple the senator, Kefauver took the state. Later in that same month, Kefauver administered a sound thrashing to Stevenson in Minnesota, where Stevenson had been supposed to win. But once more the victory was hollow, for Kefauver did not have the backing of the state's political leaders, and the surprise defeat that Stevenson suffered roused him to a hard fight. Kefauver won principally in the states where he was unopposed. Stevenson won some of his own battles, particularly those in Florida and California. These made him the leading candidate and effectively doomed Kefauver's chances. By late July, Kefauver had only 200 delegates, compared to over 400 for Stevenson.

The *coup de grâce* was administered to Kefauver by his own state party convention. Kefauver was always to be too strong in his own state to be defeated for the Senate, but his political enemies were numerous and powerful enough to deny him the state delegation's whole-hearted support for the presidency. His civil rights position had earned him the enduring animosity of many white West Tennesseans, and the blacks of Tennessee were not organized into cohesive and significant forces as they were twenty-five years later. Clement and Kefauver had always been potential rivals, although they sought to maintain a show of amiability. Clement had declared himself for Adlai Stevenson in 1955. He harboured his own ambitions, which lay athwart the road that Kefauver wanted to follow. And, to complicate affairs still more, Albert Gore had ambitions for a place on the national ticket. Tennessee suffered from an embarrassment of riches. Inside the party ranks, support for the competing candidates was often fluid. Many of Kefauver's backers were also attached to Clement, and, if they seemed to put the senator first, that might be no more than temporary.

Early in January 1956, Buford Ellington and Herbert Walters, state Democratic chairman, hoisted a brightly colored balloon; Clement, they announced, would have the Tennessee delegation's full support as a favorite son candidate for the presidential nomination. Clement said the idea was all news to him, but it is difficult to believe that Ellington and Walters had kept him in complete ignorance. Kefauver was painfully embarrassed. Gore maintained a wary neutrality. Privately he wrote Kefauver, clearly withholding his support. The delegation would be under Clement's control, even though it would have Kefauver members, and Kefauver had little choice but to announce that he would avoid a county-by-county fight with the Clement forces. His only hope was to effect some kind of mutual accommodation.

Late in January, Clement announced that he would not seek the favorite son candidacy, and his renunciation earned him the praise of some Democrats. He avoided by this move a clear direct confrontation with the Kefauver machine (if such a tight word can be applied to such a loose organization), but in fact Clement and his group were undoubtedly committed to the idea of an uninstructed delegation; such a development would be fatal to Kefauver's chances. In the meantime, Kefauver wired the governor applauding his refusal of the favorite son designa-

tion as an act of generosity, and Charles Neese, a major Kefauver lieutenant, endorsed Clement for the post of keynoter. Both sides denied
that a "deal" had been made, but that was not the way things looked.
The two men were carefully feeling their way to an uneasy adjustment,
while Gore continued to watch his own chances from the stage wings.
The endorsement of Clement as keynoter by Neese, one can surely assume, was made with Kefauver's knowledge and consent, but Kefauver
himself remained coy about publicly endorsing Clement's ambitions,
and the two—Clement and Kefauver—continued to be locked in their
regular posture of uneasy suspicion. Clement had been in active touch
with Adlai Stevenson for some months, and clearly Stevenson hoped for
support against Kefauver from the Tennessee governor.

While Walters continued his efforts to have Clement selected as keynoter, Truman continued to think of Clement as a foil against Kefauver.
The former President had visited the locally famous Ramp Festival in
Cocke County (an annual occasion celebrating the virtues of a variety of
wild onion and offering political hopefuls a chance to be seen in the company of country musicians), where he had again studied Clement as a
possibility. In February 1956 he praised Clement as a grand young man
who would make a good vice president. Late that year, Clement made
Truman a Tennessee colonel. The ex-President said he would not seek to
block Kefauver, but when convention time came he did try to block
Stevenson.

Clement had no walk-away in the campaign to be named keynoter.
He faced some formidable rivals, particularly Senator Bob Kerr of Oklahoma and the liberal and loquacious Hubert Humphrey. Paul Butler was
then national chairman, and while he was grateful for the services of
Clement as a stump speaker, he had not guaranteed that he would support him for the opener. He opposed both Clement and Humphrey, on
the grounds they were vice presidential possibilities, and Clement wrote
Butler denying ambitions for that spot. Herbert Walters lined up Camille Gravel of Louisiana, and the New York Times reported that Clement had the private support of Lyndon Johnson. The Missouri state
convention endorsed Clement for keynoter, after he had roused the convention with a fighting speech. It was a return engagement for Missouri; Clement had addressed the 1954 convention there.

While these maneuvers were developing, the Tennessee state Democratic convention dealt a mortal wound to Kefauver's presidential hopes.
Until shortly before the convention met, a bitter floor fight was seen as
a possibility. The opposition to Kefauver was determined to block his

endorsement by the convention. The *Tennessean* had said that of the 4,480 votes in the convention, Kefauver possessed 1,314, but the paper recognized a hard core of close to 1,100 opposing votes. Sentiment for an uninstructed delegation was widespread, and Clement himself took that position. Pressure was brought on the governor to support the Kefauver candidacy. Joseph Donahue, general chairman of Kefauver's campaign committee, wrote the governor urging him to nominate Kefauver for the presidency at the convention; a telegram of strong support for Kefauver was dispatched to Clement late in June by a group of Kefauverites, including George Dempster, Stanton Smith, Max Friedman, Steve Para, Jim Camp, Paul Christopher, and Tim Lawson, a mixture of labor leaders and politicians, many of whom divided their support of Kefauver with support of Clement, although for most of them Clement was a second choice. But the men closest to Clement, such as Joe Carr and Herbert Walters, were clearly anti-Kefauver, and James G. Stahlman, publisher of the *Banner,* who had long been a consistent Clement backer, was one of the most determined of Kefauver's enemies.

As the convention neared, the governor was in Atlantic City attending the annual governors' conference, but he planned to return to Nashville to direct the selection of the delegates and to prepare their marching orders. The fact that he had conferred in Atlantic City with James Finnigan, Stevenson's manager, could have boded no good for the senator. As it turned out, a floor fight was avoided, and neither Clement nor Kefauver attended the state convention.

Although the floor fight was avoided, in effect Kefauver lost anyway. Before the convention went into session, a resolution had been worked out and agreed to by representatives of the Clement and Kefauver groups. Ellington, Carr, and J. Frank Hobbs represented the governor, and Charles Neese, Stanton Smith, and Rudy Olgiati spoke for Kefauver. The resolution was fed to the press by Herbert Walters, whose firm but not impartial hand could be recognized in the words he announced. The resolution, adopted by the convention on June 29, declared that the delegation to the national convention would support any Tennessean as long as he had an opportunity to be nominated either for President or vice-president. The way was thus opened to Clement or Gore, but, as far as the presidency was concerned, the resolution dashed the senator's chances. He tried to put a good face on it, and the *Tennessean* put up a brave front, saying that Kefauver seemed assured of the state's thirty-two votes under this compromise, but clearly this was not so. In the end the senator did get the state's thirty-two votes for the second place on the ticket, but even that was a near thing. His failure to get a clear endorsement for the presidency from his own state put a final end to a campaign probably already doomed. Late in July, he withdrew from the battle for the presidency, leaving the field to Stevenson and Harriman, and the numerous smaller figures who continued to look for miracles.

Meanwhile the campaign for the selection of Clement as keynoter continued. Tennessee politicians and officeholders pressured friends all over the country. Clement had steered through the shoals of the racial issue with great care. He could ill afford to appear nationally as an unreconstructed Southerner, but in Tennessee he had to think of the western end of his state. In his pre-convention speeches he concentrated on attacks on Eisenhower, even though it cost him some public criticism from James Stahlman.

Butler was still lukewarm to Clement's selection as keynoter, and Walters was initially unsuccessful in getting the support of the Illinois boss, Jacob Arvey. The *Tennessean* reported that Kerr and Humphrey were preferred over Clement, until Truman returned from Europe; then it credited Truman with turning the tide in Clement's favor. But in July after earlier delays and disappointments, Clement was awarded the prize by the national committee. Votes were not made public, but it was known that Clement had the support of committee men and women from Oregon, Texas, Louisiana, West Virginia, Utah, and Alabama.

Clement professed to be surprised, as well as gratified. Such surprise could ordinarily be doubted, but he had failed to secure the prize until late in the day, and his files contain a draft of a telegram of congratulation to Kerr, a telegram that now did not need to be sent. Apparently Carr and Lipe Henslee had little hope toward the last. Now Clement, finally chosen, had only a few short weeks to prepare an address which Tennessee politicians expected would be a blockbuster. George Dempster said it would pale the Cross-of-Gold speech that lingered so endearingly in Democratic memory.

The governor now set to work in earnest. It has never been clear who worked on or wrote this important address in its initial stages. The speech turned out to be something of a let-down, and would-be claimants to authorship have not been numerous. Hilton Butler, Joe Henry, and Howard Anderson, as well as the governor's father, probably put ideas into it. Billy Graham offered suggestions. Prominent Democrats over the country were consulted, but probably Hilton Butler, aside from Clement himself, was the principal writer. Clement said that he had consulted Paul Butler, Harry Truman, Lyndon Johnson, and Sam Rayburn, sometimes in person. His selection as keynoter had evoked a characteristically ebullient salutation from Hubert Horatio Humphrey, who wrote the governor: "We are looking forward to your speech at the convention. I know that it will ring the bell and sound the victory call." Clement had sought Humphrey's advice, and had appealed to Senators Kerr, George, and Russell. His files contain suggestions and comments from Dean Acheson on the platform, particularly on foreign affairs. So the speech became an amalgam of varying suggestions, and some have faulted the results on this account.

Meanwhile Clement's hold on the Democratic party of Tennessee was strengthened. Late in July, Herbert Walters and Mrs. Albert Hill, both members of the Clement faction, were elected to the national committee, succeeding Jack Norman and Mrs. Martha Ragland, associated with Kefauver and Browning. Their choice had been backed by such Clement figures as Mrs. Charles Lockett, whose husband had dropped his partnership with Eddie Friar (after Friar parted company with Clement), J. Carlton Loser of Nashville, the powerful J. Frank Hobbs of Lawrenceburg, and Kenneth Woods of Henderson. Mrs. Ragland's supporters had included Max Friedman of Knoxville, long a Kefauver friend, Beverly Briley of Nashville, and Mrs. Cecil Branstetter of Nashville, whose husband was a prominent labor attorney there.

The delegation slated to attend the national convention contained both Clement and Kefauver men and women, but as Kefauver well knew Clement forces held a clear majority, and the delegation was bound by the unit role. Among the delegates-at-large who could be counted in the Clement camp, aside from the governor himself, were Jim Nance McCord; Herbert Walters; Joe Carr; Buford Ellington; Mrs. Lockett; former legislator Walter Haynes (who, at Haynes' urgent request, had been put on the delegation by Clement); James Bomar, Clement's influential legislative leader; his close friend, Jared Maddux; Hugh Abercrombie of Hamilton County (one of the party's wealthy men); Mrs. Hill; Kenneth Woods; James Peeler; William Baird; and Clement's aunt, Mrs. Carl Nicks. Old and sick but reluctant to leave the power centers, former Senator McKellar had hoped to go to the convention. He was too feeble to undertake the trip, but he wired Stevenson and the Memphis politician, Watkins Overton, that Kefauver was "utterly unfitted" for the vice-presidency.

Kefauver had the backing of Alfred Starr and John J. Hooker of Nashville; and of George Dempster and Max Friedman of Knoxville, but neither of these two could be counted as definitely anti-Clement. Dempster (no doubt like others) was not always certain which way to jump during the convention. Clement, of course, ran political risks by bucking Kefauver, but he could not forget that Kefauver's ambitions lay athwart his own. It was all a matter of personal rivalry, not political principle.

The convention opened in Chicago on August 13. Two sessions were held on that day, one to get organized, the other, to hear the keynote speech of temporary chairman, Frank Clement. The first session was routine and attracted little attention, but the keynote occasion was the real beginning of excitement. Clement had been preparing. The physical setting had been carefully studied. A dry run of the speech at Chicago had shown both Clement and his assistant, Douglas Fisher, that the speech was shockingly long, and Fisher was given the job of cutting it down to size. He worked at it all night and succeeded in putting forty-five minutes of the speech on the cutting-floor. During this waiting period, elaborate preparation had been made for a floor demonstration for Clement, should he manage to stampede the convention into a move in his own direction. Clement had tried out his voice in the auditorium in the afternoon and had been warned that he would have to speak against the noise of an unruly crowd. In fact, the crowd was attentive, and some critics thought Clement shouted when he did not need to.

By eight o'clock all the seats and all the standing room had been claimed. Some twelve to fifteen million TV sets were tuned to Chicago; twenty years later many of these listeners would vividly recall the words that were soon to be broadcast. Among the audience, a place of honor had been allotted to Aunt Dockie Weems, who was shortly to enjoy an experience seldom given to small-town debate and elocution teachers: a favorite pupil, a nephew, was to bring to the podium the results of days, months, and years of practice in churches, courthouse squares, and, farther back, under the summertime trees of a small Tennessee town. Clement's mother was in a box with Aunt Dockie; his father was stationed back of the platform. The hall was filled with Democratic personages: Stevenson, Harriman, Kefauver, Gore, Kennedy, Mayor Daley, Rayburn, Lyndon Johnson, Symington, and all the rest. The past, by no means dead or inactive, numbered Eleanor Roosevelt and Harry Truman.

Clement's big moment had to be shared with a film made for the occasion extolling the Democrats and their achievements, with narration by John Kennedy. The film was shown before the keynote address. Its impact was unclear, although Clement friends had not wanted it. It may

(*Top*) Keynote Speaker. (*Bottom*) Convention Balloting.

have been something of a spoiler for Clement, who otherwise would have had the evening to himself. Kennedy was to come close to spoiling Kefauver's chances as well, before the week was out. As the speech was in progress, Truman entered the hall, and Clement had to pause to recognize the former President and to allow time for the applause to die down.

The speech was designed for hearing, not reading. It is filled with conscious alliteration; it made a number of points, ticked off numerically, as Clement speeches usually did. It was short on political theory and literary value. In sum, it followed the model of most keynote speeches, which usually are more acceptable when heard than when subjected to sober reflection.

It was a fighting speech. As in earlier speeches across the country, Clement openly attacked President Eisenhower (a near saintly figure to many of Clement's listeners) and he referred to Vice-President Nixon as the "Vice-Hatchet Man." Clement prophesied the approaching exodus of the Republicans from the White House, when "the opposition party of privilege and pillage passes over the Potomac in the greatest water crossing since the children of Israel crossed the Red Sea" (Truman could be seen leading the waves of laughter that surged through the crowd) — an exodus "with generals to the left of them, generals to the right of them, and generals in front of them as these old soldiers fold their political tents and just fade away."

Clement moved on with vigorous head, arm, and shoulder movements to voice appeals based on the plight of the poor farmer, the small businessman — the standard fare of the populist platform. Following closely the notes made for the platform committee by Dean Acheson, Clement attacked the Republicans for their weak foreign policy, their failure to block Soviet diplomacy. He acknowledged that the issue of civil rights would come up in the convention, but he avoided taking any definite stand, passing quickly to an invitation to the downtrodden to consider the past efforts of the Democratic party in their behalf.

Then, in the fashion long practiced by him and his speechwriters, he moved to a ten-point indictment of the Republicans, again citing the familiar populist themes. Finally he came to the phrase, "How long, O, America, shall these things endure"; the phrase "How long" was repeated again and again, as Clement, carried along by the attention and the enthusiasm of the crowd, ran on beyond the ending that Douglas Fisher had prepared for him. At the final exhortation to "fight, fight, fight," the speaker seemed to be struggling against the increasing im-

(*Top*) Keynoter and national chairman—Clement and Paul M. Butler. (*Bottom*) Talent surplus—Butler, Clement, Carr, Gore, and Kefauver. Photographs courtesy Tennessee State Library and Archives.

pulse of the crowd to start the cheering, and the closing Clement theme-words—"Precious Lord, take my hand, and lead me on"—were drowned out in waves of applause. Clement was applauded 43 times in a speech that lasted 43 minutes, according to the *Tennessean,* and the governor was given a four-minute ovation (although no floor demonstration materialized, and the banners and balloons that had been readied for such a contingency had to be scrapped). The convention was launched, and the serious factional fights were now to come on the floor. It was to be an unusually open convention.

The speech had a mixed reception. Letters and telegrams flowed in, and Clement's staff accumulated two thick files—one marked favorable, the other, unfavorable. The favorable comments tended to come from political friends. Stevenson, in his cultivated way, said the speech was inspiring. Sam Rayburn and John Sparkman said it was a great speech. H.V. Kaltenborn said it carried him back to Bryan. Billy Graham applauded. But severely caustic criticism zeroed in on Chicago. The public, many of them, had been especially incensed at the attacks on Eisenhower. The comments that reached the governor were often rough, salty, and unrestrained. From Detroit came the query: "When did you blow your top or are you just nuts?" A listener from San Mateo, California, noted: "Have heard you and Amy McPherson. Prefer Amy. You have made a staunch Republican of me." A Tuscaloosan informed the governor: "You made a perfect jackass of yourself in your defamation of our great President." A disgruntled Kansas Democrat wired: "Your stupid speech [sic] has made me a Republican for life."

The frank use of religious themes, so familiar in Tennessee, failed to please some listeners outside the region. From Brooklyn came the word: "Shocked to hear our Lord's Gospel being used for political ends." You are the first politician in the history of this republic," wired one listener in reckless disregard of the past, "who undertakes to make Almighty God a member of a political party." As almost always is the case, the critical comments were more entertaining than the friendly observations.

Clement's detractors and some of his friends thought the speech had at worst been silly and at best a failure. The conventional judgment has been expressed in these words: "After the hall settled down, Governor Clement, eager to propel himself into the ranks of politically available, gave an old-fashioned keynote speech. He attacked not only the Republican party and the Vice President, but even the President himself. Clement spoke too long. At the forty-five minute mark, the audience was still pleased with his Biblical oratory; a half hour later they were let

Pre-convention friendship—Governors Adlai Stevenson and Clement at Cook County (Ill.) dinner, 1955. Photograph courtesy Mrs. Lucille Clement.

down. Clement had put himself well beyond the range of serious consideration for higher office."

There is a good deal to question in this statement. The *Tennessean* spoke of a forty-three minute speech. The videotape of the speech does not seem unduly long. Clement had so long been tagged by the national press as a "Bible-toting" old-fashioned, Billy Graham kind of orator that it is easy to ape these opinions. In fact, most of the speech was devoted to standard populist themes. If the Lord was noticed on occasion, this was well in the American tradition, a tradition that had faded in the intellectual community while still strong outside that charmed and narrow circle. But even some Tennesseans felt the kind of oratory that produced results in Tennessee were not usable in the North, and that may be so.

Certainly the speech did not produce the hoped-for floor demonstration, and possibly for this reason Clement's friends have always carried an air of apology for the speech. Critics remember the experiences of Bryan and Barkley; they forget the keynoters who quadrennium after quadrennium have their brief half-hour upon the stage, without being carried up to the heights of candidacy. Clement had not put himself beyond the range of national office by his speech; he did not reach that eminence, not because of the speech but because of the complicated political situations that put Kefauver, and momentarily Gore, ahead of him. Still, there can be little doubt that Chicago was a disappointment, to be succeeded in later years by other disappointments in national affairs.

The platform, with its dangers of splitting a party composed of historical but uneasy coalitions, came before the convention on Wednesday night, the fifteenth of August. The dissensions that would have been aroused by prolonged fights over seating the delegations or extracting loyalty oaths, such as had disturbed Democratic serenities in 1948 and 1952, had been avoided. The only threat of substance was the possibility of a minority report on civil rights. But the majority report, which pledged the party to continue to eliminate illegal discriminations, and which was disliked, as a compromise, by both northern and southern diehards but which had the support of both Stevenson and Truman, was rammed through the convention by voice votes, under presiding officer Sam Rayburn, who knew a good bit about railroading decisions through parliamentary bodies. Rayburn was not prepared to court any further disasters.

The following day, Thursday, was the day set for the nomination for the presidency. Stevenson, of course, was the favored candidate, since Kefauver had withdrawn himself from the running, but Harriman was still in contention, backed by Harry Truman who did not care for the man from Illinois. In the Tennessee delegation, a stormy period of shouting had produced a resolution to offer Clement as the favorite son candidate, a move which the *Tennessean* reporter interpreted as a move to help Truman keep Stevenson from the nomination, an interpretation that might seem strange in the light of Clement's past contacts with Stevenson. Doubtless Clement hoped to bargain for second place. In any case, the move was unrealistic; Clement withdrew himself as a favorite son, as did Lausche of Ohio. A number of other minor or not-so-minor candidates were put up, including Magnusson, Lyndon Johnson, Stuart Symington, and "Happy" Chandler. Senator John Kennedy nominated Stevenson, and Harriman was put forward by Governor Gary of Oklahoma.

When evening came, the Stevenson machine flattened the opposition, and Stevenson received the nod on the first ballot; shortly thereafter, he threw the convention into a frenzy by refusing, contrary to the advice of Rayburn, Johnson, and Butler, to state a choice for the vice-presidency. The matter was left to the free dealing of the convention. Rumors floated concerning Stevenson's real, if unexpressed, wishes. Clement was told later that Stevenson had turned thumbs down on a possibility of Clement for the spot, but it was widely thought that the presidential nominee did not want Kefauver for a runningmate either. In view of the past rivalry between Stevenson and Kefauver (reinforced by the correspondence that had passed between Clement and Stevenson, and possibly by the animosity of Truman to Kefauver), the senator was probably not much liked in the Stevenson entourage. Whether Stevenson decided to leave matters to the convention because of his customary indecisiveness, or for other more subtle reasons, is not clear. It has been said that Stevenson was committed to Kefauver to throw the vice-presidency open.

In any case, Stevenson's decision to leave the second-place choice to an open convention started flurries of activity throughout the convention. The verbose and ubiquitous senator from Minnesota, Hubert Horatio Humphrey, certainly nourished ambitions, but he was somewhat too stereotyped as an unreconstructed liberal. In the delegation the ambitions of Clement, Kefauver, and Gore now mounted to fever heat. Kefauver, angered by Stevenson's attitude, had decided to leave the convention, but he was talked into staying, and he spent all Thursday night moving from one delegation to another. The resolution adopted at the state convention gave a chance to all three, although Kefauver was at a disadvantage because his men and women were in the minority in the state delegation. Rayburn, as presiding officer of the convention, was dead set on getting a candidate selected for the second place during the Friday afternoon session on August 17th, and, using his gavel vigorously, he announced his discovery of a number of "unanimous consents" to shorten the procedure.

Within the Tennessee delegation, procedure at times approached pandemonium. A move to put Clement forward for the vice-presidency failed to jell. There were rumors that the delegation would be delivered to Lyndon Johnson. Alfred Starr, a Kefauver delegate, charged that plans were being formulated to stab Kefauver in the back, and William Baird was heard shouting that Kefauver was no true Tennessean. A group of labor spokesmen in Knoxville wired Clement saying: "How long, O how long, are you going to hold out against Estes who is bestes."

The Tennessean dilemma was quickly exposed before the entire country, for, as things happened, Alabama, first in the roll call for nominations, yielded to Tennessee so that Jared Maddux could place the name of Albert Gore in nomination for the vice-presidency. (Pauline Gore said later that she had been picking vice-presidential lice off her husband for a year but had evidently missed one). Maddux was a resident of Gore's section of the state, but the fact that Maddux now took the spotlight can be taken as a sure sign that Clement's hopes for the vice-presidency had gone, for Maddux was a close friend and ally of Clement (and remained so until the end of the governor's life). The nomination of Gore was also a good sign that the Tennessee delegation would desert Kefauver, if it could. As the nominations and the balloting went on, Tennessee sentiments for and against Kefauver became even more evident. Arizona yielded to Ohio, so that Lausche could nominate Kefauver, another piece of evidence that Kefauver had little appeal below that famous line drawn by Mason and Dixon. Abraham Ribicoff nominated John Kennedy.

On the first ballot, Kefauver was ahead, but he was far from a majority. Clement acquired 4½ votes from Alabama, 9 from South Carolina; Gore had 178. Kennedy showed great strength on this ballot and quickly became a serious threat to Kefauver; he got heavy support from Georgia, Louisiana, and Virginia, and he picked up votes in South Carolina. Gore had only one vote outside the South. Gore captured all of Tennessee's 32 votes, for the state (unlike some of the delegations) was bound by the unit rule, and Kefauver's friends were unable to help him.

Dramatic changes marked the second and decisive ballot. Arkansas (under the unit rule) shifted from Gore to Kennedy. Delaware (also under the rule) moved from Wagner to Kennedy. Kentucky (likewise under the rule) left Maner to go to Gore; still under the unit procedure, Mississippi deserted Gore for Kennedy. Gore was now out of the running, and a series of breaks started to Kennedy. Tennessee stuck with Gore, but when Texas and California started to build Kennedy up, the senator from Massachusetts passed Kefauver.

Before the convention, Clement forces had been in touch with Lyndon Johnson, who was courting Clement for support for one of the places on the ticket. After the convention, Mary Smith, the governor's secretary, suggested that Clement write "our boy" in Texas, and Clement wrote Johnson a formal letter expressing regret at "our inability to keep our lines of communication open."

The final crisis for Kefauver, and for the Tennessee delegation, had now arrived. Further Tennessee resistance to its senator could cost him the nomination, and Gore now released his delegates to Kefauver. Kefauver sought and secured the support of Hubert Humphrey, and the two men embraced, weeping. Tennessee, managing with some difficulty to get Rayburn's attention (Rayburn was maneuvering to block Kefauver), shifted its votes to Kefauver; the Kennedy tide began to recede steadily, and Kefauver became the nominee. That nomination concluded, little remained except to hear Stevenson's acceptance speech, a speech in the same populist vein as that of Clement's keynote speech.

The fun was all over, and the Tennessee delegation returned to the recriminations at home. A crowd that had gathered at Berry Field in Nashville to welcome the vice-presidential candidate, booed Governor Clement as he left the plane. Gore got similar treatment, though he remained as quiet as he could. Kefauver supporters were outraged at the near miss their man had suffered, and Kefauver enemies were equally bitter at the final outcome. Kefauver owed about $85,000 as a result of the battle for the nomination, and in one night, he and Noble Caudill secured pledges for the money. Subsequently a considerable number of checks came in over the legal limit of $5,000, and a second campaign was necessary to raise the money in the proper way.

The enmity to Kefauver was most strongly expressed to Governor Clement by James G. Stahlman, who, in a lengthy letter dated September 24, 1956, condemned the governor in harsh words for what he regarded as a betrayal of the life-long Clement stand that had led the *Banner* to support him.

Stahlman's letter was a reply to a letter he had received from the governor, dated August 2. His delay in replying, he said, was caused by a vacation and his need to think through the situation. To begin with, Stahlman said, the *Banner* was not interested in "bossing" anyone, or in "naming" candidates. Its interest lay solely in the good of the city, the state, and the nation, and the *Banner,* said its publisher, will continue to support the principles it considers soundest and the men qualified and likely to see those principles carried through. "It was in furtherance of this policy that the *Banner* had placed its hope, its confidence, its fullest faith in you as the man best qualified to rid Tennessee of those influences in its political life represented by the Browning-Kefauver cabal, which this newspaper has for so long considered inimical to the welfare of the people of Tennessee and to sound, honest, constitutional government here and in these United States."

Stahlman then reminded Clement of his past support and referred to a series of conferences held with him and others in an effort to protect Clement from being victimized by the efforts of Kefauver's supporters to trap the governor into a position of support for the senator. He wrote:

> At least, it was my firm understanding, fortified by your own attitude and that of those who accompanied you to that conference, namely: Jim Mc-Cord, Hub Walters, Buford Ellington, Joe Carr, and Russell Brothers, that there was general agreement with my frequently repeated contention that your future course should in no way parallel that of Estes Kefauver and or that of Albert Gore, if you entertained any ambition or hope of defeating either incumbent for his seat in the United States Senate or going on to higher political office on the national level. . . .

> Your own indignation at Stevenson's suspected attitude toward Kefauver and your freely expressed apprehension of its consequences were reflected in your conversation with me and others on Saturday morning preceding the Democratic National Convention in Chicago, when you detailed your telephone conversation with Stevenson which had taken place earlier that day.

> During the period of the Chicago convention, the public was continually assured by Les Hart and others that your control of the Tennessee delegation precluded possibility of the State's 32 votes ever going for Kefauver.

> Preceding the convention, Buford Ellington and Hub Walters attended two gatherings of Southern Democratic leaders in an effort to arrive at a joint attitude toward a platform that was not only satisfactory but non-irritating to the South. It was reported then that sentiment of that Southern group was cool, if not actually hostile, to Kefauver, whom some of them considered and still consider a "renegade." Ellington and Walters were representing you and your group's point of view at those conferences. That is the impres-

sion which was publicly left at that time and never subsequently denied by you or them.

Considering the known attitude, not only of Southern Democrats but those from other sections, particularly his associates in the Senate, toward Estes Kefauver on many issues which had made him unacceptable to the South as a Presidential candidate, and considering Stevenson's emphasis and that of the convention on the importance of the Vice Presidency, it would seem reasonable to anyone familiar with politics that the same qualities which made Kefauver unacceptable for the Presidential nomination were equally applicable to the vice presidential spot.

. . . .

No man could have been unaware of this Southern hostility toward Kefauver or of the consequences to Tennessee's prestige and good will among her sister states resulting from the Tennessee delegation's vote for him on "THE BIG SWITCH." It may have been considered the "honorable thing" to have been "bound" by the Tennessee convention's resolution to vote as the delegation did, but it is quite another thing to have interpreted that resolution without full regard to its INTENT as explained by many in your own group, unless that resolution WAS actually an "agreement" between your forces and those of Kefauver, as he and they frequently claimed, but which you and your associates repeatedly denied. Perhaps the resolution, like platforms and so many campaign promises, was never intended as anything but so much window-dressing. Certainly its generally accepted INTENT was not material when the show-down came and the cave-in occurred. As your friend, I would prefer to believe your part in this disgraceful affair due to "political immaturity," but since you are no babe in the woods politically and you had ready access to advice and counsel of many political "pros," it would be difficult to believe that you and others were innocently "mouse-trapped" by the smart Kefauver crowd. But "trapped" or "Gored," the end result is the same.

You will recall that for many months prior to the Chicago Convention, The Banner and I had endeavored to caution you against putting any reliance in any alliance with or reported support from Ex-President Harry Truman. You will also recall my many earnest efforts to persuade you not to allow your name to be mentioned in connection with the vice presidential nomination in 1956. You will likewise recall that I said to you very frankly, however regretfully on the personal basis, that if President Eisenhower were a candidate for reelection The Banner would support him, as it did in 1952, when you carried Tennessee by an unprecedented majority while Tennessee voters were repudiating Trumanism and all that it represented, by casting their votes for the Eisenhower electors.

When you were selected to keynote the Democratic National Convention, I was happy for you at the compliment paid you. The Banner likewise expressed itself in similar vein. I did not suggest one word that went into your keynote speech. I DID suggest to you that this afforded you an opportunity to address yourself to the inspiration and unification of the Democratic Party in such a manner as to assure that you would add to your stature so that you would come out of the Convention as its greatest statesman and proudest hope.

With full consideration for the fact that your keynote address would necessarily be partisan, nevertheless when I read its text on Monday afternoon before its delivery, my heart sank. The indelible imprint of Truman was inescapable. He had already projected himself two days earlier upon a course which would shortly lead to his humiliating repudiation, rejection and ejection from any further position of influence in the Democratic Party. When, in your most promising hour, you delivered yourself of utterances which belied your claims to Christian virtues of tolerance, charity, and truthfulness, in tone and temper at times almost hysterical, and while many about me in the press section tittered, guffawed and grimaced in derision, I literally and unashamedly wept for my friend who had followed the devices and desires of others, rather than the dictates of his own conscience and what should have been his better judgment. Once again, as so frequently happens, party politics had triumphed over moral and ethical considerations.

. . . .

The denouement of the following Friday was more tragic for you in the opinion of your real friends than you have apparently sensed up to now. There were those of us, not only among your newspaper supporters in all sections of the State, but thousands of men and women who had cast their lot with you in the same original hope as that which The Banner had entertained and which prompted its espousal of your first and succeeding candidacies.

To have witnessed YOUR participation in the ultimate nomination of Estes Kefauver, regardless of the interpretations of the Tennessee delegation's "obligations" under the resolution which you or your forces are credited with having engineered in the State convention, was an almost unbelievable experience.

It was unbelievable for many reasons, including the heretofore referred to declarations by you and your closest associates (including the unlamented Truman) that a last ditch fight would be made to thwart Kefauver in his ambition for either nomination. Likewise, it was unbelievable, because many, including me and The Banner, had been led to believe, from repeated protestations and assurances from you and your colleagues who represented you in the State convention, that the resolution as adopted by that meeting would keep the Tennessee delegation from ever voting for Kefauver, particularly since all and sundry were assured that *you*, as Governor and chairman of the delegation, would control the majority of the delegation, and consequently its full 32 votes through the unit rule.

This was followed by the dropping of Mrs. Martha Ragland and Jack Norman from their state and national committee posts, on the alleged grounds that your forces were routing all Kefauver influence from the committee and would have full control at Chicago and later.

But Mrs. Ragland and others prevailed. Albert Gore capitulated under threatening pressure. And without any visible or publicly audible resistance, you assumed the same role which Gordon Browning had played in 1952, by flouting the champion carpetbagger of the 20th century in the face and teeth of the other delegations from the South. It may be that you considered it politically expedient and advantageous to gamble on your succession by appointment, in the event Kefauver should become the next Vice President.

.   .   .   .

Your subsequent stultifying performance under the guise of "party unity" was disgusting and an affront to all who had relied upon your courage and your vaunted political "savvy" and strength to maintain your position against the State's and the South's worst renegade.

You have charted your own course. You have chosen new political associates. Such an alliance is revolting and repulsive to The Banner. It cannot and will not acquiesce.

.   .   .   .

My disappointment is not so much that Kefauver won the nomination. That can and will be outlived. My greatest disappointment is my loss of faith in a friend upon whose assurances and in whose background as a Tennessean and a Southerner I had reposed fullest confidence. That disappointment is shared by thousands, if the conversations, letters and other communications which have come to me and The Banner may form a safe criterion.

I am further saddened by the thought that four years of struggle, most of it in your behalf, have gone for naught. I am comforted, however, by the assurance that this, too, shall pass.

Sincerely,
James G. Stahlman

Copies of this vigorous, if sharply partisan, analysis of Tennessee politics were dispatched to Jim McCord, Hub Walters, Buford Ellington, Joe Carr, and Russell Brothers.

The governor, as conciliatory as usual in the face of harsh criticism, replied on October 4, 1956, in these words:

There are two or three things I felt I should say to you at this time, however. First of all, there were no secret deals; no commitments and no implied understandings of any type between me or anyone on our team and Senator Kefauver and his people.

Secondly, while I am not attempting to shift any responsibility whatsoever, you are entitled to know that our action at the National Convention strictly was in accord with decisions reached by such people as Governor McCord, Mr. H.S. Walters, Joe Carr, Buford Ellington and others. There was no dissension on what course we were required to follow and I think you know these men well enough to know that they are men of honor, who would not be a part of a dishonorable act even if they were asked.

My only hope is that you will take advantage of the opportunity to clear up the apparent misunderstandings. Either I have failed miserably to get across to you the true picture or else you have been given erroneous information. One fact that I am sure you have not overlooked is that all Southern Governors, with exception of the Governor of Texas, are supporting the Democratic ticket.

It is not up to me to suggest that you do anything, but if you have the opportunity to talk with such men as Governor McCord, Mr. Walters, Joe Carr, Buford Ellington, Lt. Governor Jared Maddux, Speaker Jim Bomar or others who were on the scene, I am sure you will find that, however vigorously you may disagree with the judgement that was exercised, every act was taken in good faith. In fact, I know Governor McCord would welcome the opportunity to tell you how he pleaded with me as my friend to get out of the Vice Presidential race the morning the voting took place.

So much for the view from the anti-Kefauver side of the stream. The governor and his colleagues, supposedly in control of the 32-member delegation, were brought under a barrage from the Kefauver guns. During the frantic negotiations at Chicago, the governor had been pressured steadily to back the senator's desire for the second place on the ticket. To assume that the governor "controlled" the delegation was an exaggeration, for that delegation included many of the most powerful politicians in the state, and it would be nonsense to suppose they were subject to the governor's every whim. He had to listen, as well as to lead. Nevertheless, the delegation had climbed on the bandwagon for the senator just in time to prevent a disaster for Kefauver, and Kefauver's friends, already hostile to Clement—as well as to Walters, Joe Carr, et alia—were not prepared to forgive and forget. They never have.

In the welter of controversy, Walters felt he had to say something to explain; he issued the following statement:

> In response to the many requests from newspapers in all sections of the State for a statement of what actually happened in Chicago, I am making this statement for release through State Democratic Headquarters in Nashville.
>
> All of those who believe in majority rule and adherence to the instructions of the people back home (whether you like those instructions or not) have every reason to be proud of the action of Tennessee's delegates at the National Democratic Convention.
>
> It is well known to all Tennesseans that Governor Clement has never been lined up with Senator Kefauver and that he has never supported the Governor — but to the contrary, has actively worked against the Governor.
>
> Nevertheless, they both went to Chicago under instructions from our State Convention to support any Tennessean so long as that Tennessean had a chance to win.
>
> Tennessee's delegation was kind and generous enough to endorse the Governor for President, although he was not present at the caucus and had not suggested any such action.
>
> It was the Governor's decision (after an acceptable platform had been adopted and with consent of some other interested Southerners,) to request Tennessee not to place his name in nomination for the Presidency.
>
> Thereafter, the Tennessee delegates caucused and endorsed Stevenson for President and Governor Clement for Vice President.
>
> In conformity with his lifelong record of never wilfully being an obstructionist, the Governor decided to again decline the honor of having his name placed in nomination.
>
> During this period, however, Senator Gore had asked whether the Governor would continue as a serious Vice Presidential candidate and had requested notification of the final decision.
>
> When it was finally reached, both Senators Kefauver and Gore were notified within the hour.
>
> The Tennessee Delegation then caucused again and without any recommendation from Governor Clement, by a majority vote, agreed to support Senator Gore until released and then to switch to Senator Kefauver.
>
> As Chairman of the Tennessee Delegation, Governor Clement played the game strictly according to the rules and instructions of the State Convention.

When Senator Gore released the Tennessee Delegates, the Governor immediately got the attention of Chairman Rayburn and permitted Senator Gore
to make his announcement of release. He then again got the attention of the
Chairman and officially switched the thirty-two votes to Senator Kefauver
(without which action Senator Gore's announcement would have failed to
swing the Tennessee vote to the senior Senator.)

And as to the actions of our Governor and Chairman, it can certainly be
stated without qualification that the test of a man's greatness is not what
happens but how he plays the game, and the honor and integrity he shows
under pressure. Our Governor lived up to the high standards in this case.

It was a most interesting Convention and it is my hope that the State of
Tennessee will support the nominees of our Party in November.

Clement, like the good soldier that he always was in party affairs,
campaigned for the ticket—in Pennsylvania, Florida, Kentucky, Missouri, and Tennessee. The following year, after the Democratic defeat,
Clement and Walters helped to raise money to pay the Democrats' debts.

Nonetheless, as the Democrats must secretly have expected, Eisenhower was overwhelmingly returned, his popular majority greater than
in 1952. The general did not—just yet—leave the White House, in spite
of the keynote's confident prediction. The Democratic party did retain
its control of Congress. Tennessee went along with Stahlman and the
Banner for Eisenhower and Nixon. Eisenhower and the man whom
Clement had dubbed the "Vice Hatchet Man" carried Tennessee by a
plurality of slightly less than 6,000 votes.

Stevenson took seven states—Alabama, Arkansas, Georgia, Mississippi, Missouri, North Carolina and South Carolina, states where
Kefauver's popularity was not notable. Graciously—and Biblically—
Stevenson said: "A merry heart doeth good like a medicine, but a broken
spirit drieth the bones."

9. When Man to Judgment Wakes

THE IMPEACHMENT AND TRIAL
OF JUDGE SCHOOLFIELD

During Clement's terms as governor, his state was plagued by labor strife and a pattern of violence in labor affairs, not always too clearly
perceived by the public. The violence stemmed largely from the Teamsters' union. The story of that violence has been extensively documented
by the reports of the famous McClellan committee of the United States
Senate, in which the law enforcement officials in the state of Tennessee
were contemptuously castigated. Governor Clement escaped published
criticism from this committee, but he did not escape involvement in the
labor controversies of those times.

The constitution of Tennessee provides that the governor shall take
care that the laws be faithfully executed, but these vague words fail to
describe the actual allocations of power and responsibility for law enforcement in the state. In fact, that power and responsibility rest primarily on municipal and county officials — the sheriff, the municipal police, the city and district attorneys. These are local officials, locally
chosen, except for the city police, by so much of the electorate as bothers
to vote. They are not tied closely in any way to the election of the governor, they are not responsible to him, and they are not under his control.
Normally, the governor does not interfere with these local officials, and
he does not attempt to control them, and if he did, the resulting resentment would almost certainly bring about his political defeat. Tennesseans do not welcome centralized direction.

To a limited extent the governor can use the highway patrol to sup-
plement the enforcement efforts of local officials; and to some degree the
governor can exert pressure on sheriffs and others — as Clement did at
times in liquor law enforcement — but such efforts are occasional and

spasmodic, and the governor is largely helpless in local law enforcement. Use of the patrol or the National Guard is attended with high political risk, as every governor well knows.

Violence and corruption in organized labor reached such proportions in the 1950s that the Senate of the United States created a special committee to investigate the situation and to recommend legislation. This committee, the Select Committee on Improper Activities in the Labor or Management Field, created pursuant to Senate Resolutions 74 and 221 of the 85th Congress, had a small but remarkable membership. Its chairman was Senator John L. McClellan of Arkansas, and its vice chairman was Senator Irving Ives of New York. The remaining members were John F. Kennedy of Massachusetts, destined soon to be the President of the United States; Sam J. Ervin, Jr. of North Carolina, given to concealing his expertise on constitutional matters under the guise of being just a "poor old country lawyer," and fated to become the nemesis of Richard Nixon; Senator Pat McNamara of Michigan; together with Karl Mundt, South Dakota; Barry Goldwater of Arizona, shortly to be the Republican standard-bearer; Frank Church; Homer Capehart; and Carl T. Curtis, the noted conservative from Nebraska. Until his death in May 1957, the controversial Joe McCarthy of Wisconsin was a member. The committee was overwhelmingly conservative and notably able. Its chief counsel was the young Robert F. Kennedy, on his way to the cabinet, the Senate, a presidential candidacy, and death by assassination.

The committee's three-year study of labor racketeering took it all over the country and into a variety of unions and management groups, but it put heavy emphasis on the activities of the Teamsters. In Tennessee, the committee concentrated on the Teamsters, including Teamster involvement in the attempted organization of barbers in Nashville. Committee investigators LaVern J. Duffy and James P. McShane prepared a tabulation of violent acts occurring in the five states of Kentucky, Tennessee, Georgia, Ohio, and North Carolina from 1953 until 1957. They put the total of such acts at 173, with losses of property estimated at more than $2 million. Violence took the form of assaults, dynamiting, arson, window smashing, and several types of truck sabotage, one of which was the ruination of engines by introducing syrup into the fuel. The investigators concentrated in Tennessee on Nashville, Chattanooga, and Knoxville, where violence was perpetrated by such "goons" (so designated by the committee) as "Hard of Hearing" Smitty, Corky Ellis, and Perry Canaday. Individuals of this stripe boasted lengthy police records. Canaday, for example, had a record of two arrests for disorderly conduct, two for drunkenness, an arrest for breaking barbershop windows, one arrest for assault, and one arrest for felonious conspiracy to commit murder. In its official findings, the committee stated that top Teamster officials in Tennessee had actively and enthusiastically engaged in violent acts, and it directly named Glenn Smith, president of Chattanooga Local 515, and W.J. Reynolds, president of Local 621 in Knoxville. It found that the Teamsters' national hierarchy approved and abetted the actions of its Tennessee officials; the finger was pointed directly at James Hoffa, who was finally to receive his come-uppance in the federal courts in that state.

The committee was unsparing in its criticism of local officialdom in Tennessee. It found that "law enforcement agencies at every level in Tennessee have been shockingly derelict in their civic duty toward teamster malefactions." It pointed accusing fingers at the municipal authorities of Knoxville and Nashville; at sheriffs in a number of Tennessee counties, notably Knox and Davidson; members of the state highway patrol; and members of the Tennessee Bureau of Criminal Identification. (For these last two, the governor was legally responsible.) The committee charged that the law enforcement agencies in Tennessee had accorded Teamster criminals a scandalous immunity from prosecution and noted that Teamster influence reached into local governments. And, finally, it mounted a specific and detailed attack on Judge Raulston Schoolfield.

Raulston Schoolfield was a controversial figure in the politics of Hamilton County and of the state. He had been named judge of the criminal court in Hamilton County in 1948 and elected for a full term in 1950. Events were now beginning that were to lead to his impeachment and conviction and to disbarment, but, to this day, opinion remains divided on the justice of these actions. That opinion involves, among other things, the attitudes of Tennesseans toward the Kennedy wing of the Democratic party, for Jack Kennedy was a member of the McClellan committee, and his brother, Robert, was its chief counsel. The impeachment proceedings brought a young John Jay Hooker into the limelight as the assistant prosecutor of Schoolfield; in the future Hooker would be thought of as the associate of the Kennedys in his attempts to win the governorship of Tennessee. Schoolfield had been deeply immersed in the complicated struggles of Hamilton County politics. He had run as a segregationist candidate for governor in 1954 and had been associated with the Clinton school disturbances of 1956, and Governor Clement had to be wary lest he be charged with a cheap attempt at political reprisal.

Duffy and McShane had arrived in Nashville in the middle of 1957. It shortly was a matter of public knowledge that their investigations into Teamster misdeeds would go beyond the local situation in Nashville. Senator McClellan was impatient for some sort of corrective action by Tennessee officials and late in the year he released material attacking law enforcement in the state. Robert Kennedy indicated that, if the state officials did not take some action, the federal agencies would move.

One cannot know definitely what line would have been pursued by Governor Clement had he been left free from national pressure. He indicated to friends that he would not be stampeded into unnecessary actions against a former political opponent, but he had been receiving private information on Schoolfield's activities and his background, some of it fed to him by Hugh Abercrombie, the wealthy leader of Clement forces in Hamilton County. The governor sent the attorney general, George McCanless, and the W.E. Hopton, the head of the Tennessee Bureau of Identification, to Washington to confer with McClellan and to obtain what information was available in the Committee files.

On December 23, Clement wrote Schoolfield, calling his attention to the judge's refusal to appear before the McClellan committee and asking him in effect to make some choices: he could testify before the committee; he could resign; or he could stand trial on impeachment charges. Schoolfield's "stonewall" attitude did not alter; it became increasingly apparent that the governor would have to act, and he stated publicly that he would not hesitate to call a special impeachment session if that should become necessary.

Four days later the judge counterattacked. In television appearances broadcast in Nashville and Chattanooga, Schoolfield stated that forces favorable to racial integration were involved in a plot to ruin him. He denied that he had accepted a bribe to dismiss indictments against teamsters. He attacked Clement, Kefauver, and Senator McClellan. He referred to the two federal investigators, McShane and Duffy, as creeps. He claimed that the *Chattanooga Times* was a subsidiary of the *New York Times,* which he charged with Communist-cell infamy; he stated that the *Times* of New York had been beating the tocsins for an all-powerful federal government and for the integration of the colored and white races on all levels of life. He charged that Clement had been receiving campaign funds from liquor interests. He stated that he would not resign nor recuse himself.

On December 28, the sixteen-member central committee of the state bar association met to consider a resolution calling on Schoolfield to step

out of his office temporarily. The resolution was adopted, but Schoolfield declined compliance. At the end of the month, Clement named
Jack Norman as special counsel for a state investigation of Judge Schoolfield. It was a highly significant appointment. Norman, a well-known
and highly qualified attorney, was associated with the Browning forces
within the Democratic party and hence had been lined up against the
governor politically, although his personal relations with Clement were
friendly. In 1956 he had resigned from the national committee of the
party, to be succeeded by Herbert Walters. His experience with questions of labor violence had been enriched by his service as a prosecutor in
cases involving Perry Canaday, "Shorty" Richardson, and James Gilley,
all Teamster members. Ordinarily, charges involving Judge Schoolfield
would have been the concern of Corry Smith, the district attorney in
Hamilton County, but as Smith was a widely known and bitter political
opponent of the judge, the central committee of the state bar association
suggested that he withdraw from any activity in the Schoolfield matter.
Smith complied.

While Norman's investigation was in progress during the opening
months of 1958, other events surfaced in Hamilton County. At the suggestion of Corry Smith, Harold E. Brown, the assistant district attorney in Hamilton County, resigned his office. Brown had received a contribution from Schoolfield, which he said he thought was a political
contribution. But some persons said the contribution was a payoff for an
action taken by Schoolfield as judge, and the contribution was to figure
largely in the later proceedings. Brown testified before the McClellan
committee that he had accepted $1,000 from a professional bondsman,
Sam C. Jones.

The January news also included a story of the murder of one Gill by
one Long, both said to be Schoolfield friends. Schoolfield labeled Long a
hired gunman for Robinson Freight Lines. Brown, when he had been a
policeman, had investigated the murder. (Long himself was subsequently
murdered in prison.)

The news that month carried information that Schoolfield intended
to run again for his judicial post. When he was elected in 1950, the judge
had been supported by both the leading Chattanooga newspapers, by a
good government group, by the WCTU, and, according to his opponents, a local gambling syndicate. The story discloses something of the
complicated nature of Hamilton County politics.

Schoolfield's continuance in his post was not to go unchallenged by
other interested candidates. Schoolfield himself, in addition to running

for his own office, was said to be committed to unseating Corry Smith from his job as district attorney general, and the possible opponents to Smith included Ben Cash, Ward Crutchfield, and Don Moore, all of whom had been members of the General Assembly when bills were presented to that body to take away the wide authority that Judge Schoolfield had been given over the Hamilton County grand jury. The bills had been beaten down; the scope of the judge's authority over the grand jury and his use of that authority became cardinal issues in the impeachment proceedings.

The growing controversy in the press presented questions regarding the judge's connections with the underworld of Hamilton County, Schoolfield's enemies contending that he was tied to that underworld, Schoolfield himself contending that he was actually one of that underworld's principal enemies. The controversy on this point was not illumined by the voting patterns of the 1950 election, for the judge was weak in some of the "controlled" wards, while showing exceptional strength in Lookout Mountain, the upper class section; in Red Bank, home of the middle class; and Signal Mountain, conceded, according to the *Nashville Banner,* to be dominated by coal miners and bootleggers.

In February, Teamster members Glenn W. Smith and H.L. Boling of Chattanooga, both to be figured in the forthcoming Schoolfield proceedings, were indicted by a federal grand jury on charges of filing fraudulent income tax returns for 1951. In March, the McClellan committee released a blistering attack on Teamster union violence in Tennessee, with due attention to Schoolfield. In April, Governor Clement received Norman's report on Schoolfield and was faced with the painful duty of deciding whether to call the General Assembly into special session.

Norman's report was countersigned by his assistant, John J. Hooker, Jr. (later to emerge as a principal opponent of Buford Ellington) and W.E. Hopton, director of the Tennessee Bureau of Criminal Identification. (Hopton's agency had been subjected earlier to some criticism for inactivity by the reports of the McClellan committee.) The report was sharply critical of Schoolfield; there was no evasion, no mincing words. Norman first slapped Schoolfield for his refusal to recuse himself during the investigation, a refusal which blocked the appointment of a special judge and the convening of a special grand jury, actions that would have, in Norman's opinion, greatly aided the investigation. Norman observed that he and his colleagues had no power to compel testimony, and he noted caustically that "We found immediately that strong effort had been concentrated to block the path to these sources of these facts. From then until now, we have encountered effort and feverish activity to thwart our success in finding the truth." Again, "Many persons in places of official responsibility who, to our knowledge, could have contributed greatly to this effort remained silent, proferred no help, and were elusive and evasive when questioned. Some whose sworn duty it was to detect and prevent many of the evils discovered, in the first place, refused to cooperate." Since the investigation was conducted primarily in Hamilton County, it is reasonably safe to assume that the difficulties of which Norman speaks were in that county, at the local level, rather than in state offices. But Norman did not mention names. He did say that many conscientious citizens had helped them, including a few who had fought the wrongs in Hamilton County with much courage over the preceding years.

Norman then moved to specify the offenses with which his report charged Judge Schoolfield. Those charges are numerous and detailed, expressed in the sharpest kind of language. To begin with, Norman noted that, on the day when Schoolfield ascended the bench of the criminal court in Hamilton County, he stood in contempt of that same court, having refused to pay a fine for contempt even after the contempt conviction had been upheld by the state's Supreme Court. Says the report: "The lack of judicial propriety, contempt for orderly processes, repudiation of judicial ethics, and official insolence represented by this initial attitude, has [sic] continued through his tenures of office like a red thread through a piece of white cloth."

The judge, the report charged, had formed a habit of interfering with the conduct of jury trials, by directing verdicts of not guilty, stopping the trials, and dismissing the juries. The first such action occurred on September 14, 1948. "From that date on," continued the report, "in literally hundreds of cases, in many of which the charges have been murder, rape, robbery, and other aggravated offenses, he [Judge Schoolfield] has followed the policy of interrupting the introduction of evidence in the trials of such cases and ended the prosecutions over the vigorous objection of the counsel for the State, and taken like action."

Norman charged that the judge entered orders on the minutebooks of his court

arbitrarily, corruptly and unlawfully modifying and changing the final decrees and orders of judgments entered in cases where persons had been convicted of crimes in the Court by a predecessor judge before Judge Schoolfield was even elected or assumed the duties as judge of the Court, in order to effect the release from incarceration of those persons. In nearly two thousand criminal charges involving murders, rapes, robberies, burglaries, and all types and kinds of criminal offenses, he has entered orders retiring these cases. In but an infinitesimal few of the same have these charges ever been reinstated. They have remained retired with the status of the persons charged suspended, with neither acquittal or conviction but all the time subject to being called back into Court to answer, by one man—Judge Raulston Schoolfield.

(If true, this can scarcely be what the writers of American constitutions meant by a "speedy trial.")

The judge, according to the report, was impatient with jury trials and was prone to sentence defendants upon guilty pleas, without a jury verdict, as required for conviction in cases of felony. According to the report, in approximately 8,000 cases coming before him (a stupefying number), less than 700 cases were completed by jury trial, where there were jury convictions and no probated sentences. "We were shocked," Mr. Norman and his colleagues noted, "to find that in cases where the defendants had . . . been tried before Judge Schoolfield and a jury . . . that Judge Schoolfield in arbitrary and total disregard of the known law, had actually entered orders . . . changing the offenses for which the defendants had been convicted; and changing the sentences they were to serve to different grades of felony and different sentences." Other similar kinds of arbitrary actions were described.

The report went on to criticize the judge for his "association . . . with certain persons and his insatiable desire to project himself into every political campaign and factional difference in Chattanooga and Hamilton County." This association extended to "law violators, gamblers, and racketeers . . . [including] many who have had cases involving criminal offenses in his court. This association has been open and notorious." He had accepted money, according to the report, "knowing it to have come from their illegal gambling enterprises, for protection and favor." "The sworn testimony and documentary evidence further revealed that Judge Schoolfield accepted the payment of large sums of money as bribes in consideration of which he agreed to and did in his official capacity give favorable judgment to certain persons in matters pending before him." He had, the report charged, been active in drawing law violators before his court to coerce their support in his "varied political adventures." His participation in bribery, noted the report, had included an attempt to bribe members of the General Assembly—a charge that this body was to find acutely embarrassing in subsequent proceedings.

The report dealt with Schoolfield's connection with officials of the Teamsters union, Glenn W. Smith and Hubert Leon Boling, of Local 515, the connection which had eventually led to the proceedings of the McClellan committee and eventually to the employment of Norman and Hooker and the cooperation of Hopton in the current investigation.

An intriguing by-play in this lurid recital was provided by the following paragraph: "It was interesting to note that the first person referred to above [in a preceding paragraph] as having been released on the bond signed by Judge Schoolfield was the notorious law violator and gunman, W.C. (Bill) Long, who had criminal charges against him retired by Judge Schoolfield, who had served as Judge Schoolfield's bodyguard, and was actively associated with Judge Schoolfield in his political fortunes. It is further interesting to note that soon thereafter this same W.C. (Bill) Long shot and killed Fred Gill, another notorious gambler and law violator of Chattanooga and Hamilton County, Tennessee, who had likewise been a close friend and political associate of Judge Schoolfield, and that Judge Schoolfield was a pallbearer at his, Gill's, funeral." "We pause here," the report notes satirically, "to call attention to the fact that during the time of these positive happenings, and positive associations between Judge Schoolfield and these racketeers and criminal characters, that Judge Schoolfield was continuously posing as the champion of law and order in the community and professing to be the only defense that law and order had against the onslaughts of criminals."

The report is harshly critical of Judge Schoolfield's judicial deportment, noting that he had continuously been intemperate, inattentive, impatient, and partial, and it calls his conduct improper, saying he had been "arbitrary in his actions, inconsistent in his obligations, partisan in his decisions, profane and obscene." He was charged with having confiscated private property.

This sensational recital continued. It is unnecessary to recount further details at this point. Norman and his colleagues recommended impeachment, having reported also that impeachment does not necessarily depend upon the kind of "crimes" that are described in the felony laws of the state but may depend upon actions that call for disqualification from office, even though such actions are not crimes within the meaning of felony statutes or the common law.

The report proposed thirty-one articles of impeachment, based not only on specific alleged actions, but on general behavior. The specific charges included such matters as directing verdicts of not guilty, without authority and contrary to law; changing sentences and punishments on the docket, including sentences imposed by a predecessor; suspending and delaying cases as to hold persons before his court before long periods; accepting bribes and gifts from persons before his court, including the gift of a Pontiac; associating with known gamblers and law violators over long periods of time; mixing in local politics, contrary to codes of judicial behavior; failing to testify before the McClellan committee; failing to recuse himself as a judge and as the official who selects the grand jury during the period of investigation; and indulging in private behavior inappropriate for a judge.

This striking report, and its demand for action, reached the governor in the middle of April, just at the period when primaries for county offices were shaping up and shortly before the most intense period of campaigning for the 1958 gubernatorial primary. Clement himself was not a candidate in this election, but the prospect of a special session to consider the matter of Schoolfield was embarrassing to a number of Hamilton County politicians, some of whom had had some association with Schoolfield and apparently might have liked his support for campaigns for attorney general in Hamilton County. With the judge under fire, more than normal uncertainties were added to the local campaigns. Schoolfield himself might have been a candidate for reelection.

Some hope was expressed that Clement would avoid the calling of a special session to a less unpropitious moment. He did not. On April 26, 1958, the governor issued a call for the Assembly to convene on May 6, for the purpose of considering Schoolfield's impeachment. When the House came together on that day, it was presented with a brief message from the governor, outlining the duties of the House and saying, "I feel that I have done what duty demands and what the law requires of the Governor in calling you into Special Session. . . . As you set about your task, I pray you do so in the knowledge that the eyes of Tennessee and of the nation are upon you. From this place let it be known to all the world that dignity was maintained; that honor was upheld; that justice was done."

There is no evidence whatever that Clement exerted any further influence on the House or the Senate in the subsequent proceedings. The votes were not party-line votes and there is little evidence of factional alliances at work. Both Clement leaders and Clement opponents are to be found on the same side during the hearings and the trial. Nor is there any evidence that the outcome had any influence on the future fortunes of the governor. Nevertheless, the hearings and the trial constituted a major episode in Tennessee history—one that throws a somewhat murky glow on the realities of local politics in Tennessee.

Impeachment had been little used in Tennessee and the members of the Assembly had no experience with the practice. Speaker Bomar restricted access to the floor to members of the Assembly, contrary to the ordinary loose practice during regular sessions in those days. Judge Schoolfield was in regular attendance in the gallery of the House; he did not avail himself of invitations to take a place on the floor of the House. Bomar ruled, quite soundly, that impeachment proceedings consist in bringing charges, not trying them; the House was therefore like a grand jury, although not subject to grand jury rules regarding evidence or publicity, and the hearings and the votes taken were to be public. Strict silence and propriety were conditions to be met by gallery spectators, and decorum was required on the floor as well.

The aspect of the procedure that some members of the Assembly found it most difficult to accept was that impeachment was not trial, for those friendly to the judge were inclined to want to cross-examine prosecutors and witnesses and to argue from time to time. Speaker Bomar was polite but strict in his management of the hearings, keeping them firmly on track, keeping the House steadily at work, and cutting disputes wherever possible. His performance was impressive. The most active role in questioning various aspects of the proceedings was taken by various members of the Hamilton County delegation, sometimes assisted by members from Marshall County, Sullivan, and Bradley. Any representative was allowed to question witnesses, but the House strongly supported Bomar's determination not to allow House proceedings to become the trial itself.

Norman and Hooker first read their report to the governor into the record, and following this report several days of evidence were heard: official documents, readings from the testimony given the McClellan committee, and presentation of affidavits from various persons who had been interviewed by Hooker and his staff. Norman's position was candidly stated: "I am an advocate, I am a lawyer. I get in a thing, I produce the evidence. Naturally I am prejudiced. I am one of a few lawyers that will admit that. Most of them won't, but I do. I am prejudiced on the side that I am working on and I really think every lawyer ought to admit it himself . . . but I will say this, I am not going to presume to suggest what you do about it." The use of depositions, where no cross-examination was possible, caused some flurry, but Norman stated unequivocally that depositions are in order before grand juries and that what he was offering was sworn testimony, not hearsay.

Members of the House were troubled that some of the witnesses before the McClellan committee, most notably H.L. Boling, had repeatedly taken the Fifth Amendment before that committee. They were greatly troubled by the fact that some of the evidence offered came from underworld characters whose word could not be easily credited. As Norman said of one of them, Joe Frank, when asked whether Frank had ever been convicted of felonies in Tennessee, "I don't know, Mr. Crutchfield, I wouldn't imagine he was a Sunday School teacher or he wouldn't be engaged in that kind of activity."

Judge Schoolfield had been accused of accepting a Pontiac as a gift. McKellip in questioning Hooker said: "Was Mr. Weaver questioned as to his violation of the code of ethics on giving away this Cadillac?" Said the Speaker, possibly remembering the 1954 election troubles attending the governor's acquisition of a Cadillac: "I think you wish to amend your statement to say a Pontiac." There is no record, in the *Journal*, of laughter, but there must have been some smiles.

Some members of the House wished to hear evidence from witnesses besides Norman, Hooker, and Hopton. A fifteen-member subcommittee was appointed to select such witnesses, who were to be subpoenaed by the House. The committee was chaired by McAllen Foutch, one of the most persistent opponents of Clement in the legislature, who took an active part in the proceedings of the special session. Other members included Harry Lee Senter, Damon Headden, J.I. Bell, and W.L. Barry, all prominent legislators during the Clement years. The subcommittee decision to call three witnesses was adopted by the House; the witnesses were: H.L. Boling, Glenn Smith, both connected with the Teamsters, and Corry Smith, attorney general of Hamilton County. Only Corry Smith responded: Boling was in the Campbell Clinic in Chattanooga, following major surgery for cancer; Glenn Smith could not be located, and Mrs. Smith was reported as saying to the process server: "Mr. Patterson, to tell you the truth, I don't know where he is because he called me this afternoon and said he was leaving town and didn't know when he would be back." Corry Smith was heard. He was known to be actively opposed to Judge Schoolfield, and his testimony added little to what the House had already heard.

One of the charges brought against the judge was embarrassing to the Assembly itself. It was alleged that Judge Schoolfield had been involved in an attempt to bribe members of the legislature, presumably members of the Hamilton County delegation, to suppress legislation directed against the numbers racket in operation on Lookout Mountain. The House heard testimony to the effect that Schoolfield had conspired with Joe Frank, Claude Massey, Leonard Lane, Charley Jones, and other persons in Hamilton County who at the time were engaged in illegal gambling in that county to raise $2,500 to pay legislators to suppress House Bill No. 739, which would have hindered illegal gambling in the county. The charge included the allegation that Schoolfield, Frank, and Charley Jones (referred to as Sam in the charges) traveled to Nashville, where it was alleged that Schoolfield left his two companions outside the Andrew Jackson Hotel in Nashville, entered the hotel, and later returned to his companions, saying his mission had been completed.

In view of the reflection on the Assembly, a subcommittee of five was named to investigate. What they were to study had occurred, if it occurred at all, in 1949, almost a decade before the present proceedings. The trail was stone cold. Members of the Hamilton County at that time included John Chambliss, J.B. Ragon, Ambrose Locke, and Leonard Aymon. Of these only Aymon was still in the legislature, and he was seriously ill. He did not appear before the committee; Chambliss, Ragon, and Locke all appeared voluntarily. Chambliss was a respected member of an old established family of Chattanooga; his father had been a notable member of the state Supreme Court. John Chambliss was deeply immersed in attempts to reform the local governmental structure of Hamilton County; he testified that he had introduced the anti-gambling bill in question, but that he had withdrawn it because of objections to the increased powers it had given to the county court of Hamilton. Chambliss also said he had supported Schoolfield for judge and had spoken for him, but he denied any personal friendship with him. He, Ragon, and Locke all disavowed any knowledge of any payment for suppression of the bill, although Ragon and Locke both stated that their hotel bills and some meal expenses for them, as well as for Leonard Aymon, had been paid by a Chattanooga whiskey dealer. Ragon stated that he had been a political opponent of Schoolfield.

The resolutions of the subcommittee were necessarily weak. They recommended further investigation of this particular charge should impeachment be approved, and they condemned the practice of accepting aid on hotel and other expenses. The impeachment charge based on this alleged episode was, in due course, approved, but no further investigation was undertaken by the House.

On May 15, the subcommittee of fifteen, under the chairmanship of

McAllen Foutch, was given the task of recommending whether articles of impeachment should be adopted and of preparing such articles if they so wished. The following day, this subcommittee recommended impeachment of the judge on twenty-five counts, substantially those recommended by Norman's report. In the end, the House adopted twenty-four articles, but one proposal—to impeach the judge for angry speech to a person outside the courtroom—was rejected.

All other charges were adopted by a majority vote, an ordinary majority being sufficient for impeachment. (Conviction in the Senate would require a two-thirds vote.) The charges varied in seriousness. On the whole, the majorities for adoption were substantial and sometimes even overwhelming. Those charges where the "no" votes were substantial included the allegations of acceptance of a bribe of $1,000 and the gift of a Pontiac, the failure of the judge to pay a fine for contempt, the judge's constant mixing in county politics, and an order of the judge seizing guns from pawnbrokers in Chattanooga. The alleged $1,000 bribe was regarded by some as a campaign contribution; the contempt fine had not been large; and the seizure of the guns, it was argued by some, had been seizure of property essentially without value. On the first article of impeachment, Representatives Aderholt, Crutchfield, Estes, Hull, McKellip, Moore, and Thompson voted "no," and in general these could be said to have constituted a hard core of resistance to impeachment on the remaining charges.

The charges of impeachment were now transmitted to the Senate for trial. Judge Schoolfield had been present in the gallery of the House throughout the proceedings; he had not accepted the invitation of the Speaker to take a place on the floor. Trial in the Senate would be a full-fledged adversary affair, in which the judge would defend himself. The Senate met on Wednesday, May 21, under the chairmanship of Chief Justice A.B. Neil. The impeachment had resulted in Judge Schoolfield's suspension from the bench in Hamilton County, and Neil had named J. Fred Bibb, of the criminal court in Knox County, to function in Judge Schoolfield's stead, pending outcome of the trial.

Three members of the House—John R. Jones, McAllen Foutch, and J. Alan Hanover—were made managers of the House's charges against the judge; they were assisted by Speaker Bomar ex officio. Counsel for the state were Jack Norman and John J. Hooker, Jr. Counsel for the defense were E.B. Baker and Hager Odum of Chattanooga and Excell Eaves, a resident of Rossville, Georgia, just over the state line from Hamilton County.

The opening line of the defense was a move to quash twenty-one articles on various grounds — that no crime under the statutes or the constitution had been committed; that certain alleged actions were taken, if taken, by the judge in his judicial capacity and involved judicial discretion which the legislature had no authority to question; that some of the actions had taken place, if at all, in the previous term of office, and therefore were not subject to present question; and that the articles in general were vague and ambiguous. Had the motion to quash been upheld, the charges against the judge would have been reduced to three: that he had accepted a bribe in a case involving James Spense Galloway; that he had accepted bribes in the cases of Claude Massey and Joe Frank; and that he continued hearings and made other rulings favorable to Leonard Lane. Schoolfield's attorneys also challenged the authority of the Senate on the grounds that it had not been reapportioned as required by the state constitution (which was most certainly true), and the attorneys also hinted that the actions of the Senate would be subject to appeal (a thoroughly questionable contention).

Motions to quash were overruled. This having been done, Schoolfield's written reply was filed. His response to each article of impeachment, one by one, was along the lines laid down in the motion to quash. On articles 1 and 2, for instance, the judge argued that the action involved "does not constitute a violation of the statutes or of the constitution and as Judge of the Criminal Court the action taken was done openly with no questionable motives involved therein, that this matter involved the discretionary power of the Court and is not reviewable by the Legislature and that the same does not constitute grounds for impeachment within the purview of Article 5 of the Constitution of Tennessee."

Charges of acceptance of bribes were denied outright.

On the charge of interfering in local politics, the judge averred that he had done nothing "in this respect which was not motivated by a desire on the part of the defendant to promote good, sound, honest, and constitutional government. . . . and were not done in the defendant's official capacity as Judge; wherefore defendant says he is not guilty." Article 24 dealt with the judge's failure to recuse himself while under investigation. To this he said, in part: "To pursue . . . such course . . . would place not only the defendant, but every Judge at the mercy of any irresponsible hoodlum or law violator who wished to make unfounded and untrue charges against a Judge."

In proceedings before the Senate, witnesses were to be heard by both sides. Subpoenas were delivered in a number of cases, and immunity was granted to certain witnesses so as to compel testimony from those likely to plead self-incrimination. Three persons were given such immunity: James Spense Galloway, Sam Jones, a bondsman, and H.L. Boling. Galloway and Jones appeared before the Senate; Boling had suffered a severe cancer operation; he claimed to be unable to travel to Nashville, and arrangements were made to take his testimony by deposition.

It had been alleged that Galloway, charged with the concealment of some stolen property, had paid Sam Jones $1,000, which Jones was to deliver to Schoolfield as an inducement for some kind of adjustment in the charge against him. It appeared that this money had been passed by Jones to Harold Brown, assistant attorney general of Hamilton County, who had accepted it as a contribution to Schoolfield's campaign funds. Galloway, Jones, and Brown had all testified before the McClellan committee and that testimony was read into the current proceedings. The record shows that after this transfer of funds, Galloway, by an unusual procedure, was granted a new trial; he entered a plea of guilty to a reduced charge and was paroled.

In some respects, Galloway's testimony before the Senate differed from that he gave the McClellan committee; he claimed the committee investigators had put words in his mouth, and he averred that he could not remember always what he had told the committee. He did insist that he did not know what the $1,000 were to be used for, but he allowed clearly enough that he understood he was to plead guilty to a lesser charge and that he would receive a suspended sentence.

Brown testified that he had passed the money to Schoolfield from Jones, but he denied that it was a contribution in return for a suspended sentence for Galloway. Jones testified that he had contributed to campaigns for Corry Smith, an acknowledged opponent of Schoolfield, apparently to indicate that political contributions were not new for him, but he did testify that he thought the $1,000 from Galloway were designed to bring Galloway's freedom about; he avoided the use of the word "bribe." Galloway's divergent testimony caused him to be ordered to trial for contempt of the Senate, but apparently no subsequent action was ever taken.

The case against the jurist rested heavily on the testimony of Leonard Lane, but Lane's own occupations and life were not such as to give his evidence completely creditable weight. Lane testified that he had known Schoolfield for some twenty years; during part of that time, Lane said, he himself had been actively engaged in the numbers racket in Chattanooga, along with other gambling ventures. Lane stated that after he had retired from the numbers game, his wife, Alma, had taken over. Alma Lane had died shortly before the impeachment proceedings had been started, and, as it was hinted in some quarters that her departure from this life had been assisted, proceedings to exhume her body were put under way, over the objections of her widower. Her body was, in fact, exhumed, and the papers reported that an examining physician said she had sustained a blow on the head that could have caused death. But the manner of her death, the Senate thought, was irrelevant, and no further details of her demise appeared in the Senate proceedings. Her testimony, given to the McClellan committee, that she had paid Schoolfield off during her operation of the numbers racket, was not received in the trial before the state Senate, since cross-examination was now impossible, and technically the evidence was hearsay.

Judge Schoolfield took an active part in cross-examining the witnesses ranged against him. In the case of Galloway, the judge attempted to demonstrate that the case had been disposed of by a new trial, and he suspended sentence by agreement with Cardinal Woolsey (Chattanooga has always had its share of strange names), then Hamilton County assistant district attorney. The prosecution insisted that the attorney general's office had not been represented in court when Schoolfield suspended the case against Galloway, and Woolsey testified that he had not been present at the time, but Chester Frost, clerk of the criminal court, maintained that the attorney general's office was represented.

In his cross-examination of Lane, Judge Schoolfield attempted to show that gambling had been closed down in Chattanooga during his administration. He tried to get Lane to admit that Alma Lane was mentally ill, and he sought to show that Lane had been a persistent enemy of the judge and a friend of his great opponent, Corry Smith. Schoolfield did extract an admission from Lane that cases involving Lane had been postponed because of the illness of one of his attorneys and that the cases had finally been assigned to another judge.

The most sensational of the charges against Judge Schoolfield, and the one that, through the McClellan committee, had apparently been the principal issue leading to the impeachment proceedings, was the allegation that the judge had suppressed the trial of Teamster Union members, Glenn Smith and H.L. Boling, following a payment of $18,500 (the amount was not specified in the charge). The Senate had experienced great difficulty in getting the ill Boling to the stand. At first his doctor said he was unable to appear; the Senate then agreed to take his deposition, but he refused to give it. Thereafter, the doctor having agreed that he could testify in person, he did appear before the Senate under a subpoena. His testimony put the Senate into an uproar, for Boling testified that he had heard that the $18,500 which disappeared from the union treasury had gone to Corry Smith, H.G.B. King, a union attorney, and Frank Clement. He also said that he heard part of it went to Schoolfield. The testimony could have seemed a blatant attempt to tie blame to the judge's opponents. At the time the alleged bribe was supposed to have occurred, Clement had been in the army, stationed in Georgia, although he had already announced that he would be a candidate later. All of the statement was hearsay. Boling claimed no certain knowledge, and the Senate voted to reject his testimony and to expunge it from the record.

A.O. Buck, a Nashville attorney, had been accused of receiving the $18,500. He took the stand to deny that he had received that sum from Boling. He did say that he had met with Robert Crichton in a hotel room in Chattanooga and that at this meeting Glenn Smith and another union official were present. A few days after the testimony of Boling and Buck, Glenn Smith was finally brought to the bar of the Senate. Smith testified clearly that the money in question had been given to Buck to fix the case in Schoolfield's court. The money was passed, he stated, in the James Robertson Hotel in Nashville. He stated that Buck had originally told him that the amount required would be $39,000 but that he had secured a reduction by negotiation. Smith testified that the amount was actually $20,000, to be divided into two payments. Smith testified to his contacts with Crichton, and said that, besides himself, only Crichton, Schoolfield, Eddie Friar, and Steven Stone, a Chattanooga attorney, knew about the payments. Smith admitted that in 1953 he had lied to the Internal Revenue Service about the $18,500, claiming at that time that the money was used to help out a Knoxville local union. Smith did not think of the payment to Schoolfield as bribery; he regarded it, he testified, as an out-and-out political shakedown. Smith also testified that Crichton took the initiative in suggesting monetary contributions in return for the help he was seeking from Crichton.

Smith's statements on the stand scattered firecrackers through the camps of Tennessee politics. Friar took time out from his campaign for the governorship to appear before the Senate, where he denied all knowledge of a contribution of $20,000 from the Teamsters. Crichton followed Friar to the stand. Friar had testified to his close personal and political friendship with Crichton. By this time, both had long since fallen out with Governor Clement. Crichton testified that he was acquainted with Smith (which was not surprising, since Crichton's business was trucking and he necessarily had dealings with the Teamsters.) He said he did not know Boling, although he knew who he was. He did testify that he had met in the Patten Hotel in Chattanooga with A.O. Buck and Glen Smith in 1951 when he sought the support of the Teamsters for a candidate; that candidate was Clement, who was to run for the first time the following year. He testified that he did know at that time that Boling, Smith, and other teamsters were under indictment in Judge Schoolfield's court, but he denied that he had tried to do anything for them, presumably in return for their political support. He did say that Smith later asked for his help during a visit to Crichton's Nashville office, but he said he had told Smith he could do nothing for him and was not inclined to. He asserted that he knew there was some trouble concerning a sum amounting to $18,500 because the Internal Revenue Service approached him around 1953 to see whether he knew anything about it. Crichton's testimony to the IRS agent was read into the Senate record; in that testimony he denied any connection with any payoff by Smith or Boling.

On the stand, A.O. Buck, who was a trustee for some of the Teamster funds — although as a management, not a labor, representative — denied any payoff to Crichton, and he denied receiving $18,500 for purposes of the campaign or for any other purpose. Steven Stone testified that he had no knowledge of any payment of $18,500 in any way.

The alleged payment of $18,500 or $20,000, whichever it was, if it was either, remained elusive. The state was unable to produce further evidence. The most it was able to produce was the testimony of Charles M. Pendergast of Selma, Alabama, a former Teamster official, who said he had arranged a meeting between Glen Smith and Crichton for the purpose of seeking Crichton's help in a case involving the Teamsters; but Pendergast denied any knowledge of money being offered or passed.

Testimony, equally contradictory and confused, was offered relating to other charges of bribery.

One of the more disturbing charges against the jurist concerned his alleged changing of sentences and his use of directed verdicts of not guilty without the concurrence of the state attorney or the jury. Schoolfield's defense was essentially that the use of directed verdicts had been long established and repeatedly used by other judges. The testimony and ruling were in conflict. Chief Justice Neil stated flatly that the Supreme Court of the state had ruled against the practice (and who should have known

better than the chief justice?), but Judge Tillman Grant of the second
division of the Hamilton County criminal court stated that over the
years it had become practice for judges to direct verdicts of not guilty
without the presence of juries. Schoolfield's predecessor, Judge Myers,
said he knew of no law against the practice, but Judge Grant did say that
Schoolfield had exceeded his authority. Evidence was received relating
to certain other alleged financial transactions and to behavior charged to
be inappropriate for a judge.

On July 9, 1958, Jack Norman led off in the summation of the prosecution's case. He emphasized that causes for impeachment could reach
beyond ordinary felonies to touch upon the essential fitness of the man
for the office — a point well established in Tennessee law and practice, although some of the legislators had difficulty in accepting the point. As
in the case of his original report to the governor, Norman minced no
words. On the matter of the judge's alteration of sentences, he said:

> It is fundamental and basic in the criminal law of this, and every other state
> in the Union, that a defendant can be convicted of a felony only by a Jury.
> No jury convicted this defendant of second degree murder and gave him a
> sentence of from ten to twenty years in the state penitentiary. Judge School-
> field arbitrarily and illegally entered this verdict himself without a jury. He
> not only acted illegally and arbitrarily in changing the verdict which the
> jury had actually returned, but also when he entered his judgment of mur-
> der in the second degree, with a sentence of ten to twenty years, without a
> jury verdict to this effect.
>
> Judge Schoolfield admits that he likewise changed a jury conviction of five
> years on a charge of highway robbery to a sentence of one year for petty lar-
> ceny in another case. He also admitted that he had thus changed and modi-
> fied other jury verdicts, all without the approval of a jury.

"Lane testified," he said,

> and Judge Schoolfield admits, that Lane, a notorious gambler, according to
> Schoolfield, and a man of bad reputation and criminal tendencies, as urged
> by Schoolfield, had a number of gambling charges pending against him,
> Lane, in Judge Schoolfield's court from the day Schoolfield went on the
> bench until the summer of 1950, or for a period of two years. It is peculiar
> that during the same time Lane was participating in Schoolfield's cam-
> paigns, donating money to his campaigns, renting and helping to equip
> Schoolfield's political headquarters, signed $1,000.00 notes for his friends,
> and doing other favors for Schoolfield, that the Judge never forced him to
> trial in a single one of these cases for a period of two years. Why?

"Judge Schoolfield frankly admitted," he noted,

> that he, as the presiding judge of the criminal court of Hamilton County, together with the District Attorney of Hamilton County, the City Judge of Chattanooga, and the Foreman of the Hamilton County Grand Jury, whom he had appointed, met with gamblers, bootleggers and outlaws in order to urge them to get out the vote in an election in which he was a candidate, but in which his first interest was the defeat of a candidate running for another office.

"The undisputed and uncontradicted evidence," he said,

> is that Judge Schoolfield has taken between three and four hundred cases wherein defendants had plead not guilty, and when in the process of being tried by a jury, and stopped trial of the cause, and in many instances over objection of the district attorney, as in the teamsters case, arbitrarily and illegally taken the case away from the consideration of the jury, and directed the entry of his own verdict of not guilty without concurrence of a jury.

On the illusive $18,500, he said in part:

> It further helps to understand this attitude and action on the part of Judge Schoolfield to remember that back when he first set this case for trial on July 10, 1951, that counsel for the defendant tried their utmost, as late as June 11, 1951, to get a continuance, but Judge Schoolfield refused, and stated that the case would be tried as set on July 10th. Then we find that again it just so happened that on July 6 he changed his mind and continued the trial of the case from July 10 indefinitely.

> What made him change his mind? It will be remembered that the testimony is to the effect that on the day before, — on July 5, $18,500.00 was drawn out of the bank by Glenn Smith and Judge Schoolfield's friend, H.L. Boling, and the money brought to Nashville and paid to parties "to get the case fixed."

> Again, you have one of these coincidences which seem peculiar to Judge Schoolfield's court.

. . . .

> Did the respondent have any conception of this obligation of a judge when he accompanied the district attorney general, the city judge and the man he had appointed as the foreman of the grand jury of Hamilton County, — when four of them, representing the very ultimate in the prosecution of crime — to a political meeting where they were gathered with those who were known to him, as the presiding judge as gamblers, racketeers and law violators, and when the door was guarded by the notorious outlaw, Bill

Long, whose political services the judge admits he had solicited, and while the judge, under this circumstance, among those people, and in that place, was urging these law violators how to get out the vote in the coming election.

. . . .

He scoffs and derides the unanimous opinion of his profession and his fellow judges as suggested in the Canons of Judicial Ethics, accepted by every Court in America, including the Supreme Court of Tennessee, that a judge should not accept gifts. Do I need to argue to you the propriety of such a principle? 'Yes, I received a $3,000.00 automobile, but I didn't inquire as to the identity of the donors.' Why would anybody want to give a judge a $3,000.00 automobile? What would they have in mind?

Such are significant and typical portions of an address read to the Senators that cover fifty-eight pages in the official proceedings. He summed it all up in the words,

In this impeachment proceeding, you have not seen a judge, hastening to bring into the open sunlight a review of his actions. On the contrary, you have seen a shrewd, cagey defendant invoking all the technicalities of the law to prevent an open hearing, hiding behind objections, lurking behind exceptions, persistently trying to cut away the charges, determinedly trying to limit the inquiry. Every honest man will agree that, if, in the investigation of such an official, a court of impeachment, which has nothing in view but justice, were to be stopped at every step by objections based solely upon technicalities, then arrogant and unprincipled men would escape the just penalty of violated justice. Impeachment and conviction are the principal, perhaps the only, steps whereby public security can be preserved.

The argument of James Bomar, although shorter, was no less severe. Bomar called attention to the silent witnesses, the witnesses Schoolfield could have called, he said, but who were left silent—Claude Massey, a boyhood friend of Judge Schoolfield, Jim Earl West, who was charged with raising $3,000 to buy a Pontiac for the judge, Son Skillern, the judge's parole officer (who had been present with him in the gallery of the House during the impeachment proceedings). "I hold," said Bomar, "that between the admissions of the defendant and the absent witnesses he stands convicted of the articles that have been presented here." And he attacked the jurist's behavior in these sharp words:

It is above reproach when he threatens to rough it with a lawyer practicing in his court as he did one young lawyer not too long ago? It it above reproach when he meets prospective sheriff candidates at a bootlegger's home because it is a convenient place? Is it above reproach when he uses abusive, obscene language to a man trying to carry out proper law and order because he thought it was appropriate under the circumstances? Is it above reproach when he tells an associate editor of a metropolitan newspaper that those who have opposed him have had to leave town? Is it above reproach when he uses a notorious gunman as his associate, as he did Bill Long? Is it above reproach when he frequents dives in political campaigns or when he continually uses his office as a vehicle to cast aspersions on every person who opposes him and continually refers to them with epitaphs of a degrading personal nature ranging from "inexperienced" to "half-wits?"

John J. Hooker, Jr., J. Alan Hanover, and John R. Jones also made speeches for the prosecution.

The argument for the defense was presented by Schoolfield in a lengthy reply, seconded by some of his attorneys. Schoolfield's defense was much the same as his initial plea. He claimed to have tried to lessen crime in the county. He admitted to having been a gregarious man, who believed in association with people in all walks of life. His political activities he defended as being appropriate for a judge in a state where judgeships are filled by election. He said:

> If my distractors succeed in finishing my destruction you have placed every judge in this state in peril of the same sort of attack, you have placed every hoodlum that happens to be tried in front of a judge, or who might be tried in front of a judge, in a position to defend himself by accusing the judge.

> Whoever dredged these witnesses and brought them up here went to the bottom of the sewers of Chattanooga for the source of their proof. I don't think any judge should even have to defend himself against such testimony. I think it is an insult to the judiciary to require a judge to, but having gone that far it became necessary that this case proceed to a final decision and so I say that in this case, if it had been investigated fairly and impartially, it never would have attained the proportions it has attained.

On July 11, Judge Schoolfield was found guilty by the necessary two-thirds on three counts, Articles 8, 19, and 22, and was thereby removed from the office of judge of Division I of the Criminal Court of the Sixth Judicial Circuit of Tennessee. Upon a motion that the judgment of the high court of impeachment include, in addition to removal from office, the disqualification of the judge for filling any office thereafter within the meaning of Article 5, Section 4 of the constitution of Tennessee, 19 votes were cast for disqualification, with 12 against. This was short of the two-thirds needed for disqualification.

Article 8 dealt with the gift of the Pontiac; the vote was 24 to 7. Article 19 dealt with the extensive political activities of the judge; the vote was 27 "guilty" to 4 "not guilty." Article 22, critical of his general conduct on and off the bench, was carried by a vote of 22 to 9. The last vote of 22 was a bare two-thirds of the total membership of the Senate of 33. Only 31 of the 33 senators were voting. Senator Head had been absent throughout the trial, and Senator Clifford Allen, once again a candidate for governor, had decided to absent himself during the voting. The constitution speaks of the vote necessary for conviction as two-thirds of the senators sworn to hear the case; this would have included Allen, but not Head, therefore, 32 senators. Twenty-two votes were needed for conviction. That majority—still 22—was barely missed on Article 16, which charged the judge with having illegally entered an order suspending a sentence of five years for voluntary manslaughter placed on Avenell Leonard and for probating Leonard.

In Article 23, Schoolfield had been charged with a culpable failure to appear before the McClellan committee to purge himself of the charges made against him in evidence offered that body. On this article, thirty-one senators voted to acquit; there was not one single vote for conviction. The words of Senator Dodson in his explanation of his vote undoubtedly echo the sentiments of all his colleagues: "The use of Congressional committees for 'so-called' investigation incidental to needs for Federal legislation has gone beyond the bounds of all possible legal justification in that such committees are now used for inquisitorial or Grand Jury purposes and functions. The rights and liberties of individuals are constantly invaded without opportunity on the part of the individual to offer evidence and the good name of respectable citizens maligned and the individual convicted by public information media without recourse. Under these conditions it is my opinion that such conduct on the part of the Respondent as is charged and proven, and indeed admitted, is not an offense and certainly not an impeachable offense." The resentment against federal intrusion and inadequate congressional procedure is apparent, but sharp observers could have noted the inadequacies of Tennessee procedure that had led to the current proceedings. It has never been argued that Tennessee did not suffer from illegal union activities.

On Article 24, which dealt not only with the judge's failure to testify, but with his refusal to rescue himself, only Senator Dyer voted guilty. Thirty senators voted not guilty—a surprising result.

Article 14 had dealt with the embarrassing allegation of attempted bribery of legislators. On this charge, only Senator Dyer and Senator

Dunbar voted guilty; twenty-nine senators voted not guilty. Three explanations of votes were offered, referring to the lack of convincing proof. The witnesses against Schoolfield were suspect because of their association with gambling.

On ten other counts, not guilty verdicts received majority votes. These dealt with changes in final judgment entered by the judge, the alleged contribution of $1,000 from Galloway, the alleged forced loan of Galloway to Argo, an alleged bribery by Joe Frank, contributions to the political campaign by Leonard Lane, interference with the grand jury, directed verdicts, failure to pay a fine for contempt, and the seizure of revolvers from pawnbrokers.

Senators were entitled to spread the reasons for their votes on the record. A few did; most did not. Motivations for the votes must therefore be largely guesswork. Those who did cite motives mentioned the failure of the prosecution to prove charges beyond reasonable doubt, doubts as to culpable motives on the part of the judge when sentences were suspended or verdicts changed, or doubt as to the judge's ill will in his failure to pay his contempt fine.

In addition to the two-thirds majorities attained on three counts, simple majorities for conviction were handed down on six counts. These had to do with the order modifying sentences of the judge's predecessor, a dismissal of a drunk driving charge against a friend of the judge, frequent delays and dismissals of cases without jury verdicts, and disregard of the law which forbids a judge to sign surety bonds.

Chief Justice Neil had stricken out articles 11 (dealing with the judge's failure to report campaign expenses in his 1954 campaign for the governorship) and 20 (dealing with his failure to return a car to a former client), and his action had been sustained by the Senate.

The verdicts of the Senate contrasted sharply with the judgments reached by the House in its own proceedings. But one must remember that the proceedings in the House are ex parte; only the prosecution is heard. In the trial, the judge had an opportunity to be heard, and to call and cross-examine witnesses. Whether his use of these rights influenced the senators is difficult to say. The prosecution had to rely on witnesses in some of the serious bribery charges whose public reputation was not flattering. They were not exactly pillars of good society. The evidence itself was confused, contradictory, unreliable—or could have been considered so by any senator.

It is nonetheless puzzling that the judge was convicted largely on his general behavior and the atmosphere in his court, while escaping on most of those specific charges that detailed that behavior and that atmosphere.

The highly respected and respectable *Chattanooga Times* was critical of the failure of the Senate to convict on more than a few counts. In an editorial on July 14 it analyzed the votes of the lawyers in the Senate. Ten of the senators were lawyers, the *Times* noted: Clifford Allen, Hobart Atkins, Ben Cash, James Cummings, Ross Dyer, Harlan Dodson, William D. Howell, Jared Maddux, Brooks McLemore, and Thomas P. Mitchell. "One of [these], of course," said the *Times,* "ran out on his oath and his obligations as member of the court. Clifford Allen sat for four weeks listening to the evidence and then couldn't wait four days to cast his vote." The *Times* listed a number of guilty votes by Atkins, Cash, and Dyer, and a few such votes by Dodson, Maddux, and Mitchell on charges that should have been particularly important for lawyers. And the *Times* concluded its editorial with the sharp statement: "The legal profession has lofty principles; the public expects lawyers to abide by them."

There was no evidence of party or factional alignment in the voting. Brooks McLemore had been a Clement opponent. Maddux and Dyer were Clement friends and supporters. Hobart Atkins was a prominent Knoxville Republican. Ben Cash was a Hamilton County Democrat whom Clement had courted. Harlan Dodson was a Davidson County Democrat. Clifford Allen was a bitter and determined Clement enemy.

One week before the Senate began to take the pleas and the evidence, the voters of Hamilton County had retired Judge Schoolfield from office; he was defeated for renomination, 2 to 1, by Campbell Carden. Carden carried the so-called "controlled" wards, but he lost in Soddy, the home of Son Skillern, Schoolfield's close associate and parole officer. Schoolfield had closed his campaign by attacking professional scandalmongers, saying that a block of his opposition came from the Highlander Folk School at nearby Monteagle, an institution that he, as well as others, accused of Communist taint.

The judge was doubly out of office, and he had been disbarred. But he had not been disqualified from future office and in time he was to be returned by popular vote as a sessions judge in Hamilton County, a post that can be occupied by a nonlawyer.

♪ *A rugged path to travel in*

H. Parkhurst
in J.R. Graves, *The Little Seraph*
(Memphis: Southern Baptist
Publication Society, 1874), 92

10. A Rugged Path to Travel In

THE FINAL CAMPAIGN FOR THE GOVERNORSHIP

When Clement left the governorship in 1959, he was only a few months before his thirty-ninth birthday. He was still a young man, the father of a young family. He had no large fortune. He, his wife, and three young sons moved into a three-bedroom house on Curtiswood Circle, a short street of comfortable but modest homes not far from the governor's mansion on Curtiswood Lane. The ex-governor carried heavy life insurance and held a small equity in his new home. Making a living was a necessity for him, and for the moment no political opening appeared. Return to the practice of law was inevitable.

The next four years were a rather dark period in Clement's life. He was frequently saddened and depressed — perhaps at times unreasonably — to find that some fair-weather friends now gave him little attention, thinking that his political prominence and power were now permanently gone. He was too young to suffer uncomplainingly the neglect often enough endured by the old.

He formed a law firm with two former associates, Valerius Sanford and Douglas Fisher. (Robert Clement was not a member of this firm.) He also represented an insurance firm that he helped to form, the American Educational Life Insurance Company, developed by active members of the Church of Christ (the firm has since been dissolved). His law firm dealt principally with civil cases, chiefly with insurance firms and securities dealers, supplemented by occasional practice in criminal cases. It had a sizeable practice among the country musicians who swarmed in Nashville.

The practice of law was decidedly second choice for Clement. Indeed, one of his close associates has said that he was totally disinterested in a career of that kind. But certainly he brought notable talents to the job.

273

(*Top*) Douglas Fisher. Photograph courtesy Mr. Fisher. (*Bottom left*) Valerius Sanford. Photograph courtesy Mr. Sanford. (*Bottom right*) Grant W. Smith. Photograph courtesy Mr. Smith.

He had an extraordinarily quick and tenacious memory. His gift for extempore speaking was nationally known. He had a good mind and a sound legal education, great charm and a fine appearance, and a deep love for human relationships. He was good in acquiring business, where his flair for meeting and making friends was highly valuable to his firm; and he did much of this kind of thing, leaving some of the more uncongenial labors to his uncomplaining partners. He did not like to prepare briefs, and legal research repelled him. He liked court appearances well enough, although he was haunted by the fear of making mistakes, for he had not acquired much courtroom experience in his professional career. He missed the excitement and the adulation of public office.

Clement's former campaign manager, Buford Ellington, was now governor — governor by one of the smallest pluralities in the history of the state. The machine that Ellington had built for Clement, but with his own interests always in mind, was running effectively, as Edmund Orgill had publicly feared it would, when Orgill tried to defeat Ellington and Taylor. The speaker of the House was still James Bomar. The Speaker of the Senate was now William Baird of Lebanon, a power in the Tennessee Municipal League and a friend of Clement as well as of Ellington. But the relations of Ellington and Clement were already strained for various reasons, serious and trivial. Clement thought he had made Ellington; Ellington, for his part, thought he had made Clement, and he felt that Clement had not backed him soon enough in the campaign of 1957–58. It was rumored that Ellington had been miffed because Clement had not moved out of the executive mansion promptly enough. And personality and ideology showed differences between the two. National ambition caused a further rift in Ellington-Clement relations. Jack Norman was beginning to be friendly to Clement, and at the 1960 national Democratic convention Norman backed John Kennedy, while Ellington cemented his growing friendship with Lyndon Johnson. Ellington had planned to keep Clement off of the list of delegates to that convention but was persuaded by Walters and others that this would be a gross and impossible insult. Clement went to the convention, but did not stay at the hotel in Pasadena used by the other delegates. He supported Kennedy, perhaps because he sensed that Kennedy's time had come. It was another stroke that Ellington could not forgive.

To those who were familiar with the dynamism of a Clement administration, Ellington would always seem something of a do-nothing governor. Ellington was deeply conservative; he was temperamentally disinclined to look up new tasks for government. He was thoroughly

averse to new taxation, and he was able to avoid tax issues by the booming economy of the times and the surpluses that Clement's policies had
left for him to use. But in spite of Ellington's cautious views of governmental activity, the trends noticeable in the first two Clement administrations continued without much abatement. Certainly there were no
roll-backs. The number of state employees continued to increase annually, although at a somewhat slower pace. New bond issues were voted
for educational facilities, roads, and other capital investment. Industrial
and urban development continued; local units were authorized to develop industrial parks. A coordinator of elections was established. Steps
were taken to improve the education of mentally retarded children. An
Air Pollution Control Service was established in the Department of
Public Health. Counties were authorized to provide urban-type services. A law to control the price of milk was passed. The Communist
party was outlawed in Tennessee as an immediate and continuing threat
(not a serious one, surely). And the legislature of 1959, pausing momentarily in its thoroughly serious labor, found that ring-tailed coons had
increased in those areas of Gibson County frequented by said ring-tailed
coons, that those areas are patrolled by water moccasins and gallinippers
from May until frost, and, in answer to the prayerful petitions of coon-
hunters in general and those of Gibson County in particular, extended
the benefits of coon dog training to Gibson, Crockett, and Henry counties that had hitherto been accorded elsewhere.

The return of Clement to the political ring was a foregone conclusion, but in what role was still uncertain. It was no secret to Gore or Kefauver that Clement cast speculative glances in their directions, and
Brainard Cheney had carefully studied Clement's chances against Gore.
Clement also thought of taking on Kefauver in 1960, and informed persons have claimed that Ellington made a deal with the *Tennessean* establishment that, if it would soften its opposition to Ellington, Ellington
and Walters would keep Clement from running against Kefauver. Clement, said one observer, "knew that the knife was right there in his ribs."
Whether or not this was the case (and it does not sound in character for
Walters), Clement did not try against Kefauver. The Senate ruled out,
only the governorship remained.

In the early months of 1962, the usual Democratic show took to the
roads. Ellington could not run to succeed himself; the constitutional
changes of 1953 had made self-succession impossible. Nor was he in any
position to pick a candidate, and early in 1962 he stated that he had not

attempted to choose a successor. Becoming governor was a career open to all; the air was shortly full of trial balloons.

The speculations and temptations that now appeared were naturally associated with the continuing factions within the Democratic party. One of those who succumbed to the promptings of ambition was Carl Fry, a federal employee long associated with the Kefauver organization. That organization was split from the start of the race. Fry supposedly had influence among rural voters. Gordon Browning, permanently retired from gubernatorial candidacy but far from retired from activity, was still devoted to the suppression of Clement, and he was said to be exerting pressure on the wealthy M.M. Bullard, a Newport industrialist, to run. McAllen Foutch, a long-time Browning legislative leader, was mentioned by newspapers. George Dempster of Knoxville, once a candidate against Prentice Cooper, and a backer of Kefauver first and Clement second, was put into the race briefly by some of his friends; but he had no staying power. John J. Hooker, Jr., assistant prosecutor of Judge Schoolfield, was eager to flex his running muscles. Hammond Fowler sought Kefauver's support and had to be tactfully discouraged.

In all this complicated jockeying at the starting post, it was increasingly certain that Clement would run again, and he began to collect small newspaper endorsements, even before his official announcement. The campaign of 1962, in its large number of candidates and in the splitting of the Democrats between those candidates and in the steady growth of Republican hopes, was a repetition of the campaign of 1958; it was to be typical of the Democratic primaries during the fifteen years that lay ahead.

The strong possibility that Clement would try for a third term was not entirely acceptable to some individuals in the Clement camp. Tradition in Tennessee had long held that tenure in the governorship should be limited to a few years. Chance at the office should be spread around. It was an attitude quite different from the view held of the United States Senate, to which a man could be sent for term after term, until a Senate seat became almost a vested right. One of those who felt that Clement had been governor long enough was "Rudy" Olgiati, mayor of Chattanooga. Olgiati made his own candidacy official in February 1962.

Olgiati was known as a labor union man; he was a member of the bricklayers' union. He had been born in 1901 in a small Swiss settlement, Gruentli, in the mining country of Grundy County, northwest of Chattanooga. His maternal grandparents had been born in Switzerland. He had attended the schools of Hamilton County and had studied engineering at the Chicago Technical Institute. In 1932 he had begun his political career as superintendent of parks in Chattanooga. After a period of service in the Army Corps of Engineers, he was elected a member of the City Commission of Chattanooga in 1946, and in 1951 he became Chattanooga's mayor. There he was identified with the candidacies of Clement and helped to develop the Clement machine, but even then his own ambitions aroused the suspicion of other Clement backers in Hamilton County.

As mayor of Chattanooga, Olgiati became an influential figure in the Tennessee Municipal League, and he was a prominent spokesman for city officials in their increasing claims to state financial support. Almost simultaneously with his official announcement for the governorship, Olgiati was in Nashville for a meeting of the County Services Association, the lobbying organization for Tennessee's ninety-five counties, where he endorsed a program for the cities and the counties that had been worked out by the Municipal League and the County Services Association. Olgiati had been a member of the committee that developed this program, a program that, in accordance with normal procedure, called for added taxing authority for cities and counties, the equalization of property assessment, state aid for making that assessment, the creation of vocational schools, more technical and scientific programs in college, state loans for local acquisition of waterfront sites, and various public works projects. The program bore the heavy imprint of the Municipal League's restless secretary, Herbert Bingham.

Olgiati had supported Clement in his earlier campaigns, but he now felt, with some bitterness, that Clement and Ellington should allow him his chance. Olgiati's backing of Clement in the past had assured him of Browning's continuing opposition, for Browning was not inclined to forgiveness and forgetfulness. And, as Olgiati had been a backer of Kefauver as well as of Clement, his announcement spelled an end to early attempts to limit competition inside the Kefauver organization, attempts that were no more successful than the attempts of Clement to limit competition inside his own cabinet in 1958.

Early in February a meeting of Kefauver leaders had been convened in Nashville to go over the list of possible candidates. Well-known members of the Kefauver wing of the party were on hand—Browning, of course, M.M. Bullard of Newport, Lucius Burch of Memphis, George Dempster and Max Friedman of Knoxville, and Edmund Orgill of Memphis, erstwhile candidate for governor. But unanimity eluded them.

Neither Fry nor Olgiati was present; both men firmly let it be known that they would not consent to be dumped in any anti-Clement unity move. The meeting broke up, but a committee of twenty members, headed by Barret Ashley of Dyersburg, was organized to continue attempts to melt down the competition. It was all in vain.

With Fry and Olgiati still in the field, another name was now added to the *dramatis personae*; William Farris, public works commissioner of Memphis, decided he would like to move to Nashville. A *Banner* columnist suggested that his ambitions had been fostered by persons attached to Browning and "Tip" Taylor. Farris' candidacy, as it developed, was largely a West Tennessee affair, but it helped to insure the reelection of Clement by splitting the opposition.

March was a month of decisions. Early in the month, the group that the *Banner* satirically dubbed "the Kefauver selection-for-governor committee" met again in Nashville for some futile balloting. The committee dropped Olgiati (an action that Olgiati declined to recognize); Hooker and Fry ran about neck and neck, with a slight edge to Hooker. Dempster expressed the hope that Fry and Olgiati would withdraw, but Dempster's hopes counted for little. The *Banner* averred, reasonably enough, that Kennedy forces were behind Hooker. Hooker was a personal friend of both President Kennedy and his brother, Robert, and he had served as chairman of a national committee of lawyers for Kennedy in 1960.

Kefauver's position was acutely uncomfortable. Fry had been a Kefauver friend. Noble Caudill, a long-time friend of and financial supporter of the senator, was an announced backer of Fry. Early in the month, Kefauver said he was seriously considering backing Hooker, but in the middle of the month, he decided to sit this one out. He announced he would not choose among his friends. This was likely to alienate a maximum number of those friends, but the action never had any effect on his own political fortunes; he was only a few months from sudden death.

Kefauver's neutrality was of some use to Clement. He could never have secured Kefauver's endorsement; they had been at odds too long. But the senator's neutrality freed Kefauver's friends to support Clement, if they wished. Just about a week later, Hooker withdrew, condemning "leap-frog" government in a parting shot against Clement and Ellington.

Farris' own official announcement came in the closing days of March. Some of his programs was laid forth in his statement. He said he would not raise taxes, unless (leaving himself a loophole) absolutely required to do so. He would not, he said, ask repeal of the open shop law, but (giving himself an "on the other hand") he would not veto such an appeal. He favored reapportionment. He did not think segregation would be a major campaign issue (and in this he was quite right.) He declined to surrender his position as a member of the city commission of Memphis, or to take a leave of absence. Farris was a native of Dyer County. Like so many Tennessee public men he had received a bachelor of laws degree from Cumberland University, in 1946, after having graduated from Memphis State. He was at Cumberland just a few years after Clement's two years there. Most of his life had been spent in Memphis. He had been a Browning supporter and had held office in his administration. He had occupied public office in Memphis, as personnel director and as assistant to both Walter Chandler and Edmund Orgill, service that gave him connections to both the Crump and anti-Crump groups. Eventually he had been elected to the Memphis city commission.

While the king-makers and the would-be kings were moving or being pushed around on the Tennessee chessboard, changes were taking place in the personnel of the principal anti-Clement organ, the *Nashville Tennessean*. Silliman Evans, Sr., had died in 1955; his son, Silliman, Jr., who had become his successor as publisher of the paper, had followed him in death in 1961. A second son, Amon (named for Amon Carter, of Texas, close friend of Silliman the elder) had succeeded as publisher of the *Tennessean* and now, in late March 1962, John Seigenthaler became the editor of this formidable newspaper. He had been a reporter with the paper and had been assigned to the famous 400-Club episode that had lit up a moment in the campaign of 1954. He had been associated with Robert Kennedy in the investigation of union activities in Tennessee and had helped Kennedy produce *The Enemy Within,* the book that reported union violence and chicanery of various sorts. In 1961 Seigenthaler had worked in Alabama as the personal representative of President Kennedy.

The mutual rivalry of the *Tennessean* and the *Banner* always assured Clement the opposition of the *Tennessean*. Nothing that Clement could do changed things—no matter how closely his policies followed what the *Tennessean* was assumed to stand for; the morning newspaper generally found means to put an unfavorable light on Clement and his fortunes. The unwary reader could be thoroughly puzzled by the differing versions of affairs served up by the two journals. Only when they unwillingly jibe can one be certain that the unrelenting pressure of fact has forced them into temporary agreement. The *Tennessean*'s list of potential governors in early 1962 reads differently from the *Banner*'s columns. In the morning newspaper Hilton Butler and John R. Long appear as potential candidates, along with Hammond Fowler and William Baird. Names such as these were missing from the *Banner*. As Joe Hatcher of the *Tennessean* put it in January 1962, Frank Clement was "roaming the highways and byways in search of support." He was. What Hatcher did not mention was that Clement was finding that support, and, given the Clement personality, the hunt was thoroughly exhilarating—much better than humdrum law practice.

The Clement formal announcement of candidacy came on February 28 at a press conference staged in Clement's law office in the Third National Bank Building. A few days earlier the former governor had stepped down as board chairman and director of the American Educational Life Insurance Company, saying at that time he anticipated engaging in other activities, hardly very secret by that time. At this time, his younger son, Gary, was a nine-year-old fourth grader at Glendale School in Nashville; Frank, Jr., was in the seventh grade; and Bob was finishing his last year at Hillsboro High School. Mrs. Clement (still faithful to the distasteful demands of politics), the three boys, and Anna Belle were all present as the announcement of candidacy was made. *Newsweek* took note of the Clement candidacy, observing that Clement was now forty-two and his black wavy hair was a little thinner, but that, politically, he towered head and shoulders above all the other candidates.

In his farewell address as governor in 1959, Clement had advocated the repeal of the death penalty, but now in his announcement he said merely that the Assembly should study the question, although, as it turned out, he did try without success to get the penalty repealed.

In earlier campaigns, Clement had promised repeal of the open shop law; now he clearly abandoned all attempts at repeal. Some have thought that Clement became more conservative as time went on, but be that as it may, this particular position was no more than a recognition of the overwhelming sentiment of the legislature. Repeal of the open shop was also given up by the other candidates. Farris was to take that position shortly, and even Olgiati, an acknowledged union man, cast repeal aside.

Clearly labor support was not decisive in Tennessee politics, but it was still valued. Browning had been a disappointment to labor, and labor had turned to Clement. Clement in his turn had not been able to deliver, and some labor leaders would naturally turn to Olgiati. But Clement retained strong friendships in labor ranks, and Olgiati did not have things entirely his own way. It was estimated that the membership of the AFL-CIO in the state numbered about 100,000, a formidable bloc could it have been delivered intact to any one candidate. The State Labor Council had a campaign fund of some $50,000 (no mean sum in those days). Matt Lynch continued to support Clement, while Steve Para and Charles Houk backed Olgiati, and on March 17, labor's Committee on Political Education urged the statewide convention of COPE (the political arm of the AFL-CIO) to endorse Olgiati. Para claimed the vote was unanimous, but even the *Tennessean* reported that this was a spurious last-minute unanimity. Actually, according to the *Tennessean,* the vote was about 27 to 16 in Olgiati's favor.

When the statewide convention of COPE met in April, it did in fact endorse Olgiati, but the vote was anything but unanimous. The vote, taken by voice alone, was ruled by Chairman Steve Para to be two-thirds in the affirmative, but the *Banner* and the *Tennessean* agreed that the "no" shouts were about as loud as the "ayes." These tactics, familiar enough to all students of legislative activities, had been agreed upon by COPE's executive board less than an hour before the convention was to open. Neither Clement nor Farris made any attempt to stop the steamroller, for the endorsement of COPE was admittedly weak, leaving the candidates about where they were before.

In May, Carl Fry withdrew from the campaign, not expectedly and not decisively for the eventual outcome. He was bitterly disappointed— "heart-broken," one friend thought. The *Tennessean* thought that Fry probably had the majority of the anti-Clement votes at the moment of his withdrawal, but that these votes were not enough to win. Fry had failed to get the endorsement of the pro-Kefauver informal committee, that vote going instead to Hooker. Caudill, devoted to Fry, had been unable to win Kefauver's support. Neither Fry nor Olgiati would yield to Hooker. Olgiati had come close to withdrawal, but the COPE endorsement encouraged him to stick it out. Fry's retirement was pushed along by his failure to win newspaper endorsements (they had been going steadily to Clement) and by the slow pace of financial aid. Candidacies wither like late autumn leaves when financial backing does not show up. Fry's experience was typical.

The withdrawal of Fry left Noble Caudill without a candidate. He wrote Kefauver that he did not know Farris and could not support Olgiati, who was too pro-labor to get the financial backing of the businessmen who were Caudill's friends and sources of supply. Caudill began the swing to Clement that resulted in a public announcement of support that Kefauver found "terribly" surprising and "somewhat" shocking.

Truth is, Kefauver must have been seriously upset, and a little time was required before Caudill and Kefauver could work back to something like their old relationships. At one point, Caudill complained that he must have missed Kefauver's signals.

In the meantime Clement was honing his local and state organization. It was an organization built up originally by Clement and Ellington on the remnants of the former McCord machine with the help of old Crump allies. But what looked like leapfrog government, and was so attacked by opponents, actually cloaked some lively antagonism between Clement and his former campaign manager. Ellington announced in the spring of 1962 that he would not endorse any candidate, an announcement that had to be viewed as a repudiation of Clement because the remaining candidates were of course anti-Clement and partially pro-Kefauver. Whatever Ellington's own personal ambitions may have been, he could have expected little help in that quarter. Ellington thus took some risks with his own future. But he did not confine himself to a decision to remain neutral; he warned his top officials that they would have to resign if they intended to take active roles in the upcoming campaign, and he took a sharp public stand against solicitation of state employees. Here he assumed a stance dear to reformers, but one entirely at odds with the long-observed practice of Tennessee state and local campaigns. Possibly his instructions were no more than window-dressing. In any case, no attention was paid to him. The collection went on as before.

Clement had the old and battle-hardened organization to build on. Ellington himself was out of it. Crichton was dead, Jeanne Bodfish had disappeared from state politics, and Eddie Friar had no influence left — although his animosity to Clement was alive and well. James Alexander of McKenzie was made state campaign manager. His residence in West Tennessee could be expected to help in cutting down William Farris in the only section of the state where he was well known. In East Tennessee, the faithful and powerful Herbert Walters could be counted on to bring support from Democrats and Republicans alike. Through May and June the rosters of county organizations were fleshed out with old and new names. Father-in-law Nelson Christianson headed affairs in Houston County. Other familiar names included J.I. Bell, legislator from Hardin County, W.F. Register in Blount, Kirby Matherne in Haywood, Winfield B. Hale, Jr., in Hawkins County, and George Lewis and John Heiskell in Memphis. Supporters not on the county committees included W.L. Barry and earlier supporters, Jared Maddux and James Bomar. One of the most prominent backers, not new to either

Clement or Ellington, was J. Howard Warf, the controversial "boss" of Lewis County. The Jack Normans, Senior and Junior, came into the Clement camp.

New names began to appear, some of them destined to become better known. Franklin Haney developed a Youth-for-Clement movement, a connection that was to result in Frank Clement, Jr., becoming Haney's manager when Haney ran for governor in 1974.

By 1962, the blacks had become more self-consciously active and independent. Negroes accounted for some 200,000 votes in the state. Clearly the black vote was worth considering — more so than the labor vote. Clement's Memphis tours courted the blacks. Clement wrote such black leaders as A.W. Willis, Russell Sugermon, Ben Hooks, J.H. Turner, and H.T. Lockard. The reports fed back to campaign headquarters detail some of the encounters with black voters. "No, sir," said one, when asked if he was an attorney, "I'se just a little ole school teacher. I'se for your man." (Impossible to tell whether the dialect was real, satiric, or merely the repetition of a stereotype.) Said another, according to the optimistic report: "Lordy Mercy, look who is here. Let me shake the hand of the best looking Governor Tennessee ever had." (This one carries the unmistakable ring of truth.)

Black voters had a representative organization in the Tennessee Voters Council, and in June the candidates appeared before the Council, at Fisk University in Nashville, to beseech support. Clement secured the council's endorsement, getting 61 votes to 26 for Olgiati and 11 for Farris. Clement declared that he would be happy to appoint a commission charged with improving race relations, and he stated that he would ask the legislature to study the issue of capital punishment. In the history of Tennessee, whites as well as blacks had been executed, but had there been an "affirmative action" system on execution, the number of black deaths would have been less or the number of whites considerably greater.

The black endorsement had been given somewhat grudgingly. The Reverend Ben Hooks of Memphis, who combined the practice of law with his role as minister of the gospel, said he backed the council's decision but called it a choice among evils. (This somewhat bitter candor did not keep Clement from extending a judicial appointment to Hooks in his third term.) Avon Williams, militant black attorney in Nashville, who was then vice-president of the council, said after the balloting that the council hoped to line up 175,000 to 200,000 blacks for Clement. Clement and his two rivals posed for a picture with A.W. Willis, secretary of the council, Reverend Charles F. Williams, its president, Reverend Frank R. Gordon of East Tennessee, Russell Sugermon, and Avon Williams.

Tennessee's campaign finance laws of that day were completely unrealistic and consistently ignored. The statutes had set some ridiculously low limits for campaign expenditures — hardly enough to buy billboard displays — and no one gave the restrictions the slightest heed. The cost of a campaign for the governorship in those pre-inflation days had been estimated by some persons at about a quarter of a million. But even this was an amount that not all could reach. The burning deserts of Tennessee politics were strewn with the bones of politicians who failed to locate the fiscal waterholes. Big donors were always in short supply and nothing has ever stopped, then or now, the flow of cash from the pockets of the state's jobholders, large and small.

"The Tax Department is being shaken down all around Commissioner Butler." In some such words, Joe Hatcher described the lively solicitation of funds from state employees, all Ellington orders to the contrary notwithstanding. Mr. Hatcher also vented the rumor that Commissioner Butler (one of the original discoverers of Clement and a veteran speechwriter for more than one occupant of the big chair in the Capitol) was already preparing the opening campaign speech for the governor. True or not, it was not unlikely.

Prolonged arm twisting for money from jobholders was hardly necessary. They had reason to think that Clement might well be back, and they would have been recklessly unmindful of their own interest not to have their contributions recorded in the right places. And there is good reason to suppose that many of them would have contributed out of friendship, loyalty, and conviction.

But such things were not left to chance. Whatever Ellington may have said, whether or not Commissioner Butler helped to produce the rain of small change that Hatcher sighted, the official correspondence indicates beyond any doubt that officials high and low collected contributions and kept track of them. Whether reprisals were ever taken against the holdouts cannot be established (doubtless they were few in any case), but it would be folly to suppose that monetary friends were not remembered whenever possible. To one pathetic letter written in 1956 about a reprisal for failure to contribute, the governor's administrative assistant stated: "Governor Clement had always insisted that all election contributions be strictly voluntary and that no employee be fired or denied any of his rights for reasons of not making political contributions." But the letter does not offer much concrete help, and whatever the chief executive's feelings may have been, reprisals could not have been completely prevented.

Money dribbled in from state employees in individually modest amounts, $5 to $25 per person. It came from correctional institutions — prison guards and the like, from highway crews, from the highway patrol, and other sources not always recorded in detail. But tallies were sometimes kept by name. Funds flowed in from other sources, but, as records were not reported, it is impossible to say how much was received or expended. The recorded amounts were seldom large. Contributions of the four-digit order were rare. Contributions of $100 were fairly frequent, and occasional sums of $500 came in. If any free and big spending angels hovered over the campaign trail, they have left no trace in the official records. The *Banner* said that big money, more than the $50,000 originally available, was being spent on Olgiati by labor, according to an unidentified informant (a UFO of journalism). The newspaper said Teamster officials admitted contributing to Olgiati.

According to the rituals of Tennessee campaigns, an official opening is celebrated with a speech on policies long after the campaign is really well under way. The Clement opener was held in Gallatin on June 23; before he spoke, Clement put himself in the proper mood by listening to gospel music. The *Banner* thought the friendly crowd in the courthouse square was one of the largest audiences in the state's political history; estimates ranged from 6,000 to 11,000 persons. Clement referred to the past political associations of Gallatin; to the opening of his 1952 political campaign there, to the birthplace of his mother just across the line in Kentucky, and to the fact that both his grandfather, Will C. Goad of Scottsville, Kentucky, and J.A. Clement of Dickson, Tennessee, had pled cases in Sumner County.

He referred to his spectacular victory of 1954 and noted that the anti-Clement campaign of innuendoes and half-truths was starting up again. Then he listed the earlier promises that he had kept: the improvement in purchasing procedures, the mental health program, the disappearance of political road-building, the lifting of the threat of mortgages on the modest homes of the needy, the one-cent gas tax to cities, the programs for the handicapped and exceptional (that is to say, retarded) children, the tenth month of salaries for teachers, industrial development — an impressive record. He also listed prison reform, although in fact this was one area that Clement never succeeded in reforming. Then he returned to his old formula: ten points in a "program of progress."

As always, Clement's ten points called for more spending; there was

Campaign style that TV killed—the 1962 Gallatin opener. Photograph courtesy Mrs. Lucille Clement.

no mention of the increase in taxation that would inevitably follow and just as inevitably weaken his popularity. Both Clement and his public repeatedly ignored the necessary connection between getting and spending.

Tennessee's number one priority, said the candidate, is education. He promised increases for the teachers. He would secure statewide educational television. He would seek improvement in the retirement system. He denied the allegation coming from his opponents that his past allocation of educational funds from the sales tax has been offset by reductions in other educational revenues. He promised further developments in mental health and care for the retarded, including out-patient clinics. In his third point, he attended to youth and noted that Tennessee was the first state in the South to set up a system for juvenile probation. He promised reorganization of the Department of Corrections so that juvenile rehabilitation would have its separate program.

Then he ticked off proposed benefits for the aged, improvement of public health, the shutdown of poor farms, subsidies for nursing homes, the expansion of grants for the aged and the disabled. Roads were, as always, to be improved. Local governments were to benefit from state aid, with due regard for decentralization. Tourists were to be encouraged (tourists, although the governor did not say so, were, according to an ancient joke, more profitable than cotton and easier to pick), the Game and Fish Commission was to remain independent, and TVA was to be supported. Industrial development was to be boosted. Repeal of the closed shop law was formally and definitely abandoned.

No mention of impending tax increases was allowed to mar this rosy vision of the future. There was no suggestion that the General Assembly might not go along, although in fact the legislature was ripening for the independence it was to regain within the next decade. The ten points were scarcely innovations; it was more of the same, a program of promise with all the major groups touched, from youth to decline.

Now began the hectic round of visits to all corners of the state. The former governor's still striking presence, in spite of a slightly greater girth and somewhat heavier features, was enhanced by white suits and a white Stetson, the political hallmarks of his later years. In these 1962 forays he was often accompanied by his oldest son, Bob, by autumn to be a freshman at UT. Bob's customary role was to read for the audience the list of benefits the particular locality had secured during the preceding Clement incumbencies, a performance that the audience found appealing enough to enable the forty-two-year-old father to say as he did at Dover in July, "As a father I'm naturally pleased for the wonderful reception you've given my son, but on August second, don't forget it's ole Frank that's running for governor." It was a good act, its effectiveness enhanced by the youth and personality of both the Clements. As Lucille suggested to her husband, it spared the father's overworked voice. Family pride was displayed and nurtured in one courthouse square after another.

Clement has always wanted one of his sons to follow him in politics. Robert was the natural choice, for Frank and Gary were too young to be schooled in the trying trade of politics. And Bob—out of both interest and affection—followed his father. His childhood distaste for public attention soon gave way to interest in his father's career, and at an early age he began following his speeches whenever he could tag along.

The pace was as frenetic as always; nothing was neglected. Reports of some representative's visits in April and May give the flavor of the campaign. "Made the usual calls at the courthouse," said the account of a visit to Ripley, "shaking hands with all. Called on officials. [Name withheld], attorney, wants to support FGC along with Sheriff [name withheld], but is opposed to the other faction there. [Name withheld] suggested that Frank make Sheriff [name withheld] his campaign manager. . . . Called on Judge C.S. Carney. (I was impressed with this man. I would suggest everything to be cleared through this man). . . . Send picture of Clement family to Patricia Garrison, 144 Elm Street, Ripley, Tennessee. Teenage girl. My observation of this tour is that the most important to be done is to bring all factions together. They all seem to be for FGC, but state that they cannot go with this and that faction. Very important that this be given top consideration."

Bringing peace to local wars was always a necessary and troublesome task for the state organization. "We sincerely appreciate your efforts to work with the several counties where factional problems exist," wrote Anna Belle in July 1962 to a western county well-wisher. "Please keep us advised and whenever possible, we try hard to take suggestions and work the problems out. As you know, in one or two counties it is almost an impossibility and we must take our chances on doing the best with the situation as it exists. Thanking you for just being our friend, I am. . . ."

While Clement was opening at Gallatin, Olgiati, following the same formula of staging the first official appearance in a small town, took off at Winchester. Farris had already opened his campaign at Lebanon, where he had once lived, as had Clement, as a student. Farris and Olgiati both had trouble outbidding the former and soon-to-be governor, and

Bob, Lucille, Frank Clement—Campaign 1962. Walters in background. Photograph courtesy Bob Clement.

they had to resort to personal attack. Also they had to attack each other, an embarrassment to them both. At Lebanon, Farris declared, "I say in all candor, there is only one opposition to Frank Clement's taking another Cadillac ride to Capitol Hill, and that opposition is William Farris." The reference to the Cadillac was a hopeless beating of a thoroughly dead horse; the Cadillac had been worked for all it was worth eight years earlier, with an astounding lack of success (as the *Tennessean* staff was willing to concede in private). Farris' crowd at Lebanon was small; the *Tennessean* estimated it at between six and seven hundred. Those few hundred may have been as much interested in shade as in speech; shade on that blistering June day was in short supply in the Lebanon central square.

Farris promised to get rid of professional politicians (a wild promise that would cause no second thoughts in the mind of anyone who knew the least thing about political life.) He lumped Clement and Olgiati together, and did not fail to note that Olgiati had been a long-time backer of Clement. In introducing Farris, Alfred T. MacFarland, a former state revenue commissioner, said Farris was unmarred by scandals, "tarnished colonels and bright Cadillacs." Without mentioning names, MacFarland was building up Billie Sol Estes as a political issue. Estes, then in trouble with the law and later to be convicted of fraudulent business operations in Texas, had been one of the ten young men of the country named as "outstanding" the same year that Clement received this accolade. Clement had made Estes one of his colonels, and he and his father had invested money (not very profitably) in some of Estes' business ventures.

Farris allowed that he was in complete sympathy with the program of the Tennessee Education Association (to have been otherwise would have been suicidal), and he said he would make vocational education available for the young people of Tennessee who needed it. He promised to get new industry (nothing new here) and abandoned all hope of repeal of the open shop law. He promised trained professional personnel for the mental health institutions and promised to replace the professional politicians in the correctional institutions. (Here he was offering a genuine improvement, if he could have brought it off.) He promised the passage of a little Hatch Act to assure a genuine merit system in state ranks, again a thoroughly laudable objective, but one without much popular appeal.

Throughout the speech, refusing to abandon hope for a defeat of his old rival, Browning sat on the platform, enduring the 90-degree heat.

He had refused to back Olgiati, for Olgiati's past support of Clement was a barrier he could not surmount. At Winchester, Olgiati faced the problem of reconciling his candidacy with his former support of Clement. The Chattanooga mayor's present opposition was based on his own (quite justifiable) personal ambition, but some noble sentiment is required by political conventions— sentiment that few would bother to believe in private. Olgiati offered the "calloused hands of a former bricklayer to build a greater Tennessee brick by brick." It was not a bad metaphor, if one could forget that bricks had not been felt in the mayor's professional hands for quite a number of years. The candidates' desperate search for appealing issues was as richly disclosed in Olgiati's remarks as in those of Farris and Clement. Olgiati also promised vocational education and industrial development. He likewise wanted qualified people in the field of mental health; neither he nor Farris could deny Clement the credit for having developed mental program. He promised a "balanced" road program; what this could have meant remained unspecified. He offered a balanced labor program, no repeal of the open shop law, an advisory board for welfare, and a professional welfare commissioner, all topped off with a prison rehabilitation program. A major portion of his opening speech was devoted to attacks on Clement. Both he and Farris, although they gave some thought to each other's ruin, seemed from the outset to recognize that Clement was the man to defeat. Olgiati made no mention of Farris at Winchester. He read a telegram from Kefauver promising to vote for Olgiati.

As a footnote to these opening cannonades, Carl Fry announced that he had regained his old job as state executive director of the Agricultural Stabilization and Conservation Committee for Tennessee. Late in June, the voters of Nashville and Davidson County approved the consolidation of the two units, and the *Tennessean* was left free to concentrate on a gubernatorial primary that it had characterized as "lacklustre."

In the stunning sunlight of the Tennessee summer, the campaign now warmed up. A typical day for Clement covered Livingston, Huntsville, Oneida, and Clinton. The next day he reached Maynardville, at 10 A.M., Rutledge at noon, Sneedville at 3 P.M., and Morristown at 7:30 P.M. During his speech in Polk County a small airplane flew over the area dropping leaflets that attacked Clement with crude drawings and vicious comments. Printed on the leaflet were the words: "Remember August Lewis," but Mrs. Lewis and her daughter, Augustine, who were supporting Clement, stood near him during his speech. No part of the state was neglected; no small center, untouched. A large group of country

Anna Belle Clement in 1963. Photograph courtesy Tennessee State Library and Archives.

music stars accompanied Clement in his forays through the state. The once and future governor exuded confidence. When a Shelby Countian told him that she was a neighbor of Farris, Clement replied with a ready wit: "I hope he's a good neighbor, because he is going to be living there for four more years."

The *Tennessean*, freed from its preoccupation with the form of local government in Davidson County, attacked Clement with news stories, editorials, and cartoons. Bissell caricatured the candidate with jet black hair, a gap in a mouthful of big teeth, and thickened lips, a degredation of the features that all of Clement's opponents had perceived as a threat. Tom Little portrayed him tightly wrapped up in taxes, bonded debt, Billie Sol, tape recorders (Clement was said to have had one concealed under his desk), spying, truckweights, shakedowns, broken promises, and Cadillacs. In one cartoon, Clement was pictured as King Frank I sitting on a big bag of dollars, with Billie Sol Estes peeking around the corner. Farris commenced to hit out at both Clement and Olgiati, tying Clement to Estes and Olgiati to Hoffa. Olgiati indignantly denied the connection, but Olgiati never liked to oppose any labor man publicly. Olgiati had in fact never been tied to the Teamsters during all the investigations of the McClellan Committee. Farris tried to picture himself as free from any machine, an honest, independent man on his own.

But it was quite clear to the *Tennessean* and to other observers that the combined efforts of Olgiati and Farris would put Clement in the governor's chair once more, although naturally little of this was aired publicly. In the second week of July, the *Banner* recorded (its glee no doubt tinged with anxiety) that a meeting was held between Olgiati and Farris, evidently in the offices of the *Tennessean*, identified by Olgiati as their host. Olgiati declined to describe what went on at the meeting, but it seems evident that a withdrawal of one of the two was suggested. Neither would budge. The *Banner* alleged that the polls, which showed Clement far in the lead, had led to the abortive session between the two. A week later, Clement observed in Wilson County, relaxing into a humor not typical of his style, that "the publisher later said they were discussing recipes for blueberry pie. I thought that was sweet that they were getting together and I think it's terrible that they've fallen out again."

Toward the end of July, James Hoffa was indicted in Nashville on various federal charges. Brainard Cheney, who once was a member of the Clement staff but who, dissatisfied with Ellington, was now supporting Olgiati, repeatedly attempted without success to get Olgiati to re-

'–I Just Want To Serve You'

Billie Sol Estes peeks over King Frank's money bag; Little, *Tennessean.*

Father and son campaigners, Jackson, Tennessee. Photograph courtesy Bob Clement.

pudiate Hoffa. The *Banner* ran a cartoon showing Olgiati with his hands mixed up in Hoffa's dough; Hoffa was hiding under the kitchen table. As a sidelight on all these goings-on, a widely known former member of Congress, currently running for sheriff in his home county, was arrested on a charge of counterfeiting.

The day of decision was just around the corner when a *Tennessean* newswriter admitted, without saying so specifically, that Clement was the likely choice. Wayne Whitt in the issue for July 28 described the split of the Kefauver organization between Olgiati and Farris, with some of the Kefauver forces moving to Clement. Two years earlier, the organization had turned in a landslide for the senator. Now the district leaders for Kefauver were all like Isaiah's sheep, every one to his own way.

Earlier in this same week, the influential industrialist, Noble Caudill, who with the Nashville banker, Sam Fleming, had long given Kefauver moral, political, and financial support, announced that he would support Clement. Charles Houk, labor backer of Kefauver, had announced that the senator would campaign for Olgiati; he did not do so, although he stated he would vote for the mayor. Orgill of Memphis, closely tied Kefauver for years, was supporting his fellow Memphian, Farris. Gordon Browning had been a Farris man from the beginning. Olgiati could claim the backing of George Dempster of Knoxville, Barret Ashley of Dyersburg, Mrs. Tom Ragland, and Eugene Joyce, the former Oak Ridge law partner of Frank Wilson, a Kefauver manager. The cracks in the Kefauver organization from Shelby County to Sullivan were visible to the naked eye.

On the first of August, the *Tennessean* launched a comprehensive attack on Clement, probing his weaknesses with relentless passion. He was charged with absenteeism. He was said to have increased the number of state employees by 40 percent. Bonded indebtedness had gone up on the order of $5 million. In spite of campaign vows, the sales tax was raised to three cents. The state's insurance business had been handed over to friends, and without regard to promises to conduct state business in a goldfish bowl, insurance awards had been covered up. Clement, said the paper, had parted company with men and women who had served him as campaign managers, treasurers, secretary of state, administrative assistants, and commissioners. He was a bad personnel manager. Much of what the paper said was true — on its face. The other side of the ledger was left unexplored. The voters on the following day again registered their verdict, one that was foreseen in the news report of Wayne Whitt.

"Stay Outa My Kitchen, Boys! I'm Cookin' Up Somethin' Big!"

Olgiati's labor ties lampooned; Knox, *Banner.*

On the morning of August 3, the *Tennessean* reported the nomination of Clement. With 2,428 precincts in, out of a total of 2,687, Clement had a commanding lead, clearly out of reach of either of his rivals. At this time, Clement had 266,204 votes; Olgiati was second with 187,528; and Farris had accumulated 169,869. (Only the day before the *Tennessean* had claimed that Farris was coming up fast.) In the very early returns from rural East Tennessee, Clement and Olgiati had appeared to see-saw; but by the time the first ten boxes were reported, Clement took a lead that he maintained steadily thereafter in the First Congressional District. In the Second he ran behind Olgiati. Farris did badly in East Tennessee; he carried only eight counties in the whole state, including five in Middle Tennessee. He carried Shelby by a plurality, not a majority. In Hamilton he came in third, where Olgiati carried his home county by 21,000 votes to 16,000 for Clement. But Olgiati had only a plurality in his home county; Clement and Farris together had bested him. Clement carried Davidson, but only by a plurality. Knox County gave Olgiati a majority.

Olgiati's strength lay in Hamilton and Knox counties and in the mountains and valleys north, south, and west of Knox. Clement carried the counties, generally, of Upper East Tennessee and great stretches of Middle and West Tennessee, including his own home county and the home county of Gordon Browning, which, in 1954, was the only county that Browning carried. The final official tally stood at:

Clement	309,333
Olgiati	211,812
Farris	202,813

Two unknowns had votes of less than 2,500 each. Four write-ins were recorded — one, in Cumberland County, for General Vogel, chairman of the board of the Tennessee Valley Authority.

Clement had 43 percent of the vote; Olgiati, 29; and Farris, 28. This was a sharp come-down from the overwhelming vote of 1954, but it was a far better showing than Ellington turned out in the three-cornered race of 1958. Majority votes were produced in 45 of the state's 95 counties. Clement had 33 of these majorities; Farris, only 1 (Dyer, where he was born); Olgiati, 11, all of them in East Tennessee. His biggest majority was given in Anderson County, where he had 71 percent of the total vote. The little mountain county of Johnson gave Clement 74 percent, but the record county was Lewis, where Clement had a majority of 76 percent. Lewis was dominated politically by Howard Warf, who was shortly to become a cabinet member in spite of some determined opposition. Clement's home county of Dickson gave him 61 percent of the vote, and his other majorities were rather widely distributed among the three Grand Divisions.

It would not be quite true to say that neither Olgiati nor Farris laid a glove on Clement, but they delivered nothing approaching a knockout. Had it been a two-way race between Clement and either of the other two, conceivably Clement could have lost, but even that possibility is highly doubtful. Some of the vote for Farris was unquestionably as anti-Olgiati as it was anti-Clement. Had Farris not been in the race, Olgiati's pro-labor stance, and his refusal to repudiate Hoffa, would have cost him votes. Clement was only 7 to 8 points short of a majority. But all of this is mere speculation, intriguing but unnecessary. Clement was in. Nonetheless, the narrowness of his margin, compared to 1954, could be seen as a warning. "Fortune, veiled in obscurity" was soon to attack Clement also.

Outside the main tent, the Republicans had again performed in their pitiful little sideshow, with no suggestion of the political victories that lay just ahead in Tennessee history. Hubert Patty had received about 52,000 votes for the nomination for governor, to 12 for someone named Fred Smith, and 36 for General Vogel, who was not a candidate. The Republican primary was held in 29 counties; in the remaining 66 units, the game was called—for lack of a quorum.

The day after the election, Joe Hatcher noted that there had been no major upset in the state. The old "pro's," he thought, were in charge from the upper east to the Mississippi, and he commented that Clement held on to much of the old organization that carried him to victory in 1952 and 1954. The well-oiled engine was tended, in his opinion, by such maintenance men as "Hub" Walters, Howard Warf, Hugh Abercrombie, Jimmy Peeler, and Jim Lanier. In Memphis, Hatcher dutifully glimpsed traces of the old Crump machine in the persons of John Heiskell, John Lewis, and "Buddy" Dwyer. There is little reason to quarrel with Hatcher's assessment in the growing dawn of August 3, but a wry smirk is appropriate for his statement that Clement's victory appeared certain from the start, according to the polls. It was a belated admission.

In the same issue, the editorial page noted the paper's continued opposition to the nominee. "His record, despite his election," read the editorial," has not been a good one. . . . It is hoped for the future progress of Tennessee that his record will improve and that his coming administration will be an enlightened one." History must judge whether this last term would prove to be enlightened, but it must record that the opposition of the morning newspaper continued unabated.

No doubt Clement, the *Tennessean*, and practically everyone else now considered that the contest was over. In fact, a sharp challenge remained. Speculation on the makeup of Clement's new cabinet was well under way when, on October 6, William Anderson opened his bid for governor as an independent candidate with a sharp attack on Clement at Waverly. Independent candidacies are far from uncommon in Tennessee, but they are usually hopeless. Anderson had been considered a possibility before the primary but had not moved. His unexpected independent candidacy had to be interpreted as opposition to Clement's success in August. Anderson was a retired naval commander. He had won the status of an authentic hero by commanding the nuclear-powered submarine, the *Nautilus,* as it made its historic way under the North Pole in 1957. Possibly the dark waters of Tennessee politics presented another dare to the commander.

Anderson's attack on Clement before a crowd of some 500 homefolks (estimates by courtesy of the *Tennessean*) was exceptionally virulent. He accused Clement of shaking down bootleggers, law violators, state employees, and businessmen to finance the most expensive campaign in Tennessee history. The *Tennessean* reported only silence from the audience during ten minutes of the twenty-one minute speech. Applause did come during the last part of the speech, which included a proposed drive to make Tennessee the capital of peaceful atomic development, a dream that had never ceased to stir the state's ambitions since the first devastating drop of the new horror on Hiroshima. Anderson then trotted out the old formula of more industry, more saving by efficiency, and more benefits, including the payment of the prevailing wage on all state contracts.

Independents do not make the grade in Tennessee. When Jim McCord, handicapped by old age but with a good reputation, ran as an independent, he acquired over 136,000 votes, clearly aided by a protest against Ellington. Anderson, however, managed to secure 203,765 votes in November 1962 against Clement's 315,648. The Republican, Patty, rolled up 99,884 after a token campaign, almost double what he had in the sparse Republican primary. Slightly over 1,400 votes threw away their franchises on E.B. "Banana" Bowles, a Knoxville grocer, who was also listed as an independent. Bowles' rather eccentric political career had included some time in the state Senate. The *Banner* said his candidacy was a joke, and Bowles had tried to withdraw.

Altogether Clement had a comfortable majority, but the heavy vote for Anderson and Patty should have been viewed as at least partly a heavy ground swell of opposition to Clement and, perhaps, to Ellington. Patty carried four small counties in East Tennessee, but Anderson carried eight counties in East and Middle Tennessee, including his home county, Humphreys, near Clement's home, and, significantly, Hamilton, Olgiati's base. Clement's margin was uncomfortably thin in several congressional districts. November that year was a portent of troubles to come.

♪ Work, for the night is coming,
Under the sunset skies;
While their bright tints are glowing,
Work, for daylight flies.
Work till the last beam fadeth,
Fadeth to shine no more;
Work while the night is darkening,
When man's work is o'er.

ANNA LOUISE COGHILL, 1836–1907

11. Under the Sunset Skies

THE FINAL TERM

Clement now entered his final term. He and Ellington, in spite of their differences, had been close enough that this third term could be considered part of a continuum in the executive office lasting close to twenty years. Clearly the two men were quite different. Ellington was a conservator — not an innovator — a man who watched expenditures jealously. Clement was a restless although cautious explorer for new worlds, and a spender.

The transition from Ellington's first to Clement's final term was sticky, for many of the original Clement team had served with Ellington and were now returning to Clement, under Ellington's jealously suspicious eye. No formal transition team was named, but certain key figures cautiously and secretly aided Clement, risking their own immediate futures in the uneasy weeks from November to January.

In late November, Clement announced a significant appointment, giving to the press the information that his sister, Anna Belle, would be administrative assistant to the governor. Anna Belle had attended McMurray College in Abilene, Texas, for one year, on a speech scholarship; like her brother, she had studied elocution with Aunt Dockie, and she had placed in state oratorical contests. After that one year in college permitted by the family's resources, she had gone to work. In 1942 she had been employed by the state Tire and Sugar Rationing Board, of the Office of Price Administration, and from 1947 to 1952 she served as a secretary for an automobile firm in Nashville, waiting confidently, to the sceptical amusement of her employers, for her brother's race for the governorship. She had worked in the 1952 campaign as Ellington's secretary, and she served as Ellington's secretary when he was commissioner of agriculture (and dispenser of patronage) during Clement's second term. She acquired skill in the management of people—as president of the Davidson County Women's Club, as vice-president of the Davidson County Young Democrats Club, and as a member of the state Democratic Committee. In childhood she suffered the accidental loss of one of her eyes, but she became a tall and striking woman, abundantly possessed of the charm that was a Clement family trait, and she shared with her brother the ability to make and keep friends. In all the submerged tensions between Ellington and her brother, she remained on good terms with Ellington, and even the *Tennessean*, no friend to her brother, always treated her well, or so she thought, at least. Without any exaggeration of her own capacities, she was able to assure her brother that she could handle the responsibilities he intended to give her.

There was little or no criticism of the appointment, although the influence of her father in Clement's first two administrations had drawn some fire, particularly from Browning, who conveniently forgot his own dependence on his brother, F.L. Browning, whom he used as his administrative assistant. The Tennessee voter does not seem to find an official's use of his family an improper action; if anything, family loyalty is likely to be applauded.

Edward F. (Eddie) Jones was invited to become Clement's press relations representative. Butler had apparently been Clement's first choice for the post, but Butler did not want the job. Jones had been a reporter on the *Nashville Banner*. He was employed by Hilton Butler in 1956 as a public relations officer for the department of safety, where he wrote speeches for Butler and for Clement. He had first met the governor on a personal basis in 1956, although he had encountered him as a reporter before then. Through the influence of Congressman J. Carlton Loser of the Fifth District, Jones spent some time in Washington in congressional staff work, and after that experience came back to Nashville to work for Butler, who by that time had become commissioner of revenue. Jones worked for Clement in the 1962 campaign. In order to do so, he was compelled to resign his post with the state, for Ellington refused to give leaves to employees who wanted to work for Clement. In that campaign, Jones was chief press representative for Clement, and, at Clement's request, he prepared an analysis of the duties appropriate for the chief press relations representative in the governor's office. The guidelines of Jones were adopted and subsequently observed when he became a member of the governor's staff in 1963.

The days of numerous staff agencies in the governor's office were still in the future. In 1963 Anna Belle Clement and Jones were the principal persons in the governor's headquarters. The division of work was not highly formalized, but, in addition to being the principal coordinator of patronage questions, Anna Belle served as staff chief, coordinating the work of the others. Several assistants were given special assignments. One of these was Colonel Billy Shoulders. Roy Nicks served in the governor's office for a time during the third term, and Noble Caudill became an important trouble-shooter for the governor, concerning himself especially, but not exclusively, with the increasingly troublesome questions of racial relations. He became an important political counsellor for the governor.

Douglas Fisher, Clement's law partner during the interim years, became a personal adviser to the governor, principally involved in his old job of analyzing legislation; but he served under a consulting contract, not, as in earlier years, as a state employee. He retained his private legal practice. Mary Smith was the governor's personal secretary, one of the most important posts in the office, as every executive knows.

The whole staff worked harmoniously; there were no major conflicts.

The governor's relations with the press were basically good—as they always had been. Clement was affable. He liked people—even reporters. Press conferences did worry him some, and he and Jones prepared for them carefully, trying to think up the questions that would be asked and working up "spontaneous" answers. The *Tennessean* reporters, Bill Kovach and, later, Larry Daughtrey, naturally gave Clement as hard a time as any opposition could. Fred Travis, veteran representative of the *Chattanooga Times,* was a tough but fair interrogator. Dana Ford Thomas of the *Knoxville New-Sentinel* favored long and complicated questions, and Clement, prompted by Jones, occasionally discombobulated Thomas by simply answering "yes" or "no" to overly lengthy queries. Jones thought the press conferences—about one each month—were not held frequently enough, but the governor disliked conferences when he had nothing new to announce.

The constitutional offices caused no trouble and had no surprises. Joe Carr remained as secretary of state, and the durability of William Snodgrass as comptroller was once more demonstrated. James Alexander,

(*Top*) Clement with his parents and Truman. Photograph Walters Papers, UT Library, Special Collections. (*Bottom*) Democratic history—Jim Nance Mc-Cord, Frank Clement, Prentice Cooper, UT, Nov. 21, 1964. Photograph courtesy UT Library, Special Collections.

who had managed the Clement campaign, became the state treasurer. Clement always reposed complete confidence in his cabinet. Each commissioner was expected to run his department with a minimum of interference or supervision. They did not meet often as a body. The choosing of the cabinet for the final term followed well-established patterns. The new term brought few new faces, but announcements came more slowly than in the earlier terms. Clement had repeatedly emphasized in his earlier terms that he had sought men and women for the cabinet, not vice versa, but there was no lack of candidates for cabinet posts in the third term. Cabinet technicians included Commissioner of Public Health Hutcheson and Commissioner Baker in Mental Health—holdovers from earlier years. Some deputy commissioners—such as Joe Johnson—were primarily technicians, even if skilled in human relations as well. Political considerations for appointment remained paramount at the top levels in the departments of corrections, revenue, highways, and agriculture, although experience had provided most of these commissioners with expertise in administration as well as in political affairs.

In the middle of December, Clement announced the proposed appointment of Howard Warf, the powerful political leader and superintendent of schools of Lewis County, as commissioner of education. The appointment aroused clearly expressed opposition from educators, who saw Warf as a "boss" not entirely acceptable to professionals. But Warf had strong claims on Clement's attention. Although he had wanted a cabinet post in the earlier years, when Clement had passed him over in favor of Quill Cope, Warf had swallowed his disappointment and had continued to work for Clement and Ellington. In the 1962 primary, Lewis County gave Clement his highest county majority. Ellington, who also had reason to feel grateful to Warf, actually appointed Warf to the education post before Clement took the oath, since Commissioner Joe Morgan, following a line of succession that became common in the state, left his cabinet position as Ellington's commissioner of education to take the presidency of Austin Peay College at Clarksville.

W.F. Moss remained in the cabinet as commissioner of agriculture, a holdover from Ellington. Early in January, Keith Hampton, who had been corrections commissioner for Ellington, was named commissioner of personnel. Hampton had always been one of the most political of politicians; his appointment indicated clearly that the technical considerations leading to such persons as Boling and Snodgrass would not be followed in the department of personnel. Hilton Butler, in great measure the discoverer of Clement, the old backer of Jim McCord and foe of

Browning, moved into the slot of safety commissioner from his Ellington job as comissioner of revenue. He had grown tired of Revenue.

Harry S. Avery was named commissioner of corrections. He was a member of a political family of Alamo, the brother of J.B. Avery, Sr., who had been named to the state Court of Appeals by Clement in an earlier administration. Harry Avery had been a member of the Assembly and of the constitutional convention of 1953. He had worked with the Board of Fire Underwriters. Prison reform and the betterment of prison life was a cherished ambition of the governor, but the area was one that friendly observers saw an an area of failure. One of the reasons for the failure, according to these commentators, was the lack of professionalization in prison administration. Apparently Clement did not realize that prison reform could not be attained under old-style political direction.

The incoming governor was able to persuade Noble Caudill to accept the post of commissioner of welfare, temporarily, and with the promise of giving him one of his best young men as his assistant. Roy Nicks (then only twenty-six, and without political experience) was sent to that post, and from there succeeded Caudill as commissioner after Caudill had fulfilled his promise of short-term occupancy.

Early in December, long before the cabinet was complete, the governor-elect announced his choices for speakers of the two houses of the Assembly. He backed James Bomar for speaker of the Senate and W.L. Barry, a youthful member of the legislature from Henderson and Madison counties, as speaker of the House. The governor was not entirely a free agent in making these selections, and indeed even this early the approaching independence of the legislature might have been detected by the discerning. Barry had been a floor leader in the House for Ellington. A protegé of James Bomar, he had campaigned for the post of speaker for 1963; he had only one rival, Alan O'Brien of Springfield, who was handicapped by injuries received in a recent fire. Clement and Barry were acquainted, but had not been, and never became, intimate friends. Clement might have had difficulty passing Barry over, but there is no indication that he ever thought of doing so. The two cooperated effectively.

David Givens of Somerville became the floor leader in the House. He had begun his legislative career in 1956 and had known the governor slightly in the second term. Givens had not sought the job as floor leader. He was approached on the subject by Speaker Barry, and having shown interest he was selected to serve as floor leader in the sessions of 1963, 1965, and 1967, after Ellington had returned as governor. James

Cummings, once a Browning leader, also served as a floor leader in 1963.

Legislative methods in 1963 were similar to those of the past. Plans for action were laid in morning meetings in the governor's office, although Clement was not always present. The speakers and the floor leaders were assisted by Secretary of State Carr and by Douglas Fisher, together with the commissioners whose departments were concerned in the proposals being considered. The group worked hard; it had a virtual veto over all proposals, unless the governor was already committed.

As the roster of the cabinet was gradually filled out, the General Assembly convened. The next four years were to be important in legislative history, for important tax issues were to arise, the issue of reapportionment had to be met once more since the reluctant moves of the Ellington years failed to satisfy the federal courts, and in the last two years of the four an independent legislature began to emerge.

Ellington had often been characterized both by friends and enemies, as a do-nothing governor. Probably the comment was not unknown to him, for on January 10, he appeared before a joint session of the General Assembly to provide the legislators with a final report on his administration. It was a recital of achievements, with some nods of recognition to problem areas. He observed that the department of corrections had been plagued with low morale, failure to control some inmates, and irregularities in some institutions. He claimed that corrective measures had been taken. He also acknowledged that a recent audit had shown that not all was well in the department of revenue and said that he and Commissioner Butler had taken remedial measures. Then he listed (the usual recital) the increased expenditures for education, including capital investment, new mental health facilities over the state, the first steps to medical care for older persons, a new state park, the expansion of industry, and the maintenance of a working capital of $25 million that had been turned over to him at the end of Governor Clement's second term. And he said, prophetically, in closing: "Thank you—and undoubtedly I will have the opportunity to see you again."

The inauguration took place on January 15, in temperatures that were hovering around twenty degrees above zero. The past inauguration address of Clement, in the opinion of the *Tennessean*, had been in a lengthy, "rug-chewing evangelistic style," but the paper said Clement had promised to keep the 1963 inauguration remarks within ten minutes. Ellington led off, with a brief statement in which he claimed for himself an effort do to the very best he knew how to do. The Clement inaugural statement had been prepared by Joe Henry. Clement had called him on a

Sunday morning and asked him for speech to be delivered the following day. Henry wrote a proposed speech and sent it to the governor, without consulting further with him. The speech as delivered by the new governor was not calculated to make Ellington happy, for, although Clement did not mention Ellington, he gave the impression that the administration he was succeeding had been coasting. In characteristically florid words, Clement said: "Time is a river of passing events. The challenge we face in Tennessee lies in an acute realization that today is tomorrow's past, and floating gently down the placid waters of the flowing river of complacency and contentment leads only to the landing dock of a fool's paradise." "There must be," the new executive claimed, "a constant movement toward a higher, and nobler and better way of life."

It was a good summary of the Clement philosophy, but the words were gall to Ellington. The break between Clement and Ellington was deepened by the speech and its philosophy; it was never healed. Ellington spent the next four years partly in private employment with the L&N Railroad (a surprising association considering his past ties to the truckers) and partly in the national government under his old friend, Lyndon Johnson (until Mrs. Ellington and her husband both found Johnson's personal and administrative style insupportable); but Ellington's undercurrent of opposition to Clement, clearly enough known to professional politicians, was never to abate.

Clement's philosophy called for expanded programs and expenditures. The budget appeared before the Assembly on January 22; it set a record with its proposed expenditures of $1.2 billion. Reaction to the budget, since this was the giving stage, was generally favorable, but the comments made by legislators to newspaper reporters were subdued by the shadow of higher taxation. The budget called for an increase in expenditure of $61 million over a two-year period, an amount not covered by the existing tax structure. The budget message was filled with vigorous demands and earnest promises. "The most precious resources of our state are its human resources," the governor announced, with the old oratorical ring in full-throated operation. Public education was the state's most expensive undertaking, but one of the best investments that could be made. Noting the shift of rural population to the cities, the governor recommended the establishment of a system of area vocational and technical schools, "to offer training to high-school drop-outs, to high school graduates and to adults as well." He recommended the establishment at the University of Tennessee of an Industrial Research Advisory Service, a scheme clearly modeled on the long established Mu-

(*Top*) Friends and cornerstones — Clement and Andy Holt, UT, Nov. 27, 1965.
(*Bottom*) Commencement, UT, June 2, 1963. Photographs courtesy UT.

nicipal Technical Advisory Service and one reminiscent of the efforts of universities such as those in North Carolina and Kentucky to furnish a climate that would attract industry. He proposed the creation of an Aerospace Engineering Institute at Tullahoma to offer doctorates in the program of the University of Tennessee.

And then he turned to the public schools: a fifty-cent per child increase in textbook appropriations (he had started the free text program back in his first term); substantial increases in the operation and maintenance and supply of instructional material of schools, new classrooms and other school buildings, and a two-step raise for teachers, to a total of $900 for each teacher during the biennium. But there was a sour note on teachers' salaries; the governor noted that since the beginning of the foundation program in 1947, there remained 32 school systems in 18 counties that had appropriated no additional funds for teacher pay. The state was carrying the added burden for about one-fifth of the state's area, presumably areas where in truth the property tax could not manage a great deal more, although the governor did not say so.

Education was, as usual, to get the big slice, but highways were to be accorded an increase, and the governor proposed that the maximum monthly welfare check be raised from $55 to $65. The increase for welfare would amount to slightly less than $2 million, compared to over $72 million for education. An increase in the number of highway patrolmen was suggested, and public health and mental health were to share in the upgrading. Clement offered no large new revenue grants to local governments, but he recommended, as they wanted him to, an expansion of their authority to impose taxes on their own.

The governor forecast added prison and correctional facilities, and he suggested that the legislature reconsider the death penalty, although he said he would submit no bill. He was beginning to feel the burden of the clemency power: "I have had," he said, "the unforgettable experience of standing at the last road of possible detour from the electric chair for eight condemned human beings, and subsequently of watching the clock tick away the lives of six of them."

Departing from themes that carried heavy costs, the governor recommended the creation of an office of executive secretary of the Supreme Court, the enactment of the Uniform Commercial Code, the establishment of a special law revision commission, with an adequate staff. Then he moved on to the necessity of new revenue, but for the moment he withheld the grim details.

Eddie Jones, quite justifiably thinking the Clement proposals were in line with the governmental theories of the opposition newspaper, showed details of the budget, even before Clement's speech, to Bill Kovach, reporter for the *Tennessean*, and asked him for support. Kovach saw nothing unreasonable in the suggestion and put the issue up to his supervisors, but he had to return to Jones with the word that the paper would continue in opposition to Clement, notwithstanding the character of the budget proposals.

Since expanded benefits were hardly controversial, it was evident that the principal struggle in the legislature would be over the ways of paying the bill. The expanded budget had been the result, not only of Clement's own political philosophy, but of the intense pressures brought to bear on him. Expectations and demands were constantly rising, fuelled in part by an inflation that was steady, although not yet galloping. The legislature itself was pushed hard by the lobbies, particularly the education establishment — the TEA and the universities — and the local governments represented by the Tennessee Municipal League and the County Services Association. The floors of the legislature were still open to nonmembers, and TEA representatives packed the hallways and flowed onto the floor of the legislative chambers themselves.

The choices among revenue sources were severely circumscribed. The personal graduated income tax had been ruled unconstitutional many years before, and the tax was given no consideration. The whole idea of the income tax was highly unpopular with voters. The general sales tax had already been raised in Clement's second administration from two to three cents; neither the public nor the Assembly were yet ready for a higher rate. All that was left was a broadening of the sales tax. One week after the budget message, the governor let the tax shoe drop. "Mr. Speaker," read the letter from the governor's office, "I am directed by the Governor to transmit to you a message in writing. Secretary, Mary Smith."

The chief clerk of the House read the message to the members; in slightly less than three pages the governor put the painfully inevitable before the reluctant solons. The revenue proposals contained in the message included a broadened base for the sales tax — on utilities (water, electricity, gas, telephone), for an estimated yield of $8.25 million; on laundering and drycleaning, a $990,000 charge on keeping clean; and on repairs on tangible personal property, for another $4.5 million. After the local units received their cuts of this increase, the yield to the state could account for $12,640,000. Then came the nibbles, although they were big enough to be felt: increased taxes on cigarettes and distilled spirits and a rise in the excise tax, topped off with a doubled charge on drivers licenses and an increase in the cost of motor vehicle license plates.

No new ground was plowed up. The general sales tax still carried the principal burden, business was hit through the excise tax, the appetites for liquor and cigarettes still looked inviting, and the motorist was asked to shoulder some smallish added loads. The tax structure of the state had been regressive; it was to remain so.

The outcry was prompt; the euphoria of the expanded budget was stifled. The *Tennessean*, without, naturally, offering any alternatives, promptly attached a high taxes tag to the governor. Its cartoonists for months thereafter pictured Clement in a checked suit marked with the words, "Sales Tax." Sales was printed "$ales." At one of the well-attended struggles in the UT stadium between Kentucky and Tennessee, for possession of the elusive pigskin, when Clement tried to introduce the governor of Kentucky to the fans, he was resoundingly "booed"; close friends thought the derision was a result of the tax proposal. The public attitude on that occasion was a harsh, and accurate, augury of the future.

The Tennessee Valley Authority, devoted to the low electricity rates that always seemed more important than flood control and navigation, took an official position against a sales tax on electricity; the Clement opposition had a rare and valued opportunity to treat the governor as anti-TVA. In those days, before the rate increases of the late 1970s, a pro-TVA stance was essential for a governor. Governor Clement had taken occasion to mix with President Eisenhower over the Dixon-Yates controversy concerning TVA and had generally pictured himself as friendly to the huge Authority, as indeed he probably was.

Clement had faced what other tax-raising governors had always faced: limited sources. It is true that the truckers could have been hit again; they were not, although Senator Hobart Atkins, Republican of Knox County, assayed a futile move in that direction. But adverse criticism and opposition by other legislators was largely untempered by suggestions for other means of raising revenue, although some of the opposition tried to pass some of the new burdens for teacher pay on to the localities. Both procedurally and logically, the broadened tax was tied to the big appropriation measures — the general education bill and the general appropriation bill. The *Tennessean* claimed that Clement strategy was to pass the appropriation bills first and the tax measures later. But actually both tax and spending bills passed through the Assembly in a tie-up that was clear to everyone. Pressure was not needed on appropria-

'Ain't Nobody Against Us But the People'

Clement is pictured as laying violating hands on the sacred TVA; Little, *Tennessean.*

tions; it was applied vigorously on the tax bills. In the end both taxing and spending were approved.

The appropriation bills were passed quickly and overwhelmingly. A four-hour public hearing was held on the education appropriation bill; no opposition appeared. After fifteen minutes of consideration, the Senate, in the middle of February, passed a general education bill, the initial appropriation for education, for $370 million by a vote of 33 to 0. A short while later the Senate passed the general appropriations bill with like unanimity. The full membership of the Senate approved. One day later, the House passed the general education bill by 95 to 0 (the House has 99 members). One week later the House passed the general appropriations bill by 93 to 3. Passage of bills by large majorities, once compromises have been made, is by not means unusual, even in highly independent legislatures, and spending bills, where everyone gets something, are likely to be popular. But what was not significant, perhaps, was the speed with which the decisions were taken.

The overwhelming adoption of the spending bills made some kind of tax increase inevitable, and it is difficult to see how legislators expected to raise the money except through the sales tax. Nevertheless the passage of the tax bills was difficult, and the governor had to marshall all his persuasive weaponry. A temporary failure of nerve within the cabinet itself was countered by a dramatic confrontation between the governor and his cabinet at the mansion on Curtiswood Lane, where Clement, refusing to turn back, shamed his followers into line by a carefully planned and professionally staged show. A phalanx of executive troops stormed the legislative chambers. The *Tennessean* cataloged the pressure activities of Howard Warf, Keith Hampton, Bill Litchford (the peripatetic and more-or-less self-appointed troubleshooter for governors), Joe Carr, Labor Commissioner Bill Parham, Harlan Mathews, Commissioner of Revenue Don King, William Snodgrass, Greg O'Rear (the huge man who headed the highway patrol), and "Sonny" Humphreys (the popular president of Memphis State). Reluctant senators, said Joe Hatcher, were standing on the governor's plush carpets listening to lectures on patronage. True or not, the account sounds convincing. The administration had its way, but not without some "squeakers." The administration was supposedly strong in the Senate, but some of the Senate votes were so close that the House contest was delayed for a week. In the end, the administration carried the House comfortably.

Party lines meant little in the decision. Some Republicans voted for the taxes; some against. Some of those who voted against the added taxes represented poor counties, but patterns were obscure. Among the twenty-one Democratic votes in the House against the principal sales tax bill were substantial numbers from the metropolitan counties, and the adverse vote included persons like John Peay, Louis Pride, and M.T. Puckett, who were among the group that shortly began the struggle for an independent legislature. Throughout the voting in the House, "Mr. Jim" — the veteran legislator from Cannon County, James Cummings — led the majority as one amendment after another was firmly laid to rest on the table. Mr. Jim had a habit of being on the winning side.

Another hot potato — reapportionment — was now thrust upon the attention of the Assembly, and, necessarily, upon the governor. The issue had been building up for years. The eastern portion of the state — the heartland of Republicanism — had been underrepresented for decades, and the metropolitan areas, all of them, were more and more clearly the object of discrimination as they grew through the continual flight from Tennessee farms. Gerrymandering was fairly common, such as the coupling of Republican Henderson County with Democratic Madison in West Tennessee. Tennessee's normally Democratic governors were aided to office by rural machines, and their control of the Assembly had been exercised through rural blocs. Mr. Jim's favorable assessment of Clement had been conditioned by his judgment that Clement had always been fair to the smaller counties.

Governors were loathe to tinker with the system that had nurtured them. As Clement once said, in a rare burst of humor, the whole issue reminded him of a poem he saw in a volume entitled *Ruthless Rhymes for Heartless Homes:*

Little Willie, with all his sashes,
Fell in the fire and was burned to ashes.
By and by the room grew chilly,
No one wanted to stir up Willie.

In his first two administrations, Clement resisted attempts to force him into a stand in favor of reapportionment. Pressured to call special sessions to deal with the matter, he refused, quite properly saying that the Assembly had clearly shown it would do nothing, whether in regular or special session. Critics of the governor could point to his inaction, but a political realist would have to admit that he was powerless. Even the gesture that Clement made by asking for a study of the matter by the Legislative Council was voted down. The legislature would not act.

In Tennessee, the Republicans have always had their chance at power when the Democrats split. East Tennessee Republicans now forged an alliance with big city Democrats, particularly in Davidson and Shelby counties, and tried their luck in the courts. Chancellor Steele in Davidson County (originally appointed by Clement) held the legislative apportionment in violation of the state constitution and ordered a remedy; he was overruled by the state Supreme Court, which took the view, then almost universally held, that no judicial remedy was available. Action was now started in the federal district court, which began by holding that no judicial remedy was available, but when the appeal reached the Supreme Court of the United States, that body, in the epoch case of *Baker* v. *Carr,* reversed past holdings and held that the federal courts could take jurisdiction. The case triggered a massive restructuring of state legislative bodies and a rearrangement of congressional districts within the states throughout the country.

In the ensuing resistance to this and subsequent decisions, Governor Ellington had called the legislature into special session in May 1962 to reapportion legislative seats. This session put in motion the machinery for the call of a constitutional convention to consider reapportionment and other matters, and it passed a reapportionment act that remedied some inequities. That act failed to receive federal court approval; the judges called it a crazy quilt, unexplainable in terms of geography or demography. The plan was allowed for the 1963 General Assembly with which Clement was now dealing, but further reapportionment was called for. So the session of 1963 was put back in front of the drawing board.

The federal district court, which supervised the reapportionment activity of the General Assembly, had intimated that it might agree to a plan if at least one house of the legislature was reasonably consonant with the distribution of people; but the 1963 session failed even this test. The act was challenged, and the court adopted the proposals of the challengers, throwing out the work of the 1963 legislative session. Meanwhile challenges to reapportionments in other states has led to a decision in the United States Supreme Court that *both* houses of legislatures had to be districted on the basis of population, and in June 1964 the federal court with jurisdiction over Tennessee ordered reapportionment of both houses on a population basis not later than June 1, 1965.

This time the governor called a special session for 1965. This session also dealt with congressional seats. The reluctance of the rural forces to face the reapportionment issue was sometimes backed by business spokesman who feared labor union influence in the large cities. Clement signed the 1965 legislative reapportionment on May 28, 1965, but it was to take several more attempts by the Assembly before it was held in compliance with the fundamental law both of Tennessee and of the United States.

Governor Clement continued his agonizing appraisal of the death sentence. For three decades the number of executions had been dropping; the figure stood at 47 in the years between 1930 and 1939; in the next ten years, 37 people took that last walk to the chair; in the next ten, only 10 were executed; in 1960, 1 only, and then the parade of condemned men was halted for some twenty years. As it turned out, the switch was never thrown during the remainder of Clement's life.

The governor had come to disbelieve in the capital sentence. He refrained, however, from legislative arm-twisting, and, perhaps partly because of his abstention, the Assembly maintained the sentence as a part of the law. It is far from certain, however, that any amount of executive pressure could have changed things. David Givens, the administration floor leader, had made it clear to Clement that he could not agree to repeal of the penalty, and Clement had told him to vote his convictions. Representative Charles Galbreath, of Davidson, introduced a bill to abolish the penalty and publicly called for the governor's endorsement. In late March, Clement gave the endorsement, and the bill was promptly reported out of committee, only to meet a resounding defeat on the House floor, 60 to 29. At that time, four men sat on death row, and other death sentences were pending before the state Supreme Court. On March 26, after the legislators had gone home, Clement announced that he would grant stays of execution for the four men until the federal courts had ruled on an appeal by a convicted rapist, Clayton Dawson. The governor's statement was announced just thirteen days before black, nineteen-year old Freddie Green of Memphis was scheduled to die for murder. Dawson had appealed on the ground that the statute under which he had been convicted had been enacted by a malapportioned and therefore unconstitutional legislature. At the time of the stay, the governor was quoted as saying that when the courts had acted he would obey his oath of office and enforce the law.

In addition to passing the controversial tax measures, the General Assembly of 1963 ground out myriad statutes designed to implement the welfare and humanitarian policies of the state and to tighten fiscal and administrative practices. The names of floor leaders Givens and Cummings, Maddux and Flippen appeared on one administration bill after another as they swept through the busy Assembly. Without fundamentally altering the judicial structure, the Assembly puts its approval on judicial improvements that Clement had promised. Research assistants were provided for judges of the Supreme Court. An Advisory Commission on the Administration of Justice was authorized. Salaries of lower court judges were raised. An Executive Secretary to the Supreme Court was established. A Law Revision Commission was created. A retirement system for judges and attorneys general was authorized. The Uniform Commercial Code was adopted. A Police Training Institute was created.

Again fulfilling a campaign pledge, the governor sponsored a statute creating an alcoholism commission in the Department of Mental Health. A re-education center for emotionally disturbed children was established. The State Board of Education was authorized to develop a statewide system of area vocational-technical schools. The powers of the comptroller of the treasury were enhanced. State agencies were required to report to him any shortages of money or other acts of malfeasance. He was empowered to inspect and examine books and to summon witnesses, a power to be shared with the commissioner of revenue. The comptroller was authorized to conduct audits of any governmental entity when he thought it necessary. An Office of Local Government was created under the comptroller and a Local Government Advisory Commission was established.

Developments in the field of higher education were wide-ranging. The promised Space Institute of the University of Tennessee was authorized, to be located at Tullahoma. A student loan scheme, to be administered by the Tennessee Education Loan Corporation, was created and a board of directors named. The Industry-Government-Law Center was established in the University of Tennessee. A statewide system of educational television was authorized.

Continuing a trend started with the earlier changing of the name of Memphis State College to Memphis State University, the legislature now lifted East Tennessee State College to the status of a university. Hitherto, the legislature had left the internal structure of universities largely to their own boards. The creation of the Center for Industry-Law-Government and of the Space Institute represented something of a move away from autonomy. The Center was justified as a means of channeling administrative requests from the governor himself — but it is highly doubtful whether the idea came from the governor — and the action put one added bureaucracy between the governor and the working intellectuals of the faculty.

Legislation created a Staff Division for Industrial Development in the governor's office and transferred to it the functions relating to industrial expansion that had been lodged in the Department of Conservation and Commerce; a tendency to enlarge the governor's office was begun. The same tendencies were at work here that had led to the burgeoning of the executive office of the President of the United States — with results that were not always satisfying.

The local units got substantially what they wanted when the Assembly authorized them to impose local sales taxes, after popular referenda. Bingham had persuaded the governor to tack this authorization onto the broadened sales tax base, so as to avoid the opposition of the metropolitan press.

On some matters the legislature balked. The old issue of increasing the truck weight allowance was raised; this time the truckers lost. A bill to repeal the price-fixing on liquor was defeated. Proposals to provide for a run-off in races for the governor were never allowed to get to the floor. On March 22, about two and one-half months after it convened, the legislature went home, accompanied by the usual sighs of relief across the state. "Good riddance," said the *Tennessean*. The *Knoxville News-Sentinel* summed up the session in sour words, saying the whole effort was a sorry one: "Like most of its predecessors, this one wasted a terrific amount of time and tax-payer money. On the average it worked a three-day week, and it deliberated and debated on very few issues." The *Chattanooga Times* remarked the continued deterioration of state government. Its rival, the *News-Free Press,* dubbed the legislature, "the handmaiden of the governor." The *Memphis Commercial Appeal* and the *Press-Scimitar* united in their poor view of legislative performance.

Newspaper — and public — dissatisfaction with the Assembly was nothing new in Tennessee affairs; it was the normal reaction to the tensions and frustrations of a legislative session. In years past, some Kentucky wit, noting that the Kentucky constitution required the legislature to meet not less than once in two years for no more than sixty days, had suggested that it would be better if the body got together not more than once in sixty years for no more than two days. The same feeling was prevalent in Tennessee — and had been for some time. It is not easy to see why the public was dissatisfied, except on one or two points. People evidently thought the legislature ought to do more debating, and it ought to be independent. It was supposed to be a deliberative body; therefore, let it do more deliberating. How could it be independent and deliberative, and at the same time so hasty?

A few members of the legislature agreed with the papers. Some sixteen members of the House and Senate, forming a group to work for a more independent Assembly in 1965, elected Senator Cartter Patten of Chattanooga and Representative John Peay of Clarksville co-chairmen. Senator Tom Shriver, generally thought of as friendly to Governor Clement, was made chairman for Middle Tennessee. The group advocated a cut-off date for the introduction of bills, the setting of daily calendars at least three days in advance, annual sessions, permanent offices, and the election of members of the Legislative Council by the members of the legislature. Eventually, most of these things were to come to pass; in 1977, the Legislative Council was abolished, but in the meantime the legislature did become independent, and the first evidence of the crumbling power of the governor was to surface in the Assembly's next session in 1965.

Before the legislature had adjourned, Rudy Olgiati was defeated for mayor of Chattanooga, and his political career was brought to an end.

In May, the governor named his father as special temporary judge of the Supreme Court for the second time.

In the interim between the sessions of 1963 and 1965, Governor Clement was faced with both crises and opportunities. Fights for control of the local Democratic organizations and the Young Democratic Clubs continued through 1963. A city election in Memphis was interpreted as a defeat for Clement. The sudden death of Estes Kefauver eliminated from Tennessee politics a souce of opposition to Clement and led him into the two defeats for the Senate that marked the end of his political career. The growing militancy of blacks gave him trouble but led him to make changes in state policy. Trouble in the prisons faced him with difficulties that disturbed him, but for which no solutions were ever found. Strikes plagued him during 1963.

In the immediate aftermath of the initial desegregation decisions, Clement had turned his back on massive resistance as a tactic. His action should have earned him the gratitude of the blacks, and to some extent it did. Clement received black support in subsequent campaigns, but more than one black gave that support grudgingly, openly labeling Clement the lesser of the evils they faced. Clement was a sensitive man, and he probably felt that his cautious, but politically expensive approaches to justice for Negroes were ill rewarded. In fact, it was all he could have reasonably expected. The Negroes of the United States, having broken the pattern of "separate but equal," have never shown any sign, in the ensuing years, of being satisfied. During Clement's last administration they vigorously and often militantly pushed for added recognition of their needs, and their cause was brought repeatedly to Clement's attention by close advisers in his own intimate circle.

In the early sixties the blacks sought the desegregation of public facilities such as motels and restaurants. They prosecuted their quest by seeking favorable legislation and, at the same time, by direct action of various sorts. Legislation was attempted at both state and federal levels; the introduction and enactment of federal civil rights legislation produced reactions in state politics. All through the country, marches and "sit-ins" demanded the opening of restaurants and motels to black patrons. White sympathizers aided the Negro cause, and, in some cities, owners gave in—sometimes voluntarily. A few places had practiced some desegregation in the fifties. One such was the Allen House in Nashville. Another was the Mountain View in Gatlinburg; in the middle fifties it was accepting black guests in conventions held in the off season. By the early sixties, desegregation was gaining acceptance; in the early summer of 1963, the majority of the Nashville hotels, motels, and restaurants agreed to desegregate.

School segregation was gradually breaking up during the Ellington administration. Although Ellington had declared himself a dedicated segregationist, the settlement of the issue was left to the local authorities, as Clement has advocated. Chattanooga and Hamilton County had desegregated in 1962. This desegregation was made under court order, and court actions continued as some blacks were dissatisfied with the pace of change. Some systems desegregated voluntarily, as in Putnam, White, Overton, and Clay counties. Late in 1962 the state School for the Blind started to admit blacks. Violence largely subsided, although the threat of disturbance still hung over certain areas, particularly in the southwest area of the state. Nevertheless, the pace of school desegregation was slow.

On September 30, 1963, Governor Clement signed an order establishing a commission on human relations, although the commission was not activated until the following January. He assigned the commission the task of encouraging and promoting fair and equal treatment and opportunity for all persons, of conducting research and making reports, and of coordinating and assisting local governmental agencies on human relations. The powers of the commission were broad but vague, typical of many governmental agencies operating in areas where public acceptance is not sure, and its members did not always agree on program and personnel. Clement named twenty-one members to the board. The chairman was Reverend Sam R. Dodson, Jr. (white); the vice-chairman, A.W. Willis (black). The commission included Chancellor Madison Sarratt of Vanderbilt; Labor Commissioner W.H. Parham; Personnel Commissioner Keith Hampton; Reverend Ben Hooks of Memphis, a black minister and lawyer; labor leader Matthew Lynch; Education Commissioner Howard Warf; Edward Boling, who had now become a vice president of the University of Tennessee; Commissioner Mrs. C. Frank Scott; and Commissioner Harlan Mathews. The roster was a mixture of public officials and private leaders, black and white. A.W. Willis and Ben Hooks had both been very active in the Tennessee Voters' Council, the leading political organization for blacks, and both had been active in the 1962 election. It was inevitable that the commission members, many of them, would not be content with mere coordination, study, and research. They would want more power and quicker results.

President Kennedy was murdered in November 1963. Lyndon Johnson, now President, promptly began the push for civil rights that was to be one of the most striking policies of his administration. Voting by blacks had already been reinforced and was to spread; what was now at issue was jobs and open accommodation, public and private. The federal Civil Rights Act of 1964 had as its main thrust the requirement for desegregation of public accommodations and the prohibition of racial discrimination in employment. The Tennessee Commission on Human Relations took a public position in favor of the federal act while it was under consideration, and it proposed for Tennessee a code of fair practices, based on similar codes that began to appear in other states. The commission asked the governor to sign the code.

Barring passage of legislation by the General Assembly, the governor could have done little about the desegregation of private establishments, but he could have influenced the employment and contract policies of the states. The governor was pressured to participate in the battle over the passage of the federal act of 1964. As this issue coincided with his first campaign for the United States Senate, he found himself in a predicament. His own feelings seem to have been ambivalent. In any event, he refused to sign the proposed code, and the refusal cost him some of the support of the blacks. In 1965 he was to take further steps to improve their employment by the state.

The state was plagued by prison trouble during 1963 and 1964. Inmates escaped from some of the juvenile detention institutions, and in 1964 a revolt broke out in the prison at Petros. The governor knew that improvement was needed in the prisons, but he thought almost entirely in the terms of physical facilities. He never found it possible to put professionals in charge of the prisons, if indeed he was conscious of the need. In the meantime as the population of the state grew, so also grew the number of prisoners. In 1953, 896 persons were received by the prisons from the courts. By 1967, when Clement left office, this figure was 1,313, an increase of 47 percent. In 1967, Tennessee prisons housed 2,980 inmates, compared to 2,474 in 1953. The burden had grown, although as yet not intolerably.

Politically, 1964 was a busy year. The governor made his first unsuccessful try for the Senate of the United States. The national presidential nominating conventions were held that summer. As governor, Clement was again in control of the Tennessee Democratic delegation. This time a few blacks were included in the delegation, but otherwise nothing of any great importance transpired, for the restless Texan, Lyndon Johnson, had the nomination firmly packaged and delivered.

The August primary of 1964 had seen Clement's first defeat for public office. Ross Bass became the Democratic nominee for the Senate seat that had been briefly occupied by Herbert Walters, following Kefauver's death. In the general election, Bass defeated Howard Baker, Jr. The governor's enemies sensed a decline in the Clement name and image, and they and others who could not be considered persistent enemies of the governor saw an unusual opportunity to forward their own ambitions. The natural arena for these ambitions was the 1965 session of the General Assembly. The initial battle would be joined over the election of the speakers.

James Bomar had decided to withdraw from the legislature. He would not, therefore, continue as Speaker of the Senate, although, legally, the Senate can select a non-member as Speaker. William Barry announced his candidacy for a second term in the House post. A temporary flurry among House members on behalf of M.T. Puckett subsided with Puckett's withdrawal (under intense pressure, according to the *Tennessean*), and Barry was left without rivals. Clement should have acted quickly to cinch the election of Jared Maddux who wanted to return as Speaker of the Senate, but for some reason he delayed. Before he got around to supporting Maddux, Frank Gorrell of Nashville announced, and the battle was on. The consequences for the governor were to be dramatic and fateful.

When the legislature convened on January 4, it was evident that the senatorial contest would be vigorous, with the outcome uncertain. The governor's prestige, following his defeat by Bass, was endangered. Pressure was applied on behalf of Maddux, in a fight that was uphill all the way. Gorrell had the promise of backing from twelve of the twenty-five Democratic senators, and, for the moment the Republicans stood aside, watching the Democrats fight it out. Gorrell was also counting on the support of Senator Charles O'Brien of Shelby County; the *Tennessean* claimed that the twelve, plus O'Brien, had given public pledges to Gorrell.

As the Democrats caucused on January 4, to nominate a candidate for the speakership, Senator O'Brien disappeared. He did not show up for the tally; as a result, Gorrell and Maddux were locked in a tie, 12 votes each. The vote disclosed little recognizable pattern. East Tennessee was represented mainly by Republicans, who watched the Democratic squabbling with an eye to their own gain. Senator Ray of Sullivan, a county that had often spoiled East Tennessee Republican purity, sided with Maddux. The Shelby delegation split, an event unthinkable in Crump's day. Hamilton and Davidson counties, which furnished some of the important members of the group pushing for legislative independence, went with Gorrell, showing some evidence of that rivalry between the metropolitan areas and the rest of the state that has influenced some legislation contests in the 1960s and 1970s.

Senator O'Brien remained absent, presumably ill and under a doctor's care. The deadlock continued—day after day. The Senate could not organize, and the legislature remained idle. Talk of a compromise candidate arose, and Maddux approached Gorrell to get his agreement on a third party. Gorrell refused to budge. Toward the end of the hectic week, Senator O'Brien withdrew from Gorrell's cause and gave his support to the idea of a compromise candidate.

Senator O'Brien's action helped the Clement forces to push the choice of the Speaker out of the hands of the Democratic caucus onto the floor of the Senate, where a deal with the Republicans could give victory to Maddux and the Clement allies. The Clement faction, as their *quid pro quo,* agreed to give the Republicans more places in the county election commissions. Traditionally, Republicans in Tennessee had a chance at power only when the majority party factional fights came to actual splits in the party. Through all the constant tinkering with the structure of the state and local election commissions, while the Democratic factions struggled for supremacy, the Republicans had been relegated to a minority position, even in those counties that normally went Republican. Now, this was to be altered with a structure that was to last from 1965 to the Blanton administration of the middle seventies.

Clement and his backers agreed, in return for Republican support of Maddux, to give Republicans a majority on the election commissions of those counties that went Republican in the presidential elections. The bargain was made—and carried out. Maddux became the Speaker, and the Republicans subsequently got their election commissioners. On the floor of the Senate, seven of the eight Republicans voted for Maddux; only Senator Hobart Atkins of Knox County abstained, for reasons that were not noted. Senator Fred Berry, Republican of Knox, explained his vote by saying that he had secured a promise that "my party and the people of Knox County would in all things be treated fairly."

The *Tennessean* editorialized indignantly about this "last shameful episode of the Clement administration" and stated that people would not "soon forget the shock and disgust of this historic occasion." The truth is that the pople as a whole were, as usual, rather uninformed, not too much interested, and likely to forget the whole thing in a hurry. The quarrels of politicians almost always seem more important to them than to the voters. Senator Gorrell became a Clement supporter before the end of Clement's political career, which, indeed, had only two more years to run. Gorrell backers were even given some committee chairmanships shortly after the Senate was organized.

The Senate finally fitted with a Speaker, the legislature was ready to do business; as usual, one of the most crucial items was the budget. The governor, continuing the tradition of expanded spending and expanded services, brought in a record biennial budget, calling for an expenditure of $240 million more than in the preceding biennium. The two major items of expenditure, as always, were highways and education, but mental health, corrections, and public welfare also received major chunks of money. New levels of operation were forecast for almost every department. Clement said his proposals would raise teacher salaries to a new minimum of $4,100 in the second year of the biennium. He also forecast the completion of the vocational schools that he had promised in the 1962 campaign, and that had been started in 1963.

The governor's money bills were passed with the usual overwhelming celerity. It took approximately one month to carry the appropriations through the legislature, but there was no serious fight. No new sweeping tax proposals disturbed the prevailing harmony. Authorized indebtedness leaped: $20.5 million for state institutions of learning, $47 million for highways, $9 million for prisons, $4.5 million for parks and recreation, $9 million for mental health.

But the governor did not always have his own way; and some observers thought he was less attentive to legislative relations than he had been in past years, although he had always been more attentive to individual legislators than Ellington managed to be. Both Ellington and Clement had become increasingly reluctant to enforce the death penalty, and now, in 1965, Clement made one last try to get the penalty suppressed. This time he went before the House and in an emotional appeal asked for the removal of this terrible burden from his shoulders—in vain. The Senate voted to abolish the punishment, but the House would not go along. In that chamber, the bill was tabled by 48 to 47. Speaker Barry voted to table; Ray Blanton, who in later years as governor refused to enforce the penalty, voted against tabling.

But Clement, and after him Ellington, found grounds to stay sentences and neither ever allowed another individual to go to death. In 1965, Clement commuted the sentences of five men, condemned for crimes of rape, murder, rape attempt and murder, and murder during robbery. In 1978, four of these men were still in prison; one was out on parole.

The governor attempted to secure the passage of a mild minimum wage bill; he lost. The House passed the bill 47 to 46, but this was less than the majority required by the constitution. The governor's close advisers, Noble Caudill and Roy Nicks, had wanted the legislation, and many of Clement's usual opponents voted for it, but the rural bloc, generally on Clement's side, would have none of it.

The Assembly passed a bill designed to raise the price of milk. Clement vetoed it, and the veto stuck, although the Assembly members had been entertained by the provision of a dairy bar on the eighth floor of the Hermitage. For those who did not like milk with their cheese and crackers, beer was available.

A proposed repeal of the liquor price-fixing law died. The truckers lost another bid to increase the weight of the vehicles that were already pounding the roads apart. A bill to provide primary run-offs to put an end to plurality governors never escaped the deadly clutches of the Local Government Committee. Death by suffocation by committee was also meted out to a strip mining reclamation bill and automobile inspection. Some improvements in workmen's compensation were enacted. A weak lobbying registration act was passed. Auto graveyards were restricted (not to be noticeably enforced in the years that followed).

The legislature continued to raise the status of the institutions that had once been normal schools. Middle Tennessee State College and Tennessee Polytechnic were crowned universities. In the meantime the process of creating two-year community colleges, begun in Ellington's first administration, was continued.

The legislature was remarkable for the return of blacks to membership in a decade when, in the country as a whole, blacks were seeking to assert their rights by both violent and nonviolent action. A.W. Willis of Shelby County became the first black legislator since Reconstruction days.

The media accorded the Assembly its usual dubious marks. In a feature story, the *Tennessean,* recounting the triumphs and a considerable number of failures, stated that the "third House" — the lobbyists — enjoyed a field day; the story mentioned the manufacturers, the Farm Bureau, the soft drink bottlers, the dairy interests, meat interests, and hotel-motel operators. Said Charles Galbreath, "Everybody has a lobby up here but the public."

The legislature, having gone home, was called back into special session by the governor to deal with reapportionment once more. In the interval between the regular and special sessions, Aunt Dockie Weems died. She was seventy when she succumbed to a heart attack at home in Dickson, on April 15, 1965. Her effect on her nephew's career had been decisive; he himself stated his deep conviction that his speaking ability had made him governor.

The General Assembly came back into special session on May 10, 1965, to have another try at reapportionment. Pressured by the courts, the Assembly could no longer maintain the old power relationships. But it tried. The congressional redistricting that emerged from the conference between House and Senate committees and that was enacted into law showed a population variation from a low of 341,468 people in the Sixth District (Democratic country) to a high of 453,298 in the Second (Republican terrain). The Sixth stretched along the Highland Rim to the north, west, and south of Nashville. It was to become acquainted with Republicans in the future, not yet even dimly seen. The Second was solid in its Republicanism; since the Civil War, no Democrat has ever succeeded there. The First, another fortress of Republican power, was left with 441,516 people. The Third, where Republicans and Democrats fight it out, was awarded 415,385. The metropolitan areas were isolated as much as feasible. Davidson County, with its 399,743 people, made up the Fifth District.

Not everything could be made safe for the Democrats. Knox County Democrats had to be abandoned to the Republicans of the Second District. The Democrats of Sullivan could not be divorced from their Republican neighbors. Toward the west, Henry County was put in the Eighth District, causing the *Tennessean* to ponder the chance of a Republican victor in the Seventh, and the splitting off of the suburbs of Memphis from the central city would add potential Republican voters to the neighboring districts.

An opposition bloc of some thirty House members fought the conference committee report, backing a minority plan developed by Senator Hobart Atkins, who had been one of the litigants in *Baker* v. *Carr*. The opposition was made up principally of members from the metropolitan counties, both Republican and Democrat. Their efforts were consistently beaten to the ground by a majority representing the old rural bloc that had so long dominated the state legislature. In the Senate, a nucleus of 12 senators—2 Republicans and 10 Democrats—mostly metropolitans, fought the majority plan, and as that majority had only one vote to spare in the Senate, the future end of rural domination could now be glimpsed.

The majority also passed a reapportionment of the Assembly, and in the process they divided the urban counties into districts (although the constitution of the state then quite clearly outlawed such a division); in 1966 that portion of the act was invalidated by the Tennessee Supreme Court. Once more the minority opposition was based on metropolitan memberships. In the Senate, two Republicans and five Democrats vainly opposed the steamroller. But once again, the end of rural domination was foretold, in spite of this last victory.

Joe Hatcher saw in the deeds of the special session the imprint of Clement's fingers. But, almost certainly the legislature would have come up with these results whether the governor aided or abetted. Hatcher also saw a continuing deal between Clement and the Republicans; there is little evidence to support such a view. Hatcher from now on referred frequently to the Clement-Republican combine, and this line may have damaged Clement in the Senate race that lay ahead in 1966.

In November a three-judge federal court (Miller, Phillips, and Gray) defenstrated the congressional redistricting law—but only in spirit. They held the act unconstitutional, although they declined to issue an immediate remedy, indicating that the redistricted 1967 legislature should have a chance to measure up by improving on the unconstitutional realignment. The judges appeared to assume that the reapportioned legislature might behave itself, but that in any case it should be given a chance. As a matter of fact, the legislature did not act as the court felt it should, and eventually the court imposed its own scheme of congressional reapportionment. It was all part of a decade or so of a court-legislature tug of war. Earlier that same month, the same court but somewhat different judges (that time, Miller, Boyd, and Weick) had approved the legislative redistricting act (although the 1970 census would require further adjustment).

Meanwhile the reapportionment battle, seemingly endless, moved to a new arena, one prepared in the Ellington administration. In 1962 a special session of the Assembly had been convened following the decision in *Baker* v. *Carr*. The special session cranked up the machinery for another constitutional convention, designed to do what it could to save the rural bloc. The convention membership itself was based on the maldistribution of seats in the old legislature. This convention — the call having been issued by popular vote — convened in July 1965. By that time, the Supreme Court of the United States had decisively ruled that *both* houses of the state legislatures had to be based on population. The convention provided that apportionment should be based on population, with a stipulation that it could be based on something else, provided the Supreme Court changed its mind or had its mind changed, but, knowing this to be unlikely, the convention went on to other affairs. Among other things, it provided that counties could be split into districts for representatives and senators, thus validating what the earlier special session had already approved. The voters approved this arrangement in 1966, undoing what the state high court disallowed a few weeks earlier. Suburbanites were thus allowed to vote against the central cities, and Republican chances were somewhat strengthened. Clement's noncommittal speech to the convention was seen by some political observers as a sign of his coming candidacy for the Senate.

Two groups — labor and the blacks — occupied the attention of the governor and his aides in the final years of the Clement administration. For blacks, the setting had shifted some since the early days of Clement's career. When the governor had first come to office, blacks were still politically subservient. Equal — or unequal — separation was the rule. The slow arrival of school desegregation and other changes had created a now different climate. The governor was called upon to respond to demands that grew increasingly insistent. Tennessee was caught up again in the racial violence of the time.

In 1963 and 1964, Clement made cautious approaches to the involvement of Negroes in his administrative family. Blacks were included in the 1964 slate of delegates to the national Democratic convention. At Clement's suggestion, without doubt, Keith Hampton, commissioner of personnel, had instituted a survey in 1963 of black employment in state offices. Clement was gesturing in the direction of civil rights, but he made few dramatic moves, and aggressive black leaders expressed disappointment. As 1965 wore on, the governor intensified his efforts to hire blacks, pushed to these actions by the gentle insistence of Noble Caudill, who, having transferred to the governor some of the strong loyalty he had given Kefauver, had become briefly his commissioner of public welfare, then state treasurer, and now a special assistant to the governor. The departments were asked for reports on black employment, and a kind of "affirmative action" program began, quite aside from any pressure from the national government.

Caudill sent frequent memoranda to his chief, making suggestions and providing detailed reports. "Harlan Mathews and I," he wrote in early April 1965, "met with the Negro leaders, Russell Sugerman [sic] and A.W. Willis, Tuesday afternoon, April 5, and brought them up to date on what we are doing on economic opportunity." The two black leaders, politically powerful in Shelby County, felt—and Caudill and Mathews agreed—that blacks should be put on the highway patrol. The four agreed that some special effort had to be made to recruit blacks for all departments. The blacks wanted some kind of commission established by executive order to help find solutions to black difficulties; the memorandum was vague as to expectations. Blacks still wanted a code of fair practices. They wanted greater state pressure on local school desegregation. They wanted—and the two white officials seemed to agree —more black judicial appointments. And they wanted blacks on some elections commissions.

Although Noble Caudill was quite aware of the political implications of his proposals ("I do not get the feeling yet that we are really reaching the people," he once wrote the governor), he exhibited a genuine sympathy for the needs of Negroes, and he kept shoving the governor into satisfying those needs. The question of a black judge was kept on the front burner. Late in April 1965 Caudill advised the governor that Ben Hooks of Shelby County was keenly interested in a judgeship—either in a probate or in a criminal court. The blacks were not interested, Caudill said, in the circuit courts, which in the larger circuits dealt entirely with civil issues. For blacks, the action was in the probate and the criminal courts. A.W. Willis supported Hooks, and Caudill passed on to the governor the startling suggestion that Clement name Avon Williams to a judgeship. Williams had become increasingly demanding, and his relationships with Clement were touchy. But he, along with Hooks and

(*Top*) Mr. Speaker Barry. Photograph courtesy Mr. Barry. (*Bottom left*) Devoted adviser—Noble Caudill. Photograph courtesy Mr. Caudill. (*Bottom right*) Manager and Treasurer—James Alexander. Photograph courtesy Tennessee State Library and Archives.

Willis, had supported Clement in the past, although often with well suppressed enthusiasm, for Clement would never move as far and as fast as they would have liked.

In the end, Clement appointed Reverend Hooks (who was a minister as well as a lawyer) to the judgeship of the Criminal Court, Division Four of Shelby County, the first black ever to fill that post. Clement had always studied his judicial appointments with great care and had always moved after consultation with the local bar, but in this case he acted without that advice. This by itself occasioned a local tempest of short duration, for the bar had began to consider consultation a vested right. The appointment was apparently a good one, and the bar shortly acquiesced. Quite clearly the appointment was politically motivated, for the governor still contemplated a race for the Senate, but most judicial appointments in the United States are at least partly political. Public and private motivations were always mixed together in the governor's actions. He was always a political man. In later years Hooks became a member of the Federal Communications Commission and later executive director of the NAACP.

The appointment of blacks to the state bureaucracy did not move rapidly, and Caudill kept pressing the matter through 1964, 1965, and 1966. The usual obstacles were encountered. Blacks had difficulty in passing the examinations for the highway patrol. They had trouble getting adequate backing for business ventures, and the governor's staff tried to help in this area. In 1966 the governor ordered an increase in the number of black members of draft boards.

Civil rights demonstrations were staged in West Tennessee in 1965 and 1966, centering in the counties north and east of Memphis. Blacks were pressing, particularly in Haywood, Hardeman, and Tipton counties, for betterment in their situations with respect to schools, voting, service in restaurants, admission to swimming pools, and improvement in employment. Local leaders and forces were accompanied by participants from outside the state who were regarded widely as outside agitators by local whites. Some violence erupted, although never at the pitch reached in Birmingham and other Alabama communities. The dangers in the western communities occupied the governor and his staff during the last two years of Clement's time in office, but no final solution was ever attained. Controversy continued, although violence subsided.

Labor difficulties continued to plague the administration. In his second term, the governor had participated in the settlement of a long and bitter strike of the L&N railroad. Now, in his final term, a lengthy and

Clement and future voters. Photograph courtesy Tennessee State Library and Archives.

Bolivian visit—At San Andres University, La Paz, 1955; UT party chief
Robert S. Avery at extreme right. Photograph courtesy UT Library, Special
Collections.

violent labor dispute between the Teamsters and the Murray Ohio Manufacturing plant was staged in Lawrenceburg. On labor disputes, as in desegregation cases, the governor's policy had been to stay neutral as far as he could and to leave maintenance of law and order to local officials. But when local disputes got out of hand, the governor could not avoid intervention, and this proved to be the case in Lawrenceburg.

In December 1964 the National Labor Relations Board conducted a referendum in the Murray Ohio plant (which manufactured bicycles) to select a bargaining agent, a certification coveted by the Teamster local. The Teamsters lost. Thereafter, they filed eight objections to the election with the NLRB; five of these were disallowed by the regional board, upheld later by the national board. A further hearing was ordered on the remaining three points. On March 3, 1965, shortly after the order was issued calling for the hearing, mass picket lines were set up at the plant to prevent the majority of the employees from entering for work. The local chancery court by injunction limited the number of pickets, prohibited mass picketing, intimidation, and violence. The injunction was disregarded. From March 3 to April 12 the plant was closed; not even officers or supervisors were permitted to enter.

By April 12 the situation was so tense that the sheriff of Lawrence County and the vice-mayor of Lawrenceburg called on Governor Clement for aid, and Clement directed the highway patrol, under the direction of Greg O'Rear, to enter the town and enforce order. O'Rear was no novice in such affairs; he had led the highway patrol into Clinton in the segregation crisis of the preceding decade.

O'Rear's brother was involved in the picketing; Lawrenceburg was O'Rear's home town. When the brother, a man almost as huge as Greg himself, attempted to cross the line set up the troopers in a confrontation with the pickets, he, on O'Rear's specific orders, was arrested, along with other pickets. The two brothers had been much attached to each other, and it is said that, when the arrest was made, Greg O'Rear turned his head to the wall and burst into violent weeping.

The plant reopened; on April 23, a press release from the governor's office stated that the patrol would shortly be withdrawn. A meeting between the governor and both sides to the dispute had led to an agreement to maintain order. Mass picketing was dropped. The governor's actions received widespread commendation from the business community, but a number of labor unions expressed opposition. Clement went into his final election contest with that disapproval hanging over him.

The first election success of the governor, back in 1952, had been aided

Greg O'Rear in consultation, Lawrenceburg, 1965. Photograph courtesy
Tennessee State Library and Archives.

Picket line—Lawrenceburg, 1965. Photograph courtesy Tennessee State Library and Archives.

by Browning's mistake in allowing his friends to arrange a profitable business deal with the state. Browning and his friends had followed what was all too clearly the established practice in state contracting. Clement himself was now caught up in a tide of newspaper criticism dealing with the same sort of practice. This time it was insurance. The opposition press obtained lists of dealers who did business with the state, and it was not hard to discover a close correlation between these firms and the backers of the Clement faction in the Democratic party. It was not exactly a new custom that was here disclosed, but it was not a feature of government that could be praised. All the same, defenders of the practice, including Joe Carr, said openly that, since insurance rates were standard over the state, rewarding one's friends was a time-honored and defensible practice. The public received this further lesson in civics without much excitement.

The last year of Clement's term was marked by his final campaign for the national Senate, and the likelihood of that campaign undoubtedly influenced his policies as governor. Aside from this election, probably the most important single action of 1966 was the calling of the special session of that year to deal with the tax structure and to arrange for a disposition of the surplus that had accumulated as the result of past taxes and a booming economy.

The tax problem was an old one—the discriminatory taxation of railroads. Assessments for the general property tax were in the hands of locally elected assessors, who undervalued real property to degrees that varied dramatically from county to county. The assessment of utilities, on the other hand, lay with the Public Service Commission, which tended to keep their values closer to actuality. Inevitably, the railroads were victimized, and at last, the two principal lines, the Southern and the L&N, turned to the courts—federal and state. The railroads won their cases; some adjustments were now essential. Once again the judiciary had compelled the executive and legislative branches to acknowledge an abuse, an abuse they never had the will to deal with on their own.

The distribution of the state's surplus by the special session of 1966 gave one more twist to the strained relations between Clement and Ellington. The fiscal policies of Clement during his second term had provided Ellington with a comfortable surplus that he could use to continue the expansion of services between 1959 and 1963. In Clement's last term he decided to spend his own surplus rather than leave it to his successor. That successor turned out to be Ellington again, although in the spring of 1966 when the special session took place, Clement could not have known that John J. Hooker, Jr., or someone else, would not be governor. Certainly Hooker thought he would be the choice. Ellington's narrow margin of victory in 1958 could not fail to give his opponents hope. Perhaps, therefore, we cannot attribute Clement's call for the special session as a deliberate sabotage of Ellington, although it is reasonably certain that such a thought, however vagrant, must have flitted through his astute mind. We can be sure that his distribution of the surplus was related to his intention to have another try at the Senate seat once occupied by Estes Kefauver. And Clement was no man to leave money lying around unspent; he still had things he wanted to do.

On March 1, 1966, the governor issued his call for the special session to begin on March 14 to consider a constitutional amendment to allow property tax classification and to dispose of a surplus expected to reach $25 million. Actually, the surplus turned out to be $37 million, counting $20 million still to come. He asked the lawmakers to hike teacher pay, to expand welfare and mental health programs, and to put additional money into highways. Nothing revolutionary; just more of the same. That the governor expected trouble was evident in his opening oratorical blast. "Let the political winds howl; let the election year storm rage," he said, baring his head to the tempest. "Let us . . . do those things which should be done."

Dividing the multi-million dollar melon took eighteen days. In the end the administration again dominated the legislature, although more was allocated to teacher retirement than Clement had proposed. Teacher retirement netted $3,200,000, another $6.6 million went for a $250 annual pay hike for teachers, and higher education faculty obtained $1.8 million. Mental health got a boost of $4.1 million, and highway construction received $9 million. The minimum pay of low-paid state employees was lifted with $3.2 million and another $3.2 million was set aside to improve the welfare benefits of 80,000 Tennesseans. New aerial mapping of property for improved assessment was allocated $1.6 million, and $4.3 million was set aside for debt retirement. A loan fund of $900,000 was set up to aid cities and counties that might encounter distress as the result of the decision to stop discrimination against railroads.

The legislature turned down the governor's request for a constitutional amendment to permit the classification of property for taxation and the development of a general homestead exemption. It did propose a constitutional amendment for homestead exemption for the elderly. But

Municipal power—Signing act for industrial building bonds. (Left to right) Herbert Bingham, Clay McCarley, Edward Lindsey, Willis Maddox, William Baird, John R. Long. Photograph courtesy Tennessee State Library and Archives.

the furor over constitutional amendment was thoroughly futile. No constitutional amendment has ever passed by the route the legislature took, not since 1870, for the majorities required for approval of the legislative proposals by referenda were impossibly high.

While the special session was busy dividing up the surplus, John J. Hooker, Jr., was preparing his first candidacy for the governorship. (He had considered trying in 1958, but the time was not ripe.) As Ellington was to be a candidate, Hooker had little choice except to appear as candidate opposed to the Clement-Ellington faction; it was not his first appearance in opposition to that faction. His campaign made something of the charge against "leap-frog" government, but without effect, for Ellington secured the nomination, riding still on the old organization first built in the early fifties on the remnants of the McCord machine.

Clement had not favored Ellington for a second term. Ellington had studiously neglected to extend courtesies to Clement during his first term, and Clement felt the slight. Clement was interested in seeing the singer, Eddie Arnold, a close friend, run for the governorship and even approached him on the matter, but Arnold preferred musical approval to the uncertainties of politics.

In the years immediately before the campaign of 1966, Ellington had been in Washington, as head of the Office of Emergency Planning, where he had been placed by Lyndon Johnson, whose presidential ambitions Ellington had supported for years. Serving Johnson was no sinecure; he was demanding on the attentions of Ellington in ways that became insupportable. It is reported by friends of Ellington that he determined to seek the governorship as a means of withdrawal from proximity to a domineering President. In the opinion of many, he came back to Tennessee a changed man, having acquired some of the arrogance of Johnson. He was absent from the state as the General Assembly gradually turned to an attitude of independence of the executive, and he came back to a legislative situation new to his experience. The attitude of independence was to increase substantially in the Assembly, as Ellington's final term went on.

Contrary to the situation in the "squeaker" of 1958, Ellington defeated Hooker decisively in a two-way race in August 1966. Hooker narrowly carried Shelby County, and a band of counties roughly on the western, southern, and eastern edges of the Highland Rim and the Cumberland Plateau. He lost all the other metropolitan counties. East Tennessee gave its counties primarily to Ellington, no doubt an expression of Ellington's alliance with the Republicans that was to be so fateful for Frank Clement. In the general election of November, Ellington carried every county in the state; the Republican party was completely disorganized as to the governorship. Its strength was concentrated on the Senate race, where Clement suffered his final political disaster.

♪ *For the tide is swiftly flowing*
And I long to greet the blest,
Where the wicked cease from troubling
And the weary are at rest.

HUBERT P. MAIN
in J.R. Graves, *The Little Seraph*
(Memphis; Southern Baptist
Publication Society, 1874), 66–67

12. For the Tide Is Swiftly Flowing

CAMPAIGNS FOR THE SENATE

"O Fortune, variable as the moon, always dost thou wax and wane." So the medieval poem, the *Carmina Burana,* celebrates the reversals of destiny. In two years Clement, toward the end of his short life, suffered devastating defeats at the hand of an unpredictable and fickle electorate.

In the early morning hours of August 10, 1963, the thinly stretched aorta of Estes Kefauver burst; in a few moments he was dead. He had been taken to the hospital in preparation for heart surgery, but, according to reports, the operation had been delayed to permit Nancy Kefauver to get there. She reached her husband's side too late to see him alive.

Kefauver's death precipitated an immediate crisis in Tennessee politics. His organization had always been a loose one, appropriate to Kefauver's own personality and campaign style. His followers were a heterogeneous mixture of old-fashioned populists, international do-gooders, and vigorous proponents of the welfare state. There was no heir apparent; there never had been. Like other Tennessee politicians, Kefauver tried to stay out of other people's races, but there were times when the demands of friendship compelled him to support, however reluctantly, candidates who had worked for him. This was the case with Olgiati and should have been the case, by the compulsions of gratitude, with Browning.

For Clement the sudden opening of a Senate seat presented a two-fold opportunity: he could name a temporary successor, and he could become a candidate in the next general election for the two years remaining in Kefauver's term. Back in 1952, flushed with the victory of that summer, many of the young people around Clement had looked forward with some confidence to the moment when he could be chosen President of the United States. They paid small heed to the difficulties faced by any candidate from a small and relatively weak one-party state. Clement was too bright not to realize that his chances at the top spot were limited, but he could reasonably hope for election to the Senate. Indeed a governor has no place else to go by the electoral route; election to the national House would be a comedown. Clement had seriously considered running for the Senate from time to time. Kefauver and Gore had both worried about Clement's mounting popularity and his evident ambition. But for various reasons, Clement never came to the point of challenging either of them. Now Kefauver was gone, and the way was open.

Clement's bid for his third term as governor had aroused determined resistance from some of his friends, let alone his long-time foes. His election, just a few months before Kefauver's unexpected death, had been achieved in the primary by no more than a plurality, and he had faced the subsequent challenge of an independent in the general election. He could not succeed himself, and private life was always distasteful to him. It was either the Senate or a federal appointment. Although this could not be foreseen at the moment, Lyndon Johnson was to be in the White House before long, and Clement and Johnson were not close friends. Nor in fact was he close to the Kennedys, who were tied to political forces allied to the *Nashville Tennessean.* So only the Senate remained.

If Clement thought of becoming a candidate in 1964, his immediate problem was the selection in 1963 of an interim senator who would not become a rival in '64. He could have resigned as governor and have been appointed by his successor. Rumors of such an arrangement, by no means unusual in American history, were naturally thrown about. But Clement was only eight months into the first year of his term. The voter's memory is short, but in 1964, when the Kefauver seat would be up "for grabs," he could have held it against the governor had Clement left the place for which he had so recently been chosen. The risk of a resignation of the governorship in 1963 was clearly too great.

The governor did not lack for advice, solicited or not. As might have been predicted, Nancy Kefauver was suggested, most notably by the *Tennessean.* Russell Brothers, long time close friend and backer of the governor, was mentioned. A telegram came in suggesting Noble Caudill. Sam Fleming, a Kefauver friend, was proposed. But, no more than ten days after Kefauver died, the governor named Herbert Walters— "Mr. Hub"—to the Senate of the United States.

At the governor's office, members of the press assembled for an announcement. Behind closed doors, while the press waited, the governor asked Mr. Walters if he would care to go to the Senate. An immediate and favorable reply was given, and the governor then proposed that the group move into the next room to face the newsmen. The first person to enter the press room was Robert S. Clement, and, as this occurred, Eddie Jones noticed that one newsman, eager for a scoop, got up to leave the room, probably to report that the elder Clement had been selected for the Senate. Quickly Jones intercepted the reporter and prevented an embarrassing mistake.

The appointment gave full rein to political cynics. Mr. Walters was a widely experienced Democrat, of the conservative wing, with close ties to the Republican powers of his home area in East Tennessee. By any standard of party service and leadership he was fully entitled to the appointment, but he was old and not well. Of all the candidates who might have been chosen, he was one who could be thought of as a stand-in for the governor until the election of 1964 would roll around. Such a role would not have been completely distasteful to him, for quite aside from his health he had the deepest attachment to Frank Clement and that strongly emotional tie was certainly reciprocal. Senator Walters was not in the upper house much longer than the time needed to acquire the title of "Senator," but whatever sacrifice of his own ambitions may have been involved, that sacrifice was offered in vain, for the governor was not to succeed him.

Walter's appointment was applauded by conservatives throughout the party. A contrary sentiment was expressed in a *Tennessean* cartoon where Clement, appearing in the dollar sign suit that was used against him repeatedly, was pictured pulling the appointment from under Kefauver's big coonskin cap. The next day, the cartoonist showed a huge dollar sign arm putting a diminutive Walters in Kefauver's chair. Walters took the oath as senator on August 7. The fights of 1964 and 1966 were now in preparation.

The battle was not long in shaping up. A private letter from Frank Ahlgren, editor of the *Commercial Appeal,* told Clement in middle December of 1963 that Ross Bass would be a candidate and would announce after the first of the year. In that month, Milton M. Bullard of Newport also announced; his candidacy turned the primary of the coming August into a three-cornered race. As a sort of side-issue, Senator Albert Gore was up for a renewal of his mandate, and Ellington thought awhile before he decided against a trial against him. In the end, Gore had an easy time of it, and the really dramatic and significant battle took place around the two-year Senate term.

In March 1964 Joe Hatcher reported after a visit to Kefauver's "unbeatable" machine in the First Congressional District that the Bass campaign was gathering steam. Ross Bass, a former postmaster, had gone to the lower house of Congress in 1955, when Pat Sutton left that seat to try to defeat Kefauver. On closer examination the enthusiasm perceived by Hatcher seemed less than heated, for Kefauver's followers were not completely happy with Bass. It was rumored that some of them had tried to talk Kefauver's former manager, Frank Wilson, into running, but, if so, Wilson evidently preferred the steady and less emotionally charged work of the federal bench to the political snakepit.

The Kefauver machine was by no means as unbeatable as Hatcher liked to imply. Bullard and Bass split it in two. With Kefauver dead, some of his former friends drifted to Clement, an easy enough shift since Clement's welfare state visions were not far from Kefauver's ideals. The hard-core Kefauver remnants maintained a vigorous hatred for Clement; they feared that Bullard, a wealthy, self-made, and fairly unknown man, would succeed in electing Clement, but they could not get him to withdraw. He had the backing of such notables as George Dempster of Knoxville and Edward Ward Carmack of Middle Tennessee. Gordon Browning, always mindful of the disaster of 1954, supported Bullard, as did that old anti-Crump battler, Lewis Pope. Bullard was rich enough to finance his own campaign, but a self-financed candidate can also be a self-deceived candidate.

It was unusually difficult to detect substantive issues in the 1964 race. Clement talked about Bass's "absenteeism" in the House of Representatives, not an enthralling subject for the normally apathetic Tennessee electorate. Bass called attention to Clement's frequent trips outside the state, an equally dull subject. Clement was always in demand as a speaker in and out of the state. In the 1950s he had traveled in Latin America in the interest of the Cordell Hull Foundation. In the 1960s his calendar was still crowded. But the public was not much concerned with "absenteeism" on the part of either candidate, and the issue fell flat. Clement always carried the burden of having raised taxes; the memory of the latest rise was green enough in 1964. Of course, Clement had raised benefits as well, but beneficiaries are not uniformly grateful. The tax issue damaged the governor.

One issue went largely unreported. It was widely known that the governor had been victimized by drink. Alcohol is a widespread American curse, more widespread than the public is willing to admit; the list of American politicians who have suffered from it is long and impressive. Only in the seventies have public personalities had the courage to recognize and defeat the enemy; one thinks of Wilbur Mills, Betty Ford, Herman Talmadge. But the list of victims goes far back. That Daniel Webster was addicted was well known; jokes were made. General Grant's whiskey was the subject of criticism (although Lincoln wanted to give some to less aggressive generals); Andrew Johnson was accused of drunkenness on the day of his inauguration as vice president. Kefauver's friendly biographers have not hesitated to mention the steady drinking that became part of the senator's daily routine.

In 1964, and before, addiction to liquor was not publicly attributed to candidates, even by their opponents, but rumors and stories always sweep through the state. Often the stories of the governor's trouble were humorous, tolerant, and friendly, but they were, all the same, damaging, and deeply tormenting to his sincere and often loving friends. Some of them still speak with deepest regret of the tragic self-destruction that was unfolding. Some may have reflected on the road that the American politician must travel through pressure, tension, disappointed hopes, and disillusionment.

Clement, of course, had no national record, although he was widely known as a brilliant public speaker throughout the country. Bass had to attack Clement on his record as governor; his stock in trade consisted of the state's low rank in education (neglecting the long record of consistent support that Clement had given to education at all levels); the lag in interstate road construction (in disregard of the lavish appropriations for highways in the state); and the "shakedowns" and "political dictatorship." The shakedowns can be well documented, for Clement was counting on the votes and the finances of state employees, as all governors before and since have done as a matter of course. The charge of "dictatorship" was purely spurious. Clement had maintained control of his own machine, as every politician does and must do, but the notion that he was a "dictator" will not fit with the realities of Tennessee affairs.

Both Bass and Clement reached for black support. Both got into trouble, for both had to temper their support of steadily mounting black demands with the undoubted fact that whites greatly outnumbered blacks in Tennessee and that an unknown, but certainly very considerable number, of those whites was not prepared to meet black aspirations. The governor had earned some credits with the blacks over the years. He had turned his back firmly on massive resistance to integration, using his veto powers when individual legislators got out of hand. He had maintained order in Clinton, even if belatedly and reluctantly, and in the process had upheld school integration there, although publicly claiming that his sole interest was in law and order. He had started to employ blacks for something more than menial jobs. In April 1963 he had appointed Willard Bowden, a black man, to the State Pardons and Paroles Board. In early May he had appointed Dr. Harold D. West, Negro president of Meharry Medical College, to the state Board of Education. These were appointments made several weeks before Kefauver's unanticipated death.

But, in the 1960s, the blacks began to move from the battle against *de jure* segregation to demands for quick and special benefits for blacks to erase the effect of an unjust past. Clement did not move fast enough and far enough to suit them. At the same time, any movement at all was too fast and too far to content the die-hard whites. Bass had the same trouble. His perch on the prickly fence that is the customary seat of the powerful in a democracy was increasingly uncomfortable. He had signed the famous — or infamous — Southern Manifesto, that futile and unrealistic defiance signed by most of the southern leaders of Congress in the wake of the desegregation orders of the federal courts. Then he had appeared to back off; he was quoted as saying he had signed because of political pressure. Then, in December 1963, as his candidacy seemed certain, he claimed, according to the unfriendly *Banner,* that he had been misquoted. The *Banner* quoted him as saying he was unequivocally for segregated schools.

In his nine years in the lower House, Bass had gained a reputation as friend of labor. The *Banner* said he had earned the title of "Labor's Little Darling," a usage probably confined to that newspaper. Labor had grown partially disenchanted with Clement, for the legislature had given little heed to the governor's labor proposals. Since 1962, when Olgiati had been a candidate, labor had been split on the governor. In September 1963 Clement's faithful labor ally, Matthew Lynch, had taken control of the Tennessee Labor Council from Steve Para and Charles Houk, who had supported Olgiati, but Lynch could not assure the governor of labor's support. Bass still had reason to expect backing from much of the rank-and-file.

Bass waited until February 17, 1964, before making his plunge into candidacy official. Then he dove in, but a number of Kefauver men and women watched uncertainly from the bank. Sam Neal of Carthage,

William Farris of Memphis, and Bill Wilson of Knoxville were present for the Bass announcement; but Mrs. Martha Ragland was not present, nor were Noble Caudill, Edmund Orgill, or Rudy Olgiati. John J. Hooker was on hand—and a number of labor leaders. Barrett Ashley of Dyersburg, George Dempster of Knoxville, and Gordon Browning—all old Kefauver allies—had already declared their support for Bullard. Bullard also received the backing of Bruce Shine, a former field secretary for Kefauver.

Clement held off his own official announcement, and perhaps he was actually of two minds about running. He was, after all, only a few months into his third term. Meanwhile, endorsements began to flow his way. The executive committee of a Negro organization, the Tennessee Federation of Democratic Leagues, headed by Robert Lillard, in early May urged Clement to run. Newspaper endorsements started to build. In the middle of May, the *Columbia Daily Herald,* the *Dickson County Herald,* the *Bristol Herald-Courier,* and the *South Pittsburgh Hustler* called for his candidacy. They were quickly followed by endorsements from all three Grand Divisions.

Bass opened his campaign officially on June 6 at Shelbyville. Bullard followed on June 12 at Woodbury, invading Middle Tennessee. Clement, who had announced formally on May 13, opened officially on June 20, speaking to a crowd in Gallatin (a town he favored for openers) estimated at between 4,000 and 5,000.

Bass sought to identify himself with Kefauver and spent most of his half-hour opener on an attack on Clement. The unpopular sales tax on utilities got heavy attention. Bass did what he could to label Clement as anti-TVA. And then, with the glaring inconsistency not unknown to political campaigns, he skinned the governor for an alleged do-nothing attitude on education. Bass strongly supported Lyndon Johnson's poverty program, promised improved housing, upheld a vigorous national defense policy, and called for a cut in foreign aid. Clement's political machine was attacked, along with the funds he was getting from state employees, and he was hit for his failure to say who would succeed him as governor, if Clement were to become senator. That last point was possible because the new Senate would come into office in November, and there would be no speaker of the Senate to succeed until the new body had met and organized. Possibly Joe Carr, as secretary of state, would succeed. This point, of a certain value to the constitutional lawyers, had little popular interest.

Bullard's opener was an attack on Clement and Bass. Bass, said the candidate from Newport, was a political coward who had ignored black voters; Clement was derelict for failing to follow the recommendations of his own Commission on Human Relations, which urged him to sign a code of fair practices. Bass was given a black mark for failing to tell the voters of Tennessee that he had signed the infamous Paper of White Supremacy—presumably the Southern Manifesto. Bullard confessed to some reservations about the federal civil rights bill of 1964, then pending, but he said that it would be passed and that efforts would have to be made in the future to improve the bill's sections on public accommodations and jury trials. He scattered support over a variety of current and future nostrums, medical aid for the aged, farm programs, TVA, the poverty program, improvements in Appalachia; he added his support for a constitutional amendment permitting prayer in the public schools. Then, having distributed largesse with the usual political abandon, while asking that he be sent to the Senate as a businessman, he raked the governor, fore and aft. Clement, an anti-machine politician, he said, had built his own machine. Only a few token vocational schools had been provided. The little man had been hurt by the tax on electricity and water. State employees had been cruelly shaken loose from their money. Blacks had never had their code of fair practices. Even the old Cadillac of the early fifties was rolled by once again. And he closed: "So send a businessman instead of a politician to Washington. Together let's break Frank Clement's machine. Thank you."

Clement's June 20th opener, in what was to be the usual intense period of harrowing travel over the state, braved heat at 97 degrees in the Gallatin square. The governor dubbed his two opponents the "Colonel" and the "Congressman" and said he hoped they knew they were running for the Senate, not the governorship. The colonel, he said, had no record, except one of doing business with the state before Clement became governor. The congressman, he remarked, in ten years in the House had introduced fifty-five bills of which three had been passed. The remainder of Clement's time was a defense of his own record as governor. He defended the notion of a governor running for the Senate, citing the precedents of Sevier, Roane, and Frazier. To the charge that he had not resigned to run, he noted that Bass also had not resigned. Speaking to labor (some months before the Lawrenceville strike), he told the crowd that not a single national guard bayonet had been drawn in a strike during his tenure. He said little about the current civil rights issue, although he did attack Bass for not insisting on jury trials in civil rights

Grasping

The *Tennessean*'s view of Clement's senatorial ambitions; Little, *Tennessean*.

enforcement proceedings, a point of controversy during the passage of the civil rights act of that year.

The Clement campaign was managed by James Alexander, who had resigned as state treasurer. Alexander had funds collected from state employees and from recipients or would-be recipients of state contracts and purchases—attorneys, automobile and auto parts dealers, insurance men, bankers. Road contractors chipped in heavily. Druggists, food wholesalers, building contractors, and architects were among those counted. Considerable amounts were collected and spent locally, and contributions in kind were significant. While financial management in this campaign was probably not as loose as was the case with Kefauver affairs, the whole affair was somewhat haphazard. Expenditures were incurred less according to need than to availability. The total cost to the Clement organization is unknown, for no reporting was required, but estimates range from $250,000 to $650,000. Half a million may be about right.

Bass probably spent about a quarter of a million. Bullard put up his own money, chiefly, and said he was prepared to go up to $600,000, but few know how high his costs went. The strongest financial backing that Bass could draw on was provided by organized labor. It has been estimated that labor put more than $50,000 into the Bass funds, beginning with a reported initial gift of $10,000 from COPE. Even so, labor support for Bass was not unanimous, for the State Labor Council was headed by Matthew Lynch, a Clement friend. Bullard charged that the Kennedy family channeled $30,000 to Bass through John J. Hooker, Jr., but the report was denied. Bass may have had support from some of the federal employees in the state. President Kennedy had been gunned down by his assassin, Lee Harvey Oswald, by this time, and Lyndon Johnson was in power; but the Kennedy influence may have remained strong enough to aid Bass, as Bullard seemed to think. Bullard had a weak organization, ran a weak campaign, and came in third.

Probably the most significant feature of the contest was the enhanced importance of the black voter and the impact of the civil rights issue. During the campaign, the proposals that later emerged in the Civil Rights Act of 1964 were under congressional scrutiny. As the statute was finally enacted, it forbade discrimination on a racial basis in the provision of accommodations such as restaurants and motels. The attorney general was authorized to take civil action on behalf of any person denied equal access to those accommodations. Offenders could be cited for contempt of court, and fines and imprisonment could be imposed without juries. The denial of the right of jury in contempt proceedings was a sore point on which many Southerners, who would have found other provisions manageable, balked.

Bass, as a member of the lower House, had voted for the House version of the civil rights bill, but he did not play up that vote in his campaign, for there was plenty of opposition to the bill in his home state. Senators Gore and Walters both took exceptions to some provisions of the bill, and Bullard, as a candidate, emphasized his disquiet with the sections of the bill dealing with public accommodations and the denial of jury trial in contempt proceedings.

Clement, unsure of his position, sought guidance among a wide range of advisers, including academic leaders, without finding any satisfactory way out of a situation that no politician could find safe. Most of his advisers counseled a slow and cautious advance of civil rights knowing full well that nobody would be happy with the results. The governor criticized Bass for his vote approving the denial of jury trial in contempt procedures and he steadfastly refused to sign a state code of fair practices, saying some sections of the proposed code would violate state purchasing law. Apparently, what was at issue here was an early version of the argument over "affirmative action" and "reverse discrimination," an argument that would intensify in the 1970s.

All three candidates perched as firmly on the fence as they could manage, but, to the blacks, Bass looked the most likely to alight on their side, and undoubtedly his subsequent victory owed much to the black vote.

The primary on August 6 was a devastating blow to the governor. Many of his advisers had sensed that the race would be severe, and some of them must have foreseen defeat. Bass secured an absolute majority, with a vote of 330,213 to 233,245 for Clement, and 86,718 for Bullard. Had Bullard not been in the race, a considerable number of his votes would undoubtedly have gone for Bass. The election must therefore be considered a clear repudiation of the governor's ambitions for the Senate. Bullard carried only two counties—his home county, Cocke, and, strangely, Cannon County, where he had given his opening speech and where Jim Cummings was the acknowledged leader.

Bass carried almost all of Middle Tennessee, plus some of the heavily peopled counties of East Tennessee, and a considerable portion of West Tennessee beyond Kentucky Lake. He carried every one of the metropolitan counties. Clement had to be content with the smaller counties of East Tennessee and some of the counties of the West. In Middle Tennessee, where he had enjoyed great strength in earlier years, he carried

Lewis County, still doubtless under the strong and friendly influence of Commissioner Warf, and he carried a few counties on the Cumberland Plateau and in the Sequatchie Valley. The governor lost his home county. The governor must have been deeply shocked, for he had not been able to believe some of the warnings that came from his close friends. He could not understand that, when he loved people as he did, they did not always love him. But whatever his private despondency, he was never a poor sport in public. "This is a new experience for me," he said; "All my life, I've gotten almost everything I asked for, it seems like. I hope the people will unite behind me for the next two years." Clement pledged support to the man who had defeated him.

Post-mortems on the election must have been conducted with all the attention a Roman augur might give to chicken livers—and with almost as little precision. The black vote was certainly noted, and Clement continued to woo that vote during the remainder of his term. In the whole state, the black population was only 16.5 percent of the total, down sharply from the 23.8 percent it had been in 1900. In three metropolitan counties—Shelby, Davidson, and Hamilton—it was 36, 19, and 20 percent; in Knox, it was 9 percent. In no county of East Tennessee, other than Knox, was the percentage as high as 5 percent. Aside from the metropolitan counties, the black population was heaviest in certain counties of West Tennessee and a few counties to the north and south of Nashville. But the black voter had become more aggressive, and, though some black leaders stuck with the governor, large numbers of blacks unquestionably cast ballots for Bass. That trend is clear from the precinct returns in metropolitan areas. The reverse trend—the white backlash, unpublicized and silent but detectable—appears in the majorities given the governor in counties to the north and east of Memphis, counties where King Cotton had ruled in past decades over a slave and tenant population. But even if no blacks had voted, Bass might still have beaten the governor. The black vote was important, but it was not the sole answer.

The governor's friends have explained the defeat partly on the ground that many voters wanted Clement to remain governor and partly on the animosities that gradually develop toward any officeholder. The second line of reasoning carries some conviction; the first, very little, although some thousands may have decided that Clement was too ambitious and should stay in the job he had sought in 1962. And there were the Republicans to be accounted for. Under Tennessee practice, they could move around freely. But whether this movement benefited Bass is not so clear.

The results in some counties indicate that Republicans had gone into the Democratic primary to vote for Clement and had returned to the Republican ranks in the general election to vote for Howard Baker. Some of the Clement Democrats probably found Bass less to their liking than Baker when the November choices were made.

While the three-cornered duel of Bass, Bullard, and Clement—the congressman, the colonel, and the governor—was going forward, Senator Gore was conducting his own easy-going primary campaign. He had been moving in a conservative direction recently, voting against the civil rights bill and against the proposed federal tax reduction, and perhaps this made him more immune to attack from the right. The *Tennessean* was quarreling with him. He had no significant opposition, spent comparatively little on the campaign, and did not work hard. He was nominated without difficulty. The potential threat from Ellington had not materialized, and Clement was fully occupied elsewhere. The blacks ostracized him, but they had no alternative.

In the Republican ranks, however, frenetic activity was evident. Howard Baker, Jr., won the Republican nomination for the Senate, with the active support of his father-in-law, the powerful and highly articulate, not to say verbose, Senator Everett Dirksen from Illinois. The Republicans of Tennessee were said to be prepared to spend over a million dollars in the interest of Republicans in Tennessee, including Barry Goldwater for President, Howard Baker, Jr., against the Democratic nominee—whether Bass or Clement—and Representative Dan Kuykendall, who planned to take on Gore. Baker had no significant opposition, and Kuykendall had none at all in the Republican primaries. No such primaries were held in a considerable number of Tennessee counties, but this foretold nothing of the nature of the contest in the general election.

When that election rolled around, Johnson, Bass, and Gore duly received the customary accolades, but the size of the Republican vote was a warning of things to come. Clearly the Republican party was on the way to a revival, and Tennessee was due to become something of a two-party state; in presidential elections the state had already formed a habit of deserting the Democratic establishment when the occasion warranted. Johnson won, with a popular vote of 634,000, but 508,000 Tennesseans opted for Goldwater. Gore won with a majority of about 80,000, but, nonetheless, 493,500 voters spoke up for the Shelby County Republican, Kuykendall. Bass had 569,000 votes, but Baker was in sight of him with 517,000. Prophets could have risked something on the outcome of the votes in 1966 and 1970. Republican strength for the Senate seats was as usual concentrated in the East, but the Republican candidates carried a substantial bloc of territory in West Tennessee. Unfortunately for them, they could not manage to carry Shelby and Davidson counties; the old slave areas that they did carry had too sparse a population to bring victory. But the election brought hope all the same.

Clement swallowed his disappointment and began to prepare for a return bout, two years away. Through the remainder of his final term, his policies were moulded by his senatorial ambitions. He stepped with caution around the troublesome issues of reapportionment and constitutional revision. He managed to retain control of the state Senate by deals with the Republicans. He avoided further increases in taxation; a burgeoning economy helped to build a surplus that he could divide in the late spring of 1966.

Noble Caudill fed advice to the governor on his political future, which Caudill realized was in jeopardy. "Now, governor," he wrote, "this is not easy to say, the majority opinion is that you have your work really cut out for you in the next eighteen months to really stay in public life." He urged Clement to get around more, to be more leisurely and less hurried, to set up schedules in each county. Above all, he kept urging Clement to court the black vote.

Clement had to rebuild his organization. Old age and death had taken the toll of the organization that his opponents had called a "dictatorship." Ellington, who looked more and more like a candidate for a second term as governor, would take over some of the old organization, and Clement could not count on a combined campaign with his former manager. When Clement ran his last race, Lon Varnell became the campaign manager, and Caudill was made finance chairman.

After Clement announced again for the Senate (on May 31, 1966), he made Roy Nicks his campaign coordinator. Nicks had come into the Clement organization as a civil servant, after beginning his career as a fellow of the Southern Regional Training Program in Public Administration. He was a member of that cadre of young professional administrators that distinguished the Clement and Ellington years from their predecessors. In due course he had become a valuable member of the subcabinet under the commissionership of Caudill, whom he then succeeded as commissioner of welfare. Nicks was highly regarded, and he was acquiring experience in political affairs, but he had not come up through the ranks of the county and state political machine, and his appointment, in the minds of some, was an indication of political weakness in the Clement organization.

(*Top*) Roy Nicks, cabinet officer, political adviser. Photograph courtesy Tennessee State Library and Archives. (*Bottom*) Press representative—"Eddie" Jones. Photograph courtesy Mr. Edward F. Jones.

Nicks was aware that the coming campaign would be a severe test. He was keenly appreciative of the need for information, and he commissioned a private study of Clement's record in past elections, attempting to spot the areas of weakness. The study showed Nicks and his colleagues a few counties where Clement had always shown strength, but it also showed that these counties were poor, limited in population, and less well educated. They could never give Clement enough support to carry the state. The counties that carried strength were counties that Clement could not depend on through thick and thin. Sometimes Clement had won there, sometimes not.

Bass was not a strongly popular candidate, even among the political enemies of Clement. Like Browning, he had a quick temper that sometimes gave an edge to his opponent. In April 1966 at a Washington dinner organized to give support to Democrats throughout the country, Senator Bass and his wife, Avenell, occupied chairs at the head table. The master of ceremonies, Patty Cavin, a TV commentator, seeking to give some humor to the occasion, introduced guests with some rather lame verse and when the turn of Bass and his pretty wife came, she announced:

> He's known in the Senate as big-mouth Bass,
> What's more, he has a pretty lass.

> The Senator from Tennessee, Ross Bass, Avenell's husband.

The feminism, the verse, or the pun was too much for the senator. According to the *Banner,* which clearly enjoyed telling the story, Bass threw down his napkin and, in rapid order, announced: "I'm no big mouth—I didn't want to come—I think I'm going to leave—I'm leaving." Avenell remained at the table, even, as the *Banner* put it, "through a few thousand words of exhortation dropped by Hubert Horatio Humphrey." The episode caused some newspaper flurries, with more wit of the same quality. "Ross is Cross—Verse is Worse," noted the *News-Sentinel.* The *Chattanooga News-Free Press* came up with: "Bass not Amused. He Feels Abused." Ridicule is dangerous for a candidate. Whether the incumbent senator was seriously hurt, it is impossible to say, but anyway the short-lived episode helped to add a little color to a campaign that remained rather humdrum and colorless.

The Negroes were split between Clement and Bass. In early April, both Bass and Hooker, running for governor against Ellington, had received endorsements from the Tennessee Voters Council, but some East Tennessee members of that body, which claimed to represent 100,000 black voters, were publicly critical of the way in which the endorsement was adopted, noting that Clement had not been invited to present his views. Some of the dissenters talked of supporting a ticket of Clement for the Senate and Hooker for governor. Other blacks announced support for Ellington, and attorney H.T. Lockard, a black squire of Shelby County, became an Ellington manager. (Lockard later occupied a post in Ellington's office, after Ellington had become governor a second time.) Throughout the campaign, Clement emphasized publicly his support for Negro aspirations. He noted that he had been the first southern governor to put blacks into highway patrol uniform. He had hired a Negro secretary for his own office and had appointed Judge Ben Hooks to the criminal court in Shelby County, the first black judge since reconstruction days.

Clement's opening address in Murfreesboro delivered on June 25, featured proposals for benefits to various groups in the voting community, very much in the pattern that all candidates for public office follow. In Clement's case, the benefits proposed were to accrue to the aged and to low-income groups. He suggested increases in social security payments, tax exemptions for low-income families, increases in the minimum wage, and increased assistance to disabled veterans. Bass's program for benefits tended to overlap Clement's, as he also advocated an increase in the minimum wage. He spent a good bit of his time attacking Clement for his tax increases. Whether or not he coupled increased benefits with tax increases in his own mind was not too apparent.

Both men stayed clear of the race for governor between Ellington and Hooker, another illustration of the lack of closely coordinated factional politics in Tennessee. Ellington and Clement were by this time quite thoroughly separated from each other in their campaigns (although not in the public mind), and Bass tried to keep his distance from Hooker. Hooker was as clearly anti-Clement, as he was anti-Ellington, but he naturally concentrated on Ellington. The campaign called for the usual strenuous travel schedule for the candidates, but the newspapers gave relatively short shrift to the senatorial contest, concentrating its first page attention on the governorship.

The primary election of August 4 terminated Bass' short term as senator, and, as it turned out, probably spelled the end of his political career. Clement was the recipient of a come-back, but it was not a strong one. He had acquired 384,000 votes, to 366,000 for Bass; not only was the majority narrow, but little doubt existed that some of the Clement strength had come from Republican crossovers into the Democratic

THE GRAND DIVISIONS OF TENNESSEE
(as of 1980)

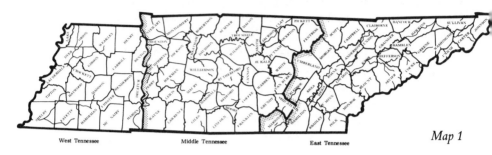

West Tennessee   Middle Tennessee   East Tennessee   *Map 1*

THE POLITICS OF VICTORY

Democratic Primary, 1952
Counties carried by Clement (shaded)

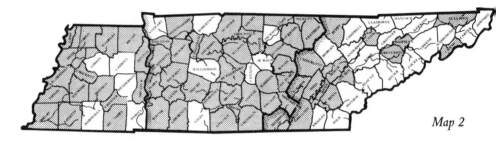

Map 2

Democratic Primary, 1954
Counties carried by Clement (shaded)

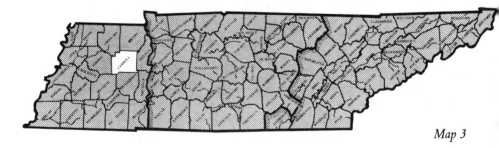

Map 3

Democratic Primary, 1962
Counties carried by Clement (shaded)

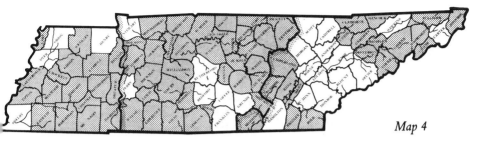

Map 4

THE POLITICS OF DEFEAT

Democratic Primary, 1964
Counties carried by Clement (shaded)

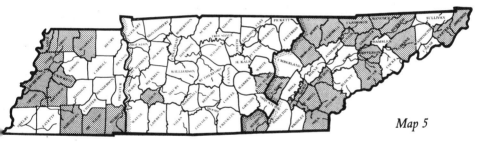

Map 5

Democratic Primary, 1966 (temporary victory)
Counties carried by Clement (shaded)

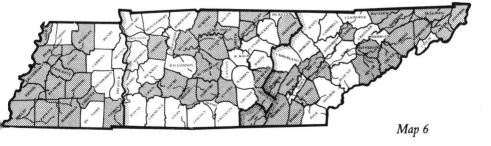

Map 6

General Election, 1966
Counties carried by Clement (shaded)

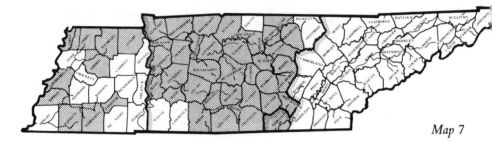

Map 7

Senatorial Election, 1966
Counties lost by Clement in the primary
but carried in the general election (shaded)

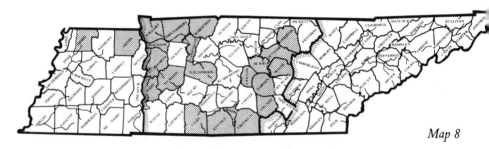

Map 8

Senatorial Election, 1966
Counties carried by Clement in the primary
but lost in the general election (shaded)

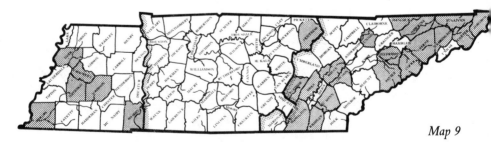

Map 9

party. For example, Clement carried most of the counties of Upper East Tennessee as well as counties in the Great Valley. At the same time, Bass carried some of the traditional Republican areas of the Second Congressional District, including Knox County. Clement carried Hamilton, Davidson, and Shelby counties, where labor and black votes were significant but where significant enemies of those forces were also concentrated. He carried most of the counties west of the Tennessee River, but he lost six of those counties, including Carroll, where Browning still lived, and he lost large chunks of Middle Tennessee, where he should have shown strength.

In the meantime the Republicans had been conducting their own quiet little clambakes in various parts of the state. Howard Baker, Jr., benefiting from the publicity he had built up in the 1964 race against Bass, had defeated Kenneth Roberts handily, 122,617 to 36,043. The votes were generally small, and in some counties, no Republican primary for the senatorial nomination was held at all. Only in Knox County did the total Republican vote exceed the round figure of 13,000.

Given the past history of Tennessee where senatorial races were concerned, it is not surprising that large numbers of persons both in and out of the state assumed that Baker would be no match for Clement. From Hubert Humphrey came a telegram of congratulations, that said in part, "We look forward to your election to the United States Senate this fall. . . . I know you will make a mighty fine Senator from the Volunteer state which has a history of sending their [*sic*] best." Whether Humphrey recognized the slight to Bass is doubtful. A fellow FBI agent from the years long past wrote congratulations, with the intriguing words: "I remember distinctly the time I got you to go with me to interview one of the "boys" in that stinking third rate hotel on the near north side [of Chicago]."

Representative Joe Evins, a veteran of the lower house, wrote the governor, addressing him as "my friend and future colleague." A warm letter came from the governor's cousin, Frank Goad, of Scottsville, Kentucky, who, nonetheless, recognized obliquely the dangerously low margin that the governor had secured over Senator Bass. The governor's longtime Dickson County friend and backer, J.E. "Droopy" Edwards, now an official of the Ford Motor Company in Nashville, wrote the governor in interesting detail. He predicted strong labor support and thought the blacks were unlikely to shift to the Republicans. The average voter, he thought, was sick of Johnson's Great Society. Numerous individuals, he said, had told him that Frank had again become the old

Clement—surrounded by people, out on the sidewalk shaking hands and speaking words the voters liked to hear. The governor he said had won without pressure groups, without the endorsements of big labor and the blacks. But he worried about getting the vote out.

From Nancy Kefauver came a friendly and gallant letter: "Dear Frank: I learned of the success of your campaign on the eve of my departure for Europe on official business. You again have proved what determination can achieve. You and your family must anticipate an interesting and challenging term of office. With best wishes, Nancy Kefauver."

Gore promised full support. Some labor endorsement was forthcoming. *Labor,* a national weekly representing some eighteen unions in the railroad and airlines field, devoted its issue of October 15 to lead articles supporting Clement. It cited, as reasons for support for Clement, the planks in his platform that advocated increases in income tax exemptions, improvements in social security benefits, the creation of a cabinet post for consumer protection, backing of TVA, support for equal rights, and support for American troops in Vietnam. The Vietnam War was becoming increasingly unpopular, but opposition had not yet reached the panic stage. Clement's position was consistent with the views to be expected from a former state commander of the American Legion. All the same, complete labor endorsement was not forthcoming; the workers' organizations were as usual split, and as usual their endorsement was not decisive. Still, the lack of whole-hearted labor support was a weakening factor in the total situation.

Black support was also less than overwhelming. The emerging issue of open housing was troublesome, for Clement, like many another white man, could have accepted open housing in principle while disliking it in practice. Clement did contrive to get the endorsement of the Tennessee Voters Council on October 1. Howard Baker managed to delay the endorsement for some seven hours, although in the end he failed to swing the group away from official backing of the governor— although the endorsement of Clement was not unanimous. Baker declared, in what the *Tennessean* called a forthright manner, that he would not have backed the open housing section of the civil rights act because of the way in which it was worded; then he added, "This does not mean I oppose the equality of man." He said open housing was morally right. Clement was, in the words of the *Tennessean* "reluctant"; he did not take a clear position. The blacks were unhappy, but they had few options. The West Tennessee delegation went quickly into the Clement camp. "The Republicans," said one spokesman for this group, "crossed the line in August to kill our candidates. We've got to have some way to rebel."

The remaining issues before the Voters Council included the creation of a department of urban housing and development, the possible repeal of 14-B of the Taft-Hartley Act, and the raising of the minimum wage. Both candidates favored improvements in the minimum wage. Baker said he was opposed to the repeal of 14-B and proposed massive federal effort to overcome the blight on the central cities. Clement's position on these two issues was unclear. The Council endorsed Clement; they were not happy about it. Ellington was refused endorsement.

Officially, the Democratic party closed ranks. Some observers think that Ellington made secret arrangements with Republicans to ditch Clement, and that this arrangement played a part in his defeat. Officially Ellington endorsed Clement late in October. Ross Bass stated that he had scheduled some speeches in support of Clement, and in this month, Clement was endorsed by his old opponent, Gordon Browning. Clement's staff had urged him to seek the support of the *Tennessean,* which had always supported Democratic nominees against Republicans. Clement vigorously rejected any notion of bending the knee to Amon Evans, the publisher, but he was eventually persuaded to call on Evans for a private talk. The conference seemed to go off amiably, and the *Tennessean* lent support. Clement also garnered the support of the *Commercial Appeal.* As the campaign warmed up in the final days of October, Clement began to secure some official labor support. Some Clement friends worried that Hubert Humphrey might come into the state to work for the Democrats. They advised that such a move be discouraged, and Clement said he had no such plans. Local Democrats were glad that Lyndon Johnson did not visit the state.

Generally the campaign was rather low key. Baker opened formally at the Grand Ole Opry House in Nashville on September 22, with the assistance of country musicians led by Archie Campbell. Some 1,000 supporters heard his forty-five minute speech, in which he promised a campaign on the issues rather than on personalities. He took time then and later to attack Clement for his failures in state affairs, saying that Tennessee was last in education and short on municipal facilities of various sorts. Later in the short campaign, Baker attacked Clement for dodging the issues, but his own speeches managed to encompass the customary collection of inconsistencies. He declared himself not to be a states-rights man in the classic sense, leaving a vague implication of progressive emotions. His one clear position — which he followed up in his later political career — was that in favor of federal revenue sharing. He was for unity of purpose in Vietnam—a position not unlike that of Clement—but neither he nor his opponent had any clear suggestions to make for a solution to this increasingly troublesome burden for the United States.

Clement's opener, on October 4, was as indecisive as that of Baker. He pledged to be a progressive voice in the Senate (no one would think of promising to be a retrogressive voice), and he brought forth his primary campaign package of higher social security, income tax and minimum wage benefits, together with improvements on the whole gamut of American problems. He was as usual questioned about his stand on open housing; he took refuge in a general statement that all citizens should have equal rights, but that the rights of some should not be pushed to the extent of damaging others. The truth was—as Clement had made clear to Amon Evans in their private talks—he did not know where he stood on the open housing question, a position he held in common with large numbers of his white constituents. Later in the campaign, Clement began to move toward a position critical of the Vietnam War, but of course, no more than others, had he any satisfactory suggestion for concluding the conflict. The campaign signaled the continuing decline of the old-style stump speaking in the rural courthouse squares; television was taking its place. Baker was highly effective on TV; Clement was, as always, photogenic, but he must have missed the stimulus that audiences gave him.

On November 8 the electorate gave the governor his second and final defeat. Clement trailed Baker by almost 100,000 votes, a devastating statistic. Of the four metropolitan counties, Clement carried only Davidson. Shelby County, once the citadel of the Democrats, gave Baker a comfortable majority. Hamilton County was overwhelmingly in the Baker camp, and Knox even more so. Baker's victory was based on the solid support of East Tennessee, straight up the Cumberland Plateau to the edge of the Highland Rim, plus majorities in Shelby County and an impressive number of counties to the west of the Tennessee River in West Tennessee. A few counties in Middle Tennessee ate into the Clement vote. In many instances, Baker carried these counties by only modest majorities, but in the past no Republican contestant for the Senate would have stood much chance there.

Why did the Tennessee voters, who had three times made Clement the chief executive, turn him down so decisively as a senator? No more than informed speculation can be offered in answer to this question. One reason might be found in the tendency voters probably have to weary of a politician who goes to the well too often. Clement won his last victory in a three-cornered race where his opposition included a former friend. In retrospect some of his other friends felt that he should have been content with two terms as governor. Others found the cause for his defeat in the inevitable disappointments a governor must deal out to many supporters who expect more than he can deliver. Long periods in office, in this view, breed enemies, not friends. Quite clearly the blacks, and some of organized labor, were luke-warm in their backing of the governor, although they had little choice of other routes to follow. Clement had acquired the reputation of being a taxing governor. Certainly his actions in broadening the sales tax had played a part in the Senate race of 1964, and, even though voters tend to forget such matters, resentment against the tax may have played a role still in 1966.

The governor's close friend, "Droopy" Edwards had warned him that the voters were tiring of Johnson's Great Society. Clement had never been closely tied to the Johnson administration and indeed had in the past quietly sided with the Kennedy faction at times, but the growing reaction to Johnson, his Great Society, and his war, may well have increased the Republican vote. Clement was certainly one of the spenders; perhaps some of the electorate made a connection between the spender in Nashville and the one in Washington.

And, finally, there was a definite Republican plan to vote for Clement in the primary, putting Bass to pasture and deserting Clement for Baker in the general election. The Republicans were open about the plan. When these votes were backed up by the undoubted Bass votes that went for Baker as a backlash against Clement and when these votes can be added to all the other possible reasons for deserting Clement, the sum was the 100,000 verdict delivered in November. As it turned out, Clement's political career had come to a close.

The defeat was an unbelievable shock to Clement. He had been unable to contemplate the possibility of a Republican victory. At night, near or on election day, at a meeting either in the governor's office or his home (memories are not clear on this point), Grant Smith, who was to be Clement's law partner in the future, told the governor that, in his opinion, he had been defeated. The governor's oldest son, Bob, was present, and, probably, Roy Nicks and Harlan Mathews. The governor asked whether Smith could be right, and his son, Bob, agreed that the election had been lost. Clement could not accept the opinion. He reached up to a nearby library shelf, took down a copy of one of Robert

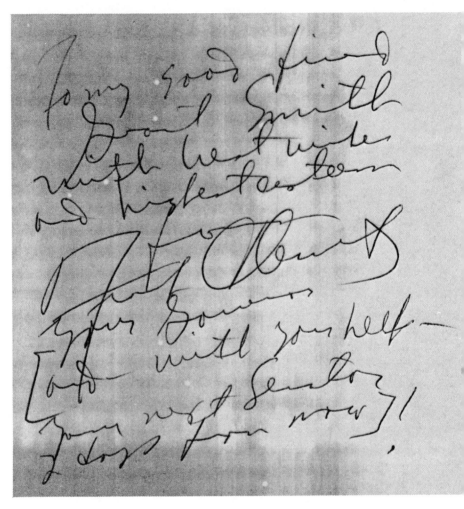

Clement autograph, prophesying election to the Senate. Used by permission of Grant W. Smith.

White's volumes on the messages of the governors of Tennessee, auto-graphed it with the words "your future Senator" and gave it to Smith. The aftermath of this confident prediction was devastating.

But this was all in private. Publicly, the governor was gallant in de-feat. Letters of condolence, encouragement, and post-election analysis poured in; to all of them he made a grateful and courageous reply. "In defeat," wrote one correspondent, "you can receive comfort from Eccle-siastes 9–11: 'I returned, and saw under the sun, that the race is not to the swift, nor the battle to the strong, neither yet bread to the wise, nor yet riches to men of understanding, nor yet favor to men of skill; but time and chance happen [eth] to them all.'" Jared Maddux wrote:

> I join your many thousands of loyal friends across the State in stating that we could not be more sorely disappointed had the loss of the election hap-pened to us. You deserved to win. As we all know, politics is a very jealous mistress, and a very fickle lover. I am reminded of what Governor Bob Tay-lor said in Knoxville when he was about eighty years old. Some newspaper man asked him if he would give a statement as to what he thought about politics as a career for young men. Governor Taylor responded by saying he would be pleased to accede to the request, and stated that "after having served in the Tennessee Legislature, the House of Representatives in Wash-ington, the Governor's office in Tennessee, and the United States Senate, I have reached the conclusion that politics is a son-of-a-bitch." How true.

> I hope the levity hereinabove expressed will make you feel better. Your many friends are still just as loyal and just as proud of you as they ever were. Personally, my association with you in government has been truly a reward-ing experience, and I shall not soon forget, but will long remember, your many courtesies and kindnesses to me.

The analyses bore down heavily on the dissatisfaction with the John-son administration and the urban riots of the sixties. Maddux engaged in a sharp exchange of correspondence with newscaster Frank McGee who had quoted Tom Anderson, a prominent conservative, as saying Clement was a Bible-toting, whiskey-drinking hypocrite. McGee made a conciliatory reply which Maddux reported to Clement, voicing some suspicion that he had received a form letter. In fact, McGee had been do-ing what other broadcasters do regularly, reaching for the sensational and "newsworthy" without regard to the possible damage. The letters breathed a confidence for the future that was probably not justified by the actualities of politics, and which, in any case, was aborted by the tragic end of Clement's life, now just three years away in the (as yet) clouded future.

Clement's reply to Maddux carries a note of valediction:

Dear Jared:

My long-time, close association with you has enriched my life and although
I was not privileged to have a brother, you more nearly fill that spot for me
than any friend I have and I am grateful for your unquestioned loyalty along
with the many, many ways you have assisted me through the years.

With appropriate irony, fate gave Baker what was denied Clement.
Baker as senator was to attain national prominence, rising to minority
floor leader of the Senate, where he was able to wield considerable influence over the policies of President Carter and attain a prominence great
enough to make him a believable candidate for the presidency. In 1981 he
became majority leader in the Senate. Some of this would certainly have
been denied Clement had he been the winner in 1966. He would have
been just another senator in the majority party, with little chance of becoming floor leader or presidential candidate. Indeed it is questionable
whether he would have been happy in the Senate; Clement could have
found the work of the Senate irksome. It was no longer a chamber
where oratory flourished; the days of Clay, Webster, and Calhoun were
long since gone. No longer would he have occupied the center of the
stage, as he had in state politics. But neither such considerations nor the
continued affection of his friends could fully reconcile him to defeat, and
he suffered moments of deep despondency as he left the governor's office
to return to the private career that never greatly interested him.

♪ Precious Lord, take my hand,
Lead me on, let me stand.
I am tired, I am weak, I am worn;
Through the storm, through the night,
Lead me on to the light;
Take my hand, precious Lord, lead me home.

THOMAS A. DORSEY

13. Lead Me Home

THE END OF LIFE

On the night of November 4, 1969, the life of Frank Clement came to an end in a two-car collision on Franklin Road. The accident occurred about 7 P.M., a short distance from the conjunction of Tyne Boulevard with Franklin Road, when Clement, alone in his car, swerved out of his lane and struck a car driven by David Carlton, vice president of Crest Chemical Company, who was also driving alone. Mr. Carlton suffered a broken leg in the accident. The former governor sustained massive chest injuries and was dead on arrival at General Hospital. Very probably he died at once at the scene of the accident. Mrs. Clement was at the time hospitalized in Virginia and the two older sons were out of town, Robert in the army and Frank, Jr., at Memphis State University. The youngest son, Gary, went to General Hospital. Later in the night, on instructions from Robert S. Clement, the body was taken by ambulance to Dickson.

The last human being who talked to Clement was probably David Alexander, who was representing him in the divorce suit that Mrs. Clement had filed earlier in the year. Alexander thought that a reconciliation was pending. He had talked to Clement several times during that last day, and in the afternoon Mrs. Alexander had invited the former governor to take a simple supper with them that evening in their home on Curtiswood Lane, on the street where the governor's mansion is located.

Alexander had last talked to Clement about six o'clock. As the Alexanders waited for Clement to arrive, they were stunned to hear over the evening news that their guest had been killed. As the Clement car ran into the front and side of the other car, it had been headed south toward Brentwood; the former governor should have been traveling north. Shortly after the fatal accident, Mr. Alexander went to Clement's home in Brentwood to examine his desk and there he found a small gift evidently intended for Mrs. Alexander. It seems likely that as Clement drove north he remembered that the gift had been left behind and turned back south to get it. The tragic accident then followed. Noble Caudill heard of the news of the death of his good friend and former boss on a newscast in a motel in Valdosta. Clement's law partner, Grant Smith, was informed by a telephone call from Mary Smith. Rapidly the shocking news spread across the state.

After his retirement from the governorship in 1967, Clement had again entered the practice of law. His former law partners, Val Sanford and Douglas Fisher, had by this time made other professional connections, and Clement's final partner was Grant W. Smith, a younger man who had worked in the later Clement campaigns. He acquired a new home near Franklin Pike in the Brentwood area, a comfortable and attractive structure, fairly large but unpretentious. Clement's relation with his young partner was one of mutual regard and friendship. Each day when Clement came to the office he shook hands formally with his partner as a means of starting a friendly and productive day. But his heart was not in private business; he would never cease to long for public activity.

Clement did not accept his defeat by Baker as the end of his political career, and there is plenty of evidence that he intended to make a try for a fourth term as governor, a move that would not have been completely without precedent. Browning ran for governor seven times. Had Clement been elected, he would have had a fourth term, three of them for four-year periods. But a service that long would have been unusual in Tennessee affairs, in a state where electors are chary of giving governors more than two terms, and it seems doubtful that Clement could have succeeded. As matters turned out, the Democratic candidate in 1970 lost on a rising tide of Republicanism, and Clement, had he become the nominee, might have suffered the same fate. He was politically active in the last three years of his life and was a delegate to the national convention of 1968, but he did not attend. During those last two years, he was mentioned as a possible ambassador in South America, and speculation was raised that he might succeed C.C. Humphries as president of Memphis State. But these were little more than the usual rumors that float around public figures.

Frank Clement was amply endowed with that indefinable quality that we call "charisma." A quiet child, somewhat withdrawn in manner, he had developed as a young man into the kind of person "who never knew a stranger." But his personality and his politics made unforgiving enemies as it made devoted friends. Those who were unfriendly to him were little inclined to credit him with sincerity; for them the qualities that endeared him to so many were regarded as "put-on." His friendliness, genuine and welcome to some, was regarded with suspicion and scepticism by others. In truth, his personality demanded the friendship and companionship of others to an intense degree; he was not happy in solitude; his friendly approach to other beings was too constant to have been feigned. And, by the same token, he could not thrive without attention. Private life was therefore unacceptable to him, and he made no secret of his insistence on the excitement and adulation of a public career.

The constitution of the United States separates church and state; politics puts them together. Rare indeed is the American politician who has never used religious appeals. Clement's religious feelings were as much the subject of dispute as any of his character traits. The Eastern Establishment, the political enemy, and many newspaper men could not credit him with religious sincerity. For them such religious expression was merely a feature of the "Bible belt" that was automatically condemned. Clement's behavior was not, in this view, the kind that can be demanded of a religious person. But these views are faulty. The church —and the Christian religion—are not unused to sinners; nor is the world unused to compromise between the ideals of Christianity and the sordid affairs of political life. Clement was a sincerely religious man, in an emotional rather than an intellectual sense. Some of his close associates, themselves religious believers, accorded his evangelical approach to Christianity the benefit of credibility. He was, in the words of one of them, a Godly man in his extroverted fashion. His critics found his use of religious themes and religious appeals in politics offensive, but Clement had sense on his side when he saw religion as an integral factor in policy and politics. We might dismiss Clement's early attachment to religion as the emotional response of a boy raised in a sincerely religious family; his continued attachment to his beliefs during his manhood are entitled to respect, if not necessarily to agreement.

The governor made frequent reference to religious belief; he prayed, both as a child and as a mature politician. To many of his critics his use of religion seemed deliberate and insincere. In religious affairs the "truth" may be strictly in the eye of the beholder. To the unbelieving observer the politician's religion is likely to seem all craft and calculation. To the believer the politician's religion must seem as genuine as the voter's. But the man who remembers his own childhood conversion clearly is unlikely to cast doubt on the sincerity of Clement's childhood beliefs. Such conversion is a deep-seated characteristic in the long history of Christianity, and, if some children are converted because their contemporaries are joining the church, others are moved by an emotional experience of a far more personal and moving nature.

Even Clement's enemies would testify to his sharp intelligence. He clearly exhibited marks of brilliance. He was quick to perceive the core of controversial issues. He had the photographic memory that ran through the Goad family. Certainly he was articulate beyond the average. Although his academic career was no more than normally satisfying up to his entrance into law school, his record in law college was solid, even if not brilliant. But Clement could not be described as an intellectual. He was not literary or bookish. Apparently he read about as little as the ordinary politician who seeks information from persons rather than books. His was a life of activity, not contemplation. In his practice of law, it was the human relationship that attracted his attention, not the close study of legal hairsplitting. The preparation of legal briefs was not for him. Had Clement been a genuine intellectual he would have sought to develop a theoretical philosophy to surround and support his political actions. He did not. His goals, when announced, were benign, but vague.

Clement's family attachments were strong. His mother's religious feelings supported him. His deep love for his father was always evident, based on a regard that persisted through the strict discipline that his father exercised over him when he was a boy. The mutual loyalty of Clement and his sisters is a testimony to a closely knit family that survived the crushing discouragement that the Great Depression imposed on the Clement household.

The governor was little inclined to bear grudges. Some politicians operate on the principle: don't get mad, get even. Clement did neither. He seemed to have a genuine, not merely a political, inclination to conciliation. Certainly it was a trait that paid political dividends; more than one enemy was converted into a supporter before Clement's life came to a close. Consultation with others was a basic feature of his behavior. But, of course, conciliation and consultation did not always work. Browning remained an opponent consistently throughout Clement's career, in spite of certain unpublicized and quiet courtesies that Clement accorded him after Browning's last defeat. The relationships with Ellington deteriorated over the years, their rivalries too great a strain for an alliance based more on convenience than compatibility.

Devoted friends of the governor have praised him as an outstanding administrator. If he was so, it was because he liked to delegate and expected his aides to carry out their responsibilities on their own. He had no great taste for pettifogging details, and his interests did not lie in the minutiae of administrative theory and practice. He did little to change the generally well-designed administrative machine that he inherited from his predecessors, for it needed little change. Two administrative approaches deserve to be remembered. He had a strong sense that administrative capacity was needed in fiscal affairs; he saw to that consistently, and he put his fiscal aides over other administrative subordinates, both executive and legislative. Secondly, he introduced into the government of the state a cadre of young technically trained persons—without close attention to political connections—relied upon them, and forwarded their careers. Perhaps that change in administrative staffing patterns would have developed anyway, under the pressure of events, but Clement is entitled to the credit for the innovation, one that has become a permanent fixture of succeeding administrations.

Aside from this important matter, Clement displayed no interest in any sharp professionalization of the civil service. It is significant that political figures often headed the personnel department. Clement needed a technician in fiscal affairs; reform and improvement in personnel administration meant little or nothing to him, and he played the patronage game as devotedly as any politician, although it is true that in certain technical areas, such as mental and public health, he sought technicians, not politicians, and he protected his technicians from too great a political interference.

The cabinet was not much used as a collectivity. Clement relied heavily on his legislative leaders and a few close advisers such as Mathews, Snodgrass, Caudill, and Boling, and his speech writers. His immediate family, particularly his father and his sister Anna Belle, were always politically useful. Mathews was close to the governor, who enjoyed his company during moments of escape from politics.

Clement had a sense of the uses to which the specialists in the university community might be put, but his contacts with the intellectual leaders in that community were not close. He was screened from them by university administrators and staff who served him well, but he had no close associates in the professoriate. But he is well remembered as a staunch backer of university programs.

Clement's own rise to power, as he himself candidly recognized, was due to his oratory. His other undoubted, even remarkable, abilities would never have obtained for him the eminence which his speech captured for him even in his twenties. "I knew I shouldn't have come here," one of his listeners once said. "I was against him all summer, and now he's sold me all over again." His oratory was of the old school, orotund, florid, at times grandiose beyond the tastes of moderation. Sublimity is difficult to maintain. Like declarations of love, it can easily shift into the ridiculous. But Clement loved the purple passage. He never worried about appearing ridiculous. He knew his audience, and he knew they delighted in his art. His speeches do not survive reading well; they depended on his physical appeal and the nuances of his voice, assets that he knew how to use to the greatest advantage. But, in a sense he was trained in a speech-making culture that was to die with the advent of television (where his final rival, Howard Baker, was always a good performer) and the dispersal and decline of the courthouse square. He was a performer whose show improved as he felt the response of his audience; they stimulated each other. The impersonality of the tube was not his medium. But those, inside and outside Tennessee, who heard him speak and liked what they heard (not everyone did) remember him, and seem likely to do so while they survive.

As governor, Clement did what most other governors do, if they do much at all: he responded to crises as they arose. But he was an activist, and, though he was cautious and at times reluctant, he did build a record of accomplishment. He served his terms during a time when the state was developing and expanding, particularly in commerce and industry, and he widened the scope of state activity as he broadened the tax yield. That expansion was congenial to his nature; had he had the misfortune to be chief executive during times of retrenchment, he would have found the role most unrewarding. When he spoke, as he did at times when he was a boy, of his ambition to be governor, he would speak vaguely of a desire to do things for people. That desire was genuine enough, no matter how much his aim at the executive power was motivated by personal drives. He was happy to spend, and he had the courage to raise taxes to make that spending possible. There can be little doubt that the taxes hurt him politically, even though the spending was greeted with pleasure by recipients who did not always respond with votes.

The state's spending was directed toward three primary objects: education, welfare, and highways. These have long been the three great burdens on the tax resources of the state of Tennessee; they still are. Clement spent freely on all three, but he did not succeed in greatly altering the status of the three in relation to other states. In the late 1970s the demands of education are as persistent as they were in Clement's time. Governors and legislatures have not diminished the continuing demands made upon them by the highway and education lobbies.

A mark of the Clement policy was the friendliness displayed to the organized municipalities of the state. The rise of municipal power in the politics of Tennessee begins with the first administration of Clement, even though Clement's own analysis of his political needs placed heavy emphasis on the backing of the rural machine that was in power in state politics in 1952. The Tennessee Municipal League and many of its principles were duly grateful to the governor, but they never ceased their demands on him. One step forward led only to another; no governor since Clement's time, and even before, has failed to hear the demands of cities and counties for increased benefits from the state.

It so happened that Clement had to deal with the opening crises of racial desegregation. It is not easy to tell how he felt about blacks. They had played no more than a minor part in the hometowns of his childhood. On his own he would have done little, in all probability, to challenge the standard attitudes of the South on race relations. But he was not a rabble-rouser and he was not a Negro-hater. Indeed his friendliness to people in general reached out to both blacks and whites. The orders of the Supreme Court in the fifties were met with some reluctance and with considerable moderation; the governor easily irritated the extremists on both sides. As the blacks became increasingly impatient in the 1960s, they lost faith, some of them, in Clement, and they contributed to the two defeats he sustained at the close of his career. Clement's disasters were the disasters common to men who wish to make haste slowly; to some of the most rabid of the conservatives, he became a "poltroon"; to the more demanding of the blacks, he was a time-serving politician.

Clement's strategy on school desegregation was a delicate procedure based principally on inactivity. Desegregation, he said, was a matter for the localities. He thus shifted the responsibility to the local school authorities who presumably would act only when pushed by the courts. Only with the greatest reluctance did the governor provide paramilitary backing for hard pressed local police. Moreover, he proposed the passage of delaying legislation that turned out to be unconstitutional in part.

On the other hand, he put a stop to some extremist local legislation. Perhaps he can be faulted for not becoming a civil rights crusader; but he was the governor of a state that was deeply divided on the course of action to be pursued, and of a state where the belief in local autonomy is one of the most powerful impulses in political life. Of course he did not succeed in satisfying the increasingly insistent blacks; he tried once more in his last term to bring them cautiously into the political mainstream, but he never moved fast enough to satisfy all of them. No more did other white politicians, north or south. Ten years after Clement's death, the status of the black is as troublesome to the white as ever.

Clement never willingly took much lead in securing the reapportionment of the legislature. It is highly doubtful whether he could have accomplished anything if he had. That was a matter that had to come, unfortunately, through the courts. Nor did he take any steps in the nature of party or electoral reforms. He played the political game according to the time-established formula of factional politics; it was a game generally good to him, until the disasters of the senatorial contest.

Like other governors before and after him, Clement responded to the times; he did not make them. What happened to the state of Tennessee and its people would have happened anyway. Notable as they momentarily seem, governors cannot make or remake the society; probably the same thing may be said of the more powerful national leader, the President.

In Clement's time, the state and its economy were going through a vigorous expansion. From 1950 to 1965, public school enrollment increased by 35 percent. The number of teachers jumped from 1952 to 1967 from 24,000 to 36,000. The number of those teachers with masters' degrees increased in those years from 11 percent of the total to 20 percent; the number with bachelors' degrees moved higher, from 48 percent to 68 percent. The average salary of these teachers advanced from about $2,400 to $5,700. Even when allowance is made for the slow deterioration in the dollar they were paid, they were still over 100 percent better paid at the end of Clement's last term than when he began. The average spent per pupil advanced from 1950 to 1967 by 154 percent. More students were going to school longer. In 1950 the median year of school completed was 8.4. In 1970, this figure was 10.6. In both years the whites had completed about two more years than the blacks; their relationship did not change.

In spite of their connection to rural interests, governors have generally been eager to promote the commercial and industrial development of the state; by that route come payrolls and tax rolls. Clement was as eager for that development as any one else; his correspondence is full of attempts great and small to boost state industry. And the state was becoming industrial, along with the rest of the country. In 1950, some 759,000 Tennesseans had been employed in nonagricultural establishments; 250,000 of these had worked in manufacturing. By 1967, nonagricultural establishments accounted for 1,219,000 persons, of which 436,000 were in manufacturing. This was a sizeable jump. Emphasis to this development was lent by the fact that in 1950, 31 percent of Tennessee's population was classed as rural farm; in 1970, 8 percent. This was a drastic decline, although the farm interests were still powerful politically.

But Tennessee was also persistently moving in the path of a developing welfare and bureaucratic state. The number of state employees grew steadily from 21,000 in 1955 to 45,000 in 1967. A single year of the Clement-Ellington period from 1955 to 1967 failed to show an increase in the number of state jobholders (the figures before 1955 are not available). That was the period 1956 and 1957, when there was no jump. In every other year increases of from 4 percent to 11 percent are recorded. The lowest increases are in some of the Ellington years, but increases there were, all the same.

The revenues of the state zoomed steadily higher. In 1950, they were $238,860,000; in 1967, $962,743,000. They mounted steadily during the Clement years, born on the tides of higher taxes and a cheapening dollar. Even accounting for the declining dollar, they are higher. The expenditures mounted in the same way, for the state was not building up a permanent surplus, although yearly surpluses above the estimates were characteristic of the Clement administration. Part of the material prosperity of the state's treasury came from the expanding contributions from the national government. The per capita revenue of the state jumped from $85 in 1955 to $229 in 1967. The per capita debt jumped from $30 in 1950 to $67 in 1967, an advance of 162 percent. It was a debt that continued to grow steadily after Clement's time.

And with these advances in taxation and debt, the state was constantly increasing the scope of its services and its regulation. Although Clement participated fully and with conviction in at least some of this development, he could not have influenced it greatly one way or another. The state was going the way that the country was going, for better or for worse.

He had always wanted to be a "humane" governor. No one can deny him this achievement. The blind remember him with affection. He was able to stir others — even some of those he let go to the dread chair in the penitentiary were reconciled to him. If he failed with prison administration, it was not through ill will. Those stricken in the mind could have thanked him for better care, had they possessed the reason to respond.

The normal fate of a politician in a democratic society is repudiation. One may reflect on Woodrow Wilson, Winston Churchill, Lyndon Johnson, and on the lesser figures, known principally to Tennesseans, of Prentice Cooper, Jim Nance McCord, Gordon Browning. For Clement, rejection, like victory, came early in his all-too-brief career. Suppressing inward hurt and amazed disbelief, he bore his defeats with outward gallantry, maintaining some personal ties across the divisions of political dispute. His achievements in a time of good fortune were substantial enough to deaden the deeply felt disappointments of the final years.

*   *   *   *   *

And so—all this behind him—the governor came home at last to Dickson County. Frank Clement was buried on November 6th, his father's birthday. Services were held in the small First United Methodist Church in Dickson; it was filled to overflowing. Crowds stood outside the building. The major political figures of Clement's lifetime were there: former Senator Walters, the incumbent United States Senators Gore and Baker, members of the national House of Representatives, longtime political allies and former opponents, such as Jared Maddux, James Bomar, Frank Gorrell, Governor Buford Ellington, and most notably, Gordon Browning, wasted by the ravages of Parkinson's disease. Clement's family was there, with the exception of his wife, hospitalized outside the state. The congregation sang "Amazing Grace"; a quartet sang, once more, the hymn that Clement had loved and so often used, with its final prayer,

> Precious Lord, . . .
> through the storm, through the night, . . .
> take my hand, Precious Lord,
> lead me home.

Truck loads of flowers and a long line of cars moved to the small cemetery at the side of Highway 70-S, east of Dickson. The congregation flowed around the funereal canopy and among the markers of the other dead, as Clement's flag-draped coffin was borne by Legionnaires to the grave. His father and mother braved the mourners and the persistent cameras to follow him to the spot where his broken body was committed to the Tennessee's earth's "encircling arms." In due course, his grave was marked by a small bronze plate, inscribed with the record of a brief life's ambition and achievement:

> **Frank Goad Clement**
> **1920–1969**
> **Governor of Tennessee**
> **1953 — 1959 — 1963 — 1967**

Notes

DIRECTIONS FOR USE OF NOTES

Following the customary references in these notes, added citations are shown in parentheses. These added citations refer to folders of correspondence and papers in my research files, which have been housed in the Special Collections of the James D. Hoskins Library of the University of Tennessee, Knoxville. My research files also include my notes on books, articles, and similar material, and on newspapers, as well as my correspondence dealing with this research. Where the normal citations refer to material readily available, such as newspapers or official records, no citations to my research files are shown. Citations of letters to or from me will be found in my correspondence unless otherwise indicated.

Correspondence and similar material in my research files have normally been arranged in folders by subject matter identified by folder titles shown within the parentheses in the notes, except in instances where the folder refers to copies of papers duplicated from collections such as the Kefauver papers or the Walters papers. The great bulk of the correspondence comes from the Clement papers in the Tennessee State Library and Archives; at the time I worked with this material, it had not yet been permanently classified, and it seemed best that instead of referring to temporary locations in the State Library I refer to my own copies of this material classified by subject matter and housed at UT. Researchers are free to consult my research files in the UT Library, where more complete descriptions and instructions for their use have been provided. If necessary, researchers can locate material in the State Library and other collections through the names and dates provided in my citations.

Ellipsis marks are used to separate phrases in the note references. Usually, but not always, these correspond to ellipses in the text.

Additional unpublished notes to this work are filed in the State Library and Archives, in Special Collections, UT, and the Memphis State University Library.

SHORT TITLES FOR REFERENCES

(Browning files) refers to copies of letters found in the Browning collection of the Tennessee State Library and Archives, Nashville.

(Corres.-Browning) refers to copies of letters found in the Clement collection of the Tennessee State Library and Archives.

(D) is used to identify copies of papers housed at the Clement birthplace in Dickson, Tennessee.

(Davidson) refers to copies of letters of Donald Davidson in the collections of the Vanderbilt University Library, Nashville.

(Gore papers) refers to copies of letters in the collection of Senator Albert Gore's papers in the library of Middle Tennessee State University, Murfreesboro.

(JUL) refers to copies of letters of Brainard Cheney in the collections of the Vanderbilt University Library (formerly the Joint University Libraries) and are cited by permission of Mr. Cheney.

(Kefauver papers) refers to the Kefauver collection in Special Collections, Hoskins Library, University of Tennessee, Knoxville.

(Corres.-Kefauver) refers to correspondence in the Clement papers of the Tennessee State Library and Archives.

(Walters) refers to papers of Senator Herbert Walters in Special Collections, Hoskins Library, University of Tennessee.

(Corres.-Walters) refers to letters in the Clement papers of the Tennessee State Library and Archives.

All other references to papers and correspondence are to copies of papers in the Clement collection of the Tennessee State Library and Archives; these copies are filed by subject matter as indicated in the notes and are stored in Special Collections, Hoskins Library, University of Tennessee, where additional identification is provided.

CH refers to the Capitol Hill column in the *Nashville Banner.*

P refers to the Politics column in the *Nashville Tennessean.*

Interview tapes and transcripts: These—with some exceptions—are filed with Special Collections, Hoskins Library, University of Tennessee, in the Tennessee State Library and Archives, and in the Clement oral history collection at Memphis State University.

The interview tapes of Dr. Stephen D. Boyd in the Tennessee State Library and Archives have been used and cited with Dr. Boyd's permission.

CHAPTER 1.

page

5 "Nathan, Isaac, and Stephen": Letter, J.D. Melton to LSG, May 15, 1976, based on family Bible records supplied to Melton by Sam Cooper, descendant of Daniel Buchanan (Data on Clement-Goad family).

"still found": *Benton County Marriages, 1832–1957,* Florence Elliott Hillis, ed. (n.p., 1962) shows Clements in the county. Additional details of the Clement families are contained in Jonathan K.T. Smith, *Genealogical Gleanings in Benton County, Tennessee* (Memphis, n.p., 1974).

6 "Daniel Buchanan": Jonathan Kennon Thompson Smith, *Historic Benton: A People's History of Benton County, Tennessee* (Memphis, n.p., 1975) contains information on Daniel Buchanan, including his occupation of lands. Daniel Buchanan is also mentioned as a "strong man" in what became Houston County in the *Goodspeed History of Houston* (Nashville: Goodspeed Pub. Co., 1886; rpt. 1972), 978. His brother, Christopher is also mentioned. Also letters from Kennon Smith to FGC, June 19, 1956, and Jan. 19, 1957 (Data on Clement-Goad family). See also Jonathan K.T. Smith, *Benton County* (Memphis: Memphis State Univ. Press, 1979), 23, 27.

"James Archibald Clement . . . August 1, 1853": Letter, Robert S. Clement to Mrs. R.O. Sherer, Aug. 17, 1955 (Data on Clement-Goad family); letter, Melton to LSG, May 15, 1976 (Data on Clement-Goad family), the information being based on family Bible records supplied in 1955 to Melton by Sam Cooper, a descendant of Daniel Buchanan; Jill K. Garrett and Iris H. McClain, *Dickson County, Tennessee Cemetery Records,* (n.p., 1967) 95.

8 "six other children": *Tennessee: A History* (New York, 1933), IV, 595. One child was W.A. Clement, whose mental collapse as a result of an incurable head wound turned Frank Clement's attention to mental problems. Interview, Robert S. Clement, March 25, 1975. *Biographical Directory, Tennessee General Assembly, 1796–1967* (Preliminary, Tennessee State Library and Archives) Cheatham County, Dickson County, 18.

"state Senate": *Biographical Directory,* 18. J.A. Clement later represented Dickson, Houston, Humphreys, and Stewart counties as senator in 1913 and 1915; see lists in *Tennessee Acts, Public,* 1913 and 1915.

"Agnes Anne Work": Gravestone, Union Cemetery, Dickson; Garrett and McClain; *Cemetery Records,* Pt. I, 142; Stanley J. Folmsbee, Robert E. Corlew, and Enoch L. Mitchell, *History of Tennessee* (New York: Lewis Historical Publishing Co., 1960), IV, 868.

8 "Dock Shipp": *Historical Sketches of Hickman County, Tennessee,* comp. Jill K. Garrett (n.d., n.p.), 125.

"11th Tennessee Infantry": *Family and Military Records from Spence's History of Hickman County, Tennessee,* by Kate Derryberry Leeper, 154. See Folmsbee et al., *History of Tennessee,* IV, 868. See W. Jerome D. Spence and David L. Spence, *A History of Hickman County, Tennessee* (Nashville: Gospel Advocate Publishing Co., 1900), 471.

10 "school teacher . . . county superintendent of schools": Interview, Robert S. Clement, March 25, 1975; *Historical Sketches, Hickman County,* 126; Robert Ewing Corlew, *A History of Dickson County* (Nashville: Tennessee Historical Commission and the Dickson County Historical Society, 1956), 228; Folmsbee et al., ibid., IV, 870–72.

"first woman": Interview, Robert S. Clement, March 25, 1975; Corlew, *Dickson County,* 159, 228.

"state librarian . . . state superintendent of schools": Robert S. Clement thought his mother was a candidate for state librarian (ibid), but I could not verify this candidacy from official records; the story is given in Folmsbee et al., *History of Tennessee,* IV, 869; letter, Robert S. Clement to LSG, May 25, 1976.

"December 1899": *Tennessee: A History,* 595.

"forty-seven": Gravestone; *Tennessee: A History,* 595; Folmsbee et al., *History of Tennessee,* IV, 868; interview, Robert S. Clement, March 25, 1975. See *Biographical Directory,* 18. After her death, J.A. Clement married Florence Kellam, ibid.

"Robert Samuel Clement": Interview, Clement, ibid.

"died in the 1950s": ibid.; *Tennessee: A History,* 595. Jesse Archie died in 1954. Joseph Malcolm died in 1957; Folmsbee et al., *History of Tennessee,* IV, 870.

"her life in the state service": Ida Agnes Clement Nicks was, like Aunt Dockie, a teacher of elocution. She taught in Aunt Dockie's school for part of her life; interview, Ida Nicks, Oct. 18, 1978.

"as a page . . . four dollars a day . . . Hubert Fisher . . . Hill McAlister": Interview Robert S. Clement, March 25, 1975.

12 "returning that night . . . liquor question . . . 100 percent of the votes": ibid.

"along Goose Creek . . . Taylors, Burrows, Roarks, and Wrights . . . for the law . . . country newspapers . . . Idle Roark": Ibid.; interview, Judge Frank Goad, Aug. 20, 1976.

"at Lafayette in 1889": Letter, Frank R. Goad to FGC, July 2, 1954.

"to Scottsville": Interview, Judge Frank Goad, Aug. 20, 1976.

13 "sudden heart attack . . . acquired real estate": Interview, ibid.

"the Halbrook": This old commercial hotel has been converted into a

13   museum as a memorial to Gov. Clement. Exhibits are displayed on
      the ground floor; the second floor has been converted into residen-
      tial quarters, occupied for some years by Gov. Clement's parents.
      See description of hotel as a museum in file-Family Letters.
      "August 20, 1919": Marriage license record; see also Folmsbee et al.,
      History of Tennessee, IV, 869.

15   "Vermont": The family were in Vermont from Oct. 1923 to May
      1924; letter, Anna Belle O'Brien to LSG, Nov. 10, 1978; interview,
      Robert S. Clement, March 25, 1975.
      "residence in Kentucky . . . bookkeeper": Statement by Anna Belle
      Clement in Clement papers; letter, Paul H. Sanders to FGC, Jan. 16,
      1955 (both in Family Letters).
      "born in Kentucky": Anna Belle was born in Scottsville on May 6,
      1923; *Tennessee Blue Book,* 1977–1978, p. 57. Emma Gene, who be-
      came Mrs. Bruce Peery, was born in Scottsville on March 16, 1925;
      letter, Anna Belle O'Brien to LSG, Nov. 10, 1978. Anna Belle Clem-
      ent became Mrs. Charles H. O'Brien by her third marriage.
      "Goebel Goad . . . Emma Goad Johnson": Interview, Judge Frank
      Goad, Aug. 20, 1976.
      "abnormally large head . . . any sense at all": Interview, Robert S.
      Clement; March 25, 1975.

16   "protective attitude": Ibid.
      "most of the decisions": Interview, Anna Belle O'Brien, March 25,
      1975.
      "to the Baptists": Interview, Robert S. Clement, March 25, 1975; in-
      terview, O'Brien, ibid.
      "dry-cleaned . . . in the Green River": Interview, Robert S. Clem-
      ent, ibid.

17   "Bible-toting": These words were used from time to time during the
      campaigns; see also letter, Jared Maddux to Frank McGee, Nov. 10,
      1966 (1966 Campaign). *Newsweek,* March 12, 1962, called him
      "Bible-quoting" (1962 Campaign).
      "challenged the teacher": This story has often been told by the Clem-
      ent family. Interview, Robert S. Clement, March 25, 1975; letter,
      FGC to David F. MacPherson, Aug. 18, 1954 (Family Letters); also
      transcripts of tapes on a proposed autobiography in the file-Proposed
      Autobiography.
      "Bowling Green": Interview, Robert S. Clement, ibid.
      "on Park Street": Statement by Anna Belle Clement in file-Family
      Letters. See also letter, Estelle Drake to FGC, Jan. 28, 1955 (Family
      Letters).
      "Bowling Green home was given up": Statement, Clement, ibid.
      "W.A. Clement": ibid.

17 "little else . . . 75 cents per night . . . for about $300": This descrip-
tion of the early family hardships is found in the statement by Anna
Belle Clement in file-Family Letters.

18 "freshman high school year": Information on the official transcript
for Frank Clement from Dickson High School (Academic Records).

"in 1933, James A. Clement died": Gravestone, Union Cemetery,
Dickson; *Cemetery Records*, 95.

"never wanted his sons to practice law": Interview, Anna Belle
O'Brien, March 25, 1975.

"took in boarders . . . Frank peddled newspapers": Memorandum,
Brainard Cheney to Anna Belle Clement, Oct. 13, 1955 (Family
Letters). See also *Nashville Banner*, March 17, 1958. (Hereafter re-
ferred to as *Banner*.)

19 "final two high school years": Dickson County High School transcript (Academic Records); see also Stephen Dean Boyd, "The
Campaign Speaking of Frank Clement in the 1954 Democratic Primary: Field Study and Rhetorical Analysis", diss., Univ. of Illinois, 1972, 17.

"particularly one player": Interview, Anna Belle O'Brien, March 25,
1975. See Kesterson press release, n.d. (Young Democratic Clubs);
see *Banner*, Aug. 8, 1952; interview, Mrs. Lucille Clement, Sept. 4,
1980.

"Dockie Shipp Weems": Boyd diss.; also interview, Anna Belle
O'Brien, ibid.

"Dickson Normal School . . . of 800 . . . ceased existence": Corlew, *Dickson County*, 160–65.

"honor student": Corlew, ibid., 160–65.

"Joe Weems" B. 1888, d. 1950; see *Cemetery Records*, Part I, 154. The
date of birth is given as 1887 in Folmsbee et al., *History of Tennessee*,
IV, 872.

"Vanderbilt School of Expression": *Banner*, April 15, 1965.

20 "*Life* and *Time*": Ibid., April 15, 1965; see also Folmsbee et al., *History
of Tennessee*, 871.

"County Judge of Dickson": Joe B. Weems was county judge of Dickson from 1918 to 1934; he was succeeded by W.M. Leech, who became a cabinet member for Clement; Leech served as county judge
from 1934 to 1950; he was succeeded by James A. Weems—"Jimmy"
Weems, Clement's cousin—who served from 1950 to 1958. Corlew, *Dickson County*, 227; *Tennessee Blue Book*, 1957–58, p. 152.

"Tennessee Interscholastic Literary League": Records of the Division
of Continuing Education, Univ. of Tennessee (Speaking Contests).

"District III . . . much in evidence": Records, ibid.

21 "evenings": Boyd, 17.

21 "reading other speeches": Interview, Anna Belle O'Brien, March 25, 1975.

"first in District III . . . second prize . . . Stuart Maher": Records, UT Continuing Education (Speaking Contests). In these records, Maher's first name is given as "Stewart"; Maher became a geologist for the state of Tennessee.

"exactly the same paragraph": Telephone conversation, Stuart Maher, March 8, 1980.

"baseball": Interview, Charles Lockett, Jan. 25, 1980.

22 "gospel hymns and country music": Interview, Anna Belle O'Brien, March 25, 1975.

"singing out loud": *Tennessean*, April 5, 1963.

"Anna Belle": Interview, Anna Belle O'Brien, March 25, 1975.

"his promise": Interview, Robert N. Clement, May 6, 1976.

"to right wrongs": Interview, Anna Belle O'Brien, March 25, 1975.

CHAPTER 2.

23 "it was well understood": Among the other difficulties that plagued the family, it was discovered that Robert Clement, the father, had contracted tuberculosis; it was said in the *Tennessean* that a family conference determined that only Frank could be fully educated. *Tennessean*, Nov. 5, 1969. Also, interview, Anna Belle O'Brien, ibid.

"Presbyterian auspices": Winstead Paine Bone, *A History of Cumberland University, 1842–1935* (Lebanon, Tenn., 1935), 15, 36.

24 "Joe Evins": Interview, Ernest L. Stockton, Jr., June 4, 1976.

"five Dickson boys": ibid.; *Phoenix*, 1938 (Cumberland Univ. Data).

"Jimmy Weems": Ibid.

"Dortch Oldham": *Phoenix*, 1938.

"Ramon Davis": Interview, Ernest L. Stockton, Jr., June 4, 1976. Spelled "Raymond" in the *Phoenix*, 1938.

"James Bomar": *Phoenix*, 1938; interview, Stockton, ibid.

25 "Gordon Browning spoke there": *Phoenix*, 1938. Browning also attended the law school there; William Raymond Majors, "*Gordon Browning and Tennessee Politics*" (diss. Univ. of Georgia, 1967), 15.

26 "religious emphasis week": 1937 Catalog; interview, Ernest L. Stockton, Jr., June 4, 1976.

"prescribed liberal arts curriculum": Comments on the courses pursued by Clement are based on the official transcripts.

"photographic memory": All close observers of Clement comment on his phenomenal memory; for example, interviews, David Alexander, Feb. 28, 1978, and Harold Read, Nov. 25, 1974. Among the

26   Goads, Clement's grandfather, Will Goad, and his uncle, Goebel
      Goad, each possessed a similar memory. Whether members of the
      Clement family possessed this trait is not known.
      "long trip to Erin": Interviews, Ernest L. Stockton, Jr., June 4, 1976;
      Lucille Clement, Sept. 14, 1980; Robert N. Clement, May 6, 1976.
      "Ralph T. Donnell": Interview, Ralph T. Donnell, June 4, 1976.
      "Tennessee Forensic League": Ibid.
      "president of the freshman class . . . member of the student council":
      Interview, Ernest L. Stockton, June 4, 1976.
      "to avoid placing Frank Clement . . . Weems lost": Interview,
      Ralph T. Donnell, June 4, 1976.
28 "a brilliant student": Weems was apparently a highly capable man.
      He served as an officer in World War II, where he suffered the
      tragic experience of having all his men killed around him. The ex-
      perience scarred him deeply. He served as county judge of Dickson
      County and died of cancer in 1975. Weems had a distinguished ca-
      reer as a law student at the University of Virginia; see Folmsbee et
      al., *History of Tennessee*, IV, 874. Interview, Ernest L. Stockton, Jr.,
      June 4, 1976.
      "his father or grandfather": The experience of the three generations
      indicates the changes in society. J.A. Clement could become a law-
      yer by reading in a law office and hanging out his shingle, but by
      the time his grandson was making a start, entrance to the profes-
      sion was becoming more difficult.
      "Dave Alexander": Interview, David Alexander, Feb. 28, 1978.
29 "he and Lucille eloped": Interview, Lucille Clement, Sept. 4, 1980;
      letter, Anna Belle O'Brien to LSG, Nov. 10, 1978. Copies of the
      marriage records are in the file-Birth, Death, Marriage Data.
      "first experience in public speaking": Letter, FGC to National Invita-
      tional Debate Tournament, Vanderbilt Univ., March 2, 1964 (Speak-
      ing Contests).
31 "profitless undertaking": The account of the Clement courtship and
      early married life is based on an interview with Lucille Clement,
      Sept. 4, 1980. Compare also interview, Robert N. Clement, May
      6, 1976.
      "he recalls": Interview, David Alexander, Feb. 28, 1978.
      "his memory says": Ibid.
32 "young Clement couple": Interview, Lucille Clement, Sept. 4, 1980.
      "not interested in becoming a profound student": Interview, David
      Alexander, Feb. 28, 1978.
      "A rumor": Clement frequently made this claim himself; see cam-
      paign brochure in the 1952 campaign; also letter, FGC to Richard
      Hansen, Sept. 24, 1953 (Bio Data).

32 "telephone call": Interview, Buford Lewallen, March 18, 1975.

33 "officer in charge": Story told to LSG by Scott Alden, former FBI direc-
    tor at Knoxville.

    "she would have to leave when": Interview, Anna Belle O'Brien,
    March 25, 1975; see also file-Family Letters.

    "three months": Separation Qualifications Record, signed, Capt. T.L.
    Kubach (D) (Military Records).

    "an FBI agent": Ibid. Clement said he had a minor role in the capture
    of Basil Banghart of the Touhey gang in 1942, but there was little
    spectacular about his short period of service; see Proposed Auto-
    biography Data, notes prepared when the governor thought of
    writing an autobiography.

34 "military service came to him unsolicited": FBI agents were normally
    given deferments, through the prestige of J. Edgar Hoover. In ad-
    dition, Clement was eligible for some deferment through marriage.
    The symbols on his military records indicate that he was drafted.

    "His military records": Military Record and Report of Separation;
    (D) (Military Records). Report of Separation from the Armed
    Forces (D) (Military Records).

    "as a private": Statement of service, signed by Capt. W.F. Saunders,
    Jr. (D) (Military Records).

    "he was promoted": Ibid. Enlisted Record signed by Kenneth J.
    White. The records are not always consistent internally.

    "Military Police School": Letter, FGC to Henry J. Dalimonte, Sept. 5,
    1956 (Military Service); verified by Statement of Service, Dec. 8,
    1958 (D) (Military Records), and Enlisted Record, signed by Capt.
    Kenneth J. White (D) (Military Records). During 1944, FGC and
    his father made some attempts to secure a transfer for him into the
    judge advocate general's office or into intelligence service; letter,
    FGC to Martin V. Coffey, Feb. 26, 1944 (D) (Military Service); let-
    ter, Wirt Courtney to Robert S. Clement, May 24, 1944 (D) (Mili-
    tary Service); letter, Robert S. Clement to Lt. Col. Joseph C. Jack-
    son, Aug. 9, 1944 (D) (Military Service).

    "in basic training . . . second lieutenant . . . Camp Bullis, Texas
    . . . first lieutenant . . . commanding officer": 1958 Statement of
    Service (D) (Military Records).

    "Fort Sam Houston": Report of Separation, 1946 (D); *Separation
    Qualification Record* (D); 1958 *Statement of Separation* (See file-
    Military Records).

    "highest rank . . . next to highest rank": Information from Colonel
    Joe Shepherd, formerly ROTC, UT.

35 "statements of defenders": Attacks by columnist Joe Hatcher on
    Clement's military record are contained in the *Tennessean*, May 11,

35 July 13, and July 19, 1952. In one column, Hatcher refers to a list of affidavits read out by "Honest Eddie" Friar from persons defending Clement's record. The Hamilton County Veterans for Browning attacked Clement's war record—ibid., July 10, 1952; Clarence Evans attacked Clement's lack of combat experience—ibid., July 17, 1952. These attacks were made at the height of the 1952 campaign. In July 1952, A.D. Walker, who had been executive officer of the 770th Military Police Battalion at Fort Sam Houston, signed an affidavit praising Clement as one of six outstanding second lieutenants. Walker stated that Clement sought no favors and that he had repeatedly volunteered for overseas duty. Walker said he was kept where he was needed most. Walker stated that he had given Clement the highest ratings he had ever recorded for any man under his command (Military Records).

"Buford Lewallen": Interview, Buford Lewallen, March 18, 1975.

"general counsel": See *Banner*, March 2, 1949.

"consent and influence": Joe Hatcher in the *Tennessean*, May 11, 1952.

"Herbert Walters": Statement made by Senator Walters to LSG.

"already launched": Letters, H.C. Smith to Walters, Jan. 24, 1942; Frank Riley to Walters, May 25, 1942; Walters to Benton Trundle, June 26, 1942; form letter, Joe Carr to county managers, July 14, 1942; resolution, Hamblen County Democrats, May 27, 1944 (all in file-Walters).

36 "McKellar": McKellar to Walters, June 25, 1942; McKellar to Walters, Aug. 9, 1942 (all in file-Walters).

"Cooper": Letter, Prentice Cooper to Walters, June 29, 1942; telegram, Cooper to Walters, Aug. 7, 1942 (all in file-Walters).

"Stewart": Letter, Stewart to Walters, Aug. 18, 1942; letter, Walters to Mary James Cottrell, July 27, 1948 (all in file-Walters).

"McCord": Letter, Louis R. Schubert to Walters, June 8, 1944 (Walters); letter, Joe C. Carr to Walters, June 18, 1944 (Walters).

"appeals": Letters, Robert L. Taylor to Walters, Oct. 29, 1949; Clifford D. Pierce to Walters, Feb. 9, 1950; Clifford D. Pierce to Walters, May 23, 1950; Clifford Allen to Walters, Jan. 29, 1952 (Walters).

"close touch": Letters, Walters to FGC, Nov. 10, 1949; FGC to Walters n.d. but 1949 (Walters).

"Korean War period": Letters, FGC to Walters, n.d. but 1950; FGC to Walters, Dec. 14, 1950 (Walters).

"early law practice": Letter, Walters to FGC, Feb. 12, 1948 (Walters).

"niece": Letter, Fred E. Wankan to Walters, Oct. 21, 1949 (Walters).

"until 1950": Clement resigned effective April 1, 1950; *Banner*, Jan. 16, 1950.

36 "new found friend . . . high school commencement time" Inter-
        view, Andrew D. Holt, July 9, 1976.
37 "would not take fees": Letters, FGC to Everett Norman, April 19,
        1950; FGC to W.M. Hunter, April 29, 1950 (both in Speeches and
        Speech-Policies). Clement gave small amounts of money to various
        churches during these early years: letters, FGC to Rev. S.D. Organ,
        Methodist, Dickson, May 6, June 6, 1946; FGC to Rev. W.H. Wise-
        man, Erin, Aug. 31, 1946 (Religious Activities). A list in the Clem-
        ent files shows small contributions totaling over $1,000 in gifts to
        churches and charities between May and the following April in one
        of these years, but no year is given (Religious Activities). Inter-
        view, Robert N. Clement, May 6, 1976.
     "presidency of the Young Democrats Clubs": Bio-data file; Joe
        Henry's contacts with Clement date from this time; interview, Joe
        Henry, Sept. 30, 1975.
     "up and down history . . . Joe Carr, Lipe Henslee, and Sam Coward":
        Interview, Joe C. Carr, Sept. 16, 1975. Letter, Coward to FGC, June
        28, 1951 (Pre-1952).
     "Sam Coward": Numerous letters from Dr. Coward are found in the
        Clement files, e.g., Coward to FGC, March 19, 1952 (1952 cam-
        paign); see also Banner, Sept. 25, 1952.
39 "Joe Henry": Interview, Joe Henry, Sept. 30, 1975.
     "Charlie Lockett": Interview, Charles Lockett, June 29, 1980.
     "one of the alternate delegates": Tennessee had 28 votes at the 1948
        convention. The delegates-at-large included Mrs. Albert Hill of
        Nashville, prominent in the party during the Clement administra-
        tions; Mrs. Edith Susong, newspaper publisher from Greeneville;
        John W. Harton of Tullahoma, at one time state treasurer; and
        Charles Stainback of Somerville, who was to be prominent in the
        later segregation fights. Congressional district delegates included
        Russell Kramer, prominent lawyer of Knoxville; Cecil Sims of
        Nashville; James A. Peeler, Jr., of Covington; and Representative
        Joe Evins of Smithville. Frank Clement was an alternate delegate-
        at-large, Tom Elam, later prominent as a UT trustee from Union
        City, was a district alternate; Democracy at Work, being the Official
        Report of the Democratic National Convention, July 12 to July 14, 1948,
        published by the Local Democratic Political Committee of Penn-
        sylvania, 369–70. It is surprising that no governor or candidate for
        governor was a member of this delegation.
     "state commander of the American Legion": Banner, March 2, July
        20, and July 25, 1949. The convention was held in Chattanooga
        July 24 to July 27, 1949; there was no opposition to Clement.
        Other candidates for Legion positions included Joe Henry, Cayce

39 Pentecost, Harlan Dodson; ibid., July 25, 1949. Sam Morris, a Clement friend, was the Chattanooga commander of the Legion; ibid., CH, July 25, 1949.

"district commander": Letter, Donald M. McSween to Herbert Walters, Feb. 20, 1948 (Walters).

40 "Donald McSween of Newport": McSween was the state commander of the Legion in 1948; letter, McSween to FGC, Jan. 17, 1950 (Pre-1952); *Banner*, CH, June 14, 1949. McSween became a cabinet member under Clement. In earlier years, Prentice Cooper had been state commander; *Banner*, Aug. 27, 1949.

"Roane Waring": Hatcher said Waring, "Kingmaker from Memphis," had moved to get Clement made state commander of the Legion "without regard to his service record"; *Tennessean*, P, May 11, 1952.

"held off acceptance": *Banner*, March 2, 1949.

"scrupulously absented himself": Letters, FGC to Barton Dement, Jr., Murfreesboro, June 8, 1950; FGC to Kyle King, Greeneville, June 9, 1950 (Pre-1952); see also *Banner*, CH, Nov. 17, 1949.

"Valerius Sanford . . . law school at Vanderbilt": Interview, Valerius Sanford, Sept. 29, 1977.

"reporting regularly": Letters, FGC to Miss Gibbs (signed "Soldier Boy"), Oct. 30, 1950; Valerius Sanford to FGC, Sept. 23, Oct. 27, 1950; FGC to Miss Gibbs and "Mike," Oct. 29, 1950 (all in Legal Career).

"Bishop Mattie Lou Jewell": Interview, Valerius Sanford, Sept. 29, 1977.

"reentered active service": *Report of Separation* (D) (Military Records); see *Banner*, Aug. 21, 1950.

"very high rating": *Report of Separation,* signed by Virgil P. Foster, Jr., Lt. Col. MPC, Director of Instruction, Provost Marshall General's School, 8801-2 Technical Service Unit, Camp Gordon, Ga., Dec. 20, 1951 (D) (Military Records). Clement's release from the army was reported in the *Banner*, CH, Dec. 21, 1951.

41 "off post from time to time": Interview, Joe C. Carr, Sept. 16, 1975; *Banner*, CH, March 26, 1951.

"had placed his name": *Banner*, CH, June 5, 1950.

"withdraw his name": Letters, Jack Norman to FGC, June 24, 1950; FGC to Jack Norman, Chairman, State Democratic Executive Committee, June 26, 1950; Norman to FGC, June 29, 1950 (Pre-1952).

"publicly declared himself": Letter, Jared Maddux to FGC, Oct. 26, 1950 (Pre-1952). On responses to his early announcement, letter, Jared Maddux to FGC, Oct. 26, 1950. Sanders Anglea, Nashville

41   politician, offered support (Anglea was then in the state House of
      Representatives); letter, Anglea to FGC, Oct. 26, 1950 (Pre-1952);
      as did Reader Parker, district attorney general for area composing
      Dickson, Houston, Humphreys, Robertson, Stewart, and Sumner
      counties; letter, Parker to FGC, Oct. 26, 1950 (Pre-1952); Joe Henry
      said Browning was singing his swan song; letter, Henry to FGC,
      Nov. 17, 1950 (Pre-1952). A pledge of support came from Sam Rid-
      ley of Smyrna; letter, Ridley to FGC, Dec. 6, 1950 (Pre-1952). Jim
      McCord was friendly but noncommittal; letter, McCord to FGC,
      Nov. 21, 1950 (Pre-1952). See also *Banner,* CH, Aug. 29, 1950; news
      story, Sept. 14, 1950; CH, Sept. 16, 1950.

CHAPTER 3.

42   "announced in 1950": Clement's announcement was reported in the
      Banner, Sept. 14, 1950.
      "held the private opinion": Letter, Hammond Fowler to FGC, Dec.
      14, 1950 (Pre-1952).
      "taken out of the state": When I talked to Robert S. Clement about
      this rumor, he did not claim directly that Browning influence or
      influence of Browning supporters had been exerted to draw Clem-
      ent into the army again, but I think he suspected it. Also interview,
      Buford Lewallen, March 18, 1975.
43   "only a few succeeded": John Sevier, 1796–1801, 1803–9; William
      Carroll, 1821–27, 1829–35; Robert Love Taylor, 1887–91, 1897–99.
      Andrew Johnson, governor from 1853 to 1857, was the military
      governor of Tennessee from March 1862 to March 1865. Browning,
      governor from 1937–39, was again in office when Clement an-
      nounced in 1950.
      "suddenly quit the job": Stanley J. Folmsbee, Robert E. Corlew and
      Enoch L. Mitchell, *Tennessee, A Short History* (Knoxville: Univer-
      sity of Tennessee Press, 1969) 171–72. Louise Davis, *Sam Houston's
      Tragic Marriage, from the pages of the Nashville Tennessean,* n.p.d.;
      Henry Bruce, *Life of General Houston, 1793–1863* (New York:
      Dodd, Mead, 1891), ch. 5.
      "populist governor": Folmsbee et al., *Tennessee, Short History,* 394–97,
      428–33.
      "four Whigs": Newton Cannon, James C. Jones ("Lean Jimmy
      Jones"), Neil S. Brown, William B. Campbell.
      "city dwellers . . . substantial planters": Folmsbee et al., *Tennessee,
      Short History,* 193–94.
44   "Whig-Republicans": William G. Brownlow, DeWitt Clinton
      Senter.

44 "Whig-Democrat": John C. Brown.

"Lean Jimmy Jones": Born in 1809; became governor in 1841.

"few ridge counties": Interview, W.L. Barry, Nov. 2, 1977. The Clement family had settled along these western ridges near the Tennessee River but not in Republican territory.

"Republican party shown strength in Shelby County": In the late 1970s, Shelby County has been divided between the central Memphis area, black and Democratic, and the outlying areas, white and Republican.

"Republican presidential candidates": See Folmsbee et al., *Tennessee, A Short History*, 455. See also Lee S. Greene and Jack E. Holmes, "Tennessee: A Politics of Peaceful Change" in William C. Harvard, ed., *The Changing Politics of the South* (Baton Rouge: Louisiana State Univ. Press, 1972), 165–200.

"1901 was faulty": Henry N. Williams, "Legislative Reapportionment in Tennessee," *Tennessee Law Review* 20 (April 1948), 235–45.

"could seize and hold power . . . Paul Cantrell . . . Burch Biggs" Burch Biggs in Polk County, Hilary Howse in Davidson, Paul Cantrell in McMinn, Crump in Shelby, e.g. See V.O. Key, Jr., *Southern Politics in State and Nation* (New York: Knopf, 1949), 65; Greene and Holmes, 169.

45 "Luke Lea": Majors, 9; Folmsbee et al., *Tennessee, A Short History*, 488–91.

"Austin Peay": Peay and Lea were bosses that wielded statewide influence; Peay is associated with the 1923 administrative reorganization which has been seen as a weapon for giving the governor boss-like power; see David D. Lee, *Tennessee in Turmoil: Politics in the Volunteer State, 1920–1932* (Memphis: Memphis State Univ. Press, 1979). Folmsbee, et al., *Tennessee, Short History*, 492–96.

"Ed Crump": A considerable literature has developed around Crump. See William D. Miller, *Mr. Crump of Memphis* (Baton Rouge: Louisiana State Univ. Press, 1964); Gerald M. Capers, Jr., "Memphis, Satrapy of a Benevolent Despot," in Robert S. Allen, ed., *Our Fair City* (New York: Vanguard, 1947); rpt. in Capers, *The Biography of a River Town: Memphis: Its Heroic Age* (New Orleans: The Author, 1966).

"attempting to spot winners": See Majors, 43. Crump's techniques are discussed in James B. Gardner, "Political Leadership in a Period of Transition: Frank G. Clement, Albert Gore, Estes Kefauver, and Tennessee Politics, 1948–1956", diss. Vanderbilt Univ., 1978.

"Tom Stewart": Joseph Bruce Gorman, *Kefauver: A Political Biography* (New York: Oxford Univ. Press, 1971), ch. 3; Gardner, ibid., ch. 3.

"direct primary": Folmsbee et al., *Tennessee, Short History*, 438; Lee

45   Seifert Greene, David H. Grubbs, Victor C. Hobday, *Government in Tennessee,* 3rd ed. (Knoxville: Univ. of Tennessee Press, 1975), 51.

"continuity of factions": Factions within the Democratic party are discussed at various points in Folmsbee et al., *Tennessee, Short History.* It should not be assumed that these factions have too much to do with ideology; they are mostly power combinations to serve the ambitions of individual candidates. In recent decades, connections can be traced from Cooper-McCord-Clement-Ellington-Clement-Ellington, and from Browning to John J. Hooker, but many candidates do not fit easily into any group, and the connections seem to me to break up with the election of Republican Dunn and Democrat Blanton. Most twentieth-century Tennessee politicians have some tinge of populism, and it is not easy to see one faction as liberal and the other as conservative.

"not strictly up for purchase": See William Buchanan and Agnes Bird, *Money as a Campaign Resource: Tennessee Democratic Senatorial Primaries, 1948–1964* (Princeton: Citizens' Research Foundation, n.d.).

"feel free to endorse": Public and party officials make no pretense to impartiality in party affairs; party committee members, both state and national, are clearly known to belong to party factions and to be partisans of individual candidates. Compare interview, Anna Belle O'Brien, May 5, 1975. The governor's control over the state party committee is limited by local forces; interview, ibid.

46   "pluralities": Ellington's plurality in 1958 was particularly narrow; all attempts to provide for runoff elections have so far been beaten down, and it must be assumed that the candidates like the free-for-all character of the primaries and the chance of being the winner that the plurality system encourages.

"no party platforms": It is impossible to discover a party stand on any issue in Tennessee; platforms are the exclusive prerogative of individual candidates.

"young Estes Kefauver . . . Governor Prentice Cooper": Charles L. Fontenay, *Estes Kefauver: A Biography* (Knoxville: Univ. of Tennessee Press, 1980), 85–87. Kefauver served as commissioner of finance and taxation under Cooper for four months in 1939; *Tennessee Blue Book,* 1942–43, p. 8.

"I do not believe in that": Reported to the author by Mrs. James Todd, the delegate from Davidson County to whom the remark was made.

47   "Browning's case": Browning was thirty-four years old when he went to the House of Representatives for the first time. His youthfulness at the time of the 1922 election was subsequently forgotten in the attention paid to Clement's youthfulness thirty years later.

47 When Browning first entered Congress, Clement was still a two-year-old toddler. See Majors, ch. 2.

"general counsel": The office of general counsel has some political overtones, and holders of that office are likely to have some sort of career in politics, either as officeholders or as active participants in party affairs.

"no office": Friar advised Clement to stay out of local political contests for fear of making enemies; Harold H. Martin, "The Things They Say about the Governor," *Saturday Evening Post,* Jan. 29, 1955, p. 50.

"immediately clear as to his own plans": Many Tennesseans felt that a governor was entitled to a courtesy second term, but a third term was felt by many to be too much. Browning had, in fact, served one term of two years, before being defeated by Prentice Cooper, and now was in his second consecutive term. But Browning had as much desire to stay in public office as Clement had, and remained interested in politics throughout his life. Even when he was old and ill, he could be counted on to be present at Democratic jamborees.

48 "flitted through Browning's thinking": Majors thought Browning had his eye on the Senate even when he was in lower house; Majors, 56; letter, Whit LaFon to FGC, May 14, 1951 (Pre-1952). Letters, Col. Raymond L. Prescott to Gov. Gordon Browning, Nov. 10, 1951, and reply, Nov. 19, 1951; Lucius Burch, Jr., to Gov. Gordon Browning, Feb. 7, 1951, and reply, Feb. 10, 1951 (Browning files).

"fiery temper": Browning's replies to critical letters were often sharp; see letter, Browning to Frank E. Knight, Feb. 15, 1951 (Browning files).

"twelve rather routine years": Majors, ch. 2.

"longing eye on a senatorship": ibid., 56.

"Weak Hill McAlister": Crump fell out with McAlister, Browning, Senator Tom Stewart, and, late in his career, with Clement. He and Cooper sometimes disagreed sharply. This record of disputes dims somewhat the claims made by so many writers that Crump's power was absolute or nearly so.

"bitter shoot-out": The no-holds-barred struggle between Browning and Crump in Browning's first term is described by Majors, ch. 5.

"county unit election law": The act established a county-unit vote for each county in the primaries for governor, United States senators, and members of the Railroad and Public Utilities Commission, and placed a limitation on the size of the county unit vote, so that the metropolitan counties, including Shelby, were at a disadvantage; *Public and Private Acts of Tennessee, Extra Sessions,* ch. 2, 1937.

48 "Many political leaders": See Majors, ch. 5.

"found the act unconstitutional": *Gates et al.* v. *Long et al.,* 113 SW 2d 388 (1938); 172 Tenn. 471 (1938).

"a mild-mannered, soft-spoken, irascible, and determined": Author's characterization based on personal acquaintance; numerous stories are told about Cooper's quick temper and vindictive behavior. After his marriage, he changed considerably. He was an honest and intelligent man, unusually cultured compared to other governors of his time.

"imposition of a personal income tax": Majors, 81, 120.

"had been ruled unconstitutional": *Evans,* v. *McCabe,* 164 Tenn. 672 (1932).

"state's first general sales tax": Folmsbee et al., *Tennessee, Short History* 469.

"denied a third term": The causes of a defeat for an incumbent governor cannot be determined, but Tennessee governors who have been associated with tax increases have often been defeated; interviews, Jim Cummings, Nov. 4, 1974; Joe C. Carr, Sept. 16, 1975; Robert S. Clement, March 25, 1975.

49 "Estes Kefauver slipped into the Senate": The 1948 senatorial campaign is described by Gorman, ch. III; see also Fontenay. See also David M. Tucker, *Memphis Since Crump: Bossism, Blacks, and Civic Reformers 1948–1968* (Knoxville: Univ. of Tennessee Press, 1980), ch. 3.

"created for the first time": Greene, Grubbs, Hobday, 127; Lee, ch. 3.

"Educational appropriations were improved": Majors, 120.

"rural-road building": Compare the *Banner,* March 8, 1949; Majors, 164.

"the railroad lobby": In this period, the railroads were fighting a principally defensive action against the growth of bus and truck traffic; the Browning-Clement campaign turned into a battle behind the scenes between the railroads and the truckers. Browning fought truck weight increases. In 1949 a bill in the Assembly proposed an increase in allowable truck weight from 42,000 to 54,000 pounds. Browning actually appeared before the legislature to "beg" that the bill be defeated. It was defeated in the House of Representatives; see *Banner,* March 29, 30, April 4, 1949.

"control of the state debt": Greene, Grubbs, Hobday, 187–88.

"pay-as-you-go philosophy": Browning had a horror of increased state debt, based, one would suppose, on the debacle of the Caldwell-Horton days. See John Berry McFerrin, *Caldwell and Company: A Southern Financial Empire* (Chapel Hill: Univ. of North Carolina Press, 1939; rpt. Nashville: Vanderbilt Univ. Press, 1969). See also

49   Folmsbee et al., *Tennessee, Short History,* 492–96. Apparently, Brown-
      ing wanted to pay for capital expenditures out of current surplus, a
      safe policy, but one that would have slowed development.

"military companions from the two world wars": Majors, 18. One of
      Browning's military friends was that flamboyant Tennessean,
      Luke Lea, who very nearly involved Browning in his plot to cap-
      ture the Kaiser; ibid., 17.

"the game of patronage": The *Banner* described Browning's patron-
      age activities in the opening months of 1949. See, e.g., *Banner,*
      CH, Jan. 22; and March 1, 1949. At the same time, Browning ap-
      parently did not try to build an extremely tight machine, perhaps
      because he had so detested the machine of Crump; compare Gard-
      ner, 152ff; Majors, 173–75.

50 "reorganized the primary election system": *Banner,* Jan. 26, 1949. Joe
      Henry was left off the election committee in the legislature because
      he had managed the campaigns of McCord and McKellar. After a
      hard battle in the legislature, Browning's election laws passed;
      ibid., Jan. 27 and Feb. 2, 1949. Browning took control of the elec-
      tions boards in May 1949; ibid., May 10, 24, 26, 1949. See Majors,
      164–67.

"G. Hilton Butler": Butler was born in 1898 near Fort Gibson, Missis-
      sippi, and was educated at Millsaps College. He entered the news-
      paper profession and became Nashville manager and later Wash-
      ington correspondent for the *Memphis Commercial Appeal.* At one
      time he was managing editor of the *Army and Navy Journal.* He was
      a member of the publicity staff of the Democratic National Com-
      mittee in 1932 and 1936. He studied law at George Washington
      University and in 1939 was admitted to the bar of Tennessee. He
      became director of safety under Governor Prentice Cooper and was
      later made executive assistant to Cooper (where rumor has it that
      he frequently bore the tempermental wrath of the governor).
      Among other duties, he helped to write speeches for Cooper. But-
      ler had served in World War I (and was to return to duty in World
      War II). Under McCord he was named acting adjutant general,
      state director of selective service and adjutant general. *Tennessee
      Blue Book,* 1939–40, p. 27, and 1945–46, p. 27. Butler lost his post
      with the government when Browning became governor in 1949;
      Banner, Jan. 1, 1949.

"dislike for large crowds": Interview, Fred Travis, correspondent for
      the *Chattanooga Times,* Sept. 26, 1977.

"I want you to get in on this": Interviews, Brainard Cheney, Feb. 11,
      1975; Robert S. Clement, March 25, 1975. Also letter, Cheney to
      Sen. Richard Russell, March 2, 1952 (JUL).

50 "free lance writing": Interview, Cheney, ibid.

"one of the first men": Ibid.

"key technician": Cheney was used particularly for research; Joe Henry was known as a phrase-maker of talent.

"into private employment": Joe Cordell Carr, born 1907, at Cookeville, was named for Cordell Hull, for whom his father had served as a campaign manager; interview, Carr, Sept. 16, 1975. He was a page in the Senate in 1923, page in the House, 1925; bill clerk in the House, 1929–31; assistant chief clerk of the House, 1933; re-elected to that post in 1935; reading clerk of the House, 1937; chief clerk of the House, 1939; *Tennessee Blue Book,* 1939–40, p. 21. He became secretary of state in 1941; ibid., 1942–43, p. 29, resigning to go into military service in 1944, ibid., 1945–46, p. 24. Mrs. Carr succeeded him as secretary of state, by appointment and subsequent election, remaining in the office until her husband's return from service, when she resigned, in 1945, and he returned to the office; ibid., 24. His term ran to 1949, when James Cummings was elected secretary of state; ibid., 1949–50, 25. Carr was associated with the Cooper-McCord faction in the Democratic party; Cummings, at this time, was associated with Browning. During the time Carr was out of office, he was in the insurance business; see *Banner,* CH, Feb. 14, 1949.

"Young Democratic clubs": Carr helped organize the Young Democratic Club of Tennessee in 1932 and served as secretary; he became president in 1934. He served as national secretary of the Young Democrats from 1935 to 1937 and was elected president of the Young Democratic Clubs of America in 1941; *Tennessee Blue Book,* 1945–46, p. 24. He was influential in securing the presidency of the Young Democrats of Tennessee for Clement; interview, Carr, Sept. 16, 1975.

"Frank Hobbs": Interview, Carr, ibid.; Frank Hobbs was at one time chairman of the Democratic state committee, an ally of McCord and Crump; *Banner,* CH, Jan. 26, 1949.

"major speechwriter": Interview, Joe Henry, Sept. 30, 1975.

"had managed . . . campaign . . . McCord": *Banner,* Jan. 26, 1949.

"did not clearly commit himself": McCord had been friendly but noncommittal in 1950; letter, Jim McCord to FGC, Nov. 21, 1950 (Pre-1952).

"Whit LaFon": Letters, LaFon to FGC, May 14, 1951; FGC to LaFon, May 19, 1951 (Pre-1952).

"Albert Gore . . . national House of Representatives": Gore was in the lower house from 1939 to 1953.

51 "campaign manager of Clifford Allen": Letter, Donald M. McSween

51 to FGC, Jan. 17, 1950 (Pre-1950); interview, Joe C. Carr, Sept. 16, 1975; letter, Donald M. McSween to Malcolm Hill, Nov. 14, 1951 (Corres.-McSween).

"R.G. Crossno": Letter, Crossno to FGC, Sept. 13, 1950 (Pre-1952).

"Jared Maddux": Letters, Maddux to FGC, Oct. 26, 1950, April 28, 1951 (Pre-1952).

"Jimmy Weems": *Banner*, CH, Jan. 15, 1952.

"Ramon Davis": Ibid., CH, June 11, 1952. Letter, Davis to FGC, June 15, 1951 (Pre-1952).

"released from active duty": *Banner*, CH, Dec. 21, 1951.

"took pains": Letter, Ellyn Warth to FGC, May 8, 1951 (Pre-1952). Ellyn Warth reported on a conversation with Silliman Evans. Evans said he hadn't formed an opinion on Clement because he hadn't been anywhere where he was preaching.

"Capitol Chevrolet Company": See data sheet (Family letters). Letter, Anna Belle Clement to FGC, Oct. 25, 1951 (Pre-1952).

"observations": Letter, ibid., Nov. 23, 1951 (Pre-1952).

"joined two women's organizations": Ibid., Oct. 25, 1951 (Pre-1952).

"Those gals": Ibid.

"urged to counteract": See letters, FGC to Sanders Anglea, July 3, 1951; FGC to Don McSween, July 5, 1951; "Bert" to "Frank," March 13, 1951 (Pre-1952).

52 "candidacy that involved opposition to McKellar": Leslie T. Hart, *Banner* columnist, said in 1950 that Browning wanted to run for the Senate and wanted Gore eliminated as a possibility; *Banner*, April 11, 1950; McKellar's announcement, thought Hart, might have turned Browning's ambitions back to the governorship; ibid., June 22, 1951.

"Browning's own camp . . . possible candidates": Fred Travis in the *Chattanooga Times,* Jan. 23, 1952; see also *Banner*, CH, March 26, 27, Nov. 19, 1951.

"surveying the field" Travis, *ibid.* Leslie Hart discussed Browning's indecision in his *Banner* column, CH March 27, June 20, 1951.

"battle with Crump": Letters, Browning to Mrs. Bennie C. Hall, June 16, 1952; Browning to Charles E. Marsh, Jan. 8, 1952; Browning to Col. G. Hurst Paul, May 16, 1952 (Browning files).

"own bottom": *Tennessean*, P, Feb. 10, 1952. Hatcher said Crump set up a coalition of McCord, Mitchell, and Fowler (Fowler for the Railroad and Public Utilities Commission); before that the coalitions had included: Cooper, Stewart, Hudson; Cooper, McCord; McCord, McKellar.

"Herbert Bingham": Bingham, a native Tennessean, was born in 1917 and attended the Webb School in Bell Buckle, Tenn.; he re-

52 ceived his A.B. at Southwestern College, Memphis; and he did
graduate work at Vanderbilt and the University of Chicago. He
joined the Tennessee Municipal League as executive secretary in
1946; biodata supplied by Tennessee Municipal League (TML).
"Baird": Letters, Baird to FGC, Sept. 11, 1951 (TML).

53 "Cards": See file—TML. See *Banner*, May 1, 1952.
"Allen": Browning and Clement backed the TML; letters, Baird to Edward Friar, Jan. 18, 1951; FGC to W.D. Baird, Jan. 29, 1952 (TML).
Banner, May 2, 1952. Also letters, Browning to S.F. Polk, April 18,
1952; Browning to D.W. Moulton, Dec. 8, 1950 (Browning files).
"backing of the railroads": On early political activity of the railroads,
see Folmsbee et al., *Tennessee, Short History*, 366–68. Railroads had
the habit of keeping numerous local lawyers as retainers; James A.
Clement was retained in this way, and his family traveled on passes.
On Browning's railway support, interview, Stephen D. Boyd with
Buford Ellington, Aug. 18, 1971; see also *Banner*, March 29, 1949.
James Bomar, in 1949, led a fight in the legislature for increasing
the truck weight; ibid.
"Super Service Motor Freight Company": See Harold H. Martin, 50,
51. Martin says a "kitty" of $300,000 was collected from highway
contractors and that Crichton added $140,000 of his own. This
seems too high.
"the most ruthless lobby in the state": Interview, Brainard Cheney,
Feb. 11, 1975. On Clement's support of TEA, letter, FGC to Frank E.
Bass, April 9, 1952. (1952 Campaign).
"the blacks": Clement picked up support from blacks who were later
significant; letters, John Willard Bowden to FGC, saying he and
Ben Hooks were interested in him, July 29, Dec. 10, 1951; FGC to
Bowden May 8, 1952 (Negroes I). Some warnings were sent to
Clement not to court black support too openly in West Tennessee;
letter, Robert Felsenthal to FGC, March 21, 1952 (Negroes I).
"the endorsement of labor organizations": Letter, Charles Houk to
FGC, n.d. (Pre-1952); see *Banner*, CH, Dec. 6, 1951; see also *Banner*,
May 9, 1952. Steve Para, legislative representative for the Brotherhood of Railroad Trainmen, was an early supporter of Clement;
letter, Para to FGC, Nov. 15, 1950 (Labor Problems). Browning
claimed to support the union shop; letter, Browning to A.T. Edwards, June 10, 1952 (Browning files).
"was equivocal": Letters, FGC to W.B. Woolsey, July 15, 1952; A.T.
Edwards to FGC, June 4, 1952 (1952 Campaign).
"Veterans of Foreign Wars": See *Banner*, CH, Oct. 3, 1949.
"county judges" Letters, W. Lunn McKeel to FGC, July 18, 1951;
Hugh Lee Webster to Judge W.M. Leech, Aug. 13, 1951; H.M.

53   Fulbright to Judge James A. Weems, Nov. 7, 1951 (Pre-1952). Leech sent a letter to some 36 county judges (Pre-1952).

"Forrest Ladd": *Banner,* March 7, 1952.

"Charles Everhart": Letter, C.M. Everhart to FGC, Feb. 25, 1951 (Pre-1952).

"Harlan Dodson": Letter, K. Harlan Dodson to FGC, June 18, 1951 (Pre-1952).

"Mark Hays": Letters, Mark Hays to FGC, March 19, 1951; FGC to Hays, Oct. 6, 1951 (Pre-1952).

54   "George T. Lewis" "Roane Waring" Letters, George T. Lewis, Jr. to FGC, June 16, 1951 (Pre-1952); Lewis to FGC, March 20, 1952 (1952 Campaign); *Banner,* March 7, 1952.

"the discoverer of Clement": Letter, Leslie T. Hart to LSG, Sept. 7, 1973. Interview, Leslie T. Hart, Oct. 25, 1973. Harold H. Martin says Hart brought Crichton and Clement together; see Martin, 50. He also says Crichton put the Clement law firm on his payroll; ibid.

"as far back as 1949 . . . education . . . family . . . Legion activities . . . public speaking": See Hart in the *Banner,* Sept. 19, 1949, and thereafter—e.g., March 2, Sept. 2, 7, 28, 1949.

"selling hamburgers": Ibid., CH, Sept. 19, Oct. 3, 12, 1949.

"established by Luke Lea": See Folmsbee et al., *Tennessee, Short History,* 440–41.

"Caldwell fortunes": See McFerrin.

"to capture the Kaiser": This bizarre bit of swashbuckling is described in T.H. Alexander, "They Tried to Kidnap the Kaiser", *Saturday Evening Post* Oct. 23, 1937, pp. 5–6, 84–89. The origin of this article is the result of Browning's generosity. T.H. Alexander, an author and friend of Browning, needed funds for an operation for one of his children; Browning and his friends gave him this story so that he could sell it in order to pay for the surgery; see interview, Alexander, Feb. 28, 1978. See also Luke Lea, "The Attempt to Capture the Kaiser", *Tennessee Historical Quarterly,* XX (Sept. 1961), 222–61.

"purchased by Silliman Evans . . . aid of a loan" *Tennessean,* June 27, 1955.

55 "opposition to Boss Crump": Ibid.

"provided they had some hope of success": The *Tennessean* backed Kefauver for the Senate only when Evans was convinced that Kefauver had a fighting chance; Gorman, 39–40; see also Gardner, 49.

"fundamental opposition": The *Tennessean* editorially endorsed Browning on March 9, 1952.

"grudging approval": E.g., the *Tennessean* approved editorially of Clement's early cabinet appointments; Ibid., Jan. 16, 1953.

55 "third place": Ibid., P, April 6, 1952. On June 27, 1952, Hatcher saw
Clement starting downhill; ibid., P, June 27, 1952.

"not as contemptuous": Interview, Stephen D. Boyd with Joe
Hatcher, Aug. 16, 1971.

"Clifford Allen": Allen ran for governor in 1950, with Donald M.
McSween as his campaign manager, but in 1951 McSween told
Allen he was for Clement and had been pledged to him for several
years. Letter, McSween to Malcolm Hill, Nov. 14, 1951 (Corres.-
McSween). Allen was reported to have tried to get Clement to
withdraw; Banner and CH, Nov. 9, 1951. Also letters, Bud Harwell
to FGC, 1951; Cayce L. Pentecost to FGC, June 26, 1951 (Pre-1952).
Also letter, McSween to FGC, March 25, 1952 (1952 Campaign).

"Clifford Pierce": Browning considered Clement, Allen, and Pierce
all to be Crump men, and this helped to make Browning a candidate once more. He felt he had to battle Crump. Interview, Fred
Travis, Sept. 26, 1977. See also Banner, CH, June 22, Aug. 23, 1951.

56 "hand-shaking tours": Clement described his hand-shaking tour in a
letter to Paul Andrews, Jan. 14, 1952 (1952 Campaign). In Feb.
1952, he said he had been shaking about 1,000 hands each day; he
said his hand was calloused; letter, FGC to Bert Bates, Feb. 16, 1952
(1952 Campaign). He started his hand-shaking tour in Jan. 1952;
see Hart in the Banner, Jan. 11, 1952. The tour continued through
January and February. Allen started his hand-shaking tour in January 1952; Tennessean, Jan. 17, 1952. Clement's "flesh-pressing" forays are described in the Banner, CH, Jan. 11, 15, 31, Feb. 5, 6, 13,
1952.

"a third term": Browning announced in March; Tennessean, March 2,
1952.

"Jack Norman": Majors, 174. After Browning's ultimate defeat, Norman became a Clement backer. On Norman's earlier connections
with Browning and Kefauver, see William Goodman, Inherited Domain; Political Parties in Tennessee (Bur. of Public Administration,
Univ. of Tennessee, 1954), 72.

"John J. Hooker, Sr.": Majors, 174. John J. Hooker, Jr., was to become an opponent of the Clement-Ellington faction.

"McAllen Foutch": Foutch was a Smithville attorney. He was born at
Alexandria in DeKalb County on June 14, 1909. He was elected to
the 1943 legislature as direct representative from that county and
returned for 1945, 1947, and 1949. He was elected speaker of the
House in 1949; Tennessee Blue Book, 1949–1950, p. 16. Although he
supported Clement on some matters, Foutch has to be considered
one of the leaders of the Clement opposition.

"James Cummings": Cummings was born Nov. 8, 1890, at Wood-

56 bury, Tenn., and remained a citizen of that small town until his death in 1979. His association with politics began when, as a young man, he was made a confidant of Gov. Malcolm Patterson. He was law clerk to A.H. Roberts, before Roberts became governor. Interview, Cummings, Nov. 4, 1974. He started his long legislative career as a member of the 66th General Assembly, 1929–31. In Browning's administration, Cummings was sometimes considered "the man to see," *Banner*, CH, Jan. 4, 1949. Cummings and Beasley were sometimes called the "legislative twins," ibid., Jan. 7, 1949.

57 "Charles Wayland": *Banner*, May 1, 1952. Wayland was a member of a prominent political family in Knox County. He was born in Birmingham on Feb. 28, 1909; *Tennessee Blue Book*, 1949–50, p. 23. Wayland was a district campaign manager for Browning in 1948. He became Browning's administrative assistant, succeeding Browning's brother, F.L. Browning, when the latter died. Later he became Commissioner of Highways under Browning; *Knoxville News-Sentinel*, April 20, 1951. Wayland was also Browning's campaign manager in 1950; *Banner*, CH, May 12, 1950. The rumor of Wayland's possible candidacy for the governorship was aired in Hart's CH column; *Banner*, March 27, 1951; Letter, Donald M. McSween to FGC, March 29, 1951 (Pre-1952).

"campaign manager for Ellington": This occurred in the 1966 campaign when Ellington was elected to his final term.

"*dramatis personae*": Among the friends of Browning who sooner or later shifted to Clement or Ellington were James Cummings, Jack Norman, Charles Wayland, and Tom Johnson. Clement's ever-conciliatory attitude toward opponents made the shifts easier.

"January 23, 1952" *Banner*, Jan. 23, 1952; Paul T. David, Malcolm Moos, and Ralph M. Goldman, *Presidential Nominating Politics in 1952* (Baltimore: Johns Hopkins Univ. Press, 1954), VOL. I, *The National Story*, 35; *Tennessean*, Jan. 24, 1952. See also Gardner, 211ff.; Gorman, ch. viii, ix; Fontenay, 192.

"Charles Neese" *Tennessean*, Jan. 1, 1952.

"federal judgeship": Neese was appointed federal district judge of the eastern district of Tennessee in 1961; he had practiced law in Paris and Nashville from 1938 to 1961; he served as Senator Kefauver's administrative assistant from 1949 to 1951; *Who's Who in America, 1978–79*. Neese was Kefauver's campaign manager in 1948; see Gardner, 211; see Fontenay, 190ff.

"Mrs. Tom Ragland": *Tennessean*, Jan. 1, 1952. (Mrs. Ragland's first name is Martha, and citations sometimes show this name).

"private annoyance": David et al., 36; Truman disliked Kefauver because of the damage he had done to the Democratic party by his

57   crime investigation; Gardner, 213; Gorman, 129–30. See Fontenay,
      193–94.

      "number of important presidential primaries": David et al., 35–41; 55–
      61; Gardner, ch. VI, Gorman, ch. IX; Fontenay, ch. 10.

      "Florida primary": David et al., 61; Fontenay, 201–204.

      "the front runner": David et al., 65; Fontenay, 209.

59   "of 1948": This convention was boycotted by prominent Tennessee
      conservatives, including Crump, McKellar, Tom Stewart, and
      John Mitchell. Herbert Walters, in poor health, stayed home. *Ten-
      nessean*, P, March 6, 1952.

      "Strom Thurmond": See Emile B. Ader, *The Dixiecrat Movement: Its
      Role in Third Party Politics* (Washington: Public Affairs, 1955).

      "flurry of support for Browning . . . put this movement to rest": Joe
      Hatcher in "Politics," *Tennessean*, Jan. 16, 1952; news story, ibid.,
      Jan. 11, 1952. Letters, Gordon Browning to Edwin T. Nance, July
      12, 1952, and reply to letter from Nance, July 7, 1952; Browning to
      Col. Henry Buck, Jan. 10, 1952 (Browning files).

      "constantly heckled Clement": E.g., see editorial, *Tennessean*, May 11,
      1952; letter, Coleman A. Harwell, vice president and editor of the
      Tennessean, to FGC, May 14, 1952. (1952 Campaign).

      "announcing his support for Kefauver": *Tennessean*, May 18, 1952; see
      also Politics column in this issue.

      "convenience, not friendship": Interview, Robert S. Clement, March
      25, 1975. Robert Clement said some of Clement's advisers wanted
      the place to go to Judge Weldon White; ibid. Interview, Anna
      Belle O'Brien, May 5, 1975.

      "not been acquainted personally": Interview, Robert S. Clement,
      ibid. Ellington had expressed interest in Clement to Eddie Friar; let-
      ter, Friar to Ellington, Feb. 8, 1952 (Bodfish, Friar, Crichton).

      "if the rural areas were carried": Clement had city connections
      through his work with the Railroad and Public Utilities Commis-
      sion; interview, Stephen Boyd with Buford Ellington, Aug. 18,
      1971.

60   "Born in Mississippi": In 1952, Ellington was 45 years old. He was
      married to Catherine Cheek of Lewisburg; they had two children.
      For eight years, he had been director of the Marshall County Farm
      Bureau. He had served in the General Assembly in the 1949 session
      as direct representative from Marshall County. He owned the El-
      lington General Mercantile Company of Verona, a country store,
      and a 145-acre farm in the Verona community. He was a Methodist.
      At the time he was made campaign manager he had been for four
      years field representative of the Tennessee Farm Bureau Federation
      service program, from which he resigned to work for Clement.

60   Press release, April 15, 1952 (1952 Campaign); *Banner,* April 15, 1952.

"General Assembly": See *Banner,* CH, Feb. 8, 1949.

"conferred in Dickson . . . Robert Clement, Hilton Butler, Joe Carr, and, possibly, Leslie Hart": Interview, Robert S. Clement, March 25, 1975.

"Robert Clement remembers": Ibid.

"an indefatigible worker": Interview, Douglas Fisher, June 28, 1977.

"three hundred telephone calls": Ibid.

"A campaign committee": Interview, Anna Belle O'Brien, May 5, 1975.

"ran a tight ship": Ibid.

62 "Anna Belle": Ibid. Anna Belle Clement, then unmarried, had not known Ellington before the campaign. The campaign headquarters consisted, to begin with, of two rooms in the Hermitage Hotel in Nashville.

"Eddie Friar . . . Brainard Cheney": Interview, Cheney, Feb. 11, 1975. Friar's correspondence shows his efforts in 1951 and early 1952; letters to Ellington, Feb. 8, 1952, and to Z.D. Atkins, Jan. 31, 1952 (Bodfish, Friar, Crichton); Robert S. Clement to Friar, Dec. 15, (Bodfish, Friar, Crichton). Also letter, Friar to FGC, Sept. 5, 1951 (Bodfish, Friar, Crichton). Letters, Cheney to Robert Penn Warren, Feb. 24, 1952 (JUL); Feb. 4, 1953 (JUL).

"research man": Interview, Fred Travis, Sept. 26, 1977; see also interview, Stephen Boyd with Ellington, August 18, 1971.

"Hilton Butler" "Joe Henry" "effective phrasemakers": Interview, Travis, *ibid.* Also interview, Stephen D. Boyd with Buford Ellington, August 18, 1971, and author's interview with Joe Henry, Sept. 30, 1975.

"from earlier campaigns": *Banner,* Nov. 29, 1952.

"speech writing style": Interview, Stephen D. Boyd with Douglas Fisher, August 14, 1971.

"depart effectively from a prepared text": Stephen Dean Boyd, "The Campaign Speaking of Frank Clement in the 1954 Democratic Primary: Field Study and Rhetorical Analysis", diss. U. of Illinois, 1972, 37–42.

"could cost $250,000": Interview, Glen Nicely, Aug. 24, 1977; interview, Agnes Bird, Sept. 20, 1977; compare Buchanan and Bird, 86.

"of the railroads" "frankly said": Interview, Stephen D. Boyd with Buford Ellington, August 18, 1971; interview, Boyd with Joe Henry, Sept. 30, 1975. See also Boyd, "Campaign Speaking", p. 80.

"raised a great outcry": *Banner,* CH, July 8, 9, 15, 16, 18, 21, 1952.

"small, unpublicized contributions": Letters, Fred Berry to FGC,

62   Sept. 17, 1953; Ernest Crouch to FGC, Feb. 4, 1952; Cowan Oldham
      to FGC, Jan. 15, 1952 (Campaign Funds, 1952).

      "he got trucker money": Ellington in retrospect saw the campaign as
      a struggle between the railroads and the trucking industry; inter-
      view, Boyd with Ellington, ibid. Crichton was a very heavy con-
      tributor.

      "fabulous sums": Browning said the trucking interests offered him
      $150,000, which he declined, and that those interests gave Clem-
      ent that much; *Tennessean*, June 14, July 8, 1952. See also *Banner*, July
      31, 1952.

      "in kind": Letter, FGC to Raleigh Patton, March 12, 1952 (Campaign
      Funds, 1952). Individual contributions ranged from $10 to $1,000;
      letter, W.B. Whitson to FGC, Feb. 19, 1952 (Campaign Funds,
      1952).

      "on May 24": *Banner*, May 24, 1952; *Tennessean*, May 7, 25, 1952.

64   "Gargantua": Letter, Joe Henry to FGC, Nov. 7, 1951 (Pre-1952).

      "John Heiskell . . . Forrest Ladd . . . George T. Lewis": *Banner*,
      March 7, 1952.

      "to blow his breath": *Banner*, May 24, 1952; *Tennessean*, June 4, 14,
      1952. Hatcher had noted Crump's backing of Clement as early as
      March; ibid., P, March 9, 1952.

      "liar, pipsqueak, a demagogue": *Banner*, CH, June 17, 1952.

      "a loud-mouthed traducer of character": Tennessean, May 25, July 8,
      1952.

      "pliable puppet": Ibid., May 25, 1952.

      "too green": Ibid., June 3, 1952.

      "opened officially": *Banner*, June 2, 1952; the plans had been announced
      in the *Banner*, CH, May 5, 1952. The speech is reproduced in Wil-
      liam L. Davis, "Corruption vs Morality: A Rhetorical Analysis of
      the Campaign of Frank Goad Clement for Governor of Tennessee,
      1952," M.A. thesis, Wake Forest Univ., 1972.

      "sixteen-point program": See *Tennessean*, June 1, 1952. Hatcher said
      Clement's speech sounded like it had been written by Willie
      Gerber; *ibid.*, P, June 3, 1952.

65   "The pace was gruelling": *Tennessean*, July 13, 1952.

      "changing his sweaty clothes": Interview, Boyd with Anna Belle
      O'Brien, Aug. 25, 1971.

      "gospel hymns and country music": Interview, Anna Belle O'Brien,
      March 25, 1975; interview, Boyd with Buford Ellington, Aug. 18,
      1971.

      "Precious Lord": See *Tennessean*, July 13, 1952.

      "his mother urged him": Statement by Clement found in the file-
      Proposed Autobiography.

65 "highway system": Press release from Buford Ellington, April 17, 1952 (1952 Campaign).

"new taxes": Letter, FGC to Douglas S. Lambeth, May 5, 1952 (1952 Campaign).

66 "his administration had a good record in mental health": See *Tennessean*, editorial, July 17, 1952.

"Cumberland Properties": See *Banner*, CH, Aug. 17, 1951; Majors, 183–88.

"Karl Martin and R.S. Doggett": *Banner*, CH, Aug. 30, 1951.

"friends and backers of Browning": Ibid. Martin had managed Browning's East Tennessee campaigns in 1948 and 1950; ibid., March 14, 1952.

"W.N. McKinney": Ibid. CH, Aug. 30, 1951.

"the man to see": Ibid. Others reputed to be "men to see" at various times included F.L. Browning, the governor's brother, and James Cummings.

"J. Marshall Ewing, Andrew Ewing, and J.H. Talbot": Ibid., Aug. 30, 31, 1951.

"denied they had any connection with the enterprise": Ibid., CH, Aug. 31, 1951.

68 "Throughout September": Ibid., Sept. 4–7, 10, 11, 14, 19, 1951.

"Clifford Allen": Ibid., Sept. 27, 1951; letters, Allen to Browning, Sept. 25, Oct. 10, 1951 (Browning files). Allen had attacked Browning for raising taxes; letter, Allen to Browning, Jan. 22, 1951 (Browning files).

"Attorney General Beeler": See *Banner*, CH, Sept. 9, 27, 1951; Beeler's unfavorable opinions were subsequently published in ibid., Aug. 4, 1952.

"he went ahead": Ibid., CH, Oct. 27, 1951.

"George Dempster": Ibid., Nov. 17, 1951. Dempster was defeated by a landslide victory of Prentice Cooper in the Democratic primary of Aug. 1, 1940.

"Elmore was": Ibid. Elmore, in any case, was a Republican, and the defeat of Elmore was more the result of a contest between Dempster and Elmore than a reflection of state politics.

"the hotel for $625,000": *Banner*, March 4, 1952. The hotel matter was discussed repeatedly by the *Banner* in the opening months of 1952.

"the *Banner* headlined": March 14, 1952.

"scooped by the morning newspaper": *Tennessean*, March 14, 1952. The *Tennessean*, as the morning newspaper, beat the *Banner* to the streets by a few hours; the *Tennessean*'s treatment of the story was defensive.

68 "God-send to the Clement forces": As Robert S. Clement says, anything that takes more than 30 minutes to explain will defeat you;
interview, Robert S. Clement, March 25, 1975.

"the state was getting a good deal": *Chattanooga Times,* Jan. 23, 1952;
Tennessean, March 15, 1952.

"willingly conceded that the arrangement": Interview, Joe Carr,
Sept. 16, 1975; interview, Joe Mynatt, Oct. 2, 1975; Clement was
reported to have admitted privately in later years that the deal was
not bad for the state; interview, Fred Travis, Sept. 26, 1977.

"he had not known who the owners were": *Banner,* CH, Feb. 23,
1952; *Tennessean,* Feb. 9, 23, 1952.

69 "promising an early investigation": Speech at Newbern, reported in
the *Banner,* July 16, 1952.

"could not track a bleeding elephant": Ibid., June 28, 1952.

"without ever locating a battle": *Ibid.;* see also ibid., July 18, 1952. The
Hamilton County Veterans for Browning attacked Clement's war
record; *Tennessean,* July 10, 1952. See also ibid., P, July 13, 1952. For
Clement's defense, see ibid., July 19, 1952.

"the right end of a horse . . . collars and muzzles": *Banner,* CH, June
18, 1952.

"purchasing": See, e.g., *Tennessean,* July 19, 1952.

"the military police": In both World War II and the Korean War,
Clement served in the military police; see ch. 2.

"move had developed": Minutes, Board of Trustees, Univ. of Tennessee, Oct. 20, 1950.

"several normal schools": Memphis State had been established in 1912
under the General Education Act of 1909 as West Tennessee Normal School. *Tennessee Blue Book,* 1977–78, p. 192. The normal
schools were converted into teachers' colleges following passage of
the General Education Law of 1925; Greene, Grubbs, and Hobday,
289.

"strong support of Crump": Statement, Professor Sprunt to LSG during the late 1940's. For a typical story, see *Banner,* CH, Dec. 30,
1950.

70 "good for both institutions": Minutes, Board of Trustees, Univ. of
Tennessee, Oct. 20, Dec. 3, 4, 1950.

"In October": Ibid., Oct. 20, 1950.

"first week of December": Ibid., Dec. 3, 4, 1950.

"Many of the faculty worried": Contrary to what seems to have been
the case in the UT Medical School at Memphis, members of the faculty at Knoxville, particularly those in the social sciences, were
afraid of Crump, although it was by no means easy to spot any
pressure from the Memphis boss. I believe that President Hoskins

70   had also feared Crump; he once told me that he had taken care never to meet Crump, and I was present on one occasion when Maj. Thomas Allen, a member of Crump's organization, had spoken most brutally to Hoskins, compelling him to withdraw from Edward J. Meeman an invitation to speak in Memphis at a meeting sponsored by the University. Faculty members had also been angrily attacked by Gov. Cooper, who was regarded by some as dominated by Crump (Prof. William E. Cole and Prof. W.B. Jones, both sociologists). Members of the Knoxville faculty always were concerned about the burden of a medical school on a budget that was never generous; personal recollections of the author. Hoskins was opposed to the merger with Memphis; letter, James D. Hoskins to FGC, April 15, 1952 (UT Affairs).

71   "kill the proposal": Interview, Andrew D. Holt, July 9, 1976; bills introduced by the Shelby delegation plus some Browning backers were reported out from committee in the House without recommendation and without subsequent action and tabled in the Senate by narrow votes; *House Journal,* 1951, pp. 346, 365, 725, and *Senate Journal,* 1951, pp. 1147–54. (The House and Senate journals are cited throughout by short title).

"Memphis State University": *Public Acts,* 1957, ch. 4.

"assail the plan": *Banner,* April 8, 1952. Letter in a political advertisement in the *LaFollette Press,* April 18, 1952 (1952 Campaign); letter, FGC to H.H. Sutton, LaFollette, Tenn., May 26, 1952 (1952 Campaign). Clement released a statement dated April 8, 1952, saying he was against the UT-split, as it was mistakenly called (1952 Campaign). The *Banner* story on Clement's opposition was reproduced as a campaign flier (1952 Campaign). Actually, in my opinion, the failure to consolidate the two schools was a blow to UT, which could have by this means acquired an institution that later became a rival.

"one of Crump's pet schemes": *Tennessean,* July 19, 1952. Allen said Crump schemed to move UT to Memphis; there was never much chance of this, and no evidence that Crump ever contemplated any such thing. In fact, it is not certain that Crump had much to do with the whole project.

"pardon record": Clement attacked Browning's paroles and pardons at a speech in Bradley County, June 20, 1952, and again at Pulaski, July 15, 1952. Letter from Clifton Bridges (presumably to FGC), n.d.; see also *Banner,* CH, April 29, 1949; Majors, 181.

"according to one newspaper": The *Franklin Review Appeal,* July 17, 1952, attacked Browning for his pardon of a rapist who repeated his crimes (rpt. as campaign flier; see file-1952 Campaign).

71 "Browning's defense": Browning justified the pardon on the ground that Gerber, a Memphis attorney allied to Crump, had caused the imprisonment of an innocent man, ibid.

"pardoning power of God Almighty": *Banner,* CH, July 14, 1952.

72 "number of official cars": Ibid., April 16, 1952, story reproduced as a campaign flier. The car issue was featured in cartoons; see ibid., April 18, 1952. See report of the charges in the *Tennessean,* e.g., June 12, 1952. Browning had been somewhat sensitive to the abuse of state-owned cars; letter, Gordon Browning to Paul Sloan, April 12, 1952 (1952 Campaign). The car issue was a serious bone of contention in 1979, as the term of Governor Lamar Alexander opened, and reappeared in 1980.

"increased number of state employees": *Tennessean,* June 11, 1952. Browning defended himself on cars and employees, ibid., June 12, 1952.

"more doorkeepers than legislators . . . sole purpose": Interview, Robert S. Clement, March 25, 1975; see also *Banner,* CH, April 13, 1949.

"advice of Clement's father": Interview, ibid.

74 "doorkeeper pay list": Ibid. When Clement became governor, he successfully pressured the assembly into an abandonment of these excessive appointments, against some legislative reluctance—letters, Jim Camp to FGC and Harold T. Brundage to FGC, Dec. 3, 1952 (Legislative Relations); circular letter to members of the Assembly from FGC, Nov. 28, 1952 (D) (Doorkeeper Issue).

"Polk County": Interview, Dr. Roy Lillard, July 2, 1976; see also unpublished paper, Dr. Roy Lillard, "Some Aspects of Polk County Politics," Dec. 1958, pp. 9, 12, 14, 25 ff. Dr. Lillard quotes Bill Davidson and Harold Twitty, *Collier's,* "Terror in Tennessee," Sept. 8, 1951, pp. 16–17.

"voted secessionist": In the second vote on secession, June 8, 1961; see Lillard paper, p. 12.

"copper industry controlled": Interview, Roy Lillard, July 2, 1976.

"Burch Biggs and his sons": Ibid.; see Lillard paper, ch. IV.

"Washington establishment": Biggs was pro-Cooper-McCord-Kefauver, and anti-Browning, Lillard, ibid.

"no effective voter registration": Voter registration had been established as early as 1889; see *Acts of the State of Tennessee,* 1889, Ch. 207, and Joseph H. Cartwright, *The Triumph of Jim Crow: Tennessee Race Relations in the 1880s* (Knoxville: Univ. of Tennessee Press, 1976) 233. Registration laws, however, did not cover the more rural areas of the state, and enforcement was highly decentralized and subject to abuse and lax administration.

75 "Republicans were still numerous enough": Interview, Roy Lillard, July 2, 1976.

"turn of the aging Biggs": Ibid.

"Good Government League": Accounts of this development are contained in *Chattanooga Times* articles during 1948; ibid. Davidson and Twitty, quoted in paper by Lillard.

"R.E. Barclay,": A Democrat; interview, Lillard, ibid. See also various articles of the period in the *Chattanooga Times.* See also Lillard paper, p. 27, quoting Davidson and Twitty.

"to send in troops": Interview, Lillard, ibid.; Lillard paper, p. 27.

"August Lewis . . . defected": Interview, ibid.; paper, ibid., p. 29.

"murdered from ambush": Interview, ibid.

"murders near Turtletown": *Tennessean,* March 9, 10, 1958.

76 "had been urged": Telegram, *Cleveland Daily Banner* to Browning, May 12, 1951 (Browning files).

"maybe not then": *Chattanooga Times,* March 16, 1951.

"abolish Polk County": Interview, Roy Lillard, July 2, 1976; Lillard paper, p. 27.

"campaigned in Polk": *Banner,* July 3, 4, 1952. Clement blamed Browning for the Polk disorders.

"written by Brainard Cheney": Interview, Cheney, Feb. 11, 1975. The speech is rpt. in Davis, thesis cited.

"surrounded by armed men": *Banner,* July 4, 1952; letter, A.F. Curbow, to FGC, April 22, 1953 (Polk County); interview, Cheney, ibid.; interview, Anna Belle O'Brien, May 5, 1975.

77 "who couldn't spell fear": Interview, Robert S. Clement, March 25, 1975. See also material prepared for autobiography in Clement files.

"boy was a good campaigner": *Tennessean,* July 4, 1952.

"criticized Clement": Ibid., July 13, 1952.

"family was anxious": Anyone who has observed the impulses to violence present in Tennessee politics could believe readily in the danger.

"Clifford Pierce": Pierce's program was a series of vague generalities; see *Tennessean,* July 19, 1952.

"Allen is a demagogue": Ibid. May 25, 1952.

"Tennessee Waltz": Ibid., June 1, 1952. Browning said he got started with the waltz in a contest with Allan Shivers on New Year's Eve, 1951; letter Browning to Rev. W.T. Parrett, Dec. 31, 1951 (Browning files).

"refrained from backing": Morris Cunningham in the *Commercial Appeal,* March 9, 1952.

"he approved Clement": Ibid.; see also *Banner,* March 7, 1952.

77 "Shelby County organization": The group included John Heiskell, Forrest Ladd, and George Lewis. The committee kept its distance from McKellar, possible thinking McKellar would lose. Crump wanted a friendly governor in case McKellar was elected and died, and the governor had to name his successor; Harry Woodbury in the *Commercial Appeal,* March 9, 1952; also letter, George T. Lewis, Jr. to FGC, March 20, 1952 (1952 Campaign). See also *Tennessean,* P, March 9, 1952. Initially, Crump had not been for Clement, thinking him too young. Herbert Bingham and William Baird, representing the Municipal League, visited Crump to get his backing for Clement, possible as early as 1951; interview, Herbert J. Bingham, Oct. 9, 1974.

"ran a cartoon": *Tennessean,* June 25, 1952.

"Another showed Crump": Ibid., March 30, 1952.

"showing Willie Gerber . . . obtained the job": *Tennessean,* June 22, 1952.

"talkative little stooge": Ibid., July 19, 1952.

"was still valuable": Some of Clement's friends were disturbed by the Crump endorsement and feared it might hurt; this feeling appeared among people opposed to McKellar and in favor of Gore; letter, Donald M. McSween to FGC, March 25, 1952 (1952 Campaign). Others of the Clement people, on the other hand, favored McKellar; letter, Donald M. McSween to Kenneth D. McKellar, April 9, 1952, with copy and added information to FGC (1952 Campaign).

80 "some labor support": Some of the railroad unions supported Browning because of his ties with the railroad interests; endorsement of Brotherhood of Railway and Steamship Clerks, Freight Handlers, Express and Station Employees; *Tennessean,* July 20, 1952.

"what they wanted": An anticlosed shop law had been passed during the McCord administration and organized labor had sought its repeal and had unsuccessfully contested its constitutionality; see Greene, Grubbs, and Hobday, 329.

"sent troops": *Banner,* CH, May 31, 1950. Browning had also called out the National Guard at Alcoa in 1937–38, after three people had been killed. Thereafter the Guard had not been called until the Enka action; ibid. Senators Hubert Humphrey and James Murray of the Senate Labor Committee had investigated the use of the Guard at Enka; ibid., CH, June 17, 19, July 1, 1950.

"radical labor support": *Tennessean,* June 11, 1952. See also *Banner,* May 24, 1952.

"he defended his actions": *Banner,* May 24, 1952.

"hog-callin' and peafowl pickin'": *Tennessean,* July 13, 1952.

"a debate": Ibid., July 16, 1952.

80 "a great promiser": Attacks on Allen for this attitude were mounted
early by the *Tennessean*; see P, Jan. 23, 1951; on Allen, see Majors,
176.

"tax reductions . . . full earmarking . . . four big superhighways . . .
soldiers' bonus" *Tennessean*, May 18, June 1, 27, July 4, 5, 1952; on
the textbook issue, see also *Banner*, CH, Feb. 22, 1949, and Allen
campaign card. Allen's later political career, which finally put him
in the national House of Representatives for a short while before his
death, was characterized by this same kind of reckless promising.

"cartoon showing Allen": *Tennessean*, July 16, 1952.

"Crump had offered": Ibid., March 15, 1952.

"says bad people live in it": Ibid.

"wanted Allen to stay": Ibid., P and news story, June 20, 1952.

"Clement forces worried": Letter, Don McSween to FGC, March 25,
1952 (1952 Campaign).

"campaign manager in 1950": *Banner*, CH, May 16, 1950.

"in November, 1951 . . . public quarreling with Allen": *Banner*, Nov.
27, 1951; letter, Donald McSween to FGC, March 29, 1951 (Pre-1952).

"some support": Allen was backed by the Nashville Labor League for
Political Education (AFL), the Stovemounters International state
council, and District 155 of the Machinists; *Tennessean*, May 13,
1952. He received the backing of a number of other locals; ibid.,
May 22, 1952.

81 "chairmanship of Browning": Davis, Moos, and Goldman, eds., *Presidential Nominating Politics*, Vol. III, *The South*, section on Tennessee
based on reports by William Goodman, pp. 179–80.

"by the unit rule": David et al., Vol. I, 136.

"backing of the delegates": Goodman, 179, 181. See also Gorman, ch.
ix; Gardner, ch. VII.

"He had campaigned": Kefauver announced officially on Jan. 23,
1952; he entered a number of primaries; see Gorman, 134–40.

"front runner": David et al., 65; Gorman, 148.

"Florida primary": Gorman, 136–40.

"had been split . . . Dixiecrat": V.O. Key, *Southern Politics in State
and Nation* (New York: Knopf, 1949), 329–44.

"loyalty oath": David et al., 116–17.

"to stop Adlai Stevenson": Ibid., 112 ff.

"Averill Harriman": See, e.g., ibid., 113.

"from Texas and Mississippi": Ibid., 132–33. See Fontenay, 214–20.

"Virginia, South Carolina, and Louisiana": David et al., 136–49; Fontenay, 220–23.

82 "was compelled to cast": See David et al., 145; Fontenay, 221.

"it hurt him politically": Majors, 190–93; see Goodman, *Inherited Do-*

82   *main:* 68–75. The *Banner*, of course, criticized Browning, July 23,
     1952; the fact that Senator Humphrey defended Browning (re-
     ported in ibid., Aug. 2, 1952) would have been no especial help to
     Browning in Tennessee, where Humphrey was not exactly a hero.
     For defense of Browning, see *Tennessean*, July 29, 1952, including
     praise by the *Chattanooga Times.*

     "Kefauver, too, was hurt": Gorman, ch. x.

     "endorsed Browning": Kefauver also took the blame for Browning's
     actions at the convention; Majors, 193. See *Tennessean*, July 31,
     Aug. 1, 1952; telegram of condolence, Kefauver to Browning,
     Aug. 8, 1952 (Browning files); Kefauver press release on address in
     Memphis, Aug. 1, 1952 (Browning files).

     "firmly held the other": *Tennessean*, July 13, 1952. Willie Gerber was
     the reputed hatchet man of the Crump organization.

     "Democratic primary of August 7, 1952": The voting figures are
     given in *Fifty Years of Tennessee Primary Elections, 1918–1968,* comp.
     Shirley Hassler, State Election Coordinator, n.d. I have also had ac-
     cess to a study of the Clement votes commissioned by Roy Nicks in
     the senatorial election of 1966; this study is referred to here as the
     Nicks study. A copy of this study has been placed with the Clement
     files in the Special Collections of the University of Tennessee
     library. See also Anne H. Hopkins and William Lyons, *Tennessee
     Votes: 1799–1976* (Knoxville: Bureau of Public Administration,
     Univ. of Tennessee, 1978), 280–81.

     "in East Tennessee": Nicks study, Map III.

83   "hound dog": Letter, Gale O. Delias to FGC, Aug. 11, 1952 (Party Line
     Crossing).

     "Middle and West Tennessee": Nicks Study, Map III.

     "Hardin and Hardeman": Ibid., Map IV.

     "lost Polk": A Clement manager in Polk claimed people were afraid
     to serve as poll watchers; *Banner*, Aug. 7, 1952.

     "John Edwards": *Tennessean*, Aug. 8, 1952.

84   "vote for Gore": Personal recollections of author. Gore said his wife
     thought up the slogan; Albert Gore, *Let the Glory Out; My South
     and Its Politics* (New York: Viking, 1972), 78–79.

     "carried out independently": Various combinations of candidacies ap-
     peared over the state. In some places, the same groups supported
     Clement and Gore, but there was no formal or informal statewide
     tie. Candidacies in Tennessee usually tend to independence, and
     Gore, shrewd and cold-blooded, was never inclined to tie up with
     potential losers. Gore had strong past alliances with Browning,
     had managed campaigns for him, and had been in his cabinet;
     Gore, 53.

CHAPTER 4.

85 "with the words": Letter, FGC to John G. Heiskell, Oct. 15, 1953
(Misc. Correspondence).

"campaigned together": *Tennessean*, Sept. 27, 1952; see also ibid.
throughout Oct. 1952.

"Ellington was made chairman": Ibid., Sept. 1, 11, 1952; *Banner*, Sept.
15, 1952. Gore agreed to Ellington; *Tennessean*, Sept. 1, 1952.

"Springfield": *Tennessean*, Sept. 17, 1952.

"Two Memphis groups": Ibid., P, Oct. 17, 1952; telegrams, FGC to
John Heiskell, Gore to William Barr, Oct. 14, 1952, asking work
for national ticket (1952 Campaign).

"He bolted to Eisenhower": *Tennessean*, ibid.

86 "to prepare": In the late fall of 1952, Clement put in a long day; rising
at 5:30 A.M. in Dickson, he left at 6:30 for Nashville, chauffered by
Rick Morgan. At 7:30 he was at the Hermitage Hotel (Morgan
took Bob to school, Robertson Academy, where he was in the 3rd
grade.) Clement began reading correspondence at 7:35; at 8:15 his
secretary arrived; at 9:00 he started appointments. Each day he saw
around 40 people. His assistants saw others. Clement worked until
about 10:30, when he started back to Dickson. See *Banner*, CH,
Nov. 25, 1952.

"the exact date": As is not infrequently the case with this particular
document, the constitution of Tennessee is rather vague about the
date of inauguration. Art. VII, sec. 5 says, "The term of office of
the Governor and of other executive officers shall be computed
from the fifteenth of January next after the election of the Governor." But Art. III, sec. 4 in 1953 said: "The governor shall hold his
office for two years, and until his successor shall be elected and
qualified." The General Assembly had been in the habit of setting a
date for the weekend after Jan. 15 for the ceremony, and the outgoing governor would sometimes serve for a few days after that date.

"in his early musings": Interview, Anna Belle O'Brien, March 25,
1975.

87 "began to tour": *Banner*, Sept. 29, 30, Oct. 1, 2, 6, 14, 29, 1952.

"his condition worsened . . . weeping bitterly": Interviews, Noble
Caudill, Jan. 22, 1975; Anna Belle O'Brien, March 25, 1975.

"youthful acquaintance with Governor Patterson . . . He never
fumed about it": Interview, James Cummings, Nov. 4, 1974.

88 "W.N. Estes": Born near Dresden in 1891, Estes had been a teacher at
the secondary school level. He entered the insurance business and
later investment work, forming his own company eventually in
Nashville. In 1937 Browning asked him to organize the Depart-

88   ment of Local Finance and to assist in the debt reorganization pro-
      gram. *Tennessee Blue Book, 1951–1952,* 25.

      "Cedric Hunt": Hunt was born in 1899 in Jackson, Tennessee. He had
      served as page in the State House of Representatives, had held vari-
      ous clerkships in the Senate, and had been chief clerk of the Senate
      for five sessions. Ibid., 26.

      "equally taken for granted": *Tennessean,* P, Dec. 3, 1952.

      "no evidence of a coattail effect": Although conducted along partisan
      lines, elections to the General Assembly are highly localized
      events, a condition emphasized by the fact that many decisions are
      made in the primaries, for both the governorship and membership
      in the legislature. Factions form but they are not clearly delineated
      and are not always known to the voters. Gubernatorial candidates
      do not exacerbate their own troubles by interfering in local
      choices. Particularly when a new governor is chosen, his legislators
      may be an unknown quantity to him.

      "technical competence": Technical competence, of course, could be
      and was shown by some political figures, but Clement was innova-
      tive in emphasizing such competence in certain areas; in others, he
      neglected it as much as his predecessors had.

89   "he used a friendship": Interview, Andrew D. Holt, July 9, 1976.

      "executive secretary": Holt was executive secretary of the TEA from
      1937 to 1950; see *Leaders in Education* (5th ed., New York: R.R.
      Bowker, 1974), 506.

      "administrative assistant to the president": Holt occupied this post
      from 1950 to 1953, when he was made one of the vice presidents of
      UT; ibid.

      "according to faculty rumor": Recollections of the author. There
      may have been nothing at all in this rumor, but it is certainly true
      that Brehm feared that Holt would succeed him before he was
      ready to retire. Brehm placed some limits on Holt's activities, par-
      ticularly his contacts with the legislature, which was exactly the
      spot where Holt could have been most useful (author's recollec-
      tions of conversations with Holt during Brehm's presidency).

      "technical qualifications": Holt had been an elementary and high
      school teacher in West Tennessee, and professor of education at West
      Tennessee State College from 1930 to 1937. *Leaders in Education.*

      "comprehensive dissertation": Andrew David Holt, *The Struggle for a
      State System of Public Schools in Tennessee, 1903–1936* (New York:
      Teachers College, Columbia Univ., 1938).

      "not a technician alone": Holt had been an active participant in poli-
      tics as a matter of necessity (and probably of choice) by reason of his
      post with TEA. Everett Derryberry told the author on one occasion

89 that Holt had worked against Prentice Cooper's candidacy for governor, and after the primary tried to make up with Cooper, who was not the most forgiving man in public affairs. Cooper had told Holt: "We got along without you during the primary, and we will continue to get along without you." Holt had been slated to become president of Tennessee Polytechnic, but Cooper appointed Derryberry instead. It is ironical that Derryberry remained at Polytechnic until his retirement, while Holt became president of UT eventually. Dr. Holt denies the accuracy of this story.

"to become commissioner of education": Interview, Andrew D. Holt, July 9, 1976.

"I've got a job": Ibid.

"Holt proposed Quill Cope": Ibid.; for the appointment of Cope, see *Banner*, Dec. 6, 1952.

"a Tennessean": Cope was born in White County, Tennessee, on March 28, 1912. *Tennessee Blue Book*, 1956, p. 68.

90 "No political clearance": This is Holt's opinion; interview, Holt, July 9, 1976. It is always possible that private inquiries are made, but politics was certainly not a major consideration. Holt says Clement had not known Cope, even by name; ibid.

"Howard Warf": Letter, FGC to Howard Warf, Dec. 16, 1952 (Major Appointments). Warf bided his time and maintained his loyalty to Clement.

"he had been left free from political pressure": Interview, Andrew D. Holt, July 9, 1976.

"budget director": There was a rumor that the new governor's father would be budget director—a clear failure to understand Clement's purposes; see *Banner*, CH, Dec. 17, 1952, and *Tennessean*, P, Dec. 18, 1952.

"attention was called to Harold Read": Clement's channel to Read was through Fred Page, a Nashville accountant; interview, Harold Read, Nov. 25, 1974; interview, William Snodgrass, Jan. 22, 1975.

"keep in touch": Interview, Read, ibid.

"budget director of the University": Read became budget director in December 1950.

"was interviewed by Robert Clement . . . budget director during the transition": Interview, Harold Read, Nov. 25, 1974.

"died in November": *Banner*, Nov. 15, 1952.

"made no attempt": Interview, William Snodgrass, Jan. 22, 1975.

"provided him with every facility": Interview, Harold Read, Nov. 25, 1974.

"completely cooperative": Interview, William Snodgrass, Jan. 22, 1975. Letters, FGC to Gordon Browning, Nov. 7, 1952 (Corres.-

90   Browning); Gordon Browning to FGC, Nov. 13, 1952 (Corres.-
      Browning).
91   "a former student": Snodgrass was born in Sparta, Tennessee, on Sept.
      15, 1922. He graduated from David Lipscomb College in Nashville
      in 1942, attended the University of Pennsylvania in 1943, and grad-
      uated from the University of Tennessee in 1947 with a B.S. in ac-
      counting. He did graduate work at UT and served in the Bureau of
      Business Research there. *Tennessee Blue Book,* 1960, p. 60.
      "Municipal Technical Advisory Service": Snodgrass became a consul-
      tant in MTAS in 1951.
      "no connection with party politics": Interview, William Snodgrass,
      Jan. 22, 1975; Snodgrass thinks he received a routine political check
      for the position; ibid. Snodgrass had formed a close friendship with
      Howard Bozeman of Knoxville, a supporter of Clement, who be-
      came county judge of Knox County; ibid.
      "tended to dominate the conversations . . . not highly favorable":
      Interview, Robert S. Clement, May 15, 1975.
      "last major appointment": Snodgrass was appointed Jan. 10, 1953;
      Banner, Jan. 10, 1953. Joe Hatcher had reported a rumor that Clem-
      ent's father was to be made budget director (*Tennessean,* P, Dec. 17,
      1952), but he corrected this in his column the next day.
      "Read thought": Interview, Harold Read, Nov. 25, 1974.
92   "gained Clement's full confidence . . . a key figure": Interview, Wil-
      liam Snodgrass, Jan. 22, 1975.
      "came to occupy": Before Snodgrass, the budget director had been lit-
      tle more than a bookkeeper; Clement increasingly referred adminis-
      trative decisions to Snodgrass and expanded his influence over
      cabinet members, a move that was resisted by some, notably com-
      missioners Leach, McCord, and Hutcheson. Snodgrass' relations
      with Glen Nicely, who became Clement's administrative assistant,
      were good; ibid. Memorandum, FGC to department heads, March
      5, 1954 (Corres.-Snodgrass).
      "never subjected to unwanted political pressure": Interview, Snod-
      grass, ibid.
      "Clement promptly endorsed her": *Banner,* Nov. 28, 1952.
      "Mrs. Bodfish came from a family": Her father was Jay G. Stephen-
      son, active in political affairs. See ibid., June 4, 1952.
      "a trained accountant . . . willing and quick learner": Interviews,
      Harold Read, Nov. 25, 1974; William Snodgrass, Jan. 22, 1975.
      "limited commitment": *Banner,* Nov. 26, 1952.
93   "one of Snodgrass' staunchest backers": Interview, William Snod-
      grass, Jan. 22, 1975.

93 "he acknowledged": Interview, James Cummings, Nov. 4, 1974; Cummings had been and was to remain a power in the Assembly.

"succeeded Clement as counsel": Ibid., Feb. 24, 1950. Friar had managed John Mitchell's campaign for the Senate; ibid.

"ole buddies": Telegram, n.d., Friar to FGC (Bodfish, Friar, Crichton); letter, FGC to Friar, Aug. 6, 1952 (Bodfish, Friar, Crichton); letter, Friar to FGC, March 21, 1951 (Pre-1952).

"adjutant general": Interview, Joe Henry, Sept. 30, 1975.

"he had sought the men": See *Banner*, Dec. 11, 12, 1952.

94 "Buford Ellington": Ibid., Nov. 18, 1952.

"the rivalry of Friar": To begin with, Ellington and Friar were both used on patronage matters; ibid., CH, Nov. 20, 1952.

"principal patronage dispenser": Ellington was a rival with Friar for this role, and his success helps to account for Friar's later break with Clement. Most administrations were criticized for having a "man to see," but they all find the arrangement necessary.

"an elected delegate": *Banner*, Nov. 27, 1952.

"Nicely was a former newsman": Ibid. See also *Tennessee Blue Book*, 1956, p.30; *Tennessean*, Dec. 21, 1952.

"he had not been acquainted with Clement": Interview, Glen Nicely, Aug. 24, 1977.

95 "administrative assistant": Nicely became administrative assistant to the governor on July 1, 1953.

"commissioner of safety": *Banner*, Dec. 1, 1952.

"It's a Girl": Ibid., Dec. 9, 1952.

"woman to a cabinet post": Ibid., Dec. 8, 1952; *Tennessean*, Dec. 8, 1952. Clement was fulfilling a campaign promise; see news release, n.d. (1952 campaign). *Banner*, March 14, 1952.

"resident of Paris": Ibid., Dec. 8, 1952.

"vice-president of the Young Democratic Clubs": Ibid.

"graduate of Cumberland . . . political ambitions of his own": Ibid., Dec. 12, 1952.

"hyperactive patronage dispenser": The Clement files contain numerous letters from McSween on patronage questions.

"state campaign manager for Clifford Allen": *Banner*, May 16, 1950.

"publicly differed": Ibid., Nov. 27, 1951.

97 "William Parham": Ibid., Dec. 11, 1952.

"Trades and Labor Council": Ibid. See also *Tennessee Blue Book*, 1954, p. 99.

"had managed Clement's campaign": *Banner,* Dec. 11, 1952.

"possible conflicts of interest": It was then—and still is—a common practice in Tennessee to name as regulators of certain business areas

97   people who have had experience, and therefore interests, in that
      area. This is not widely perceived in the state as involving any im-
      proper conflict. The post of commissioner of banking and insur-
      ance is a prime example of this practice. Joe Hatcher had charged
      that Crump, who was in the insurance business, had regularly
      picked commissioners of insurance, starting with the administra-
      tion of McAlister. *Tennessean*, P, Dec. 14, 1952. The pressure exerted
      by insurance businesses on the cabinet appointment is illustrated by
      letters in the file-Dept. of Insurance.

"brunt of sharp attacks": *Banner*, Dec. 18, 1952. Letter, Joe W. Henry,
      Jr., to Arch K. Northington, Sept. 16, 1957; Allen to FGC, Aug. 30,
      1957; and press release by Northington Aug. 29, 1957 (all Corres.-
      Clifford Allen).

"Crump played no part": *Tennessean*, P, Dec. 19, 1952; the *Tennessean*
      news story, Dec. 19, 1952, on Northington made no mention of
      Crump influence.

"William Luttrell": *Banner*, Dec. 11, 1952.

"Dr. Hutcheson": Ibid., Dec. 19, 1952; *Tennessean*, Dec. 19, 1952.

"spoke approvingly": *Tennessean*, P, Dec. 2, 1952; editorial, Jan. 16,
      1953.

98 "Jim Camp": *Banner*, Dec. 13, 1952; *Tennessean*, Dec. 5, 1952.

"Carl Hardin": *Banner*, Dec. 13, 1952; *Tennessean*, P, Dec. 3, 1952.

"Charles Everhart": *Banner*, Dec. 13, 1952; Everhart had been a sort of
      floor leader of the opposition to Browning; *Tennessean*, P, Dec. 3,
      1952.

"trucking firm": *Tennessean*, P, Dec. 3, 1952.

"Fleming Hodges": *Banner*, Dec. 13, 1952.

"Forrest Ladd": Ladd was a Crump man; *Tennessean*, P, Dec. 3, 1952.

"Jared Maddux": *Banner*, Dec. 13, 1952; *Tennessean*, P, Dec. 3, 1952.

"early in December": *Banner*, Dec. 13, 1952.

"talk of a floor fight": *Tennessean*, P, Dec. 17, 21, 1952; *Banner*, CH,
      Dec. 14, 1952; *Banner* news story, Dec. 15, 1952.

"definitely dampened": *Banner*, Dec. 30, 1952; *Tennessean*, Dec. 31,
      1952. Letters, Camp to FGC, Dec. 20, 1952; FGC to Camp, Dec. 15,
      1952; Camp to FGC, Dec. 13, 1952 (Corres.-Jim Camp).

"Kefauver machine": *Tennessean*, Dec. 31, 1952.

"withdrew": Ibid., Jan. 5, 1953. A *Tennessean* editorial approved the
      selection of Maddux and Bomar, Jan. 6, 1953.

"from Hardin": *Banner*, Dec. 15, 1952; *Tennessean*, Dec. 15, 1952; let-
      ter, Donald A. McSween to Carl Hardin, Sept. 10, 1952 (Legisla-
      tive Relations).

"assistant clerk . . . clerk of the House": *Banner* Dec. 13, 1952; *Ten-
      nessean*, P, Dec. 3, 1952.

98 "comptroller of the treasury . . . former district commander": Ibid.

"James Bomar . . . Hoyt Bryson . . . Harry Lee Senter": *Tennessean*, P, Dec. 3, 1952.

"middle of December": *Banner*, Dec. 15, 1952.

"floor leader": Ibid., Dec. 29, 1952; *Tennessean*, P, Dec. 30, 1952. Bryson, a UT alumnus, had led the fight against uniting Memphis State to UT; *Banner*, CH, Nov. 29, 1952.

"independent person": *Tennessean*, P, Dec. 3, 21, 30, 1952.

"did not always agree": Letters, Hoyt Bryson to FGC in July 1956; FGC to Hoyt Bryson, June 18, July 18, 1956 (Legislative Relations).

"not to remain": Bryson did not run for reelection in 1954.

99 "Johnson was interested": Interview, Joe Mynatt, Oct. 2, 1975.

"he and Clement": *Tennessean*, P, Dec. 21, 1952.

"legislative council": Interview, Joe Mynatt, Oct. 2, 1975.

"aid of political scientists": At this period, the author, then head of the Dept. of Political Science at UT, was seeking ways to increase contacts between that department and state officials, and, learning of the project for a legislative council, he offered such assistance as the department could give to Tom Johnson. Johnson's response was most positive, and Professor William Goodman spent some time with Johnson in Nashville, helping to work out the legislation to establish the council. Johnson was always quick in later years to give Goodman and the department credit, and he became a friend of the author.

"became law": *Banner*, April 1, 1953; *Public Acts,* 1953, ch. 215. (Acts of the legislature are referred to by short title throughout these notes.)

"resigned his seat": Interview, Joe Mynatt, Oct. 2, 1975.

"the opposition": Johnson was very much an independent, but he had been a Browning floor leader in 1951. Mynatt thought Johnson may have known Clement in the Legion; ibid.

"basic disposition": Interview, Robert S. Clement, March 25, 1975.

"became a useful tool": The council was dominated by the legislative leadership, allied, of course, to the governor, but officially Clement and Ellington maintained a hands-off attitude toward the council; interview, Joe Mynatt, Oct. 2, 1975. The council's studies were coordinated with representatives of the governor such as W.L. Barry, "Bo" Roberts, and Douglas Fisher, during the Clement-Ellington years; interview, Joe Mynatt, Oct. 2, 1975.

"elected Maddux . . . nominating speech": *Senate Journal* 1953, p. 12; *Banner*, Jan. 5, 1953.

100 "name be withdrawn": *Banner*, ibid.

"nominated Bomar": Ibid.

"Judd Acuff": Ibid.

100   "Bodfish, Friar, and Walker": *Senate Journal,* 1953, pp. 31, 32, 33. *Banner* Jan. 7, 1953.

      "to deliver an accounting": *Senate Journal,* 1953, pp. 40–80. See also *Tennessean,* Jan. 9, 1953.

101   "religious service": *Senate Journal,* 1953, pp. 141 ff.

      "had cooperated fully": Interview, Harold Read, Nov. 25, 1974.

      "were frigid": *Tennessean,* Jan. 16, 1964.

      "either coming or going": *Senate Journal,* 1953, p. 141.

      "list his promises . . . This I have done": Ibid., 141 ff.

      "stubbornly defended": Ibid., 147–48.

      "retributive justice": Ibid., 143.

      "lacking in specific content": Ibid., 149–59.

      "Snodgrass": *Banner,* Jan. 10, 1953.

102   "Ramon Davis": Ibid., Feb. 12, 1953.

      "Local bills": The number of local bills was to diminish somewhat after the amendment of the constitution in 1953.

      "embarrassing investigation": Hatcher referred to the investigation as a wildcat whose tail was being held by political figures; *Tennessean,* P, Jan. 22, 1953; see also *Banner,* Jan. 16, 1953.

      "antisubversive affairs": Clement had been involved in this way during his Legion activities, but he showed signs of caution about getting too heavily committed to anticommunist hunts; see an evasive letter on the issue of the Highlander Folk School, FGC to W.A. Swift, Dec. 31, 1953 (Highlander Folk School); letter, FGC to Mrs. J.M. Haynes, Feb. 14, 1953 (Subversion). Clement was a signer of a petition against admitting Red China to the United Nations; letter, S.T. Liang to FGC, Nov. 9, 1953 (Subversion).

      "Sterling Roberts": *Senate Journal,* 1953, p. 510.

      "used his position": *Banner,* Jan 16, 1953.

      "Some hearings": See ibid., Jan. 22, Feb. 4, 1953.

      "Mrs. Winston Caldwell": *Tennessean,* Jan. 11, 1953; *Banner,* Jan. 22, 1953.

      "Mrs. Eric Bell": *Banner,* Feb. 10, 1953.

      "Sims Crownover": *Tennessean,* Feb. 1, 1953; Roberts called Crownover's statement "unfortunate"; see also *Banner,* Jan. 27, 1953.

103   "a father who had served": *Tennessee — A History,* IV, 590.

      "Donald Davidson": *Banner,* Feb. 10, 1953.

      "quizzing of faculties": Personal recollections of the author. Acuff was quoted in the press as making an attack on UT because a teacher of Russian history, Sam Barron, was using a Russian-style text; *Tennessean,* March 4, 1953; Barron and J. Wesley Hoffmann, head of the history dept., were attacked by Acuff on the floor of the House of Representatives; *Tennessean,* March 9, 1953.

103 "used a textbook": Personal recollections of author; see also *Senate Journal*, 1953, p. 505; *Banner*, March 3, 1953.

"Chapter One": *Public Acts*, 1953, ch. 1. Hoyt Bryson's name is listed as sponsor of the act.

"only Clifford Allen": History of the League in file-TML.

"statute provided": *Public Acts*, 1953, ch. 1.

106 "was overwhelming": *Banner*, Feb. 18, 1953. Baird expressed the thanks of the League to Clement; letter, William D. Baird to FGC, Feb. 26, 1953 (TML).

"asking more state money": *Tennessean*, editorial, Jan. 13, 1953; *Banner*, Jan. 9, 1953; letter, FGC to Judge MacFarrar, Shelbyville, Feb. 11, 1953, (D) (Tax Policy). See also "State Legislative Efforts" (TML).

"budget message": Audiotape, State Library and Archives.

"Clement was thinking": *Tennessean*, Jan. 12, 1953.

"rejection of any new taxes": *Senate Journal*, 1953, pp. 373ff.

"NO NEW TAXES" *Banner*, Feb. 25, 1953.

"his disquiet": *Senate Journal*, 1953, pp. 375–76.

"waste and corruption": Ibid., 377–78.

111 "separate department . . . improvement of purchasing . . . union shop . . . reform of the election laws . . . industrial development": *Senate Journal*, 1953, pp. 379ff.

"no commitment": *Senate Journal*, 1953, p. 385; see editorial in the *Tennessean*, Feb. 2, 1953.

"signature of floor leader": *Public Acts*, 1953, ch. 1.

"Chapter 3" "signature of Bryson": Ibid., ch. 3.

"55,980 pounds . . . weights on . . . license fees": Ibid.

"passed the House": *Banner*, Feb. 26, 1953.

"on third reading": Ibid., Feb. 26, 27, 1953. Sen. Harry Lee Senter's attempt to return the bill to committee was defeated; *Banner*, Feb. 25, 1953.

"No hearings": Crump criticized the lack of hearings and that may have led to more care on other bills; *Tennessean*, P, March 4, 1953. See *Banner*, Feb. 28, 1953.

"worked openly": *Banner*, Feb. 26, 1952; *Tennessean*, P, March 1, 1953.

112 "showed clearly . . . McAllen Foutch and Tom Johnson": *Banner*, Feb. 26, 1953. *House Journal*, 1953, 506–8.

"Harry Lee Senter": *Banner*, March 3, 1953.

"parties were split": *Senate Journal*, 1953, 450. The Shelby delegation was also split; *Tennessean*, P, March 1, 1953.

"on his desk": *Banner*, March 3, 1953; *Tennessean*, March 4, 1953; a *Tennessean* editorial on March 4, 1953, said the delay by Clement was insincere.

"called for a veto": *Tennessean*, March 3, 1953.

112 "Crump was critical . . . sharp rejoinder": Telegram, FGC to E.H.
     Crump, March 1, 1953 (D) (Correspondence-E.H. Crump); *Ban-*
     ner, Feb. 28, 1953; see *Tennessean*, P, March 1, 1953.

"echoed the criticism": *Banner*, March 3, 1953; *Tennessean*, March 4,
     1953. For Charles Everhart's counterattack on the *Tennessean*, see
     Banner, March 3, 1953. See statement issued by Clement (Trucks).

"had put forward earlier": See *Banner*, Feb. 22, 1949.

"stolen from him": Browning also claimed that Clement stole the
     idea from Allen; *Tennessean*, July 8, 1952.

114 "somehow counted": Interview, Harold Read, Nov. 25, 1974; inter-
     view, William Snodgrass, Feb. 11, 1975.

"Clement was strongly impelled": Interview, Read, ibid.

"financial quackery": *Tennessean*, P, March 17, 1953; see also *Banner*,
     Feb. 28, 1953; *Tennessean*, March 1, 1953; interview, William Snod-
     grass, Feb. 11, 1975.

"informed Crump": *Banner*, Feb. 28, 1953.

"backing Walter Chandler": *Tennessean*, P, Aug. 2, 1953.

"source of opposition": Hoyt Bryson, quoted in the *Banner*, March 19,
     1953.

"charges were made": *Tennessean*, March 12, 1953.

"based on promises": Ibid., March 15, 1953; ibid., P, March 17, 1953;
     see report of Clement's letter to teachers, *Banner*, March 16, 1953,
     and his speech to the teachers, *Banner*, March 27, 1953.

"adequate margin": *Banner*, March 19, 1953; *Tennessean*, March 19,
     1953; ibid., P, March 19, 1953. On the bitter fight in the House, see
     Banner, March 18, 1953.

"constitutional minimum": *Banner*, March 19, 1953; *Tennessean*,
     March 20, 1953. See *Public Acts,* 1953, ch. 35.

"split both parties":*Tennessean,* March 20, 1953. James Cummings
     voted against the bill, as did Ben Cash of Chattanooga; Cash was
     particularly critical of the financing of the textbook law. Sen. Long
     said he voted for the bill because of the danger to the passage of the
     general education bill if the textbook issue got in the way. The *Ten-*
     nessean carried pictures showing the intense lobbying for the bill.
     The Shelby delegation voted against the bill, reflecting Crump's
     opposition to the financial arrangements.

"could not deliver": The attempt to modify the anti-closed-shop law
     failed in all subsequent legislatures. See *Banner,* March 7, 1953.

"was not repeated": *Tennessean,* March 23, 1953; ibid., P, March 25,
     1953.

"have alienated": Interview, Joe Henry, Sept. 30, 1975.

"Some Negroes opposed": This opposition was expressed in 1955
     when the issue came up again in a letter to FGC on a letterhead of the

114. Colored Voters League of Greater Chattanooga, Jan. 24, 1955 (Labor Problems).

"tabled the measure": *Banner,* April 8, 1953; *Tennessean,* April 9, 1953.

"Chester Coker": *Tennessean,* April 9, 1953.

"Speaker Maddux . . . Jim Camp . . . metropolitan vote": Ibid.

115 "controlled the three-man board": Ibid., editorial, April 4, 1953; see also *Banner,* CH, Jan. 26, 1949; news story, Jan. 27, 1949; for a story on Browning's gradual seizure of the election machinery, see *Banner,* CH, May 24, 26, 1949.

"had increased the size": *Tennessean,* editorial, April 4, 1953. On Browning's 1949 changes, see also *Banner,* CH, Jan. 26, 1949; *Banner,* Jan. 27, 28, 1949; ibid., CH, Jan. 28, 1949; *Banner,* Feb. 2, 1949.

"increased to eight members": *Public Acts,* 1951, ch. 120; *Tennessean,* editorial, April 4, 1953. Browning worked with the John Jennings-Dayton Phillips faction of the Republican party, which, like the Democrats, was split between factions, partly ideological, partly personal. See also *Banner,* CH, Jan. 31, Feb. 2, July 2, 1949.

"78 to 1 . . . 30 to 1": *Banner,* April 7, 1953. Cf. *Banner,* CH, Jan. 8, 1953; *Senate Journal,* 1953, p. 1380, *House Journal,* 1953, p. 1682.

"provided for the election": *Public Acts,* 1953, ch. 88. See *Banner,* March 28, April 1, 1953.

"Guy Smith-Carroll Reece": *Tennessean,* P, April 1, 1953; see also *Tennessean,* April 3, 1953; see also *Banner,* CH, March 7, 1953.

"friends of the governor": *Tennessean,* May 5, 1953; *Banner,* April 9, 1953.

"Republican member": *Tennessean,* May 5, 1953; see also ibid., April 8; P in April 9, 10, 1953; and *Banner,* April 9, 1953.

116 "Mr. Hub": Mr. Walters' friendship with East Tennessee Republicans is clearly shown from his own files. Walters was a friend of the Guy Smith-Carroll Reece faction; *Banner,* March 7, 1953.

"tried to maintain": Letters, FGC to Mrs. Mary Ferrell, Dec. 31, 1954; FGC to Howard Patrick, May 3, 1956; FGC to Sam Monger, Jr., March 28, 1957 (Election Commissions).

"one candid correspondent": Letters [name withheld] to FGC, Feb. 2, 1953; [name withheld] to FGC, July 18, 1953 (Election Commissions).

"state board's choices": *Tennessean,* May 5, 1953.

"an all-time record": *Banner,* April 11, 1953. The rapid passage of the appropriations is described in ibid., March 25, 1953.

"the *Tennessean* listed": *Tennessean,* March 7, 1953, editorial; P, April 12, 1953; see also *Banner,* April 11, 1953.

"Mental Health": *Public Acts,* 1953, ch. 27.

"motor title law": Ibid., ch. 167.

116 "the revision": Ibid., chs. 160, 161, 163.

"the Blind": Ibid., ch. 13.

117 "mere rubber stamp": *Tennessean*, P, April 5, 1953; see also column in *Tennessean*, March 4, 1953; in his column on March 12, 1953, Hatcher claimed that the legislature used to deliberate, and that it did not now know what was in the appropriations bill.

"wildest spending orgy": Ibid., P, April 1, 1953. Hatcher criticized the increase in the state debt in his column on March 26, 1953.

"Nashville Civitan Club": *Tennessean*, July 1, 1953.

"Browning and Clement": Letters, Raymond Denney to FGC, April 9, 1952; FGC to Mrs. Tom Ragland, Oct. 10, 1949; FGC to Ernest Stockton, Oct. 10, 1949 (1953 Const. Conv.). Memorandum, FGC to Les Hart, Sept. 27, 1949; letters, FGC to Mrs. Tom Ragland, July 15, 1949; FGC to Dawson Frierson, Oct. 8, 1951 (all in 1953 Const. Conv.). Pierce also backed the convention; *Tennessean*, Aug. 1, 1952. See also MS of a speech by FGC to the League of Women Voters (1952 Campaign).

"he favored some revision": Letter, FGC to Mrs. C.P. Kelly, President of the League of Women Voters, Chattanooga, July 16, 1952 (1952 Campaign).

"a bias in favor": Ibid.; also letter FGC to Rev. Tom P. Carriger, Erwin, Tenn., March 17, 1953, in reply to Carriger to FGC, March 3, 1953 (1953 Const. Conv.). See report of speech before the municipal league, *Banner*, June 9, 1953.

"had worked hard": Personal recollections of author. See also Greene, Grubbs, and Hobday, 26–27; Tip H. Allen, Jr., and Coleman B. Ransone, Jr., *Constitutional Revision in Theory and Practice* (University: Bureau of Public Administration, Univ. of Alabama, 1962), 35, 42–43, 69. Copies of letters between Denney and various delegates are in file-Denney Papers-Const. Conv. 1953.

"Cooper campaigned": Personal recollections of author; see also Allen and Ransone, 71; *Banner*, April 4, 17, 1953.

"for his re-entry": Hatcher said the story was that Clement hoped to route Cooper into a race for the U.S. Senate; *Tennessean*, P, April 21, 1953.

"Denney ran a poor third . . . caught in a crossfire": Letters, W. Raymond Denney to A.A. Kelly, April 22, 1953; Denney to Hiram Holtsford, April 15, 1953 (Denney letters—Const. Conv. 1953); Allen and Ransone, 69–70; see also *Tennessean*, April 21, 1953; and ibid., P, April 21, 22, 1953.

118 "by a margin of one vote": See *Banner*, April 21; ibid., CH, April 22, 1953.

"on the floor": The *Tennessean*, in an editorial commented that Clem-

118 ent had said he would keep hands off the convention, April 18, 1953.

"the governor's term . . . an item veto . . . a sharp restriction": Greene, Grubbs, and Hobday, 27–30. Commenting on the issue of the item veto then before the convention, Joe Hatcher said there had not been a free, deliberative legislature in twenty years; *Tennessean*, P, May 14, 1953.

"patronage": The pressures on Clement for jobs began, of course, even before he was inaugurated; see *Banner*, CH, Nov. 20, 1952.

119 "Rube McKinney": Ibid., Aug. 30, 1951, June 3, 1952.

"elder Clement was influential": Robert Clement was always very close to his son; he was a significant figure in all the campaigns, and although he was not *the* patronage director, he was certainly consulted on many patronage matters—for example, interviews, Harold Reed and William Snodgrass; letter, W.W. Tucker to FGC, Nov. 7, 1952 (Patronage-General); and reply of Robert S. Clement to Tucker, Nov. 13, 1952 (Patronage-General).

"rivalries and rows": For example, letters, O.O. Frogge to FGC, March 26, 1953, and reply, March 31, 1953 (Patronage-Local Organizations); Dink L. Gibson to J.C. McCallen, March 26, 1953 (Patronage-Highways); Robert H. Polk to FGC, April 8, 1953; (Patronage-Local Organizations); Pat Smith to FGC, Aug. 14, 1953; FGC to J. Edward Hyder, Sept. 21, 1953; FGC to Rev. A.W. Buchanan, Nov. 7, 1953 (the last four in Patronage-Local Organizations). Sometimes the local committees were asked to meet to compose differences; for example, letters, FGC to C.T. Haggard, July 22, 1953; Glen Nicely to Bill McNeil, Sept. 15, 1953 (Patronage-Local Organizations). At times the committee met with the governor; for example, letter, Marshall Priest to FGC, Feb. 7, 1953 (Patronage-Local Organizations). Glen Nicely used a system of local clearance for recommendations made by cabinet officers; memorandum, Nicely to FGC, Nov. 2, 1953 (Patronage-State Library and Archives). Occasionally, at least, members of local committees tried to interfere in merit appointments; letter, [name withheld] to Dr. R.H. Hutcheson, Aug. 9, 1954 (Public Health).

"wired one local supporter": Telegram, [name withheld] to FGC, May 1, 1953 (Patronage-Local Organizations); letter, [name withheld] to FGC, Oct. 28, 1953, and reply, FGC to [name withheld], Nov. 2, 1953 (Patronage-State Library and Archives).

120 "Both senators": Letters, FGC to Albert Gore, June 8, 1953 (Patronage-Fed.-Cong. Pressure); Estes Kefauver to W.W. Luttrell, Dec. 16, 1954 (Patronage-Highway Patrol).

"well-known members": Letters, Joe L. Evins to FGC, Dec. 15, 1952;

120   Percy Priest to FGC, April 20, 1953; FGC to Joe L. Evins, May 19,
        1953; FGC to Jere Cooper, March 9, 1954; Carroll Reece to FGC,
        Dec. 10, 1954; Sam Rayburn to FGC, June 10, 1955, and reply, June
        16, 1955 (Patronage-Fed.-Cong. Pressure).

     "mayors, councilmen": Letters, A.L. Bender to FGC, March 4, 1953;
        FGC to Judge Cummings, March 26, 1953 (both in Patronage-
        Highways); FGC to Mayor Ben West, Aug. 3, 1956 (Patronage-
        Action by FGC).

     "all offered": Examples of the appeals from private citizens are in let-
        ters, Paul Kruesi to FGC, Sept. 7, 1954 (Mr. Kruesi was a prominent
        Chattanooga industrialist who had been a member of the UT
        Board) and reply, FGC to Kruesi, Sept. 16, 1954; Sam McAllester to
        FGC, Sept. 21, 1954 (all in Major Appointments).

     "Poor man": Memorandum, Ellyn Warth to Buford Ellington, un-
        dated, but probably 1954 (Patronage-Highways).

     "did not put warnings": Interview, Joe Henry, Sept. 30, 1975. Henry
        said Clement subscribed to the old adage—if you are going to cut a
        man, don't let him see you sharpening the knife.

     "legislators": For example, letters, [name withheld] to FGC, June 15,
        1953 (Patronage-Highways). [Name withheld] to Buford Elling-
        ton, April 24, 1955 (Legislative Relations); Jim Camp, senator
        from White County, was especially active in patronage matters—
        letters, Camp to Buford Ellington, March 9, 1954 (Patronage-
        Highway Patrol); Camp to Glen Nicely, May 5, 1953 (Corres.-Jim
        Camp); Camp to Nicely, June 13, 1953 (Corres.-Jim Camp); Also
        letters, Jared Maddux to FGC, Oct. 16, 1964 (1964 Campaign);
        James Bomar to FGC, March 15, 1955 (Corres.-James Bomar); Ben
        Cash to Jared Maddux, Oct. 21, 1953 (Legislative Relations).

     "lost friends": Letter, FGC to Hoyt Bryson, April 1, 1954 (Patronage-
        Local Organizations).

     "a post for himself": On jobs for legislators, letters, Paul A. Phillips to
        FGC, April 29, 1953; Weldon Burrow to FGC, Sept. 1, 1955 (Legisla-
        tive Relations).

     "highways": The files are filled with patronage letters dealing with
        highway building (for example, file on Patronage-Highways).
        One memorandum said: "We think Mr. [name withheld] should
        have a job as he is in need of one." But Commissioner Leech
        thought it bad policy to turn local road building over to the politi-
        cal factions; letter, W.M. Leech to FGC, April 6, 1953 (Patronage-
        Highways).

     "agriculture": For example, letter, FGC to John Perry Whitten,
        March 9, 1954 (Patronage-Cons. and Ag.).

120 "finance and taxation": For example, letter, J.L. Hutcheson to FGC, May 16, 1955 (Patronage-General).

"highway patrol": Clement was sometimes pressured on promotions, discharges, and transfers within the patrol.

"welfare . . . employment security": For example, letter, FGC to Fred I. Womack, Oct. 27, 1953 (Patronage-Local Organizations). Also memorandum, Glen Nicely to Commissioner McSween, June 19, 1953; letters, Charles G. Tomerlin to FGC, May 23, 1953; FGC to Mrs. Frank E. Smith, July 9, 1953; Donald M. McSween to James Crawford, Oct. 15, 1953; FGC to George H. McDowell, Aug. 17, 1954; memorandum, McSween to FGC, undated (all in Patronage-Employment Security).

"conservation": Letters, Rev. William H. Blue to FGC, March 24, 1953; Pat McCulley to FGC, May 5, 1953; S. Briscoe Justice to J.N. McCord, Aug. 6, 1953; Hugh G. Marshall to FGC, Aug. 14, 1953; also letter, Guy L. Smith to FGC, June 15, 1953 (all in Patronage-Cons. and Ag.).

121 "federally imposed merit systems": For example, letters, Sam W. Carmack to FGC, Sept. 19, 1952; William H. Orgain to FGC, April 1, 1953; Edith G. Gragg to Christine Reynolds, April 23, 1953; FGC to Rev. Wilmer B. Robbins, Aug. 24, 1955 (all in Patronage-Welfare). Also letter, FGC to T. Leroy Neblett, Dec. 17, 1954 (Public Health).

"wrote a supplicant": Letter, [name withheld] to FGC, May 20, 1953 (Patronage-Employment Security).

"Clement replied": Letter, FGC to [name withheld], May 30, 1953 (Patronage-Employment Security).

"sound truck driver": Memorandum, Donald M. McSween to FGC, no date (Patronage-Employment Security).

"Boards and commissions": Letter, Cayce L. Pentecost to FGC, March 16, 1954 (Patronage-Action by FGC); jobs as games wardens were in heavy demand. Clement often said he did not control patronage in the Game and Fish Commission—for example, letter, FGC to Gon Z. Robinson, Nov. 27, 1953 (Game and Fish Commission). On contacts between Chester Parham and the Board of Education, letter, FGC to Chester Parham, July 20, 1953 (Major Appointments); telegrams, FGC to Parham, July 16, 1953, and reply, July 16, 1953 (Major Appointments.) Appointments to the Game and Fish Commission were a matter of intense interest to sportsmen, who wanted adequate regional representation. Clement promised to keep appointments to the commission out of politics.

"Posts of honor": Letters, S. Harry Busch to FGC, Nov. 27, 1953; Will

121   Cummings to FGC, Oct. 14, 1953; Charles T. Rhyne to Donald Mc-
       Sween, Feb. 21, 1953 (all in Patronage-Colonels).

       "queried one candid candidate": Letter, [name withheld] to FGC, June
       23, 1954 (Patronage-Colonels).

       "acknowledging this unabashed inquiry": Letter, Glen Nicely to
       [name withheld], June 28, 1954 (Patronage-Colonels).

       "Harry Truman and Alben Barkley": See ch. 8; letters, Barkley to
       FGC, Jan. 11, 1954 (Patronage-Colonels); Truman to FGC, Nov. 6,
       1956 (Corres.-Truman).

       "careful analyses": Memorandum, Bob Morgan to Nicely, Ellington,
       Carr, Friar, Henry, Dec. 30, 1953 (Patronage-Colonels).

       "wanted a limit set": Memorandum, Morgan to FGC, Nov. 7, 1953
       (Patronage-Colonels).

122   "dismissals had to be made": Some of the dismissals were undoubtedly
       punitive. Hatcher catalogued some of the early firings— Tennes-
       sean, P, Jan. 16, 1953. Also, for example, memorandum, Nicely to
       Carl Peterson, June 18, 1953 (Patronage-Cons. and Ag.).

       "bitterly expressed": For example, letter, [name withheld] to Glen
       Nicely, April 4, 1953 (Patronage-Local Organizations). Dismissals
       were made for political reasons and as the result of checks on loy-
       alty; for example, memorandum from Ellington to governor's of-
       fice, Nov. 10, 1954; and an accompanying letter, [name withheld]
       to FGC, Nov. 8, 1954 (Patronage-Local Organizations).

       "only fair way to do it": Letter, [name withheld] to FGC, Dec. 23, 1954.

       "checked with Friar": Letter, W.M. Leech to Gene Calloway, Feb. 11,
       1953 (Patronage-Highways). Hatcher regarded Friar as the "hatchet
       man" in the early days: see Tennessean, P, Jan. 16, March 3, 1953.

       "friendly letter to the jobseeker": Letters, FGC to [name withheld],
       March 26, 1953 (Patronage-Highways); FGC to [name withheld],
       Feb. 21, 1953; FGC to [name withheld], April 14, 1953; FGC to [name
       withheld], Aug. 17, 1953 (last three letters in Patronage-Delegation);
       sometimes these letters were dated in batches.

       "not hesitate to override": For example, memorandum, FGC to Friar,
       Feb. 26, 1953; letters, FGC to W.W. Luttrell, Feb. 25, 1954
       (Patronage-Action by FGC); FGC to Judge Will Cummings, March
       26, 1953 (Patronage-Highways); memorandum, FGC to W.M.
       Leech, Jan. 12, 1954 (Patronage-Highways). Occasionally, Clem-
       ent intervened in salary increase issues; see letter, FGC to James W.
       Henry, May 27, 1953; memorandum, FGC to W.M. Leech, Jan. 12,
       1954 (Patronage-Highways).

       "could become peremptory": Letter, FGC to Joel Rogers, abruptly and
       curtly terminating Rogers as associate director, Bureau of Aero-
       nautics, Jan. 15, 1953 (Patronage-Highways).

122 "he demanded": Memorandum, FGC to Glen Nicely, March 26, 1953, referring to a hotel and restaurant inspector in Chattanooga (Patronage-Action by FGC).

"is not dismissed": Memorandum, FGC to Friar, March 26, 1953 (Patronage-Action by FGC). In Dec. 1953, Joe Hatcher said waivers on promotion were forced on 11 highway patrolmen; *Tennessean*, P, Dec. 22, 23, 1953.

"Work out something for him": Memorandum, FGC to Ellington, Sept. 3, 1954 (Patronage-Action by FGC).

"unusually close attention": Interview, Anna Belle O'Brien, May 5, 1975; interview, Douglas Fisher, June 28, 1977; interview, Valerius Sanford, Sept. 29, 1977.

123 "lawyers and other judges": Clement was usually careful to consult bar and bench—for example, letters, H.W. Laughlin, Jr., to FGC, May 12, 1953; FGC to Tom Murray, member of Congress, June 2, 1953 (Judicial Appointments). For a case in which Clement disregarded bar recommendations, see *Tennessean*, P, Nov. 20, 1953.

"the chief justice": Memorandum, FGC to Glen Nicely, Nov. 3, 1954 (Judicial Appointments).

"appointments of Republicans": See, for example, *Banner*, CH, May 1, 1963.

"paid to geography": For example, letters, FGC to H.W. Laughlin, Jr., June 2, 1953; Grooms Herron to FGC, May 23, 1953 (both in Judicial Appointments).

"pressure on him as 'severe'": Letters, FGC to Andrew T. Taylor, May 22, 1953; FGC to H.W. Laughlin, Jr., June 2, 1953 (Judicial Appointments). Considerable pressure was applied for and against Buford Lewallen in 1954 (Judicial Appointments).

"he withdrew his name": Telegram, Andrew T. Taylor to FGC, May 20, 1953; letters, FGC to Taylor, May 22, 1953; Tom Murray to FGC, May 11, 1953 (all in Judicial Appointments). Taylor received numerous endorsements. See *Banner*, CH, May 13, 21, 1953; list provided Taylor by FGC, June 9, 1953 (Judicial Appointments).

"John E. Swepston": Rumors of a probable vacancy surfaced in 1953: letters, Neil Robertson to FGC, June 11, 1953 (Judicial Appointments). On the recommendations, when the vacancy occurred, letters, Charles C. Gillespie to FGC, April 9, 1954; FGC to Gillespie, April 16, 1954; John E. Swepston to FGC, April 22, 1954; FGC to Swepston, April 27, 1954 (Judicial Appointments).

"acceptance of Joe Hatcher . . . appointment of Lois Bejach . . . had Crump's approval": *Tennessean*, P, April 15, 1954.

"David Pack": Memorandum, FGC to Glen Nicely, Nov. 3, 1954; letter, FGC to Pack, Nov. 5, 1954 (both in Judicial Appointments). On

123   recommendations for Pack, letters, Hamilton S. Burnett to FGC,
       Nov. 21, 1954; Chancellor Ben Robertson to Chief Justice A.B.
       Neil, Oct. 30, 1954; Robertson to FGC, Oct. 30, 1954; telegram,
       Donald McSween to FGC, Nov. 2, 1954 (all in Judicial Appoint-
       ments). Pack was "cleared" with Herbert Walters, Attorney Gen-
       eral McCanless and Chief Justice Neil; letter, Walters to FGC, Nov.
       1, 1954 (Judicial Appointments). The reason for the temporary
       character of the initial appointment of Pack is not clear. See inter-
       view, David Pack, Feb. 28, 1978.

       "J.B. Avery": On Avery appointment, letters, FGC to S. Homer Ta-
       tum, April 16, 1953; J.B. Avery, Sr., to FGC, April 7, 1953, a letter
       with embarrassingly fulsome thanks (Judicial Appointments). See
       also Banner, CH, March 23, 1953; news story, March 24, 1953. Pres-
       sures for appointments to trial courts are exemplified by letters,
       FGC to Jesse L. Rogers, Nov. 22, 1954; Estes Kefauver to FGC, Nov.
       24, 1954; C.W. Wright (Scott County manager for Clement) to
       FGC, Nov. 27, 1954; Ray Schubert (Morgan County manager) to
       FGC, Nov. 27, 1954; Sam Jones to FGC, Nov. 30, 1954 (all in Judicial
       Appointments). At times the governor received applications for ju-
       dicial appointments; letter, [name withheld] to FGC, May 8, 1953
       (Judicial Appointments). Clement regularly sent out form letters
       thanking people for their approval of his appointments. At times
       the letters went astray, and one such letter came back to the gover-
       nor from East Tennessee with a written comment: "Wrong form let-
       ter; I don't give a [word(s) withheld] who's judge in West Tennes-
       see;" written note on returned copy of letter, FGC to [name with-
       held], June 4, 1953 (Judicial Appointments).

       "car dealers, oil and gas vendors, bankers, insurance salesmen, archi-
       tects": Letter, [name withheld] to FGC, Nov. 13, 1954; memoran-
       dum, Franklin Pierce to FGC, May 19, 1954 (both in Contracts). An
       award of insurance to a cousin of Sam Rayburn was made on Ray-
       burn's request; letters, Sam Rayburn to FGC, June 10, 1955; FGC to
       Rayburn, June 16, 1955 (Patronage-Fed.-Cong. Pressure). On ar-
       chitects, letter, Ben Cash to Jared Maddux, Oct. 21, 1953 (Legisla-
       tive Relations).

       "share of state funds": For example, letters, [name withheld] to Glen
       Nicely, June 20, 1953; [name withheld] to FGC, Dec. 14, 1953;
       [name withheld] to FGC, Nov. 2, 1953 (Contracts).

124   "the governor's replies": For example, letters, FGC to [name with-
       held], March 11, 1954; FGC to [name withheld], May 8, 1953; FGC to
       [name withheld], Nov. 29, 1954 (Contracts).

       "pledged an investigation": A Tennessean editorial supported the in-
       vestigation, Jan. 12, 1953.

124 "Senate Joint Resolution No. 12": Ibid., Jan. 14, 1953.

"all duly catalogued": Ibid., P, Jan. 15, 1953.

⟩ "strong majorities": *Senate Journal,* 1953, p. 99; *House Journal,* 136–39.

"investigating committee . . . Hatcher praised": See *Banner,* Jan. 16, 1953; *Tennessean,* P, Jan. 18, 1953.

"editorially labeled": *Tennessean,* editorials, Jan. 16, 18, 1953.

"by only one day": The report is found in *Senate Journal,* 1953, pp. 295 ff.

"to express shock": *Tennessean,* P, Feb. 6, 1953; he had said on Feb. 1, 1953, that the examination of the Memorial Hotel issue was a near flop; see also news story, Feb. 5, 1953, and P, Feb. 10, 1953.

"committee reported": *Senate Journal,* 1953, p. 296.

"transaction was criticized": Ibid., 301 ff.

"Martin and Doggett": Ibid., 305 ff; see *Tennessean,* P, Feb. 6, 1953.

125 "collusive and fraudulent practices": *Senate Journal,* 1953, p. 312.

"mismanaged and misused": Ibid.

"dummy companies . . . accommodation addresses . . . collusive and fictitious bidding . . . closed specifications . . . excessive purchases . . . unnecessarily high prices": Ibid., 312 ff.

"Department of Conservation . . . park system": Ibid., 327.

"improper sales practices . . . forgery . . . fraud and collusive bidding . . . Knoxville furniture company": Ibid., 327.

"former commissioner of conservation": Ibid., 333.

"Department of Purchasing . . . penal institutions": Ibid., 333–39.

126 "claim too much": Events in the 1970s indicated that the old custom of tempering contracts by considerations other than low bids was still alive.

"insurance for state operations": See ch. 5.

"chancery court": *Banner,* March 19, April 15, 1953; *Tennessean,* April 7, 1954.

"started moving out": *Tennessean,* Aug. 28, 30, Oct. 14, 1953. The former owners of the hotel had asked the court to enjoin the state from moving, ibid., Sept. 1, 1953. See also *Banner,* Aug. 27, Sept. 1, 1953.

"court took evidence": See *Banner,* Sept. 25, 1953, Feb. 9, 10, 11, March 19, 31, April 3, 1954.

"beyond the powers": *Tennessean,* Aug. 27, 1954; *Banner,* Aug. 26, 1954.

"under receivership": *Tennessean,* Nov. 21, 1953.

"Browning maintained": Majors, 205.

127 "something else again": Betty [Gentry] to Lowrey, n.d. (Highway Department). This file contains information on highway pressures generally.

"without opposition": *Banner,* March 3, 1953.

"Dr. C.J. Ruilman": Ibid., Feb. 19, 1953.

127 "claimed": See ibid., June 5, 1954.

"allegations of 1975-76": Purchasing practices in the Blanton administration resulted in some indictments and convictions.

"ordered an investigation": *Tennessean,* Jan. 16, 1953; the paper said
Joel Boyd Williams had started an investigation at an earlier date.
See *Banner,* CH, April 24, 28, July 13, 1953.

"and forgotten": By the general public but probably not in Polk
County, where it is still difficult to get some people to talk freely
about the matter.

"informed sheriffs": *Banner,* June 25, 26, July 6, 11, Aug. 17, 1953. See
also ibid., CH, Nov. 25, 1953. See also *Tennessean,* July 3, 1953.

128 "arranged to sell": *Banner,* April 24, 28, May 1, Oct. 13, 1953; letter,
Rep. L.C. Aymon, Sr., to FGC, April 14, 1953, and reply, April 27,
1953 (Legislative Relations).

"regarded suspiciously": For example, the issue of an engineering
program at Memphis State; letters, A.D. Holt to Harlan Matthews,
Oct. 29, 1963; A.D. Holt to FGC, Oct. 30, 1963 (UT Affairs).

"Dr. R.B. Wood . . . Acuff Clinic": The history of the hospital project is based largely on a report prepared by Lee S. Greene, assisted
by Robert Dupree and Robert Wood (son of Dr. R.B. Wood), "A
Report on Certain Problems Connected with the University Memorial Research Center and Hospital," submitted to the Hospital
Committee of the Board of Trustees, Knoxville, 1960. The idea
originated about 1947; *Tennessean,* P, Jan. 1, 1953. Local support included Legion backing: letter, Claude L. Machamer to Gordon
Browning, Oct. 14, 1948; reply, Nov. 27, 1948 (Univ. Hospital Issue). See also "Report," 3-4. On support of Acuff Clinic, letter,
Herbert Acuff to Gov. Browning, Jan. 7, 1949 (Univ. Hospital
Issue).

"Tennessee Medical Association": Letter, W.M. Hardy to Gov.
Browning, Jan. 20, 1949 (Univ. Hospital Issue).

129 "rabies is not a circumstance": Letter, Gordon Browning to Albert
Gore, Feb. 14, 1949 (Univ. Hospital Issue). Browning told Gore
that the hospital proponents were fearful that the proposed Oak
Ridge hospital that Gore had written about would be only for
treatment.

"the Board of Trustees": The principal opposition within the Board
came from Col. Harry S. Berry. Letters, J.P. Hess to FGC, Feb. 27,
1953; Clyde B. Austin to FGC, Jan. 10, 1953 (Univ. Hospital Issue).
See also "Report", 6.

"mobilization": The Knoxville Area CIO Council backed the project;
see Resolution, March 3, 1953, sent to FGC by letter of Joe Cummings (Univ. Hospital Issue). The local American Legion backed

129 the project: letter, Charles Siegal to FGC, March 5, 1953 (Univ. Hospital Issue). Also letter, Paul Gragg, secretary, Northeast Tennessee Industrial Union Council, to FGC, March 11, 1953 (Univ. Hospital Issue). A memorandum, no date, signed by Friar, refers to a "terrific collection of witnesses" for the project, with a covering letter to FGC, July 24, 1953, signed by George Dempster and other Knoxville leaders (Univ. Hospital Issue).

130 "initial impulse": Compare *Banner,* CH, Jan. 1, 1953.

"leading proponent": Letter, Sam J. McAllester to FGC, Sept. 3, 1953, and reply, Sept. 16, 1953 (Univ. Hospital Issue).

"George Dempster . . . Howard Bozeman": Letter, George R. Dempster to FGC, Dec. 9, 1953 (Univ. Hospital Issue).

"stage-managed": Notes for and minutes of this meeting, July 29, 1953; also Confidential Notes concerning meeting of Atomic Hospital Commission, Oct. 30, 1953 (all in Univ. Hospital Issue).

"Clement announced": Statement of FGC, no date; also letters, Col. C.S. Reeder to FGC, Oct. 15, 1953; and reply, Nov. 10, 1953; W.R. Snodgrass to FGC, Oct. 29, 1953; Reeder to FGC, Dec. 2, 1953 (all in Univ. Hospital Issue).

"was built": The hospital was accepted in 1956 by the University; letter, Sam. J. McAllester, Sr., to FGC, July 28, 1956 (Univ. Hospital Issue).

"frequently sought": For example, letter, FGC to C.E. Brehm, on behalf of a friend of Camille Gravel, July 12, 1956 (UT Affairs); at this time, Gravel, a Louisiana politician, had been supporting FGC as keynoter for the 1956 Democratic convention. Browning received similar letters, for example, on July 17, 1952 (Browning files).

"rarely developed": Telegram, Glen Nicely to H.T. Lockard, Jan. 5, 1956 (UT Affairs).

"courteously but vaguely": For example, letter, FGC to [name withheld], Nov. 2, 1956 (UT Affairs).

"undue favoritism": Andrew Holt said there was no trace of this kind of influence in UT; interview, Andrew D. Holt, July 9, 1976.

"for locating jobs": For example, letter, FGC to Dean N.C. Beasley, April 20, 1953 (MTSU).

"would-be academicians": Letter, FGC to Dean Meek, April 21, 1954 (UT-Martin).

"were not completely immune": For example, letter, FGC to Paul Meek, April 21, 1954 (UT-Martin); FGC to Meek, Sept. 7, 1954 (UT-Martin); Burgin E. Dossett to Mrs. O.A. Jared, Feb. 2, 1954 (East Tenn. U); FGC to Dean N.C. Beasley, April 20, 1953 (MTSU).

131 "substantial qualifications": Among the Clement-Ellington figures who advanced in the educational field, the following should be

131   mentioned: Edward Boling, President, and Joe Johnson, Vice-
       President of UT; Roy Nicks, Chancellor of the system of state re-
       gional universities and community colleges; Peter J. Pere, at one
       time, assistant to Nicks. Boling, Johnson, and Nicks possess earned
       doctorates, and all had some experience at the teaching level. Pere
       had successfully completed advanced degrees.

       "largely unappeased": The faculties have struggled for an increased
       role in the selection of administrators for over 30 years, with some
       successes and some defeats; personal recollections of the author. In
       the 1960s and 1970s, the trend has been toward increased faculty
       participation, but it would be a rash man who would maintain that
       the results have always been satisfactory. See letter, Prof. R.D.
       Present to FGC, Dec. 14, 1957 (UT Affairs).

       "valued prizes": Interview, Harold Read, Nov. 25, 1974. For exam-
       ple, series of letters supporting Knoxville industrialist and former
       football star "Breezy" Wynn for the UT Board; dated late 1958 and
       early 1959 (UT Affairs).

       "pressures": Interview, Andrew D. Holt, July 9, 1976; for example,
       telegram, Organization for Expansion of UT-Martin Branch to
       FGC, April 13, 1953; letters, Organization to FGC, April 14, 1953;
       Hafford C. Paschall, Jr., rep. from Henry County, to FGC, April 19,
       1953; FGC to Wayne Fisher, April 28, 1953; Fisher to FGC, APRIL 30,
       1953; Wassell Randolph to FGC, July 31, 1953; Thomas H. Allen to
       FGC, Aug. 4, 1953 (all in UT Affairs). See *Banner*, Sept. 17, 1953.
       Also letter, Mrs. Joe. B. Tilson to FGC, Sept. 27, 1956; telegrams,
       Carroll Reece to FGC, Dec. 12, 1957, and Z. Cartter Patten to FGC,
       Dec. 17, 1957 (all in UT Affairs).

       "Holt": Interview, Holt, July 9, 1976. Letter, Andrew Holt to FGC,
       Dec 21, 1957 (UT Affairs).

       "administrative assistant": *Banner,* June 18, 1953.

       "succeeded Nicely": Ibid.

       "as his counsel": Interview, Douglas Fisher, June 28, 1977.

       "Franklin Pierce": *Tennessee Blue Book,* 1956, p. 48.

       "Safety": *Banner,* July 2, 1953.

       "Keith Hampton": Ibid., July 14, 1953.

       "dynamited": See resolution by Nashville Building and Construction
       Council, Sept. 9, 1953 (Labor Problems).

       "barber shops": *Tennessean,* Dec. 19, 1953.

       "Weakley County": Telegram, Hillary Freeman to FGC, July 10, 1953
       (Labor Problems).

       "Oak Ridge": Telegram, S.R. Sapirie to FGC, July 8, 1954 (Labor
       Problems).

131 "declined": Telegram, Glen Nicely to E.A. Wende, July 16, 1954
(Labor Problems).

"black dissatisfaction": Letter, W.E. Harlan, President, Mid-State
Colored Fair, Murfreesboro, to FGC, July 22, 1954 (Negroes I).

"Whites became vocal": Letter, [name withheld], President, Donelson Men's Civic Club to FGC, March 19, 1953 (Negroes I).

CHAPTER 5.

133 "Rudy Olgiati" *Tennessean,* P, Sept. 24, 1953.

"Prentice Cooper": Ibid., Nov. 15, 1953.

"Clifford Pierce . . . Clifford Allen": Ibid., Dec. 13, 1953.

"Carl Fry": *Tennessean,* Jan. 17, 1954.

"McAllen Foutch, Walter Haynes, John R. Long": Ibid., P, July 19,
1953; see also *Banner,* CH, Aug. 18, 1953.

134 "abandon politics": *Memphis Press-Scimitar,* May 23, 1953.

"given money freely": For example, letter, FGC to Rev. S.D. Organ,
June 6, 1946 (Religious Activities).

"lay preacher": Martin, 48.

"evangelist Billy Graham": Letter, for example, Graham to FGC, Aug.
20, 1953 (D) (Corres.-Graham). Clement actively supported Graham's "Crusades" and often appeared in public with him; for example, letter, W.H. Bryant to FGC, Nov. 8, 1954 (Corres.-Religious
Figures). Baylor University gave Clement and Graham honorary
doctorates on Nov. 6, 1954; letter, W.H. Bryant to Stephen A.
Mitchell, Nov. 8, 1954 (Degree from Baylor). Clement frequently
spoke in churches in and out of the state; for example, letter, FGC to
Rev. Wayne Dehoney, March 26, 1954 (Corres.-Religious Figures);
letter, FGC to Henry G. Perry, Sept. 20, 1954 (Religious Activities).

"Ira North": Interview, Ira North, Oct. 2, 1975.

"Graham's crusades": Letters, Maxey Jarman to FGC, April 1, 1953
(D); FGC to Jarman, Sept. 16, 1953 (D) (Corres.-Graham). Jarman
gave $1000 to one of the crusades; letter, Jarman to FGC, Sept. 18,
1953 (D) (Corres.-Graham). Also letters, FGC to Henry G. Perry,
American Tract Society, Sept. 20, 1954 (Religious Activities); FGC
to Rev. Graham, Oct. 21, 1954 (Corres.-Graham). Clement solicited friends for funds for Graham; letters in (D) (Corres.-Graham).

"Clement time schedule": See Martin, 50.

"many a letter": letters in 1956 Conv. file. Hatcher speculated early on
Clement's interest in the Senate; *Tennessean,* P, March 3, 1953.

"George Dempster and Rudy Olgiati": *Banner,* Feb. 2, 1954. Letter,
Dempster to FGC, July 16, 1953 (1954 Campaign).

135 "circularized his cabinet": The results of this poll are in the files at
     Dickson, Tennessee (D) (Poll of Cabinet on Senate Race).

     "Clement's financial backers": *Tennessean*, P, July 19, 1953; Hatcher
     repeated the statement on Oct. 23, 1953.

     "declined to say what": *Banner*, Sept. 9, 1953. Clement never made
     any secret of the fact that he intended running for something
     whenever he could. As early as 1954, there were rumors that Clem-
     ent might challenge Gore eventually; see ibid., CH, Feb. 3, 1954.
     In an undated letter to Gore (but probably sent in late 1953), Whit
     La Fon said Clement's stock had sunk to a new low, a poor proph-
     ecy, as it turned out; letter, La Fon to Gore (Gore papers).

     "run for political office": Letter, FGC to Floyd A. Green, May 11, 1966
     (Misc. Out-State Corres.).

     "Ellington announced": *Banner*, Jan. 6, 1954; *Tennessean*, Jan. 7, 1954;
     ibid., P, Jan. 7, 1954; Hatcher again said Clement's financial back-
     ers insisted on the gubernatorial campaign, refusing prospects of a
     race for the Senate.

     "took himself out": *Banner*, CH, Dec. 30, 1953.

     "Browning's announcement": *Banner*, Jan. 20, 1954; *Tennessean*, Jan.
     20, 1954. Hatcher (ibid) in P said Browning would not ally himself
     with Kefauver in this election. He charged that Clement forces had
     tried to get Browning to run against Kefauver, but this seems very
     hard to credit. Hatcher implied that Browning was offered cam-
     paign funds, if he would take such a step.

     "not to run": Majors, 204. Browning had shown signs of running in
     the summer of 1953; letter, George R. Dempster to FGC, July 16,
     1953 (1954 Campaign); interview, Robert S. Clement, March 25,
     1975.

     "babies he had kissed": *Banner*, CH, Jan. 20, 1954. It was Browning's
     seventh campaign for the governorship; ibid., April 21, 1954.

     "determined fighter": Majors, ch. 10, quoting letter, Browning to
     Gilmer Richardson, Sept. 15, 1952.

136 "fiscal caution": See report of Civitan speech by Browning, *Tennes-
     sean*, July 1, 1953; *Banner*, Jan. 20, 1954.

     "made his candidacy official": *Banner*, Feb. 1, 1954. Crump said he
     would back Clement; ibid., CH, Feb. 1, 1954.

     "newspapers": Among the smaller newspapers that endorsed Clem-
     ent, as reported in various issues of the *Banner*,, were the *Shelbyville
     Times-Gazette*, the *Clarksville Leaf-Chronicle*, the *Johnson City Press
     Chronicle*, and the *Maryville-Alcoa Daily Times*.

     "*Commercial Appeal*": Reported in the *Banner*, Feb. 8, 1954.

     "*Times*": Reported in *Banner*, July 12, 1954. The *Times* said Clement

136   had a generally good record, although it was critical of the lack of hearings on the truck-weight bill.

"stuck to the ex-governor": Majors, 207–208. The *News-Sentinel* said Browning was running a revenge campaign; reported in *Banner*, July 26, 1954. The *Press-Scimitar* did not back anyone; Majors, 207–208.

"Bill Baird . . . Rudy Olgiati": *Banner*, Feb. 2, 10, 1954.

"Tennessee Municipal League was highly pleased": Cf. letter, Herbert J. Bingham to FGC, May 13, 1957 (TML).

"McCord": As commissioner of conservation.

"A few defections": Ellington thought Clement should have broken with Friar sooner. Clement had a sense of loyalty. Ellington said Friar wanted to dominate the cabinet. Interview, Stephen Boyd with Ellington, Aug. 18, 1971.

"winter of 1953–54": Martin, 54.

"Brothers": Ibid., 55.

"national Democratic committee": *Banner*, July 26, 1956; also file-1954 Campaign. See *Banner*, May 25, 1954.

"Hugh Abercrombie": Cf. interview, Travis, Sept. 26, 1977; see *Banner*, June 10, 1954. Letters, Hugh Abercrombie to Buford Ellington, Aug. 25, 1954; Hugh Abercrombie to FGC, Dec. 22, 1954 (County Organizations).

137   "Will Cummings": Cummings had backed Clement in 1952; *Banner*, June 9, 1952.

"Wilkes Thrasher": *Tennessean*, April 18, 1954; William Wilson managed Browning's campaign in the Second District. Ibid., P, April 18, 1954.

"Charles Lockett": See *Banner*, July 26, 1954. Lockett later became Knox County manager for Ellington; *Banner*, June 23, 1958. Interview, Lockett, June 25, 1980.

"J.N. Doane": Doane is a cattleman and local political power in Jefferson County.

"Sam Ridley": *Banner*, July 15, 1954. Ridley had been a supporter of Clement before the first term; for example, letter, Ridley to FGC, Dec. 6, 1950 (Pre-1952).

"Jim Alexander": Alexander later became a campaign manager for Clement.

"would attempt": Browning thought people were more interested in Crump than they actually were; Majors, 199.

"had not always approved": Crump was critical of the initial financing of the free textbooks, and he found the Cadillac episode distasteful.

137 "had been seen together": *Tennessean,* Dec. 5, 1953; ibid., editorial,
Dec. 5, 1953; ibid., P, Dec. 8, 1953; *Tennessean,* Dec. 11, 1953.
"backing of Clement": *Banner,* CH, Feb. 1, 1954.
"Allen and Pierce": *Tennessean,* Dec. 13, 1953.
"deficit financing": *Tennessean,* including P, regularly referred to it as
deficit financing; see, for example, *Tennessean,* P, Oct. 14, 1953, Jan.
27, 1954.

138 "out of the surplus": *Banner,* June 5, 1954.
"in 1954 and 1955 ": *Brown* v. *Board of Education,* 347 U.S. 483 (1954)
and 349 U.S. 294 (1955).
Browning tended to take the first option": Majors, 206. See also *Tennessean,* June 1, Aug. 1, 1954.
"Clement, the second": Ibid., July 28, 1954; Hatcher accused Clement of hedging, ibid., P, July 30, 1954.

140 "would not be allowed": Majors, 206.
"state had not been ordered": *Tennessean,* July 28, 1954.
"Judge Raulston Schoolfield . . . entered the race for the governorship": *Banner,* June 22, 1954.
"at Trenton": Ibid., June 4, 1954; *Tennessean,* June 4, 1954.
"Clifford Pierce": *Banner,* CH, June 3, 1954.
"Wilkes Thrasher . . . was present": *Banner,* June 4, 1954.
"Gene Steele": Ibid.
"political holiday": Ibid., June 5, 1954; see also June 14, 1954.

141 "idea of toll roads . . . truckers . . . debt policies of Clement . . .
testify against thee . . . Browning observed . . . asserting that he
started": *Banner,* June 5, 1954. Browning made attacks on the
trucks through the campaign; see *Tennessean,* May 13, 1954; also
Browning flyer (1954 Campaign). Clement defended himself on
the truck-weight issue—June 26, 1954, speech at Johnson City
(1954 Campaign).
"Clement's opening salvo": *Banner,* June 5, 1954.
"a new state institution to treat alcoholics . . . lavish old age pensions": *Tennessean,* P, April 11, 1954. No promises were made on
means of paying; *ibid.*

142 "dignified campaign": *Banner,* June 5, 1954.
"endorsed TEA's 4-point program": See ibid., April 9, June 5, 1954.
"calm and cautious waiting": Ibid., June 5, 1954; see also ibid., May
15, 1954.
"the peroration": Ibid., June 5, 1954.

144 "attracted little notice": Reports are found in ibid., Sept. 9, 14, 15, 16,
1953.
"did not do so": Compare ibid., CH, March 30, 1954.
"repeal of the right-to-work law": Browning was endorsed by the

144   Brotherood of Railway and Steamship Clerks, Freight Handlers, Express and Station Employees, AFL. *Tennessean,* P, April 27, 1954.

"promised to try again": *Banner,* June 5, 1954.

"Enka plant . . . broad swipes at agitators": Browning defended his action at Enka as being necessary to protect lives and property. *Tennessean,* March 1, 1954.

"TEA had a new program" The teachers wanted a hike in the sales tax; ibid., P, April 13, 1954.

"TEA program": *Banner,* May 8, 1954. Clement sent letters to various interest groups to indicate what he had done for them (1954 Campaign).

"fifty-one mayors": Ibid., June 5, 1954.

145   "attacked them": Ibid.

"Clement wanted to raise the sales tax": *Tennessean,* July 11, 1954.

"this was all propaganda": *Banner,* July 17, 1954.

"same charge": *Banner,* CH, June 15, 1954.

"asserted that he had given": *Banner,* July 21, 1954; *Tennessean,* July 22, 1954; see opening charge by Browning, ibid., July 21, 1954.

"using his savings": *Banner,* July 27, 1954. Telegram, FGC to E.H. Crump, March 1, 1953 (Corres.-Crump).

"without any noticeable effect": Cf. interview, Boyd, with Joe Hatcher, Aug. 16, 1971.

146   "admiration for his father": See *Banner,* June 29, 1954.

"Pappy Clementine": Ibid., June 5, 30, 1954.

"any court higher than a j.p. . . . $240 was a fortune . . . credit rating": Ibid., June 30, 1954.

"too large a role in state affairs": *Tennessean,* May 29, 1954; ibid., P, June 6, 1954.

"insurance policies": *Tennessean,* editorial, June 5, 1954; *Banner,* June 5, 1954; *Tennessean,* May 29, June 1, 4, 1954; ibid., P, June 6, 1954.

"governor released information . . . business was routed to political allies" *Banner,* June 10, 1954.

"Mrs. Reynolds": Ibid., July 2, 1954.

147   "he derided McCord . . . Lucille and the young boys": Browning's attacks on McCord were brutal: he said that McCord was a vote trader and that the old man was in love and had his mind on something else; ibid., July 2, 1954.

"ways of provoking": Interview, Boyd with Ellington, Aug. 18, 1971.

"remove Olgiati": *Banner,* July 13, 1954.

"flocked openly": Ibid., July 15, 1954.

"pressured some sheriffs": Clement promised to continue his crackdown on gambling and racketeering in West Tennessee; *Banner,* June 29, 1954.

147 *"Times* declined": An offer had been made to the *Chattanooga Times.*
      Banner, July 12, 1954. Interview, Travis, Sept. 26, 1977.
    "Photographs were made . . . governor later claimed": (Proposed
      Autobiography).

148 "studying the photographs": Ibid.
    "tired of making payoffs": *Tennessean,* P, July 15, 1954.
    "parole violation": *Tennessean,* July 11, 1954.
    "club was padlocked": *Banner,* July 10, 1954.
    "off-the-bench remarks": Ibid., July 12, 1954.
    "categorized Judge Hicks": A *Tennessean* editorial backed the 400-
      Club story, July 16, 1954. Interview, Travis, Sept. 26, 1977.
    "endorsing Clement . . . deplored": *Banner,* July 12, 1954.
    "brought into open view": Fred Travis in the *Chattanooga Times* un-
      der a story dated July 17, 1954, said that the *Times* reported the
      break last winter; Travis said that Clement objected to Friar's inter-
      ference in purchasing and the break, he continued, was complete in
      January although not actually final until April. Travis said that
      Browning and Friar had formed an alliance and said that capital
      sources thought that Friar was feeding material to Browning.
      Clement's attitude was to keep quiet unless one of the three an-
      nounced for Browning. Jeanne Bodfish had announced retirement
      from politics.
    "Browning announced": *Tennessean,* July 17, 1954.
    "imagination leaped far beyond": Martin, 50.

149 "before the women voters": *Banner,* June 4, 1952.
    "Friar's ambitions": See Martin, 54. Letter, FGC to Friar, Jan. 28, 1954
      (Bodfish, Friar, Crichton).
    "to promote his own influence": *Banner,* July 21, 1954.
    "influence . . . alleged use": Martin, 55.
    "quietly left political life": Cf. Gardner, 432–33.

150 "Dear Eddie . . . Dear Bob": Letters, FGC to Friar, Jan. 28, 1954; FGC
      to Crichton, Jan. 28, 1954 (Bodfish, Friar, Crichton).
    "a bit short on specific charges": FGC to Friar, Jan. 28, 1954 (Bodfish,
      Friar, Crichton). Cf. interview, Robert N. Clement, May 6, 1976.
    "communication to Crichton": FGC to Crichton, Jan. 28, 1954 (D)
      (Bodfish, Friar, Crichton).
    "a long statement": See file (D) (Bodfish, Friar, Crichton).

151 "once said . . . supported no one": *Banner,* Aug. 3, 1954.
    "news conference": *Tennessean,* July 26, 1954; *Banner,* CH, July 26,
      1954.
    "asked facilities": Telegram, Friar to FGC, July 26, 1954 (Bodfish,
      Friar, Crichton). The correspondence files show a friendly letter
      from Crichton to FGC dated April 15, 1954, which seems odd tim-

151   ing in view of reputed breaks before that date (Bodfish, Friar, Crichton).

"dissolved his law partnership": *Banner,* July 26, 1954.

"Crichton disappeared": In Sept. 1954, Joe Carr succeeded Crichton as treasurer of the Democratic State Executive Committee; ibid., Sept. 13, 1954.

"to impeach": Some small moves were made in this direction; *Tennessean,* Aug. 24, 1954. Also letter, Eddie Harmon to FGC, Aug. 28, 1954 (Bodfish, Friar, Crichton).

"disappointed": Cf. letter, G.F. Lewis to FGC, Dec. 3, 1956. Also letters, FGC to A.F. Curbow, April 27, 1953; Harold J. Webb to FGC; Mrs. August Lewis to FGC, Oct. 1, 1954; Mrs. W.A. Lewis to FGC, Dec. 7, 1954; John Standridge to FGC, March 17, 1955. (All letters in file-Polk County.)

"A poem": File-Polk County.

152   "appeared again": *Banner,* July 21, 1954; *Tennessean,* July 21, 24, 1954.

"peace was maintained": See *Tennessean,* Aug 5, 6, 1954.

"Lucille Clement was exhausted": *Banner,* Aug. 11, 1954. Mrs. Clement was at Mayo's for diagnosis of headaches.

"counties and small towns": Schedules in file-1954 Campaign.

"in a white suit": Interview, Boyd with Anna Belle O'Brien, Aug. 25, 1971.

153   "Contributions": For example, a list prepared for Glen Nicely, Sept. 1, 1954 (Campaign Funds-1954).

"half a million dollars": *Tennessean,* P, Jan. 13, 1954.

"employee shakedowns": Ibid., May 11, 20, 23, 1954; see also *Banner,* CH, May 15, 18, 1954.

"issued a memorandum": Memorandum, FGC to department heads, May 18, 1954 (Campaign Funds, 1954). See story, *Banner,* May 19, 1954; *Tennessean,* May 16, 1954; ibid., P, May 20, 23, 1954; also letter, FGC to W.R. Coate, Sr., July 14, 1954 (Campaign Funds, 1954).

"contributions were tabulated": For example, checking of registrations, memorandum, Mrs. Watson to Robert D. Morgan, Sept. 22, 1954 (1954 Campaign).

"Most of the newspapers": The *Commercial Appeal* said Browning was embittered and hidebound; *Banner,* June 8, 1954; for names of endorsing papers, see ibid., various issues during early and middle 1954.

"stubbornly predicted": See, for example, *Tennessean,* P, May 30, Aug. 1, 4, 1954.

154   "Bryson . . . Mansfield": Losses or retirements in the Senate included Sen. Everhart, J.K. Long, Jim Camp, Sterling Roberts. House losses or retirements included Bryson, Harry Mansfield. Foutch re-

154   turned to the Senate. Both houses were strongly pro-Clement. Ibid., Aug. 12, 1954.

"a man of upright personal life": Interview, David Alexander, Feb. 28, 1978.

"he outlived": Browning died in 1976.

"more cordial relations": Barry said Browning later in life became friendly with Robert S. Clement and visited his home several times. Interview, W.L. Barry, Nov. 2, 1977.

"Pat Sutton": Hassler, *Primary Elections,* 37–38; see also Buchanan and Bird, 22–32.

"Senator Gore": Gore refused to get involved in the Kefauver-Sutton contest; letters, James E. Charlet to Gore, July 10, 1954; Gore to Charlet, July 17, 1954; W.M. Barr to Gore, July 9, 1954; Gore to Barr, July 17, 1954; Gore to Forrest Ford, July 17, 1954; Gore to Edward J. Meeman, July 17, 1954 (Gore Papers). Kefauver's friends (Orgill, Tom Robinson, Meeman, Al Richey) were reported to fear Kefauver might lose; letter, W.M. Barr to Gore, July 20, 1954 (Gore Papers). Gore had also refused to take a stand in the governor's race; letter, Gore to Paul Robinson, July 30, 1954 (Gore Papers).

155   "before the general election": *Banner,* CH, Oct. 20, 1954.

"Ross Bass": *Banner,* Aug. 7, 1954.

"Boss Crump": *Tennessean,* Oct. 17, 1954.

"worked for Bozeman": Memorandum for FGC to be used in speeches for Bozeman, Oct. 18–19, 1954 (Corres.-Bozeman). Gore also supported Bozeman and tried to help him; letter, Gore to Michael J. Kirwan, Sept. 28, 1954. (Gore papers).

CHAPTER 6.

157   "was in demand": Clement made a deep impression with his speech to the Democratic National Committee in Indianapolis; it led to immediate talk as to his possible use as keynoter in 1956; *Banner,* CH, Sept. 20, 1954; see also *Banner,* Feb. 15, 1955.

158   "to leave his office": Letter, J.B. Walker, Jr., to FGC, July 1, 1953 (Cabinet Appointments).

"Ramon Davis": Davis succeeded Walker on June 30, 1955.

"offered William Snodgrass": Interview, Snodgrass, Jan. 22, 1975.

"never a professional politician": Although in later years, Snodgrass sometimes appeared at meetings staged as party rallies or conferences, he was never comfortable in the role.

"He advised": Interview, Snodgrass, Jan. 22, 1975.

"as students . . . as an instructor": Ibid.

"fiscal officer for Union Carbide": Recommendation of Boling, let-

158   ter, Clark E. Center, vice president of Carbide and Carbon Chemicals, to FGC, Sept. 28, 1954 (Corres.-Boling).

"allegiances were unknown . . . he was not asked . . . would be his own man": Interview, Edward J. Boling, June 25, 1975. Boling's selection was made known in early fall; *Banner,* CH, Oct. 4, 1954.

160 "vice president . . . president": Boling became vice president, Sept. 1, 1961, and president, Sept. 1, 1970.

"Harlan Mathews": Interview, Snodgrass, Jan. 22, 1975. Mathews entered the state service as a planner but was moved to the budget staff; interview, Mathews, Jan. 23, 1975.

"Joseph Johnson": Interview, Joseph Johnson, Aug. 16, 1977.

"Roy Nicks": Nicks joined the Department of Finance and Administration in 1959.

"Gerald Adams": Adams entered state service in June 1962 upon completion of Southern Regional Training Program; letter, Adams to LSG, April 2, 1980.

"Vanderbilt": Interview, Harlan Mathews, Jan. 23, 1975.

"Southern Regional Training Program": The early beginnings of this program are described in Lee S. Greene, "Regional Research and Training in Public Administration," *Public Administration Review,* VII, 4 (Autumn 1947), 245–53, and *Graduate Education and Research in Government in the South* (Atlanta: Southern Regional Educational Board, 1954), report written by Lee S. Greene and Richard Leach.

"Johnson": Johnson, after various high level educational experiences, became executive vice president and vice president for development of the University of Tennessee in 1973.

"Nicks": Nicks, after filling high level posts in state government and in the University of Tennessee, became chancellor of the Board of Regents of the State University and Community College System of Tennessee in 1975.

"has never run": Rumors developed at one time that Nicks might run for governor, but nothing of the sort occurred.

"Bomar remained": *House Journal,* 1955, p. 16.

"Maddux was reelected": *Senate Journal,* 1955, pp. 12–13.

"quickly died": *Tennessean,* Dec. 12, 30, 1954; ibid., P, Dec. 22, 1954.

"vainly urged": Letters, Bryson to FGC, May 27, 1954; FGC to Bryson, May 15, 1954; FGC to Bryson, June 2, 1954 (Corres.-Bryson).

"had offered to help": Letter, Bryson to FGC, May 27, 1954 (Corres.-Bryson).

"in patronage matters": Letter, Camp to Commissioner Z.D. Atkins, Feb. 5, 1957 (Corres.-Camp).

"ran unsuccessfully": Letter, Camp to FGC, April 21, 1956 (Corres.-Camp).

160 "Eugene Collins": Interview, Eugene Collins, Sept. 18, 1975.

"protege of Hoyt Bryson . . . gone to school . . . low-keyed and inexpensive venture . . . Collins decided": Ibid.

161 "Rudy Olgiati, Hugh Abercrombie, Ben Cash, J. Fred Johnson, Leonard Aymon": Ibid. Also letter, Ben Cash to FGC, Nov. 29, 1954 (Corres.-Collins).

"surrounding counties": Interview, Eugene Collins, Sept. 18, 1975.

"slight acquaintance": Collins had met Clement in 1952. Clement gave him an appointment to attend a meeting of the Southern Regional Education Board; ibid.

"Clement felt impelled": The invitation to Collins to be floor leader was extended at a meeting with Clement and Ellington; Collins thought Joe Henry may also have been present; ibid. It is significant that Ellington was sitting in on legislative as well as executive appointments.

"would back an increase": Clement's opponents charged him with considering or planning an increase.

"Damon Headden": Collins himself suggested the arrangement of stepping aside; Headden was eventually picked for the role of leader on the tax; interview, Eugene Collins, Sept. 18, 1975.

"a little strain for a few days . . . all the publicity . . . abandoned his legislative career": Ibid.

"to work hard": Interview, Joe Mynatt, Oct. 2, 1975. Ellington was Clement's liaison with Collins and gave him aid when needed.

163 "daily early morning conferences . . . the firm control . . . dropped off to sleep . . . during one of his speeches . . . about 80 percent": Interview, Eugene Collins, Sept. 18, 1975.

"Senate Joint Resolution Number One": *Senate Journal,* 1955, pp. 17–19.

164 "he left no successor . . . in some disarray": Cf. Tucker, ch. 4.

"represent all interests": It was rumored that Crump took care to get a delegation that would appeal to various groups; for example, the delegation, it was said, would include at least one drinker and one nondrinker.

"solidly loyal": Walters' attachment to the governor went back to the days when Walters had helped to make him general counsel to the Railroad and Public Utilities Commission.

"elected to the state Senate": *Senate Journal,* 1955, pp. 36, 39.

"by party action": *Banner,* Oct. 19, 20, 21, 1954.

"refused to seat him": *Senate Journal,* 1955, pp. 35–40; *Banner,* Jan. 5, 1955.

"ministers of the gospel": Art. IX, sec. 1; the provision was taken over from the constitution of North Carolina.

164 "seated": *House Journal*, 1955, pp. 54–57.

"Clifford Allen": *Tennessean*, Jan. 28, 1955; *Banner*, Jan. 27, 28, 1955.

"clear enmity": Clement's well-known propensity to forgive was delayed for Allen and probably would not have been welcomed at
first. Clement was rarely sarcastic in his letters, but in at least one
he exploded to Allen; letter, FGC to Allen, Feb. 17, 1954 (Corres.-
Allen). In later years, thanks to Clement's courtesy, Allen became a
friend of Clement; interview, Robert N. Clement, May 6, 1976.

"January 18, 1955": *Tennessean*, Jan. 19, 1955.

"two hours and eight minutes": *Banner*, Jan. 11, 1955; *Tennessean*, Jan.
12, 1955. The intensity of the speech is evident on the sound records
maintained in the State Library and Archives; *Senate Journal*, 1955,
pp. 72–147.

165 "new revenue": *Senate Journal*, 1955, p. 140; *Tennessean*, Jan 12, 1955.

"a new high": Cf. *Banner*, March 2, 1955.

"Holt remained evasive": Comment by Douglas Fisher written on
the letter, Andy Holt to FGC, Dec. 28, 1954 (UT Affairs). Clement's
relations with UT were good, but he was critical of some of UT's
salaries, noting that the salary of J.J. Walker, the treasurer of UT,
exceeded the salary of the treasurer of the state; notes for a letter,
typed and signed by FGC but possibly not sent, July 5, 1955 (UT Affairs).

"to ask for a rise": *Tennessean*, Jan. 18, 1955.

"TEA came out for an increase": *Banner*, Jan. 15, 1955. Individual teachers supported increases in taxes and expenditure; e.g., telegram,
Ruby Delashmit to FGC, Jan. 19, 1955; letters, Carol D. Bailey to
FGC, Jan. 20, 1955; FGC to Mrs. James Cunningham, Jan. 25, 1955
(all in Teacher Salaries).

"had expressed resentment": *Banner*, July 17, 1954.

"Ellington had disliked the idea": Ibid., CH, Dec. 15, 1954.

"memento": The cards are undated but appear to be sent in 1955, although they could have been sent in 1957 (Teacher Salaries).

"clan gathered": *Tennessean*, Jan. 19, 1955.

"striking exception of Gordon Browning": *Banner*, Jan. 18, 1955.

"Ross Bass . . . Billie Sol Estes": Ibid., Jan. 4, 1954, Jan. 17, 19, 1955.

168 "died aborning": Ibid., Jan. 28, 1955.

"Clifford Allen": See ibid., Jan. 28, Feb. 7, 1955; *Tennessean*, Jan. 28,
Feb. 15, 1955.

"proposed a three-cent sales tax . . . hike in motor vehicle license
fees": *Tennessean*, Feb. 1, 3, 1955; *Banner*, Feb. 4, 1955.

"dumped into the general fund": See *Tennessean*, Feb. 17, 1955.

"McCord . . . backed the increase": *Banner*, Feb. 7, 1955.

"Jim Cummings . . . came over": Ibid., CH, Feb. 11, 1955.

168 "around a two-thirds majority": *Tennessean*, Feb. 11, 1955.

"on February 10": *House Journal*, 1955, p. 621; *Tennessean*, Feb. 11, 1955.

"February 16": *Senate Journal*, 1955, p. 588; *Tennessean*, Feb. 17, 1955; *Banner*, Feb. 16, 1955.

"Ben Cash": *Senate Journal*, 1955, p. 589.

"Clifford Allen": Ibid.

"all of the added one cent": *Tennessean*, Feb. 17, 1955; *Banner*, Feb. 18, 1955.

"had persuaded his colleagues": *Tennessean*, Feb. 18, 1955; *Senate Journal*, 1955, pp. 586–87; *Banner*, Feb. 18, 1955.

"Senate backed down": *House Journal*, 1955, p. 773.

169 "unanimity was the rule": See *Banner*, Feb. 25, March 2, 4, 1955.

"made a gesture to labor": *Tennessean*, Feb. 25, 1955.

"revision of the open shop law . . . Minimum railway crew": See *Banner*, CH, Feb. 25, *Banner*, Feb. 1, 26, 1955, *Tennessean*, Feb. 25, March 4, 1955.

"carefully emphasized": The *Tennessean* suggested that not much pressure was applied, Feb. 26, 1955. Pressure would not have produced results anyway because the proposals were too controversial; interview, Eugene Collins, Sept. 18, 1975. For opposition, telegram, L. Elmore to FGC, Jan. 25, 1955; Commander, v.F.W., Newport to FGC, Jan. 26, 1955 (both in Labor Problems). Proponents' correspondence in file-Labor Problems.

"anti-injunction law . . . in a popular storm": *Tennessean*, March 4, 1955; interview, Collins, ibid. The experience rankled in Henry's mind long afterward; interview, Joe Henry, Sept. 30, 1975. See *Banner*, March 7, 1955; CH, March 8, 1955.

"a general annexation law": The annexation law was one of the outstanding achievements of the Clement years; it broke the log-jam on municipal expansion, but in the quarter-century since the passage of the act, suburban forces have gradually weakened the law. The original act is *Public Acts*, 1955, Ch. 113. Professor Wallace Mendelson of the Department of Political Science, the University of Tennessee, acted as a consultant to the Tennessee Municipal League in the preparation of the legislation. See also Greene, Grubbs, and Hobday, 259–60. It cannot be supposed that Clement personally had much to do with the annexation law, but he is entitled to credit for having been a friend to the cities during this period. Also interview, Collins, ibid.; see *Banner*, March 2, 1955; *Tennessean*, Feb. 25, 1955.

"began to come alive": See *Banner*, Jan. 12, 22, 25, 1955.

"even the Municipal League felt easy": The league never backed apportionment strongly; the fight was left to the big cities. The

169 league had done well with the legislatures beginning in 1953 and had no interest in changing the ground rules.

"Douglas Fisher": Interview, Douglas Fisher, June 28, 1977. Clement's deliberation on judicial appointments sometimes led to hopes that had to end in disappointment and trouble. Ellington tried to avoid such trouble by quick and decisive actions on judicial appointments.

"named his father": *Banner,* April 27, 1955. The governor checked the proposed appointment with Chief Justice Neil before announcing it; letter, FGC to Chief Justice A.B. Neil, April 25, 1955 (Judicial Appointments).

"little opposition": Letters of approval came in — Claude S. Reeder to FGC, April 28, 1955; Judge J.B. Avery to FGC, April 28, 1955; Lewis C. Payne to FGC, May 2, 1955 (Judicial Appointments).

170 "Wardlaw Steele": *Banner,* CH, May 11, 1955; news story, May 17, 1955.

"to hold": See Ibid., July 6, 1955; Nov. 22, 1955. Steele was overruled by the state Supreme Court in *Kidd* v. *McCanless,* 200 Tenn. 273 (1956); cert. denied by the Supreme Court of the United States, 352 U.S. 920 (1956). See *Banner,* April 5, 1956.

"chapter 181": *Public and Private Acts,* Jan. 4, 1915 to March 31, 1916, ch. 181, regular sess., 1915.

"Seldon L. Maiden . . . T.K. Reynolds": House Bill No. 94; transmitted to Senate, March 8, 1915; reported out of Senate Committee on Penitentiary without recommendation, by J.A. Clement, chairman, March 23, 1915; passed Senate on third reading, March 26, 1915, with 20 ayes, 11 noes. *Senate Journal,* Jan. 4–May 17, 1915.

"Clement voting for repeal": On March 26, 1915, Clement moved to table motion to reconsider; passed.

"following a highly publicized crime": Interview, Robert S. Clement, March 25, 1975.

"once more instituted": By *Public Acts,* Jan. 1–Apr. 10, 1917, ch. 14. J.A. Clement was no longer in the Senate.

"Since 1915": List in file-Executions.

"85 colored men and 39 white men": From July 13, 1915, to Nov. 7, 1960; figures in file-Executions.

"With tears": Interview, Harlan Mathews, Jan. 23, 1975; also interview, Anna Belle O'Brien, Oct. 26, 1978.

"for he felt": Tapes for a proposed autobiography (Proposed Autobiography); interview, Ira North, Oct. 2, 1975.

"to talk to him": Interview, Eugene Collins, Sept. 18, 1975.

171 "always said": File-Proposed Autobiography; interview, Ira North, Oct. 2, 1975.

171 "by chance": File: Proposed Autobiography.

"Eddie Collins": *Tennessean,* Jan. 5, 1954.

"governor was pressured . . . William Baird": Letter, William Baird to FGC, July 8, 1955 (Pardons and Paroles).

"a delay for Sullins": Telegrams, Evins to FGC, July 31, 1955; FGC to Joe L. Evins, no date (Pardons and Paroles). Clement told Evins that Sullins admitted to him in the presence of the deputy warden that he (Sullins) had lied when he claimed he had instructed Kirkendall not to kill Collins. Clement had prepared a reprieve for both men from Aug. 1, 1955 to Sept. 1955, but the reprieve was not issued. The sentence was carried out on Aug. 1, 1955.

"Billy Graham was present": Telegram, FGC to Evins, no date (Pardons and Paroles).

"in his own words" File-Proposed Autobiography; also interview, Ira North, Oct. 2, 1975.

172 "Silliman Evans": The biographical material on Evans in largely taken from the story in the *Tennessean,* June 27, 1955; see also *Banner,* June 27, 1955.

173 "been a power": The following story was told to the author by UT President C.E. Brehm: On the occasion of a Democratic clambake in Nashville, Evans made a speech. He pounded the table and said, "I own the Democratic party of Tennessee." This he followed with: "I own the senator from Tennessee." Kefauver, who was sitting at the head table, said nothing. Once again Evans pounded the table, shouting, "I own the governor of Tennessee." Browning got up, and, saying "Silliman, you go too far," he left the party. Whatever his faults, Browning had a sense of dignity of the governorship.

"mouthpiece of Luke Lea": See McFerrin, 87.

"Once Kefauver had demonstrated": Evans had told Kefauver he would get his support, once he had gone out and shaken some 500 hands successfully; see Gardner, p. 49.

"Cordell Hull died": *Banner,* July 23, 1955.

"I.D. Beasley died": Ibid., Oct. 26, 1955.

"had attended Cumberland University": Ibid.

"died in September of 1956": Ibid., Sept. 8, 1956.

174 "Mrs. Albert Hill": Ibid., Oct. 4, 1956.

"Senator McKellar": Ibid., Oct. 25, 1957.

"died in 1958": Ibid., Jan. 21, 1958.

"strike of the L&N": See *Tennessean,* March 19, April 2, 3 ff., 1955; also analysis, Doug Fisher to FGC, March 16, 1955 (Strikes).

"Southern Bell Telephone Company struck": See *Tennessean,* March 19, 1955; April 2, 1955.

174 "court action": Injunctions were issued by Judge Richard Dews and Chancellor T.A. Shriver, but they seemed ineffective; memorandum, Douglas Fisher to FGC, March 16, 1955 (Strikes).

"Clement . . . Governor Wetherby": Telegram, Lawrence W. Wetherby to FGC, March 17, 1955 (Strikes). Clement also contacted twelve southern governors, offering to arrange a conference on the strike; telegram, FGC to the governors, April 13, 1955 (Strikes). Because of the L&N strike, disorder spread to the coalfields (telegram, C.R. Griffith, President, Southern Appalachian Coal Operators Association to FGC, April 13, 1955, in file-Strikes), and Clement requested FBI intervention in the coal fields; telegram, FGC to J. Edgar Hoover, April 18, 1955 (Strikes). Clement broadcast on April 19, 1955, saying his powers were rather limited and that he had not been asked for local aid (Strikes); Clement, like most governors, was reluctant to use state forces without local requests.

"arbitration": Telegrams, John E. Tilford, President of the L&N, to FGC, April 20, 1955; Lawrence W. Wetherby to FGC, March 17, 1955 (Strikes).

"discharge all employees": Telegram, FGC to the officials concerned, May 6, 1955 (Strikes).

"strikes came to an end": The L&N strike was settled in May; statement of Tilford, May 23, 1955 (Strikes). See *Tennessean,* May 21, 1955. For an account of the strike, see Maury Klein, *History of the Louisville and Nashville Railroad* (New York: Macmillan, 1972), 478–85.

"Bomar and Maddux": *Banner,* Dec. 7, 1956.

"Jim Cummings had indicated some interest": *Tennessean,* Jan. 7, 1957. Maddux already had enough signatures of senators to put him in. Also interview, Jim Cummings, Nov. 4, 1974.

"without resentment or fuss": The game, as Cummings understood it and played it, allowed the governor to pick the speakers; interview, Cummings, ibid. *Banner,* Jan. 7, 1957.

"Senate floor leadership": *Banner,* Jan. 8, 1957.

"Republican candidates for speaker withdrew": *Senate Journal,* 1957, p. 14.

"his law practice": Interview, Eugene Collins, Sept. 18, 1975; letter, Eugene N. Collins to FGC, May 3, 1956. (Legislative Relations).

"Damon Headden": Indicated by sponsorship of bills; see *Public Acts, 1957.* Also letter, Damon Headden to FGC, April 10, 1957 (Legislative Relations).

"Ross Dyer and Lyndon Jennings": The floor leader selections do not appear in the Journals but can be detected by the frequency of their sponsorship of legislation. Dyer eventually became a justice of the state Supreme Court. *Banner,* Jan. 8, 1957.

175 "expired in January": See *Tennessee Blue Book, 1957–58*, p. 62.

"announced his candidacy for governor": *Banner*, Jan. 14, 1957; see also *Tennessean*, P, Jan. 1, 1957.

"attacked Clement . . . Bob Crichton": *Banner*, Jan. 14, 1957.

"a page . . . his father . . . clerk . . . trustee for Putnam County": Interview, Joe C. Carr, Sept. 16, 1975.

"final two terms": In the interim, Carr was in the insurance business; *Banner*, CH, Feb. 14, 1949.

"his wife had served": Interview, Joe C. Carr, Sept. 16, 1975.

"He and Lipe Henslee": Interview, Joe Carr, Sept. 16, 1975; also interview, Robert S. Clement, March 25, 1975.

"Ramon Davis": Davis had succeeded Walker, who resigned because of ill health; *Banner*, June 9, 1955.

"wanted more money": See *Tennessean*, Oct. 30, 1956, and *Tennessean*, P, Nov. 15, 1956. Frank Bass of the TEA advocated a state income tax, an unpopular proposal in Tennessee; *Banner*, April 18, 1957.

"series of conferences": *Tennessean*, P, Nov. 15, 1956.

176 "bond issue . . . equalize property assessments . . . industrial development . . . increased power to levy local taxes": Ibid.

"This attempt was to fail": Ibid., Jan. 2, 1957. Blacks were speaking up against repeal of the anti-closed shop law, for blacks had been frozen out of unions. Other opposition was felt; telegrams, Happy Day Cleaners to FGC, Jan. 25, 1955; V.F.W., Newport, to FGC, Jan. 26, 1955 (Labor Problems). There was, of course, pressure for repeal; e.g., telegram, Aubrey L. Brown, union leader, to FGC, Jan. 27, 1955 (Labor Problems).

"pointing to other achievements": Notes for speech to the state CIO convention, June 17, 1955 (Labor Problems).

"minimum wage on state employment": Letter, Lacy Suiter to FGC, June 27, 1956 (Labor Problems).

"rehabilitation programs": Letter, FGC to Mrs. Frank Brice, Secretary, Knoxville Labor League for Political Education, Feb. 21, 1956. (Labor Problems).

"he had observed": Cf. memorandum, Ed Boling to FGC, Nov. 5, 1956 (TML).

"he warned": Clement said the TEA might force a 4 cent sales tax no later than two years in the future. Letters, FGC to Morris Cunningham, Feb. 6, 1957 (TEA); FGC to Doyle J. Blackwood, Feb. 27, 1957 (TEA); pressure was exerted on Clement to call a special session in 1956 to distribute a supposed surplus; letters, T. Robert Acklen to FGC, May 2, 1956; Douglas Henry to FGC, May 3, 1956; FGC to G.C. Crider, May 8, 1956; FGC to Edward C. Murray, May 21, 1956 (Leg-

176　islative Relations). The Municipal League also pushed Clement continually for benefits.

"was not to be put off": Brainard Cheney, who disliked the TEA lobby, referred to the 1957 struggle as a hard, mean fight; interview, Cheney, Feb. 11, 1975. See, e.g., *Tennessean,* Jan. 17, 27, Feb. 21, 1957.

"introduce a bill": *Banner,* Jan. 8, 1957.

177　"spelled out his general program": *Tennessean,* Jan. 17, 1957; *Senate Journal,* 1957, pp. 81–123.

"$125 million": *Banner,* Jan. 16, 1957.

"annual increase": *Senate Journal,* 1957, p. 117; *Tennessean,* Jan. 17, 1957; *Banner,* Jan. 16, 1957.

"was building up": *Banner,* Jan. 8, 1957. Clement resisted the idea of a special session on reapportionment in 1956 saying it would do no good; letter, T. Robert Acklen to FGC, May 2, 1956 (Legislative Relations).

"asked for a study": *Senate Journal,* 1957, p. 95; *Banner,* Jan. 16, 1957. Clement said that the matter was one primarily for the legislature; letter, FGC to William R. Morris, Feb. 8, 1956 (Reapportionment).

"in 1955": Letter, FGC to Jesse L. Rogers, Nov. 13, 1956 (Reapportionment). Some pressure was exerted on Clement for a special session on reapportionment and the allocation of excess revenues; letters, Maclin P. Davis, Jr., member of the Assembly, to FGC, May 10, 1956; negative reply, FGC to Davis, May 24, 1956 (Reapportionment). Also petition, Elmer W. White, member of the Assembly, to FGC, no date (Reapportionment). Individual moves toward reapportionment were made in 1953 and 1955 but were quickly sidetracked.

"railway minimum crew law . . . federal social security": *Banner,* Jan. 16, 1957.

"split the Assembly": See, e.g., ibid., Jan. 29, 31, Feb. 4, 7, 11, 1957.

"Shelby delegation split": *Banner,* Jan. 31, Feb. 1, 5, 1957.

"Snodgrass and Boling": Ibid., Feb. 1, 1957.

"suffered a heart attack": Ibid., Feb. 7, 1957.

"into the Senate Chamber": Ibid., Feb. 11, 12, 1957.

178　"led the TEA fight": Ibid., Feb. 7, 1957; Sen. Edward C. Murray of La-Follette was very active on behalf of the TEA. Murray and Allen had both opposed the sales tax in years past. See *Banner,* Jan. 26, Feb. 1, 1957.

"A bloc of Republicans": Ibid., Feb. 6, 1957.

"weaker in the House": Ibid., Feb. 8, 1957.

"conference committee . . . was heavily dominated . . . compromise was necessary": Ibid., Feb. 13, 1957. See also editorial, *Tennessean,* Feb. 21, 1957.

178 "drafted by Clement's floor leader": *Banner,* Feb. 19, 1957.

"overwhelming majorities": Ibid., Feb. 20, 1957. The compromise was attacked in a *Tennessean* editorial, Feb. 21, 1957.

"overages were produced": *Banner,* Aug. 14, 1957.

"the minimum crew bill": *Tennessean,* P, March 1, 1957; *Banner,* March 6, 1957.

"open shop repeal": *Tennessean,* P, March 1, 1957.

"killed off": *Tennessean,* March 10, 1957; ibid., P, March 12, 1957; *Tennessean,* March 14, 15, 1957; see also *Banner,* March 12, 13, 1957.

"good deal of worried attention": See *Tennessean,* P, Sept. 17, 1957. Cf. letter, Brainard Cheney to Russell Kirk, Jan. 8, 1958 (JUL).

"Gore's speeches had content": Memorandum, Brainard Cheney to Speech Committee, Feb. 8, 1955 (Speech Technique).

179 "on early notice": *Banner,* Dec. 1, 1956, Jan. 14, 1957.

"no clear choice": *Tennessean,* Oct. 30, 1957. In some places, Clement forces had asked for an early decision; ibid., P, April 16, 1957. A fiction was promoted that Clement backers would support his choice; *Banner,* May 8, 1957.

"hard-working Ellington": Interview, Anna Belle O'Brien, May 5, 1975.

"Glen Nicely": *Banner,* Jan. 14, 1957; Nicely's comment in later years was that everyone wanted to be governor; interview, Nicely, Aug. 24, 1977.

"Joe Henry . . . Joe Carr . . . Hilton Butler . . . William Leech": The lists of the *Banner* and the *Tennessean* varied somewhat. See *Banner,* Jan. 14, 1957; *Tennessean,* Oct. 30, 1957; ibid., P, Nov. 27, Dec. 3, 1957.

"Maddux . . . Bomar": *Banner,* Jan. 14, 1957.

"Olgiati": Ibid. Ben West, mayor of Nashville, was also mentioned, *Tennessean,*, P, Jan. 15, 1958; *Banner,* Jan. 15, 1958. Olgiati finally endorsed Ellington, ibid., CH, July 2, 1958.

"Tip Taylor . . . Prentice Cooper . . . Raulston Schoolfield": *Banner,* Jan. 14, 1957.

"using Boling . . . warned Boling": Interview, Edward J. Boling, June 25, 1975.

"failure to give him": Travis said that Clement had been coy about backing Ellington; Ellington then took the bull by the horns and announced at a morning news conference. That afternoon Clement endorsed Ellington and tried to leave the impression that he had always planned to do so; interview, Fred Travis, Sept. 26, 1977. The *Tennessean* was saying Ellington was the official candidate at the end of 1957, Dec. 31, 1957, and ibid., P, Jan. 7, 1958.

179 "he determined to force the issue": Cf. *Tennessean,* Oct. 30, 1957; and
   ibid., P, Dec. 3, 1957.
180 "Memphis Rotary Club": *Tennessean,* Oct. 30, 1957; *Banner,* Nov. 5,
   1957.
   "Prentice Cooper . . . Tip Taylor . . . Glen Nicely": See *Banner,* Jan.
   11, 1958.
   "studied contempt . . . statement of nonsupport": Ibid.
   "formal candidacy": Ibid., Feb. 18, 1958.
   "promptly endorsed": Ibid., Feb. 25, 1958.
   "Ellington's ties": Ibid., CH, Feb. 25, 1958.
   "Joe Evins": *Banner,* Jan. 31, 1958.
   "Evins decided against trying": *Tennessean,* Oct. 22, 1957; *Banner,*
   CH, Feb. 25, 1958. The *Banner* writer said Browning forces had
   tried to get Evins to run.
   "In supporting Ellington": *Banner,* Feb. 25, 1958.
   "almost intact": Ibid., CH, March 21, 1958.
   "J.N. Doane . . . Judge Sue Hicks . . . Howard Warf . . . Ross
   Dyer . . . Jimmy Peeler": Ibid., CH, Feb. 24, 1958. Dr. Agnes
   Bird says that Ellington succeeded pretty well to the Clement organization; interview, Agnes Bird, Sept. 20, 1977.
   "Herbert Walters": *Banner,* Feb. 25, 1958.
   "formal endorsement": Ibid., CH, March 5, 1958.
   "he declined to run . . . was unacceptable": See ibid., Feb. 25, 1958.
181 "Prentice Cooper furnished no answer": *Banner,* Feb. 25, 1958.
   "Clifford Allen was already in the race": Allen announced in February; *Tennessean,* Feb. 5, 1958.
   "were dismissed": *Banner,* CH, Feb. 25, 1958.
   "urged to the race by Kefauver": Various Kefauver friends supported
   Orgill, according to the *Banner,* March 12, 14, 1958.
   "had been elected mayor": Tucker, 71–78.
   "member of a small group": Tucker, ch. 3.
   "had solicited Kefauver's interest": Ibid., 46–47.
   "Orgill had helped": Ibid., ch. 3.
   "the reform of local government": Personal recollections of author.
   See also Tucker, passim.
   "William C. Wilson . . . Mayor Frank Gray": *Banner,* March 12, 1958.
   "Lucius Burch, Jr. . . . George Crider": Ibid., CH, April 8, 1958,
   quoting *Commercial Appeal.*
   "eyed the Orgill waltz": *Banner,* CH, March 24, 1958; see also ibid.,
   April 12, 1958.
   "would make it on his own": *Banner,* April 26, 1958; see also ibid.,
   March 28, 29, 1958.

181 "formally committed himself": Ibid., April 26, 28, 1958; see also ibid., April 4, 1958.
182 "Lon Cheney . . . thought he detected": Interview, Cheney, Feb. 11, 1975.
"old-fashioned segregationist": He stated this position in his opener at Columbia; *Banner,* June 14, 1958; the statement was also made at Pulaski; ibid., July 30, 1958.
"The *Banner* columnist said": Ibid., CH, July 22, 1958.
"at a talk": Personal recollection of the author.
"could not have survived": Ibid.
"an acknowledged segregationist": *Banner,* June 7, 1958.
"Orgill tried to tag Ellington": Ibid., April 28, 1958; see also ibid., July 12, 1958.
"unequivocal stand against new taxes": See, e.g., ibid., June 14, 1958.
183 "I have a little shadow": Ibid., May 2, 1958.
"Edmund G. Estes Kefriar": Ibid., July 24, 1958.
"Orgill's ties": See *Tennessean,* P, May 22, 1958; *Banner,* CH, May 13, 1958; see also ibid., Aug. 1, 1958.
"Carl Fry": Ibid., May 13, 1958.
"Lucius Burch": *Banner,* ibid. See also ibid., April 8, 1958, quoting the *Commercial Appeal* on Burch's backing of Orgill.
"Noble Caudill": *Banner,* May 13, 1958.
"with Sam Fleming . . . financial supporter": Caudill and Fleming each contributed $12,500 annually to Kefauver for a number of years. Caudill often picked up the checks for Kefauver's political expenses. On one occasion, he had allowed Kefauver to occupy an extra bedroom in his suite in Boston and had told him to stay as long as he wished after Caudill had checked out. Caudill was surprised to get a bill of about $700 from the hotel; he was told that the senator had entertained the mayor and city council of Boston at breakfast.
"for a long period": Interview, Noble Caudill, Jan. 22, 1975.
"Frank Wilson . . . had managed": *Banner,* CH, May 13, 1958. Wilson later became judge of the federal district court in Chattanooga.
"Mrs. Martha Ragland . . . Jim Camp . . . Max Friedman": *Banner,* Ibid. Friedman supported Clement at times, as did Jim Camp. Mrs. Ragland was generally with the anti-Clement forces.
"One of the rumors": Ibid., CH, May 22, 1958.
"Prentice Cooper would withdraw": Ibid.
"denied it . . . what he did": Ibid., May 24, 1958; *Banner,* June 5, 1958.
185 "Newspaper reports indicated": Cf. Buchanan and Bird, 33–34.

185 "attacking Clement, Ellington, and Orgill": *Banner,* June 7, 1958.
"Nicely withdrew": Ibid., CH, June 10, 1958. Nicely became Taylor's
state manager; *Banner,* July 1, 1958.
"in his opener": Ibid., June 21, 1958.
"he said that Taylor gave . . . Taylor said": Ibid., July 12, 1958.
"Friar said Ellington was owned . . . also charged": Ibid., June 21,
1958.
"announced his support of Orgill . . . his name could not be removed": Ibid., July 22, 1958. See also Hassler, *Primary Elections,* 25,
26.
"to come in first": The election produced one of the closest votes in
Tennessee history; see *Banner,* Aug. 8, 1958. The results were in
doubt all night; interview, Travis, Sept. 26, 1977.
"certain regional pattern": Hopkins and Lyons, 309.
186 "The *Banner* said": Aug. 8, 1958.
"White backlash": This is, of course, a personal judgment of the author, for no record is kept of voters' private reasoning.
"were probably not voting": A personal judgment of the author;
careful studies of voting in these counties have not been made, but
the upsurge of black voting was still to occur.
"lopsided majorities": See *Banner,* CH, Aug. 20, 1954. For voting
maps, see Hopkins and Lyons, 306–307.
187 "only twenty-five counties": Hassler, 27.
"Glen Nicely and Mrs. Christine Reynolds": *Banner,* CH, Aug. 18,
1958.
"the second Mrs. Jim Nance McCord": *Banner,* June 27, 1958.
"no friend to Ellington": See column by Fred Travis in *Knoxville Journal,* Jan. 19, 1981.
"Taylor might go": *Banner,* Aug. 30, 1958.
"Ellington and Taylor": Ibid., CH, Sept. 12, 1958. The feelings between Ellington and Taylor had not been bitter. Ellington thought
Orgill was his principal opponent. Interview, W.L. Barry, Nov. 2,
1977. Ellington had a poor opinion of Allen; he spoke little of Orgill and had no contact with him; ibid. Barry thought that if Allen
had not been in the race, Orgill would have won; ibid.
"his name be removed": *Banner,* CH, Sept. 19, 1958.
"he would support Ellington": *Banner,* Sept. 10, 1958.
"blasted away at all notions of independence": Ibid., Oct. 2, 1958.
Gore had declined, as usual, to get involved in the gubernatorial
hassles in the primary; letter, Gore to Edmund Orgill, April 14,
1958 (Gore Papers).
"openly in his memoirs": Gore, *Let the Glory Out,* 114.

187 "Jim Nance McCord announced": *Banner,* Oct. 7, 1958. McCord had supported Cooper in the Senate race; ibid., CH, July 11, 1958.

"sharply opposed by many": Carl Jones of Johnson City urged McCord not to run; *Banner,* Sept. 23, 1958; Herbert Walters tried to keep McCord from running; letter, Walters to Harry Avery, Sept. 29, 1958 (Walters).

"to give the voters a new chance": *Banner,* Oct. 7, 1958. Nicely was party to the independence move; ibid., CH, Nov. 4, 1958.

"attacked machines": *Banner,* Oct. 7, 1958.

188 "seventy-nine years old": Ibid., Oct. 6, 1958.

"Ellington was elected": Allen backed Ellington; ibid., Oct. 31, 1958; the *Commercial Appeal* had supported Taylor; in the general election it backed Ellington; *Banner,* CH, Nov. 3, 1958.

"East Tennessee counties": *Banner,* Nov. 5, 1958. See Hopkins and Lyons, 308–309.

CHAPTER 7.

189 "before 1820 . . . increasingly impossible . . . horde of black free people": Folmsbee, Corlew, and Mitchell, *Tennessee, Short History,* 223–227.

"most numerous in West Tennessee": Ibid., 217.

"In 1818": Ibid., 216.

"Free Negroes . . . progressively more difficult": Folmsbee et al., *Tennessee, Short History,* 222.

"emancipation harder . . . immigration of free blacks . . . require the deportation of": Ibid., 226.

190 "The first referendum": Greene, Grubbs, and Hobday, 16; Folmsbee et al., *Tennessee, Short History,* 318–19.

"in favor of leaving it": Greene et al., 16; Folmsbee et al., *Tennessee, Short History,* 320–22.

"in favor of . . . the Union": Greene et al., 17; Folmsbee et al., *Tennessee, Short History,* 322.

"possessed the state": See Folmsbee et al., *Tennessee, Short History,* ch. 19.

"its military governor": Greene et al., 17; Folmsbee et al, *Tennessee, Short History,* 342.

"but intervention never came": Folmsbee et al., *Tennessee, Short History,* ch. 20.

"were given grudgingly": Folmsbee et al., *Tennessee, Short History,* ch. 20.

"such period as the legislature should direct": On the constitution,

190 see Folmsbee et al., *Tennessee, Short History,* 374–77; Greene et al., ch. 2.

191 "until 1978": See *The Journal of the Debates of the Constitutional Convention, State of Tennessee,* 1977; Introduction, Proposals 1 and 5.

"living together": TCA, 36-402, *Acts,* 1822, ch. 19, sec. 1; *Acts,* 1870, ch. 39, sec. 1. Interracial marriage was prohibited, TCA, 36-402. The position of the Negroes is extensively treated in Cartwright, *The Triumph of Jim Crow: Tennessee Race Relations in the 1880s;* Alrutheous Ambush Taylor, *The Negro in Tennessee, 1865–1880* (Washington: Associated Publishers, 1941).

"child of color could not inherit": TCA, 31-306; *Acts,* 1825, ch. 15. (Former usages in numbering the Tennessee Code have been followed here).

"Colored insane": TCA, 33-602; *Acts,* 1865-66, ch. 4, sec. 2; on the deaf, see TCA, 49-3106.

"few Negroes made their way": See, e.g., Mary U. Rothrock, ed., *The French Broad-Holston Country: A History of Knox County, Tennessee* (Knoxville: East Tennessee Historical Society, 1946).

"in the hospitals": As in the Knoxville General at one time. The state's charitable institutions were segregated, and Clement was aware that the black facilities were often inferior; e.g., letters, Quill E. Cope to Mrs. Earl F. Olson, April 24, 1953; Lindsey P. Pherigo to FGC, May 19, 1953 (Schools for the Deaf and Blind). Desegregation of state charitable facilities faced opposition; letter, [name withheld] to FGC, March 19, 1953 (Negroes I).

"on the Knoxville police force . . . somewhat rudimentary civil service examinations": Personal recollections of the author as chairman, Knoxville Civil Service Board.

192 "local elective offices": Personal recollection of the author. See also Mingo Scott, Jr., *The Negro in Tennessee Politics and Governmental Affairs* (Nashville: Rich Printing Co., 1964), ch. IX.

"joined in the singing": Interview, Mrs. Anna Belle O'Brien, March 25, 1975.

"blacks were not invited": See story in *Knoxville News-Sentinel,* March 10, 1948.

193 "LaFollette": David James Brittain, "A Case Study of the Problems of Racial Integration in the Clinton, Tennessee, High School," diss. New York Univ., 1959, p. 36.

"Austin High": Cf. Connie Pat Mauney, *Evolving Equality: The Courts and Desegregation in Tennessee* (Knoxville: Bureau of Public Administration, Univ. of Tennessee, n.d.), 5.

"class action suit": Cf. interview, Horace V. Wells, Jan. 17, 1975.

193 "was held up": Ibid.

"Clement was urged": Some persons urged southern officials to prepare for the decision that was coming, to see if peaceful change
could be effected; e.g., letters, Alfred Mynders (*Chattanooga
Times*) to FGC, on behalf of the Southern Regional Council, May 7,
1953; William G. Nunn to FGC, May 23, 1953, asking about plans
(Segregation through 1956).

"non-committal": Clement worked out a standard reply that said
Tennessee was improving Negro schools but was otherwise non-
committal. Letters, FGC to Mynders, May 19, 1953; FGC to William
G. Nunn [editor of a black journal], June 2, 1953 (Segregation
through 1956). Clement in these letters took the view that most
blacks were happy with the existing situation.

"in May 1954": *Banner,* May 15, 1954; cf. implication of the story in
Tennessean, May 19, 1954. Cf. Horace V. Wells interview, Jan. 17,
1975.

"calmly enough": *Southern School News,* Sept. 3, 1954, p. 14.

"Attorney General Roy Beeler": *Banner,* May 21, 1954.

"wait-and-see statement": Ibid., May 15, 1954. Also Clement's opening campaign speech in Lebanon, June 5, 1954 (Segregation
through 1956).

194 "he ran": *Southern School News,* Sept. 3, 1954, p. 14.

"On June 10, 1954 . . . white professors of mathematics . . . would
not change": Ibid.

"Reverend Charles M. Williams . . . petitioned the Davidson County
School Board . . . was refused": Ibid.

"Middle Tennessee State College . . . Memphis State": Ibid.; see also
ibid., Oct. 1, 1954, p. 13.

"watchful and uncommitted": Ibid., Nov. 4, 1954, p. 16; letters,
Brainard Cooper to FGC, Aug. 19, 1954, and reply (Segregation
through 1956).

"become a part": *Southern School News,* Oct. 1, 1954, p. 13.

195 "took the same position": Ibid.

"public schools of Oak Ridge": Ibid., Feb. 3, 1955, p. 1.

"was introduced": Ibid., Jan. 6, 1955, p. 14.

"all from Middle and West Tennessee": Ibid., March 3, 1955; *Banner,*
Jan. 13, 1955.

"Justin Thrasher": *Banner,* Jan. 13, 31, 1955.

"against 1600 whites": Round number, *Southern School News,* Sept. 3,
1954, p. 14.

"to 1800 whites": Ibid.

"6660 to 116": Ibid.

"out of the Senate education committee": Ibid., March 3, 1955, p. 15.

195 "state's police power": Ibid., Feb. 3, 1955, p. 16; hearings on Stainback bill, *Banner*, Feb. 9, 1955.

"higher rate of illegitimate births . . . tuberculosis among blacks": *Southern School News*, March 3, 1955, p. 15.

196 "6 to 1 . . . McAllen Foutch . . . Landon Colvard . . . Dr. J.H. Gammon . . . Mrs. C.M. Hayes . . . Avon Williams": Ibid. (Gammon incorrectly shown as Cammon in source).

"he sought the views": Letters, Halbert Harvill (Austin Peay) to FGC, Jan. 10, 1955; J.M. Smith (Memphis State) to FGC, Jan. 10, 1955; Q.M. Smith (Middle Tennessee State College) to FGC, Jan. 12, 1955; Everett Derryberry (TPI) to FGC, Jan. 24, 1955; Burgin Dossett (East Tennessee State College) to FGC, Jan. 11, 1955; Quill Cope from C.E. Brehm (Univ. of Tennessee), Jan. 13, 1955 (all in file-Segregation through 1956).

"unfriendly to the bill": Ibid.

"Nashville pastors": Letters, Robert S. Lee, for the Nashville Pastors' Association, to FGC, Feb. 8, 1955 (Segregation through 1956). Clement had suggested contacts with legislature, FGC to Lee, Feb. 12, 1955; Larry Eisenberg to FGC, Feb. 14, 1955 (all in Segregation through 1956).

"buried the bill": *Southern School News*, April 7, 1955, p. 16. See also *Tennessean*, Feb. 28, 1955.

"to be present": Stainback called this a personal affront. *Banner*, March 1, 1955; *Southern School News*, April 7, 1955, p. 16.

"His bill was dead . . . passed both houses . . . Tipton County . . . Sumner County": *Southern School News*, April 7, 1955, p. 16.

197 "vetoed every one": Ibid.; *Banner*, March 15, 1955; *Tennessean*, March 15, 1955. Gore has praised Clement's stand; see Gore, *Let the Glory Out*, 88–89.

"also failed": *Southern School News*, April 7, 1955, p. 16.

"he wrote": Ibid.; *Senate Journal*, 1955 (message dated March 14, 1955), 1320–23.

"sent letters": Letters, FGC to Governor Boggs (Delaware), March 15, 1955; reply, Lawrence W. Wetherby, Governor of Kentucky, to FGC (said that FGC was right), March 21, 1955; James E. Folsom said Clement was right, letter to FGC, March 21, 1955. Clement also sent letters to U.S. senators and nine representatives from Tennessee. Percy Priest approved, letter to FGC, March 28, 1955 (all in Segregation through 1956).

"irate Memphian": Letter, [name withheld] to FGC, Jan. 7, 1955; also letter, Martha Peel to FGC, Feb. 8, 1955 (both in Segregation through 1956).

"Ministers": Rev. H. McDonald Nelson to FGC, March 8, 1955; Rev.

197   L.D. Kennedy to FGC, March 9, 1955 (Segregation through 1956);
       also letters, H.D. Bollinger to FGC, March 18, 1955; A.C. Miller to
       FGC, March 23, 1955 (Segregation through 1956).

198   "*Courier-Journal* commented favorably": Letter, FGC to Barry Bing-
       ham, with clipping attached, April 6, 1955 (Segregation through
       1956).

       "Governor Lawrence Wetherby" Letter to FGC, March 21, 1955 (Seg-
       regation through 1956).

       "stop at nothing": Letter, FGC to Sam Morris, Dec. 9, 1954 (Segrega-
       tion through 1956).

       "May, 1955": *Brown* v. *Board of Education,* 349 U.S. 294 (1955).

       "Cope told him": Memorandum, Quill E. Cope to Douglas Fisher,
       June 6, 1955 (Segregation through 1956). See also *Tennessean,* April
       19, 1956.

       "who told him": Letter, McCanless to Cope, June 16, 1955 (Segrega-
       tion through 1956). Cope passed information on to the schools;
       memorandum, Cope to county, city and special district superinten-
       dents, June 17, 1955 (Segregation through 1956).

       "Marion County": *Southern School News,* May 4, 1955, p. 10.

       "Federation for Constitutional Government": Ibid., Aug. 1955, p. 1.

       "organization for resistance": Ibid., p. 16; June 1956, p. 6.

199   "criticized by Eugene Cook": Letters, FGC to Gene Cook, Aug. 2,
       1955, and reply Aug. 31, 1955; FGC to Cook, Sept. 6, 1955 (Segrega-
       tion through 1956).

       "began to prepare plans": On June 15, 1955, a special and non-
       publicized session of the State Board of Education was held to con-
       sider a suit filed by five Negroes for admission to Memphis State
       College. Clement did not attend "because of pressing official du-
       ties." Cope stated that a meeting had been held with presidents of
       five state colleges and Tennessee A&I to determine a plan for transi-
       tion to desegregation. A plan was adopted providing for gradual
       desegregation, but only after courts had ruled Tennessee segrega-
       tion laws unconstitutional. Minutes, Called Meeting, State Board
       of Education, June 15, 1955 (Segregation through 1956); at the end
       of 1955, no Tennessee school systems were planning integration for
       that fall, but it was clear that plans for integration were being
       made. *Southern School News,* Sept. 1955, p. 13.

       "issued his order": *Banner,* Jan. 4, 1956. Cf. Horace V. Wells, inter-
       view, Jan. 17, 1975.

       "supporter of Gordon Browning": *Banner,* July 2, 1949.

       "should begin": Ibid., Jan. 4, 1956.

       "leadership . . . realized quite clearly": Interview, Horace V. Wells,
       Jan. 17, 1975.

199 "A.A. Canada . . . Tennessee Society to Maintain Segregation": *Banner,* Jan. 19, 1956.

"moved into Nashville": Ibid., Jan. 23, 1956. Clement's stance with this delegation was widely approved; letter, Cuyler Dunbar (senator from Montgomery and Robertson counties), to FGC, Jan. 25, 1956 (Segregation through 1956). Also letters, Rev. Henry Atkins to FGC, Jan. 25, 1956; Rev. R.L. Freeman to FGC, Jan. 25, 1956; Rhoda C. Edmeston, Scarritt College Department of Bible and Department of Missions, to FGC, Jan. 25, 1956; Chancellor Harvie Branscomb to FGC, Jan. 26, 1956; Thomas Wardlaw Steele, Jan. 26, 1956; Wilson Wyatt to FGC, Jan. 25, 1956; Lee Sanders, President of the Nashville Trades and Labor Council, to FGC, Jan. 27, 1956; R.Q. Vinson, Memphis Cotton Makers' Jubilee, Jan. 27, 1956; telegrams, Mrs. I.H. Patton, President of the Chattanooga Teacher's Association, to FGC, Jan. 26, 1956; Charles C. Diggs, Jr., to FGC, Jan. 27, 1956 (Diggs is the black member of Congress convicted in the late 1970s for taking kickbacks from staff members) (all in file-Segregation through 1956). Rabbi Silverman was present at the meeting with segregationists on Jan. 23, 1956, at which a religious tone was set; letter, Rabbi N.M.B. Silverman to FGC, Jan. 25, 1956 (Segregation through 1956). Some of the people calling on Clement had also been active in desegregation movements in other states; letters, Bill Pennix to FGC, Jan. 28, 1956 (Segregation through 1956). For further approvals, letters, M.A. Wright, Southern Regional Council, to FGC, Jan. 28, 1956; Sue Spencer, UT School of Social Work, to FGC, Jan. 30, 1956; Dave Alexander to FGC, Jan. 27, 1956; Nashville Chapter of National Council of Negro Women, Jan. 31, 1956. See also H.T. Lockard, President of Memphis Chapter of NAACP to FGC, Feb. 6, 1956. (All letters are in file-Segregation through 1956.) Letter, Rev. Robert McCan to FGC, Feb. 17, 1956 (D) (Clinton). Eric Sevareid approved, broadcast, Feb. 14, 1956 (Segregation through 1956).

200 "Donald Davidson and fifteen other persons": *Banner,* Jan. 27, 1956; Sims Crownover was the attorney for this group, ibid., Feb. 27, 1956.

"Southern Manifesto": Ibid., March 12, 1956; *Tennessean,* March 13, 1956.

"refused to sign": On Gore's attitude, letters, Lucius E. Burch, Jr., to Gore, March 23, 1956; Hewitt P. Tomlin, Jr., to Gore, March 26, 1956, and reply, March 28, 1956; Gayle Malone to Gore, March 27, 1956, and reply, March 29, 1956; Gore to Robert L. Taylor, March 28, 1956; Sims Crownover to Gore, April 19, 25, 1956, and Gore's sharp reply, April 23, 1956 (all in Gore papers).

200 "all signed": *Banner,* March 13, 1956.

"town's elite": Interview, Horace V. Wells, Jan. 17, 1975; *Southern School News,* Sept. 1956, p. 3.

"anticipated trouble": Interview, Horace V. Wells, Jan. 17, 1975.

"Meetings were organized": Interviews, Wells, Jan. 17, 1975; Buford Lewallen, March 18, 1975.

"On that day . . . could be members of teams . . . to attend social events": *Southern School News,* Sept. 1956, p. 3.

201 "had greatly influenced him": *Banner,* Jan. 31, 1957. For Pound's confused notions on economics, see James F. Knapp, *Ezra Pound* (Boston: Twayne, 1979), 146–51.

"racist attitudes toward Jews": *Banner,* Jan. 31, 1957.

"appeared in town": *Southern School News,* Sept. 1956, p. 3; interview, Buford Lewallen, March 18, 1975.

"more threatening": *Southern School News,* Oct. 1956, p. 15; interview, Lewallen, ibid.

"held a mass meeting": *Southern School News,* Sept. 1956, p. 3.

"arrested Kasper": Ibid.; interview, Horace V. Wells, Jan. 17, 1975.

"transition from one sheriff to another": Interviews, Wells, Jan. 17, 1975; Lewallen, March 18, 1975.

"had not had time . . . was small . . . sweeping injunction . . . tore the order up": Interview, Horace V. Wells, Jan. 17, 1975.

204 "went to the school . . . harangued a crowd . . . police arrested": *Southern School News,* Sept. 1956, p. 3.

"Admiral Cromelin": Interview, Horace V. Wells, Jan. 17, 1975.

"was scheduled for Friday": Ibid., Jan. 17, 1975.

"Labor Day": Ibid., Jan. 17, 1975.

"home guard": Ibid.

"to describe": Interview, Buford Lewallen, March 18, 1975.

"Enka plant": See *Banner,* June 24, 1950.

"dodged the issue": On Clement's reluctance, cf. interview, Joe Henry, Sept. 30, 1975; Interviews, Horace V. Wells, Jan. 17, 1975; Buford Lewallen, March 18, 1975.

"A rally was scheduled . . . he did not appear . . . Arthur A. Canada . . . Jack Kershaw": *Southern School News,* Oct. 1956, p. 15.

205 "three telegrams": Sept. 1, 1956 (D) (Clinton). *Banner,* Sept. 1, 1956.

"by special plane": *Southern School News,* Oct. 1956, p. 15; interview, Horace V. Wells, Jan. 17, 1975. Letter, Woodward to FGC, Sept. 1, 1956 (D) (Clinton); interview, Buford Lewallen, March 18, 1975.

"some twenty persons . . . Van Nunally . . . Carr . . . McCanless . . . said Henry . . . McCanless backed him up . . . Henry flatly refused . . . he remembered later": Interview, Joe Henry, Sept. 30, 1975.

206 "Saturday evening": *Tennessean,* Sept. 2, 1956.

"recalled Wells years later": Interview, Horace V. Wells, Jan. 17, 1975.

"nearly eight feet tall": O'Rear was 6′8″; *Tennessean,* April 25, 1965.

"had started for Clinton": Interview, Joe Henry, Sept. 30, 1975; see *Banner,* Sept. 3, 1956.

"633 battle-equipped men, 7 M-41 tanks, and 3 armored personnel carriers": *Southern School News,* Oct. 1956, p. 15. Judge Lewallen said there were enough troups to fight the "Battle of the Bulge"; interview, Buford Lewallen, March 18, 1975.

"set up road blocks": Interview, Joe Henry, Sept. 30, 1975; interview, Horace V. Wells, Jan. 17, 1975.

"Nine out of every ten cars": Interview, Henry, ibid.

"prohibited outdoor assemblies": *Southern School News,* Oct. 1956, p. 15.

"troops at Clinton": Charles Lockett was a colonel in this organization; *Banner,* Sept. 3, 1956; *Tennessean,* Sept. 2, 1956; interview, Joe Henry, Sept. 30, 1975.

"where they prayed": Interviews, Robert S. Clement, March 25, 1975; Ira North, Oct. 2, 1975.

"always maintained": *Banner,* Aug. 9, 1957. Telegram, Glen Nicely to Walter Winchell, Sept. 6, 1956; also letter, FGC to Mrs. Wendell Williams, Oct. 8, 1956 (both in file-Clinton).

"receiving written orders": Interview, Joe Henry, Sept. 30, 1975.

207 "they were well behaved": Ibid. Also letter, Mayor W.E. Lewallen to FGC, Sept. 12, 1956 (D) (Clinton).

"a side trip to nearby Oliver Springs": *Southern School News,* Oct. 1956, p. 15; *Banner,* Sept. 6, 7, 1956. Newsmen from the East were attacked at Oliver Springs; the Guard did not try to protect them. *Banner,* Sept. 6, 1956.

"125 of them": Interview, Joe Henry, Sept. 30, 1975. See *Tennessean,* Sept. 4, 1956.

"said Henry to Loye Miller": Interview, ibid.

"attended class on the first day after Labor Day": *Southern School News,* Oct. 1956, p. 15; see *Banner,* Sept. 6, 1956.

"was up to 324 . . . 394 . . . left for home that weekend . . . middle of the following week": *Southern School News,* Oct. 1956, p. 15.

"Clement and the sheriff exchanged . . . letters": A news story quoted Woodward as saying that he had not asked for help. *Clinton Courier-News,* Aug. 22, 1957. Letter, Glad Woodward to FGC, Sept. 7, 1956 (D) (Clinton); telegram, FGC to Woodward, Sept. 8, 1956 (D) (Clinton).

"This takes the cake": (D) (Clinton).

"sought an injunction . . . denied the petition . . . had been ren-

207   dered void . . . in contempt of his court": *Southern School News,*
      Nov. 1956, p. 6.

208   "found him not guilty": *Tennessean,* Nov. 21, 1956.
      "free-wheeling speech of thirty minutes": *Southern School News,* Dec.
      1956, p. 5.
      "a piece of polemic writing": *Banner,* Jan. 31, 1957.
      "Harrassment of black children": Ibid., Nov. 27, 1956.
      "staying out of school": *Southern School News,* Dec. 1956, p. 5, and
      Jan. 1957, p. 6.
      "put candidates in the field": Ibid., Jan. 1957, p. 6; interview, Horace
      V. Wells, Jan. 17, 1975.
      "were arrested for contempt": *Southern School News,* ibid.
      "sent a letter . . . Brownell": *Banner,* Dec. 3, 1956.
      "Reverend Paul W. Turner": Interview, Wells, Jan. 17, 1975.
      "rose in his pulpit": Ibid.; *Tennessean,* Dec. 10, 1956.

209   "Reverend Turner, Sidney Davis . . . Leo Burnett": Interview, Wells,
      ibid.
      "Brittain closed the school indefinitely": *Southern School News,* Jan.
      1957, p. 6. *Banner,* Dec. 4, 1956.
      "enforcement of his injunction . . . for violation of his injunction":
      Southern School News, Jan. 1957, p. 6.
      "were defeated": *Banner,* Dec. 5, 1956; *Southern School News,* Jan.
      1957, p. 6.
      "a pitiable contrast": *Southern School News,* Jan. 1957, p. 7; *Banner,*
      Dec. 6, 1956. One of the defendants, John Gates, died in March
      1957 at Eastern State Mental Hospital; *Banner,* March 19, 1957.
      "Donald Davidson . . . Jack Kershaw . . . Sims Crownover": Let-
      ter, Crownover to FGC, Sept. 19, 1956, and reply, Oct. 1, 1956;
      letter, transmitting speech, Kershaw to FGC, Oct. 6, 1956 (Segre-
      gation through 1956).

210   "the Fugitives . . . great eminence": See Louise Cowan, *The Fugitive
      Group: A Literary History* (Baton Rouge: Louisiana State Univ.
      Press, 1959).
      "sharply critical of TVA": See his study of TVA in *The Tennessee,* Vol. II,
      Rivers of America Series (New York: Rinehart, 1948).
      "wrote to W.T. Couch": Letter, Davidson to W.T. Couch, Oct. 13,
      1948 (Davidson).
      "he wrote in late 1953": Letter, Davidson to Dr. Crabb, Dec. 15, 1953
      (Davidson).

211   "the chairman": Letterhead as of May 26, 1956.
      "Vice-chairman . . . Dudley Gale": Ibid.
      "he wrote": Letter, Davidson to Thomas J.B. Walsh, Sept. 2, 1956
      (Davidson).

212 "wrote Davidson": Letter, Davidson to Walsh, Dec. 24, 1956 (Davidson).

"wrote one irate citizen": Letter, [name withheld] to FGC, Jan. 19,
1956.

"artful dodger": Editorial in the *Hamilton County Herald,* Jan. 1956,
Vol. 44, No. 3.

"Wilkes Thrasher, Jr.": Telegram, Thrasher, Jr., to FGC, Oct. 8, 1956
(Segregation through 1956).

"nigger lover": Letter, [name withheld] to FGC, Dec. 2, 1956 (Segregation through 1956).

"No reply": Ibid.

"was submitted to federal judge Miller . . . Negro groups attacked":
Southern School News, Dec. 1956, p. 5.

"admitted two blacks . . . had already been graduated": Ibid., Oct.
1956, p. 15.

213 "if decisions were left up to local boards": Ibid., Dec. 1956, p. 5.

"dodged the issue": Ibid.

"Quill Cope stated clearly": *Tennessean,* Dec. 4, 1956. In 1955, Clement, speaking to the Tennessee Congress of Parents and Teachers at
Chattanooga, said Cope and he took the position that segregation
was a local problem; *Tennessean,* April 19, 1956.

"some of his staff": Interview, Brainard Cheney, Feb. 11, 1975.
Cheney did not write this speech. The manuscript notes for the
speech in the files indicate that Clement himself worked on the
speech (MS of the Segregation Speech). Cheney thought the speech
had a sobering effect on a legislature "with blood in their eyes";
Cheney to Robert Penn Warren, Jan. 18, 1957 (JUL). Cheney
thought the speech was politically, racially, and "Christianly" a
sound speech; letter, Cheney to Julia Peterkin, Feb. 4, 1957 (JUL).
According to Nicely, Clement would veto any bill requiring abolition of school system. (A group met with Nicely representing the
Methodist Board of Education, League of Women Voters, Nashville Ministerial Alliance and others, *Tennessean,* Jan. 5, 1957.) Already in 1955, Clement's policy of letting local units decide had
been established; letter, FGC to Mrs. F.W. Peel, Dec. 15, 1955 (Segregation through 1956). Clement's policy was based on Cope's advice; memorandum, FGC to Quill E. Cope, Dec. 15, 1955 (Segregation through 1956).

"began the governor": *Senate Journal,* 1957, p. 34. See *Banner,* Jan. 9,
1957.

216 "as his voice dropped to a quiet close": *Senate Journal,* 1957, p. 46; the
speech can be heard on audiograph records in the State Library and
Archives.

216 "was fully dispersed": *Southern School News,* Feb. 1957, p. 8.

"telegram": To FGC, Jan. 9, 1957 (Segregation-1957ff.).

217 "UT scientists": Letter, Gerald R. Pascal to FGC, Jan. 17, 1957, for-
warding statements primarily from prominent members of the
chemistry department. (Segregation-1957ff.).

"without significant dissent": *Southern School News,* Feb. 1957, pp. 8,
9. Passed House of Representatives with only two dissenting votes
on two of the measures, *Banner,* Jan. 17, 1957; Senate put minor
amendments on bills, *Banner,* Jan. 23, 1957. Committee votes on
the bills secured approval, with a few passes. Allen voted against
the pupil assignment bill; Allen and Murray voted against the voluntary segregation bill. In the House, the vote was almost unanimous on every bill. Hearing witness Crownover wanted interposi-
tion; Lillard supported integration; Preston Valien opposed the
bills; *Tennessean,* Jan. 16, 1957. The acts include: power to boards to
transport in TCA-49-2201, *Public Acts,* 1957, ch. 10; transfers and
admissions from outside in TCA-49-1701, *Acts,* ch. 9; power of
boards to provide separate schools for children whose parents voluntarily select them, *Acts,* ch. 11; operating schools jointly; TCA-
49-410ff. in part, *Acts,* ch. 12; power to assign children, etc., TCA-
49-1741ff. in part, *Acts,* ch. 13; permitting contacts with schools in
other states, TCA-49-1764, 49-215, *Acts,* ch. 90. For cases, see
TCA-Vol. 9, pp. 231ff.

"given extensive hearings": *Southern School News,* Feb. 1957, p. 8.

"segregation by sex": Introduced by Sen. Harlan Dodson, Jr., Nashville; passed, *Public Acts,* 1957, ch. 98; TCA, 49-230.

"regulating and curbing": They defined barratry, required filing of
information and required registration with the secretary of state.
Southern School News, April 1957; see *Banner,* Jan. 10, Feb. 26, 28,
1957. The laws were disregarded; see *Banner,* May 13, 1957. See *Public Acts,* 1957, ch. 104, ch. 151, ch. 152.

"their validity": The state school preference law was ruled unconstitutional by Judge Miller in the fall of 1957; *Kelley* v. *Nashville Board
of Education; Southern School News,* Oct. 1957, p. 6; *Banner,* Sept. 6,
1957; *Southern School News,* May 1964, pp. 3–8.

218 "music capital of Appalachia": House Resolution No. 38, *Public Acts,*
1957, pp. 1488–89.

"House Resolution No. 1": *Public Acts,* 1957, pp. 1437–42.

"Senate Resolution No. 3": *Public Acts,* 1957, pp. 1573–78. See also
Banner, Feb. 27, 1957.

"a statement": *Southern School News,* July 1957, p. 2.

"twelve black students": Ibid.

"Nashville made plans": Ibid., Feb. 1957, p. 8.

218 "Parents School Preference Committee": Ibid., July 1957, p. 2.

219 "troublesome interloper": He was repudiated by Kershaw. *Banner,* Feb. 11, 1957.

"he announced . . . Knoxville school board to resign": *Southern School News,* July 1957, p. 2.

"Thomas P. Gore": Gore had been associated with segregationists; *Banner,* Feb. 11, 1957; *Southern School News,* Aug. 1957, p. 1.

"on that same day": *Southern School News,* Aug. 1957, p. 1.

"verdicts of guilty": Ibid.; *Banner,* July 23, 1957.

"had been dropped": *Banner,* July 18, 1957.

"subsequently sentenced": *Southern School News,* Nov. 1957, p. 3; *Banner,* June 1, 1957.

"placed on probation": *Southern School News,* Dec. 1957, p. 9.

"was bombed": Ibid., Oct. 1957, p. 6; *Banner,* Aug. 11, Sept. 17, 1957.

"in that city": *Banner,* Aug. 11, 1957.

"publicly disagreed": *Tennessean,* Oct. 2, 1957; *Banner,* Sept. 27, Oct. 2, 1957. Clement was a member of a committee that called on Eisenhower to mediate the Little Rock matter; letter, Chief Justice A.B. Neil to FGC, Sept. 30, 1957 (Segregation-1957ff.).

"dynamite explosion": *Southern School News,* Nov. 1958, p. 14. For earlier threats there, see *Banner,* Nov. 7, 1957.

220 "Eisenhower declared . . . Clement . . . was annoyed . . . runaround, heave-ho, and pass-the-buck": *Southern School News,* Nov. 1958, p. 14.

"inciting to riot": See also *Banner,* Aug. 11, Sept. 12, 13, 17, 1957.

"Raulston Schoolfield": *Southern School News,* Dec. 1958, p. 13; *Banner,* Oct. 23, 1958.

"escorted to the county line": *Southern School News,* Nov. 1958, p. 14.

"Athens police chief": Ibid.

CHAPTER 8.

221 "Joe Carr": Interview, Joe C. Carr, Sept. 16, 1975. Lipe Henslee worked for Clement's selection; Carr, ibid.

"Herbert Walters . . . worked assiduously": Letters, Herbert S. Walters to FGC, March 15, 1956; (1956 Conv.). Tom Stewart to Gov. Ed Johnson of Colorado, March 21, 1956 (D); (1956 Conv.); Walters to FGC, May 10, 1956 (1956 Conv.).

"Alben Barkley's": Alben W. Barkley, *That Reminds Me* (Garden City, N.Y.: Doubleday, 1954), 200–202; James K. Libbey, *Dear Alben: Mr. Barkley of Kentucky* (Lexington: Univ. Press of Kentucky, 1979), 94–95.

"worked hard": Letters, Brainard Cheney to John J. Henry, Babson's

221   Washington Forecast, Aug. 15, 1955; Babson official to Douglas
      Fisher, Aug. 24, 1955 (both in 1956 Conv.). Letters, "Lon" Cheney
      to Mrs. Richard Coe, *McCall's Magazine,* Oct. 4, 1955; Christine
      Sadler to Brainard Cheney, Oct. 17, 1955; and reply, Oct. 21, 1955
      (1956 Conv.). Efforts with *McCall's* were unsuccessful; letters,
      Christine Sadler to Cheney, Nov. 4, 1955; Cheney to Sadler, Nov.
      8, 1955 (1956 Conv.). Clement friends over the state supported his
      national ambitions; e.g., letter, Fred Hixson to FGC, Oct. 2, 1954
      (1956 Conv.). Democratic leaders outside the state encouraged
      Clement; e.g., telegram, Joseph Gluck to FGC, Nov. 10, 1954 (1956
      Conv.). Also letter, Herbert Walters to FGC, Sept. 14, 1955 (D)
      (Corres.-Walters). Cheney said "we" were grooming Clement to
      be Stevenson's running mate; Cheney to Paul Brooks, June 25, 1955
      (JUL).
      "interest magazine publishers" E.g., letter, Brainard Cheney to
          Helen Strauss, Nov. 8, 1955 (1956 Conv.).
      "biographies and autobiographies": E.g. Cheney to Strauss, ibid.
          Also letter, Cheney to Flannery O'Connor, Oct. 14, 1956 (JUL).
      "speeches had content": Letter, Brainard Cheney to Speech Commit-
          tee, Feb. 8, 1955 (Speech Technique).
      "an orator bloomed": Cf. Martin in the *Saturday Evening Post.*
      "Indianapolis [to] Missouri": Clement's speech in Indianapolis roused
          great enthusiasm and caused talk of him as vice-president. Tele-
          gram, Joseph Gluck to FGC, Nov. 10, 1954 (1956 Conv.). Some
          thought Clement might be used to stop Kefauver; letter, Fred Hix-
          son to FGC, Oct. 2, 1954 (1956 Conv.). For thanks for Clement's
          role, letter, Stephen A. Mitchell to FGC, March 26, 1954 (1956
          Conv.). On Michigan, Oct. 1954, letter, Newman Jeffrey to Glen
          Nicely, Sept. 16, 1954 (Out-state Campaigns). On Jefferson-
          Jackson Day dinner in Hartford, Conn., Feb. 26, 1955, telegram,
          John M. Bailey to FGC, Feb. 10, 1955 (Out-state Campaigns). On
          Jackson Day banquet, Springfield, Mo., Jan. 1956, letter, M. Ray
          Daniel to FGC, Jan. 19, 1956 (Out-state Campaigns). On American
          Legion "Back to God" TV program, Feb. 1956, letter, Charles A.
          Speed to FGC, Feb. 10, 1956 (Out-state Campaigns). On Ohio
          Jefferson-Jackson Day dinner, May, 1956, letter, Frank J. Lausche
          to FGC, May 23, 1956 (Out-state Campaigns). On the 1954 speech
          to the Democratic Club of the District of Columbia, letter, A.C.
          Smith to Douglas Fisher, Oct. 1, 1954 (Speeches and Speech Policies).
222   "Indianapolis and Springfield": On the Springfield speech, letter, J.
          Warren Head to FGC, July 13, 1956 (Out-state Campaigns).
      "hints of the vice-presidency": Letters, Gluck and Hixson to FGC,
          cited above.

222 "he said" Martin, p. 22.

"cornball governor": *Time,* Sept. 27, 1954, pp. 17–18.

"against corruption . . . did not always find": Gorman, ch. 5, ch. 8; Fontenay, ch. 9.

"Truman was uncertain": David, Moos, Goldman, *Presidential Nominating Politics, The National Story,* 34–41.

"January 23, 1952": David et al., 35–36.

"on the capitol": Letter, Gordon Browning to Lyle B. Cherry, Jan. 25, 1952 (Browning files).

"a nice man and a good Senator": David et al., 36. See also Gorman, 114–16.

223 "coonskin cap": Merle Miller, *Plain Speaking: An Oral Biography of Harry S. Truman* (New York: Berkley Publishing, 1973), 349.

"were preferential only": David et al., 65.

"the sole candidate": Ibid.

"could count more delegates": Gorman, 140, 154.

"Stevenson was not absolutely certain": Ibid., 154.

"unlikely alliance": Friendly relations had been maintained early in Clement's career with Kefauver, and Clement had given him some support; letters, Kefauver to FGC, Nov. 30, 1948; June 12, 1950 (Corres.-Kefauver).

"Kefauver was isolated": David et al., 145–47.

224 "under a cloud": Browning's ties with Kefauver hurt him in both 1952 and 1954; letters, T.D. Oxford to Browning, May 2, 1952; Moore Blankenship to Browning, Sept. 27, 1952; Dolly Red Spain to Kefauver, July 28, 1952 (Browning files). Ed Smith of the *News-Sentinel* wrote Browning in 1950 that attempts were being made to split Kefauver and Browning; letter, Smith to Browning, Sept. 2, 1950 (Browning files).

"some party leaders": When Paul Butler became Democratic chairman at the end of 1954, he said Stevenson would have to fight for the nomination. Charles A.H. Thomson and Frances M. Shattuck, *The 1956 Presidential Campaign* (Washington: Brookings, 1960), 24.

"public and official": Ibid., 28–32.

"threw his own hat in": Ibid. See also Gorman, 216. Kefauver announced officially on Dec. 16, 1955; Fontenay, 248.

"Harriman held off officially": Thomson, 65.

"Governors who longed . . . Rayburn's eye": Ibid., 32.

"weak on organization . . . fourteen primaries . . . Adlai Stevenson . . . was conceded . . . to enter New Jersey . . . only candidate": Ibid., 34.

"write-ins": Ibid.

224 "Kefauver took the state": Ibid., 32–35; 37–45; 48–61; Fontenay, 249–51.

"sound thrashing to Stevenson in Minnesota": Thomson, ibid.; Fontenay, 251–55.

"roused him to a hard fight": Thomson.

225 "had only 200 delegates": Ibid., 63.

"political enemies were numerous": Cf. *Tennessean,* Aug. 14, 1955; ibid., P, Oct. 4, 1955, Jan. 11, 1956.

"many white West Tennesseans": E.g., letters, T.R. Lasley to FGC, March 27, 1956; W.D. Hastings to FGC, Aug. 1, 1956 (1956 Conv.).

"maintain a show of amiability": Clement and Kefauver had mutual friends who tried to reconcile their ambitions; letter, Tim Lawson to FGC, Jan. 9, 1956 (1956 Conv.).

"had declared himself for Adlai Stevenson": At a governor's conference in 1955, Clement called a news conference and said he would back Stevenson. Cf. letter, FGC to Stevenson, Dec. 15, 1956 (Corres.-Stevenson). This was probably aimed to counteract an early different announcement from Shivers; *Tennessean,* P, Aug. 13, 1955; see also Gardner, 550.

"Albert Gore had ambitions": Gore describes those ambitions in *Let the Glory Out,* 88ff. See also Gardner, 553.

"were also attached to Clement": Noble Caudill was a Kefauver man who became attracted to Clement. When he wanted to join Clement, he checked with Kefauver, who showed some reluctance; Caudill, interview, Jan. 22, 1975. Also letter, Jack Norman to Herbert Walters, March 21, 1956 (D) (1956 Conv.). Also telegrams to FGC from George Dempster, Stanton Smith, Max Friedman, Steve Para, Jim Camp, Paul Christopher, Tim Lawson, June 26, 1956 (D) (1956 Conv.); M.C. Plunk to FGC, June 27, 1956 (1956 Conv.).

"be no more than temporary": Cf. interview, Agnes Bird, Sept. 20, 1977.

"full support as a favorite son": *Banner,* Jan. 7, 1956. For an unfavorable view of this move, see Ed Smith in the *Knoxville News-Sentinel,* copy sent to FGC (1956 Conv.); letter, FGC to Edward B. Smith, Jan. 12, 1956 (1956 Conv.); see also *Tennessean,* P, Jan. 10, 1956.

"all news to him": *Tennessean,* P, Jan. 11, 1956. See also *Banner,* Jan. 7, 1956. Cf. Gardner, 576–78.

"a wary neutrality": *Banner,* Jan. 7, 1956.

"clearly withholding his support": Letter, Gore to Kefauver, April 17, 1956 (1956 Conv.). A copy was sent to Clement; see reply, FGC to Gore, April 23, 1956 (1956 Conv.). Gore supported Clement for keynoter; letter, Gore to Paul Butler, May 23, 1956 (D) (1956 Conv.). See also Gardner, 567–68, 570, 594.

225 "he would avoid a county-by-county fight": *Banner,* Jan. 11, 1956.

"he would not seek": Ibid., Jan. 25, 1956.

"earned him the praise": Ibid. Also letter, Thomas A. Shriver to FGC, Feb. 2, 1956 (1956 Conv.).

"were undoubtedly committed": Cf. Gardner, 586.

"Kefauver wired the governor": Telegram, Kefauver to FGC, Jan. 24, 1956 (1956 Conv.).

226 "endorsed Clement": *Tennessean,* Jan. 26, 1956; see Gardner, 585.

"denied that a deal had been made": *Banner,* Jan. 26, 1956; see Gardner, 586.

"Kefauver himself remained coy": Gardner, 585–87.

"in active touch with Adlai Stevenson . . . hoped for support": Letters, Stevenson to FGC, Dec. 10, 1955; FGC to Stevenson, Dec. 15, 1955; Stevenson to FGC, Jan. 16, 23, May, 1956 (Corres.-Stevenson). Letters, Stevenson to FGC, March 20, 1956 (D); (1956 Conv.); FGC to Stevenson, March 28, 1956 (D) (1956 Conv.).

"a foil against Kefauver": For Truman contacts, letter, Truman to FGC, Oct. 17, 1953; FGC to Truman, Oct. 30, 1953; FGC to Truman, mentioning a talk between Clement and Mayor Daley, June 6, 1955; Truman to FGC, visit between them in New Orleans, Nov. 15, 1955; James W. Shaffer to Truman, including Clement's Springfield speech, Feb. 2, 1956 (all in Truman Lib.). Clement said he was entirely dependent on what Truman wanted, keynoter and anything else, FGC to Truman, March 2, 1954; Truman to FGC, wedding gift to Margaret, April 26, 1956; Truman to FGC, privately saying FGC would make the "very best keynote speaker . . . don't you let anyone try to work up a disagreement between you and me because there is none," March 6, 1956 (all in Truman Lib.).

"a grand young man": *Banner,* Feb. 2, 1956.

"made Truman a Tennessee colonel": Letter, HST to FGC, Nov. 6, 1956 (Corres.-Truman).

"he did try to block Stevenson": Gorman, 250.

"Senator Bob Kerr": Gardner, 628.

"Hubert Humphrey": Ibid., 626.

"Paul Butler": See Ibid., 625.

"He opposed both Clement and Humphrey": *Banner,* May 25, 1956. Letters, George F. Rock to Tom Stewart, May 5, 1956; Herbert S. Walters to FGC, May 10, 21, 1956 (1956 Conv.).

"wrote Butler": Letter, FGC to Paul M. Butler, May 29, 1956 (D) (1956 Conv.).

"Camille Gravel": Camille Gravel had known Clement since 1954. Letter, Gravel to FGC, Dec. 13, 1954 (Miscellaneous Out-state Correspondence). *Banner,* April 21, 1956; letter, Camille Gravel to

226   "Hub" Walters, May 27, 1956 (D) (1956 Conv.). On campaign to
       be keynoter, Carr interview, Sept. 16, 1975.
       "Lyndon Johnson": *Banner,* April 30, 1956.
       "Missouri state convention": Ibid., May 25, 1956; on one speech, let-
       ter, Gov. Phil M. Donnelly to FGC, Sept. 20, 1954 (Keynote
       Speech). The speech before the 1954 Democratic State Convention
       is in the file Out-State Campaigns. On the 1956 convention, letter,
       Mary E. Chapman to FGC, June 1, 1956 (Keynote Speech).
       "fight was seen as a possibility": Ibid., June 26, 1956; *Tennessean,* June
       17, 20, 26, 27, 1956. Fontenay says little about the Tennessee Dem-
       ocratic convention; probably the Kefauver candidacy for President
       was already dead by the time that convention took place.
227   "Kefauver possessed 1314": *Tennessean,* June 17, 1956; *Banner,* June 27,
       1956.
       "1100 hundred opposing votes": *Tennessean,* June 17, 1956.
       "Clement himself took that position": *Banner,* CH, June 26, 1956;
       Banner, June 27, 1956.
       "urging him to nominate Kefauver": Letter, F. Joseph Donahue to
       FGC, Feb. 27, 1956 (1956 Conv.).
       "telegram of strong support for Kefauver": *Tennessean,* June 27, 1956.
       Dempster pushed for Kefauver, ibid., June 20, 1956; railroad
       worker spokesmen tried to get Kefauver and Clement together,
       telegram, M.C. Plunk (Madison County Democratic chairman) to
       FGC, June 27, 1956 (1956 Conv.). Telegram, Dempster and others to
       FGC, June 26, 1956 (D) (1956 Conv.).
       "James G. Stahlman": Letter, Stahlman to FGC, Sept. 24, 1956 (Corres.-
       Stahlman).
       "in Atlantic City": *Tennessean,* June 26, 1956.
       "with James Finnigan": Ibid. Adlai Stevenson courted Clement; let-
       ters, Stevenson to FGC, Jan. 16, 23, 1956 (Corres.-Stevenson).
       "neither Clement nor Kefauver": Gardner, 614.
       "Kefauver lost anyway . . . a resolution had been worked out": *Ban-
       ner,* June ᴛ 7, 1956; *Tennessean,* June 28, 1956.
       "represented the governor": *Banner,* June 27, 1956.
       "spoke for Kefauver": Ibid.
       "would support any Tennessean": Ibid., July 2, 1956; *Tennessean,* June
       28, 29, 1956.
       "a good face": *Tennessean,* June 28, 1956. See Gardner, 612–18.
228   "he withdrew": *Banner,* Aug. 1, 1956.
       "pressured friends": E.g., letter, Joe L. Evins to FGC, May 23, 1956 (D)
       (1956 Conv.). Joint letter, signed by Tennessee delegation to the
       House of Representatives to Paul M. Butler, May 31, 1956; letter,
       Williston M. Cox to FGC, saying he had written Speaker Rayburn,

228 May 29, 1956; telegram, George R. Dempster to Paul Butler, June 12, 1956 (all in Keynote Speech).

"ill afford": Gardner, 628–29.

"Butler was still lukewarm": *Tennessean,* July 10, 1956.

"Jacob Arvey": Letter, Herbert S. Walters to FGC, May 29, 1956 (D) (1956 Conv.). Jacob M. Arvey wrote a friendly but reserved letter after selection to FGC, July 31, 1956 (Keynote Speech).

"Truman returned from Europe": *Tennessean,* July 10, 1956.

"turning the tide in Clement's favor": Ibid.

"delays and disappointments": Gardner, 625–30.

"by the national committee": *Banner,* July 10, 1956; *Tennessean,* July 10, 1956. Gore telegraphed approval; Gore to FGC, July 10, 1956 (Gore papers).

"it was known": *Tennessean,* July 11, 1956; also letter, Calvin Rawlings (Utah) to FGC, Aug. 27, 1956 (Keynote Speech). Clement subsequently made Rawlings a colonel. Letter, Rawlings, to FGC, July 19, 1956 (Keynote Speech).

"files contain a draft": (D) (1956 Conv.).

"Carr and Lipe Henslee": Gardner, 630.

"George Dempster said": Letter, George R. Dempster to FGC, July 6, 1956 (Keynote Speech).

229 "Butler . . . Henry . . . Anderson": Joe Henry later said that the speech was not his, but that Clement had written it himself; letter, Henry to LSG, Sept. 21, 1977. Fisher said Hilton Butler wrote most of the speech. Interviews, Douglas Fisher, June 28, 1977; Joe C. Carr, Sept. 16, 1975. Cf. Gardner, 641–43.

"Billy Graham": Fragmentary notes (D) (Keynote Speech).

"Butler . . . Truman . . . Johnson . . . Rayburn": Letter, FGC to Paul Butler, Aug. 6, 1956 (D) (1956 Conv.). Butler was asked for consultation, telegram, FGC to Butler, July 12, 1956 (D) (1956 Conv.). Telegram, FGC to Lyndon Johnson, July 12, 1956 (D) (1956 Conv.). Clayton Fritchey (Democratic National Committee) was consulted on foreign affairs, Israel and the Middle East, bipartisanship, and the "give-away program" as it pertained to natural resources; telegram, FGC to Clayton Fritchey, July 30, 1956 (D) (1956 Conv.). Letters, Truman to FGC, July 26, 1956; FGC to Truman, July 26, 1956; FGC to Truman, July 30, 1956 (Truman Lib.).

"who wrote the governor": Letter, Hubert H. Humphrey to FGC, July 30, 1956 (Keynote Speech).

"had sought Humphrey's advice": Telegram, FGC to Humphrey, July 12, 1956 (D) (1956 Conv.).

"Senators Kerr, George, and Russell": Telegram, FGC, to Kerr, July 12, 1956 (D) (1956 Conv.). Telegrams, FGC, to Walter F. George and

229   Richard Russell, July 26, 1956 (Keynote Speech). George and Russell responded in a lukewarm vein; telegrams, George to FGC, July 30, 1956; Russell to FGC, July 28, 1956 (Keynote Speech). Clement had earlier contacts with Russell; letter, Erle Cocke, Jr., to FGC, Sept. 7, 1954 (Keynote Speech).

"Dean Acheson": Draft (confidential) of platform plank by Acheson (1956 Conv.).

"some have faulted the results": Interview, Douglas Fisher, June 28, 1977. Jones implies that Butler was a major author of the speech but says probably Joe Henry was a principal author. Very likely Robert S. Clement put thoughts in it. Interview, Edward F. Jones, June 29, 1977.

"were elected": *Banner*, July 26, 1956; *Tennessean*, P, July 27, 1956.

"backed by such Clement figures": *Tennessean*, P, July 27, 1956.

"Mrs. Ragland's supporters": Ibid.

"Clement forces held a clear majority": List (1956 Conv.). Gore speaks of fierce rivalry between Clement and Kefauver in *Let the Glory Out*, 91.

"at Haynes' urgent request": Letter, Walter M. Haynes to FGC, April 10, 1956. (D) (1956 Conv.).

"McKellar had hoped to go": Letters, K.D. McKellar to Herbert Walters, July 16, 1956 (D) (1956 Conv.); K.D. McKellar to FGC, July 31, 1956 (1956 Conv.).

"wired Stevenson . . . Watkins Overton": Telegram, McKellar to FGC, Aug. 17, 1956 (1956 Conv.).

"Alfred Starr . . . John J. Hooker": List (1956 Conv.).

230   "Two sessions": Thomson, 138.

"physical setting": Gardner, 641.

"Douglas Fisher": Interview, Douglas Fisher, June 28, 1977.

"Fisher was given the job . . . all night . . . for a floor demonstration": Ibid.

"tried out his voice . . . would have to speak against the noise": Interview, Fred Travis, Sept. 26, 1977.

"thought Clement shouted": Clement thought the crowd would be milling around; ibid.

"all the seats . . . all the standing room": Thomson, 140.

o   "twelve to fifteen million TV sets": Ibid.

"to Aunt Dockie Weems . . . Clement's mother . . . father": *Tennessean*, Aug. 14, 1956.

"with a film": Kennedy's narration was the same general partisan appeal as the keynote speech. In the proceedings, it takes up 11 pages; the Clement speech took 13; *Official Report of the Proceedings of the Democratic National Convention,* Chicago, Aug. 13–17, 1956, pub-

230   lished under direction of the Democratic National Committee, 37–47, 48–61. See also Thomson, 141.

232   "something of a spoiler": For opposition to the film, letters; Herbert S. Walters to FGC, May 21, 1956 (D) (1956 Conv.); FGC, to Paul Butler, Aug. 6, 1956 (D) (1956 Conv.).

"to allow time": Interview, Fred Travis, Sept. 26, 1977.

"openly attacked President Eisenhower": *Proceedings,* 48–51; also copy of speech in file-Keynote Speech.

"Vice-Hatchet Man": *Proceedings,* 49.

"head, arm and shoulder movements": *Proceedings, 48ff.* Clement had worked on the speech, practicing gestures, etc. Interview, Joe C. Carr, Sept. 16, 1975.

"How long, O, America,": *Proceedings,* 57–58.

"ran on beyond the ending": Clement said that the *Chicago Tribune* said in reply to "O, Lord, how long?" — one hour and twenty-six minutes. Letter, Edward F. Jones to James H. Troman, Jan. 5, 1966 (Keynote Speech).

234   "according to the *Tennessean* . . . a four-minute ovation": *Tennessean,* Aug. 14, 1956.

"had to be scrapped": Interview, Fred Travis, Sept. 26, 1977.

"accumulated two thick files": See collection in the State Library and Archives; file-Keynote Speech.

"Stevenson": *Tennessean,* Aug. 14, 1956.

"Sam Rayburn . . . John Sparkman": Ibid. Hubert Humphrey approved cautiously; letter, Humphrey to FGC, Sept. 6, 1956 (Keynote Speech).

"H.V. Kaltenborn": Letter, H.V. Kaltenborn to FGC, Aug. 31, 1956 (Keynote Speech).

"Graham": Letter, Graham to FGC, Aug. 20, 1956 (D) (1956 Conv.).

"came the query . . . California . . . A Tuscaloosan . . . Kansas Democrat . . . From Brooklyn . . . wired one listener": Telegrams, [names withheld] to FGC, Aug. 13, 14, 1956 (Keynote Speech).

"been silly . . . a failure": Henry didn't think the speech was "tops", but thought that many had expected too much from it; interview, Joe Henry, Sept. 30, 1975. Caudill was apologetic about it; interview, Noble Caudill, Jan. 22, 1975. Travis thought the speech was terrible, that the delivery was bad; he thought that Clement would have done better to deliver speech ex tempore and that the old fashioned oratory had gone out; interview, Fred Travis, Sept. 26, 1977. Cummings didn't think the speech went well; interview, James Cummings, Nov. 4, 1974.

236   "for higher office": Thomson, 141; interview, Agnes Bird, Sept. 20, 1977. See also Fontenay, 271.

236 "a forty-three minute speech": *Tennessean,* Aug. 14, 1956.

"not usable in the North": Caudill was apologetic about the use of the phrase, "Precious Lord, take my hand and lead me on." He said that times had changed. Interview, Noble Caudill, Jan. 22, 1975. Also interview, James Cummings, Nov. 4, 1974; he said that the speech was good for Tennessee but not for Chicago.

"was rammed through": *Proceedings,* 332; Thomson, 148.

237 "backed by Harry Truman": Harry Truman's animosity toward Kefauver was a long standing one.

"produced a resolution": *Tennessean,* Aug. 15, 1956; also, press release, Aug. 14, 1956 (D) (1956 Conv.). See Gardner, 655–56.

"hoped to bargain": Gardner, 655–56.

"Clement withdrew": *Banner,* Aug. 16, 1956; Cf. *Tennessean,* Aug. 16, 1956. Clement wrote Truman later saying that he had no choice but to withdraw; letter, FGC to Truman, Aug. 21, 1956 (Truman Lib.).

"Lausche of Ohio": Thomson, 150.

"Magnusson . . . Johnson . . . Symington . . . Chandler": Ibid.

"Senator John Kennedy": Ibid.

"Governor Gary": Ibid., 151.

"flattened the opposition": Fontenay, 268.

"first ballot": *Proceedings,* 417–18; Thomson, 153.

"by refusing": *Banner,* Aug. 16, 17, 1956; *Tennessean,* Aug. 17, 1956; *Proceedings,* 420; Thomson, 152.

"Clement was told later": Letter, D.W. Gilmore to FGC, July 31, 1956 (1956 Conv.).

"did not want Kefauver": Thomson, 149.

"it has been said": Fontenay, 268.

"decided to leave": Gardner, 662–63.

"spent all Thursday night": Interview, Fred Travis, Sept. 26, 1977.

238 "approached pandemonium": *Tennessean,* Aug. 17, 1956, story by Wayne Whitt.

"failed to jell": Ibid.; Fontenay, 271.

"would be delivered to Lyndon Johnson": *Tennessean,* Aug. 17, 1956.

"charged that plans were being formulated": Ibid. See also ibid., Aug. 18, 1956; Fontenay, 271.

"was heard shouting" (because he refused to sign the "Southern Manifesto"): *Tennessean,* Aug. 17, 1956.

"Estes who is bestes": Telegram, John Essary, Lucille Thornburg, and others to FGC, Aug. 17, 1956 (1956 Conv.).

"yielded to Tennessee . . . Jared Maddux": *Proceedings,* 427–429. See also *Banner,* Aug. 17, 1956. Gore was seconded by Sen. Mike Monroney of Oklahoma and delegate Laurie C. Battle of Alabama; *Pro-*

238 *ceedings,* 429–31; Thomson, 146. Gore said he had trouble getting Clement to say what he would do; *Let the Glory Out,* 94.

"Pauline Gore": Interview, Fred Travis, Sept. 26, 1977. Gore has said he thought Stevenson would support him; *Let the Glory Out,* 92.

"delegation would desert Kefauver": The delegation was dominated by anti-Kefauver delegates. Interview, Fred Travis, ibid. See list of delegates (1956 Conv.).

"Abraham Ribicoff": *Proceedings,* 435–37; Thomson, 156.

"the first ballot": Thomson, 157.

"Georgia . . . Louisiana . . . Virginia . . . South Carolina": Gorman points out that Texas had played along with Kennedy. Rayburn's rulings had seemed to favor Kennedy, and it was speculated that he thought Tennessee was going to switch to the senator from Massachusetts. Gorman, 259. *Proceedings,* 464–65.

"had only one vote": *Proceedings,* 464–65; Thomson, 158.

"Arkansas shifted": *Proceedings,* 467; Thomson, 158; see Gore, *Let the Glory Out,* 94.

"Delaware moved": *Proceedings,* 467.

239 "Kentucky . . . left Maner": Ibid., 469.

"Mississippi deserted Gore": Ibid., 470; Thomson, 159.

"Clement write 'our boy'": Memorandum, Mary Smith to "Leota" (Corres.-Lyndon Johnson).

"formal letter": Letters, FGC to LBJ, Aug. 21, 1956, and reply, Aug. 29, 1956 (Corres.-London Johnson). Clement hinted at the same idea in a letter to Billy Graham; letter, FGC to Graham, Aug. 23, 1956, in response to Aug. 20 letter from Graham (D) (1956 Conv.).

"Gore now released his delegates": *Proceedings,* 476; Thomson, 161; see Gore, *Let the Glory Out,* 94. On Aug. 21, 1956, Gore wrote FGC to thank him for his support (1956 Conv.).

"embraced, weeping": Interview, Noble Caudill, Jan. 22, 1975; Fontenay, 273.

"Rayburn was maneuvering": Fontenay, 275–76, gives an account of the deception practiced on Rayburn.

"shifted its votes": Thomson, 161; *Tennessean,* Aug. 18, 1956; cf. *Banner,* Aug. 17, 1956.

"in the same populist vein": *Proceedings,* 504–11. Barkley's lengthy address in 1948 was quite like Clement's. See *Official Report of the Democratic National Convention,* Philadelphia, July 12–14, 1948.

"booed Governor Clement": *Tennessean,* Aug. 19, 1956; interview, Fred Travis, Sept. 26, 1977.

"Gore got similar treatment": Gore issued a defensive statement; see *Tennessean,* Aug. 20, 1956.

"$85,000": Interview, Noble Caudill, Jan. 22, 1975.

239 "Noble Caudill secured pledges": Ibid.

"a second campaign": Ibid.

"lengthy letter": Letter, Stahlman to FGC, Sept. 24, 1956 (Corres.-Stahlman).

244 "voting took place": Letter, FGC to Stahlman, Oct. 4, 1956 (Corres.-Stahlman).

245 "he issued": (D) (1956 Conv.). Clement explained in detail to Truman why the Tennessee delegation proceeded as it did; letter, FGC to Truman, Nov. 2, 1956, and received a conciliatory reply, Nov. 8, 1956 (Truman Lib.). Clement and Stahlman remained friends; interview, Joe C. Carr, Sept. 16, 1975.

246 "Party in November": A copy of this statement is in file (D) (1956 Conv.).

"campaigned for the ticket": Stevenson asked for the help of Clement; e.g., telegram, Stevenson to FGC, Nov. 2, 1956 (D), and favorable reply, Nov. 3, 1956 (D) (1956 Conv.). Letters, James A. Finnegan to FGC, Aug. 24, 1956, dealing with regional visit with Stevenson and Kefauver; Stevenson to FGC, Sept. 4, 1956 (Corres.-Stevenson).

"Pennsylvania . . . Florida . . . Kentucky . . . Missouri . . . Tennessee": on Pennsylvania, Letters, Emmy Guffy Miller to FGC, Nov. 24, 1956; Florida, James M. Milligan to FGC, Nov. 29, 1956; on Kentucky, Carl D. Perkins to FGC, Dec. 6, 1956; on California, Harlan Hagen to FGC, Dec. 21, 1956; on Missouri, W.R. Hull, Jr. to FGC, Dec. 22, 1956 (all in Out-state Campaigns). Much of this speech-making was in aid of congressmen. Clement had always done a good deal of this and had been active in the 1954 election; e.g., letter, Newman Jeffrey to Glen Nicely, Sept. 15, 1954; memorandum, Doug Fisher to FGC, Sept. 10, 1954; letter, John L. Smith to FGC, Oct. 30, 1954 (all in Out-state Campaigns).

"helped to raise money": E.g., letters, Walters to FGC, May 15, 1957 (D); Butler to Walters, Nov. 26, 1957 (D) (1956 Conv.).

"a broken spirit drieth the bones": Thomson, 319.

CHAPTER 9.

247 "McClellan committee": See *Final Report of the Select Committee on Improper Activities in the Labor or Management Field, 86th Congress, Second Session, Report No. 1139, 1960.*

248 "largely helpless": Interview, W.L. Barry, Nov. 2, 1977.

"Select Committee": See *Hearings before the Select Committee on Improper Activities in the Labor or Management Field,* 85th Congress, First Session, parts 1–18 (Washington: U.S. Government Printing

248 Office, 1957). See also *Interim Report,* 85th Congress, Second Session, Report No. 1417 (Washington: U.S. Government Printing Office, 1958).

"of barbers": See *Hearings,* part 18; *Banner,* Sept. 5, 1957.

"LaVern J. Duffy . . . James P. McShane": *Interim Report,* 331. See *Banner,* June 15, July 22, Nov. 29, 1957.

"at 173": *Hearings,* Part 18, p. 7055. (Unless otherwise noted, Hearings hereafter refers to Part 18).

"$2 million": *Hearings,* 7069; *Interim Report,* 331.

"syrup into the fuel": *Hearings,* 7068.

"goons": *Interim Report,* 331.

"Hard of Hearing Smitty . . . Corky Ellis . . . Perry Canaday": Ibid., 331, 338, 339.

"had a record": Ibid., 339, 367.

249 "Glenn Smith . . . W.J. Reynolds": Ibid., 366.

"James Hoffa": Ibid., 367.

"shockingly derelict . . . Knoxville and Nashville . . . Knox and Davidson . . . state highway patrol . . . Bureau of Criminal Identification": Ibid., 368.

"scandalous immunity . . . reached into local governments": Ibid., 369.

"Judge Raulston Schoolfield": Ibid., 370.

"in 1948": *House Journal,* First Extraordinary Session, Eightieth General Assembly, 1958, p. 197.

"elected for a full term": Ibid.

"opinion remains divided": E.g., interviews, J.J. Mynatt, Oct. 2, 1975, Joe Henry, Sept. 30, 1975.

"associate of the Kennedys": Personal recollections of the author.

250 "was impatient": *Banner,* Dec. 19, 1957.

"he released material": Ibid.

"he would not be stampeded": Clement probably would not have acted, except under pressure from the McClellan committee; interview, Barry, Nov. 2, 1977. See also rough draft of a letter to various publishers and editors (Stahlman, Ahlgren, Meeman, and others, n.d.) (D); notes in Clement's handwriting, indicating what he expected to do (D) (Schoolfield Impeachment).

"had been receiving private information": See (D) file-Schoolfield Impeachment.

"Hugh Abercrombie": Ibid., confidential memorandum of telephone conversation, Abercrombie to FGC, Dec. 19, 1957; also notes on telephone conversation with Jake O'Brien, Dec. 19, 1957.

"George McCanless . . . W.E. Hopton": Letter, Sen. John L. McClellan to FGC and George McCanless, Dec. 24, 1957; telegram,

250   FGC and McCanless to Sen. McClellan, Dec. 19, 1957 (D) (Schoolfield Impeachment); *Banner,* Dec. 19, 21, 1957.

"Clement wrote Schoolfield": Letter, FGC to Judge Raulston Schoolfield, Dec. 23, 1957 (D) (Schoolfield Impeachment). Clement had taken the advice of persons who met with him for four hours; persons present were: P.R. Olgiati, Ceylon B. Frazer, Charles G. Morgan, James Cummings, Damon Headden, Ross Dyer, Jim McCord, W.E. Hopton, Hilton Butler, William Snodgrass, L.B. Jennings, George F. McCanless, James Bomar, Jared Maddux, and Corry Smith (D) (Schoolfield Impeachment). The character of this group attests to the seriousness of the issue. Ceylon Frazer was the chairman of the State Judicial Conference. See *Banner,* Dec. 24, 1957.

"he stated publicly": *Banner,* Dec. 24, 1957.

"Schoolfield stated": Ibid., Dec. 27, 28, 1957.

"as creeps . . . was a subsidiary . . . all-powerful federal government . . . integration": Ibid., Dec. 28, 1957.

"liquor interests": Ibid.

251 "The resolution was adopted": Ibid., Dec. 30, 1957.

"Jack Norman": Letter, FGC to Jack Norman, Sr., Dec. 31, 1957 (D) (Schoolfield Impeachment); *Banner,* Dec. 31, 1957.

"with the Browning forces": Cf. letter, FGC to James G. Stahlman, Jan. 2, 1958; and reply, Jan. 2, 1958 (D) (Schoolfield Impeachment). See *Banner,* Dec. 31, 1957.

"resigned from the national committee": *Banner,* Jan. 1, 1958.

"Perry Canaday . . . "Shorty" Richardson . . . James Gilley": Ibid., Dec. 31, 1957.

"Smith complied": Ibid., Dec. 31, 1957, Jan. 1, 1958.

"resigned his office . . . some persons said": Ibid., Jan. 2, 1958.

"Brown testified": Ibid.

"Schoolfield friends . . . investigated the murder": Ibid., Jan. 4, 1958.

"was subsequently murdered": Ibid., Jan. 4, 9, 16, 1958.

"to run again . . . Chattanooga newspapers . . . good government group . . . WCTU . . . local gambling syndicate": Ibid., Jan. 8, 1958.

252 "was said to be committed . . . Ben Cash . . . Ward Crutchfield . . . Don Moore . . . had been members . . . bills were presented . . . connections with the underworld . . . tied to that underworld . . . underworld's principal enemies": Ibid., Jan. 10, 1958.

"controlled" wards . . . coal miners and bootleggers": Ibid.

"were indicted": Ibid., Feb. 13, 1958.

"blistering attack": Ibid., March 24, 25, 1958.

252 "received Norman's report": Ibid., April 15, 1958.

"subjected earlier to some criticism": *Interim Report*, 344ff., 368, 369.

"refusal to recuse himself": The report is printed in the *House Journal, First Extraordinary Session, 1958,* supp. 194–674; the refusal to recuse is noted on p. 196; the Norman report is referred to hereafter by page citations to the *House Journal,* supplemented by references to the typescript of the Norman report which is in the files at Dickson.

"We found immediately": *House Journal,* 196.

253 "refused to cooperate . . . did not mention names . . . many conscientious citizens": ibid., 197.

"he stood in contempt . . . piece of white cloth . . . directing verdicts of not guilty": Ibid., 198.

"taken like action": Ibid., 198–99.

"from incarceration of those persons": Ibid., 199.

254 "he has entered orders": Ibid., 199.

"was impatient with jury trials . . . 8000 cases coming before him": Ibid., 199–200.

"had actually entered orders . . . changing the offenses": Ibid., 200–201.

"grades of felony and different sentences . . . arbitrary actions were described": Ibid.

"insatiable desire to project himself": Ibid., 201.

"law violators, gamblers, and racketeers . . . open and notorious": Ibid., 202.

"He had accepted money": Ibid., 203.

"money as bribes . . . in matters pending before him": Ibid., 202.

255 "Glenn W. Smith . . . Hubert Leon Boling": Ibid., 204.

"W.C. (Bill) Long shot and killed Fred Gill . . . pallbearer . . . Gill's funeral": Ibid., 206–207.

"continuously posing as the champion of law and order . . . intemperate, inattentive, impatient, and partial . . . profane and obscene": Ibid., 207.

"confiscated private property": Ibid., 209.

"recommended impeachment": Ibid., 217–18.

"proposed thirty-one articles of impeachment": *House Journal,* 218; the *House Journal* says 32 such articles, but the typescript shows 31; Typescript (D).

"directing verdicts of not guilty": Typescript, 44–45, 88–90.

"changing sentences and punishments": Ibid., 41–43, 86–87.

256 "suspending and delaying cases": Ibid., 46, 91–92.

"accepting bribes and gifts": Ibid., 47–54.

"gift of a Pontiac": Ibid., 59–60.

"associating with known gamblers and law violators": Ibid., 77–78.

256 "mixing in local politics": Ibid., 81–83.

"failing to testify": Ibid., 31–32.

"failing to recuse himself": Ibid., 33–34.

"indulging in private behavior inappropriate for a judge": Ibid., 61–62, 68–69.

"reached the governor" *Banner*, CH, April 15, 1958.

"Some hope was expressed": Ibid., April 21, 1958.

"issued a call": *Banner*, April 26, 1958.

"that justice was done": *House Journal*, 9.

"any influence on the future fortunes of the governor": Olgiati carried Hamilton County in 1962, and Ross Bass carried it in 1964 in the primaries. Baker defeated Clement there in the general election of 1966, but all these results can be explained on numerous bases other than the Schoolfield matter.

257 "restricted access": *House Journal*, 12–13.

"in regular attendance": See, e.g., *Banner*, May 7, 1958.

"did not avail himself of invitations": *House Journal*, 13; *Banner*, May 8, 1958.

"were inclined to want to cross-examine . . . Hamilton County delegation . . . Marshall County . . . Sullivan . . . Bradley": *Banner*, May 9, 1958.

"House strongly supported Bomar's": See, e.g., *House Journal*, 481ff., 848–49.

"to presume to suggest": Ibid., 327.

258 "H.L. Boling . . . Fifth Amendment": Ibid., 355–56.

"in that kind of activity": Ibid., 379.

"McKellip . . . to say a Pontiac": Ibid., 395.

"fifteen-member subcommittee": Ibid., 39, 611.

"Harry Lee Senter . . . Damon Headden . . . J.I. Bell . . . W.L. Barry": Ibid., 39; see also *Banner*, May 16, 1958.

"three witnesses": *House Journal*, 682, 683.

"Only Corry Smith responded": *Banner*, May 15, 1958; *House Journal*, 707ff.

"major surgery for cancer": *House Journal*, 703, 704.

"didn't know when he would be back": Ibid., 704.

"attempt to bribe members": Ibid., 365ff.; See also *Banner*, June 17, 1958.

259 "Joe Frank . . . Claude Massey . . . Leonard Lane . . . Charley Jones": *House Journal*, 365–68, 374–79; see *Banner*, May 9, 1958.

"to raise $2,500": *House Journal*, 367.

"House Bill No. 739": Ibid., 379.

"saying his mission had been completed": Ibid., 368.

259 "John Chambliss . . . J.B. Ragon . . . Ambrose Locke . . . Leonard
Aymon": Ibid., 41–46, 808–811.

"only Aymon": *Tennessee Blue Book,* 1957–58, p. 24; *House Journal,*
808; see *Banner,* May 8, 1958.

"state Supreme Court": *Tennessee Blue Book,* 1942–1943, p. 103.

"attempts to reform": *House Journal,* 809.

"had introduced": Ibid., 43, 809.

"he had supported Schoolfield": Ibid.

"He, Ragon, and Locke all": Ibid., 41–46, 808–12.

"Ragon and Locke": Ibid., 44, 45, 810, 811; see *Banner,* CH, May 16,
1958.

"political opponent": *House Journal,* 44, 810.

"condemned the practice": Ibid., 46, 812.

"was, in due course, approved" Article 14; Ibid., 109–11, 1143–46.

"the subcommittee of fifteen": Ibid., 39.

260 "following day . . . twenty-five counts . . . twenty-four articles":
Ibid., 49–80.

"was rejected": Ibid., 558–76, 894–95.

"the majorities . . . substantial": Ibid., 49–80.

"a bribe of $1,000": Ibid., 86, 1120–22.

"gift of a Pontiac": Ibid., 96, 1130–32.

"failure of the judge to pay a fine": This became 18 in final form; Ibid.,
1152.

"constant mixing in county politics": Nineteen in final form; *House
Journal,* 1152–55.

"seizing guns": Ibid., 1157–59.

"it was argued by some": Ibid., 900–903.

"Aderholt, Crutchfield, Estes, Hull, McKellip, Moore, and Thompson": Ibid., 50; *Banner,* May 16, 1958.

"to have constituted a hard core of resistance": See votes and debates
recorded in *House Journal.*

"Wednesday, May 21": *Proceedings of the High Court of Impeachment in
the Case of the People of the State of Tennessee* v. *Raulston Schoolfield,
Judge* (1958), 1. The trial actually began on June 10.

"J. Fred Bibb": Ibid., 3–4. Judge Bibb ran court strictly and formally;
see *Banner,* May 28, 1958.

"managers": *Proceedings,* 61.

261 "move to quash": Ibid., 62–63; transcript of Senate proceedings in the
State Library and Archives, Vol. III. See also *Banner,* June 10, 1958.

"reduced to three": *Banner,* June 10, 1958.

"it had not been reapportioned": Ibid.

"a thoroughly questionable contention": Ibid.

261 "reply was filed . . . was along the lines" *Proceedings,* 62–75.
"does not constitute grounds for impeachment": Ibid., 63–64.
"were denied outright": Ibid., 64.
"not done in the defendant's official capacity": Ibid., 71.
"unfounded and untrue charges": Ibid., 74–75.
"James Spense Galloway . . . Sam Jones . . . H.L. Boling": Ibid., 76–80. See *Banner,* June 11, 12, 1958.

262 "Jones to Harold Brown": *Banner,* June 12, 1958.
"Galloway, Jones, and Brown": Transcript, 401ff., 421ff; *Banner,* June 12, 1958.
"was granted a new trial": *Banner,* June 13, 1958.
"differed": See also ibid., June 11, 1958.
"put words in his mouth": Transcript, 261; *Banner,* June 11, 1958.
"he allowed clearly enough": *Banner,* June 11, 1958.
"Brown testified": Transcript, 401ff.; *Banner,* June 12, 1958.
"Jones testified": Transcript, 421ff.; *Banner,* June 12, 1958; see also *Chattanooga Times,* June 13, 1958.
"ordered to trial for contempt of the Senate": Transcript, 567; *Banner,* June 13, 17, 1958.
"he himself had been actively engaged": Transcript, 581, 587ff., 596; *Banner,* June 13, 1958. See also *Chattanooga Times,* June 14, 17, 1958; *Banner,* June 3, 1958.

263 "his wife, Alma, had taken over": Transcript, ibid.; *Banner,* June 13, 1958; *Chattanooga Times,* June 14, 17, 1958.
"had died": Transcript, ibid.; *Banner,* ibid.
"it was hinted in some quarters": *Banner,* ibid.
"proceedings to exhume her body": Ibid., June 24, 1958.
"exhumed": Ibid.
"papers reported": Ibid., June 26, 1958.
"was irrelevant": Ibid.
"she had paid Schoolfield off": Ibid.
"was not received": Ibid.
"took an active part": See Transcript, *passim.*
"case of Galloway": *Banner,* June 13, 1958.
"attorney general's office had not been represented": Ibid.
"Woolsey testified . . . Chester Frost": Ibid.
"his cross-examination of Lane": Transcript, 633ff., 643, 706ff.; *Banner,* ibid.
"Alma Lane was mentally ill": Transcript, ibid.; *Banner,* June 13, 1958.
"Lane had been a persistent enemy": Transcript, ibid.; *Banner,* June 13, 1958.
"an admission from Lane": Transcript, ibid.; *Banner,* June 13, 1958.
"was the allegation": Transcript, 1167ff; 1237ff. *Banner,* June 19, 1958.

264 "he refused to give it": Transcript, 679ff., 1059; *Banner,* June 17, 18, 1958.

"an uproar": *Banner,* June 19, 1958.

"Boling testified": Transcript, 1178ff.; *Banner,* June 19, 1958.

"in Georgia": *Banner,* June 19, 1958.

"Senate voted": As a result, the testimony is missing from the published record.

"to deny": Transcript, 1237ff.

"he had met with Robert Crichton . . . Glenn Smith and another union official": Ibid., 1245ff.

"Glenn Smith was finally brought to the bar": Ibid., 1417ff., 1466, 1472, 1773ff.; *Banner,* June 24, 25, 1958.

"to fix the case in Schoolfield's court": Transcript, ibid.; *Banner,* June 24, 25, 1958.

"James Robertson Hotel in Nashville": Transcript, ibid.; *Banner,* June 24, 25, 1958.

"$39,000": Transcript, ibid.; *Banner,* June 24, 1958.

"$20,000": Transcript, ibid.; *Banner,* June 25, 1958.

"contacts with Crichton": Transcript, 1466ff.; *Banner,* ibid.

"only Crichton, Schoolfield, Eddie Friar, and Steven Stone": Transcript, ibid.; *Banner,* June 24, 1958.

"he had lied to the Internal Revenue Service": Transcript, 1773ff.; *Banner,* June 25, 1958.

"out-and-out political shakedown": Transcript, 1472; *Banner,* ibid.

"Crichton took the initiative": Transcript, 1429.

"Friar took time . . . to appear before the Senate": Ibid., 1660ff.; *Banner,* June 24, 1958.

265 "he was acquainted with Smith . . . he did not know Boling": Transcript, 1672ff.

"he had met": Ibid., 1689–90.

"he denied . . . Smith later asked for his help": Ibid., 1672ff.

"Internal Revenue Service approached him": Ibid., 1672ff., 1693ff.

"denied any payoff to Crichton": Ibid., 1728ff.; *Banner,* June 19, 1958.

"testified that he had no knowledge": Transcript, 1751–59.

"Charles M. Pendergast": *Banner,* July 8, 1958.

"was offered": Ibid., July 1, 1958.

"Schoolfield's defense": *Proceedings,* 306–10.

"stated flatly": Transcript, 1133; see also *Chattanooga Times,* June 19, 1958.

266 "Judge Tillman Grant . . . stated": *Banner,* July 8, 1958; also testimony of H.G.B. King, Transcript, 1357ff., but see Transcript, 1513ff., 1526ff.

"Judge Myers": *Banner,* July 8, 1958.

266 "Schoolfield had exceeded his authority": Ibid.
     "without a jury verdict . . . without the approval of a jury . . .
     Why?" *Proceedings,* 218.
267 "another office . . . without concurrence of a jury": Ibid., 231, 241.
     "peculiar to Judge Schoolfield's court": Ibid., 254.
268 "how to get out the vote . . . What would they have in mind? . . .
     whereby public security can be preserved": Ibid., 263–64, 265,
     268.
     "silent witnesses": Ibid., 269–80.
     "with raising $3,000 . . . Son Skillern": Ibid., 269–80.
     "presented here": Ibid., 277.
269 "ranging from 'inexperienced' to 'half-wits'": Ibid., 277–78.
     "John J. Hooker, Jr., J. Alan Hanover, and John R. Jones": Ibid., 281–
     303.
     "lengthy reply . . . it has attained": Ibid., 304–44, 321.
     "on three counts": Ibid., 346–47; *Banner,* July 11, 1958.
     "was thereby removed": *Proceedings,* ibid.
     "short of the two-thirds": Ibid., 347.
270 "24 to 7 . . . 27 guilty to 4 not guilty . . . 22 to 9": Ibid., 346.
     "Senator Head had been absent": Ibid., 2.
     "had decided to absent himself": *Banner,* July 11, 1958.
     "not one single vote for conviction": *Proceedings,* 346.
     "'certainly not an impeachable offense'": Ibid., 195–96.
     "only Senator Dyer voted guilty": Ibid., 197–98.
     "only Senator Dyer and Senator Dunbar voted guilty": Ibid., 175–78.
271 "changes in final judgment": Ibid., 346.
     "$1000 from Galloway . . . alleged forced loan . . . alleged bribery
     . . . contributions to the political campaign . . . interference with
     the grand jury . . . directed verdicts . . . failure to pay a fine . . .
     seizure of revolvers": Ibid., 346.
     "the failure of the prosecution": Ibid., 139, 140, 155, 161, 175, 178.
     "doubts as to culpable motives": Ibid., 138.
     "judge's ill will": Ibid., 186.
     "order modifying sentences . . . dismissal of a drunk driving charge
     . . . frequent delays and dismissals . . . forbids a judge to sign surety
     bonds . . . dealing with the judge's failure . . . failure to return a
     car": Ibid., 346.
     "largely on his general behavior": See articles 8, 19, and 22 in *Proceed-
     ings*; results noted on p. 346.
     "atmosphere in his court": Ibid.
272 "editorial on July 14": *Chattanooga Times,* July 14, 1958.
     "Brooks McLemore": Senator representing Chester, Henderson,
     Madison counties.

272 "Maddux and Dyer": Maddux was a firm friend of Clement. Dyer represented Lauderdale, Crockett, and Dyer counties. He was subsequently a member of the state Supreme Court.

"Hobart Atkins": Hobart Atkins was a prominent litigant in the case of *Baker* v. *Carr*. He died in 1965.

"Clifford Allen": After serving in the national House of Representatives, Clifford Allen died on June 18, 1978.

"defeated for renomination": *Chattanooga Times,* June 4, 1958; *Banner,* June 4, 1958. Carden was a great-grandson of Gov. William B. Campbell of Tennessee; *Banner,* June 4, 1958.

"he lost in Soddy": *Banner,* June 4, 1958.

"Highlander Folk School": Ibid., June 3, 1958. Schoolfield's segregationist stand probably alienated black voters; *Banner,* June 4, 1958.

CHAPTER 10.

273 "heavy life insurance . . . a small equity": Interview, Joe Henry, Sept. 30, 1975.

"frequently saddened": Interview, Collins, Sept. 18, 1975; interview, Henry, ibid.; interview, Valerius Sanford, Sept. 29, 1977; interview, W.L. Barry, Nov. 2, 1977.

"Valerius Sanford and Douglas Fisher": Interview, Douglas Fisher, June 28, 1977; interview, Sanford, ibid. See also *Banner,* Feb. 28, 1962.

"American Educational Life Insurance Company": Interview, Sanford, ibid.; *Banner,* ibid.

"country musicians": Interview, Sanford, ibid.

"totally disinterested": Interview, Joe Henry, Sept. 30, 1975. Brainard Cheney wrote Gordon Clapp (who had joined Lilienthal in a consulting firm) suggesting that they employ Clement; letter, Cheney to Clapp, April 29, 1957 (JUL).

275 "in acquiring business . . . uncomplaining partners . . . to prepare briefs": Interviews, Douglas Fisher, June 28, 1977; Valerius Sanford, Sept. 29, 1977.

"he was haunted": Interview, Sanford, ibid.

"Clement thought . . . he had made Clement": Interview, Edward F. Jones, June 29, 1977.

"not moved out": Interview, Fred Travis, Sept. 26, 1977.

"Norman backed John Kennedy . . . Lyndon Johnson . . . Ellington had planned . . . persuaded by Walters": Ibid.

"did not stay . . . supported Kennedy": Ibid.

"deeply conservative": In the group that worked with Clement

275   and Ellington, Ellington was widely regarded as a "do-nothing" governor.

276   "continued to increase annually": *Tennessee Statistical Abstract, 1977* (Knoxville: Center for Business and Economic Research, Univ. of Tenn., 1977) 468.

"New bond issues": See, e.g., *Public Acts,* 1959, chs. 18, 19.

"authorized to develop industrial parks": Ibid., ch. 169.

"coordinator of elections": Ibid., ch. 148.

"mentally retarded children": Ibid., ch. 143.

"Air Pollution Control Service": Ibid., ch. 270.

"to provide urban-type services": Ibid., 1961, ch. 166.

"to control the price of milk": Ibid., ch. 203.

"The Communist party": Ibid., ch. 287.

"benefits of coon dog training": Ibid., 1959, ch. 183.

"no secret to Gore or Kefauver": Letters, R.R. Tipton, Sr., to Gore, June 12, 1954; Gayle Malone to Gore, Aug. 6, 1954; H.W. Asquith to Gore, Aug. 16, 1954 (Gore papers).

"had carefully studied": Interview, Brainard Cheney, Feb. 11, 1975; also letter, W.W. Wilkerson to Herbert Walters, Dec. 9, 1959 (Walters); memorandum, Cheney to Butler, Henry, Fisher, Fajardo (Clement's Speech Committee) on the Indianapolis Jefferson-Jackson Dinner Speech, Feb. 8, 1955 (Speech Technique).

"informed persons have claimed": Interview, Cheney, ibid.

277   "to choose a successor": *Tennessean,* P, Jan. 23, 1962.

"Carl Fry": Ibid., Jan. 3, 1962; *Tennessean,* Jan. 4, 1962; *Banner,* CH, Jan. 3, 1962.

"was split": *Banner,* CH, Jan. 3, 4, 1962.

"among rural voters": Ibid., Jan. 23, Feb. 7, 1962.

"be exerting pressure": *Banner,* Jan. 3, 1962, quoting columnist Ed Smith in the *Knoxville News-Sentinel.*

"McAllen Foutch": *Banner,* CH, Jan. 18, 1962.

"against Prentice Cooper": Cooper disastrously defeated Dempster in the primary of 1940.

"into the race briefly": *Banner,* Jan. 18, 1962.

"his running muscles": Ibid., CH, Jan. 18, 1962; *Tennessean,* P, Jan. 3, Jan. 28, 1962. The *Tennessean* columnist Hatcher also mentioned as possibilities County Judge Lunn McKeel, Alf MacFarland of Lebanon, John Long, Jared Maddux, and Hilton Butler; P, Jan. 3, 23, 1962.

"discouraged": Letter, Fowler to Kefauver, Feb. 15, 1962 (Kefauver papers).

"small newspaper endorsements": See, e.g., *Banner,* CH, Feb. 27, 1962; *Banner,* April 19, 1962; CH, May 9, 14, July 16, 1962.

277 "Rudy Olgiati": *Banner,* CH, Jan. 18, 1962; *Tennessean,* P, Jan. 3, 1962; *Tennessean,* Jan. 27, 1962.

"in February 1962": *Banner,* Feb. 8, 1962.

"bricklayers' union": Ibid.

"Gruentli . . . born in Switzerland . . . schools of Hamilton County . . . had studied engineering . . . superintendent of parks": Ibid.

278 "City Commission . . . Chattanooga's mayor": Ibid.

"had been worked out": Ibid., Feb. 8, 1962; CH, Feb. 9, 1962.

"added taxing authority . . . equalization . . . vocational schools . . . programs . . . state loans": ibid., Feb. 8, 1962.

"should allow him": Interview, Eugene Collins, Sept. 18, 1975.

"Browning's continuing opposition": *Banner,* Feb. 5, 1962.

"to limit competition": Ibid., CH, Feb. 1, 1962.

"were on hand": Ibid.

279 "to be dumped": *Banner,* Feb. 5, 1962.

"twenty members": *Banner,* CH, Feb. 12, 26, May 22, 1962.

"William Farris": Ibid., Feb. 19, 1962.

"columnist suggested": Ibid., Mar. 27, 1962.

"satirically dubbed . . . edge to Hooker": Ibid., March 5, 1962.

"expressed the hope": *Banner,* March 5, 1962.

"Kennedy forces . . . national committee of lawyers for Kennedy": Ibid., March 9, 1962.

"financial supporter": Interview, Noble Caudill, Jan. 22, 1975.

"considering backing Hooker": *Tennessean,* March 6, 1962.

"sit this one out": Ibid., March 17, 1962; *Banner,* CH, March 16, 1962. Kefauver telegram to Olgiati, Caudill, Charles Gore, Steve Para, E.W. Carmack, Carl Fry, W.W. Faw, Joe Bean, Charlie Houk, M.M. Bullard, Mrs. Tom Ragland, "Red" Jesse, Dan Mc-Kinnis, Charlotte Allen, March 14, 1962 (Kefauver papers).

"Hooker withdrew": *Tennessean,* March 22, 1962. Amon Evans had wanted Hooker and was angered because Hooker could not get the nod; interview Brainard Cheney, Feb. 11, 1975. Hooker's with-drawal intensified the struggle within the Kefauver camp; *Tennessean,* March 25, 1962. Cf. *Banner,* CH, March 14, 1962. Also ibid., March 21, 22, May 22, 1962.

"closing days of March": *Tennessean,* P, March 29, 1962; *Banner,* CH, March 27, 1962; ibid., news story, March 29, 1962.

"would not raise taxes . . . would not veto . . . favored reappor-tionment . . . major campaign issue . . . declined to surrender": Ibid.

280 "from Cumberland": *Tennessean,* P, March 29, 1962.

"held office . . . public office in Memphis . . . personnel director . . . assistant . . . city commission": Ibid., March 29, 1962; *Ban-*

280   *ner,* March 29, 1962. Farris had not supported Kefauver in 1960; ibid., CH, April 20, 1962.

"died in 1955 . . . followed him . . . became the editor": *Banner,* March 21, 22, 1962.

"*The Enemy Within*": Robert F. Kennedy, *The Enemy Within* (New York: Harper, 1960); see acknowledgment of Seigenthaler, p. xiv.

"personal representative": *Banner,* March 22, 1962.

"the morning newspaper": *Tennessean,* Jan. 3, Feb. 23, March 2, 1962.

281   "in search of support": Ibid., P, Jan. 3, 1962.

"Clement's law office": *Banner,* Feb. 28, 1962; *Tennessean,* Feb. 28, 1962.

"had stepped down": *Tennessean,* Feb. 23, 1962.

"fourth grader . . . seventh grade . . . Hillsboro High School": Press release, Feb. 28, 1962 (1962 Campaign).

"the announcement of candidacy": *Tennessean,* March 1, 1962.

"head and shoulders": *Newsweek,* March 12, 1962, p. 36.

"should study the question": *Tennessean,* March 1, 1962.

"open shop law": *Banner,* Feb. 28, 1962; *Tennessean,* Feb. 28, 1962.

"take that position": *Banner,* March 29, 1962.

"in labor ranks": *Banner,* CH, March 17, 1962.

282   "100,000": Ibid., June 2, 1962.

"$50,000": Ibid., Feb. 21, 1962, *Banner,* June 2, 1962.

"Matt Lynch": *Tennessean,* P, March 15, 1962; the paper said Lynch favored no endorsement; given Olgaiti's ties this was an endorsement for Clement. Lynch remained a friend of Clement. He was finally forced out of the state leadership of the union movement in Tennessee in 1979.

"Steve Para . . . Charles Houk"; Ibid.

"Committee on Political Education": *Tennessean,* March 18, 1962.

"spurious . . . in Olgiati's favor": *Tennessean,* P, March 20, 1962.

"was ruled": *Tennessean,* April 15, 1962; *Banner,* CH, April 16, 1962.

"by Cope's executive board": *Tennessean,* April 15, 1962.

"admittedly weak": Ibid., P, April 17, 1962.

"Fry withdrew": Ibid., May 16, 1962; also *Banner,* CH, May 21, 22, 1962.

"heart-broken": Letter, Noble Caudill to Kefauver, May 16, 1962 (Kefauver papers).

"not enough to win . . . failed to get": *Tennessean,* P, May 16, 1962.

"unable to win": Letter, Caudill to Kefauver, Jan. 21, 1962 (Kefauver papers).

"stick it out": *Tennessean,* P, May 16, 1962; *Tennessean,* May 16, 17, 1962.

"slow pace": Ibid.

282 "the swing to Clement": Letters, Caudill to Kefauver, May 31, 1962, Caudill to Kefauver, July 23, 1962 (Kefauver papers). See also two undated 1962 letters from Caudill to Kefauver in Kefauver papers, Box 115, Series 1, Elections 2, 1962 Governor's Race.

"somewhat shocking": Letter, Kefauver to Noble Caudill, July 20, 1962 (Kefauver papers).

283 "could work back": Letter, Kefauver to Caudill, Sept. 6, 1962 (Kefauver papers).

"must have missed": Letter, Caudill to Kefauver, July 23, 1962 (Kefauver papers).

"as a repudiation": *Tennessean,* April 11, 1962; *Banner,* April 10, 1962.

"he warned": *Tennessean,* April 11, 1962.

"public stand": *Tennessean,* April 11, 1962; *Banner,* April 10, 1962.

"to build on": Some of the Clement personnel are listed in *Banner,* CH, May 25, June 6, 22, 1962.

"James Alexander": *Banner,* May 10, 1962.

"Herbert Walters": Walters always maintained close friendships with East Tennessee Republicans.

"Christianson": *Banner,* CH, June 6, 1962.

"James I. Bell . . . W.F. Register . . . Kirby Matherene . . . Winfield B. Hale, Jr.": Ibid., June 22, 1962.

"George Lewis . . . John Heiskell": *Tennessean,* P, Aug. 3, 1962.

"W.L. Barry . . . Jared Maddux . . . James Bomar": Maddux and Bomar had been long-time backers; Barry was comparatively new.

284 "J. Howard Warf": *Banner,* Aug. 3, 1962.

"Jack Norman": Letter, FGC to Jack Norman, Sr., Feb. 16, 1962 (1962 Campaign).

"Franklin Haney": *Banner,* CH, June 21, 1962; *Tennessean,* July 25, 1962. In 1978, Haney supported Jake Butcher for governor against Robert Clement; Haney had loans from Butcher's bank; speech of Robert Clement to the political science graduate students and faculty in the spring of 1978.

"some 200,000 votes": Buchanan and Bird, 55.

"courted the blacks": Campaign report, April 4, 1962, unsigned (1962 Campaign). Blacks had sometimes expressed dissatisfaction with the lack of attention given them in the first administrations; letters, W.E. Harlan to FGC, July 22, 1954; Joe Albright to Glen Nicely, June 6, 1955 (Negroes I).

"A.W. Willis . . . H.T. Lockard": On Sugermon's support of Clement, memorandum, Ben Weisberger to Anna Belle Clement and Doug Fisher, June 15, 1962 (1962 Campaign). Also letter, Ben Weisberger to Jim Alexander, July 13, 1962. Similar overtures were made in other counties; letters, Rev. J.D. Steele to FGC, April 26,

284 1962; G.B. Abernathy to Jim Alexander, June 12, 1962; Ed Bass to FGC, Aug. 1, 1962 (Negroes I).

"I'se for your man": Remarks reported in campaign report, April 5, 1962 (1962 Campaign).

"Tennessee Voters' Council . . . candidates appeared": *Tennessean*, June 10, 1962; *Banner*, CH, June 11, 1962; *Southern School News*, July 1962, 3.

"council's endorsement":' *Tennessean, Banner*, ibid. Agnes Bird said the blacks she knew were pro-Clement; Clement, she said, was smooth-tongued and had performed for the blacks under pressure; interview, Agnes Bird, Sept. 20, 1977.

"to appoint a commission": *Tennessean*, June 10, 1962; *Banner*, CH, June 11, 1962.

"black deaths would have been less": A record of executions is kept in the "Black Book" in the offices of the Board of Pardons and Paroles. See also a list in file-Executions.

"minister . . . choice among evils": *Tennessean*, June 10, 1962; Hooks was a Republican; interview, Agnes Bird, Sept. 20, 1977. Dr. Bird said that black Republicans generally went along with Clement and Ellington.

"the council hoped": *Tennessean*, June 10, 1862.

"posed for a picture": Ibid. Segregation as an issue was skipped by all three leading candidates; *Southern School News*, July 1962, 3. A fourth, very minor candidate, L.A. Watts of Memphis, said he would do all he could to maintain segregation; *Southern School News*, Aug. 1962, 10.

285 "ridiculously low limits": See Buchanan and Bird, 16.

"quarter of a million": Cf. Buchanan and Bird, 86; interviews, Glen Nicely, Aug. 24, 1977; Agnes Bird, Sept. 20, 1977.

"Hatcher described": *Tennessean*, P, June 15, 1962. See also *Tennessean*, April 25, June 4, 1962.

"was already preparing": Ibid.

"the official correspondence": Interview, Joseph Johnson, Aug. 16, 1977.

"administrative assistant stated": Letters, [name withheld] to FGC, Oct. 2, 1956; Glen Nicely to [name withheld], Oct. 9, 1956 (Campaign Funds, 1954).

286 "individually modest amounts": See list of State Vocational Training School employees in file-Campaign Funds, 1962.

"prison guards": See letters, [name withheld] to Keith Hampton, July 9, 1962; [name withheld] to Keith Hampton, June 11, 1962; [name withheld] to Keith Hampton, July 7, 1962 (Campaign Funds, 1962).

286 "highways crews": E.g., letters, [name withheld] to Jim Alexander, Aug. 7, 1962, [name withheld] to Jimmy Alexander, July 9, 1962, [name withheld] to Alexander, July 5, 1962 (all in Campaign Funds, 1962).

"highway patrol": Letter to James Alexander on letterhead of Union City Insurance Agency, Aug. 8, 1962 (Campaign Funds, 1962).

"were rare": E.g., letter, [name withheld] to Anna Belle Clement, July 26, 1962 (Campaign Funds, 1962).

"were fairly frequent": Letters in file-Campaign Funds, 1962.

"occasional sums": E.g., Letters, [name withheld] to FGC, July 13, 1962, [name withheld] to "Joe," July 27, 1962 (Campaign Funds, 1962).

"big money": *Banner,* CH, July 23, 1962; see also *Banner,* July 18, 1962. Cf. interview, Brainard Cheney, Feb. 11, 1975.

"Teamster officials admitted": *Banner,* July 18, 1962.

"in Gallatin": Ibid., June 23, 1962.

"gospel music": Interview, Anna Belle O'Brien, March 25, 1975.

"estimates ranged": *Banner,* CH, June 25, 1962.

"had pled cases . . . he had kept . . . ten points": *Banner,* June 23, 1962.

288 "education . . . for the aged and disabled": Ibid. Clement wanted to start a college student loan fund; ibid., July 19, 1962. An alcoholism commission was created by *Public Acts,* 1963, ch. 52.

"to be improved . . . TVA": Ibid., June 23, 1962.

"Industrial development . . . definitely abandoned": Ibid.; also July 20, 1962, for the abandonment of open-shop repeal.

"hectic round . . . white Stetson": Clement made over 100 campaign speeches; Ibid., July 30, 1962; also *Tennessean,* July 12, 1962.

"often accompanied": *Banner,* June 29, July 6, 1962.

"the list of benefits": Ibid., July 16, 17, 18, 1962.

289 "ole Frank": Ibid., July 18, 1962; a typical statement of benefits was that made in Clay County; ibid., July 16, 1962.

"overworked voice": Interview, Robert N. Clement, May 6, 1976.

"to follow him": Ibid.

"the account . . . top consideration": Report on visit to Ripley, no date (1962 Campaign).

"wrote Anna Belle": Letters, Anna Belle Clement to Jerry D. Kizer, July 14, 1962; Herbert Walters to Anna Belle Clement, May 11, 1962; Wright Frogge to Jim Alexander, May 12, 1962; O.O. Frogge to James Alexander, May 12, 1962; Rosier Crabtree to James Alexander, May 12, 1962; Anna Belle Clement to Mrs. J. Frank Hobbs, Dec. 13, 1962 (all in 1962 Campaign).

"at Winchester": *Tennessean,* June 24, 1962.

289 "had already opened": *Tennessean*, June 17, 1962; *Banner*, CH, June 18, 1962.

291 "Farris declared": *Tennessean*, June 17, 1962.

"to concede": Interview, Stephen Boyd with Joe Hatcher, August 16, 1971.

"was small": *Tennessean*, June 17, 1962.

"that blistering June day": Ibid.

"Farris promised . . . Alfred T. MacFarland": Ibid.

"Billie Sol Estes": Ibid.; Hatcher had noted earlier that *Time* magazine had run a picture of Clement seated between Estes and Douglas Stringfellow. Stringfellow was a Utah member of Congress whose self-proclaimed war record had been exposed as a fraud. The picture had been taken at Seattle during a gathering of the ten outstanding young men of 1953; *Tennessean*, P, May 23, 1962. The *Tennessean*, June 3, 1962, had carried a story by Nat Caldwell on Estes' association with Clement. See also ibid., April 2, 4, 9, May 18, 1962. According to the *Banner*, the *Chattanooga Times* had carried a story of the business association of Robert S. Clement and Frank Clement with Estes, with nothing improper shown. Russell Brothers was also a participant in the business ventures, as was Bruce Peery, Clement's brother-in-law; *Banner*, May 1, 1962. Olgiati also mentioned the Estes connection; ibid., May 29, 1953. See also *Tennessean*, July 17, 1962. Estes was convicted of swindling in Nov. 1962; ibid., Nov. 8, 1962.

"had been one": The awards were for the year 1953.

"one of his colonels": *Banner*, May 29, 1962.

"invested money": *Tennessean*, May 1, 28, 1962. For statements regarding the business relations of the Clements with Estes, see file, Corres.-Billie Sol Estes.

"in complete sympathy": *Tennessean*, June 17, 1962.

"vocational education . . . replace the professional politicians": Ibid.

"little Hatch Act": Ibid.; see also *Banner*, July 7, 1962.

"on the platform . . . 90-degree heat": *Tennessean*, June 17, 1962.

292 "calloused hands": Ibid., June 24, 1962.

"vocational education . . . balanced road program": Ibid.

"balanced labor program . . . prison rehabilitation program": *Banner*, June 25, 1962.

"attacks on Clement . . . He read a telegram": Ibid.

"regained his old job": *Tennessean*, June 24, 1962.

"lacklustre": Ibid., June 29, 1962; also editorial, ibid., June 18, 1962.

"A typical day . . . The next day": Ibid., July 12, 1962.

"flew over the area . . . stood near him": *Banner*, June 28, 1962.

"country music stars": Ibid., July 7, 1962.

294 "a degradation of the features": *Tennessean,* July 14, 21, 1962.

"taxes, bonded debt, Billie Sol": Ibid., July 15, 1962.

"to have had one concealed": Cartoon in ibid.; see news stories, ibid., May 14, 15, 1954; editorial, ibid., May 16, 1954.

"King Frank I": Ibid., July 24, 1962.

"Clement to Estes": Ibid., May 28, July 11, 27, 1962.

"Olgiati to Hoffa": *Banner,* July 23, 1962; *Tennessean,* July 20, 25, 1962.

"indignantly denied": *Tennessean,* July 25, 1962. The Teamsters did support Olgiati; see *Banner,* July 2, 11, 1962.

"picture himself": Data from a political advertisement in Smith County.

"*Banner* recorded": *Banner,* July 11, 12, 13, 1962. The *Press-Scimitar* suggested that either Olgiati or Farris withdraw; *Banner,* July 12, 1962.

"the polls": *Banner,* CH, July 12, 1962.

"I think it's terrible": *Banner,* July 17, 1962; see also July 13, 1962.

"was indicted": Ibid., July 23, 1962.

"dissatisfied with Ellington . . . to repudiate Hoffa": Interview, Brainard Cheney, Feb. 11, 1975.

297 "showing Olgiati": *Banner,* July 23, 1962.

"was arrested": *Tennessean,* July 27, 1962; *Banner,* July 26, 1962.

"Wayne Whitt": *Tennessean,* July 28, 1962; the *Banner,* Aug. 1, 1962, notes Whitt's prediction of a Clement win, in an article in the *Washington Post.* Fred Travis also predicted the Clement victory; *Banner,* July 20, 1962.

"he would support Clement": *Banner,* July 19, 1962. Letter, Noble Caudill to Estes Kefauver, July 23, 1962 (Kefauver papers).

"he did not do so": *Tennessean,* May 31, July 28, 1962.

"from the beginning": Browning was on hand for Farris' opening; he could never forgive Olgiati for having been tied to Clement in the past.

"George Dempster . . . Eugene Joyce": *Tennessean,* July 28, 1962; see also *Banner,* Aug. 1, 1962.

"a comprehensive attack": *Tennessean,* Aug. 1, 1962.

299 "reported the nomination": Ibid., Aug. 3, 1962.

"coming up fast": Ibid., Aug. 2, 1962. Also, *Tennessean,* P, July 26, 1962.

"had appeared to see-saw . . . he maintained": *Tennessean,* Aug. 3, 1962.

"he ran behind . . . final official tally": Hassler, *Primary Elections,* 14, 15. See also *Banner,* Aug. 3, 1962. See Hopkins and Lyons, 322–23.

300 "Joe Hatcher noted": *Tennessean,* P, Aug. 3, 1962.

300 "was tended . . . a belated admission": Ibid.
"read the editorial": *Tennessean,* Aug. 3, 1962.
301 "William Anderson": Ibid., Oct. 7, 1962.
"considered a possibility": *Banner,* June 2, Aug. 15, 1962.
"authentic hero . . . in 1957": *Tennessean,* Oct. 7, 1962.
"by courtesy . . . then trotted out": Ibid.
"managed to secure": On the early returns, see ibid., Nov. 7, 1962;
Hassler, *Fifty Years of Tennessee Elections 1916–1966* (n.d., n.p.),
hereafter cited as Hassler, Elections, 12; *Banner,* Nov. 7, 1962. Anderson subsequently ran for the House of Representatives; see *Tennessean,* P, March 2, 1964. See Hopkins and Lyons, 324–25.
"a token campaign": *Banner,* Nov. 5, 1962.
"had tried to withdraw": *Banner,* CH, Oct. 16, 1962.

CHAPTER 11.

303 "certain key figures": Interview, Joseph Johnson, Aug. 16, 1977.
"administrative assistant": *Banner,* Nov. 29, 1962.
"McMurray College": Bio-data (Family Letters); interview, Anna
Belle O'Brien, March 25, 1975; *Banner,* Nov. 29, 1962.
"had placed": Records, Division of Continuing Education, UT
(Speaking Contests).
"gone to work": Interview, Anna Belle O'Brien, March 25, 1975.
"Tire and Sugar Rationing Board": Bio-data (Family Letters).
304 "Ellington's secretary": Interview, Anna Belle O'Brien, May 5, 1975;
Banner, Nov. 29, 1962.
"Davidson County Women's Club . . . Democratic Committee":
Bio-data (Family Letters).
"accidental loss": Interview, Anna Belle O'Brien, March 25, 1975.
"remained on good terms . . . little or no criticism": Ibid., May 5,
1975.
"Eddie Jones": *Banner,* Jan. 4, 1963.
"Butler did not want the job . . . some time in Washington": Interview, Edward F. Jones, June 29, 1977.
"worked for Clement . . . guidelines were adopted": Ibid.
305 "principal persons . . . Noble Caudill": Ibid.; interview, Anna Belle
O'Brien, Oct. 26, 1978.
"personal advisor . . . under a consulting contract": *Banner,* CH, Jan.
9, 1963.
"personal secretary": Interview, Edward F. Jones, June 29, 1977; interview, Mary Smith, Oct. 19, 1978.
"did worry him some . . . trying to think up questions": Interview,
Jones, ibid. See, e.g., preparation for question session in file-

305   Reapportionment, and other notes for press conferences in file-Newspaper Relations.

"Bill Kovach . . . Dana Ford Thomas": Interview, Jones, ibid.

"discombobulated Thomas": Ibid.

"once more demonstrated": *Tennessean,* Nov. 13, 1962.

"James Alexander": Ibid., Jan. 2, 1963.

307   "did not meet often": Interview, Joseph Johnson, Aug. 16, 1977; interview, Roy Nicks, May 6, 1976.

"came more slowly": *Banner,* CH, Dec. 24, 1962.

"candidates": For a list of such candidates, file (D) (Cabinet appointments). E.g., letters, Moreau P. Estes to FGC, Aug. 2, 1962; Harlan Dodson, Aug. 10, 1962; Clyde M. York to FGC, Aug. 22, 1962; Herbert Walters to FGC, n.d.; Clyde M. York to FGC, Aug. 23, 1962; James E. Edwards to FGC, Aug. 27, 1962; Andrew T. Taylor to FGC, Sept. 21, 1962; Reagor Motlow to FGC, Nov. 2, 1962; Herbert Walters to FGC, Nov. 30, 1962; Thomas Wardlow Steele to FGC, Dec. 13, 1962, All in (D) (Cabinet Appointments). Clement had to turn down a number of significant figures; interview, David Pack, Feb. 28, 1978.

"Hutcheson . . . Baker": Cf. interview, Joseph Johnson, Aug. 16, 1977. *Tennessean,* Dec. 1, 1962.

"Joe Johnson": Interview, Johnson, ibid.

"Howard Warf": *Banner,* Dec. 18, 1962; *Tennessean,* Dec. 28, 1962.

"opposition from educators": Ibid., P, Nov. 16, 1962; news stories, Jan. 4, 5, 1963.

"had wanted a cabinet post": Ibid., P, Nov. 16, 1962; news story, Dec. 19, 1962; letter, Carlton Scruggs, Jr. to FGC, Aug. 21, 1958 (Cabinet Appointments).

"had continued to work": *Tennessean,* Nov. 16, Dec. 19, 1962; interview, Anna Belle O'Brien, Oct. 26, 1978.

"actually appointed Warf": *Tennessean,* Aug. 4, Nov. 13, Dec. 28, 1962; *Banner,* Dec. 27, 1962.

"a line of succession": Quill Cope, e.g., became president of MTSU.

"to take the presidency": *Tennessean,* Nov. 13, 1962.

"Moss remained": *Banner,* Dec. 18, 1962; *Tennessean,* Dec. 19, 1962.

"Keith Hampton": *Banner,* Jan. 5, 1962.

"most political of politicians": Interview, Joseph Johnson, Aug. 16, 1977. Olgiati and Farris had slated Hampton for discharge; *Tennessean,* Aug. 4, 1963.

308   "safety commissioner . . . grown tired of Revenue": *Banner,* Jan. 7, 1963; *Tennessean,* Aug. 4, Dec. 19, 1962.

"member of the Assembly": *Banner,* Jan. 11, 1963.

"constitutional convention of 1953": Ibid.

308 "Board of Fire Underwriters": Ibid.

"saw as an area of failure": Interview, Joseph Johnson, Aug. 16, 1977. See *Governor's Penal Institutions Improvement Commission,* Report, Dec. 1, 1954, especially p. 44, and Legislative Council Committee, *Penal System Study,* Nov. 15, 1960. Dr. W.B. Jones of UT was the principal researcher and writer of both these studies.

"did not realize": Interview, Joseph Johnson, Aug. 16, 1977.

"commissioner of welfare": *Tennessean,* Jan. 15, 1963; interview, Noble Caudill, Jan. 22, 1975. David Pack became commissioner of highways; interview, Pack, Feb. 28, 1978.

"Roy Nicks": Interview, Noble Caudill, Jan. 22, 1975. See *Banner,* Aug. 2, 1963; interview, Roy Nicks, May 6, 1976.

"backed James Bomar . . . W.L. Barry": *Tennessean,* P, Nov. 13, news story, ibid., Nov. 14, Dec. 8, 1962. See *Banner,* Jan. 7, 1963.

"floor leader": Interview, W.L. Barry, Nov. 2, 1977.

"A protegé": *Tennessean,* Dec. 8, 1962; interview, Barry, ibid.

"Alan O'Brien": *Tennessean,* Nov. 13, 1962, Jan. 7, 1963; interview, Barry, ibid.

"had not been . . . never became": Interview, Barry, ibid.

"floor leader": Interview, David Givens, Sept. 27, 1977; *Tennessean,* Jan. 7, 1963.

"career in 1956 . . . of 1967": Interview, ibid.

309 "floor leader in 1963": Ibid.; *Tennessean,* Jan. 7, 1963.

"morning meetings . . . being considered": Interview, Givens, ibid.

"appeared before a joint session": *Tennessean,* P, Jan. 11, 1963; *House Journal,* 1963, pp. 51–60.

"plagued with low morale": *House Journal,* 1963, p. 54.

"not all was well": Ibid., 55.

"prophetically": Ibid., 60.

"rug-chewing evangelistic style": *Tennessean,* Jan. 15, 1963.

"Joe Henry": Interview, Joe Henry, Sept. 30, 1975.

310 "landing dock of a fool's paradise": *Tennessean,* Jan. 16, 1963; *House Journal,* 1963, pp. 71–73.

"L&N Railroad": Ibid., Nov. 18, 1962.

"insupportable": Interview, Andrew Holt, July 9, 1976.

"undercurrent of opposition": The *Tennessean* gave publicity to the dissension between Clement and Ellington; see *Tennessean,* March 7, 8, 1964; ibid., P, March 11, 1964. Also interview, W.L. Barry, Nov. 2, 1977.

"it set a record . . . comments made by legislators": *Tennessean,* Jan. 23, 1963.

"area vocational and technical schools": *Senate Journal,* 1963, p. 79.

"Industrial Research Advisory Service": UT administrators had been

310 much concerned that the institution do all it could to support industrial research, partly because it felt the necessity for convincing the legislature that UT had the welfare of the state in mind. The structure of the Advisory Service was developed by a faculty committee headed by the author, but whether that structure was appropriate to the problems of industrial research was dubious in his mind then — and continued to be so. For the governor's proposal, see *Senate Journal*, 1963, p. 79.

312 "Aerospace Engineering Institute": Ibid., 80.

"$900 for each teacher": Ibid., 81.

"a sour note": Ibid.

"highways": Ibid., 86-87.

"welfare check": Ibid., 88.

"highway patrolmen": Ibid., 84.

"share in the upgrading": Ibid., 84-86.

"an expansion": Ibid., 90-91.

"reconsider the death penalty . . . of six of them": Ibid., 89-90. In his first two terms, six men had been executed; two death sentences were commuted; *Banner*, Jan. 19, 1963.

"executive secretary of the Supreme Court": *Senate Journal*, 1963, p. 92. Clement's proposals for the judiciary had been forecast in a speech to the Nashville Bar Association in Dec. 1962; *Banner*, Dec. 8, 1962.

"Uniform Commercial Code": *Senate Journal*, 1963, p. 92.

"law revision commission": Ibid.

313 "showed details of the budget": Interview, Edward F. Jones, June 29, 1977.

"asked him for support . . . had to return to Jones": Ibid.

"ways of paying": See *Tennessean*, Jan. 22, 1963.

"Secretary, Mary Smith": *Senate Journal*, 1963, p. 118.

"a broadened base . . . motor vehicle license plates": Ibid., 118-121; *House Journal*, 1963, pp. 125-27; cf. *Tennessean*, Jan. 30, 1963; *Banner*, Jan. 29, 1963.

314 "high taxes tag": *Tennessean*, Feb. 1, 1963; also cartoon, ibid., Feb. 5, 1963; and editorials, ibid., Jan. 30, Feb. 6, 1963. The *Tennessean* said Clement sawed off his shotgun so as to scatter his tax shot as widely as possible.

"in a checked suit": E.g., cartoon in the *Tennessean*, Feb. 18, 1963. See also ibid., Feb. 5, 1963.

"close friends": Letter, Joe L. Williams to FGC, Dec. 5, 1964 (1964 Campaign).

"official position against": Ibid., Jan. 30, 1963; the Tennessee Valley Public Power Association also opposed the tax; ibid., Feb. 2, 1963.

314 "assayed a futile move": *Banner,* Feb. 5, 1963; *Tennessean,* Jan. 30, Feb.
       6, 1963.
     "Clement strategy": *Tennessean,* Feb. 13, 1963.
316 "applied vigorously": *Tennessean,* P, Feb. 13, 1963.
     "no opposition appeared": *Tennessean,* Feb. 6, 1963.
     "33 to 0 . . . with like unanimity": *Senate Journal,* 1963, p. 196.
     "95 to nothing": *Banner,* Feb. 14, 1963. Final passage occurred on Feb.
       21, 1963; the legislation is *Public Acts,* 1963, ch. 39.
     "93 to 3": *Banner,* Feb. 21, 1963; *Public Acts,* 1963, ch. 41.
     "dramatic confrontation": Interviews, William Snodgrass, Feb. 11,
       1975; Harlan Mathews, Feb. 2, 1975; W.L. Barry, Nov. 2, 1975.
     "stormed the legislative chambers": *Tennessean,* P, Feb. 13, 1963. Also
       interview, Joe Mynatt, Oct. 2, 1975.
     "said Joe Hatcher": *Tennessean,* P, Feb. 13, 1963.
     "was delayed for a week": *Tennessean,* Feb. 14, 1963; *Banner,* Feb. 13,
       1963.
     "the House comfortably": *Banner,* Feb. 21, 1963; *House Journal,* 1963,
       pp. 281ff.
317 "from the metropolitan counties": *Banner,* Feb. 21, 1963.
     "John Peay . . . Louis Pride . . . M.T. Puckett": Ibid.; *House Journal,*
       1963, pp. 281ff.
     "firmly laid to rest": *Banner,* Feb. 21, 1963.
     "Republican Henderson County": Interview, W.L. Barry, Nov. 2,
       1977.
     "his judgment": Interview, James Cummings, Nov. 4, 1974.
     "stir up Willie": Speech in the files of Edward F. Jones.
     "resisted attempts . . . he refused": Letter, FGC to Mrs. C.P. Kelly,
       League of Women Voters, Chattanooga, July 16, 1952 (Campaign
       1952). Also letter, T. Robert Acklen to FGC, May 2, 1956 (Legisla-
       tive Relations); press release, Jan. 14, 1964 (Reapportionment).
     "was voted down": See letter, Maclin P. Davis to FGC, April 30, 1956
       (Reapportionment).
318 "held the legislative apportionment . . . overruled by the state Su-
       preme Court": See Greene, Grubbs, Hobday, 81–86; *Kidd* v. *Mc-*
       Canless, 200 Tenn. 273 (1956).
     "no judicial remedy . . . For a history of this case, see Richard E.
       Cortner, *The Apportionment Cases* (Knoxville: Univ. of Tennessee
       Press, 1970).
     "the call of a constitutional convention": Greene et al., 85.
     "a crazy quilt": *Knoxville News-Sentinel,* June 23, 1962, quoted in ibid.
     "1963 session failed": Cf. *Tennessean,* March 4, 19, 1963; ibid., P and
       news story, March 20, 1963.
     "on the basis of population": *Reynolds* v. *Sims,* 377 U.S. 533 (1964).

318 "in June, 1964": Greene et al., 85; *Banner,* June 27, 1964; *Tennessean,*
June 29, 1964.

"a special session": Clement had held off calling such a session in 1964;
press release, Jan. 14, 1964 (Reapportionment).

"business spokesmen": Letter, Neely B. Cobble to FGC, April 9, 1965
(Reapportionment).

"on May 28, 1965": *Public Acts,* First Extra Session, 1965, p. 32.

319 "agonizing appraisal": *Banner,* Jan. 19, 1963.

"was halted for some twenty years": Greene, et al., 120.

"maintained the sentence": See remarks of Charles Galbreath on governor's role in maintaining the sentence; *Tennessean,* March 8, 1963.

"he could not agree . . . to vote his convictions": Interview, David
Givens, Sept. 27, 1977.

"to abolish the penalty": See *Tennessean,* March 8, 1963.

"60 to 29": Ibid., March 21, 1963.

"four men sat on death row . . . stays of execution": Ibid., March 27,
1963.

"unconstitutional legislature": See *State ex rel. Dawson* v. *Bomar* (1962),
209 Tenn. 567; *Dawson* v. *Bomar* (1963) 322 Fed. 2d 445; cert.
denied (1964) 376 U.S. 933.

"would obey his oath": Clement finally commuted the death sentences of five persons to 99 years.

"Research assistants": *Public Acts,* 1963, ch. 82.

320 "Administration of Justice": Ibid., ch. 83.

"were raised": Ibid., ch. 85.

"Executive Secretary": Ibid., ch. 86.

"Law Revision Commission": Ibid., ch. 74.

"retirement system": Ibid., ch. 206.

"Uniform Commercial Code": Ibid., ch. 81.

"Police Training Institute": Ibid., ch. 173.

"Alcoholism Commission": Ibid., 52.

"re-education center": Ibid., ch. 55.

"vocational-technical schools": Ibid., ch. 229.

"to report to him": Ibid., ch. 88.

"to inspect and examine books": Ibid., ch. 94.

"summon witnesses": Ibid., ch. 128.

"to conduct audits": Ibid., ch. 93.

"Office of Local Government": Ibid., ch. 205.

"was authorized": Ibid., ch. 100. *Banner,* March 19, 1963. Clement
worked to get federal aid for the Space Institute; *Tennessean,* June
19, 1963.

"A student loan scheme": *Public Acts,* 1963, ch. 227. The scheme went
into operation in August; *Banner,* Aug. 2, 1963.

320 "Industry-Government-Law Center": *Public Acts,* 1963, ch. 207.
   "educational television": Ibid., ch. 168.
   "now lifted East Tennessee State College": Ibid., ch. 67.
   "highly doubtful whether the idea came from the governor"; The
      project came, in the author's opinion, from Snodgrass, Robert
      Hutcheson, and Howard Bozeman.
   "Staff Division for Industrial Development": *Public Acts,* 1963, ch.
      169.
321 "authorized them": Ibid., ch. 329, see *Tennessean,* March 21, 1963.
   "Bingham had persuaded": Interview, Herbert Bingham, Oct. 9,
      1974.
   "this time the truckers lost": *Tennessean,* March 7, 1963.
   "repeal the price-fixing": Ibid., March 12, 1963.
   "run-off": Ibid., March 15, 1963.
   "Good riddance": *Tennessean,* P, March 22, 1963.
   "in sour words": *Knoxville News-Sentinel,* March 24, 1963.
   "continued deterioration": Quoted in *Tennessean,* P, March 26, 1963.
   "handmaiden of the governor . . . united in their poor view": Ibid.
   "sixteen members . . . members of the Legislative Council": *Tennes-
      sean,* March 24, July 12, 1963. Also letters, Grover R. Rann to FGC,
      Sept. 14, 21, 1964; Ray R. Baird to FGC, Nov. 20, 1964 (all in Legis-
      lative Relations).
322 "the Legislative Council was abolished": The Council dissolved itself
      in 1977.
   "was defeated for mayor": *Tennessean,* March 13, 1963.
   "for the second time": Ibid., May 7, 1963.
   "continued through 1963": *Tennessean,* P, July 2, 7, 1963.
   "A city election in Memphis": *Tennessean,* Nov. 12, 1963.
323 "public facilities": E.g., actions in Nashville; *Banner,* May 13, 14,
      1963; *Tennessean,* June 11, 1963.
   "marches and sit-ins": E.g., *Tennessean,* May 2, 1965.
   "majority of Nashville hotels": Ibid., June 11, 1963.
   "had desegregated in 1962": *Southern School News,* Jan. 1963, p. 5.
   "were dissatisfied": E.g., ibid., Oct. 1962, p. 4; March 1963, p. 3.
   "Putnam": Ibid., Feb. 1963, p. 7.
   "White, Overton, and Clay": Ibid., Aug. 1963, p. 8; Dec. 1963, p. 1.
      Voluntary desegregation occurred in other districts around the
      state; ibid., Sept. 1963, p. 16; April 1964, p. 6.
   "School for the Blind": Ibid., Jan. 1963, p. 5.
   "pace of school desegregation": See various issues of *Southern School
      News,* 1963. But Tennessee was moving faster than most of its
      neighbors; ibid., May 1964, p. 3-B.
   "commission on human relations": The executive order creating the

323 commission was dated Sept. 30, 1963; see also letter of Anna Belle Clement to A.W. Willis, Oct. 1, 1963 (Negroes I). The commission was not activated until Jan. 1, 1964; compare *Southern School News,* Jan. 1964, p. 1; Feb. 1964, p. 5. See also press release of that date (Negroes I). The establishment of the commission had been under consideration in earlier years; letters, Glen Nicely to Rabbi William B. Silverman, April 4, 1956; Edward F. Jones to Margaret C. McCulloch, July 10, 1963; A.W. Willis, Jr. to FGC, Sept. 6, 1963. An early version of the commission order is found in the Clement files dated May, 1963. Clement had resisted the proposal for a commission in earlier years; letter, FGC to Mrs. Clifton Rogers, Oct. 16, 1956. (All in Negroes, I.)

"but vague": *Southern School News,* Jan. 1964, p. 15.

"did not always agree": Memorandum, Noble C. Caudill to FGC, June 7, 1965 (Negroes II).

324 "Harlan Mathews": For membership of the commission, see *Southern School News,* Jan. 1964. See also lists of members in file-Negroes I.

"took a public position": Letters, Sam R. Dodson, Jr. to FGC, March 24, 1964; FGC to James W. Cassell, March 31, 1964 (Negroes I).

"code of fair practices": See *Tennessean,* May 15, 1964. For comments on the proposed code, memorandum, Mrs. C. Frank Scott to Col. Billy Shoulders, May 14, 1964 (Negroes I); see also minutes of Commission on Human Relations in file-Negroes I.

"asked the governor": Minutes of the Commission on Human Relations; see also *Tennessean,* April 26, 1964.

"to have been ambivalent": Clement asked various people for views on the civil rights issue; e.g., Edward Boling to FGC, May 20, 1964 (Negroes I); interview, Edward F. Jones, June 29, 1977. See various proposals in file-Negroes I.

"he refused to sign": *Tennessean,* May 15, June 18, 1964.

"by prison trouble . . . juvenile detention institutions": See *Banner,* May 23, 1963; *Tennessean,* May 23, Oct. 29, 30, 1963.

"in the prison at Petros": *Banner,* Nov. 28, 1964.

325 "physical facilities . . . never found it possible": Interview, Joseph Johnson, Aug. 16, 1977. On patronage in the prisons, see file-Patronage-Prisons.

"In 1953 . . . By 1967": *Tennessee Statistical Abstract,* 1977, p. 490.

"In 1967": Ibid.

"a few blacks were included": List of delegates in file-1964 convention; see also *Tennessean,* April 3, 1964.

"saw an unusual opportunity": A group for a more independent legislature began to arise in 1964; John Peay and Cartter Patten were leaders in the movement; e.g., letters, Grover R. Raun to FGC,

325   Sept. 14, 21, 1964; Roy Baird to FGC, Nov. 20, 1964 (Legislative
       Relations).
       "to withdraw": *Banner,* May 26, 1964; *Tennessean,* May 26, 1964.
       There was talk that Bomar might run for governor; interview,
       W.L. Barry, Nov. 2, 1977.
       "the House post . . . M.T. Puckett": Interview, Barry, ibid. See also
       Tennessean, P, Dec. 11, 1964; *Tennessean,* Jan. 3, 1964. Letter, Wil-
       liam L. Barry to FGC, Nov. 20, 1964 (Legislative Relations). Barry
       conferred with Clement on committee appointments; letter, Wil-
       liam L. Barry to FGC, Nov. 23, 1964 (Legislative Relations).
       "according to the *Tennessean*": Jan. 3, 1965.
       "for some reason he delayed": Interview, W.L. Barry, Nov. 2, 1977.
       "Frank Gorrell": *Tennessean,* P, Nov. 10, Dec. 23, 1964; *Banner,* Jan. 4,
       1965.
326   "applied on behalf of Maddux": *Tennessean,* Jan. 3, 1965.
       "from twelve": *Banner,* Jan. 4, 1965.
       "twelve, plus O'Brien": *Tennessean,* Jan. 5, 1965.
       "Senator O'Brien disappeared": *Banner,* Jan. 4, 5, 1965; *Tennessean,*
       Jan. 5, 1965.
       "sided with Maddux": *Banner,* Jan. 4, 1965; *Tennessean,* Jan. 6, 1965.
       "Shelby delegation split": *Banner,* Jan. 4, 1965; *Tennessean,* Jan. 6,
       1965.
       "went with Gorrell": *Banner,* Jan. 4, 1965.
       "remained absent": Ibid., Jan. 4, 5, 1965; *Tennessean,* Jan. 6, 1965.
       Copy of letter, Charles O'Brien to Temporary Chairman Flippen,
       n.d. (Legislative Relations).
       "Talk of a compromise": *Tennessean,* Jan. 6, 1965; *Banner,* Jan. 6, 1965.
       "a deal with the Republicans": *Tennessean,* Jan. 13, 1965; also inter-
       view, W.L. Barry, Nov. 2, 1977. *Banner,* CH, Jan. 13, 14, 1965.
       "more places": *Tennessean,* March 20, 1965.
       "a minority position": Greene, Grubbs, Hobday, 54.
327   "a majority": The new arrangement became law by *Public Acts,* 1965,
       ch. 12. The act was passed on Jan. 28, 1965; see *Senate Journal,* 1965,
       p. 112; *House Journal,* 1965, p. 146. See *Banner,* CH, Jan. 26; ibid.,
       news, Jan. 28, 1965.
       "Maddux became the speaker": *Banner,* Jan. 12, 1965; *Senate Journal,*
       1965, pp. 20–22. Thank-you note, Maddux to FGC, Jan. 16, 1965
       (Legislative Relations).
       "Hobart Atkins . . . abstained": *Tennessean,* Jan. 13, 1965; *Senate Jour-
       nal,* 1965, p. 22.
       "be treated fairly": *Tennessean,* Jan. 16, 1965; *Senate Journal,* 1965,
       p. 22.
       "editorialized indignantly": *Tennessean,* Jan. 13, 1965.

327 "a Clement supporter": Interview, W.L. Barry, Nov. 2, 1977.

"some committee chairmanships": Gorrell became chairman of an important committee; *Banner,* Jan. 13, 14, 1965.

"record biennial budget": *Banner,* Jan. 27, 1965; *Tennessean,* Jan. 27, 1965.

"new minimum": *Tennessean,* Nov. 13, 1963; *Banner,* Jan. 27, 1965.

"vocational schools": *Banner,* Jan. 27, 1965.

"usual overwhelming celerity": *Tennessean,* Feb. 24, 25, 1965.

"indebtedness leaped": *Public Acts,* 1965, chs. 68, 69, 70, 71, 72.

328 "less attentive to legislative relations": Interview, W.L. Barry, Nov. 2, 1977.

"one last try": *Banner,* Feb. 9, 1965; *Tennessean,* March 18, 1965.

"removal of this terrible burden": *House Journal,* 1965, p. 937. Also the *Tennessean,* March 5, 11, 16, 18, 1965.

"48 to 47": *House Journal,* 1965, p. 1012.

"Speaker Barry . . . Ray Blanton": Ibid.

"commuted the sentences": *Knoxville News-Sentinel,* March 19, 1965; *Tennessean,* March 19, 1965. The last execution under Clement and Ellington was that of William Tines, Nov. 7, 1960; see *Tennessean,* April 22, 1962.

"four of these men": Letter, Robert F. Kronick to LSG, Sept. 1, 1978.

"he lost": *Tennessean,* March 20, 1965; also letter, Roy Nicks to Advisory Commission members, Department of Public Welfare, March 5, 1965 (Labor Problems); *Tennessean,* March 11, 20, 1965.

"Noble Caudill . . . Roy Nicks": Interview, W.L. Barry, Nov. 2, 1977.

"rural bloc": See *Tennessean,* March 11, 1965; also interview, Barry, ibid.

"vetoed it": *Banner,* March 8, 1965; *Tennessean,* March 10, 11, 1965; Caudill wrote Clement praising the veto, saying it would help him to get his public image improved; memorandum, Noble C. Caudill to FGC, March 9, 1965 (Negroes II).

"dairy bar . . . beer was available": *Tennessean,* March 20, 1965.

"proposed repeal": Ibid.

"lost another bid": *Banner,* March 2, 1965; *Tennessean,* March 5, 1965.

"provide primary run-offs": *Tennessean,* Feb. 25, 1965. Clement said he did not attempt to block a run-off; letters, FGC to J.T. Rainey, March 3, 1965, in reply to Rainey to FGC, Feb. 25, 1965 (Family letters).

"strip mining reclamation bill . . . automobile inspection": *Tennessean,* March 20, 1965.

"workmen's compensation": Ibid.

"weak lobbying registration act": Ibid.; *Public Acts,* 1965, ch. 187.

328 "Auto graveyards": *Tennessean,* March 20, 1965; *Public Acts,* 1965,
        ch. 197.

     "were crowned universities": *Tennessee Blue Book,* 1977–1978, p. 193;
        Public Acts, 1965, ch. 30.

329 "the process of creating": See *Tennessee Blue Book,* 1977–78, p. 195.

     "A.W. Willis": Scott, 195–98.

     "Said Charles Galbreath": *Tennessean,* March 20, 1965.

     "into special session": Ibid., Dec. 1, 1963; cf. letter, Walter Chandler
        to FGC, Jan. 6, 1965 (Reapportionment); memorandum, FGC to leg-
        islature, May 6, 1965 (Reapportionment); Proclamation (copy in
        file-Reapportionment).

     "Aunt Dockie Weems died": *Banner,* April 15, 1965.

     "his deep conviction": *Tennessean,* April 5, 1963.

     "showed a population variation": *Senate Journal, First Extraordinary
        Session,* 1965, pp. 52–53, 63–64.

     "Third": Letter, Paul R. Leitner to FGC, March 16, 1965 (Reappor-
        tionment).

     "the Fifth District": *Senate Journal, First Extraordinary Session,* 1965,
        p. 52.

330 "Henry County": *Tennessean,* May 28, 1965.

     "splitting off of the suburbs of Memphis": See *Senate Journal, First Ex-
        traordinary Session,* 1965, p. 52.

     "backing a minority plan": Ibid., 55–61.

     "by a majority": See press release in file-Reapportionment; also ques-
        tionnaire for press conference in this file.

     "passed a reapportionment . . . into districts": *Tennessean,* May 26,
        1965.

     "was invalidated": Ibid., May 17, 1966.

     "vainly opposed the steam roller": *Senate Journal, First Extraordinary
        Session,* 1965, p. 34.

     "Joe Hatcher saw": *Tennessean,* P, May 27, 1965.

     "Clement-Republican combine": Hatcher used this idea in early June
        1965 and in following issues.

     "three-judge federal court": *Tennessean,* Nov. 20, 1965; *Baker* v. *Clem-
        ent,* 247 F. Supp. 886 (1965).

     "eventually the court": *Baker* v. *Ellington,* 273 F. Supp. 174 (1967),
        overruling ch. 4, sec. 1, *Public Acts,* ex. sess., 1965.

331 "the same court . . . had approved": *Tennessean,* Nov. 16, 1965; *Baker*
        v. *Carr,* 247 F. Supp. 629 (1965).

     "cranked up the machinery": Greene, Grubbs, Hobday, 31; *Public
        Acts,* ex. sess., 1962, ch. 2.

     "convened in July 1965": Greene et al., 31; *The Journal and Debates of*

331   *the Constitutional Convention,* 1965, Introduction, v. Cf. letter, Clyde M. York to FGC, Dec. 2, 1963 (Reapportionment).

"counties could be split": Greene et al., 31. Proposal 3, *Journal and Debates,* Introduction, viii; Proposal 5, Introduction, viii. Cf. letter, John Walters to FGC, May 7, 1965 (Reapportionment). Also letters, Walter Chandler to FGC, May 8, 1965, and reply, May 14, 1965 (Reapportionment).

"approved this arrangement": Greene et al., 31.

"by some political observers": *Tennessean,* P, Aug. 5, 1965.

"to demands": Blacks began to make patronage demands; letters, Wilfred R. Warren to FGC, Oct. 25, 1962; Jim Alexander to Wilfred R. Warren, Nov. 1, 1962 (Negroes I).

"Blacks were included": *Tennessean,* April 3, 1964; list of delegates in file-1964 Convention.

332 "of black employment": Memorandum, Hampton to heads of departments and agencies, Oct. 21, 1963 (Negroes I). Also list for Employment Security in file-Negroes I. Memorandum, W.H. Parham to FGC, March 24, 1966: letter, M.A. Bryan to FGC, March 24, 1966; memorandum, Arnold Malone to FGC, May 3, 1966 (all in Negroes II).

"special assistant": Interview, Noble Caudill, Jan. 22, 1975.

"frequent memoranda": Memoranda, Noble Caudill to FGC, Jan. 6, April 7, June 1, 1965, July 18, 1966 (Negroes II). Clement was sympathetic to Caudill's views; interview, Roy Nicks, May 6, 1976.

"he wrote": Memorandum, Noble Caudill to FGC, April 7, 1965 (Negroes II).

"the highway patrol": Ibid. Also memorandum, Col. Elmer V. Craig to Eddie Jones, Sept. 23, 1965 (Negroes II).

"code of fair practices . . . greater state pressure": Undated resolution in file-Negroes II; Scott, 176.

"white officials seemed to agree . . . on some election commissions": Memorandum, Caudill to FGC, April 7, 1965 (Negroes II).

"he once wrote the governor": Memoranda, Caudill to FGC, June 8, 23, 1965; notes for items for Caudill to discuss with the governor, June 23, 1965 (Negroes II).

"a genuine sympathy": Also interview, Agnes Bird, Sept. 20, 1977. Memorandum, Noble C. Caudill to FGC, Oct. 19, 1965 (Negroes II); in this memorandum, Caudill worried about Ku Klux Klan activities and he supplied the governor with supporting data.

"Late in April, 1965 . . . probate and the criminal courts . . . supported Hooks . . . startling suggestion": Memorandum, Noble C. Caudill to FGC, April 20, 1965 (Negroes II).

334 "Reverend Hooks": Hooks' statement of his qualifications, letter,
Ben L. Hooks to FGC, May 5, 1965 (Negroes II).

"local tempest of short duration": E.g., letter, Joe Moody to FGC,
May 17, 1965 (Negroes II). See *Commercial Appeal* story in file-
Negroes II.

"in passing the examinations": Memorandum, Commissioner Hilton
Butler to FGC, Dec. 14, 1964 (Negroes I); also notes of office staff,
as well as of Mathews and Snodgrass, April 13, 1965 (Negroes II).

"business ventures": Notes of Caudill to discuss with governor, June
28, 1965. (Negroes II).

"draft boards": Memorandum, FGC, to Arnold Malone, Director, Selective Service, May 3, 1966 (Negroes II).

"demonstrations": Memorandum, Caudill to FGC, Aug. 2, 1965 (Negroes II).

"Haywood, Hardeman, and Tipton": Nicks was assigned the job of
investigating disturbances; memorandums, Roy S. Nicks to FGC,
April 8, 28, 1965; Caudill to FGC, April 29, Aug. 2, 1965 (Negroes
II). On registration and voting rights of blacks in Fayette and Haywood counties, see Steven F. Lawson, *Black Ballots: Voting Rights in
the South 1944–1969* (New York: Columbia Univ. Press, 1976),
228, 269, 410 n. 57. Also memorandum, Noble Caudill to FGC,
March 31, 1965 (Negroes II). Some details on black complaints in
West Tennessee are found in Scott, 139–43.

"restaurants": For information on attacks on blacks in restaurants,
statement by Rev. Fred L. Shuttleworth, Southern Conference
Educational Fund, May 1965, referring to Somerville (Negroes II);
also letter, Eileen Hanson, Hyde Park Lutheran Church of Chicago to FGC, May 3, 1965; also memorandum, John A. Dyer to FGC,
July 21, 1965, reporting on western counties (Negroes II).

"from outside the state": See, for example, telegram, James Farmer to
FGC, July 22, 1965 (Negroes, II); letter, Eileen Hansen to Clement,
supra.; Tennessean, Aug. 9, 1965.

"Some violence erupted": See memorandum, Caudill to FGC, Aug. 2,
1965; letter, James E. Smith, Tipton County CORE to John J. Doar,
Assistant Attorney General, U.S. Department of Justice, June 25,
1966; letter, Smith to FGC, asking for protection, June 25, 1966 (all
in Negroes II); see *Tennessean,* Aug. 7, 1965.

337 "conducted a referendum": Statement of the Murray, Ohio, Manufacturing Company to its shareholders, April 30, 1965 (Strikes). A
long feature on this strike was published in the *Tennessean,* April
25, 1965.

"The Teamsters lost . . . plant was closed": Statement, ibid.
(Strikes).

337 "called on Governor Clement": Telegrams, Harold Brown and William C. Powell to FGC, April 12, 13, 1965 (Strikes).

"to enter the town": Statements of FGC, April 17, May 11, 1965 (Strikes).

"was involved": George O'Rear; *Tennessean,* April 25, 1965.

"a man almost as huge": George O'Rear was a mere 6'3"; Ibid.

"was arrested": Ibid.

"would shortly be withdrawn": Press release, April 23, 1965 (Strikes). But troopers were back in early May after further Teamster violence; *Tennessean,* May 12, 1965. In July, the NLRB trial examiner held that the Teamsters did not represent a majority; ibid., July 9, 1965.

"business community": Letters, William A. Harwell to FGC, April 27, 1965; Vice Mayor William G. Powell to FGC, April 27, 1965; C.E. Fritschle (Kingsport Press) to FGC, April 29, 1965; R. Bates Brown, Sr. to FGC, April 29, 1965; Edwards S. Abernathy to FGC, April 29, 1965; Carl A. Steidtmann to FGC, April 30, 1965; E.C. Snoddy to FGC, April 30, 1965 (all in Strikes).

"labor unions": Telegram, Communications Workers, Local 3895 to FGC, April 23, 1965; Teamster Local 984 protested—telegrams, M.R. Holliday to FGC, April 22, 1965; Linton O'Brien, Tennessee Building and Construction Trade Council, April 18, 1965 (all in Strikes).

340 "insurance": *Tennessean,* Sept. 4, 10, 1965.

"including Joe Carr . . . a time-honored and defensible practice": Ibid., Sept. 4, 1965.

"deal with the tax structure . . . a disposition of the surplus": *Banner,* March 1, 1966. Cf. *Tennessean,* Jan. 12, 1964.

"from county to county": Greene, Grubbs, Hobday, 175–77.

"turned to the courts": *Banner,* Feb. 2, 15, 1956.

"won their cases": Ibid., Feb. 15, 1966.

"one more twist": Interview, Joe Mynatt, Nov. 2, 1975; interview, Noble Caudill, Jan. 22, 1975.

341 "Certainly Hooker thought": Statement made by Hooker to a group of UT faculty at which the author was present.

"consider a constitutional amendment": *Banner,* March 1, 1966; *Tennessean,* March 2, 7, 1966; *Senate Journal, Second Extraordinary Session, Eighty-Fourth General Assembly,* 1966, pp. 16–17.

"hike teacher pay . . . expand welfare . . . mental health programs": *Tennessean,* March 7, 16, 1966; *Senate Journal,* ibid., 21–32.

"baring his head to the tempest": *Senate Journal,* ibid., 27; *Tennessean,* March 16, 1966.

"teacher retirement": *Tennessean,* April 1, 1966.

341 "obtained $1.8 million": *Banner,* April 1, 1966.

"$4.1 million . . . $9 MILLION . . . $1.6 million . . . debt retirement . . . A loan fund": *Banner,* April 1, 1966.

"turned down the governor's request": *Tennessean,* March 30, 1966.

343 "to be a candidate": *Banner,* April 12, 1966.

"leap-frog government": *Tennessean,* April 13, 1966. See also *Banner,* April 21, 1966.

"riding still on the old organization": Ellington used this organization in 1966, while Clement was building a group of his own for the Senate campaign.

"approached him": Interview, Robert N. Clement, May 6, 1976.

"supported for years": Ellington had been for Johnson in 1960; interview, Fred Travis, Sept. 26, 1977.

"friends of Ellington": Interview, Andrew Holt, July 9, 1976. Mrs. Ellington found Johnson difficult; interview, Harlan Mathews, Feb. 2, 1975.

"a changed man": Interview, W.L. Barry, Nov. 2, 1977; interview, David Pack, Feb. 28, 1978.

"in August, 1966": Ellington's majority was much better than Clement's over Bass.

CHAPTER 12.

345 "he was dead . . . too late": Gorman, 369; *Banner,* Aug. 10, 1963.

"young people around Clement": Interview, Herbert Bingham, Oct. 9, 1974; see quotation from Joe Henry in *Banner,* Nov. 29, 1952.

346 "seriously considered": See *Tennessean,* P, Sept. 17, 1957.

"Kefauver and Gore . . . both worried": See letters, Earl S. Ailor to Gore, Dec. 2, 1957; Grover C. Stockton to Gore, Dec. 9, 1957; W.P. Cooper to Gore, Jan. 13, 1958; J.E. Burke to Gore, Jan. 21, 1958 (all in Gore papers).

"from some": Interview, Joe Henry, Sept. 30, 1975.

"was he close to the Kennedys": Clement had flirted with the Kennedy ambitions, but had no strong alliances there; he did have a liking for John Kennedy, interview, Anna Belle O'Brien, March 25, 1975.

"Nancy Kefauver was suggested": News story, *Tennessean,* Aug. 11, 1963ff.; editorial, Aug. 13, 1963. See also *Banner,* CH, Sept. 20, 1963. See letter, C.C. Haun to FGC, Aug. 18, 1963 (Corres.-Walters).

"Brothers . . . was mentioned": Letter, Delroy Williams to FGC, Aug. 21, 1963 (Corres-Walters).

"Noble Caudill": *Tennessean,* Aug. 11, 1963. See telegram, Cranston Pearce to FGC, Aug. 20, 1963 (Corres.-Walters).

346 "Sam Fleming": *Tennessean,* Aug. 15, 1963.

347 "the governor asked Mr. Walters": Interview, Edward F. Jones, June 29, 1977; also letter, FGC to Walters, Oct. 30, 1964 (Corres.-Walters).

"governor then proposed . . . Eddie Jones noticed . . . intercepted the reporter": Interview, Jones, ibid.

"close ties to the Republican powers": Buchanan and Bird, 47. For material on Walters' career, see *Banner,* Aug. 20, 1963.

"whatever sacrifice": Hatcher maintained that Clement pushed Walters aside; see *Tennessean,* P, April 9, 1964; see also *Tennessean,* April 28, 1964.

"was applauded by conservatives": Buchanan and Bird, 47. Letters, FGC to Jim McCord, Aug. 20, 1963; Robert L. Taylor to H.S. Walters, Aug. 20, 1963; Clyde M. York to FGC, Aug. 20, 1963; James L. Bomar to FGC, Aug. 21, 1963; Jared Maddux to Walters, Aug. 23, 1963 (all in Corres.-Walters).

"*Tennessean* cartoon": *Tennessean,* Aug. 20, 1963.

"the cartoonist showed": Ibid., August, 21, 1963.

"Frank Ahlgren": Letter, Frank Ahlgren to FGC, Dec. 16, 1963 (1964 Campaign). See also *Banner,* CH, Aug. 13, 1963.

"Milton M. Bullard": *Tennessean,* Jan. 11, 1964. See also *Banner,* Aug. 30, Dec. 18, 1963, Jan. 9, 1964.

348 "he decided against": *Tennessean,* Dec. 27, 1963; *Tennessean,* P, March 24, 1964; *Banner,* Jan. 17, March 23, 1964.

"had an easy time": Buchanan and Bird, 69.

"was gathering steam": *Tennessean,* P, March 6, 1964; *Banner,* Dec. 20, 1963, Feb. 1, 17, 1964.

"Bullard and Bass": Buchanan and Bird, 49; also *Banner,* Jan. 11, 1964; cf. *Banner,* CH, Feb. 18, March 4, 1964; *Banner,* April 16, 1964.

"could not get him to withdraw": Buchanan and Bird, 49.

"George Dempster . . . Edward Ward Carmack": Ibid., 49, 52; *Banner,* April 23, 1964.

"Gordon Browning": Buchanan and Bird, 49; *Banner,* CH, Feb. 18, 1964.

"Lewis Pope": Buchanan and Bird, 49; *Banner,* April 23, June 16, 1964.

"finance his own campaign": Buchanan and Bird, 49, 50.

"'absenteeism'": *Tennessean,* July 23, 1964; *Banner,* June 23, July 22, 23, 1964.

"Clement's frequent trips": Ibid.

"tax issue": See *Tennessean,* May 13, 14, 15, July 18, 1964. Cf. letter, Mack Draper to Albert Gore, Feb. 10, 1955 (Gore papers). Clement defended his taxes in the campaign; *Tennessean,* July 12, 1964. Also, interview, Joseph Johnson, Aug. 16, 1977.

349 "friendly biographers": See Fontenay.

"even by their opponents": Very little public mention of Clement's problem surfaced; occasionally Browning mentioned it obliquely; *Tennessean,* May 22, 1962.

"state's low rank": Buchanan and Bird, 51.

"lag in interstate road construction": Ibid.

"state employees": E.g., *Tennessean,* May 24, 25, 31, 1964. The *Tennessean* quoted a contribution story in the *Press-Scimitar; Tennessean,* June 4, 1964. The new stories continued.

"black support": Clement black support is described in the *Banner,* June 22, July 15, 16, 1964.

"earned some credits . . . Willard Bowden": *Banner,* June 11, 1964; Scott, 186.

350 "Dr. Harold D. West": *Southern School News,* June 1963, p. 8; *Banner,* May 7, 1963.

"Southern Manifesto . . . appeared to back off": Buchanan and Bird, 48.

"as saying": *Banner,* Dec. 20, 1963.

"had been misquoted": Ibid.

"unequivocally for segregated schools": Ibid.

"*Banner* said": *Banner,* CH, Feb. 17, 1964.

"had taken control": *Tennessean,* Aug. 26, Sept. 12, 1963.

"he dove in": *Banner,* Feb. 17, 1964; ibid., CH, Feb. 18, 1964.

"Sam Neal . . . John J. Hooker": Ibid., Feb. 18, 1964.

351 "Barret Ashley . . . Gordon Browning": Ibid.; *Banner,* May 29, 1964; Buchanan and Bird, 49.

"Bruce Shine": *Banner,* CH, March 24, 1964.

"Tennessee Federation of Democratic Leagues": Ibid., May 4, 1964.

"called for his candidacy": *Banner,* May 15, 16, 1964; ibid., CH, May 18, 1964.

"three Grand Divisions": *Banner,* CH, May 21, 22, 28, June 1, 3, 9, 1964.

"at Shelbyville": *Banner,* June 6, 1964.

"at Woodbury": Ibid., June 13, 1964.

"announced formally": Ibid., May 13, 1964.

"in Gallatin": Ibid., June 20, 1964.

"with Kefauver": Ibid., June 6, 1964.

"got heavy attention": *Tennessean,* June 7, 1964; *Banner,* June 6, 1964.

"anti-TVA": *Banner,* June 6, 1964; *Tennessean,* June 13, 21, 1964.

"do-nothing attitude on education . . . cut in foreign aid": *Banner,* June 6, 1964.

"Bullard's opener": Ibid., June 13, 1964.

352 "Bass was given a black mark": Ibid.; also *Banner,* CH, June 17, 1964.

352 "it would be passed . . . cruelly shaken loose": *Banner,* June 13, 1964.
"June 20th opener": *Tennessean,* June 20, 1964.
"the Colonel and the Congressman": Ibid., June 21, 1964; *Banner,*
June 20, 1964.
"three had been passed": *Banner,* June 20, 1964.
"not a single national guard bayonet": Ibid.

354 "James Alexander": *Tennessean,* June 2, 1964. Buchanan and Bird, 53.
"had funds collected": Buchanan and Bird, 61–69.
"from $250,000 to $650,000": Ibid., 58.
"a quarter of a million": Interviews, Glen Nicely, Aug. 24, 1977;
Agnes Bird, Sept. 20, 1977.
"labor put more than $50,000": Buchanan and Bird, 59.
"the report was denied": Ibid., 59–60.
"came in third": Bullard was far behind.

355 "was a sore point": Gore, Walters, Bullard, among others. See, e.g.,
Banner, April 29, June 11, 13, 1964. See also Bullard attack on Bass;
Banner, CH, June 17, 26, July 4, 5, 1964.
"House version": Buchanan and Bird, 51.
"did not play up": *Banner,* June 24, July 3, 21, 1964.
"both took exceptions": Ibid., April 10, 25, 1964.
"jury trial in contempt proceedings": Buchanan and Bird, 52.
"advisors . . . academic leaders": Replies, e.g., of Edward J. Boling,
May 20, 1964, and Noble Caudill, April 13, 1964 (Negroes I).
"a slow and cautious advance": Boling's letter, e.g. Also proposals by
Bowden, Douglas Fisher, Andrew Holt (prepared for Holt by Dr.
Robert S. Avery), Ben Grove (Negroes II).
"criticized Bass": *Banner,* July 1, 21, 1964.
"refused to sign": See Buchanan and Bird, 55; *Banner,* June 18, 1964.
"owed much to the black vote": Interview, Agnes Bird, Sept. 20,
1977; Buchanan and Bird, 55.
"devastating blow": *Banner,* Aug. 7, 1964.

356 "'new experience for me'": Ibid.
"pledged support": Ibid.
"had become more aggressive": Ibid.
"precinct returns in metropolitan areas": Ibid.
"to remain governor": E.g., interview, Edward F. Jones, June 29,
1977.
"on the animosities": Eugene Collins thinks accumulated grievances
played a role. Interview, Collins, Sept. 18, 1975. Taxes hurt him;
letters, Dan M. Laws, Jr., to William H. Parham, Aug. 20, 1964,
and Paul C. Sims to FGC, Sept. 21, 1964 (1964 Campaign). Clement
was booed at the Kentucky-UT game, possibly because of taxes;
letter, Joe L. Williams to FGC, Dec. 5, 1964. John C. Hodges to

356 FGC, on Nov. 26, 1964, wrote a letter apologizing for the booing and praising him for his desegregation attitudes (all in 1964 Campaign). Bingham thought that the spread of the sales tax was the chief issue; the drinking also hurt; interview, Bingham, Oct. 9, 1974. W.L. Barry thought people wanted Clement to serve out his term as governor; interview, Barry, Nov. 2, 1977.

357 "easy-going primary campaign": Buchanan and Bird, 69; *Banner,* CH, Oct. 20, 1964.

"conservative direction": Buchanan and Bird, 69.

"voting against": *Banner,* April 29, 1964.

"was quarreling . . . did not work hard": Buchanan and Bird, 69.

"Senator Everett Dirksen": Ibid., 73. Mrs. Baker was Joy Dirksen.

"spend over a million dollars": Buchanan and Bird, 73.

"deserting the Democratic establishment": See Greene and Holmes, in Havard, 165–200.

358 "he wrote . . . to court the black vote": Memorandum, Caudill to FGC, April 6, 1965 (1966 Campaign).

"to rebuild": Interview, Anna Belle O'Brien, Oct. 26, 1978.

"Lon Varnell . . . Caudill": Letterhead of campaign organization. *Banner,* June 1, 7, 1966; interview, Roy Nicks, May 6, 1976.

"announced again": *Banner,* May 31, 1966.

"Roy Nicks his campaign coordinator": Ibid., June 1, 1966; interview, Roy Nicks, May 6, 1976.

"in the minds of some": Interview, Joseph Johnson, Aug. 26, 1977; Johnson thinks the organization in 1966 was not tight enough.

360 "a private study": Interview, Roy Nicks, May 6, 1976.

"less well educated": Nicks report.

"a quick temper": Interview, Agnes Bird, Sept. 20, 1977.

"I'm leaving": *Banner,* April 20, 1966.

" 'a few thousand words of exhortation' . . . noted the *News-Sentinel* . . . Bass not Amused. He Feels Abused": *Banner,* April 20, 1966.

"were split . . . Tennessee Voters' Council . . . were publicly critical": Ibid., April 6, 1966.

361 "Some of the dissenters": Ibid., April 21, 1966.

"became an Ellington manager": Ibid., May 6, 17, 1966.

"emphasized publicly his support": Ibid., June 25, Aug. 2, 1966.

"highway patrol uniform . . . Negro secretary": Ibid., Aug. 2, 1966.

"criminal court in Shelby County": Hooks took office in 1966. In a letter to FGC, Nov. 15, 1966, John McIntosh said Negro efforts paid off in Shelby (1966 Campaign).

"to the aged . . . low-income groups": *Banner,* June 25, 1966.

"tended to overlap Clement's": *Banner,* June 11, 1966; *Tennessean,* June 28, 1966.

361 "tax increases": E.g., see *Tennessean,* June 22, 1966.

"stayed clear": *Banner,* May 31, 1966. The Democratic organization was notably split up in this election; interview, Roy Nicks, May 6, 1976.

"his distance from Hooker": *Banner,* May 28, 1966; ibid., CH, June 13, 1966.

"short shrift": Senate campaign stories were often carried on the inside pages; the *Banner,* in the first part of July, gave little attention to Clement or Bass.

"probably spelled the end": Bass was later a rather obscure candidate for governor, and in 1979 he backed Senator Edward Kennedy for President.

"the majority narrow": Hassler, *Primary Elections,* 2; *Banner,* Aug. 19, 1966.

"from Republican crossovers": Ellington also benefitted from Republican votes; *Tennessean,* Aug. 5, 1966.

365 "mighty fine Senator": Telegrams, Hubert H. Humphrey to FGC, Aug. 5, 1966; reply, FGC to Humphrey, Aug. 8, 1966 (1966 Campaign).

"A fellow FBI agent": Letter, Stuart T. Nash to FGC, Aug. 8, 1966 (1966 Campaign).

"my friend and future colleague": Letters, Joe L. Evins to FGC, Aug. 16, 1966; and reply, Aug. 24, 1966 (1966 Campaign).

"dangerously low margin": Letter, Frank R. Goad to FGC, Aug. 13, 1966 (1966 Campaign).

"in interesting detail": Letter, J.E. Edwards to FGC, Aug. 19, 1966 (1966 Campaign).

366 "getting the vote out": Letter, ibid. Reply, FGC to Edwards, Aug. 23, 1966 (1966 Campaign).

"'Nancy Kefauver'": Letter, Nancy P. Kefauver to FGC, Aug. 27, 1966 (1966 Campaign).

"full support": Telegram, Albert Gore to FGC, Aug. 5, 1966 (1966 Campaign).

"supporting Clement": *Labor,* XLVIII, No. 4, Oct. 15, 1966; also letter, Ruben Levin to Edward Jones, Sept. 7, 1966 (1966 Campaign).

"was not forthcoming": E.g., the national COPE executive board was unfriendly; letter, Carl T. Moore to FGC, Sept. 15, 1966 (1966 Campaign).

"housing was troublesome": Interview, Edward F. Jones, June 29, 1977. Also letter, FGC to Elmo Mullins, Oct. 10, 1966 (1966 Campaign).

"the endorsement . . . he was opposed": *Tennessean,* Oct. 2, 1966.

367 "was unclear": Ibid. But at some points, Clement opposed repeal of

367   14-B; letters, FGC to O.W. Karcher, Oct. 3, 1966; FGC to Elmo
       Mullins, Oct. 10, 1966; also letters, Roy S. Nicks to Joe Worley,
       Oct. 24, 1966; Arthur H. Atwell to FGC, Aug. 19, 1966 (all in 1966
       Campaign). Clement received many letters asking for his stand on
       14-B.
       "they were not happy . . . refused endorsement": *Tennessean,* Oct. 2,
       1966.
       "Some observers": Gore, *Let the Glory Out,* 196–97.
       "late in October": *Banner,* Oct. 20, 1966.
       "Ross Bass stated": Ibid.; see also ibid., Oct. 26, 1966.
       "Gordon Browning": Ibid., Oct. 21, 1966.
       "a private talk": Interview, Edward F. Jones, June 29, 1977.
       "be discouraged": Letter, O.B. Hofstetter, Jr., to FGC, Sept. 2, 1966
       (1966 Campaign).
       "Archie Campbell": *Banner,* Sept. 23, 1966.
       "dodging the issues": Ibid., Oct. 14, 15, 1966.
       "federal revenue sharing": E.g., ibid., Sept. 23, Oct. 14, 1966.
368   "unity of purpose in Vietnam": Ibid., Sept. 23, 1966.
       "was as indecisive": Ibid., Oct. 5, 1966.
       "whole gamut . . . should have equal rights": See ibid.
       "in their private talks": Interview, Edward F. Jones, June 29, 1977.
       "to move toward": *Banner,* Oct. 13, 1966.
       "continuing decline": Interview, Robert N. Clement, May 6, 1976.
       "into the Clement vote": Hassler, *Elections,* 3.
369   "should have been content": Interview, Joe Henry, Sept. 30, 1975.
       "inevitable disappointments": Interview, Eugene Collins, Sept. 18,
       1975.
       "growing reaction to Johnson": Letters, John McIntosh to FGC, Nov.
       15, 1966; Leonard W. Edwards to FGC, Nov. 9, 1966; Judge C.S.
       Carney to FGC, Nov. 28, 1966; Thomas Motlow to FGC, Nov. 25,
       1966; E.O. Lyle, Sr., to FGC, Nov. 12, 1966 (all in file-1966 Cam-
       paign). See also *Tennessean,* editorial, Nov. 9, 1966.
       "definite Republican plan . . . about the plan": Interview, Fred Tra-
       vis, Sept. 26, 1977. Cf. interview, Robert N. Clement, May 6,
       1976.
       "had come to a close": He probably would have tried again, had death
       not intervened, but it is doubtful whether he would have been
       elected to any office.
       "he had been defeated . . . Bob agreed": Interview, Grant W. Smith,
       Oct. 18, 1978.
371   "gave it to Smith": Ibid. Clement could not believe in the possibility
       of defeat; interview, Roy Nicks, May 6, 1976.
       "condolence": E.g., letters, Eddy Arnold to FGC, Nov. 9, 1966; Dr.

371 Leonard W. Edwards to FGC, Nov. 9, 1966; E.O. Lyle to FGC, Nov. 12, 1966; James L. Bomar to FGC, Nov. 22, 1966; Mrs. R. Murray Hopper to FGC, Nov. 22, 1966; Judge C.S. Carney to FGC, Nov. 28, 1966; William C. Weaver, Jr. to FGC, Dec. 12, 1966; Judge John A. Mitchell to FGC, Nov. 10, 1966; Judge M.B. Finklestein to FGC, Dec. 7, 1966; telegram, Carl A. Jones to FGC, Nov. 9, 1966; letters, John S. Wilder to FGC, Nov. 17, 1966; Ross W. Dyer to FGC, Nov. 16, 1966; Commissioner Nat Winston to FGC, Nov. 14, 1966 (all in file-1966 Campaign).

"'to them all'": Letter, J.W. Lawson to FGC, Nov. 9, 1966 (1966 Campaign).

"Jared Maddux wrote": Maddux to FGC, Nov. 9, 1966 (Corres.-Maddux).

"a sharp exchange": Letter, Jared Maddux to Frank McGee, Nov. 10, 1966 (1966 Campaign).

"a conciliatory reply": Letter, Frank McGee to Jared Maddux, Nov. 18, 1966; copy sent to FGC by letter from Maddux, Nov. 22, 1966. Chet Huntley also quoted Tom Anderson; letter, Mrs. Thornton Taylor to FGC, Nov. 9, 1966 (all in 1966 Campaign).

372 "'through the years'": Letter, FGC to Jared Maddux, Nov. 16, 1966 (Corres.-Maddux).

"it is questionable": Cf. interview, Anna Belle O'Brien, Oct. 26, 1978.

"moments of deep despondency": Interview, Noble Caudill, Jan. 22, 1975.

CHAPTER 13.

373 "on Franklin Road": A diagram of the accident is contained in the *Tennessean,* Nov. 5, 1969. See Certificate of Death, Tennessee Department of Public Health, signed Nov. 17, 1969 by M.A. Petrone, M.D. (Birth, Death, Marriage Data).

"driving alone": *Tennessean,* Nov. 5, 1969.

"massive chest injuries": The death certificate gives immediate cause of death as intrathoracic hemorrhage as a consequence of laceration of heart. Grant Smith viewed Clement's body at General Hospital and said his face was crushed; interview, Grant W. Smith, Oct. 18, 1978.

"in Virginia": *Tennessean,* Nov. 6, 1969.

"were out of town . . . to General Hospital . . . David Alexander": Interview, David Alexander, Feb. 28, 1978.

"earlier in the year": The bill for the divorce was filed Feb. 21, 1969; an answer was filed March 21, 1969 (Circuit Court Clerk files,

373   Williamson County). The *Tennessean* noted the divorce action in a brief story on March 5, 1969; it stated no cause. According to the story, the supporting files had been withdrawn by mutual consent of the attorneys.

"was pending": Interview, David Alexander, Feb. 28, 1978. The suit was dismissed, following Clement's death, on Nov. 14, 1969 (Circuit Court Clerk files).

"that last day": Letter, Alexander to Herbert Walters, Nov. 10, 1969 (Walters).

"had invited . . . went to Clement's home": Interview, David Alexander, Feb. 28, 1978.

374   "a motel in Valdosta": Interview, Noble Caudill, Jan. 22, 1975.

"from Mary Smith": Interview, Grant W. Smith, Oct. 18, 1978.

"the practice of law": At his death, Clement left a taxable estate of $193,295.37, on which the gross estate tax was $48,668.61 (see files, County Court Clerk, Williamson County). The heirs were his widow and three sons. The Brentwood house went to his widow. The remainder of the property was principally in stocks and bonds.

"in the later Clement campaigns": Interview, Grant W. Smith, Oct. 18, 1978.

"he intended": Interview, Joe C. Carr, Sept. 16, 1975; letters, Noble C. Caudill to Herbert Walters, Nov. 8, 1969; Walters to Caudill, Nov. 11, 1969 (Walters).

"national convention of 1968": *Tennessean*, Aug. 27, 1968. He was replaced by alternate Herschel Greer.

"possible ambassador . . . president of Memphis State": Ibid., Nov. 5, 1969.

375   "benefit of credibility": Interview, James Cummings, Nov. 4, 1974; Boyd interviews, Leota Eubank, July 2, 1971, and Ira North, Aug. 12, 1971. Also letters, Brainard Cheney to Sen. Richard Russell, Nov. 4, 1954 (Corres.-Cheney); Cheney to Bruce, June 28, 1953 (JUL).

"a Godly man": Letter, Brainard Cheney to A. Lytle, Aug. 9, 1954 (JUL).

"continued attachment": Clement often referred to his religious feelings in letters to ministers; e.g., FGC to Rev. H.L. Carter, Aug. 30, 1954; Ellyn Warth to Mervin E. Rosell, May 11, 1953 (Corres.-Religious Figures).

376   "the core": Interviews, Joseph Johnson, Aug. 16, 1977; Valerius Sanford, Sept. 29, 1977; David Pack, Feb. 28, 1978; Roy Nicks, May 6, 1976.

"photographic memory": Interviews, Frank Goad, Aug. 20, 1976;

376 Harold Read, Nov. 25, 1974; W.L. Barry, Nov. 2, 1977; Harlan Mathews, Jan. 23, 1975.

"not literary or bookish": Barry thought he read more and was better educated than Ellington; interview, Barry, ibid. But Sanford said Clement was not idea-oriented, and not widely read; interview, Sanford, Sept. 29, 1977. One of Clement's teachers called him an avid reader; Boyd interview, with Mrs. Perry Baker, 1971. Clement's former secretary said he read less than he talked; read *Fortune, Wall Street Journal, Commercial Appeal, Banner,* and *Tennessean;* Boyd interview, with Leota Eubank, July 2, 1971. Anna Belle O'Brien said Clement liked to read history; interview, Anna Belle O'Brien, March 25, 1975.

"family attachments": Interview, Brainard Cheney, Feb. 11, 1975; interview, O'Brien, ibid.

"the strict discipline": Interview, O'Brien, ibid.

"to bear grudges": Interviews, Joseph Johnson, Aug. 16, 1977; Joe Henry, Sept. 30, 1975; Andrew D. Holt, July 9, 1976; O'Brien, ibid.; Douglas Fisher, June 28, 1977; Robert N. Clement, May 6, 1976.

377 "quiet courtesies": E.g., Clement and Ellington saw to it that Browning always had a patrol car at his disposal.

"have praised him": Interviews, Noble Caudill, Jan. 22, 1975; Harlan Mathews, Jan. 23, 1975.

"liked to delegate": Interviews, Joseph Johnson, Aug. 16, 1977; Mathews, ibid.; William Snodgrass, Feb. 11, 1975; Harold Read, Nov. 25, 1974. Anna Belle O'Brien thought her brother sometimes confided too much in others; interview, May 5, 1975.

"no great taste": Interviews, Mathews, Jan. 23, 1975, Feb. 2, 1975; Anna Belle O'Brien, Oct. 26, 1978; David Pack, Feb. 28, 1978.

"fiscal aides": Interview, William Snodgrass, Jan. 22, 1975. Memorandum, FGC to Edward J. Boling, March 28, 1955; Governor's Notes for Cabinet Meeting, Dec. 13, 1963 (Administrative Organization). Interview, Mathews, Feb. 2, 1975; interview, Pack, ibid.

"a cadre": Interview, Snodgrass, Feb. 11, 1975; interview, Mathews, Jan. 23, 1975.

"who enjoyed his company": Interview, Anna Belle O'Brien, May 5, 1975.

378 "candidly recognized": *Tennessean,* April 5, 1963.

"the advent of television": Cf. interviews, Dr. Ira North, Oct. 2, 1975; W.L. Barry, Nov. 2, 1977.

380 "35 percent": *Tennessee Statistical Abstract,* 1977, p. 210.

"36 thousand . . . 20 per cent . . . to 68 per cent": Ibid., 211.

"$5700": Ibid., 218.

380 "average spent per pupil": Ibid., 219.

"was 8.4 . . . was 10.6": Ibid., 222.

381 "attempts great and small": Clement rarely missed any chance to boost the state. Whenever he replied to letters from children outside the state, he would tell them to persuade their parents to visit the state.

"In 1950": *Tenn. Stat. Abs.,* 1977, p. 444.

"By 1967": Ibid.

"in 1970, 8 percent": Ibid., 6.

"45,000 . . . are recorded": Ibid., 468.

"in 1967": Ibid., 341.

"$229": Ibid., 345.

"162 percent": Ibid., 362.

382 "November 6 . . . small First United Methodist Church . . . Clement's lifetime were there . . . Amazing Grace": *Tennessean,* Nov. 7, 1969.

"Truck loads of flowers": Interview, Joe Mynatt, Oct. 2, 1975; *Tennessean,* Nov. 7, 1969.

"long line of cars": *Tennessean,* Nov. 7, 1969.

"borne by Legionnaires": Ibid.

383 "encircling arms": These words are borrowed from the inscription on the monument to Edward Carmack in front of the Capitol in Nashville.

Bibliography

NEWSPAPERS AND MAGAZINES

I have relied primarily on the *Nashville Banner* and the Nashville *Tennessean*, with some use of the *Chattanooga Times*. The *Dickson County Herald* was used for the short period that covered Clement's birth. I paid particular attention to the column named "Politics" by Joe Hatcher in the *Tennessean*, and the column named "Capitol Hill" in the *Banner* written by Leslie Hart and his successors. Occasional reference has been made to the *Commercial Appeal*, the *Knoxville News-Sentinel*, and to county or city weeklies. The monthly newspaper, *Southern School News*, specializing in race and segregation questions during its years of publication, was a highly useful source of information on events in Tennessee and its neighbors on racial matters, for the monthly contained details not readily available elsewhere, and its accounts could be relied on for accuracy and objectivity.

The newspapers supplied a day-by-day continuity that could not be acquired from the reading of the documents and letters. The columns supplied personal details that are often not contained in news stories—both entertaining and enlightening details that give the flavor of political maneuvering. They also offer interpretations and predictions, but neither the interpretations nor the predictions can be accepted without substantial reservations. The columnists are unabashedly biased, and only on rare occasions do they bother to admit the wild inaccuracy of some of their predictions. I thought this was particularly true of the late Joe Hatcher, who never—or so it seemed to me—was at all disturbed by the wide distance between some of his predictions and the subsequent turn of events. But, by combining two opposing columnists, it is possible to catch a glimmer of actuality, and the columnists do provide insights that do not emerge from documents.

The *Tennessean* was consistently anti-Clement, the *Banner* consistently pro-Clement. These positions must always be considered. When I have quoted newspaper opinion, I have identified the source and generally noted the bias of that source. My own judgments have been freely used and are, I believe, clearly marked.

Clement was made the subject of a number of magazine articles. Most of these are not especially illuminating. Some of them are at least partially muckraking in character. The governor's activities were noted in national news magazines from time to time, often with snide references to his religious beliefs or his evangelistic oratorical style.

BOOKS

Anderson, Margaret. *The Children of the South*. New York: Farrar, 1966.

Buchanan, William, and Agnes Bird. *Money As a Campaign Resource: Tennessee Democratic Senatorial Primaries, 1948–1964*. Citizens' Research Foundation Study, No. 10. Princeton, N.J.: Citizens' Research Foundation, 1966.

Cortner, Richard C. *The Apportionment Cases*. Knoxville: Univ. of Tennessee Press, 1971.

Fain, John Tyree, and Thomas Daniel Young, eds. *The Literary Correspondence of Donald Davidson and Allen Tate*. Athens: Univ. of Georgia Press, 1974.

Folmsbee, Stanley J., Robert E. Corlew, and Enoch L. Mitchell. *History of Tennessee*, 2 vols. New York: Lewis Historical Publishing Co., 1960.

————. *Tennessee, A Short History*. Knoxville: Univ. of Tennessee Press, 1969. 2d ed., 1981, by Corlew, incorporating revisions by Folmsbee and Mitchell.

Fontenay, Charles L. *Estes Kefauver: A Biography*. Knoxville: Univ. of Tennessee Press, 1980.

Goodman, William. *Inherited Domain: Political Parties in Tennessee*. Knoxville: Bureau of Public Administration, Univ. of Tennessee, 1954.

Gore, Albert. *The Eye of the Storm: A People's Politics for the Seventies*. New York: Herder and Herder, 1970.

————. *Let the Glory Out: My South and Its Politics*. New York: Viking, 1972.

Gorman, Joseph Bruce. *Kefauver: A Political Biography*. New York: Oxford Univ. Press, 1971.

Graham, Hugh Davis. *Crisis in Print: Desegregation and the Press in Tennessee*. Nashville: Vanderbilt Univ. Press, 1967.

Greene, Lee S., David H. Grubbs, and Victor C. Hobday. *Government in Tennessee*. Knoxville: Univ. of Tennessee Press, 1975, 1982.

Hill, Howard L. *The Herbert Walters Story*. Kingsport: Kingsport Press, 1963; rpt. Morristown: Morristown Printing Co., 1963.

Kennedy, Robert F. *The Enemy Within*. New York: Harper, 1960.

Key, V.O., Jr. *Southern Politics in State and Nation*. New York: Knopf, 1949.

Lee, David D. *Tennessee in Turmoil: Politics in the Volunteer State, 1920–1932*. Memphis: Memphis State Univ. Press, 1979.

Long, Herman H., and Vivian W. Henderson. *Negro Employment in Tennessee State Government: A Report from Nashville Community Conference on Employment Opportunity*. Nashville: Tennessee Council on Human Relations, 1962.

Miller, William D. *Mr. Crump of Memphis.* Baton Rouge: Louisiana State Univ. Press, 1964.

Scott, Mingo. *The Negro in Tennessee Politics and Governmental Affairs, 1865–1965.* Nashville: Rich Printing Co., 1965.

Thomson, Charles A.H., and Frances M. Shattuck. *The 1956 Presidential Campaign.* Washington: Brookings, 1960.

Tucker, David M. *Memphis Since Crump: Bossism, Blacks, and Civic Reformers, 1948–1968.* Knoxville: Univ. of Tennessee Press, 1980.

Wilson, Theodore Brantner. *The Black Codes of the South.* University: Univ. of Alabama Press, 1965.

Wright, William E. *Memphis Politics: A Study in Racial Bloc Voting.* New York: McGraw-Hill, 1962.

ARTICLES

Denney, Raymond W. "The Tennessee Constitutional Convention 1953." *Tennessee Law Review* 23, (1953), 15–23.

Ewing, Cortez A.M. "Early Tennessee Impeachments." *Tennessee Historical Quarterly* 16 (1957), 291–334.

Felsenthal, Edward. "Kenneth Douglas McKellar: The Rich Uncle of the T.V.A." *West Tennessee Historical Society Papers* 20 (1966), 108–22.

Greene, Lee S., and Jack E. Holmes. "Tennessee: A Politics of Peaceful Change" in William C. Havard, ed. *The Changing Politics of the South.* Baton Rouge: Louisiana State Univ. Press, 1972.

Kitchens, Allen H. "Political Upheavals in Tennessee: Boss Crump and the Senatorial Election of 1948." *West Tennessee Historical Society Papers,* 16 (1962), 104–26.

Kovach, Bill. "Racism Wasn't the Issue in Tennessee." *Reporter* (Sept. 24, 1964), 37–38.

Majors, William R. "Gordon Browning and Tennessee Politics, 1949–1953." *Tennessee Historical Quarterly* 28 (1969), 166–81.

Martin, Harold H. "The Things They Say about the Governor!" *Saturday Evening Post* (Jan. 29, 1955), 22–58.

Miller, William D. "The Browning-Crump Battle: The Crump Side." *East Tennessee Historical Society's Publications* 37 (1965), 77–88.

Parks, Norman L. "Tennessee Politics Since Kefauver and Reece: A 'Generalist' View." *Journal of Politics* 28 (Feb. 1966), 144–68.

Parmentel, N.E. "Tennessee Spellbinder." *Nation* (Aug. 11, 1956), 113–17.

Schreiber, F. "Frank Clement: Tennessee's Political Evangelist." *Coronet* (July 1956), 97–101.

Valien, Preston. "Expansion of Negro Suffrage in Tennessee." *Journal of Negro Education* 26 (1957), 362–68.

Walton, Brian G. "The Second Party System in Tennessee." *East Tennessee Historical Society's Publications* 43 (1971), 18–33.

DISSERTATIONS AND THESES

Bird, Agnes Thornton. "Resources Used in Tennessee Senatorial Primary Campaigns, 1948–1964." Diss., Univ. of Tennessee, 1967.

Boyd, Stephen D. "The Campaign Speaking of Frank Clement in the 1954 Democratic Primary: Field Study and Rhetorical Analysis." Diss., Univ. of Illinois, 1972.

Brittain, David James. "A Case Study of the Problems of Racial Integration in the Clinton, Tennessee High School." Diss., New York Univ., 1959.

Bronaugh, Mae M. "The Crump-Browning Political Feud — 1937–1938." Thesis, Memphis State Univ., 1959.

Davis, William L. "Corruption vs. Morality: A Rhetorical Analysis of the Campaign of Frank Goad Clement for Governor of Tennessee, 1952." Thesis, Wake Forest Univ., 1972.

Diamond, Michael Jerome. "The Negro and Organized Labor as Voting Blocs in Tennessee, 1960–64." Thesis, Univ. of Tennessee, 1965.

Gardner, James B. "Political Leadership in a Period of Transition: Frank G. Clement, Albert Gore, Estes Kefauver, and Tennessee Politics, 1948–1956." Diss., Vanderbilt Univ., 1978.

King, Roger Earl. "The Tennessee Legislative Council Committee: Reflection of Political Realities." Thesis, Middle Tennessee State Univ., 1968.

Locke, Jerry Ross. "The Politics of Legislative Reapportionment in Tennessee: 1962." Thesis, Univ. of Tennessee, 1963.

Majors, William R. "Gordon Browning and Tennessee Politics." Diss., Univ. of Georgia, 1967.

McCoy, William J. "The Tennessee Political System: The Relationship of the Socioeconomic Environment to Political Processes and Policy Outputs." Diss., Univ. of Tennessee, 1970.

Whitaker, John Ulna, Jr. "Influence of the Governors on Education in Tennessee, 1937–1957." Thesis, Univ. of Tennessee, 1958.

I wish to acknowledge in particular the assistance I have received from the studies of Dr. Boyd, Dr. Gardner, Dr. Majors, and Mr. Fontenay.

PUBLIC DOCUMENTS

I have used the *Public Acts of Tennessee* and the journals of the General Assembly extensively. The journals are a barebones account of the proceedings in the legislature, recording only actions and votes, no debates and no reports of committee hearings. The journals can be used to examine party and factional splits in the Assembly, but certain significant details (notably the names of the floor leaders in the two houses) are missing and can be secured only by inference or the use of interviews, newspaper accounts, and the like. Since 1952, the proceedings of the legislature have been taken down on audiograph disks that can be heard in the State Library and Archives; I have listened to some of these. I have made use of the *Tennessee Code Annotated* from time to time. The proceedings and debates of the periodic limited constitutional conventions of Tennessee that began in 1953 are available and have been used occasionally. I have examined in detail the proceedings relating to the impeachment and trial of Judge Raulston Schoolfield, both in typescript and as published.

CORRESPONDENCE FILES

Under my supervision, my assistants have examined the files of Clement correspondence and other papers in the State Library and Archives and in the old hotel in Dickson that now houses the Clement Foundation. The files in the State Library are unusually extensive, for Governor Clement turned almost everything in his possession over to the library. Consequently a great many political and personal items can be found there, including material from periods before he became governor. My staff examined these materials before they were catalogued under the system employed by the library. Those items that I thought would be useful were duplicated; the duplicates, classified by subject matter, have been stored in the Special Collections of the University of Tennessee Library in Knoxville, and references in the notes are to those files. The same procedure was used with respect to the much smaller collection of materials at Dickson. Generally speaking, the Dickson collection is much less useful than the material in Nashville, but certain items of a political or personal character are found in Dickson that are not in the State Library, such as Clement's military records and some sensitive political correspondence. I was given permission to examine these documents by Robert S. Clement, the late governor's father.

The Browning files in the State Library have been examined for the years immediately preceding the Clement terms. Generally speaking, political material for that period was not as rich as in the Clement papers. The Ellington papers are lacking in political material, for Governor Ellington did not turn such sources over to the State Library, and those that were retained in his possession have since been lost.

At the Vanderbilt University Library in Nashville, I and my staff have examined the papers of Cecil Sims, Brainard Cheney (with Mr. Cheney's permission), and Donald Davidson. I have been able to study some of the correspondence of Raymond Denney.

The papers of Senator Kefauver and of Senator Herbert Walters in the Special Collections of the University of Tennessee Library have been examined and used.

The papers of Albert Gore housed in the Middle Tennessee State University Library have been examined. These are only a partial collection of the papers of Senator Gore and are not especially useful for political purposes, but some items have been cited.

With the permission of the governor's father, I have obtained transcripts of Clement's academic records from the Dickson High School, Cumberland University, and Vanderbilt University. Certain other official documents, such as the governor's marriage record and death certificate, have been supplied to me, under appropriate permissions, from government departments.

INTERVIEWS

A list of interviews follows. I have used these as extensively as I could; if time permitted, a great many more could have been added. The Clement family has been generous with its time. The interviews with Robert S. Clement, the governor's father, with Mrs. Lucille Clement, his widow, with Anna Belle Clement O'Brien, his sister, and with Robert Clement, his oldest son, have been extremely valuable to me. The interview with the governor's cousin, Judge Frank Goad of Scottsville, Kentucky, was extremely enlightening on Clement's childhood years. The governor's aunt, Mrs. Ida Nicks, was gracious and informative.

I have always found the political figures of Tennessee surprisingly candid, an experience that was duplicated during my interviews. I am aware that the interviewees were reticent on some points, a circumstance that was clearly to be expected. Occasionally I was told things off the record; usually what I was told is available from other sources, but I have scrupulously kept the confidences of my interviewees, as I promised them I would. Most of the interviews were taped, and the tapes are stored in the State Library and Archives, the Special Collections of the University of Tennessee Library, and the Oral History Project of Memphis State University, where they can be consulted with appropriate permission. Transcripts of the tapes and of the interviewees' corrections are also available. A few interviews were not taped, for various reasons, but I have made careful notes of these interviews. These notes are available in the Special Collections of U.T. Library. I was refused an interview by only one person. In some cases my written requests for interviews elicited no response.

The interviews were open-ended and somewhat unstructured. In almost all cases, I prepared questions before the interview, and these questions were generally followed, but I departed from them when the course of the interview led away from them.

Most, but not all, of the people interviewed were friendly to Clement; I made an attempt to include some political opponents as well as some persons who could be thought neutral. I regret that Senator Walters and Donald Mc-Sween died before I could see them, but their correspondence has made up for some of that loss. By the time I was well into this project, Governor Browning and Judge Jimmy Weems were already too ill to be approached.

In the course of preparing a dissertation, Dr. Stephen Boyd conducted a number of interviews with former associates of Governor Clement; he courteously granted me permission to use the tapes of these interviews, which are housed in the State Library and Archives. I found these tapes most useful, and wish to express my indebtedness to Dr. Boyd.

David Alexander, February 28, 1978
W.L. Barry, November 2, 1977
Herbert Bingham, October 9, 1974
Agnes Bird, September 20, 1977
Edward Boling, June 25, 1975
Joe C. Carr, September 16, 1975
Noble Caudill, January 22, 1975; October 16, 1978
Brainard Cheney, February 11, 1975
Mrs. Lucille Clement, September 4, 1980
Robert S. Clement, March 25, 1975; May 15, 1975
Robert N. Clement, May 6, 1976
Eugene Collins, September 18, 1975
James Cummings, November 4, 1974
Ralph T. Donnell, June 4, 1977
Douglas Fisher, June 28, 1977
David Givens, September 27, 1977
Frank Goad, August 20, 1976
Leslie Hart, October 25, 1973
Joe Henry, September 30, 1975
Andrew D. Holt, July 9, 1976
Robert Hutcheson, September 10, 1974
Joseph Johnson, August 16, 1977
Edward F. Jones, June 29, 1977
Buford Lewallen, March 18, 1975
Roy Lillard, July 2, 1976
Charles Lockett, June 25, 1980
Stuart Maher, March 8, 1980
Harlan Mathews, January 23, 1975; February 2, 1975
J.J. Mynatt, October 2, 1975
Glen Nicely, August 24, 1977
Ida Nicks, Oct. 18, 1978
Roy Nicks, May 6, 1976
Dr. Ira North, October 2, 1975

Anna Belle Clement O'Brien, March 25, 1975; May 5, 1975; October 26, 1978
David Pack, February 28, 1978
Avondale Rawls, October 10, 1974
Harold Read, November 25, 1974
Valerius Sanford, September 29, 1977
Grant Smith, October 18, 1978
Mary Smith, October 19, 1978
William Snodgrass, January 22, 1975; February 11, 1975
Ernest Stockton, June 4, 1977
Fred Travis, September 26, 1977
Horace Wells, January 17, 1975

Appendix: Major Officials
of the Clement Administrations

(Dates refer entirely to the Clement years; some of these persons also held office in other administrations)

Comptroller of the Treasury: Jeanne Stephenson Bodfish, 1953–54; William Snodgrass, 1955–59; 1963–67

Treasurer: J.B. Walker, 1953–55; Ramon Davis, 1955–59; James Alexander, 1963–67

Secretary of State: G. Edward Friar, 1953–57; Joe Cordell Carr, 1957–59, 1963–67

(From this point, names of the departments or other agencies are shown with head of that department under varying titles)

Military: Joe W. Henry, 1953–59; Van D. Nunally, 1963–67

Accounts: John F. Nolan, 1953–59

Budget: William Snodgrass, 1953–55; Edward J. Boling, 1955–59

Finance and Administration: Harlan Mathews, 1963–67

Personnel: Ramon Davis, 1953–55; Sam T. Whited, 1955–59; Keith Hampton, 1963–67

Standards and Purchases: William Luttrell, 1953; Franklin Pierce, 1953–59; W. Grundy Quarles, 1963–67

Property Administrator: Porter Dunlap, 1953; Raleigh Robinson, 1954–57; Clayton Dekle, 1958–59

Veterans' Affairs: James L. Crider, 1953–59; Joe F. Hudgens, 1963–67

Mental Health: C.J. Ruilman, 1953–59; Joseph J. Baker, 1963–65; Nat Winston, 1965–67

Agriculture: Buford Ellington, 1953–58; W.F. Moss, 1958–59, 1963–67

Conservation: Glen Nicely, 1953; Jim Nance McCord, 1953–59; Donald M. McSween, 1963–67

Education: Quill E. Cope, 1953–59; J. Howard Warf, 1963–67

Employment Security: Donald M. McSween, 1953–59; Mrs. C. Frank Scott, 1963–67

Finance and Taxation: Z.D. Atkins, 1953–57; B.J. Boyd, 1958–59

Highways and Public Works: W.M. Leech, 1953–59

Highways: David M. Pack, 1963–67

Institutions (changed to Corrections, 1956): Keith Hampton, 1954–59; Harry S. Avery, 1963-67

Insurance and Banking: Arch E. Northington, 1953–59; Albert Williams, 1963–67

Labor: William H. Parham, 1953–59; 1963–67

Public Welfare: Christine C. Reynolds, 1953–59; Noble Caudill, 1963; Roy Nicks, 1963–65; Herman Yeatman, 1965–67

Safety: G. Hilton Butler, 1953, 1963–64; William Luttrell, 1953–54; Greg O'Rear, 1965–67

Public Health: R.H. Hutcheson, 1953–59; 1963–67

Revenue: Donald R. King, 1963–67

Index

(This index does not cover notes.)

Lead Me On has been composed on the Compugraphic phototypesetter in twelve-point Bembo with one-point line spacing. Centaur was selected for display and furnished from the VGC Photo Typositor. This photographic rendition is accepted as the nearest to the original Centaur letter form. The book was designed by Jim Billingsley, set into type by Metricomp, Inc., printed offset by Thomson-Shore, Inc., and bound by John H. Dekker & Sons. The paper on which the book is printed bears the watermark of S. D. Warren and is designed for an effective life of at least three hundred years.

THE UNIVERSITY OF TENNESSEE PRESS : KNOXVILLE